Hitler's Germany

Praise for the first edition:

> "This is an important new textbook on the Nazi period which is geared to intermediate and advanced undergraduates and will also interest general audiences ... this book is a real winner and deserves wide use."—Bruce Campbell, *German Studies Review*

Hitler's Germany provides a comprehensive narrative history of Nazi Germany and sets it in the wider context of nineteenth- and twentieth-century German history. Roderick Stackelberg analyzes how it was possible that a national culture of such creativity and achievement could generate such barbarism and destructiveness.

This second edition has been updated throughout to incorporate recent historical research and engage with current debates in the field. It includes:

- an expanded introduction focusing on the hazards of writing about Nazi Germany
- an extended analysis of fascism, totalitarianism, imperialism, and ideology
- a broadened contextualization of antisemitism
- discussion of the Holocaust including the euthanasia program and the role of eugenics
- new chapters on Nazi social and economic policies and the structure of government as well as on the role of culture, the arts, education, and religion
- additional maps, tables, and a chronology
- a fully updated bibliography.

Exploring the controversies surrounding Nazism and its afterlife in historiography and historical memory, *Hitler's Germany* provides students with an interpretive framework for understanding this extraordinary episode in German and European history.

Roderick Stackelberg is Robert K. and Ann J. Powers Professor of the Humanities Emeritus at Gonzaga University. His publications include *The Routledge Companion to Nazi Germany* (2007) and, with Sally A. Winkle, *The Nazi Germany Sourcebook* (2002).

Hitler's Germany

Origins, interpretations, legacies

Second Edition

Roderick Stackelberg

Routledge
Taylor & Francis Group

LONDON AND NEW YORK

First published 1999
by Routledge
270 Madison Ave, New York, NY 10016

Simultaneously published in the UK
by Routledge
2 Park Square, Milton Park, Abingdon, Oxon OX14 4RN

Second edition published 2009

Routledge is an imprint of the Taylor & Francis Group, an informa business

Typeset in Garamond by
Book Now Ltd, London
Printed and bound in Great Britain by
CPI Antony Rowe, Chippenham, Wilts

British Library Cataloguing in Publication Data
A catalogue record for this book is available from the British Library

Library of Congress Cataloging in Publication Data
Stackelberg, Roderick
Hitler's Germany: origins, interpretations, legacies/Roderick Stackelberg.—
2nd ed.
    p. cm.
Includes bibliographical references.
1. Germany—History—1933–1945—Historiography. 2. National socialism—Philosophy. 3. Hitler, Adolf, 1889–1945. 4. Holocaust, Jewish (1939–
1945)—Causes. 5. Political culture—Germany. 6. Collective memory—
Germany. I. Title.
DD256.48.S73 2008
943.0′86072—dc22   2008007859

ISBN10: 0–415–37330–1 (hbk)
ISBN10: 0–415–37331–X (pbk)

ISBN13: 978–0–415–37330–2 (hbk)
ISBN13: 978–0–415–37331–9 (pbk)

Contents

Illustrations

Maps

Tables

Figures

Preface to the second edition

The purposes of this book remain as described in the preface to *Hitler's Germany* when it was first published in 1999: to provide an accurate and reasonably complete narrative account of the period of Nazi rule, the events leading up to it, and its aftermath; and equally importantly, to provide an interpretive framework that makes some sense out of this extraordinary episode in German and European history. Scholarship, however, does not stand still, and any text that promises a synthesis of the latest research and recent historiographical debates must be periodically updated.

In this second edition I have incorporated many of the suggestions made by five anonymous Routledge readers, three of whom had used the first edition in their own classes and two of whom had not. I have also tried to respond to criticisms and suggestions made in the largely favorable published reviews of the first edition. My major change has been to expand Chapter 9 on "Society, culture, and the state in the Third Reich" into two chapters, now entitled "Economy, society, and the state in the Third Reich" and "Education, culture, religion, and eugenics in the Third Reich," respectively. The second edition now also contains a detailed chronology, maps and tables, and, of course, an updated (though still very selective) bibliography.

One reviewer of *Hitler's Germany*, a specialist in nineteenth-century German history, wrote that the first edition left him with the impression "that German history was propelled by an inherent teleological drive toward Nazism." To some extent, I suppose, such an impression is unavoidable in a work that consciously sets out to search for clues to the origins of Nazism in the past rather than to provide a general history of Germany. This criticism nonetheless surprised me as I had explicitly rejected the notion of historical determinism in my introduction: "History is always contingent and open-ended and there are many possible outcomes at any given time." I had emphasized how wrong it would be to conclude, as some still mistakenly do, that Hitler was "elected" to office or that Hindenburg had no choice but to appoint him to head the German government in 1933. Indeed, I continue to hope that by generating awareness of the ideological and political forces that brought the Nazi movement to power, my book will encourage civic engagement in the present to prevent a recurrence of such destructiveness in the future. Historical patterns do recur, even if they never repeat themselves in the specific form of their original occurrence. One point of reconstructing history according to Ranke's principle, "wie es eigentlich gewesen ist" ("as it actually occurred"), is surely to promote a sense that we are not powerless to affect our own destiny in the present. The aim of my book is to encourage civic activism and engagement, not to dampen these essential democratic virtues by portraying history as teleologically determined. The lesson of Nazism is contained in its historical specificity, not its historical inevitability.

My intellectual debts are too numerous to list them all on this page. However, I do want to give special thanks to my colleague and successor at Gonzaga University, Kevin O'Connor, for scrupulously reading the entire manuscript and offering very helpful comments and suggestions. A specialist on Soviet history, Professor O'Connor also brought a European-wide perspective that balanced my occasional tendency to focus too narrowly on developments within Germany. I also wish to acknowledge the invaluable assistance of Theresa Kappus and Anji Mertens of the Interlibrary loan services at Gonzaga's Foley library as well as the help I received from Sandy Hank and the staff at Gonzaga's Faculty Services in preparing the manuscript. As always, my greatest debt is to my wife Sally Winkle who contributed to the successful completion of this project in every imaginable way.

This book was originally dedicated to my students, whose interest, appreciation, and intellectual curiosity gave me the incentive to write. It is to them and to present and future generations of students that I dedicate this second edition as well.

Roderick Stackelberg
Spokane, WA, April 2008

Chronology

1871	January	Unification of Germany and founding of the German Empire under Kaiser Wilhelm I and Chancellor Otto von Bismarck
1888		Wilhelm II becomes Kaiser
1889	20 April	Adolf Hitler born in Braunau am Inn in Austria
1914	August	Hitler welcomes the start of World War I in Munich
1916	August	Field Marshal Paul von Hindenburg appointed commander in chief of German forces with General Erich Ludendorff as his chief of staff
1917	November	Russian Revolution; Bolsheviks under Vladimir Ilyich Lenin seize power
1918	19 February	Germany signs peace treaty with independent Ukraine
	14 March	Treaty of Brest-Litovsk imposes punitive peace on Russia
	May	Civil war in Russia
	October	German government under Prince Max von Baden sues for peace with western powers
	November	Revolution in Germany
	9 November	Abdication of Kaiser Wilhelm II; proclamation of German republic
	11 November	German government emissaries sign armistice at Compiègne ending World War I
	30 December	Founding of German Communist Party (KPD) in Berlin

1919	5–11 January	KPD-supported Spartacus uprising crushed in Berlin; German Workers' Party (DAP) founded in Munich
	6 February	National Constitutional Assembly convenes in Weimar
	2 March	Founding conference of Third International (Comintern) in Moscow
	23 March	Benito Mussolini organizes new Fascist movement in Italy
	2 May	Bavarian government of soviets (workers' councils) crushed by Reichswehr and Free Corps in Munich
	28 June	Signing of Treaty of Versailles by German government
	1 July	Mussolini issues Fascist manifesto
	31 July	Adoption of liberal Weimar constitution by National Assembly
	12 September	Hitler joins the DAP in Munich
1920	24 February	DAP adopts "Twenty-five-Point Program" and changes its name to the National Socialist German Workers' Party (NSDAP)
	11 March	Hitler leaves the army
	12–17 March	Kapp Putsch fails in Berlin
	15 March–20 May	Communist insurrection in Ruhr industrial region
1921	29 July	Hitler becomes chairman of NSDAP
1922	16 April	Germany recognizes Soviet Russia in Treaty of Rapallo, angering the radical right
	24 June	German Foreign Minister Walter Rathenau assassinated by Free Corps members
	August	Fascists clash with communists in Italy
	30 October	Mussolini asked to head Italian government in Italy after threatening a "March on Rome"
1923	11 January	French and Belgian troops occupy Ruhr to collect reparations
	27 January	First Nazi Party Congress in Munich
	June–November	The Great Inflation in Germany

	12 August	Gustav Stresemann becomes German chancellor and ends passive resistance to the French occupation
	20 October	Authoritarian Bavarian government under Gustav von Kahr breaks relations with liberal national government in Berlin
	29 October	*Reichswehr* ousts elected SPD–KPD government in state of Saxony
	9 November	Hitler and Ludendorff launch "Beer Hall Putsch" in Munich on the "Day of the Republic"
	15 November	Introduction of new currency ushers in end of Great Inflation
	23 November	KPD and NSDAP banned
1924	1 April	Hitler sentenced to minimum term of five years in prison for high treason with eligibility for parole in six months
	9 April	Dawes Plan reschedules German reparations
	20 December	Hitler released from prison
1925	27 February	Hitler refounds the NSDAP
	25 April	Hindenburg elected German president
	July	Publication of first volume of *Mein Kampf*
	16 October	Germany recognizes western borders in Treaty of Locarno
	9 November	Formation of NSDAP protection squad (SS)
1926	14 February	Bamberg Conference; Hitler rejects any change to "Twenty-five-Point Program" and establishes full control over NSDAP
	8 September	Germany admitted to League of Nations
	1 December	Goebbels named *Gauleiter* of Berlin
1927	10 March	Speaking ban on Hitler lifted in Prussia
1928	6 January	Himmler named *Reichsführer SS*
	20 May	Nazis receive only 2.6 percent of the vote in Reichstag elections
	28 June	Hermann Müller (SPD) heads coalition government in Germany
1929	9 July	Nazis join Nationalists (DNVP) in opposing Young Plan to reschedule reparations payments
	24–29 October	Stock market crash in New York

	22 December	Referendum to block Young Plan defeated
1930	23 January	Wilhelm Frick becomes first Nazi to hold state office in Germany as interior minister in Thuringia
	30 March	Heinrich Brüning becomes chancellor of government based on presidential authority rather than parliamentary majority
	30 June	French troops evacuate Rhineland five years ahead of schedule
	16 July	Brüning overrules Reichstag to impose budget under Article 48 of the Weimar constitution
	14 September	Nazis become second-largest party in Reichstag elections with 18.3 percent of the vote and 107 seats
1931	20 June	Hoover moratorium on reparations and war debts
	14 July	Financial crisis closes banks in Germany (reopen three weeks later)
	29 August	Austrian government forced to drop plans for customs union with Germany
	11 October	Hitler joins Nationalists (DNVP) in giant Harzburg Front rally aimed at supplanting Brüning's government with a nationalist regime
1932	7 January	Chancellor Brüning declares Germany will not resume reparations
	27 January	Hitler gains enthusiastic reception by industrialists in Düsseldorf
	22 February	Hitler announces his candidacy for president
	13 March	Hitler with 11 million votes prevents Hindenburg from getting an absolute majority in the first round of the presidential election
	10 April	Hindenburg re-elected president in run-off against Hitler
	13 April	Brüning prohibits paramilitary units from marching in uniform
	30 May	Brüning resigns as chancellor and is replaced by Franz von Papen
	16 June	Ban on Nazi storm troopers lifted
	20 July	Papen suspends SPD government in Prussia and declares martial law
	31 July	Nazis double their strength and become largest party in Reichstag with 37.4 percent of the vote and 227 seats

	13 August	Hitler refuses post of vice-chancellor in Papen's government; Hindenburg refuses to appoint Hitler chancellor
	30 August	Hermann Göring elected president of Reichstag
	November	Transit strike paralyzes Berlin
	6 November	Nazis lose 35 seats in Reichstag election, while Communists continue to gain
	21 November	Hitler again refuses to join the government without full power
	4 December	General Kurt von Schleicher named Reich chancellor
1933	30 January	Hitler appointed Reich chancellor with Papen as vice-chancellor
	6 February	Nazi government introduces press censorship
	22 February	Formation of SA, SS, and Stahlhelm auxiliary police in Prussia
	27 February	Fire destroys Reichstag
	28 February	Hitler suspends basic civil liberties (Decree for the Protection of People and State)
	3 March	KPD leadership arrested
	5 March	Nazis win 43.9 percent of Reichstag vote, enough only for a simple majority with the Nationalists; Communist Party banned
	12 March	By order of Hindenburg, the black–red–orange republican flag replaced by the Imperial colors black–white–red and the Swastika
	13 March	Establishment of Reich Ministry for Volk Enlightenment and Propaganda under Goebbels
	20 March	Nazis open first official concentration camp in Dachau near Munich
	21 March	"Day of Potsdam"; opening of the new Reichstag in the Garrison Church
	22 March	Establishment of a department of "Racial Hygiene" in Interior Ministry
	24 March	Reichstag passes Enabling Act giving Hitler full dictatorial power
	31 March	First law for the *Gleichschaltung* of the states
	1 April	Nazis organize one-day boycott of Jewish businesses
	7 April	Removal of Jews, Communists, Social Democrats, and liberal political opponents from the Civil Service

	25 April	"Law against the Overcrowding of German Schools and Universities" limits number of Jewish students in German schools to 1.5 percent
	1 May	Moratorium on new memberships in the Nazi Party (until 1937)
	2 May	Dissolution of labor unions and formation of German Labor Front (DAF)
	10 May	Public burning of "un-German" books in Berlin and other university cities
	21 June	Nationalist Party (DNVP) votes to dissolve
	22 June	Social Democratic Party (SPD) banned
	14 July	Nazis become only legal party in Germany; Nazis pass sterilization law "for the prevention of genetically diseased offspring"
	20 July	Concordat between German Reich and the Vatican
	25 July	General amnesty for SA and SS personnel accused of crimes against political opponents
	2 August	Auxiliary SA police force in Prussia disbanded
	25 August	Haavara (transfer) agreement between Reich Ministry of Economics and Zionist organization to facilitate emigration of German Jews to Palestine
	13 September	Reich Food Estate established
	22 September	Creation of German Chamber of Culture
	29 September	Hereditary Farm Law
	4 October	Editorial Law excludes German Jews from journalism
	14 October	Germany leaves League of Nations and disarmament conference
	12 November	93 percent approval for leaving the League in nationwide plebiscite; Nazi Reichstag elected without opposition
	30 November	Establishment of Gestapo
	1 December	"Law for the Unity of Party and State"
1934	10 January	Marinus van der Lubbe executed for setting Reichstag fire
	26 January	Germany signs nonaggression pact with Poland
	20 April	Himmler appointed "Inspector of the Gestapo"
	5 May	Jewish students excluded from examinations in medicine and dentistry

	13 June	Germany cancels mutual aid treaty with Soviet Russia
	17 June	Papen's Marburg speech
	30 June	"Night of the Long Knives"; approximately 120 persons killed in purge of Ernst Roehm and the SA
	3 July	Franz von Papen resigns as vice-chancellor
	9 July	Heinrich Himmler placed in charge of Prussian police
	22 July	Jewish students excluded from examinations in law
	25 July	Austrian Nazis fail in attempt to gain power; Austrian Chancellor Dollfuss assassinated
	2 August	Death of President Hindenburg; Hitler takes over presidency while retaining office of chancellor; Schacht appointed economics minister
	19 August	Law on Head of State approved by 88.9 percent in plebiscite
	5 September	At annual party rally in Nuremberg, Hitler announces that there will be no more revolution in Germany for a thousand years
	9 October	Assassination of King Alexander of Yugoslavia and French Foreign Minister Louis Barthou by Croatian fascists
	8 December	Jewish students excluded from examinations in pharmacy
1935	13 January	90.8 percent vote in favor of reunion with Germany in Saar plebiscite; the Saar to be returned to Germany on 1 March
	16 March	Hitler announces introduction of universal military training in defiance of Versailles Treaty
	31 March	Britain and Soviet Union agree to work for collective security in League of Nations
	11 April	Stresa conference (Italy, Britain, France)
	17 April	League of Nations condemns German rearmament
	21 May	Army Law excludes practicing Jews from military service
	18 June	Anglo-German Naval Treaty
	16 July	Reich Ministry of Churches created under Hanns Kerrl
	31 August	President Franklin Roosevelt signs neutrality act prohibiting arms shipments to countries at war

	15 September	Nuremberg racial laws deprive Jews of civil rights and prohibit marriages and sexual relations between Jews and ethnic Germans
	28 October	Mussolini's armies invade Ethiopia
	14 November	First Supplementary Decree to the "Reich Citizenship Law" defines Jews and *Mischlinge*
	18 November	League of Nations imposes economic sanctions on Italy but rejects oil embargo
	26 November	"Gypsies" and "Negroes" included in prohibition of racially mixed marriages
1936	6 February	Winter Olympics opened in Garmisch-Partenkirchen
	7 March	Nazis enter Rhineland in violation of Versailles and Locarno treaties
	24 March	Benefit payments withdrawn from large Jewish families
	29 March	99 percent vote in favor of Rhineland occupation in plebiscite
	9 May	Italy formally annexes Ethiopia
	26 May	Reich Chamber of Fine Arts requires proof of "Aryan" ancestry from its members
	8 June	Popular Front government under Leon Blum takes power in France
	17 June	Heinrich Himmler named head of Reich police
	11 July	Hitler and Austrian Chancellor Schuschnigg sign "July Agreement" to respect Austrian independence
	19 July	Right-wing forces under Francisco Franco start rebellion against Popular Front government of Spanish Republic
	25 July	Germany formally recognizes Ethiopian conquest
	1 August	Hitler opens Olympic summer games in Berlin; France declares nonintervention in Spain
	11 August	Ribbentrop named German ambassador to England
	13 September	Founding of *Lebensborn* agency for aid to single mothers
	4 October	Jewish teachers forbidden to give private lessons to "Aryans"
	18 October	Göring named to head Four-Year Plan

	1 November	Creation of "Axis" through Italo-German treaty
	4 November	Jews forbidden to use German greeting (*Heil Hitler*)
	18 November	Germany and Italy recognize Franco government
	25 November	German–Japanese Anti-Comintern Pact
	1 December	Law gives the Hitler Youth legal recognition as state institution
1937	30 January	Enabling Law extended for another four years
	14 March	Papal encyclical on "The Church in Germany" condemns racism
	15 April	Jews no longer permitted to take doctoral examinations in any field
	27 April	German warplanes kill hundreds of civilians at Guernica, Spain
	28 May	Neville Chamberlain becomes prime minister of England
	12 June	Heydrich decrees that Jews guilty of "racial disgrace" (miscegenation) are to be interned in concentration camps after serving their prison sentence
	July	Japan renews offensive in China
	1 July	Martin Niemöller arrested
	15 July	Opening of Buchenwald concentration camp
	20 October	British restrict Jewish immigration to Palestine
	5 November	Hitler outlines his plans for expansion in "Hossbach Memorandum"
	6 November	Italy accedes to Anti-Comintern Pact
	19 November	Lord Halifax visits Germany to seek British–German agreement
	26 November	Schacht dismissed as economics minister for opposing financing of Four-Year Plan
1938	25 January	Blomberg resigns as *Reichswehr* minister
	4 February	Hitler assumes direct control of armed forces through creation of new High Command (OKW); Ribbentrop becomes foreign minister; Fritsch dismissed as commander in chief of the army
	5 February	Last meeting of the Reich Cabinet

12 February	Schuschnigg forced to agree to legalize Nazi Party in Austria
9 March	Schuschnigg calls for plebiscite on independence in Austria
12 March	German troops enter Austria
10 April	Daladier forms anti-Communist cabinet in France; more than 99 percent of voters in Germany and Austria approve the Austrian *Anschluss*
26 April	Jews compelled to register all assets over 5,000 Reichsmark
May	Hitler informs his generals of his "unalterable decision to smash Czechoslovakia by military action in the near future"
6 June	Jews in Germany forbidden to buy or sell real estate
1 July	Italy introduces antisemitic laws
6 July	Marriage Law eases divorce in racially undesirable marriages
6–15 July	International conference at Evian in France fails to find a solution to the Jewish refugee problem aggravated by the *Anschluss* of Austria
23 July	Jewish doctors prohibited from treating "Aryan" patients
17 August	Jewish women and men without identifiably Jewish names ordered to add "Sarah" and "Israel," respectively, for easier identification
18 August	Resignation of Army Chief of Staff Ludwig Beck
20 August	Central Office for Jewish Emigration set up under Adolf Eichmann in Vienna
27 September	Jewish lawyers prohibited from working for "Aryan" clients
29 September	Munich Agreement transfers Sudetenland from Czechoslovakia to Germany
1 October	German troops march into Sudetenland
5 October	German Jewish passports stamped with "J" at request of Swiss government
19 October	Unemployed Jews obligated to do forced labor
28 October	Germans expel Polish Jews living in Germany after Poland revokes citizenship of all Jews living outside Poland for more than five years; 17,000 Jews caught in no-man's land before being admitted to Poland

7 November	Herschel Grynszpan, son of Polish Jewish parents expelled from Germany, assassinates German diplomat Ernst vom Rath in Paris
9 November	*Kristallnacht* pogrom against German Jews
12 November	Göring convenes conference to plan compulsory "Aryanization" of Jewish businesses; collective fine 1,000,000,000 Reichsmark imposed on German Jews; Jews forbidden to participate in cultural events outside the Jewish community
16 November	Jewish children prohibited from attending German schools

1939

21 January	Schacht dismissed as head of the *Reichsbank*
24 January	Heydrich authorized by Göring to develop comprehensive plan for Jewish emigration and to establish a Reich Central Office for Jewish Emigration
30 January	Hitler threatens annihilation of European Jews in speech to Reichstag
21 February	Jews required to surrender precious metals and jewelry
27 February	Britain recognizes Franco's regime in Spain
2 March	Cardinal Pacelli elected Pope Pius XII
15 March	Nazis occupy Prague in violation of Munich Agreement and establish Protectorate of Bohemia and Moravia
22 March	Lithuania returns port of Memel to Germany
25 March	Membership in Hitler Youth made compulsory for youths from 10 to 18
28 March	Franco enters Madrid as Spanish Civil War ends
1 April	Prime Minister Neville Chamberlain pledges to support Poland militarily against threats to her sovereignty; Germany renounces Anglo-German Naval Treaty and Nonaggression Treaty with Poland
3 April	Hitler orders preparation of plans for military attack on Poland
30 April	Soviet Union proposes military alliance with France and Britain; German Jews forced to move into designated Jewish houses
3 May	Vyacheslav Molotov named Soviet foreign minister

17 May	British "White Paper" limits Jewish immigration in Palestine
22 May	Italy and Germany sign Pact of Steel
23 May	Hitler informs his leading generals of his decision "to attack Poland at the first suitable opportunity"
1 August	Opening of Central Office for Jewish Emigration in Prague
2 August	Albert Einstein writes to President Roosevelt suggesting feasibility of atomic bomb
16 August	Germany demands Danzig (Gdansk) from Poland
22 August	France and Britain reaffirm pledge of aid to Poland
23 August	Nazi–Soviet Nonaggression Treaty signed, with secret protocol dividing Poland and eastern Europe into spheres of influence
27 August	Food rationing introduced in Germany
1 September	Germans invade Poland; Italy declares neutrality; Hitler authorizes secret euthanasia program (Aktion T-4)
3 September	Britain and France declare war on Germany
5 September	The United States declares neutrality and continues embargo of arms to warring nations
9 September	German forces reach Warsaw
16 September	Soviet forces invade Poland
20 September	German Jews required to surrender their radios
21 September	Heydrich issues guidelines for SS *Einsatzgruppen* in Poland and ghettoization of Polish Jews
27 September	Warsaw surrenders; SS Main Office for Reich Security (RSHA) established in Berlin under Reinhard Heydrich
6 October	Britain and France reject Hitler's offer of peace in return for acceptance of conquest of Poland
7 October	Office of "Reich Commissar for the Strengthening of German Ethnicity" (RFK) established under Himmler
12 October	Several trainloads of Jews from Austria and Bohemia-Moravia deported to Poland
26 October	Annexation of western Polish provinces (Wartheland); Hans Frank named to head occupied Poland (Generalgouvernement)

	4 November	US embargo on arms sales to Britain and France lifted
	8 November	Hitler escapes attempt on his life by Johann Elser in Munich
	23 November	All Jews in Nazi-occupied Poland required to wear yellow Star of David
	25 November	Sexual relations forbidden between foreign workers and Germans
	28 November	Jewish Councils (*Judenräte*) created on German orders in ghettoes of Nazi-occupied Poland
	30 November	Soviet Union invades Finland to start "Winter War"
	1 December	Deportations begin of Jews and Poles from annexed "incorporated territories" to the Generalgouvernement
	12 December	Jewish males between 14 and 60 in Generalgouvernement required to do forced labor in camps set up for that purpose
	14 December	Soviet Union expelled from League of Nations
	19 December	Conference in RSHA on plans to create a Jewish reservation in Poland
1940	2 February	First deportation of Jews from Germany to Poland
	21 February	Construction of concentration camp at Auschwitz
	13 March	Finland signs peace treaty with Soviet Union, ending "Winter War"
	17 March	Fritz Todt named to head new Reich Ministry of Munitions
	23 March	Göring prohibits further deportations into the Generalgouvernement
	9 April	Germans occupy Denmark and invade Norway
	1 May	Lodz Ghetto sealed off with barbed wire
	7 May	Resumption of "resettlement" of Jews and Poles from the "incorporated territories" into the Generalgouvernement
	10 May	Germans launch Blitzkrieg against France and Benelux countries; Winston Churchill replaces Chamberlain as prime minister
	14 May	Holland surrenders
	28 May	Belgium surrenders

4 June	Allied expeditionary force evacuated from Dunkirk
10 June	Italy declares war on Britain and France; President Roosevelt promises aid to Britain and France
14 June	Germans occupy Paris
17–23 June	USSR occupies Baltic states
22 June	French sign armistice in Compiègne
24 June	Heydrich calls for a "territorial solution" to the Jewish problem
29 June	Jewish telephones disconnected in Germany
July	German Foreign Ministry (in consultation with RSHA, the Office of the Four-Year Plan, and the Propaganda Ministry) proposes plan to deport Jews to Madagascar after peace with Britain
3 July	British naval squadron destroys French fleet in Algeria, leading to a break of diplomatic relations with Vichy France
6 July	Huge victory parade in Berlin
10 July	Authoritarian government under Marshal Henri Pétain formally established at Vichy in unoccupied France
16 July	Hitler issues orders for the preparation of "Operation Sea Lion," the invasion of Britain
19 July	Hitler makes peace offer to Britain in speech to Reichstag
22 July	British reject Hitler's peace proposal
31 July	Hitler announces plans for an invasion of the Soviet Union to his generals
26 August	First British air raid on Berlin; Hitler launches Blitz on British cities
6 September	President Roosevelt makes 50 destroyers available to Britain
17 September	Standoff in Battle of Britain forces postponement of plans to invade Britain; Madagascar Plan tabled in favor of an "eastern territorial solution"
27 September	Signing of Italo-German-Japanese Tripartite Pact
2 October	Hans Frank protests in Berlin against further deportation of Jews into the Generalgouvernement
3 October	Vichy France passes antisemitic legislation
22 October	7,500 Jews deported from southwestern Germany to Vichy France and interned

	23–24 October	Hitler unsuccessful in persuading Vichy France and Franco's Spain from joining war against Britain
	28 October	Italians invade Greece
	12 November	Soviet Foreign Minister Molotov confers with Hitler in Berlin
	15 November	Warsaw Ghetto walled off from rest of the city
	18 December	Hitler authorizes plans for "Operation Barbarossa," the invasion of the USSR
	29 December	Roosevelt describes the United States as "the arsenal of democracy"
1941	9 January	Plans for "Operation Felix," the seizure of Gibraltar, abandoned
	6 February	German troops sent to North Africa under Rommel
	March	Deportations into Generalgouvernement halted because of worsening food situation
	1 March	Himmler begins plans for expansion of Auschwitz complex to hold 130,000 inmates, including an expected 100,000 Soviet prisoners of war
	7 March	Jews in Germany now subject to forced labor
	11 March	Roosevelt signs Lend-Lease Act
	27 March	Military revolt overthrows pro-German government in Yugoslavia
	4 April	Beginning of "Aktion 14f13" for the killing of concentration camp inmates, mainly Jewish, incapable of work
	6 April	Germans invade Yugoslavia and Greece
	10 April	United States occupies Danish colony of Greenland
	13 April	Soviet Union signs nonaggression pact with Japan
	17 April	German forces occupy Belgrade; establish separate fascist state of Croatia
	27 April	Greece surrenders; Germans occupy Athens
	May	Formation of SS *Einsatzgruppen* for war against Soviet Union with assignment to kill all Jews in Communist Party or government positions
	10 May	Hitler's deputy Rudolf Hess flies to Scotland in hopes of negotiating peace with Britain in anticipation of the invasion of the USSR
	29 May	Martin Bormann appointed to ministerial rank

6 June	OKW issues the "Commissar Decree," calling for execution of captured political commissars
21 June	Himmler orders RFK to draw up a "general plan for the east" (*Generalplan Ost*)
22 June	German troops invade the Soviet Union; *Einsatzgruppen* begin roundup and execution of Jews and Communists
28 June	Wehrmacht and SS agree on selection and execution of Soviet POWs
7 July	US forces land in Iceland to prevent German occupation
15 July	*Generalplan Ost* submitted by Konrad Meyer, calling for the "evacuation" of 31 million persons from areas to be colonized by Germans
16 July	German troops take Smolensk, 200 miles from Moscow
17 July	New Ministry for the Occupied Eastern Territories established under Alfred Rosenberg
31 July	Göring authorizes Heydrich to draw up plan for "total solution" of Jewish Question in Europe
August	Eichmann visits Auschwitz and informs Commandant Höss of the planned "final solution" of the Jewish Question
14 August	Churchill and Roosevelt sign Atlantic Charter
16 August	Himmler is witness to *Einsatzgruppen* executions in Minsk; first reported killings of Jewish women and children
23 August	Hitler calls official halt to euthanasia program after church protests
1 September	All Jews in Germany over the age of six compelled to wear yellow Star of David for identification
2–5 September	Cyclon B tested for the first time on Soviet POWs at Auschwitz
4 September	Leningrad surrounded
19 September	Kiev falls to German troops
29 September	Massacre of Jews at Babi-Yar on outskirts of Kiev
2 October	Beginning of the Battle for Moscow
14 October	Deportation of German Jews to the east (first trainloads to Minsk, Riga, and Kovno) begins

	16 October	Odessa falls to German troops
	23 October	Emigration of Jews prohibited from Nazi-occupied Europe
	30 October	US destroyer Reuben James sunk by German submarine
	November	Euthanasia personnel arrive in Poland to prepare for "final solution"
	9 November	Heydrich issues invitations to various ministries for conference on "final solution," originally planned for 9 December, but postponed to 20 January
	24 November	"Model" ghetto for elderly Jews created at Theresienstadt
	26 November	Completion of construction of barracks at Auschwitz-Birkenau
	5 December	Soviets launch counterattack at Moscow
	7 December	Japanese attack on Pearl Harbor
	8 December	United States declares war on Japan; gassing of Jews in mobile gas vans at Chelmno begins
	11 December	Germany and Italy declare war on the United States
	12 December	Hitler announces coming "final solution" to Gauleiter conference in Berlin
	16 December	Hans Frank announces planned murder of the Jews of the Generalgouvernement to his staff
	19 December	Field Marshal Walther von Brauchitsch dismissed as commander of the army; Hitler assumes operational command of the army
1942	20 January	Wannsee Conference to coordinate "Final Solution of Jewish Question"
	21 January	General Rommel launches North African offensive to drive British out of Libya
	9 February	Albert Speer takes control of German war production as armaments minister
	13 February	"Operation Sea Lion" postponed indefinitely
	15 February	First transports of Jews arrive at Auschwitz
	16 March	First transports of Polish Jews to Belzec death camp under "Aktion Reinhard"
	26 March	First transports of Jewish emigrants from western Europe to Auschwitz
	28 March	Bombing raid by Royal Air Force on north German city of Lübeck

	22 April	Central Planning Committee to allocate resources established and presided over by Speer
	4 June	Reinhard Heydrich killed by Czech partisans near Prague
	7 June	US naval victory over Japanese fleet at Midway Island in the Pacific
	10 June	Czech village of Lidice liquidated in revenge for assassination of Heydrich
	21 June	Tobruk falls to German forces in North Africa
	23 June	Systematic gassing of Jews begins at Auschwitz
	1 July	Soviet Black Sea naval base at Sevastopol falls to Germans
	22 July	Beginning of deportation of Jews from Warsaw Ghetto to Treblinka
	31 August	Communist resistance network "Red Orchestra" broken up by Gestapo
	17 September	German troops reach Stalingrad
	31 October	British counteroffensive forces Rommel's Africa Corps to retreat at El Alamein in Egypt
	8 November	Anglo-American landing in North Africa
	11 November	Germans occupy Vichy France
	12 November	Allies recapture Tobruk
	16 November	Beginning of deportation of German Gypsies to Auschwitz
	17 November	Allied Declaration denouncing murder of European Jews and announcing that those responsible will be punished
	19 November	Soviets launch counteroffensive that eventually cuts off German Sixth Army in Stalingrad
1943	15 January	Roosevelt and Churchill announce policy of "unconditional surrender" at Casablanca Conference
	18 January	Soviet forces break the siege of Leningrad
	31 January	Surrender of the German Sixth Army at Stalingrad
	18 February	"White Rose" student resistance leaders arrested; Goebbels announces "total war" at mass rally in Berlin
	10 March	Rommel recalled from Tunisia

14 March	Cracow Ghetto is liquidated
19 April	Start of Warsaw Ghetto uprising
12 May	Surrender of Africa Corps at Tunis
16 May	Warsaw Ghetto uprising suppressed and ghetto destroyed
24 May	Admiral Dönitz recalls German submarines in Atlantic due to heavy losses
June	On Himmler's orders bodies are exhumed from death camps in order to obliterate evidence of Holocaust
19 June	Goebbels announces that Berlin is free of Jews
21 June	Order to liquidate remaining ghettoes on Soviet territory
5 July	Germans launch "Operation Citadel" at Kursk in central Russia
10 July	Allies land in Sicily
13 July	German defeat in the Battle of Kursk
25 July	Mussolini deposed by Fascist Grand Council
28 July	Allies launch "Operation Gomorrah," the firebombing of Hamburg
2 August	Crushing of prisoner revolt at Treblinka
24 August	Himmler named Reich interior minister
3 September	Allies invade Italian mainland; Italy signs armistice with Allies
8 September	German troops occupy northern Italy
12 September	German task force under Skorzeny frees Mussolini from Italian captivity
15 September	Mussolini established as head of Republic of Salò
25 September	Soviets retake Smolensk
13 October	Italy under General Badoglio declares war on Germany
14 October	Partial success of revolt at Sobibor as gassing operations end
16 October	Deportation of 8,360 Italian Jews to Auschwitz begins
6 November	Soviets retake Kiev
28 November	Conference of Roosevelt, Stalin, and Churchill at Teheran

1944	4 January	Soviet troops reach former Polish–Soviet border
	22 January	Roosevelt establishes War Refugee Board to assist relief and rescue of Jews
	27 January	Soviet forces break siege of Leningrad
	19 March	German troops occupy Hungary; beginning of roundup of Hungarian Jews under personal direction of Adolf Eichmann
	10 April	Soviet forces retake Odessa
	9 May	Soviet forces retake Sevastopol
	15 May	Deportation of Hungarian Jews to Auschwitz begins
	4 June	Allied forces enter Rome
	6 June	D-Day: Allied invasion of Normandy
	16 June	Hungarian government halts deportation of Jews
	22 June	Opening of Soviet summer offensive
	20 July	German military revolt fails
	23 July	Red Army liberates Lublin-Majdanek death camp
	1 August	Start of uprising of Polish Home Army (Warsaw Uprising)
	15 August	Allied landing in southern France
	18 August	Red Army reaches German borders in East Prussia
	25 August	Liberation of Paris; Romania declares war on Germany
	30 August	Soviet forces enter Bucharest
	3 September	Brussels liberated by Allied troops
	8 September	Bulgaria declares war on Germany
	12 September	Anglo-American forces reach German borders in west
	3 October	Surrender of Polish Home Army in Warsaw
	15 October	Fascist Arrow Cross government installed in Hungary by the Nazis
	18 October	Allies recognize Tito as head of Yugoslav state
	20 October	German city of Aachen falls to Allies
	3 November	British forces join in fight against Communist National Liberation Army in Greek civil war
	7 November	Roosevelt elected to fourth term as president
	27 November	End of gassing operations at Auschwitz; demolition of crematoria

	16 December	German counterattack in the "Battle of the Bulge" in the Ardennes
1945	15 January	Last German offensive in west fails; Allies resume forward march
	17 January	Red Army enters Warsaw
	27 January	Liberation of Auschwitz by Red Army troops
	30 January	Hitler's last radio speech
	4–11 February	Big Three (Roosevelt, Stalin, Churchill) meet at Yalta in the Crimea and decide on temporary division of Germany into occupation zones after the war
	13 February	Red Army takes Budapest
	14 February	Allied air raids devastate Dresden
	6 March	Allied forces take Cologne
	8 March	American troops cross Rhine River at Remagen
	19 March	Hitler orders "scorched earth" policy
	30 March	Soviet forces take Danzig
	11 April	Buchenwald liberated by Allied troops
	12 April	President Roosevelt dies and is succeeded by Harry S. Truman
	13 April	Soviet forces take Vienna
	15 April	Bergen-Belsen liberated by British troops
	16 April	Red Army launches its final assault on Berlin
	25 April	American and Soviet troops meet at Torgau on the Elbe River; United Nations conference opens in San Francisco
	27 April	Sachsenhausen liberated by Red Army
	28 April	Mussolini killed by partisans in Milan; Dachau liberated by American troops
	30 April	Hitler commits suicide in his bunker in Berlin; Admiral Dönitz appointed to succeed him
	1 May	Goebbels commits suicide in Berlin
	2 May	Soviet forces complete capture of Berlin
	8 May	Germany surrenders unconditionally
	23 May	Dönitz and other government leaders arrested; Himmler commits suicide

	July–August	Potsdam Conference confirms formation of Allied Control Council to govern Germany from Berlin
	6 August	Atomic bomb destroys Hiroshima
	2 September	Japan signs unconditional surrender, ending World War II
	20 November	Beginning of Nuremberg War Crimes trials
1946	16 October	Execution of Nazi war criminals at Nuremberg
1947	1 January	American and British zones of occupation combined into "Bizonia"
	5 June	Secretary of State George Marshall announces European Recovery Program
1948	21 March	Soviets walk out of Allied Control Council in protest against failure to create central German government
	25 June	Soviets blockade western land access to Berlin to protest introduction of new western currency and creation of separate West German state; Allies mount airlift to supply western sectors
1949	12 May	End of Berlin blockade
	23 May	Establishment of Federal Republic of Germany (FRG)
	15 September	Konrad Adenauer becomes first chancellor of FRG
	12 October	Establishment of German Democratic Republic (GDR) with Walter Ulbricht as head of the Socialist Unity Party (SED)
1951	10 April	West German parliament passes bill for rehabilitation and re-employment of civil servants removed from employment in the course of denazification
1952	10 September	The FRG and Israel sign agreement providing restitution payments to Jewish people
1953	5 March	Death of Stalin
1955	5 May	Paris Agreements give FRG full sovereignty with authority to rearm, without nuclear, biological, or chemical weapons; FRG joins NATO
	14 May	Soviet Union forms Warsaw Pact in response to German rearmament and membership in NATO
	15 May	Austrian State Treaty ends occupation

	September	Adenauer visits Moscow to open diplomatic relations between the FRG and USSR and to secure the return of remaining German POWs
1956	17 August	Communist Party outlawed in FRG
1960	23 May	Adolf Eichmann seized in Argentina and brought to Israel for trial
1961	11 April	Beginning of Eichmann trial in Jerusalem
	13 August	Construction of Berlin Wall separating East and West Berlin
1962	31 May	Execution of Eichmann
1965	21 April	West German parliament extends 20-year statute of limitation on prosecution of murder
	2 May	Full diplomatic relations established between FRG and Israel
1967	2 June	The killing of a student by a policeman at a demonstration against the Shah of Iran in Berlin precipitates militant student protests
1969	11 June	Further extension of statute of limitation on Nazi war crimes
	21 October	Willy Brandt (SPD) is elected chancellor
1970	7 December	Brandt signs treaty of reconciliation with Poland and kneels at memorial to the victims of the Warsaw Ghetto uprising
1971	3 May	Walter Ulbricht replaced by Erich Honecker as First Secretary of the SED
	3 September	Four-Power Accord recognizes special status of West Berlin
1972	17 May	The West German parliament ratifies treaty recognizing the GDR as a separate state within the German nation
1977	18 October	Leaders of the terrorist Red Army Faction (RAF) commit suicide in prison
1979	3 July	West German parliament votes to lift statute of limitation on Nazi war crimes
1982	1 October	Chancellor Helmut Schmidt (SPD) replaced by Helmut Kohl of the conservative Christian Democratic Union (CDU)

1984	6 June	Neither FRG nor GDR invited to participate in ceremonies commemorating the fortieth anniversary of D-Day landings
1985	5 May	US President Ronald Reagan joins Chancellor Kohl for a controversial ceremony at the military cemetery in Bitburg as an act of conciliation on the fortieth anniversary of the end of World War II
	8 May	West German President Richard von Weizsäcker reaffirms German responsibility for remembering the crimes of Nazism
1986–87		Historian Ernst Nolte's revisionism precipitates bitter historians' dispute (*Historikerstreit*) on the place of National Socialism in German history
1989	9 November	Opening of the Berlin Wall
1990	18 March	Elections in the GDR bring the CDU to power
	18 May	The FRG and GDR sign a treaty to unite Germany under the West German constitution
	12 September	Four victor powers and two German states sign a treaty in Moscow conferring full sovereignty on a united Germany and renouncing all German territorial claims arising from World War II
	3 October	Reunification of Germany with its capital in Berlin

Introduction: the problems of writing about National Socialism

Any new book on National Socialism, especially one presuming to provide a comprehensive history, must offer some justification for adding another volume to the hundreds of thousands of published works on this most thoroughly chronicled period in history. For 30 years I taught an undergraduate course entitled "Hitler's Germany." Although, of course, there is no dearth of material to assign in such a course (indeed, the most difficult task is to choose between the many outstanding books that are available), I was nonetheless frustrated by the lack of a brief, but comprehensive text that covered not only the period from 1918 to 1945, but also the nineteenth-century background and the post-1945 afterlife that I consider essential to understanding the Nazi[1] experience.

The purpose of this book is to provide a brief reconstruction of the history of Germany under National Socialism from 1933 to 1945 while placing this period in a larger historical context that extends from the nineteenth century up to the near present. It is intended to provide a brief but coherent narrative of the causes, the course, and the consequences of Nazism, doing justice to its antecedents in the nineteenth century and carrying the story of the impact of Nazism and its place in German public memory forward to the beginning of the twenty-first century. I believe it is useful to have within the covers of a single book not only an account of the years of the Nazi rise to power (the Weimar Republic) and the Third Reich, but also a discussion of how the history of Nazism unfolded in the wider context of German history.

History is interpretation

No historian, however, can justify his or her work solely on the basis of providing the "essential facts." Writing history is not separable from interpreting it. Even the most positivist and meticulously factual approach to history cannot avoid interpretation, if only in the selection of facts deemed worthy of presenting. In this book I present the interpretation that I believe is best suited to help generations born after the war to understand what produced this extraordinary historical phenomenon, how the Nazi regime functioned in practice, and why the Nazi dictatorship enjoyed so much popular support despite the fact that it is remembered today primarily for its massive genocidal atrocities and for the ruinous catastrophe it brought upon the German nation.

In particular I hope my book contributes to understanding key questions in any history of Nazi Germany: Why is our memory of the regime so different today than the perception of the regime in the eyes of so many of its contemporaries? How could a highly creative and progressive national culture generate such unprecedented barbarism and destructiveness? Early histories of the Third Reich tended to treat Nazism as a mysterious pathology, the incarnation of an evil force in virtuous guise that ultimately could only be accounted for metaphysically, as if the devil had directly intervened in human affairs. In view of the unprecedented horrors of the Holocaust and the irrationality of the Nazis' racial obsessions, the tendency to think of Nazism and its popular reception among Germans as beyond rational explanation is certainly understandable. Moral denunciations predominated in early accounts of the Third Reich, as if Nazism were entirely a moral problem, the triumph of evil over good.[2] After its failure and collapse in universal disgrace in World War II and after revelations of the atrocities of the Holocaust, there is no dispute about the perniciousness of Nazism. As justified as such moral denunciation may be—and surely no one could possibly deny the immorality of the Nazi regime—viewing Nazism entirely in moral or metaphysical terms does little to provide a coherent explanation for its extraordinary popularity and early successes.

History is past politics

The interpretation offered in this book is based on the assumption that politics provides the key to understanding and explaining National Socialism. In its shortest definition, history is past politics. The dialectic of historical development usually pits forces against each other, each of which perceives and defines itself as good and right. This skepticism about the analytical usefulness of moral categories is in no way meant to relativize the evil of Nazism; it is only meant to draw attention to the indisputable fact that between 1933 and 1945 many well-meaning people in Germany (and elsewhere) thought that Nazism was a positive and constructive movement. It falls to the historian to explain why this was the case. Even the most abhorrent feature of National Socialism, the virulent antisemitism that eventually led to the Holocaust, had a terrible logic of its own that the historian must try to explicate.

All interpretations are bound to generate some controversy as they provide a particular perspective that not everyone may share. That perspective is determined by the historian's values, particularly political values, which are usually, but not always, the values of the society or subgroup he or she lives in or identifies with. If the disagreement among historians is about basic historical facts, it can usually be readily resolved. But more often the disagreements between historians involve the meaning and importance of those facts. The same facts may be evaluated quite differently by different historians. "Objectivity," defined as value-neutrality, is not a given, unchanging standard against which subjective deviations can be measured. "Objectivity" is always constructed according to the conditions under which historical scholarship is practiced. Hence objective methods will generate different results depending on the perspective from which the historian is writing. That is why there are still many historical issues on which serious historians disagree, even though the basic facts are known and accepted on all sides and the contending historians are genuinely committed to sound scholarly practices and the objective evaluation of the evidence. This is particularly true for questions of historical responsibility, all the more so if the events in question, National Socialism and the Holocaust, are universally condemned. The almost universal perception today of Nazism as unmitigated evil has not diminished differences of opinion about its nature, significance, or causation.

Controversies about National Socialism

Despite, or perhaps because of, the almost universal condemnation of Hitler and his cohorts as exemplars of absolute evil, interpretations of National Socialism continue to generate heated controversy. Interpretations of Nazism are often used polemically to discredit opposing political movements and values by attributing to them some of the pernicious features of Nazism. There are examples in newspaper letters columns every day of efforts to discredit groups and movements by linking them in some way to Nazism (or the Holocaust). In the 1960s student radicals called university officials "Nazis" or "fascists" for summoning police to suppress their demonstrations and right of free speech; university officials, in turn, called the radicals "Nazis" or "fascists" for spurning civil discourse and adopting confrontational tactics. Because its ideology, ascent to power, and system of rule had so many contrasting—indeed contradictory—features, diverse movements can interpret Nazism in ways primarily designed to reinforce their own value system and policy priorities and to refute those of political opponents. "Nazism" or "fascism" have become convenient cudgels to be wielded against political attitudes or methods one is anxious to discredit. Because neutrality toward Nazism is hardly possible, interpretation of its origins, meaning, and causes has become a battleground between competing political orientations, whether of the egalitarian left, the liberal center, or the authoritarian conservative right.[3]

When communists linked fascism[4] to capitalism they genuinely believed they had pinpointed the source of the problem, but they were also deliberately seeking to discredit the capitalist system. Conversely, the Western ideological consensus at the height of the Cold War in the 1950s virtually mandated lumping the Soviet Union with Nazi Germany under the heading of totalitarianism. This was a deliberate attempt to discredit the Soviet system based on the honest conviction that Soviet and Nazi opposition to Western liberal democracy was the defining characteristic of their respective regimes. The fact that communists and fascists had fundamentally different ideological and political goals seemed almost irrelevant from the perspective of liberals who value individual freedom above all else. The political motives behind interpretations of Nazism are even clearer in the case of German nationalists who after the war sought to salvage their own conservatism by improbably linking the Nazis with what they hated most—popular democracy.

This book, however, is not about the controversies surrounding the nature of National Socialism.[5] Many of the more important scholarly controversies are dealt with in the book, to be sure, but that is not its major focus. Its major purpose is to provide a narrative survey in an interpretive framework. There are three major controversies, however, that I need to address at this stage to clarify my own perspective and interpretation.

The first, and perhaps most fundamental, controversy involves the location of Nazism on the political spectrum. In my interpretation, set forth in Chapter 1, Nazism is unambiguously a movement of the extreme right, the conservative end of the spectrum. In my view Nazism is a radical variant of fascism, the movement for national regeneration that arose in many countries to counter the perceived threat from communism and liberal democracy in the 1920s and 1930s. While very few historians place Nazism unambiguously on the left, the progressive (or egalitarian) end of the spectrum, a good number regard fascism as a mixture of left and right or a movement that is "neither left nor right."[6] Many such historians subsume Nazism under the rubric of "totalitarianism" to indicate that it is closer to communism than to other less radical forms of fascism.

A second major controversy involves the question of the German *Sonderweg*, or German exceptionalism. Should Nazism ultimately be traced to the "peculiarities of German history"[7] and culture or are its causes to be found primarily or wholly in the peculiar constellation of events in Europe after World War I? In my view, as set forth in Chapters 2–4, "the course of German history"[8] is essential to understanding the origins of Nazism and its accession to power.

A third major controversy, closely linked to the first two, involves the question whether Nazism should be understood primarily as a reaction against the forces of modernity (industrialization, democratization, rationalization, urbanization, secularization, commercialization, economic and political liberalization, social and demographic mobility, and openness to innovation and experimentation in the arts) or as an expression and radicalization of these very forces. Was it backward-looking or forward-looking or some ambiguous mixture of both? I will address each of these controversies in turn and make my own position clear.

Nazism as a movement of the right

The metanarrative in which the history and historiography of Nazi Germany is embedded is the conflict between those forces subsumed under the general headings of the "political left" and the "political right," short-hand terms that are useful in identifying basic attitudes to the ideal of human equality. Some readers will take issue with my resuscitation of a left–right distinction that some conservative publicists of the "end of history" would prefer to consign to the dustbin of history. In an era in which the two most extreme ideologies of the twentieth century—fascism and communism—have dissolved in ignominy, the distinction may no longer seem useful. We're all in the center now, the argument seems to be, and whatever differences arise between us can't usefully be understood in terms of "left" and "right." To be sure, some of the critics of the left–right distinction are themselves actively committed to right-wing policies. For them devaluation of the distinction between left and right is a way of neutralizing the reformatory challenge of the left.

The political climate in the West at the beginning of the twenty-first century does seem propitious for such a conservative initiative. The post-modern disillusionment with modern progress, the ideal of social justice, and the liberal democratic welfare state, not to mention the blow dealt to the left by the apparent eclipse of Marxism, has helped to tarnish the image of the "progressive" left. But these terms, "left" and "right," do retain their useful-ness, not only as descriptive and analytical tools for historians, but in every-day politics as well. While, for instance, concern for the preservation of the environment may today be shared by environmentalists of both the left and the right, there are still crucial differences between left-wing and right-wing solutions to this and other problems.

What is the nature of these differences? The essential difference between left and right lies in their respective attitudes toward human equality as a social ideal.[9] "Left" broadly denotes egalitarian attitudes toward human rights, social benefits, and political power (hence the left-wing partisanship for the impover-ished, disadvantaged, and otherwise excluded people of the world); "right" broadly denotes preferences for hierarchies of authority and power, whether based on birth, race, gender, ethnicity, talent, intelligence, wealth, or other traits that can be ranked on a comparative scale from inferior to superior. The more a movement deems absolute equality—legal, political, economic, or racial—among all people to be a condition worth fighting for, the further to the left it will be situated on the ideological spectrum. The more a movement considers hierarchy (and hence inequality) to be desirable and worth defending by all means necessary, the fur-ther to the right that movement will be. On the extremist fringes of this spec-trum are persons or movements who will go to any length to achieve their utopian ideal: on the left the egalitarian utopia in which the weak and the strong share equally in the benefits their society can provide; on the right the antiegal-itarian, hierarchical utopia in which the strong receive the benefits due to them by virtue of their natural superiority and the weak, however perversely defined, are viewed as dispensable, deprived of benefits, and excluded from power.

The terms "left" and "right" are most useful and least confusing when not overburdened by any criterion other than attitude toward human equality. Although historically left-wing movements have championed emancipation from oppressive government as a means to achieve greater equality and right-wing movements have defended traditional hierarchical forms of authority, the left–right distinction is *not* equivalent to the distinction between freedom and authority. Indeed, the extreme left favors authoritarian means as the optimal route to creating an egalitarian society. The communist regimes of the twentieth century have demonstrated that egalitarian goals and authoritarian means are not mutually exclusive. Conversely some libertarian movements preaching extreme individual freedom belong well on the right of the spectrum, because their ultimate goal is a society in which inequality is viewed as inevitable and is warmly embraced. What unites extremists on the left and the right is a dedication to their respective ideals so strong as to justify any means to achieve their desired ends. The essence of moderation, on the other hand, is to reject the extremist principle that the ends justify the means.

Part of the left–right confusion today is the result of the fact that self-styled American "conservatives" claim to oppose "big government" (and define "liberals" today as proponents of big government). Conservative advocacy of individual freedom appears to place them close to the champions of emancipation on the left, but their goals are very different, and it is the goals that ultimately are decisive for location on the left–right continuum. The goal of conservatives in liberal societies today is to curtail the power of government to bring about greater equality through social welfare programs and other means. In seeking to restrict the social (not the military) powers of government and in defending *laissez-faire* economics, most American conservatives today are really old-fashioned liberals, more akin to nineteenth-century liberals than to the nineteenth-century conservatives in continental Europe who championed the strong monarchical state, an established religion, and moral censorship. It is that latter conservative tradition—represented to some extent by religious fundamentalists in liberal societies today—to which Nazism and fascism are related in Chapter 1.

In liberal societies such as the United States or western Europe today most people, mainly self-styled liberals but including some who call themselves conservative, find themselves somewhere toward the center of the political spectrum. They favor personal freedom *and* social equality. Unfortunately at some point, of course, these two values must clash, as the legislation required to insure social equality must necessarily curtail the freedom from government regulation championed by supporters of *laissez-faire*. Those who opt for equality then find themselves further to the left than those who opt for freedom at the cost of equality. Of course, left–right distinctions are ideal-type models that are useful for analysis and do not necessarily correspond in every detail to a messy reality in which people can hold a left-wing position on one issue and a right-wing view on another.

Obviously, the left–right distinction is also quite different from the distinction between moderate and extreme. There are moderates and extremists on both sides of the left–right divide. Extremists are always authoritarian, intolerant, and collectivist, and usually inclined to deception and violence. These traits are not monopolies of either the left or of the right but are hallmarks of both extremes. Extremists cannot permit the deviation from or opposition to their desired ideal—whether egalitarian or inegalitarian—that individual freedom would entail. And they wish to impose their ideal on all others. If they did not seek to do so they would not be considered extremist.

The twentieth century has been a century of extremes. Communism on the left and fascism on the right share many characteristics. In totalitarianism theory, which has re-emerged to new life in the 1990s (see Chapter 17), they are treated as essentially alike. The ideals they so similarly and perversely pursued, however, were fundamentally opposed to each other. Communists wanted to create an egalitarian utopia ultimately embracing the whole world; fascists sought a utopia based on the natural and desirable inequality between individuals, peoples, and races. Communists tended to attract people who had something to gain from greater equality (hence its appeal to unpropertied workers); fascism tended to attract more people who had something to lose from rigorous implementation of the egalitarian principle (hence its disproportionate appeal to the middle and upper classes, including propertied workers). In their social policies communism disproportionately victimized the rich, the propertied, and the higher classes; fascism disproportionately victimized the poor, the "unfit," and what they defined as the "lower" races. Proponents of either system saw adherents of the other system as their worst enemies and fought them tooth and nail.

Some readers will take issue with my use of the term "counter-revolutionary" (rather than simply "revolutionary") to describe the fascist movements, including Nazism. The link to the continental European conservative tradition is in my view crucial to an understanding of fascism and to the strength of fascism in Germany. But that does not mean that fascism, and especially its German variant Nazism, did not have some distinctly anticonservative features. As I make clear in Chapter 1, these can best be understood as a radicalization of methods, many of them quite deliberately adopted from the practices of the communist foe (violence, propaganda, terror, techniques of mass mobilization, etc.). Fascists borrowed techniques from the left in order to fight the left better. The left–right distinction is defined by fundamental goals, however, which in the case of the left is to promote equality, in the case of the right to prevent it, in part by denying the existence or importance of inequality within the racial or national group, and by subordinating issues of equality to the more important goals of national rebirth and regeneration.

To label Nazism—the most radical variant of fascism—a revolutionary movement might make sense as a way of describing its ruthless and radical methods, but it obscures the fact that National Socialists employed these methods to prevent a revolutionary socialist transformation of the economy (the elimination of private property in the means of production), rather than to bring it about (despite the deliberately misleading use of "socialist" in the name of the party). That is why a better descriptive term for fascist movements is "counter-revolutionary," because it alludes to the basic fascist goal of preventing a wholesale transformation of property relations, while at the same time it acknowledges the extreme nature of the fascist project and the extent of transformation that actually took place under fascist regimes.

The German Sonderweg *debate*

In Chapter 1 I deal with questions that scholars have wrestled with for decades: What is fascism? Is Nazism a form of fascism? And how does fascism

(Nazism) relate to the other major political movements of the last two centuries? Two other questions have also generated a great deal of historical debate: Why did a particularly radical form of fascism come to power in Germany, and how is it possible that this happened in a country of such high culture, advanced technology, and long, proud historical tradition? These questions are addressed in Chapters 2–5, which deal with the historical background of German unification in 1871, the Bismarckian and Wilhelmine empires, German ideology, and World War I.

In thus going back to the nineteenth century in search of explanations for the rise and triumph of Nazism I appropriate some aspects of the so-called *Sonderweg* thesis, the notion that Germany's illiberal development was in some important ways quite different from West European models and that these differences help to explain many later events, including World War I and the German susceptibility to radical-right ideology. The *Sonderweg* thesis is discussed in more detail in Chapter 2. Its critics deny that German development was substantially different from the British model or that these differences can account for the triumph of fascism. Critics of the German *Sonderweg* come from both the right and the left. On the right, German conservatives hope by denying any "deviant" illiberal development to reclaim Germany's pre-Nazi past and thereby boost the national pride that was so badly damaged by the Nazi debacle. On the left, mainly British and American historians reject an interpretation that, by seeking the roots of Nazism too exclusively in Germany's "backward" institutions and "deviant" illiberal ideology, slights the potential for fascism in liberal capitalist societies.[10]

Chapters 2–5 seek to explain why the conflict between left and right was so fierce in Germany and why the right proved to be so strong. They are not an attempt to write an open-ended history of nineteenth-century Germany, the Bismarckian or Wilhelmine empires, or World War I. They quite consciously focus only on those aspects of German history that can provide clues to the eventual rise and triumph of Nazism. That does not mean that I believe that the rise and triumph of Nazism was the inevitable or necessary result of Germany's historical development. History is always contingent and open-ended and there are many possible outcomes at any given time. Nineteenth-century historians quite rightly object to treating nineteenth-century Germany as merely a preliminary stage to the rise of Nazism. Writing nineteenth-century history solely from the perspective of Nazism's later triumph cannot possibly do justice to the contingency and complexity of events as they occur. German history was certainly not propelled by an inherent teleological drive toward Nazism. Germany is certainly not the only nation to have developed self-congratulatory notions of its own inherent superiority to other national cultures and to have claimed the right to dominate the world on that basis. Nonetheless, Germany's historical development does provide insights that can help historians to understand and explain the German public's receptivity to Nazism. Whatever limitations the *Sonderweg* thesis may have as an all-explanatory historical trope, it retains its importance in underscoring the sense of positive exceptionalism that drove German nationalism in the nineteenth and early twentieth centuries and culminated in the Nazi conviction of German superiority to other races, peoples, and cultures.

Of course, the nineteenth-century past cannot provide anything more than a partial explanation for the triumph of Nazism in the 1930s. Far more important were the events of the interwar years discussed in Chapters 6 and 7. In that respect I am in full agreement with the critics of the *Sonderweg* who point to the Bolshevik Revolution in Russia, the defeat in World War I, the political conflicts of the Weimar Republic, and the crisis of capitalism in the Great Depression as far more significant to the triumph of Nazism than Germany's backward political development. The triumph of Nazism was neither a completely accidental aberration in German history nor was it a logical or necessary consequence of earlier German history, specifically its authoritarian, nationalist, and militarist traditions. Nonetheless, the recognition of continuities is essential to understanding the genesis of the catastrophic events of the twentieth century. That is why I devote so much space in this book to the "prehistory" of Nazism.

The modernization debate

One of the most contentious issues in the historiography of National Socialism is the question whether Nazism was an antimodern movement or a modernizing movement. This debate partly overlaps the *Sonderweg* controversy, in which the modernity of nineteenth-century Germany, relative to western Europe, was a hotly debated issue. But even proponents of Germany's "deviant development" never denied the highly efficient, dynamic, and advanced state of the German economy. It was the failure of German political liberalization to keep pace with economic liberalization that adherents of the *Sonderweg* thesis considered the key difference in Germany's development compared to Britain, France, or the United States.

Proponents of the *Sonderweg*, who saw Germany's failure to adopt such crucial features of modernity as political liberalism and democracy as the decisive flaw in its national development, tended to view Nazism as the logical culmination of this rejection of modernity. Based on the Nazis' own avowed opposition to the ideals of the Enlightenment and French Revolution, most historians assumed that the Nazis looked predominantly to the preindustrial, predemocratic, and premodern past for its social and cultural models. There is much evidence of antimodernity in the Nazi ideology of "blood and soil," which idealized a racially homogeneous agrarian lifestyle threatened by urbanization, social mobility, industrialization, the rise of an organized labor movement, and commercial exploitation perversely attributed to Jewish influence. Already in the nineteenth century politicians and publicists on the radical right drew their main support from groups such as master artisans facing economic decline because of the growth of big business.[11] The Nazis also appealed disproportionately to the hard-pressed "old" *Mittelstand*, the economically squeezed class of small proprietors (peasants, artisans, shopkeepers) who sought protection against the competition of big business and idealized a past in which they had formed the main producing group.

This view of Nazism as a reaction to modernity has come under increasing challenge, however, from historians who point out the obviously modern features of a regime that developed the world's most formidable military force in the early stages of World War II. No one can doubt the highly modern and efficient quality of the weaponry of the Third Reich, including its pioneering space technology, although Nazi rejection of "Jewish physics" may have contributed to their failure to develop nuclear weapons (see Chapter 10). The Nazis claimed to be ushering in a brave new world of scientific and technological innovation, sloughing off the detritus of the past, and reorganizing society to better meet the challenges of the future. The Nazis also sought to make use of the latest media technology to advance their essentially archaic ideological aims. American historian Jeffrey Herf coined the notion of "reactionary modernism" to designate this peculiar combination of modern and antimodern features in National Socialism.[12]

The modernization debate, like so many other historical controversies, also has political implications.[13] During the Cold War some adherents of the totalitarianism model described fascism as a "developmental dictatorship" to make the comparison to communism more plausible.[14] While a number of liberal historians agreed that modernization was an unintended consequence of Nazi rule, an outcome that contradicted the Nazis' own avowed aims, members of Germany's "new right" in the 1980s and 1990s insisted that modernization was a deliberate result of Nazi policy (see Chapter 17).[15] The political motive behind the "new right's" defense of Nazism as a modernizing dictatorship was to demonstrate that Nazism was no less progressive and no more reprehensible than Stalin's brutal modernization experiment in the USSR.

A more formidable assault on the notion of Nazism as antimodern was launched in the 1980s and 1990s under the influence of the postmodern disillusionment with the eighteenth-century Enlightenment's exaltation of human rationality. The Enlightenment's exaggerated promises of progress had proven empty in the light of the terrible catastrophes of the twentieth century. According to postmodern critiques, the homogenizing effects of Enlightenment rationalism, with its claims to universal truth and unavoidable marginalization of the nonconforming "other," contributed to the destructiveness of Nazism and the coming of the Holocaust. In this view, set forth most persuasively by the German historian Detlev Peukert (1950–90), Nazism was not antimodern so much as it was the embodiment of the "pathologies and dislocations of modernity" and the result of the "crisis of classical modernity."[16] In Peukert's view Nazi racial policy, including compulsory sterilization, eugenic abortion, euthanasia (the killing of the mentally and physically disabled), and the "final solution of the Jewish problem," exemplified a central feature of modernity, *Machbarkeitswahn* (the illusion that anything is doable), the belief that society could be renovated and social problems resolved through the application of biological principles and practices.

This interpretation highlighted the "modern," technocratic aspects of Nazi rule and suggestively linked the Holocaust and other Nazi atrocities to "scientific" eugenic schemes. However, it gravely understated the distinctly anti-modern features of both the Weimar Republic and Nazi Germany, most graphically demonstrated, perhaps, by the pervasiveness of antisemitism, which is itself historically linked to opposition to the social effects of modernization. Although it is important to understand the "logic" of Nazi racism and antisemitism and the processes by which the "pathologization" of difference and the dehumanization of anyone who did not conform to the "rational" norms of society legitimated Nazi atrocities, reducing these processes to pathological expressions of Enlightenment rationalism and modern scientific thinking distorts the roots and nature of Nazism. No doubt the instrumentalization of reason in the service of power has been an invidious and unintended legacy of the Enlightenment, but far more fundamental are the progressive values of liberty and equality to which the Enlightenment gave rise. It is in the *opposition* to these "modern," progressive values, in my view, that the roots of National Socialism must be sought.

In pointing to the modern features of the Nazi program Peukert in no way intended to offer an extenuating rationale for Nazi crimes. If he had any ulterior motive at all it was to warn against the complacency of assuming that modern industrial societies are immune to the barbarisms conveniently attributable to atavistic remnants of the past (which Nazism, in Peukert's view, was mistakenly taken to be). Peukert rejected the comforting notion that Nazi barbarism marked a relapse into the primitive past, warning that it might instead offer a preview of a potentially genocidal future. The apologetic possibilities inherent in the modernization debate were not lost, however, on conservative German revisionists who in the 1980s and 1990s deliberately played up the modern features of Nazi rule to show the regime from its best side. Their deplorable efforts to promote conservative policies by "normalizing" the history of Nazism and "relativizing" Nazi crimes led to the so-called *Historikerstreit*, a furious dispute among German historians that is the subject of Chapter 17.

The historicization of National Socialism

Neoconservative revisionists sought to take advantage of a generally perceived need for what came rather awkwardly to be called the "historicization" of National Socialism. The call for "historicization" (*Historisierung*) was first issued in a frequently cited article by the German historian Martin Broszat (1926–89) in 1985.[17] Broszat deplored the fact that historians too often failed to examine the Nazi past with the same empirical objectivity and sobriety with which they investigated other periods of history. Their moral revulsion, in Broszat's view, led them to view the Nazi experience as outside of history and impeded their efforts to understand long-range historical processes that spanned the period of the Third Reich. Numerous regional and local studies and specialized monographs revealed the complexities and contradictions of the National Socialist era, but comprehensive treatments of the period continued to suffer from a tendency to demonize the Nazi regime in a way that obscured the place of the Nazi period in German history and did little to contribute to historical explanation. Broszat disclaimed any intention of rehabilitating the Nazi regime or of mitigating moral condemnation of Hitler and his cohorts. He hoped to counteract the danger that perfunctory and stereotypical denunciations would become empty clichés without moral force or historical content and insisted that only authentic historical reconstruction could increase the sensibilities of later generations for the moral lessons and implications of the Nazi era. However, his plea for historicization could also be read as a defense of his generation's memory of the complexities and ambiguities of the Nazi era.[18]

The project of historicization became even more urgent, and even more fraught with potential pitfalls, in the wake of the movement in Germany, beginning with the so-called *Historikerstreit* of 1986–87, to "normalize" the Nazi experience and to free it of the stigma of unique criminality. This revisionism came to be associated most closely with the historian Ernst Nolte (b. 1923), whose avowed purpose was to reinterpret National Socialism in a more positive light. If the traditional strategy of German conservatives in the postwar era had been to downplay National Socialism as an historical accident, a deplorable but atypical and marginal aberration in the continuity of German history, Nolte's approach represented a bold new departure from earlier conservative apologetics. For Nolte, National Socialism was a justified, if excessively radical, response to the greater menace of Soviet communism. Indeed, the collapse of communism meant to Nolte that at least the "rational core" of National Socialism has been vindicated by history.[19] National Socialism was the only realistic alternative, he claimed, to communism, a movement that predated fascism and surpassed it in destructive intent.

It is in part to counter this kind of revisionism—dealt with in greater detail in Chapter 17—that this book was written. It seeks to combine interpretation and analysis of Nazism with a reasonably complete narrative of the most important events of the Third Reich and World War II. The bulk of the book, Chapters 8–15, deals with the years from 1933 to 1945. The last two chapters deal with the aftermath of Nazism, its place in German historical memory, and with what the Germans call *Vergangenheitsbewältigung*, the attempt to cope with and atone for the Nazi past.

The major purpose of this book is to put the Third Reich into the context of German history in an interpretive framework that makes the extraordinary events of this period comprehensible to nonspecialists but does not compromise the rigorous standards of historical scholarship nor conceal my own critical perspective from the social democratic left of the political spectrum. I hope it helps to make sense of a past in which the German radical right ran amok. I also hope it helps to ward off new episodes of radical-right rule under different circumstances and in different places, with all of the destructive consequences that this would entail.

1 Fascism and the conservative tradition

Fascist ideology, constituency, and conditions for its growth

Most historians interpret National Socialism as a radical and peculiarly German form of fascism, a movement and ideology that gained millions of adherents in many European countries in the era of the two world wars of the twentieth century. The term "fascism" was first used in early 1919 by the former socialist Benito Mussolini who had left the Italian Socialist Party in protest against their antiwar policy in World War I. The name was derived from the Latin *fasces*, the ceremonial bundle of rods and an ax that symbolized the unity and power of the Roman Empire. Mussolini turned his National Fascist Party into a militantly nationalist organization that attacked the "weakness" of liberal democracy. Its chief target, however, was the international socialist movement reinvigorated and radicalized by the Bolshevik Revolution in Russia in November 1917. In the years that followed, movements similar to Italian Fascism emerged all over Europe, particularly in Germany, Spain, Portugal, Romania, Hungary, and Croatia, but also in Poland, western Europe, Scandinavia, and even in the United States, where, however, fascist ideas never became dominant. Fascist movements inevitably differed from one another because each was dedicated to the revival and regeneration of its own particular national culture. Thus Italian Fascists evoked the glory of ancient Rome while German Nazis extolled the splendor of the medieval Hohenstaufen empire as well as the mythical past of the Nordic tribes who first settled in northern Europe. But all fascist movements shared certain political values, beliefs, methods, and common enemies.[1]

Historical antecedents

Although fascism was a twentieth-century movement that developed in the specific circumstances of Europe after World War I, its roots lie in the nineteenth century. To understand fascism, it is helpful to examine its historical antecedents and genealogy, which may be traced back to the great French Revolution that began in 1789. Out of this extraordinary convulsion there emerged the three major political ideologies that viewed the revolution in very different ways and competed for power and dominance in European countries in the nineteenth and twentieth centuries. These ideologies, though by no means monolithic or unchanging, may be broadly designated as conservative (or monarchist), liberal, and socialist, respectively. The strength of each ideology differed widely from country to country, as did its internal unity. In some countries, differences on specific policy priorities led to the formation of more than one political party within each ideological camp. Although these ideological movements and their political programs changed over time (which accounts for why the terms "conservative," "liberal," and "socialist" so frequently cause confusion today), each movement subscribed to certain fundamental goals and values that put it in conflict with the other two ideologies.

Monarchical conservatism

Today the term "conservative" is often used in a very general sense to describe a cautious political style or commitment to the status quo. "Conservatism" as the designation for a broad ideological movement in nineteenth-century continental Europe means more than merely a cautious attitude toward political change, however; it stands for a substantive political doctrine and a set of values that few "conservatives" share today. Nineteenth-century European conservatives viewed the French Revolution with loathing and disdain. French conservatives sought to reverse the changes the revolution had brought about and to restore the *ancien régime* (the prerevolutionary monarchical system). In other countries, conservatives sought to preserve the old order against the onslaught of the revolutionary ideas of liberty and equality. Conservatives favored a strong hereditary monarchy, aristocratic privilege (special rights for elite groups), and an established (i.e. state-supported) church. They believed in a divinely appointed natural order of authority and subordination. They desired a strong state that would mold character and use censorship and surveillance to uphold timeless moral and religious standards. Quite unlike most American and British conservatives today, who advocate a free market economy, nineteenth-century continental European conservatives favored an economy organized and regulated to enhance the power of the state. Indeed, social and religious conservatives who favor the legislation of morality bear a greater resemblance to nineteenth-century monarchical conservatives than do today's economic conservatives, who would probably have considered themselves liberals. European conservatives valued unity, authority, order, hierarchy, duty, and discipline, for which a powerful monarch provided the best guarantee. The main support for monarchical conservatism came from aristocrats and untitled elites who benefitted or hoped to benefit from their roles in a monarchical system, but conservatism also drew support from rural populations distrustful of changes in traditional practices or of challenges to traditional mores.

Liberalism

Liberals, on the other hand, supported the French revolutionary call for individual liberty and limitations on the arbitrary power of the monarchical state. Liberalism is historically defined by three major commitments: commitment to civil liberties or human rights, including freedom of speech, freedom of the press, and freedom of worship; commitment to a constitutional and representative form of government, entailing a separation of powers and an elected legislature; and commitment to private property and free economic activity. England developed a liberal system after the defeat of Stuart absolutism in the late seventeenth century, and the United States has never known any other system—which is one reason why many Americans have difficulty understanding European monarchical conservatism and the system of aristocratic privilege. In France, liberal institutions did not emerge until the revolution. In Germany, the liberal movement was much weaker and monarchical conservatism was correspondingly stronger than in western Europe for reasons that will be examined in more detail in Chapter 2.

Even in France the liberals' struggle against absolute monarchy was not definitively settled in the Great Revolution, as conservatives sought to salvage or restore as much of the absolutist system as seemed feasible under the changed postrevolutionary conditions. The conservative restoration after the overthrow of Napoleon in 1815 extended the struggle into the nineteenth century and led to renewed revolutionary outbreaks in Europe in 1830 and 1848. Liberalism originally defined itself by its opposition to the overweening monarchical state, which had led John Locke to enunciate his famous liberal principle: "That government is best which governs least." For early liberals the sole function of the state was the protection of life, liberty, and property (or, in Thomas Jefferson's words, "the pursuit of happiness"). Liberals advocated individual rights, a secular (nonreligious) state, equality of opportunity for all citizens, and equality under law. They sought to replace the absolutist system of privilege based on birth with a system of opportunity based on talent or merit. They believed in the possibility, indeed the inevitability, of progress, both social and technological, through the use of human reason. Liberalism drew its main support from the rising middle class of business and professional people (the *bourgeoisie*)—people of "common" birth but often of considerable wealth or property who chafed under their lack of freedom and political representation in absolutist monarchies.

Socialism

Toward the middle and late nineteenth century, as continuing industrialization led to the rapid growth of a new industrial working class and an organized labor movement, many self-styled liberals came to see socialism and the extension of democratic rights to the working class as a greater threat to their interests than to weakened monarchical absolutism. The socialist movement formed the third great political ideology of the nineteenth century. Its modern origins may be located in the radical phase of the French Revolution. For socialists, equality, even more than liberty, became the overriding revolutionary ideal. It is partly in response to socialist pressures that many countries, including the United States, eventually introduced changes that transformed free-market liberalism into the modern liberal system sometimes referred to as the "welfare state." This is one reason why in the United States the term "liberal" is commonly associated with support for the welfare state, while supporters of free-market principles are generally labeled "conservative."

The defining characteristic of socialism, as formulated by its leading theoretician, Karl Marx, is the elimination of private property in the means of production (commerce, industry, finance, agriculture, and natural resources). It is this fundamental principle that distinguishes socialism from all forms of liberalism, including the "welfare state." According to socialist belief, only the socialization or nationalization (state ownership) of wealth-creating property can assure the *economic* equality that liberal principles (equality of opportunity and equality under law) cannot guarantee because they do not prevent the strong from economically exploiting the weak in the free marketplace. Throughout the nineteenth century, socialism gained a growing constituency in Europe's increasingly organized labor movement of industrial workers and their middle-class supporters.

Most continental European socialist parties in the nineteenth century called themselves "social democratic." From their point of view, socialism was the most democratic system because it extended equal economic benefits to all members of society. After the Russian Revolution in 1917, the cataclysmic event that produced the first socialist state in history, hard-line socialists under Vladimir Lenin adopted the label "communist" to distinguish themselves from social democrats who wanted to combine a socialist economy with a democratic form of government. Lenin and Leon Trotsky abandoned Marxism's insistence on democracy, and they implicitly acknowledged this change by dropping the term "democratic" from the name of their party. Leninists believed that only an authoritarian political structure and one-party rule could successfully impose and defend a socialist economy under the conditions of early twentieth-century Europe. European Marxism was thus torn between the social democratic and the Soviet communist models, and adherents of these two different forms of Marxism became bitter foes. In the Cold War between the liberal west and the socialist Soviet Union after World War II, European social democrats in turn abandoned their commitment to socialism (the public ownership of the means of production) in favor of democratic process and welfare-state liberalism.

The left–right political spectrum

Historians usually describe the great nineteenth-century ideologies of conservatism, liberalism, and socialism with the help of a conceptual model that places these movements on a continuum from right to left in accordance to their preference for the hierarchical status quo (the right) or liberalizing and equalizing reform (the left). At the end of the twentieth century, with the eclipse of both the historical left (socialism) and the historical right (monarchical conservatism), the categories of "left" and "right" no longer seem as clearly definable as they were at the beginning of the century. The left–right distinction also seems dated today because of the new prominence of environmental issues, partially supplanting questions of economic distribution on which the left–right distinction has historically been based. A fundamental assumption of nineteenth-century industrial capitalism and its socialist critics—that continuous economic accumulation and expansion is possible—may no longer obtain today. Yet, the left–right distinction retains its usefulness for understanding the fundamental goals and values of political movements in the nineteenth and the twentieth centuries.[2]

The left–right terminology originated in the National Convention of the French Revolution. The more revolutionary factions sat to the left of the presiding chair, the more conservative deputies sat on the right. Deputies on the left favored reforms leading to greater liberty and equality; deputies on the right preferred more traditional arrangements and less radical changes. On the far left were movements that favored enforced economic equality; on the far right were Royalists who wanted to restore aristocratic privilege and the absolute power of the monarchy.

Equality was the fundamental value that determined the location of movements on the political spectrum. The greater the commitment to achieving full equality, the further to the left that movement was situated in the perception of contemporaries. The left advocated progress toward a more democratic society; the right stood for the maintenance or restoration of traditional hierarchies and social relations. On the extremes of the spectrum were those factions that advocated revolution—whether, on the left, to achieve equality and break down hierarchy or, on the right, to restore hierarchy and prevent equality.

What complicates this conceptual model, however, is the contradiction between revolutionary ends and means that emerged in practice after the Russian Revolution in 1917. For Bolsheviks (Communists) on the far left, the commitment to egalitarian social revolution was so great that any means—violence, demagoguery, terrorism, dictatorship—seemed acceptable to the achievement of their ends. This readiness to resort to extreme methods leads to the paradox, frequently observable in history, that the radical methods of revolutionaries of the left often undermined their proclaimed egalitarian and democratic goals.

Fascism as a movement of the far right

Because fascists, too, stopped at nothing in the pursuit of their ends, their methods and revolutionary rhetoric often resembled—sometimes deliberately so—those of their opponents on the extreme left. From the perspective of liberals, who value individual freedom and democratic process more than either economic equality or racial hierarchy, the similarities between extremist movements on left and right may even seem to outweigh the differences, and liberals often lump fascism and communism together under the heading "totalitarian." Because fascists often appropriated the vocabulary of socialism to enhance their appeal to industrial workers, many scholars have chosen to describe the fascist program as a mixture of "right" and "left."[3] In terms of their fundamental goals, however, the crucial determinant of location on the political spectrum if "left" and "right" are to retain their conceptual usefulness, fascism and communism belong on opposite extremes. It is helpful to conceptualize fascism as an extreme right-wing movement not only because it was dedicated to the destruction of Marxism and communism, but because of its fundamental opposition to the value of equality. Fascists regarded egalitarianism in any form, but particularly in the form of racial equality, as the source of the ruination of humankind. It was this opposition to equality and democracy and their eagerness to crack down on the left that made fascists so congenial to the traditional right-wing elites on whose help they depended to obtain power. In the perception of its contemporaries, fascism was a movement of the far right.

Location on the political spectrum is, of course, crucially dependent on the vantage point of the observer. Liberals of the Anglo-American and western European parliamentary tradition were perceived as left-wing by continental European conservatives in the nineteenth and twentieth centuries, but they were perceived as right-wing by socialists or communists. Liberals can legitimately lay claim to the center of the ideological spectrum, for although committed to equality of opportunity and equality under law, both of which were anathema to right-wing hard-liners, liberals oppose the infringement on personal liberty and freedom of choice that the left-wing effort to insure full social and economic equality necessarily entails. From the perspective of the far right before 1945, however, committed as they were to privilege on the basis of birth or race, liberalism and socialism appeared to be related to each other by virtue of their commitment to some form of equality or democracy. It is no coincidence that Nazi Germany and Fascist Italy fought against both the liberal west and the socialist Soviet Union in World War II.

After the destruction of European fascism in 1945, liberal and socialist societies were ranged against each other as mortal adversaries in the Cold War that ended with the collapse of communism and the relinquishment of Soviet control over eastern Europe in 1989–90. Because of the Cold War and its aftermath, the historical affinity of liberalism and socialism as movements that emanated from the Enlightenment and the democratic revolutions of the eighteenth and nineteenth centuries is less obvious today than it was to earlier generations. Despite their fundamental difference in respect to private property, both movements shared a commitment to the "democratic" values of the French Revolution, though liberals exalted personal liberty while socialists gave precedence to social equality. Nineteenth-century liberals were not necessarily democrats, if democracy is defined by universal suffrage. But they certainly wished to "democratize" the absolutist monarchies of prerevolutionary Europe.

Fascism, on the other hand, may be viewed as the radical culmination of the movement to resist the emancipatory and egalitarian currents that emanated from the French Revolution and were accelerated by the Industrial Revolution. Throughout the nineteenth century, conservative elites, nostalgic for the social privileges of the prerevolutionary *ancien régime*, fought a rear-guard battle against democracy; this struggle became more radical as industrialization and the growth of the labor movement increased the pressures for democratic participation and reform. Against the revolutionary ideals of liberty and equality, aristocratic conservatives invoked the traditional institutions of a strong central monarchy and privilege based on birth. Fascists embraced the aristocratic notions of pedigree and birthright and the aristocratic sense of inherited superiority. Fascists thought of themselves as reviving aristocratic warrior values in a decadent age corrupted by the democratic and commercial spirit of modernity.[4]

Continental European conservatives opposed the social consequences that industrialization invariably entailed: the transfer of wealth and power from the landed aristocracy to the industrial and commercial middle class, and the growth of an industrial working class increasingly conscious of its own specific interests. Of course, middle-class liberals and working-class adherents of socialism were increasingly at odds with each other as well in the nineteenth and early part of the twentieth centuries. But from the point of view of unreconstructed opponents of the French revolutionary tradition, both liberal and socialist movements shared an invidious dedication to liberalizing or leveling change. Fascists, the radical twentieth-century heirs to the antirevolutionary tradition, viewed liberals, notwithstanding their defense of private property, as the culprits who unwittingly or deliberately opened the floodgates to the advancing Red tide.

The relationship of fascism to traditional conservatism

This ideal-type reconstruction of the genealogy of fascism in terms of the historical conflict between right and left cannot do full justice to a complex reality in which individuals frequently change their political allegiance, and political movements share overlapping characteristics and aims. Many early fascists, including Mussolini, came from the left and brought with them—despite their disillusionment with left-wing policies—a revolutionary mentality and populist sympathies. One must be careful not to tar nineteenth-century conservatism with the fascist brush, nor to exculpate fascists by equating their more radical aims and methods with those of traditional conservatives. Fascists were certainly not conservative in the sense of wishing to defend existing institutions or return to the failed nineteenth century; rather they worked with radical fervor for a change of course that would root out the corruptions of modernity (foremost among them the movements of the left) and prepare the ground for national and racial regeneration. But one can hardly make sense of fascism if one fails to place this movement in the historical context of the long struggle waged by European conservatives against democracy of both the liberal and the socialist varieties. In an article in the Nazi Party newspaper *Völkischer Beobachter* on 6 June 1936, Hitler called himself "the most conservative revolutionary in the world."[5]

Fascists were quite different from traditional conservatives in morals and temperament, but they carried on the conservative campaign against democracy, albeit in the populist fashion required for success in an age of mass politics. Yet, it is no accident that in the countries where fascists came to power they did so with the indispensable support of conservative elites. Fascists shared with traditional conservatives not only their opposition to liberal or social democracy, but also their attachment to authoritarianism; nationalism; militarism; the aristocratic concepts of rank, pedigree, and birthright; and the martial virtues of heroism, courage, duty, obedience, discipline, and self-sacrifice. To the revolutionary triad of "liberty, equality, fraternity," conservatives and fascists juxtaposed the older triad of "authority, hierarchy, and order." It is also often forgotten, in the wake of fascist atrocities in World War II, that fascists gained electoral support by promising the restoration of "family values," traditional morality, and Christian religion.

The relationship of fascism to communism

In their fundamental goals and values, fascists and communists were fundamentally opposed to each other. Just as twentieth-century communism was ideologically linked to the nineteenth-century socialist tradition, so fascism represented a radicalized strand of the European conservative tradition. The inherent elitism of aristocratic conservatism made it difficult for conservatives to gain the kind of mass support needed to continue to wield power in an age of representative government and popular suffrage. To compete successfully with the new middle- and working-class parties that emerged in Europe in the latter part of the nineteenth or early part of the twentieth centuries, conservative groups increasingly experimented with various techniques of mass appeal, some of them pioneered by the left-wing parties they opposed. Fascists perfected these techniques to an unprecedented degree. If they bore a strong resemblance to the techniques of the radical left, this is not surprising, for fascists set out to combat communists with their own weapons. Fascists manipulated the masses by left-wing methods in order to convert them to the right. To compete effectively with socialists and communists for worker support, fascist parties adapted socialist slogans and symbols to their own ends. Fascist mobilization of the masses through propaganda, mass rallies, paramilitary formations, and orchestrated violence transgressed against traditional standards of political conduct in much the same way that communist practices did. Communists used extreme methods of mass mobilization to achieve a classless society; fascists used similar methods to create a society based on racial hierarchy.

The fascist constituency

Yet, the segment of the population from which fascism drew its maximum support turned out to be not industrial workers, who were under-represented both in fascist parties and in their electoral constituencies. Fascism attracted disproportionate support from middle-class groups, including the numerically large lower middle classes of white-collar employees and small proprietors, peasant-farmers, who feared the loss of their property and status, such as it was, if the socialist labor movement should become dominant. While the fascist mass constituency included malcontents from all classes, including nonunionized and unemployed workers, fascist movements primarily attracted groups such as small-shop owners, self-employed craftsmen, subsistence farmers, and others who feared both organized labor and the competition of big business in an unregulated economy. To occupation groups whose livelihood seemed threatened in an increasingly industrial society, fascism seemed to offer a "third way" between a socialism that favored wage-earning workers and a liberal capitalism that favored the rich. While fascists defended property rights and a competitive economy, they rejected the capitalist ethos of valuing private profit above the good of the nation as a whole. Nonetheless, fascism gained at least the tacit support of economic elites fearful of the labor movement and liberalizing social change. Fascism appealed especially to groups to whom socialism and liberalism seemed only to offer the prospect of economic and social decline.

Nationalism

Although fascists opposed modernity in the forms of democracy and liberalism, they enthusiastically embraced modernity in its nationalist form. Through nationalism, racialism, and moralism, fascists sought to counter liberal and socialist appeals to the economic interests of the middle and working classes. Here, too, fascists were the heirs of a radical nationalism that had been harnessed to the conservative cause in the latter part of the nineteenth century. Modern nationalism had originated as a democratic movement in the French Revolution. Democratic revolutionaries exalted the welfare of the nation above the narrow interests of the royal dynasty. By the end of the nineteenth century, however, nationalism had become a vehicle of conservative politics in Europe. The process by which nationalism, traditionally supported by liberals, was exploited by conservatives to weaken liberalism differed in each country, but was particularly pronounced in Germany and Italy, where national aspirations for unity had been frustrated for decades.

Nationalism lent itself readily to the struggle against liberalism and socialism. From a nationalistic perspective, these center-left movements could be condemned as selfish, materialistic, immoral, and antinational. Conservative nationalists accused liberals of giving the selfish profit motive and individual rights priority over the interests of the nation. Socialists, on the other hand, were condemned for their pursuit of the interests of a single class, the proletariat, and for their potentially treasonous advocacy of worker solidarity across national boundaries. Nationalists countered by calling for the subordination of individual and class interests to the interests of the national community as a whole.

Nationalism and racism—belief in the superiority of certain races—were particularly well suited to mobilizing mass support for illiberal ends, because they diverted popular energies from demands for reform and structural social change. Nationalists denounced liberal and socialist advocates of reform for supposedly undermining the unity of the nation by pitting individuals against each other or inciting class against class. Nationalism provided a way of integrating lower-income groups into a hierarchical social structure by offering them membership in a powerful national community as psychological compensation for the lack of material improvement in their lives. From the nationalist perspective, the tycoon and the wage laborer, regardless of the differences in their wealth and income, were by virtue of their common ethnic origins equally honored members of the national or racial community, each contributing their specific skills and services to the overriding national cause. Distributional conflicts about property and income resulting from liberal or socialist reform efforts could be made to seem petty, selfish, and antinational. Fascists exploited the demagogic possibilities of nationalism to their fullest potential. Fascism generated a kind of egalitarian consciousness of national or racial comradeship to compensate for the lack of true social or economic equality.

Preconditions for the rise of fascism

The social and economic roots of fascism lie in the nineteenth century, but it is the specific conditions of the twentieth century that made possible its rise and triumph in Italy and Germany. Fascist movements of varying strengths emerged in all European countries in the 1920s and 1930s (and in the United States as well in the form of movements like the Ku Klux Klan and the ideas of radio preacher Father Charles Coughlin). The only exception was the Soviet Union, which, however, underwent the ordeal of Stalinist dictatorship in the same period.

Thwarted nationalism

Three major factors fostered the growth of fascism in the era after the "Great War." The first factor was thwarted national aspirations. Fascism in Italy and National Socialism in Germany fed on the frustrations of nationalists who deplored the failure of their country to achieve the glorious objectives for which they had entered the war. Nowhere was disillusionment greater than in defeated Germany. But in Italy, too, which had fought on the victorious side and sacrificed millions of soldiers, nationalist disillusionment with a peace settlement that failed to award Italy its promised territorial spoils in the Balkans promoted Mussolini's cause.

Fascists and Nazis thought of themselves as continuing the war at home to a more successful conclusion. The enemies now were the internationalist, pacifist, and democratic forces that supposedly weakened and betrayed the nation in its contest with other nations. The war itself had provided a training ground for mobilizing the nation in a unified cause. The army with its ethos of discipline and unquestioning obedience served as the model for fascist organization. Disgruntled veterans returning from the front provided the manpower for fascist parties and paramilitary formations such as the Free Corps in Germany, Hitler's uniformed storm-troopers (SA), and Mussolini's *Fasci di combattimento*.

A perceived threat from the left

The second and in some ways the most important factor in the rise of fascism was the challenge posed by the Bolshevik Revolution in Russia in 1917. Fascism represented a violent backlash against the extraordinary threat that Marxist socialism seemed to present to traditional European institutions now that it enjoyed, for the first time in history, a national power base. Fascist parties were founded in the aftermath of World War I to offer workers an alternative to Marxist socialism and to lure them into the national camp; their proclaimed mission was to eliminate the radical left by "fighting fire with fire." It was mainly this anti-Marxist function that attracted the support of traditional con-servatives and even some conservative-minded liberals, who in Italy and Germany gave the fascists the aid they needed to obtain power.

Fascists were particularly valued as allies in situations where the left threat-ened to gain power. They also benefitted from the popular perception that lib-erals and traditional conservatives were too squeamish and genteel for the task of combating the revolutionary threat from the left. Where conservative elites were deeply entrenched and strong enough to suppress the left on their own, as in southeastern Europe, fascists were dispensable and fascist parties were correspondingly weak. Fascism was also weak in countries with strong liberal systems, such as western European countries and the United States, where democratic institutions proved adaptable enough to meet the challenge of the radical left without surrendering to the radical right.

Economic difficulties

Neither thwarted nationalism nor militant anticommunism might have resulted in the triumph of fascism in Italy and Germany if it had not been for a third major precondition for fascist success: economic contraction and depression. It is unlikely that Hitler would have obtained power legally if the economy of Weimar Germany had not been gravely weakened by the Great Depression. Mussolini, too, benefitted from the social strife that economic hardship precipi-tated in Italy after World War I. The services of his strike-breaking *squadristi* would not have been needed in a time of labor peace.

It is not surprising that the same conditions of scarcity and inequity that give rise to revolutionary movements on the left should also spawn counter-revolution on the right. Nothing radicalized members of the middle classes to a greater degree than the prospect of continued economic decline and the threat of a lower-class revolution. Just as economic crisis tended to radicalize wage-earning workers to the left, so people with status or property to defend were radicalized to the right. Fascism offered the promise of radical but non-Marxist solutions to the problems of capitalist economies at a time when the *laissez-faire* principles of classical liberalism seemed to hold out less and less hope for the "common man." If communists offered a way out of economic crisis through the abolition of private property, fascists offered a way out through the revival of national power.

Fascism defined

A movement as complex as European fascism resists easy definition, especially because its specific national manifestations invariably deviated to some extent from the universal "ideal type." Definitions are also complicated by the fact that fascists struggling for power against established authorities often behaved quite differently than fascists did when they had captured control of the state. The common denominator of fascist movements throughout Europe was commitment to the regeneration and rejuvenation of their own national communities, understood as communities of people related to each other by ethnicity, culture, religion, language, and homeland—in short by "blood and soil."

The rise of fascism can be best understood in the context of the great social transformations brought about by the democratic and industrial revolutions of the eighteenth and nineteenth centuries and accelerated by World War I. As a backlash movement against the humanitarian, liberalizing, and leveling tendencies of the nineteenth century, the "century of progress," fascism is easier to define by what it opposed—Marxist socialism, parliamentary democracy, constitutionalism, and political liberalism—than by what it advocated, which differed according to specific national political traditions. Whatever else it may have been, fascism was a political movement (and later a system of rule) to generate mass support by radical and violent means for antidemocratic and counter-revolutionary ends. It gained its adherents mainly among those groups that stood to lose ground as a result of the continued growth of movements identifying progress not only with technological advance, which fascists favored as well, but also with increased democratization and a more equitable distribution of material goods. Fascist ideology invoked the virtues of nationalism, authoritarianism, and militarism against the revolutionary values of liberty and equality. Because fascism promised national unity and solidarity, protection of the rights of private property, enforcement of law and order, and defense of conventional moral norms, it had special appeal to conservative elites. Fascism seemed to offer the best hope for an end to divisive class conflict and selfish individualism, a vigorous defense of the national interest, an efficient chain of command for decisive national action, and a new youthful vigor and readiness to make personal sacrifices for the national good.

If, nonetheless, there were substantial differences among the various national versions of fascism, this is in large part due to the fact that it is in the nature of all nationalisms to glorify their own inherited institutions and traditions. As a radical defense of their ethnic customs and traditions against the challenges of modernity and contamination from outside, fascism always appeared to embody the cultural traditions of the country in which it took hold. Thus Italian Fascists looked to the Roman Imperial past for inspiration, while National Socialists exalted Germanic tribalism, and leaders of the racist Ku Klux Klan idealized the "slave-holder democracy" of the pre-Civil War South. So strong were nationalist loyalties among fascists, in fact, that some French fascists joined the resistance when Germany occupied France in 1940.[6]

The radicalism of fascist movements was often linked to the scale of the perceived threat from the left. A form of racism and xenophobia was common to all fascist movements. Their search for ethnic purity and ideological uniformity led to their rejection of racial mixing and racial equality. But antisemitism often varied in proportion to the popular perception of Jews as leaders and beneficiaries of the progressive movements that fascists set out to destroy. Although the radical dynamic of fascism eventually led to the destruction of traditional institutions and class structure in World War II, this unintended denouement should not obscure the roots of fascism in the nineteenth-century opposition to liberal and social democracy. All fascist movements shared in common a determination to reverse the modern trend toward greater democratization. Insofar as traditional institutions, such as the aristocracy, proved inadequate to or uncooperative in this task, they, too, were sacrificed to fascist counter-revolution.

Why did the most extreme and virulent fascist movement emerge in Germany? And why did this radical variant of fascism succeed in gaining power in Germany while fascist movements in most other countries did not? The peculiarities of German history may help to provide answers to these questions.

2 The problem of German unity

Absolutism and particularism

A major question historians of Nazi Germany must confront is how a movement as barbaric as Nazism could have triumphed in a country of such high cultural creativity and refinement. Why, too, were the forces hostile to democracy so strong in a country that by the start of the twentieth century ranked second only to the United States in industrial strength? Are there clues in German history that may help to explain the triumph of the radical right in the years between the two world wars? Are there historical factors that can help us to understand the aggressive expansionism and destructiveness of Germany in the twentieth century?

The German *Sonderweg* (special path)

Some historians have suggested that Germany followed a course of development to modernity that differed in crucial respects from the western European model. While up to 1945 many Germans attached a positive value to these differences and proudly extolled their perceived exceptionalism, the ruinous outcome of World War II provoked a revaluation of the German *Sonderweg*. From a western perspective Germany's political development was tragically retarded by its failure to develop an effective democratic system before World War I. According to this view, the liberal movement in Germany was too weak to overcome the entrenched forces of monarchical government, the system of government in which power was concentrated in the hands of the ruler and a privileged elite dominated by the aristocracy. In contrast to the states of northwestern Europe, where absolutism was phased out by the early nineteenth century, there had never been a successful liberal revolution in Germany. In the nineteenth century most German intellectuals defined their country's national identity in opposition to the progressive (i.e. libertarian and equalitarian) ideas of the French Revolution. The *Sonderweg* thesis culminates in a major indictment of Germany's development: the German bourgeoisie failed to fulfill its historic mission of creating a liberal parliamentary form of government. The unfortunate consequence of this historic omission, so adherents of the *Sonderweg* thesis conclude, was the triumph of Nazism in the twentieth century.[1]

The *Sonderweg* thesis has been subjected to a good deal of criticism in recent years by historians who have pointed out that despite the failure of liberal revolution in 1848, the German bourgeoisie did dominate the economy and was quite successful in securing its interests through Germany's authoritarian political institutions.[2] Pinning the blame for Germany's "misdevelopment" on the preindustrial aristocratic elites who should have been displaced from positions of power is really a sophisticated way of freeing the German bourgeoisie of responsibility for the unfortunate course of German history in the twentieth century. Critics have also questioned the extent to which the mobilization of mass support for German nationalism and imperialism can be attributed to the conscious manipulations of the entrenched conservative elites, as implied in the *Sonderweg* interpretation. Finally, critics of the *Sonderweg* thesis have called for the abandonment of west European liberal democratic development as the normative standard against which German deviations are to be measured.

It would be wrong, of course, to view the richness and variety of German history solely through the prism of the Nazi experience or to exaggerate the uniqueness of German historical development. Every nation has its own exceptionalism. Yet even historians who question the notion of a German *Sonderweg*, or who criticize the liberal assumption that the English model of development is the norm against which all national traditions should be measured, do not deny the importance of historical continuities linking Nazism with the German past. The point is not whether Germany's historical development measures up to some normative standard of modernity or liberal democracy. The point is that Germany's undemocratic development can help us to understand why Germany fought two major wars with the western European countries in the twentieth century. Whether bourgeois society and development of the West is seen as normative or not, the different development of Germany helps to explain the conflict with the West that underlay the two world wars.

Most historians agree that while the triumph of Nazism was certainly not an inevitable consequence of Germany's problematic development, much less of some inherent deficiency in the German "national character," the Nazi phenomenon cannot be explained as merely the result of short-term factors or even explained away as an accidental aberration without any connections to the more distant German past. Even if the causes for the Nazi seizure of power must be sought mainly in the events of the 1920s and 1930s, the constellation of political forces that made possible the Nazi takeover was itself in part the product of earlier developments in German history. German society may not have been fundamentally different from western European societies, but we still need to account for the fact that Germany alone of the industrialized countries generated a peculiarly radical form of fascism. Though Germany was certainly not foredoomed to Nazism and emphasis on the "peculiarities" of German history should not distract historians from the general causes of fascism, there are nonetheless long-range factors that can help to explain why Germany (and Italy, too) succumbed to forms of fascism while western European countries successfully resisted the trend of the times.

Particularism and its effects

Perhaps the most obvious way in which German (and Italian) development differed from western models was the late date at which Germany and Italy became unified nation states. It was sometimes forgotten, in the outrage over the division of Germany after World War II, that Germany had been fragmented into numerous sovereign states throughout most of its history. A unitary German state has been the exception, not the rule. Before 1990 a unified and sovereign German nation state had existed for only three generations, from 1871 to 1945. (If German Austria is included, then Germany may be said to have been unified under one government only from 1938 to 1945.) Particularism, the system that left each German state free to govern itself and promote its own interests without reference to the good of the German people as a whole, has left its stamp on German history. The failure of liberalism and democracy in Germany up to 1945 is closely related to its particularist heritage. Germany's delayed unification had the effect of reinforcing existing authoritarian and antidemocratic values and institutions. The threat that regionalism and other residual particularist forces in German society presented to German unity even after formal unification in 1870–71 may also help to explain the radicalism of German nationalism in the nineteenth and twentieth centuries.

Although a vague sense of German national consciousness has probably existed for more than a thousand years among the Germanic peoples who inhabited central Europe, Germany has never had naturally defined geographical frontiers nor a state that fully coincided with the area inhabited by German peoples. From the late Middle Ages sovereignty in Germany rested with the more than 300 principalities of the Holy Roman Empire of the German nation. If its lineage is traced to Charlemagne, who revived the title of Roman emperor in the year 800 and made the German city of Aachen his northern capital, the first German Reich (empire) survived for more than a thousand years. Numerous festivals were held throughout Germany in the year 1843 to commemorate the millennial of the founding of a German state under the Treaty of Verdun of the year 843, which divided the empire among Charlemagne's grandsons, with the eastern part going to "Louis the German." Formally founded by Otto the Great in the year 962, the Holy Roman Empire achieved its greatest size and strength in the twelfth and thirteenth centuries under the Hohenstaufen emperors Frederick Barbarossa, Henry VI, and Frederick II, figures who would loom large in German national mythology up to the twentieth century. But unlike England or France, which developed strong national monarchies in the early modern period, the Holy Roman Empire emerged from the Middle Ages a weak and fragmented entity. Even the fabled Hohenstaufen emperors were unable to prevent the emerging sovereignty of territorial princes and the fragmentation of the Reich. The Holy Roman Empire, however splendid its name, was unified in name only. Aptly described by Voltaire as neither holy, nor Roman, nor an empire, this historical atavism was moribund long before its final dissolution in the wake of Napoleon's conquests in 1806.[3]

The bitter fruit of Germany's political and religious divisions was the Thirty Years' War (1618–48), which left the Empire a shadow and sealed German fragmentation and backwardness. What started as a German civil war with Emperor Ferdinand II leading the Catholic forces against the states of the Protestant Union soon turned into a war conducted by foreign powers such as France and Sweden on German soil. It took Germany more than a century to recover from the material devastations and population losses of this terrible war. The political and psychological legacy of the war lasted even longer. The Thirty Years' War lingered in popular memory as the great national misfortune that served as an object lesson in the fateful consequences of national weakness and disunity.

This historic lack of German unity, compounded by the absence of natural boundaries, left Germany prey to foreign intervention. Toward the end of the seventeenth century Louis XIV exploited Germany's internal divisions to seize territories on the German frontier, including the provinces of Alsace and Lorraine that were to be so hotly disputed in the nineteenth and twentieth centuries. Only the opposition of other European powers, notably England, kept France from annexing the entire left bank of the Rhine, at least until the Napoleonic period.

Absolutism and its effects

Germany's fragmentation compounded the oppressive and stultifying characteristics of seventeenth- and eighteenth-century absolutism. Whereas in France the rise of absolutism in the wake of the religious wars served to strengthen the central monarchy, in Germany absolutism's beneficiaries were the rulers of the many separate territories. Standing armies and centrally organized administrations, legacies of the wars that had weakened or destroyed the autonomy of the Estates (the representatives of the clergy, the aristocracy, and the urban patriciate), now served the princes as means to consolidate their rule—at the cost, to be sure, of any sense of a common German nationality, which emerged in the eighteenth century as a cultural ideal without any political reality.

Absolutism entrenched in hundreds of German principalities had enduring and debilitating consequences: it fortified the social and economic privileges of a narrow aristocratic caste, degraded the condition of the peasantry, obstructed the emancipation and political education of the middle classes, established the bureaucracy and army as the backbone of the government, and perpetuated the rigid stratification of a society in which each group had its predetermined place. Absolutist governments functioned not for the welfare of their subjects, but for the perpetuation of their own power and glory. Rigid regimes, organized according to a static conception of divinely assigned social roles, left little scope for individual initiative or popular involvement in public affairs. The proverbial German subservience to authority was firmly rooted in an absolutist tradition that endured far longer in Germany than in western Europe.

Prussia

The northern kingdom of Prussia, the largest of the German states after Austria, typified both the strengths and the weaknesses of the absolutist system.

Expanding its territory in the seventeenth and eighteenth centuries through a combination of dynastic inheritance and military conquest under its energetic ruling dynasty, the Hohenzollerns, Prussia became a power strong enough to challenge Habsburg Austria's traditional dominance in Germany. But the glory of Prussia's military exploits under Frederick the Great concealed the basic weakness of absolutism, even of the "enlightened" variety: the lack of popular involvement and identification with the monarchical state. At the very time that revolution swept away privileges based on birth in France, the privileges of the *Junkers*, the land-owning aristocracy east of the Elbe River, were reaffirmed in the Prussian Code of 1794.[4] Prussia, and later Germany as a whole, would define itself by its opposition to the democratic values of the French Revolution. The gap between the rulers and the ruled, symbolized by Frederick the Great's practice of speaking French with the peers at his court while speaking German (it was said) only to his soldiers and his horses, helps to account for the Prussian collapse in the face of the Napoleonic onslaught in 1806–07.

Yet Prussian absolutism proved remarkably impervious to the emancipatory currents that swept over Europe during the French Revolution and the Napoleonic Wars. Those areas of Germany that came under French occupation were, of course, greatly affected by the reforms that Napoleon or his agents imposed. In wide areas of western Germany the revolutionary principles of equality under law, disestablishment of religion, and careers open to talent informed changes in government and society. Even in Prussia, which survived as an independent state thanks to the intercession of Tsar Alexander I of Russia, the successes of Napoleon's citizen armies virtually forced Prussian leaders to adopt a series of reforms designed to combat public apathy and stimulate greater popular involvement in the fortunes of the monarchy. The purpose of the Prussian Reforms, however, was only to strengthen the traditional system to meet the Napoleonic challenge, and the reformist direction was abandoned after Napoleon's defeat in 1815. It was not the last time that Prussian monarchism would demonstrate its capacity for assimilating the new to reinforce the old.

The German Confederation

The victory over Napoleon strengthened the old order in Germany and in Europe as a whole. The peace settlement of 1815 was based on the principle of monarchical legitimacy, restoring traditional ruling houses to power. To be sure, the changes of the Napoleonic era left their imprint on the newly established German Confederation, reduced now to 39 states. But particularism triumphed once more, and the absolutist tradition remained dominant. Popular wishes for freedom and self-determination were ignored by the peacemakers at the Congress of Vienna, who were determined to stifle revolutionary liberalism and nationalism. Prodded by the Habsburgs' chief minister, Clemens von Metternich, the states of the German Confederation took measures to suppress the liberal movement for national unification under a representative government. Although Metternich is justifiably celebrated as the architect of a European balance of power that restored peace to a war-torn Europe, the basic goal of his conservative regime was "to root out all traces of French revolutionary ideology."[5]

The failed revolution of 1848

Both the strength and the limits of the liberal movement in Germany were starkly revealed in the revolutions of 1848–49. In that year, in A. J. P. Taylor's famous phrase, "German history reached its turning point and failed to turn."[6] The forces of monarchical conservatism, never entirely displaced from power even at the height of the revolutionary tide in the spring of 1848, reasserted their control in the end. A historic opportunity to set Germany on a democratic path was lost when Frederick William IV of Prussia turned down the Frankfurt Assembly's constitution for a limited German monarchy. Refusing to accept a crown "from the gutter," the Prussian king rejected any limitation on monarchical sovereignty. Instead he sent troops into the free city of Frankfurt to disperse the constitutional assembly and crush the liberal movement.

Historians have long debated the reasons for the failure of 1848 after such promising beginnings. Foremost among these are the lack of agreement in the liberal camp on the scope of democratic reforms and on the boundaries of a united Germany; the dependence of the liberal leadership on the support of artisan workers who did not share the liberal goal of a free, unregulated economy without protection for small proprietors; and the excessive caution of liberal leaders in failing to depose the ruling princes when they had the chance (if indeed they did).[7] The question of whether to include Austria in a united Germany was complicated by the multinational composition of the Habsburg Empire, of which only the German portion in the west was part of the German Confederation. The competition of Austria and Prussia for dominance in Germany was a major obstacle to plans both for a "greater Germany" (with Austria) and a "lesser Germany" (without Austria). Whatever the weight attached to specific causes, the legacy of absolutism and particularism proved too tenacious for the liberal movement to overcome. The proliferation of German states meant that revolution had to succeed in many different arenas and could be crushed piecemeal by the conservative reaction. The persistence of preindustrial and predemocratic values and institutions helps to explain why the constituency for liberal change was ultimately too small and disunited to sustain the revolutionary movement.

To be sure, too exclusive a focus on the failure of 1848 may well exaggerate the importance of political revolution while slighting the real changes that occurred in civil society in the course of the nineteenth century. The 1848 revolutions undoubtedly spurred the introduction of economic (and some political) changes that served middle-class interests and set the foundations for liberal capitalism and industrial takeoff in Germany. It is probably fair to say that failure of the liberal revolution in 1848 is of greater symbolic than substantive importance as an indication of how Germany's development differed from the western constitutional model. But differences there were, and these tended to grow rather than decline in the years after 1848. While economic liberalization removed obstacles to industrial expansion in Germany as it did elsewhere in western Europe, autocratic institutions remained firmly entrenched, particularly in Prussia. It was not only in Germany, of course, that members of the bourgeoisie (or economic and professional middle class) came to accept authoritarian rule and to make common cause with aristocratic conservatives against mass democracy. But nowhere in northwestern Europe were the forces arrayed against democracy so strong.

The unification of Germany under Prussia

One need not intone the moralistic clichés of liberal "default" or middle-class "abdication" of its true interests to make the point that German liberal democracy was stillborn.[8] That it remain so was the goal of the great Prussian statesman, Otto von Bismarck, who dedicated his talents to shoring up Prussian monarchical institutions against the liberal and democratic movements. Perhaps his most remarkable achievement was to have ultimately gained the assent of so many erstwhile liberals to the inherited monarchical system. He did this by shrewdly manipulating nationalist aspirations for unity to attain illiberal ends.

Named Prussian prime minister in 1862 on the strength of his record as a hard-line conservative who counseled hard-nosed realism (*Realpolitik*) to defend the interests of the Prussian monarchy, Bismarck successfully defeated the efforts of the liberal majority in the Prussian parliament to make the government more responsible to their will. The issue on which the parliament sought to make its stand was the government's demand for appropriations to expand the Prussian army. Taking advantage of the fact that the government controlled the machinery to raise revenues, Bismarck simply disregarded the refusal of parliament to approve his budget requests. The great issues of the day, Bismarck told the Budget Committee of the parliament, would be solved not by majority votes—that, he said, was the mistake of the Frankfurt Assembly in 1848—but by "iron and blood."

Bismarck eventually gained the support of most liberal nationalists by his charismatic leadership in bringing about, through a series of successful wars, the national unification that liberals had been unable to attain by parliamentary process in 1848. After Prussia's decisive victory in 1866 over Austria, which opposed the unification of Germany under Prussia, a majority of Prussian liberals retroactively approved Bismarck's high-handed treatment of parliament in the budget crisis of 1862–63. Overawed by Bismarck's stunning success on the battlefield, most liberals embraced his power politics even at the cost of parliamentary government.[9] By his policies of national unification, Bismarck got most German liberals to accept monarchical conservatism.

Nationalism triumphs over liberalism

Bismarck's success was capped by the founding of the German Empire as the war against France approached its successful conclusion in January 1871.

Liberals faced the predicament of having to choose between national unification and a truly constitutional system in which the government was responsible to the parliament. Support for Bismarck, whose use of Prussian power had made German unification possible, meant acceptance of the Prussian monarchical system, which Bismarck was determined to transfer to the newly founded *Reich*. Yet liberals found it very difficult to oppose Bismarck on constitutional grounds when this entailed, in effect, the rejection of the long-standing liberal aim of a unified German nation. Allegiance to nation now seemed to require the abandonment of liberal demands for a strong legislature and parliamentary process. When forced to choose between support for or opposition to Bismarck, most erstwhile liberals put nationalism ahead of liberal and constitutional goals. Liberals who supported Bismarck formed the National Liberal Party, whose very name suggested the priority that nationalism now received.

Before 1848 liberals and nationalists in Germany (and Italy as well) had shared a common enemy: the monarchical conservatives who sought to maintain the "legitimate" dynastic regimes of the separate German states and thus prevented both constitutionalism and unification. Liberals and nationalists shared a common goal: destruction of the absolutist and particularist regimes that blocked both representative government and national unification. That is why traditional conservatives like Metternich expended so much energy in suppressing the middle-class movements for liberalism and nationalism. Liberals tended to be nationalists, and vice versa, for how better to achieve both liberal and nationalist aims than under a national government based on popular consent? The events of 1848 revealed this project to be unattainable by democratic process or, for that matter, by revolution. Bismarck's unification of Germany under the Prussian monarchy effectively dissolved the historical connection between liberalism and nationalism in Germany and helped to transform nationalism from a democratic creed into a vehicle of conservative politics. Although Bismarck shared Metternich's monarchist values, he was far more willing to indulge German nationalism and to sacrifice the dynasties of the separate German states to German unification. Bismarckian unification committed the German nation to the values and institutions of Prussian monarchism. It marked the triumph not of liberal nationalism but of Prussian patriotism and particularism. German unification led not to the defeat of absolutism and particularism, but ultimately to their triumph in a modified and modernized form.

The German Empire

Historians sometimes refer to the unification of Germany as the expansion of Prussia, not only because unification was achieved through the force of Prussian arms, but also because so much of the Prussian monarchical system was effectively transferred to the second German *Reich*. Bismarck did permit election to the Reichstag, the German parliament, by universal manhood suffrage (elections to the Prussian *Landtag* continued until 1918 to be based on a system weighted in favor of the *Junkers*, the landed aristocracy of eastern Prussia), partly on the assumption that the mass of the German peasantry would vote conservative. He failed to foresee the rapid transformation of German society as a result of industrialization.

Ironically, it was Bismarck's hope of tapping popular resentments against an unregulated liberal economy that made him concede universal suffrage for males over the age of 25 despite his opposition to democracy. Although Bismarck came to regret this concession to popular sovereignty, it seemed of little importance in view of his success in restricting the powers of the legislature. The Bismarckian constitution created the semblance of parliamentary government without its substance. The Reichstag was limited in its powers to initiate legislation and had virtually no control over government finances, appointments, or military affairs. While in theory the Reichstag controlled the purse strings, it had no power to do so in practice, as the machinery to raise tax revenues was controlled by the government. The power to authorize war rested entirely with the executive. The Reichstag did have the right to approve legislation brought to it by the government, but it could not impose its will on the government, for the chancellor was answerable to the emperor alone and was secure in his post as long as he had the kaiser's confidence. The chancellor, in turn, appointed all government ministers without parliamentary oversight or approval. The government was not affected by the outcome of Reichstag elections as electoral results did not mandate any change in the government. Election districts created in 1872 would remain unchanged despite the growing urbanization of the country. To underscore the independence of the government from the parliament, the constitution prohibited officials from sitting in the Reichstag and put the operations of the civil service beyond parliamentary control.[10]

The *Bundesrat*, the upper chamber made up of appointed representatives of the 25 German states, played a more important role in legislation than the Reichstag. Bills were prepared in the *Bundesrat*; after Reichstag approval bills were returned to the *Bundesrat* for final approval. The *Bundesrat* was controlled by the numerically dominant Prussian delegation and through them by Bismarck, who retained his post as Prussian prime minister while serving as chancellor of the Reich. Prussia had enough votes in the upper house to block any changes to the constitution, which required a two-thirds majority. Moreover, no constitutional change was permitted in respect to rights expressly granted to any of the states without the approval of that state. Although after 1910 government ministers were required to answer questions in the Reichstag, a step toward British-style parliamentary government, the government was not required to act on any resolution passed as a result of a parliamentary interpellation. The Reichstag remained what the American ambassador to Germany in 1913 called "nothing but a debating society."[11] While debates in the Reichstag certainly influenced public opinion, the Reichstag had no control over policy.

The constitution put the institutional machinery for the containment of liberal and social democracy in place. But social and economic developments of the late nineteenth century created renewed pressures for democracy in the newly created Reich. The resultant tension and conflict help to explain the volatility and aggressiveness of the German Empire at the beginning of the twentieth century.

3 The German Empire

The containment of democracy, social imperialism, and the road to war

The empire founded under Bismarck's leadership lasted for 47 years, collapsing at the end of the first of the two great world wars of the twentieth century. The kaiser was forced to abdicate in November 1918, bringing to a close a war that was in good part the result of imperial overreach. But German imperialism was far from finished despite defeat in World War I. It would take another world war to put an end to Germany's imperial ambitions.

Historians continue to debate the degree of continuity between German aims in the two world wars. Of course, Germany fought World War II under far more radical and bellicose leadership than it did the first. Yet from a long-range perspective the two world wars form part of a Thirty Years' War in which Germany sought to reinforce its dominance in Europe and gain the status of a world power.[1] What were the sources of German aggressiveness in the twentieth century? Why did a united Germany generate such expansionist momentum? How did Bismarck's 20-year tenure as German chancellor contribute to this process?

Bismarck's foreign policy

It was not in the realm of foreign policy that Bismarck paved the way for German expansionism. Once unification had been achieved, Bismarck renounced further expansion in Europe in order not to jeopardize the survival of the newly founded Reich. His military alliances with Austria-Hungary and Russia were designed only to maintain the new balance of power on the continent and to prevent France from regaining its earlier dominance. To be sure, his successful employment of force in the wars of unification seemed to validate the axiom that "might makes right." Those splendid victories seemed to confirm the legitimacy of using power in the pursuit of self-interest. But Bismarck's *Realpolitik*, for all his cynical machinations, placed a premium on a realistic assessment of national power and on the responsibility of statesmen for the consequences of their acts. According to the principles of *Realpolitik*, policies must be judged by their outcome, not their intentions, no matter how commendable these may be. Bismarckian realism and caution were precisely the qualities that were lacking in German diplomacy in the events that led up to the two world wars.

Bismarck's domestic policies

Yet Bismarck was not entirely without responsibility for the failure of German diplomacy after his dismissal from the chancellorship in 1890. Ironically, it was his domestic policies that contributed most to the structural defects and eventual political crisis of the regime. His life's work was dedicated to the preservation of the Prussian monarchical system. He opposed not only liberal initiatives toward parliamentary government, but also the "states' rights" federalism of the newly created Catholic Center Party.

The target of his attack on political Catholicism in the 1870s (which Bismarck called a *Kulturkampf* [*culture war*]) was not Church doctrine, but rather the separatist forces that supposedly threatened the unity of the young Reich and the dominance of Protestant Prussia within it. This conflict between Church and state was precipitated by the Vatican Council's promulgation of the doctrine of papal infallibility in 1870, raising doubts about the loyalty to the Reich of the predominantly Catholic states of Bavaria, Baden, and Württemberg (all of which had fought against Prussia in 1866) as well as the Catholic provinces of Prussia in the Rhineland and in the Polish east. Once the Center Party demonstrated its loyalty to the Crown, Bismarck called off a struggle that for some liberal ideologists (but not for Bismarck) had become an anticlerical crusade. Assured of autonomy for the Church, the Center Party was in fact to become a reliable supporter of monarchical interests in the decades to come.

Suppression of the Social Democratic Party

The greatest threat to traditional monarchical institutions came not from the National Liberal Party or the Catholic Center, both of which were more or less successfully assimilated into the imperial system, but from nascent Social Democracy. Founded in 1875, the Social Democratic Party (SPD) represented the interests of the growing number of industrial workers in Germany. The SPD was to become the strongest force for democratization in Germany until its suppression by the Nazis in 1933. Revolutionary in rhetoric, especially after its formal adoption of Marxist social analysis in its program in 1891, but largely reformist in practice, the SPD sought to bring about a socialist economy through democratic and parliamentary means. While the SPD proclaimed its commitment to the public ownership of the means of production (especially large-scale industry), its immediate goal was a more democratic form of government through which the interests of workers could be pursued more effectively.

Bismarck's response to the SPD challenge was repression. In 1878, using two assassination attempts on the kaiser as a pretext for action, Bismarck gained the approval of a majority of National Liberals in the Reichstag for measures restricting the SPD's organizing and publishing activities. The party leadership was effectively driven underground. This infringement of civil liberties, coupled with the government's campaign for protective tariffs for the benefit of large-scale agriculture and industry at the expense of German consumers, further weakened the progressive wing of the liberal movement in Germany. Again Bismarck confronted German liberals with a choice that tested their commitment to liberal principles. Would they defend the right of political dissent and oppose Bismarck's antisocialist legislation? A majority of National Liberals jettisoned liberal principle out of fear of the labor movement.

Such surrender of liberal principles has been cited by some historians as evidence of the "feudalization" of the middle classes in the German Empire.[2] Whether or not members of the bourgeoisie adopted or imitated aristocratic values and cultural practices and deferred to aristocratic political leadership is a debated question. Other historians insist that the notion of "feudalization" distorts the self-confidence with which the bourgeoisie pursued its own interests. They maintain that "bourgeoisification" of the aristocracy is a more accurate description of the alignment of middle-class and aristocratic interests.[3] But that there was such an alignment is not in dispute. Bourgeois economic elites and their representatives in the National Liberal Party joined aristocratic conservatives in defense of the autocratic regime. Such a convergence of interests occurred in other countries in the late nineteenth century as well. In Germany the cooperation of large-scale industry and agriculture helped to maintain the political status quo. The economic basis for this so-called alliance of "rye and steel" lay in the mutual interest of industrialists and estate owners to exclude foreign competition from the domestic market through high tariffs. The propertied classes shared a common political goal as well, of course: the prevention of popular democracy.

German industrialization

The containment of democracy under Bismarck's leadership reinforced the growing asymmetry between Germany's economic and political development. Once the conditions for industrial takeoff had been established by political unification and the liberalization of the economy, Germany underwent economic expansion at a rate second only to that of the United States. Germany surpassed Britain in the production of iron and steel and became the world leader in the manufacture and export of chemical and electrical products. "Made in Germany" became a universally acknowledged insignia for advanced technology and high-quality craftsmanship.

German industry grew powerful through the active aid and encouragement of the government, which was directly involved in numerous branches of the economy and provided political support for the characteristically German form of big business organization, the cartel. Through the formation of cartels, businesses in the same line of manufacture or trade cooperated with each other by setting prices, establishing production levels, and allocating market shares. The German form of state-sponsored capitalism may have favored big business, but it was unquestionably efficient and productive. Yet despite the dynamism of its economy, Germany's political development remained essentially arrested at a predemocratic stage. While becoming an economic giant, Germany remained, from a western democratic perspective, a political dwarf.

The speed of industrial expansion paradoxically may have helped to impede the emergence of liberal democracy, for it created the social conditions that undermined the liberal promise of full and equal opportunity for all individuals to pursue and achieve optimal self-development. Industrialization led to the growth of an increasingly restive and urbanized industrial working class, the constituency for the growing union movement and the SPD. The typical industrial worker in central Europe at the turn of the century could not hope even after a lifetime of labor to own his or her own home or to amass enough wealth to become a member of the middle class. The growing gap between the liberal ideal of the autonomous individual and the social realities of economic concentration and inequality, urban poverty, recurring economic crisis, and class conflict made liberal ideology seem increasingly irrelevant to the social problems of the industrial age. In such circumstances socialism appealed to more and more workers. Most workers felt they had a better chance to improve their lives in solidarity with their class than by trying to raise themselves to middle-class status on their own. The individualist ethos of liberalism was weak in Germany in any case for the historical reasons outlined in the preceding chapter. The nature and form of industrialization in Germany strengthened the movement for social democracy, which in turn invited government repression that further limited the possibilities of liberalizing reform. The social forces at work in late nineteenth-century Germany made for greater polarization than in other European countries and worked against a peaceful evolution to democracy.

The pace of German industrial development intensified the threat to traditional monarchism by creating increasing pressures for democratization. The lateness of German unification meant also that industrialization in Germany coincided with the maturation of a full-fledged Marxist doctrine, which helped to make the labor movement a more fearsome and formidable foe of the existing system than had been the case at a parallel stage of industrialization in Britain decades before. For the propertied elites, the primary social question was how to integrate labor into the existing social order without ceding power to the unions or the SPD. Various strategies were put forward to accomplish this goal (in part reflecting differences among the elites), but as the labor movement grew in numbers, repression became less feasible and increasingly gave way to different integrative strategies, including demagoguery and an adventurist foreign policy designed to unify all classes in a common national purpose.

By the late 1880s it was becoming clear that Bismarck's antisocialist laws were failing to accomplish their goal of suppressing the labor movement.

Despite the legal restrictions on party activities, Social Democratic candidates received an increasing proportion of the vote in every triennial Reichstag election. Not even the innovative state-sponsored health and accident insurance and old-age pension programs that Bismarck introduced in the 1880s achieved the desired effects of weakening worker allegiance to socialism and reducing the Social Democratic vote, perhaps because Bismarck's social programs were paid for by deductions that further reduced workers' wages. The apparent bankruptcy of Bismarck's policy of repression led to growing resistance to renewal of the antisocialist legislation in the Reichstag. Many deputies feared that driving the SPD underground only strengthened the movement and made surveillance and control more difficult.

Wilhelm II and the "New Course"

Disagreement on how to deal with the workers' movement was a crucial factor in Bismarck's forced resignation in 1890. While the aging chancellor contemplated changing the constitution to eliminate universal manhood suffrage and further weaken the Reichstag, young Kaiser Wilhelm II, who had succeeded to the throne in 1888, sought to shed the regime's repressive image. He preferred to build on Bismarck's earlier paternalistic approach to the "social question," the problem of worker disaffection. His ambition was to be a *Volkskaiser*, a popular emperor, whose concern for his people would ensure their loyalty to the crown. He hoped the workers would be won over to the monarchical system by ameliorative legislation and by ending the ban on the SPD.

The conciliatory strategy of Wilhelm's so-called New Course was nonetheless also doomed to fail, because ultimately he was no more willing than Bismarck to make real concessions to democracy or worker self-determination. In any case, opposition of the Prussian *Junker* elite brought the reformist initiative of Bismarck's successor Leo von Caprivi to a halt in 1894. Under pressure from conservatives the government reverted to a more unyielding stance toward social democracy and liberalism. The Bismarckian technique of "negative integration," by which a "loyal" majority was mobilized against a minority of putative "enemies of the *Reich*" so as to create greater unity, was once again revived.[4] By the end of the decade, as electoral support for the SPD continued to grow, Kaiser Wilhelm was referring to leaders of the resurgent party as traitors to the fatherland.

Weltpolitik

The policies pursued under Wilhelm's reign were ultimately more baneful than Bismarck's policies, because they linked repudiation of liberalism and social democracy to a more dynamic and aggressive foreign policy, the concrete objectives of which were never entirely clear or consistent. Renouncing Bismarck's more static conception of the balance of power,

Wilhelmine *Weltpolitik* ("world policy") sought the consolidation of German dominance on the continent, the acquisition of colonies in Africa and Asia, and the attainment of parity with Britain as a world power. If Bismarck had viewed German unification as the end of German expansion in Europe, the mood in the Wilhelmian era was to view it as just the beginning. Under Admiral Alfred Tirpitz (1849–1930) Germany's growing navy even developed long-term contingency plans for an eventual invasion of the United States.[5] *Weltpolitik* greatly escalated the arms race and heightened the danger of war. The ineptness of German diplomacy, partly a result of Wilhelm's personal interventions, contributed to instability in Europe, as Germany's potential opponents were often kept guessing as to Germany's purposes and intent.

"Social Imperialism"

If German diplomatic goals were often unclear and unpredictable in the Wilhelmine era as a result of unresolved differences within the governing bureaucracy as well as changing international circumstances, they were also subject to mounting domestic pressures for more vigorous imperialist policies. Aggressive foreign policies are useful as a means of promoting domestic unity, for when a state is confronted with an external challenge or threat, the first imperative for the people is to rally around the flag. The doctrine of national security is a powerful integrating force. Moreover, a militant foreign policy can effectively blunt the demand for domestic reform. When the national interest or national security is at stake, agitation for a more equitable distribution of power, property, or wealth can be made to seem deliberately divisive and thus tantamount to treason.

Germany's quest for "a place in the sun," Foreign Secretary (and later Chancellor) Bernhard von Bülow's 1898 euphemism for the acquisition of a colonial empire, was conceived in part as a stratagem to deflect popular energies from domestic reform into overseas expansion. Certainly it was a policy that enjoyed great popular support among the middle classes. Imperialism held out the promise of national enrichment and spoils, which would raise the standard of living of the lower classes and reduce conflicts over the distribution of wealth and property. It could thus serve as a convenient way of exporting the "social problem" into the foreign arena. Social imperialism as a strategy to defuse popular pressures for greater material benefits and political rights was not confined to Germany, of course. But in Germany we find a heightened version of the social and political processes characteristic of the Age of Imperialism in Europe. *Weltpolitik* lent itself most effectively to the campaign to harness popular forces to monarchical interests. In the late 1890s German leaders spoke openly of the need for a *Sammlungspolitik*, a policy to gather diverse interest groups into a coherent national movement to stave off the democratic challenge.[6]

Radical nationalism

It would be simplistic, however, to view the upsurge of nationalism and popular support for imperialism and militarism in the 1890s as solely the result of manipulation by the ruling elite. The social and economic consequences of continuing industrialization created both popular pressures for greater democracy and popular reactions against such pressures. Worker disaffection led to the continued rapid growth of the SPD. Among other classes and occupational groups, however, economic resentments were frequently expressed in the call for national unity and national expansion. Aside from unskilled or nonunionized workers, it was traditional social groups, especially the *Mittelstand* of independent artisans, small-shop owners, and independent peasant-farmers, who experienced most adversely the dislocations brought about by industrialization, urbanization, economic concentration, and cyclical fluctuations in the economy.

The survival of such "preindustrial" social groups in disproportionate numbers, a result of the lateness and rapidity of German industrialization, made for an especially volatile sociological configuration in Germany in the late nineteenth and early twentieth centuries. Squeezed between big business and a growing labor movement, such lower middle-class groups provided a reservoir of widespread economic discontent that could be readily mobilized for political purposes. *Mittelstand* discontent, however, often worked to strengthen social conservatism and nationalism rather than liberalism or democracy, for the *laissez-faire* capitalism associated with liberalism left independent tradesmen and small producers unprotected against factory competition while social democracy seemed to offer the lower middle class only the prospect of proletarianization and the leveling of property, income, and status.

The 1890s emerge as a crucial transitional period, then, as Bismarckian diplomatic realism gave way to Wilhelmine illusions of German world power amid the tensions of an increasingly polarized social conflict. It was a decade in which large segments of the industrial working class were organized into unions and the SPD, while even larger segments of the middle classes joined right-wing pressure groups that exerted increasing influence on policy formation. The Agrarian League, dominated by aristocratic estate owners, mobilized peasants against economic liberalism and social democracy. The Colonial League advocated overseas expansion, while the Naval League whipped up support for the government's naval construction program and the arms race with Britain.[7] The Pan-German League's antidemocratic, antisemitic, and imperialist goals presaged the Nazi program.[8] Radically nationalist ideas were also disseminated in such influential interest groups as the German White Collar Employees' Association, the Eastern Marches Association, the *Deutschbund* (German League), the League of Industrialists, and the German Army League. Growing demagogic tendencies in the major political parties reflected these popular pressures as well. The venerable Conservative Party, pillar of the monarchical establishment, sought to parry the challenge of radical antisemitic parties by adopting antisemitic provisions in its program in 1892. The Center Party, too, responded to pressures from its socially diverse constituency by offering a rallying platform against the left.[9]

The perceived threat of the SPD promoted the growth of a "national opposition" on the right that criticized the monarchy for failing to take sufficient stringent measures to suppress democratizing trends. In the 1890s and 1900s, nationalist extremists looked back with nostalgia to Bismarck's repressive tactics.[10] On the growing right-wing fringe the government was increasingly perceived as too weak to solve the "social question" and contain the democratic threat. The governmental leaders who stepped into Bismarck's shoes had no easy task mediating the tensions and conflicts in German society while holding the line against democracy. No doubt, part of what appears as simply political incompetence in the post-Bismarckian era may be traced to the extraordinary problems faced by a government committed to the social and political status quo at a time of escalating change. The growing polarization of German society produced a crisis in German politics that the government was ultimately unable to resolve.

The origins of World War I

It is one of the ironies of history that Bismarck's nightmare of Germany having to face a hostile coalition of European powers became reality only a generation after his exit from the diplomatic stage. But the constraints that he placed on the evolution of a democratic constitution and parliamentary government in Germany helped to undermine the defensive alliance system he had so carefully constructed to avoid German isolation. The campaign against democracy developed a momentum of its own and led to the increasing militarization of German policy. *Weltpolitik* and the German naval buildup induced Britain to form the *entente cordiale* with France in 1904 and to join France and Russia in the Triple Entente in 1907. The crude attempts of the German leadership to drive a wedge between France and her allies through military threats in the diplomatic crises that preceded World War I only consolidated the anti-German alliance.

It would be misleading, of course, to portray Germany as solely responsible for the outbreak of World War I. All the combatants must share some blame for failure to stave off the war. In all countries the fear of "mob rule" and the perceived threat to property contributed to imperialism to a greater or lesser extent. The crisis of confidence in liberal values and the social conflict resulting from continuing industrialization were not confined to Germany. Nor were Germans the only ones to subscribe to the Social Darwinist notion that life is an ongoing struggle between individuals, nations, and races. The German experience was not unique so much as it was a heightened version of what occurred elsewhere in Europe as well. Germany provides a particularly compelling example of an extreme nationalist reaction to domestic pressures for reform. The German constitution proved too rigid and archaic to make possible a peaceful resolution of the social crisis. In no western European country did resistance to democracy lead to such aggressive policies abroad.[11]

The militarization of German policy was a complex and dialectical process, of course, and not merely a case of reflex reaction to democracy. Nationalism, imperialism, and militarism developed their own momentum. Diplomacy always responds to external threats, not merely to internal stimuli. Perceptions change the realities that gave rise to them in the first place, creating new realities and generating further misperceptions. Many German leaders became convinced of the peril of foreign encirclement, even if it was of Germany's own making or, as some commentators have insisted, a figment of German paranoia or a projection of Germany's own excessive ambitions.[12] Germany may have faced real foes, but German ambition and bellicosity were rooted in domestic problems, however obscured these roots may have been by nationalist rhetoric or however invisible they may be to observers who focus only on diplomatic clashes.

The "primacy of foreign policy," the principle that foreign affairs must take priority over domestic concerns, enabled conservatives to suppress civil liberties or avoid social reforms with the claim that they endangered the security of the state. In retrospect, it seems no mere coincidence that the war broke out only two years after the SPD, which had shed its revolutionary image and now stood for democratic change, had become the largest party in the Reichstag elections of 1912. For the German elites and the large segments of the population that accepted the official consensus, a short successful war provided the ideal formula for healing the nation's social divisions and damping demands for democratic change. War might provide an irrefutable argument for unity, order, discipline, and top-down authority. Victory would consolidate German dominance in Europe and reinforce the prevailing system at home.

Many German leaders, including high-ranking military officers, believed that time was running out for Germany to realize its ambitions. If war was necessary for the nation to survive in its present form, better to fight it sooner than to postpone it until Germany's enemies, particularly Russia with its enormous potential resources, became too strong. War offered a way out of both hostile encirclement and the domestic bind. There were risks, to be sure, but the prize at the end—stabilization of the monarchical regime—made the gamble seem worthwhile.

The belief that war would strengthen the regime governed the actions of German leaders in the fateful days following the assassination of the heir to the Austrian throne by Serbian nationalists in June 1914. Fully conscious that their policies might precipitate a European war, Germany's leaders encouraged Austria to take advantage of the opportunity to destroy the Serbian threat. Predisposed to favor the application of force and confident that they could win a continental war, the German leadership rejected a peaceful resolution to the crisis on any but their own terms.[13]

Overestimating German military capabilities, Germany's leaders fell victim to their own self-serving illusions of German power and righteousness. Wide sectors of the German public shared these illusions. To understand the reasons for this we need to take a closer look at German ideology.

4   Germanic ideology

Nationalism, vulgarized idealism, and antisemitism

The function of ideology

Ideology is the system of ideas, values, and beliefs that shape the outlook of a person, a group, or a society. Ideology is a way of looking at the world that explains conditions and events to make sense of a person's or a people's experiences and aspirations. Indeed, ideology is an essential component of a nation's sense of identity. As a people's self-explanation and self-justification, its dominant ideology reflects social reality and rationalizes, and thereby reinforces, existing social relationships. If this were not so, there would be no dominant consensus in favor of existing arrangements, and either these arrangements would give way to alternatives that enjoyed greater public legitimacy or ideas would change to accord more closely with the interests of dominant groups. Ideology and society are mutually reinforcing. So reciprocally conditioning and interrelated are social reality and ideology—reality and real interests creating ideology, ideology recreating social reality and reinforcing real interests—that it is often impossible to separate cause from effect.

The definition of national identity occurs on a terrain contested by various factions of the political left and right. Factions pursuing very different visions of the national purpose claim or seek to speak for the nation as a whole. Only the dominant faction succeeds in doing so; the credibility of its claim to speak for the nation as a whole is in fact a key to that faction's dominance. Discussions of national identity cannot therefore escape generalizing from the ideology or self-understanding of the dominant faction to the ideology or self-understanding of the nation as a whole.

Ideology justifies patterns of dominance and subordination, but this does not necessarily mean that dominant ideologies are consciously mendacious efforts by dominant groups to bamboozle the populace with explanations that its purveyors know to be false. Ideology can effectively reconcile people to arrangements that favor dominant groups only if it is seen to provide a truthful rendering of the world and the forces at work in it. Only if faith in its version of reality is genuine can ideology exercise the hold that it does over people's minds. Even apologists for inequitable social arrangements are not necessarily consciously trying to distort reality and pull the wool over people's eyes. The mendacity of ideologists lies in their failure to perceive or acknowledge that an ideology is a belief system, often conditioned by the political and social premises of a given social order. Ideologists are hypocritical even when they do not knowingly lie (indeed they are usually convinced they are telling the truth), if they deny, conceal, or otherwise fail to examine the usually self-serving premises on which their ideas are based.

The task of the historian is to show how dominant ideologies of the past have successfully distorted reality in the interest of certain groups. The historian must convey the plausibility and internal logic of an ideology and at the same time lay bare the usually unacknowledged interests that this ideology served. To the historian of imperialism, for instance, it is clear that the genuinely professed desire to spread the benefits of civilization and Christianity to benighted natives served as a lofty rationalization for the extension of European power and the exploitation of colonial resources. Yet the ideology of the "white man's burden" was sincerely propagated by writers unconscious of the selfish interests they helped to promote, and the notion that colonizers were serving an unselfish purpose became part of the public consciousness in Europe. Today these same ideas seem outlandish and even invidious to many people. As the victims of imperialism both in the colonies and in the homelands have become increasingly able to assert their own interests, the public consensus has radically changed, and ideas such as the "white man's burden" have lost their former persuasiveness.

German ideology

German ideology, too, the ultimately virulent combination of nationalism, racialism, and moralism that formed part of the dominant secular belief system in Germany at the end of the nineteenth and beginning of the twentieth centuries, is thoroughly discredited today. Yet it commanded widespread allegiance under the different conditions of the past. Its origins and progenitors cannot be precisely pinpointed, for it developed organically over the course of time and eclectically assimilated ideas from many sources. Not all Germans, particularly those on the left, subscribed to this ideology, of course, but it enjoyed wide currency among the dominant propertied classes.

The fact that German ideology (particularly in its radical *völkisch* variant) eventually rationalized and promoted aggression does not automatically brand its constituent elements or historical antecedents as wrong or necessarily pernicious. Ideas and beliefs can serve many purposes. After all, nationalism, the major component not only of German ideology but of the ideology of the European middle classes, could also be a democratic creed, and indeed it originated as such in the French Revolution. As the belief system of the underclasses, nationalism emerged in the French Revolution as an emancipatory ideology, aiming at the destruction of dynastic rule and its replacement with popular sovereignty. In Germany, however, even more so than in other European countries, nationalism was to become, by the end of the nineteenth century, an ideology that integrated people into a system dominated by privileged elites.

The impact of the French Revolution

German ideology reflected, rationalized, and reinforced the lack of democracy in Germany. Throughout the nineteenth century, most of Germany's leading writers and thinkers defined the identity and ideals of their nation in contradistinction to the Enlightenment and the French Revolution of 1789. The increasingly radical attempts to create a more just and perfect society in France represented a challenge to all existing regimes. Not only because of the excesses of revolutionary terror in France and Napoleonic imperialism, but also because the conditions for a democratic revolution did not exist in Germany, even reform-minded Germans, such as the great classicists Goethe and Schiller, rejected the model of the French Revolution as unsuitable to the real improvement of society. Instead they called for the only kind of change that was at least theoretically possible under the conditions of absolutism and particularism: moral perfection, or a moral regeneration within each individual. In the absence of any possibility of external revolution in Germany, the only alternative seemed to be inner regeneration. From the German perspective the French had gone about it the wrong way; they had sought to bring about a better society through political action and institutional change, when in fact human character would first have to be improved before institutions and society could be reformed.[1]

As the German states, particularly Prussia and Austria, became embroiled in war against revolutionary and Napoleonic France, even German liberalism acquired an antirevolutionary tinge. German writers like Johann Gottlieb Fichte in his famous *Addresses to the German Nation* (1807–08) attributed the wrong-headed approach of the French to their materialism. In their preoccupation with the pursuit of happiness and material improvement of their lives, the French supposedly neglected the spiritual dimension of life. Germany's mission was to regenerate the world through the spirit. The proper purpose of life was not the pursuit of material happiness, but the perfection of mind and soul. Even so sober-minded a scholar as the historian Leopold von Ranke hailed the Restoration of 1815 as the reaction of the Nordic–Germanic world against Latin revolution.

The German idea of freedom

German thinkers extolled their notion of moral freedom as far superior to the French definition of freedom in merely political terms. The German idea of freedom was to be free from the animalistic and materialistic weaknesses of human nature while the French only sought to gain freedom from the oppressive state. To be truly free in the German sense meant to be liberated from the internal bonds that prevented the full development of moral character.[2]

This idealist and apolitical conception of freedom, so characteristic of German thought, was in fact the only kind of freedom compatible with the absolutist and hierarchical systems that prevailed in most German states. A strong state may even be congenial to such a conception of freedom, for authoritarianism imposes the discipline that enables people to gain freedom from materialistic desire and temptation. If freedom to walk on the grass, for example, illustrates the western conception of freedom from government regulation or control, then not *wanting* to walk on the grass epitomized the German notion of what it means to be truly free. This notion of freedom owed much to the Lutheran and pietist traditions as expressed in Luther's famous pronouncement, "Flesh shall have no freedom." Such a notion of freedom can even turn out to be incompatible with any concrete emancipatory practice. Freedom defined exclusively in terms of spiritual conscience and moral perfection is the kind of freedom that can be enjoyed even, or perhaps especially, behind prison walls. Not only does this form of freedom not require any form of political participation, but in the light of a definition of freedom as "insight into moral necessity" political action for civil liberties or material benefits may even come to be seen as corrupting and immoral. The Lutheran notions of inner freedom and subjection to moral law (or self-induced subjection to external law) perfectly complement the Lutheran requirement of absolute obedience to secular authority. There is an undeniably heroic quality in this conception of freedom as internalization of the law, which helps to explain the great creativity of German culture. The equation of heroic self-discipline, self-denial, and self-sacrifice with the highest form of freedom provided the ideological medium in which both high culture and militant destructiveness could flourish.

German idealism

The great age of German idealism, the age of Goethe and Schiller, Kant and Hegel, gave Germany not only a heritage of great literature and philosophy, but also a legacy of quiescent political attitudes, attitudes that reflected subservience to authority and the futility of political action to effect rational reform. In the German tradition, idealism came to mean more than the conventional usage of pursuing a dream, a lofty vision, or a standard of perfection. It embraced both the Platonic philosophic doctrine of the prior and separate existence of ideas in a realm beyond temporal reality (beyond the world of appearances) and the commitment to put timeless moral ideas—ideals—into practice in the world. Corrupt temporal reality—the everyday world of politics, commerce, and human affairs—would thereby be morally redeemed and regenerated. The Kantian assumption that humans could never know ultimate reality (the ideal realm) through their intellect but only through their moral will— their courage and willingness to follow moral commandment—reinforced the practical imperative of German idealism to regenerate the world, not through reason, but through moral ideals and will.

Idealism, then, reflected both discontent with the stultifying social and political reality in Germany as well as impotence to do anything about it in the realm of political affairs. On a political level, at least, idealist thought can be interpreted as an effort to harmonize and overcome social conflicts and problems that were impervious to resolution through action in the real world. Hegelian idealism could, of course, inspire social and political activism, as in the case of Karl Marx, who, in applying Hegel's dialectic to social reality, claimed to be standing Hegel "back on his feet." The predominant effect of idealist attitudes in Germany, however, was not to mobilize energies for social or institutional reform but instead to channel them into quiescent self-improvement through education, religion, and the arts.[3]

Vulgarized idealism (*Vulgäridealismus*)

Popular forms of apolitical idealism pervaded the public consciousness in Germany in the course of the nineteenth century and served to discourage and discredit social and political reform. On a popular level idealism often degenerated into anti-intellectualism and irrationalism. Most educated Germans embraced idealism as the quintessentially German alternative to western materialism, utilitarianism, rationalism, and self-interest. Self-styled idealists prided themselves on their opposition to materialism, whether this was understood as a positivist interpretation of the world in terms of matter (a view that involved rejection of the ideal or spiritual realm as a prior or "higher" reality) or, on a more mundane level, as acquisitiveness, greed, or sensuality. "Idealism is present," wrote the influential publicist Paul de Lagarde (1827–91) in 1880, "wherever man acts out of inner needs against his own advantage, against his own comfort, against the world surrounding him."[4] Such a definition rebutted the liberal (and socialist) stress on the benignity of rational self-interest, as did Richard Wagner's (1813–83) definition of German idealism as doing something for its own sake rather than for pleasure or reward.

Idealism—the renunciation of selfishness—seemed to provide a code of heroic conduct superior to the profit-oriented commercialism of liberalism and the resentful leveling of socialism. Liberalism and socialism stood condemned as doctrines that enshrined the basely acquisitive, egotistical instincts in humankind. In their materialist aims, liberalism and socialism seemed closely related, even if these two doctrines offered quite different models of social organization. After all, both doctrines presumed to achieve a better society primarily by promoting and regulating the production and distribution of wealth and worldly goods. From an idealist perspective, the ideas of social progress and social justice merely masked the degeneracy of an era in the thrall of materialistic values.

In vulgarized idealism the absence of democracy in Germany was interpreted as a mark of German superiority. Idealism, like nationalism, became a powerful weapon in the arsenal of political conservatives who sought to discredit efforts to introduce democratic reforms. The motives of reformers who advocated the improvement of the material conditions of the lower classes could be impugned as basely materialistic. A symbiosis of nationalism and idealism was easy to attain, because both doctrines demanded the subordination of self-interest and class-interest to the good of a higher entity, the nation or the idealized moral authority of the state. Both nationalism and idealism celebrated courage and self-sacrifice. In the years before World War I, many groups preached a revival of idealism to strengthen the moral fiber of the nation. The ideology of the youth movement—a revolt of middle-class youth against materialistic urban life in the early 1900s—combined the values of nationalism, idealism, and authoritarianism.[5]

Antisemitism

Antisemitism frequently accompanied the idealist world view in its vulgarized form, if only because vulgarized idealism inherited the ancient Christian prejudice that Judaism was a materialistic religion and the Jews a materialistic people. The thread that links all historical forms of antisemitism, whether religious, economic, political, or racial, is the identification of Jewishness with materialism and immorality. For centuries Jews were held to be immoral because they stubbornly refused to accept the spiritual teachings of Christ. Jews supposedly rejected the Christian path to salvation through renunciation of the world in order to be free to pursue worldly gain for selfish ends. According to Christian antisemites, Jews perversely refused to abjure material possessions and power for the higher "kingdom within" or "beyond." Unencumbered by the Christian prohibition of usury, Jewish moneylenders, whose services were vital to Christian monarchs, grew rich through practices Christians repudiated as sinful.

Jewishness thus came to stand for worldliness, selfishness, intellectual cunning, and lack of Christian self-denial or self-restraint. The very mind-set of idealism reinforced such stereotyping, for the "idea" of Jewishness was deemed more real and significant than the evidence of empirical reality. Many self-styled idealists (such as the composer Richard Wagner and his Bayreuth Circle) saw no contradiction between their professed antisemitism and their friendship with or tolerance of individual Jews. To such ideological antisemites the danger to be averted was the corruption of German society by the "Jewish spirit." First used by the German freelance journalist Wilhelm Marr (1819–1904) in 1879 in a book entitled *The Victory of Jewry over Germandom*, the term "antisemitism" had for its adherents a distinctly positive connotation. Paradoxical though it may seem, in the nineteenth century ideological antisemitism was frequently voiced as a repudiation of commercialism and a token of selfless virtue. To self-styled idealists antisemitism seemed a mark of virtue and respectability, for it signified rejection of the selfish, profit-oriented traits that Jewishness supposedly represented.

Antisemitism was, of course, pervasive among Europeans of all classes in the nineteenth century. No predominantly Christian country was entirely free of the feeling that Jews did not belong. But in countries with liberal political systems antisemitism could not be mobilized politically to the extent that was the case in the Russian, Austrian, and German empires. Antisemitism was particularly susceptible to political exploitation and manipulation in Germany. Here the tendency to define the national identity against an ideal-type conception of Jewishness was especially pronounced. Where national consciousness is weak or insecure, historically there has been a tendency to compensate by defining the national character in contrast to some actual or mythical outside group. In the course of the nineteenth century, the Jews displaced the French as the chief foil of Germany's self-definition. To be authentically German involved commitment to idealism and rejection of "Jewish" materialism.

Antisemitism in politics

The emancipation of the Jews in central Europe in the aftermath of the democratic revolutions from 1789 to 1848 evoked more radical forms of antisemitism in the latter half of the nineteenth century, as Jews were increasingly blamed for economic crises and other dislocations of a rapidly modernizing era. Full legal emancipation of Jews did not occur in Germany until 1869, the eve of unification, when all civil disabilities resulting from religious affiliation were removed in the North German Confederation. Only four years later the first great financial crash of the new Reich triggered an outburst of virulent antisemitism. Economic, political, and racial forms of antisemitism supplanted religious antisemitism as part of the nineteenth-century trend toward secularization, which was itself widely blamed on Jewish influence. The radicalization of antisemitism toward the end of the nineteenth century was perhaps the most striking indicator of growing social and political contradictions and tensions in Germany. The willingness of conservatives to embrace antisemitism reflected their growing desperation in the face of rising pressures for a more democratic distribution of wealth and power in a rapidly industrializing society. Through a populist antisemitism conservatives sought to attract the mass support that seemed essential to retaining power in an age of mass politics.

Like the nationalism and idealism to which it became assimilated, antisemitism formed an important element of the conservative reaction to the democratic movements. Jews were blamed for the rise of the "materialistic" doctrines of liberalism and socialism, systems that supposedly enabled Jews to gain economic and political power. Liberal Judaism, not orthodoxy or Zionism, was the prime target of conservative antisemites, for liberal Jews seemed to threaten both religion and nationality, the two principles on which the German social order was based. Antisemitism was politically useful to conservatives, because it allowed them to attribute natural social developments such as the growth of the liberal and labor movements to a Jewish conspiracy (for example, in the United States the KKK blamed the civil rights movement on Jews). Conspiracy theories obviated the need to actually address the genuine problems of a rapidly changing economy in a polity resistant to change. A conspiracy theory was also required if antisemites were to provide a plausible explanation for how supposedly inferior Jews could enjoy such widespread economic and professional success.

Since Jews obviously benefitted from emancipatory movements that swept away legal constraints on Jews, there was a certain perverse logic in the antisemitic assertion that Jews undermined the traditional order for their own advantage. Not surprisingly, the Jewish community in Germany, enlarged by accelerating immigration of east-European Jewish fugitives from the repression and lack of opportunity in the Russian Empire in the late nineteenth century, overwhelmingly supported the liberal changes that made possible the ending of centuries of legal restrictions on Jews.[6] In Germany and Austria Jews played important roles in both the liberal and Social Democratic parties. The support of most politically active Jews for the parties of the left gave superficial plausibility to the assertion of antisemites that Jews inflicted liberal changes on society for selfish ends or that Jews favored socialism to gain control of the working masses. No doubt, too, most Jews opposed the militant forms of nationalism that developed in European countries in the course of the nineteenth century and that constituted such an integral part of conservative German ideology at the end of the century. Romantic nationalism, which defined nationality by membership in an organic ethnic group with roots in the tribal past, represented an obvious obstacle to the desire of many Jews to integrate into the dominant society without giving up their separate identity. But even liberal nationalism, epitomized by the Enlightenment slogan, "Everything to the Jews as individuals; nothing to the Jews as a people," had the effect of stigmatizing Jewish group identity.[7]

Their increasing visibility in careers previously closed to them made Jews a natural target for those who felt victimized by rapid industrialization. In an age in which political leaders could no longer entirely ignore the aspirations and grievances of the masses if they hoped to gain or retain power, antisemitism commended itself to unscrupulous politicians as an effective instrument of rabble-rousing to divert popular dissatisfactions into conservative channels. Antisemitism proved to be an effective way of deflecting economic discontent away from the capitalist system and on to Jews, who were held responsible for the economic fluctuations and cyclical crises of the late nineteenth century. Antisemitic conspiracy theories provided seductively simple explanations for the economic ills of the rural lower middle class. In the 1880s court chaplain Adolf Stöcker's (1835–1909) Christian-Social Party sought to mobilize worker support for monarchism through antisemitic and antiliberal appeals. The audiences he attracted, however, were mainly lower middle class. Even the prestigious Conservative Party, the party of the ruling elite, adopted antisemitic provisions in 1892 to attract disgruntled voters and strengthen its mass base.

Racial antisemitism

Antisemitism thus provided both a substantive program and a tactical weapon for the political right. The growth of racial antisemitism at the end of the nineteenth century reflected not only the vogue of eugenic theories that arose after the Darwinian revolution in biology, but also reflected the growing desperation of opponents of liberalism and democracy. Even before the Darwinian revolution focused popular attention on the importance of hereditary selection, the French racial theorist Count Arthur de Gobineau (1816–82), depressed by the declining power of the French aristocracy, had attributed the spread of democracy to racial intermarriage that corrupted the original purity of the superior "Aryan" race.[8] Gobineau's racial ideas, which bemoaned the inevitable decline of the Aryans, found more adherents in Germany than in France. Richard Wagner, Wilhelm Marr, Eugen Dühring (1833–1921), the expatriate Englishman Houston Stewart Chamberlain (1855–1927), and a host of lesser publicists popularized racial antisemitism in Germany.

In the past, Jews had been able, in theory at least, to escape persecution through baptism, conversion, and assimilation. Racial antisemitism was designed to close off this route to respectability, political influence, and public acceptance. Darwinism and the positivist temper of nineteenth-century European thought gave a pseudoscientific credibility to the racialist assumption that the cultural and psychological traits subsumed under the notion of "national character" were genetically and racially transmitted. Racial antisemitism, presumed to be based on biological "science," could be propagated as supposedly free of old-fashioned religious bigotry. Racial anti-semites argued that materialist attitudes were a function of the physical and genetic makeup of Jews and therefore not attitudes that could be eradicated through either voluntary or forced conversion to Christianity.

In practice, however, religious and racial forms of antisemitism frequently overlapped. Antisemites who called themselves Christian and rejected biolog-ical determinism had little difficulty incorporating the antisemitic discourse of the late nineteenth century, though generally speaking in terms of culture rather than race.[9] Religious and racial antisemites in Germany differed mainly in their understanding of the source of Jewish perniciousness, not in their fundamental conception of Jews as destructive of the moral order.[10] Both groups defined the "Jewish question" as arising from the uniqueness of Jews as a group, whether because of their different religious identification and/or their different ethnic origin. Many radical antisemites did, however, believe that the Christian churches had become too corrupted to effectively resist the "Judaization" of German society.[11]

This view of the Jews as alien beyond redemption was intended to forestall the increasing assimilation of Jews in the Bismarckian and Wilhelmine Empire. The spread of racial antisemitism was a symptom of the ideological transition from traditional to more radical conservatism, a transition that was not to be completed until the Nazi era. Racial antisemitism remained largely confined to the radical right-wing fringe in Germany and Austria until after World War I. Most conservative antisemites, such as the influential historian Heinrich von Treitschke (1834–96), continued to call for assimilation, as did liberal critics of antisemitism, such as the classical historian Theodor Mommsen (1817–1903). Increasingly, however, the lines between those who preached racial exclusion and those who called for full assimilation were blurred, as assimilationists, too, insisted that Jews give up their separate iden-tity. Treitschke, who coined the phrase, "The Jews are our misfortune," exhorted Jews to shed their peculiarities and adopt the manners and ideology of mainstream society. Yet there were voices on the political right who warned that continued assimilation promoted rather than counteracted the influence of Jews in German culture and society. Racial publicists like Houston Stewart Chamberlain, who published the widely read *Foundations of the Nineteenth Century* in 1899, demanded exclusion of all Jews as the only strategy commensurate with the growing threat from the left. Chamberlain also shared the anti-Catholicism of many German nationalists who viewed the Church as a foe of the national idea. In Catholic Austria, where Chamberlain lived from 1889 to 1909, the antisemitic movement was divided into Catholic and anti-Catholic factions. Owing perhaps to the growing challenge from national minorities to the dominance of the German ruling elite in the Habsburg Empire, pan-Germanic nationalism and racial antisemitism were particularly strong in Austria, where Adolf Hitler was born in 1889.

Völkisch ideology

Racial antisemitism was the hallmark of what in the late nineteenth century came to be called the *völkisch* movement. Its name is derived from the German word for people, *Volk*. Included in this broad and (before 1933) never formally unified political movement were a variety of radically nationalist and antisemitic groups on the extreme right who sought to drum up mass support for the conservative cause through quasipopulist appeals to racial and national solidarity. Racialism, like nationalism, lent itself to such demagoguery because it offered common people, even the have-nots of German society, membership by birth in a superior and exclusive community defined, in escalating degrees of vagueness, as the Germanic, Nordic, or Aryan race. Like nationalism, racialism lent itself to the struggle against the left, because it put a premium on unity and conformity rather than on individual rights or the equitable distribution of social benefits.

Common to all *völkisch* thought was the notion of a mystical blood bond between members of the same national or ethnic community. *Völkisch* ideology grew increasingly intolerant in the context of rapid industrialization, economic fluctuation and dislocation, and growing pressures for democratization in the late nineteenth century. *Völkisch* ideologues called for the creation of a regenerated "Third Reich" and assigned to Germany the mission of leading a worldwide spiritual renewal. Most *völkisch* publicists followed Wagner, Lagarde, and Chamberlain in urging a Germanized Christian faith. Others followed Dühring in rejecting the Christian religion as an Oriental superstition. *Völkisch* writers idealized the peasantry as the true guardians of the native soil, traditional values, purity of blood, and authentic folk culture, now threatened by industrialization, urbanization, and foreign influence. They juxtaposed German idealism to Jewish materialism, German culture to western civilization, and Nordic racial purity to the chaos of racial intermixing. Many *völkisch* publicists hoped for a redemptive war to revive the heroic qualities of the

German people. They rejected the ideas of 1789—liberty, equality, and popular sovereignty—in favor of unity, order, authority, and the Prussian-Germanic martial values of courage, loyalty, obedience, discipline, and self-sacrifice.

Völkisch ideologues interpreted Social Darwinism in terms of a struggle between races rather than individuals. They believed in the superiority of the Nordic or Germanic race and favored policies that would insure racial purity and Nordic predominance in Germany. They embraced eugenics (called "racial hygiene" in Germany), the science of improving a race or population group through selective breeding practices. In the era of imperialism, Social Darwinism and eugenics were not exclusively right-wing ideas, but they lent themselves to right-wing purposes. Social Darwinists stressed the need to let the struggle for existence take its course without intervention on behalf of the poor or the weak. Eugenicists deplored the tendency of proletarians to have more children than members of the educated classes. Through racial improvement German eugenicists hoped to counteract the degenerative or "counter-selective" effects of the spread of humanitarian and democratic ideas and practices. For example, the German Society for Racial Hygiene, founded by the former socialist Alfred Plötz (1860–1940) in 1905, was dedicated to the creation of optimal conditions for the maintenance and development of the German "race" in competition with other peoples. Through its links to the *völkisch* movement the cause of racial hygiene became enmeshed in antisemitism.

The most influential propagators of *völkisch* ideology were publicists and activists of the nationalist opposition to the allegedly too moderate domestic and foreign policies of the Wilhelmine monarchy. The "national opposition," as the leader of the Pan-Germans, Heinrich Class (1868–1953), called this movement in 1912, was critical of the monarchy only because they wanted a stronger monarch than William II. The radical right accused the Imperial regime of being too soft on democracy and too unwilling to employ the radical measures, such as disfranchisement of Jews, that would stem the liberal and social democratic tide.[12]

The *völkisch* opposition demanded suppression of the Social Democratic Party and an aggressive, expansionist foreign policy. Anticipating many elements of the Nazi world view, *völkisch* ideologues rejected both humanitarianism and individualism, socialism and liberalism, and called for greater sacrifices in the interest of the national community. They called for a strong, charismatic leader to exercise authority in the name of the *Volk* and to regenerate a culture supposedly corrupted by materialism, parliamentarism, and democracy. *Völkisch* propagandists denounced the Jewish presence as the ultimate cause of the supposed degeneration of Wilhelmine political culture. *Völkisch* publicists and politicians invoked the memory of Bismarck to prod the kaiser into stronger action against the SPD. Seventeen *völkisch* organizations, including the virulently antisemitic *Reichshammerbund* (Imperial Hammer League) of Theodor Fritsch (1852–1933), joined to form the umbrella organization *Deutschvölkische Vereinigung* (German Völkisch Association) in 1913.

Insofar as the regime shared the antidemocratic goals of its right-wing critics—and to a great extent it did—*völkisch* denunciations of a policy of accommodation and compromise with the left were bound to gain greater legitimacy in the eyes of the middle-class public. Nonetheless, on the eve of the Great War, traditional conservatives remained firmly in the saddle, partly, to be sure, by adopting some of the techniques and policies of their *völkisch* critics. As a result the rabble-rousing antisemitic parties that had emerged in the demagogic climate of the 1890s lost much of their constituency to Conservative cooptation a decade later. Both traditional and radical conservatives welcomed the outbreak of war in 1914 as a chance to unify the nation and eliminate democratic dissent. It was not until after the war, when Germany's defeat had weakened and discredited traditional conservatism, that radical *völkisch* conservatism would come fully into its own.

The "Ideas of 1914"

At the outbreak of war, mainstream German ideology and elements of *völkisch* extremism coalesced into the so-called "Ideas of 1914."[13] Radical nationalism had contributed to the outbreak of war; now war further radicalized German nationalism. This is a tendency inherent in war. The more war becomes (or is perceived to be) a struggle for survival, a sentiment captured in the stark alternatives of "victory or death," the more extreme its ideological manifestations are likely to be. The more desperate the struggle, the more desperate the efforts to justify it. In the vast propaganda literature generated by the war, German publicists juxtaposed German idealism to the materialism of 1789. They rejected the French revolutionary values of liberty, equality, and democracy in favor of the Germanic ideals of loyalty, duty, and spiritual regeneration. In the passions of war German ideology evolved into a Messianic cult.

While the war against Russia was widely portrayed in racial terms as a battle against the "Mongolized" and "Tartarized" Slavic hordes, the war against the west was framed in grandiose ideological terms as a struggle to determine the cultural direction of humankind and the future development of human nature. Wartime propagandists proclaimed the mission of German idealist culture to save the world from the merchant mentality of England and the shallow rationalism of France. Even so moderate a conservative as the writer Thomas Mann celebrated the superiority of German *Kultur* over western *Zivilisation* in his wartime *Reflections of an Unpolitical Man*, a work he later repudiated. If for Americans the war would be fought, in Woodrow Wilson's words, to make the world safe for democracy, for many Germans it became a war to save the world *from* the democratic and materialistic temper of the modern age. In the titanic struggle between the forces of light and darkness, good and evil, spirit and Mammon, the salvation of the world supposedly lay in the hands of the German race.

5   The First World War

The crisis of Imperial Germany

On 1 August 1914 the tensions of European society exploded into war. World War I was the great watershed of the twentieth century from which all major subsequent developments in Europe flowed. The rise of fascism and Nazism are directly related to the experience of war and to the Bolshevik Revolution that was the major legacy of the war in Russia. Of course, neither fascism nor communism was solely a product of World War I. But the war had the effect of greatly accelerating and intensifying the major trends of the preceding decades.

Legacy of the war

One such trend was the growing chauvinism and irrationalism spawned by the national rivalries of the Age of Imperialism and eventually culminating in fascism. World War I provided the experience that converted many people to fascism, furnished the model of social organization that fascists emulated, and created the conditions that made the rise of fascism possible. At the outset, at least, war was widely viewed as a vehicle of national regeneration and rejuvenation. This mind-set is of immense significance, for at the heart of fascism lay the effort to rekindle the enthusiasm for war and dedication to the nation that the Great War had originally inspired.

The war confirmed for many the axiom that the supreme law of any state is self-assertion, thus legitimating to the public the use of force to achieve political ends. Perhaps the principal legacy of the war was the tendency to define politics as *Kampf* (struggle)—a predisposition to the use of force rather than reasoned discourse to settle social, economic, or political disagreements. The adversarial habit of mind contributed to the politics of confrontation after the war. The war also provided a model for organizing a strong central state to mobilize a people for military purposes, a model that fascists upheld even in times of peace. The war strengthened the state's surveillance techniques and its ability to influence and control its population.[1] Fear and hatred of the villainous enemy induced the kind of ideological conformity and unanimity of purpose that fascists, who sought to mold society into a trained and loyal army, would seek to recapture in peacetime. The war reinforced the long-standing Prusso-German tendency to view the army as "the school of the nation."

The war also provided training in violence that hardened people to brutality and terror. As the first industrialized mass killing of the twentieth century, the war inured people to mass death: 70 million men in 36 countries were mobilized for war; at least 10 million soldiers were killed, and 20 million became invalids.[2] Most of the leading Nazi officials, including Hitler, came from a younger generation greatly affected by their experience of World War I. The earliest recruits for the fascist paramilitary formations were combat veterans returning from the front. The concept of "storm troopers," elite soldiers trained to storm the enemy lines and force a breakthrough for the regular infantry, originated in this war. Likewise, the fascist leadership principle, a legacy of both monarchism and the military tradition, was strongly reinforced by the combat experience of the war. The myth of the front experience had even greater resonance among those who had been too young to take part in the war. Young men who reached maturity at or after the end of the war provided most of the recruits for the paramilitary forces organized by right-wing parties. Displaced from the civilian workforce by returning veterans, this age cohort constituted something of a superfluous generation never fully integrated into the social fabric. Many of them sought an outlet for their frustrations in political movements on the extreme right.

War apotheosized the soldierly ethos of comradeship, unity, heroism, and self-sacrifice that would become so central to the fascist value system. The war had a leveling effect on social rank as well, bringing together men from diverse backgrounds and occupations to share the common ordeal of the trenches. The partial breakdown of class distinctions in war showed how the ethos of comradeship might facilitate the integration of disaffected workers into the national community. Survival in combat required teamwork and made differences of income and status largely irrelevant. The tendency of war to mold the disparate masses into uniform and standardized cohorts was symbolized by the vast military cemeteries in which each grave, as far as the eye could reach, was marked by a simple white wooden cross.[3]

War as a unifying force

The outbreak of war generated a surge of patriotism in all of the combatant nations. However, not all segments of German society greeted the war with equal enthusiasm. The upper and middle classes, intellectuals, and men tended to welcome the war more enthusiastically than members of the working class or women; and antiwar demonstrations, though less well attended, actually outnumbered prowar rallies at the start of the war.[4] But even members of the workers' movement who had not bought into the ideology of racial struggle viewed the war as a necessary defense against the backward Russian Empire, where workers were subject to worse conditions and had fewer rights than in Germany. Only a handful of dissidents on the left wing of the SPD opposed their party's vote in favor of war credits in the Reichstag. In Munich a recent immigrant from Austria, the young would-be artist Adolf Hitler, joined the throng that cheered the news of war.

Germany's rulers and most of the German public confidently expected a quick victory. German military leaders, although under no illusions that victory would be quick and easy, were also optimistic about Germany's ability to win a two-front continental war.[5] Not since the days of Bismarck had the regime enjoyed such widespread public support. The call to the flag seemed to override all partisan differences. The government used the national emergency to call a moratorium on political debate. "I do not know parties any longer," William II told the nation, "I know only Germans."[6] The start of World War I marked the high point of national unity that the Nazis would work so hard to restore. For conservatives, domestic peace was the gratifying corollary to foreign war. The danger to the nation mandated an end to domestic conflicts and social divisions. The war finally created the unity and patriotic consensus that conservatives had unsuccessfully sought to attain for decades. In their view, a rapid and favorable outcome would best guarantee the protection of property and power against the challenge from the left.

The Schlieffen Plan

The Schlieffen Plan, Germany's military contingency plan in case of war against both Russia and France, was designed to win a war that would be fought on both fronts. Drawn up by the General Staff under its chief Alfred von Schlieffen in 1905, this plan called for a massive assault in the west to destroy the French forces within the six weeks that their Russian allies, hampered by a backward and unwieldy infrastructure, were expected to need for full mobilization. Quick victory in the west would permit the transfer of German forces to the east in time to defeat the technologically inferior Russian army.[7]

The Schlieffen Plan was politically unwise and militarily too ambitious. Its political defects showed the excessive influence of the German General Staff on policy-making under the Imperial constitution. It also reflected the German leadership's overestimation of German capabilities. Because timing was essential to its success, the Schlieffen Plan made a peaceful resolution of the crisis virtually impossible in the last days of July 1914. Once Russia had begun mobilization to resist an Austrian invasion of Serbia, German generals could effectively argue that any delay in implementing their plan meant risking defeat in a general war. No time was left to avert war through the negotiations that the Kaiser and the German chancellor Theobald von Bethmann Hollweg (1856–1921) now belatedly hoped to bring about.

The Schlieffen Plan furnished a striking example of blindness to the political consequences of military actions. It called for the invasion of France through Belgium and Luxembourg even though Germany (through Prussia) was a signatory to the international treaty, signed in 1839, guaranteeing Belgian neutrality. The violation of Belgian neutrality united British public opinion behind the government's decision to join the war against Germany. That decision would have been taken in any case, but the Schlieffen Plan enabled the British government to make this potentially unpopular decision with full public support.

Stalemate on the western front

In the first weeks of the war the Schlieffen Plan nearly succeeded. By the time the French and British forces stopped the German assault at the Battle of the Marne in September 1914, the French government had already moved from Paris to Bordeaux. For the next three and a half years the war in the West turned into a virtual stalemate as both sides dug into well-fortified trenches that faced each other across several hundred yards of no-man's land.

Efforts on both sides to break through the stalemate resulted in hundreds of thousands of casualties. Refinement of the machine gun in the years before the war gave the defense an unprecedented advantage. It consigned to obsolescence such traditional military tactics as cavalry charges and massed infantry columns advancing into battle in march step. The Battle of Verdun that raged for almost ten months in 1916 claimed close to a million casualties on both sides, while the British suffered some 60,000 casualties on the first day of the Battle of the Somme in June of that year. Approximately 12 million soldiers lost their lives on the various fronts of this brutal war of attrition.

German war aims

In the east the German troops were more successful, defeating the ill-equipped Russians in the battles of Tannenberg and the Masurian Lakes in East Prussia in the late summer of 1914. The commanders of the victorious German forces, General Paul von Hindenburg and his Chief of Staff Erich Ludendorff, assumed the high command of the army in 1916 and ruled Germany as virtual dictators in the last two years of the war. Their appointment to the high command marks an important demarcation line as well as a connecting link between the Second Empire and the Third Reich. Unlike Hindenburg's predecessor, General Erich von Falkenhayn (1861–1922), who counseled a political solution to the war after the failure of his strategy of attrition in the Battle of Verdun, both Hindenburg and Ludendorff were committed to a military victory, German expansion, and an annexationist peace. After the war both men would play important roles in the Nazis' rise to power.

As the struggle ground on and costs and casualties mounted on both sides, neither the Germans nor the Allies were prepared to accept the kind of compromise peace that might have prevented the rise of totalitarian ideologies or regimes and a second world war. From the point of view of the ruling elites, a compromise peace would only exacerbate domestic conflict over which classes or social groups would pay for the costs of the war. Only the spoils of victory offered the prospect of continuing social peace. Thus the expansionist aims of German leaders escalated during the war. When the German invasion of France appeared on the verge of success in September 1914, the German government drew up the so-called "September Program," which called for the annexation of substantial territory from France and Belgium, the incorporation of Luxembourg, the creation of satellite regimes in rump Belgium and Holland, and the acquisition of French colonies in central Africa. Although conditions did not yet seem to warrant drawing up specific aims in the east, Chancellor Bethmann Hollweg is quoted as saying that "Russia must be thrust back as far as possible from Germany's eastern frontier and her domination over the non-Russian vassal peoples broken."[8] In order to maintain the SPD's support for the war, discussion of expansionist war aims was conducted in secret. SPD support was contingent on the assumption that Germany was fighting a defensive war. In 1916 a German peace proposal that called for the economic domination of Belgium was rejected by the Allies. Support for German expansion came from various quarters. German military leaders sought territorial acquisitions to guarantee more secure borders; Pan-Germans wanted to incorporate all ethnic Germans in an empire expanded to the east; German industrialists demanded greater access to resources. Supporters of a German overseas empire tended to view Britain as the primary enemy; backers of continental imperialism saw Russia as the major foe. German expansionist tendencies came together in the widely shared vision of a *Mitteleuropa*, a federation of central European states, including Austria-Hungary, dominated by the German Reich.

Unrestricted submarine warfare

Germany's dependence on submarine warfare against the British navy made for increasingly difficult relations with the United States, which had proclaimed neutrality at the beginning of the war. Both the Entente and the Central Powers imposed a naval blockade that adversely affected US trade, but only Britain, with its superiority in surface vessels, was able to enforce it in a systematic way. If they wished to block the British Isles, the Germans had little choice but to resort to submarine warfare, an inherently inhumane form of war because submarines cannot stop neutral vessels to search them for contraband, must attack without warning, and cannot stay in the area to rescue survivors. Submarines must proceed by stealth: if submarines reveal their location, they become easy targets for faster surface vessels. British naval superiority meant that German–American trade came to a virtual standstill while British–American trade increased. An important turning point in the war occurred in May 1915 when a German submarine sank the British passenger liner Lusitania off the coast of Ireland with the loss of over a thousand lives, including 114 Americans. This attack outraged the American public, especially since American authorities had previously certified that the Lusitania carried no military supplies (whether there was a secret military cargo, however, remains a matter of dispute). American protests persuaded the Germans to limit their submarine campaign in order not to provoke American entry into the war.

In January 1917, however, the German High Command decided to lift all restrictions on submarine warfare in a desperate effort to break out of the military stalemate. It did so in full knowledge that this decision would draw the United States into the war. The High Command nonetheless pursued the illusory hope that a total blockade of Britain would persuade the Allies to make peace on German terms before American troops could make their presence felt on the battlefields of France. High-ranking German naval officers, too, vastly underestimated the devastating effect that American participation in the war would have on German fortunes.[9] On 2 April 1917, after the loss of several ships, the United States declared war on Germany.

The American declaration of war was made easier by the overthrow of the tsarist regime in Russia a month earlier. President Woodrow Wilson's claim that this was a war for democracy would have lacked credibility if the war had been fought in alliance with the autocratic regime of Tsar Nicholas II. With American entry into the war and a liberal government temporarily in power in Russia, the war entered its revolutionary phase. The provisional government in Russia under Alexander Kerensky (1881–1970) attributed popular disaffection to the government's failure to prosecute the war against the Central Powers to a victorious conclusion. The stakes for Germany and Austria were no less great, as the very survival of the monarchical system was now at risk.

Re-emergence of opposition in Germany

Despite the false optimism of the German High Command, the prospects of victory dwindled as the war dragged on. As public awareness grew of the High Command's commitment to victory at all costs, domestic opposition to government policies re-emerged. Criticism of official policies shattered the *Burgfrieden* ("peace within the castle," the euphemism for avoiding partisan debate) that had marked the early years of the war. Signs of discontent appeared in many sectors of German society. News of the March Revolution in Russia incited sporadic unrest in Germany as well. Some naval units mutinied in the summer of 1917, and strikes broke out among factory workers, with the most serious ones occurring in January 1918. The German authorities responded by promising tactical concessions to the labor movement. Yet even at this late date, almost four years into the war, conservatives in the Prussian

Landtag defeated a bill to revoke the system of three-class suffrage in May 1918.

The SPD, which with only a few exceptions had supported war credits in the Reichstag in August 1914, was now split on the issue of ending the war. The antiwar faction formed a militant new party of opposition, the Independent Social Democrats (USPD), in April 1917. On its radical fringe members of the informal "Spartacus League" advocated civil disobedience to end the war. Left-wing pressure contributed to the Reichstag's passage in July 1917 of a "peace resolution," supported by the SPD, the Catholic Center, and the liberal parties, precisely the parties that would later support the Weimar Republic. The peace resolution called on the government to negotiate a peace without annexations or reparations.

On the right side of the political spectrum, nationalists of the Pan-German League countered by founding the German Fatherland Party in September 1917 to promote an annexationist peace. The aim of the new party, financed by army and industry, was to generate a popular base for the dictatorship of the Army High Command. With Admiral Tirpitz, the architect of Germany's prewar naval build-up, as its chairman the Fatherland Party enrolled close to a million members before it disbanded in December 1918.[10] The party's campaign against pacifism and democracy laid the groundwork for the *völkisch* counter-revolution after the war. Even antisemitism, muted for the sake of unity in the early war years, now re-emerged in the growing backlash against the antiwar movement. Even before the end of the war, the search began for domestic enemies who allegedly undermined German victory. Although 12,000 German Jews were killed in the war, charges of Jewish under-representation at the front provoked an official inquiry in 1916, the results of which, however, were never publicized. The war that was supposed to unify the country and eliminate internal conflict was now leading to increasing radicalization and polarization.

The Treaty of Brest-Litovsk

Despite the passage of the peace resolution, which sought to commit the government to purely defensive war aims, German military policy remained committed to victory and expansion. Indeed, the only effect of the peace resolution was to prompt Hindenburg and Ludendorff to drop their support for Bethmann Hollweg, who had ineffectively opposed the resolution, and increase their efforts to curb the influence of the Reichstag. The Bolshevik seizure of power in Russia in November 1917, made possible in part by the free passage across Germany of Lenin and other leading revolutionaries, gave the High Command the opportunity to exact enormous territorial concessions from the new communist regime. Germany's centuries-old dream of a *Drang nach Osten* (push to the east) seemed on the verge of fulfillment.

The Treaty of Brest-Litovsk, signed under duress by the new Russian government in March 1918, detached Poland, Finland, the new Baltic states, portions of Byelorussia (today Belarus), and the entire Ukraine from the former Russian Empire.[11] The harsh terms of this settlement, opposed in the Reichstag by the Independent Social Democrats, revealed the scope of Germany's expansionist ambitions in the east and offered a forewarning of what the Western Allies could expect if Germany won the war. Ultimately the terms of Brest-Litovsk worked against German interests by tying down close to a million troops to police the new acquisitions. A compromise peace might have released more troops for the final offensive in the west.

German defeat

This offensive in the spring of 1918 launched the High Command's final gamble for victory. However, the over-commitment of German reserves and supplies only hastened German defeat. By the fall of 1918 more than one million American troops had entered the war on the western front. The German forces soon reached the limits of their endurance and resources. On 8 August, a date General Ludendorff would call "the black day of the German army," Allied forces broke through the German lines. The last German effort to win the war at all costs had failed. All along the western front the German army was forced to retreat.

Contrary to the postwar legend that leftist politicians had stabbed the army in the back, it was the High Command itself that instructed the government to seek an immediate armistice in the fall of 1918.[12] Ludendorff himself suggested that the base of the government be broadened to obtain more favorable terms from the Allies and to force the democratic forces in Germany to accept responsibility for the defeat. "They must now deal with the mess that they have caused," he told his officers.[13] In the view of Germany's leaders a controlled revolution from above would also help to forestall a more radical one from below. On 3 October a new government with liberal and Social Democratic participation was formed under Prince Max von Baden. Its first act was to appeal to Woodrow Wilson for an armistice. The American president's statement of Allied war aims in January 1918, the Fourteen Points, offered the Germans the best hope for a generous peace. But Wilson made it clear that democratization had not gone far enough to satisfy Allied demands. If the Germans wanted an armistice, the Kaiser would have to abdicate. Under pressure from the Entente powers and American opponents of a negotiated peace, Wilson also imposed conditions that would make Germany incapable of resuming hostilities after an armistice.

This lethal threat to the monarchy and the military, coupled with the relative stabilization of the German lines after weeks of retreat, now

Map 1 The German Empire, 1871–1919, showing territorial losses following World War I.

induced Ludendorff to oppose further negotiations. His resignation as Chief of Staff on 26 October 1918 would set the stage for the stab-in-the-back legend purveyed by army officers and *völkisch* politicians after the war. But it was the collapse of the army that precipitated revolution, not the other way round. The momentum to end hostilities could no longer be halted.

Revolution

In the first week of November strikes and mutinies spread across the land. The Austro-Hungarian Empire had already fallen apart, and the German Empire now entered its final stage of dissolution. Resisting orders to set sail for a final showdown battle with the British navy, thousands of German sailors seized the port city of Kiel on 3 November and set up councils of workers and sailors on the Soviet model. By 5 November all ships in Kiel were flying the red flag. Councils of workers and soldiers sprang up in other cities as well. On 8 November the Jewish lawyer and writer Kurt Eisner, leader of the Bavarian USPD, proclaimed a Bavarian republic in Munich. Haunted by the specter of revolution, the new German government and the High Command finally persuaded the reluctant Kaiser to abdicate on 9 November. Two days later German emissaries of the new government signed the armistice at Compiègne that brought hostilities to an end.[14]

Chancellor Max von Baden announced the Kaiser's abdication to stave off chaos in strike-ridden Berlin. At the same time he tendered his own resignation, simply turning over the reins of government to members of the SPD. From the balcony of the chancellery the SPD deputy Philipp Scheidemann proclaimed the formation of a German republic. SPD leader Friedrich Ebert, later to be installed as the first president of the Weimar Republic, headed a governing council of three members each from the SPD and USPD. Once the pariahs of German politics, the Social Democratic Party outlawed by Bismarck now came into power by virtual default.

Thus democracy came to Germany by virtue of a war that was lost but that did not destroy the antidemocratic forces. The origins of German democracy were not auspicious: liberalization had been demanded by the High Command to avoid the worst consequences of military reversals in the field, yet leading officers would soon blame democracy for German defeat. Members of the new government would be labeled the "November criminals" who had supposedly stabbed the unconquered army in the back.

Many unreconstructed conservatives viewed a democratic government as but a temporary expedient to mollify the Allies until the monarchy could be restored and expansionist aims revived. They hoped for a counter-revolution to reverse the results of the war and roll back democratic gains. In the meantime democratic politicians could be made to take responsibility for accepting the terms of defeat.

For the moment the political momentum had shifted to the left, but the divided democratic forces in Germany faced an almost impossible task. They had to restore order, accept the terms of the victorious powers, and construct a viable democratic system against the opposition of powerful elites. German imperialism had been weakened but it had not been destroyed. In the polarized politics of the postwar era it would re-emerge in militant and radical form.

6 The Weimar Republic and the weakness of liberal democracy

Allied victory in World War I seemed to herald the triumph of liberal democracy in Europe. In Germany the fall of the monarchy brought to power the Social Democrats (SPD), which had been the major opposition party of the late Imperial era. A new constitution drawn up in the city of Weimar in 1919 embodied liberal and democratic principles. Yet 20 years after the armistice of November 1918 there would not be a single democracy left in central or eastern Europe. In Italy Mussolini's Fascists took power as early as 1922 and consolidated their dictatorship in 1925–26. The Weimar Republic survived, at least in form, until 1933, although normal parliamentary process had virtually ceased by 1930. It was the collapse of Weimar democracy that paved the way for the Nazi takeover in January 1933.

Periodization

The history of the Republic be divided into three major periods. Serious economic and political dislocations and civil strife marked the first phase from 1919 to 1924. During this period the government (characterized by frequently changing cabinets and party coalitions) found itself beset by revolutionary uprisings from the left and counter-revolutionary putsch attempts and a terrorist assassination campaign from the right. Separatist movements in Bavaria and the Rhineland, as well as the efforts of the victor powers, especially France, to enforce the payment of reparations as stipulated by the Treaty of Versailles, further challenged the new republic.

This period of political turmoil, inflation, and conflict with the west came to a tentative close with the defeat of Hitler's first bid for power—the "Beer Hall Putsch"—in late 1923, the rescheduling of reparation payments under the Dawes Plan in 1924, and the signing of the Locarno treaties in 1925. Economic recovery ushered in a period of relative stability from 1925 to 1929, but the strength of the Republic was ultimately deceptive. Too many enemies were arrayed against it, waiting for the opportunity to establish a more authoritarian regime. The third and final phase of the Republic, characterized by economic collapse, political polarization, bitter street-fighting, and growing authoritarianism, lasted from the onset of the Great Depression in 1930 to Hitler's appointment as chancellor in January 1933.

The assault on liberal democracy

Why was the democratic system established in Germany in 1918–19 so weak? How did the Nazis become strong enough to take and retain power in 1933–34? These are overlapping, but not identical, questions. After the onset of the Great Depression in 1930 the demise of democracy in Germany was a virtually foregone conclusion, but the triumph of the National Socialists was not. The rise of the Nazis was as much a symptom as a cause of the failure of German democracy.

In some respects the weakness of the Weimar Republic simply exemplified the general crisis of liberal democracy in Europe in the interwar years. In the unsettled and polarized political climate after World War I and the Russian Revolution liberal democracies everywhere faced challenges from the radical left and right. In the economic deceleration that began in the 1920s and bottomed out in the 1930s, liberal capitalism seemed to have played out all over Europe. The decline of *laissez-faire* liberalism had begun in the late nineteenth century, but reached its crisis point in the period between the wars. Liberal institutions such as free trade, a competitive market economy, and parliamentary government no longer seemed capable of coping with the growing problems of industrial society. These included apparently uncontrollable economic fluctuations, widespread unemployment, and bitter distributional conflicts between classes and interest groups competing for a shrinking pie.

After the Great War (and the revolutions this war precipitated in Russia in 1917) a different kind of war was waged across Europe—a war between left and right, a European civil war that was fought out in different ways and with different results in every country. The horrors of what would later be known as World War I turned a growing number of European intellectuals to Marxism as the best hope of avoiding another bloody internecine conflict between the European powers. The overriding issue in the conflict between left and right was how the benefits and burdens of modern industrial society would be distributed. The main casualty of this conflict was liberal democracy in central Europe. The increasing militancy of the labor movement, fanned by the new communist parties in Europe, drove the propertied middle classes further to the right. As popular trust in liberal democracy declined, growing numbers of people were prepared to support authoritarian solutions to social and political problems.

Even in countries like Britain and France where the liberal tradition was strong, the liberal consensus was threatened from both the left and the right. But there were factors peculiar to Germany that explain the particular virulence of antidemocratic sentiment in that country and the extremism of its National Socialist movement. In Germany, where liberalism was historically weak, the Weimar Republic could not survive the social and political polarization that was greatly intensified by the Great Depression. Because it was established in the wake of a lost war, the liberal republic faced a number of additional obstacles from the start. Weimar was coupled in the public mind with Versailles, and democracy was linked to defeat. To many Germans liberal democracy seemed like an alien system imposed by the Allied conquerors to keep Germany weak and disunited.

The Ebert–Groener Agreement

The day before the armistice was signed on 11 November 1918 a fateful bargain was struck between the new temporary head of government, the moderate Social Democrat Friedrich Ebert (1871–1925), and General Wilhelm Groener (1867–1939), who had replaced Ludendorff as Army Chief of Staff. The Ebert–Groener deal helped to insure that the transition to democracy would not end the independence of the army or the power of traditional elites. Groener pledged the cooperation and support of the army to the new SPD government on condition that no changes be made in the internal organization of the army or in the prerogatives of the officer corps. The government also pledged to take vigorous action to combat the "Bolshevik threat."

The Ebert–Groener deal helped to maintain the privileged position of the army as a virtually autonomous "state within the state." Ebert believed that the support of the army was essential to quelling disorder and preserving the new government. He did not foresee that the army itself might constitute a threat to democracy. Anxious to woo the army to the republican cause, Ebert publicly saluted the troops in Berlin for having returned from the field unconquered. He thus gave unwitting support to the "stab-in-the-back" legend disseminated by enemies of the new republic.

While the army leadership participated enthusiastically in the suppression of subversion from the left, they would pointedly fail to offer the same kind of protection against attempts to overthrow the government from the right. The government found itself in the unenviable position of relying on military leaders who were only conditionally loyal to the republican form of government, yet were able to exercise considerable influence on government policy. Whenever the High Command objected to a government measure, it announced that it could not be "responsible" for its execution. As a result the government was usually forced to heed the wishes of the High Command.[1]

The lack of fundamental social reform

As soon as power was thrust upon it in November 1918 Ebert's caretaker government sought to hold the line against the popular revolutions that had broken out in various parts of the country. In view of the anarchy that accompanied the collapse of the Imperial regime in many parts of the country, it is understandable that the majority Social Democrats gave precedence to the restoration of law and order over the implementation of social reform. Even before the war the SPD had no longer actively sought the socialization of the economy despite its formal commitment to that goal. Ebert himself seems to have preferred a constitutional monarchy to a republic in order to preserve continuity and stability. Faced by economic crisis, revolutionary unrest, a continuing Allied blockade, and the danger of Allied invasion, SPD leaders were not inclined to support any wide-ranging changes such as land reform, the socialization of industry, the creation of a popular militia to replace the *Reichswehr* (the army), democratization of the judiciary, or the dismissal of civil servants hostile to democracy. Nor was the government willing to publish documentary evidence of the role of German leaders in the outbreak of the war, which might have helped to discredit the opposition of the conservative elites to democratic change. Ebert and Philipp Scheidemann (1865–1939) feared that Allied peace terms would be even more punitive if the truth of German responsibility for the outbreak of war became known.

More far-reaching social changes might have enabled liberal democracy to strike deeper roots in German society and weather the crisis of the Great Depression. As it was, however, the social structure of Imperial Germany remained firmly in place, and the major institutions of the Republic continued to be dominated by elites hostile to democracy. The best constitution is only of limited value if democratic consciousness is lacking. Historians have aptly described the Weimar regime as a "republic without republicans" and as "the Imperial social order in republican dress."[2] Even converts from monarchism who supported the Republic did so more out of prudence (to avoid Allied intervention) than conviction.

The need to insure the cooperation of labor in a period of revolutionary turmoil did persuade industrialists to accept liberalized labor practices at the end of the war. Over the objection of heavy industry the government had already strengthened union rights in 1916 to maintain labor support for the war. On 15 November 1918 the industrialist Hugo Stinnes (1870–1924) and independent trade union leader Carl Legien (1861–1924) agreed to create a central working community to stabilize the economy in the difficult period of demobilization. The so-called Stinnes–Legien Agreement recognized union rights to collective bargaining and accepted the eight-hour workday. Only four years later, however, after the working community with labor had served its purpose, Stinnes repudiated the agreement and sought to revoke the eight-hour day. While industrialists benefitted from union cooperation, the hopes of the unions for a greater voice in economic decision-making remained unfulfilled.[3]

The limited nature of social reforms and the suppression of revolution also exposed the liberal republic to lasting attack from the far left. The example of the Russian Revolution was crucial to the fate of the Weimar Republic, not only because fear of social revolution and communism enhanced the appeal of fascism to the middle classes, but also because one of the enduring consequences of the Russian Revolution was a division of the socialist movement into advocates of a Soviet-type system and moderate socialists who rejected the

Soviet model. The bitter struggle for working-class support between the Communists and the Social Democrats further narrowed the social base of the Weimar regime. Under the circumstances, the failure of Weimar democracy is perhaps less surprising than the fact that it lasted as long as it did.

The rift on the left

The SPD's reluctance to tamper with traditional institutions and its willingness to employ armed force to suppress the revolutionary movement led to bitter conflict with the Independent Social Democrats (USPD), who had broken with the SPD and unsuccessfully tried to form a citizen army independent of the High Command. The USPD members left the governing coalition in protest against the use of army troops to put down an uprising of revolutionary sailors and soldiers in Berlin in December 1918. To the left of the USPD, the Spartacist League favored a government based on workers' councils, though without the party dictatorship that emerged in Soviet Russia. Spartacist leaders Rosa Luxemburg (1870–1919) and Karl Liebknecht (1871–1919), both of whom had been imprisoned for antiwar activities during the war, formed the German Communist Party (KPD) on 30 December 1918.

The revolutionary movement came to a head with the outbreak of the so-called "Spartacist Revolt" in Berlin in January 1919. This was not so much a revolt as it was a reaction to a preemptive move by the Ebert government against the Spartacists. On 6 January the Spartacists held a huge mass rally to protest the dismissal of the USPD deputy chief of police in Berlin. Fearing that this might be the prelude to further revolution, the government called on the army to crush the Spartacist strongholds in the city, including the offices of the SPD newspaper, *Vorwärts*, which armed Spartacists had occupied. Army units, some of whose rank and file were reluctant to join this action against the revolutionary movement, were supplemented by units of the so-called Free Corps, a volunteer military force created at the suggestion of the High Command and commanded by army officers. Recruited from soldiers discharged from the army in accordance with the terms of the armistice, these units were to become the shock troops of counter-revolution and the "vanguard of Nazism."

The Free Corps

All over Germany, nationalist officers formed volunteer units to combat the revolutionary movement that had erupted in many parts of the country in the weeks following the armistice. For the soldiers of the Free Corps the war was not over; the enemy at the front had merely been exchanged for the "enemy within." Reviving a rhyme first composed by a Prussian general in the 1848 revolution, "Gegen Demokraten helfen nur Soldaten" (against democrats only soldiers [can] help), Free Corps units proceeded with utmost brutality. They took a leading role in crushing the Spartacists in January as well as the renewed worker protests in Berlin in 1919. They also unseated left-wing governments in numerous German cities and in the Rhineland, Saxony, and Bavaria in the winter and spring of 1919. In the process the Free Corps unleashed a campaign of "white terror" against the left. Luxemburg and Liebknecht were shot in captivity in Berlin on 15 January 1919, even before the short-lived Spartacist insurgency had run its course; 600 people were killed in the first two days after the overthrow of the "Workers' Council Republic" in Munich in April 1919.[4]

Although paid by the government and organized with its blessings, Free Corps volunteers felt no loyalty to the Republic. Their ultimate objective was to "annihilate the republican gangs," as one Free Corps leader put it.[5] After fighting against western liberalism and democracy on the frontlines during the war, the veterans who joined the Free Corps would not be reconciled to a liberal and democratic system at home. The Free Corps ideology was essentially the same as that of hundreds of right-wing groups and parties (including the tiny Munich-based National Socialist Workers' Party) spawned by the disappointment of defeat. By employing Free Corps units against the revolutionary left, the SPD-run government in effect hired its own enemies to save itself from the "Red peril."

Free Corps units were also deployed to defend or acquire disputed territories on the eastern frontiers. In the hopes of salvaging at least parts of the vast eastern empire Germany had acquired at Brest-Litovsk, the High Command used Free Corps units to try to annex the Baltic nations, Latvia and Estonia, that had been part of the Russian Empire up to 1918. Free Corps units under Count von der Goltz took the Latvian capital of Riga before the Allies compelled their withdrawal in the summer of 1919. Many Free Corps veterans remained behind to fight with the White army against the Bolsheviks in the Russian Civil War. After the Versailles treaty took effect in 1919, the Free Corps movement would commend itself to army and government leaders as a way of circumventing the 100,000-man ceiling imposed on the *Reichswehr* by the Allies. Before they were disbanded under Allied pressure in 1921, the Free Corps mobilized several hundred thousand men into a dangerous counter-revolutionary force.

The Republic was thus formed more by reaction to revolution than by the revolution itself. Suppression of the revolutionary movement left a legacy of proletarian bitterness against the SPD and the Republic and created an irreconcilable gulf between moderates and radicals on the left. The hard line of the government against the revolutionary left played into the hands of its enemies on the right, who were only awaiting a favorable opportunity to overthrow the Republic.

The Weimar constitution

The revolution was "frozen" in place and the forces of popular democracy were on the defensive even before the newly elected National Assembly convened in the city of Weimar in February 1919 to draw up a constitution for the new republic. Weimar was chosen as the site of the constitutional convention to escape the disorders in the capital of Berlin. (Berlin, however, remained the capital throughout the Weimar era.) Some adherents of democracy also hoped that the choice of Weimar, where Germany's greatest writers, Goethe and Schiller, had resided, would link the new republic to Germany's humanist tradition.

In the elections to the National Assembly in January 1919, with a voter turnout of 83 percent, the Social Democrats (SPD) won a substantial plurality of 38 percent (a higher percentage than the Nazis would win in the last free election in 1932). The SPD was the primary beneficiary of public revulsion against the horrors of war and the failures of the monarchy. However, as the more radical Independent Social Democrats (USPD) received only 7.6 percent of the vote, the working-class parties fell short of the majority that many labor leaders had expected. Nevertheless, it was the SPD—along with the Catholic Center Party and the German Democratic Party (successor to the progressive wing of the liberal movement in the German Empire)—that formed the backbone of the "Weimar coalition" with a combined vote of over 75 percent in support of a new liberal constitution.

Completed in June 1919, the constitution provided for true parliamentary government. For the first time in German history, the chancellor, equivalent to the prime minister in the parliamentary systems of Britain or France, became responsible to the Reichstag, the lower house of parliament, and had to maintain a parliamentary majority in order to remain in office. As head of government the chancellor was more powerful than the president, who served as head of state. Ironically, however, the emergency powers given to the otherwise largely ceremonial office of president under Article 48 would provide a way to suspend this basic principle of parliamentary government. Article 48 gave the president authority to rule by decree in case of a crisis that threatened the Republic. Designed to protect the Republic in emergency situations, Article 48 would become one of the instruments through which the foes of the Republic destroyed the parliamentary process after 1930.

Another provision designed to strengthen democracy ultimately helped to undermine it as well. Proportional representation (which gave even the smallest parties representation in the Reichstag in direct proportion to their vote nationwide) led to a proliferation of parties and impeded the parliamentary process by making it more difficult to form governing majorities. (The framers of West Germany's postwar constitution in 1949 would learn from the Weimar experience by establishing a floor of 5 percent of the vote for representation in parliament.) The president and the members of the Reichstag were elected by universal suffrage. The Weimar government was more centralized than the Bismarckian Reich, but the states retained important jurisdictions, especially over police and education. The belated triumph of liberal principles was symbolized by the choice of the colors of 1848—black, gold, and red—for the flag of the new republic.

Even a model constitution cannot ensure the survival of democracy, however, when democratic consensus is lacking. Its liberal character made the constitution unacceptable to the elites who mourned the passing of monarchical authority. Both the German Nationalist Party (DNVP), successor to the prewar Conservatives, and the German People's Party (DVP), successor to the National Liberals, voted against the new constitution. On the left the USPD opposed the constitution for failing to effect more radical reform. Most of its members would join the Communists (KPD) when the USPD dissolved itself in 1922.

The Treaty of Versailles

The worst blow to the prestige and popularity of the Weimar assembly and the new form of government was the assembly's acceptance, under duress, of the Treaty of Versailles. In what many Germans viewed as a violation of the first of Woodrow Wilson's Fourteen Points, which pledged "open covenants openly arrived at," the treaty had been drawn up by the Allies without German participation. Yet the terms presented to the Germans were less stringent than the maximal French demands, which included the creation of a separate state in the Rhineland. The treaty was a compromise between Woodrow Wilson's principle of national self-determination and the French resolve to weaken Germany's economic capacity and great-power status. Germany lost about 13 percent of its prewar territory, mostly in the east, where a Polish state was reconstituted for the first time since 1815. A strip of land separating East Prussia from the rest of Germany gave Poland an outlet to the sea. Germany's efforts to regain control of this "Polish Corridor" and the free city of Danzig (today Gdansk) would provide the immediate cause for the outbreak of World War II.

The Versailles Treaty restored Alsace and Lorraine to France and awarded parts of Silesia to the new Polish state. The rich mining area of the Saar was placed under French control for 15 years, after which its final disposition was to be determined by plebiscite. The Rhineland was to be permanently demilitarized after a 15-year Allied occupation. Germany was also obligated to respect the "inalienable" independence of Austria. According to the terms of the related Treaty of Saint-Germain, which confirmed the partition of the former Habsburg Empire into its constituent nations, the ethnically German portion of Austria was prohibited from uniting with Germany. The Versailles Treaty also placed a ceiling of 100,000 men on the size of the once-mighty German army, while compelling the Germans to surrender both their navy and their merchant fleet; however, naval officers scuttled their vessels at Scapa Flow in June 1919 to avoid turning them over to the Allies. Most onerous of all to the German public was the obligation to pay reparations for damages caused by the war. As none of the war was fought on British soil, the British insisted that reparations include pensions and separation allowances for demobilized Allied soldiers and for families of soldiers killed in the war.

The total amount of the German debt was to be determined by a specially established commission.

To justify the demand for reparations, the Versailles Treaty required Germany to accept full responsibility for all the damage caused by the war. More than any other provision, this "war-guilt clause" united the German public in opposition to the treaty. The Allies rejected German requests for alterations in the treaty and threatened to continue their economic blockade unless the government signed. Philipp Scheidemann, who had become chancellor after Ebert was elected to the presidency in February 1919, resigned in protest against the terms of the treaty, but a majority in the Weimar assembly feared that the failure to submit would only bring Allied reprisals. On 28 June 1919 German emissaries put their signatures to what would become known in Germany as the "Versailles *Diktat.*"

The Allies might have served their own interests better by not saddling the fledgling German democracy with such highly unpopular terms. In his pamphlet, *The Economic Consequences of the Peace*, published in 1920, the British economist John Maynard Keynes accurately predicted that the treaty would lead to a renewed outbreak of war within 20 years. Versailles gave enormous impetus to the growth of the radical right in Germany. Although government leaders, too, denounced the treaty as unjust, as signatories they could hardly compete with the invective of nationalist groups without incriminating themselves. Since denunciations of the treaty by supporters of the Republic only gave added legitimacy to the attacks on the government from the right, right-wing nationalists became the primary beneficiaries of the public revulsion against Versailles.

The stab-in-the-back legend

Two myths gained wide acceptance among the German public and abetted the rise of the radical right after World War I. One was the conviction that the war had been started by Germany's enemies to destroy a dynamic economic, political, and colonial rival. The German government sponsored an historical commission to prove that Germany was not responsible for provoking the war. The second and even more dangerous myth was the conviction that Germany's humiliation had been brought about by left-wing traitors. Most Germans thought the Allies had gained through the treaty what they had not been able to win on the battlefield. Psychologically, at least, most Germans were not ready to admit that their army had been defeated. Throughout the war, the High Command had fed the German public unrealistically optimistic news about the progress of the war. The fact that, with the exception of the battles in East Prussia in 1914, none of the fighting had taken place on German soil further legitimized this myth. At the time of the armistice German troops were still entrenched in France and Belgium, and they occupied Poland, the Baltic, and the Ukraine. Hence many Germans were all too ready to believe the charge of the radical right that the humiliating end of the war was a consequence not of military defeat but of civilian defeatism. According to this view, a conspiracy of Jews and socialists had undermined the morale of the home front and stabbed the courageous army in the back. Germany could have won if it had only stayed the course. The Nazis would draw two main lessons from what they considered to have been the mistakes of the German leadership in World War I: first, internal dissent must never be tolerated, and second, surrender was never an option.

The Kapp Putsch

In 1920 the same Free Corps units that had been used by the Ebert government to suppress the Spartacist Revolt and the workers' council regime in Munich struck at the government itself. The Kapp–Lüttwitz Putsch was led by Wolfgang Kapp (1858–1922), an official in the Prussian civil service and a former leader of the wartime Fatherland Party, and General Walther von Lüttwitz (1859–1942), commander of the Free Corps units in and around Berlin. It enjoyed the support of General Ludendorff, recently returned from his self-imposed exile in Sweden. While the immediate purpose of the putsch was to reverse the government's order to demobilize certain Free Corps units in accordance with the provisions of the Versailles Treaty, its broader objective was to oust the "November criminals" and restore a powerful authoritarian regime. On the morning of 13 March, soldiers of the elite Ehrhardt Brigade, swastikas emblazoned on their helmets, marched into Berlin and occupied government offices. Ironically, the unit that had been summoned to Berlin by the government in late 1919 to help put down worker protests was now striking at the government it was supposed to defend.

The government's predicament was graphically revealed by the response of *Reichswehr* leaders to the government's request for support against the Free Corps. Chief of Staff Hans von Seeckt (1866–1936) announced the army's neutrality with the dictum, "Troops do not fire on troops." He justified his decision by claiming that army intervention against the Free Corps would encourage revolutionary forces of the left. Indeed, his soldiers did not hesitate to fire on former comrades who had joined revolutionary organizations. Nor did the army hesitate to fire on striking workers in Thuringia and the Ruhr later that same year.

President Ebert, Chancellor Gustav Bauer, and other government ministers were forced to leave Berlin for safety in Stuttgart, where the local *Reichswehr* commander remained loyal to the government. Despite significant industrial and agrarian support for Kapp's effort to establish a "national dictatorship," the putsch soon failed as a result of concerted worker opposition and the political ineptitude of the leading putschists. A general strike called by SPD members of the cabinet paralyzed the capital city and blocked the attempts of the putschists to govern. "Everything would still have been all right," one of the officers of the Ehrhardt Brigade later reminisced, "if we had just shot more people."[6] Unwilling to countenance such a wholesale slaughter of civilians and unable to gain the cooperation of government ministries or the central bank, Kapp and Lüttwitz were forced to give up their efforts four days after the start of the coup. Hitler, who had supported the coup, blamed its failure on the fact that Kapp had allowed Jews to participate in the new government as long as they shared its right-wing aims. Hitler would not make the same mistake in his own attempt to bring about a "national revolution."[7]

The continuing strength of antidemocratic sentiments in the German judiciary, virtually all of whose members were holdovers from the Wilhelmine Empire, was revealed in the double standard that the courts applied to the activities of dissidents on the right and the left. With the exception of the chief of police in Berlin, who received a sentence of five years of honorable confinement (of which he served three), none of the members of the Kapp conspiracy were punished for their efforts to overthrow the government. Lüttwitz and Kapp were acquitted. By contrast, adherents of the Bavarian socialist government of 1919 received sentences totaling more than 600 years.[8]

It would seem that the defeat of the Kapp Putsch offered an opportune moment to finally quell the antirepublican Free Corps, subordinate the army to the government, and introduce the kinds of reforms (such as the creation of a popular militia or the dismissal of antidemocratic government employees) that would strengthen the republican regime. Instead the government was forced to call upon the army and Free Corps units to suppress an uprising of industrial workers in the Ruhr. The uprising was precipitated by the government's own call for a general strike on the first day of the Kapp Putsch. USPD and KPD leaders in the Ruhr, supported by the Comintern, hoped to use this opportunity to press for the full-scale socialist revolution that had eluded them the year before.

Right-wing terrorism

Out of fear of social revolution the government thus rehabilitated the very forces that had recently sought to overthrow it. Seeckt was promoted to commander-in-chief of the *Reichswehr* and the Ehrhardt Brigade was dispatched to the Ruhr where it distinguished itself by the ferocity of its vendetta against the Reds. The government's tacit renewal of its pact with the army further alienated workers from the regime.

Government officials closed their eyes to the excesses of the Free Corps, because paramilitary formations seemed to be needed both to suppress left-wing insurgency and to defend the eastern frontiers against Polish nationalists. Since the Allies refused to permit the *Reichswehr* to operate in Silesia, Free Corps units patrolled this territory in the aftermath of the plebiscite of March 1921, which culminated in a League of Nations-sponsored partition. Even after their official disbandment by the government on Allied insistence in May 1921, Free Corps units that were not absorbed into the *Reichswehr* continued to operate, disguised as labor battalions, civil guards, or even sports clubs. Free Corps veterans were recruited as leaders of Hitler's own storm troop, the SA (*Sturm Abteilung*), which was founded as the "Gymnastic and Sports Division" of the National Socialist Party in July 1921.

The most hardened of the counter-revolutionaries, including Captain Hermann Ehrhardt (1881–1971) himself, formed vigilante bands and "people's courts" (the notorious *Femegerichte*) to mete out *"völkisch* justice" to persons they considered traitors to the fatherland. One of their objectives was to provoke an uprising on the left that could then be suppressed through force of arms and used as a pretext for eliminating the Weimar constitution. Among the prominent victims of their murderous rampage was the Finance Minister and Center Party deputy Matthias Erzberger (1875–1921), who had sponsored the Reichstag "peace resolution" in 1917 and signed the armistice in November 1918. Erzberger was gunned down in August 1921. Another victim was Foreign Minister Walther Rathenau (1867–1922), a Jewish industrialist who had headed Germany's economic mobilization in World War I but now advocated a policy of fulfilling the Allied terms. He was assassinated in June 1922. That same month Ehrhardt's right-wing terrorists seriously injured former prime minister Philipp Scheidemann by throwing sulfuric acid in his face. For the over 350 documented murders committed by *Feme* assassins in 1921–22 only token penalties were handed down by the courts.

The French occupation of the Ruhr, 1923

Early counter-revolutionary efforts to topple the government by force and to replace liberal democracy with an authoritarian regime came to a climax in Hitler's unsuccessful "Beer Hall Putsch" in November 1923. The crisis of that year again revealed the essential dilemma of the government, as its efforts to satisfy nationalist demands for a policy of resistance against the terms of Versailles only gave added legitimacy to its opponents on the radical right. The social turmoil of the immediate postwar years occurred in the context of Allied insistence on fulfillment of the terms of Versailles. These terms were meant in part to prevent a revival of German power. The French, in particular, were painfully aware of Germany's potential for resurgence—and revenge.

The reparations issue became a test of strength and will between the two governments. The London Conference of February–March 1921 had set the German obligation at 132 billion marks (about $32 billion in 1921 dollars). Historians still debate whether Germany's frequent defaults and requests for postponement of payments were more the result of inability or of unwillingness to pay. Despite continuing postwar inflation, the German economy and particularly heavy industry enjoyed a growing lead in productivity over the French between 1920 and 1923. Although the government formally agreed to fulfill the Allied terms (Rathenau's support for a policy of fulfillment was one of the reasons given by right-wing extremists for his assassination), the fundamental political will to meet the reparations payments was lacking. Fear of social revolution also worked against the kind of austerity measures that might have enabled the government to meet its reparations obligations as well as contain inflation.[9]

Matters came to a head in January 1923 when French and Belgian troops occupied the Ruhr to enforce German compliance. French suspicions of German intentions had been heightened by the Treaty of Rapallo between Germany and the Soviet Union in April 1922, in which, to the consternation of the western Allies (as well as the large Russian émigré community in Germany), the two outcast nations agreed to diplomatic relations and economic cooperation. The Ruhr occupation was not the first French attempt to impose sanctions on Germany. In 1920 the French had occupied three cities, including Frankfurt, to protest the incursion of German troops into the demilitarized Rhineland to suppress the Ruhr workers' revolt. Again in 1921 the French occupied cities in the Ruhr to compel German reparations payments. The occupation of 1923, however, was different. Not only was this an operation on a far larger scale than heretofore, but this time the French acted without the support of the British, who suspected French leaders of wanting to put German industry permanently under French control.[10]

The great inflation

The German government under businessman Wilhelm Cuno (1876–1933), whose nominally nonpartisan cabinet was supported by the parties of the Weimar coalition, issued a call for passive resistance to the French occupiers. Government employees, including railroad workers, were instructed not to carry out their jobs. To finance this operation and force the French to withdraw, the German government resorted to printing extra currency, a policy that led to the most traumatic episode of inflation in twentieth-century Europe. In August 1923 the value of the German mark against the dollar declined to five million to one.[11] On 1 November 1923 the German currency sank to its lowest level at 4.2 trillion marks to the dollar. The great inflation further alienated the middle classes from the republican regime. While inflation allowed businesses and owners of real property to pay off their debts with devalued currency, it penalized common people who depended on their liquid assets to meet their daily expenses. Savings accounts, already reduced in value by the inflationary postwar economy, were wiped out in the summer of 1923. Popular frustrations gave rise to conspiracy theories to identify the guilty parties responsible for this traumatic event. Because holders of foreign currency enjoyed privileges not available to ordinary Germans, the inflation undoubtedly exacerbated xenophobia as well. Ironically, public memory of this traumatic inflation would contribute to the decision of government leaders to pursue deflationary policies in the early 1930s, thus prolonging the Great Depression.

In the Ruhr crisis the government again found itself in the paradoxical situation of mobilizing its enemies on the right to ward off a foreign threat. Free

Corps sabotage units operated clandestinely in the Ruhr with the tacit approval of the government. The government also agreed to the plans of the *Reichswehr* to create an underground army in contravention of the terms of Versailles. Many former Free Corps veterans were recruited into the so-called "Black *Reichswehr.*" One Free Corps volunteer in the Ruhr, Leo Schlageter, became a national hero after he was executed by the French in May 1923.

By late summer 1923 the German government's confrontational strategy against the French seemed to have failed. The economy was in shambles and the authority of the government in jeopardy. Separatist movements, encouraged by the French, emerged in the Rhineland. The Communists, too, benefitted from the turmoil by increasing their popular following. Briefly outlawed by the SPD government in the aftermath of the Spartacist Revolt in 1919, the KPD had become a mass party with 350,000 members after the implosion of the USPD in December 1920. The hostility of the SPD also left the KPD more open to external influences.[12] Encouraged by the Comintern, the KPD hoped to be able to exploit the deteriorating conditions to finally stage the long-hoped-for communist revolution in Germany. Concerned by growing instability in Germany, the British demanded an end to the official policy of passive resistance and called for a negotiated solution to the crisis. Finally, on 26 September the new German chancellor, DVP leader Gustav Stresemann (1878–1929), called passive resistance to a halt.

Hitler's Beer Hall Putsch

Stresemann's "surrender" in the Ruhr provoked the radical right into renewed efforts to destroy the system of "Weimar and Versailles." Some Free Corps leaders and right-wing militants were more interested in overthrowing the government than in repelling the French. Right-wing organizations conspiring against the government were particularly active in Bavaria, where they enjoyed the protection of the authoritarian state government under the monarchist Gustav von Kahr (1862–1934). Kahr had become a virtual dictator in Bavaria in 1920 at the very time that Kapp was trying to oust the government in Berlin. Among the many right-wing conspirators who profited from the Bavarian government's hostility to the Weimar government was the man who was ultimately destined to unite the *völkisch* movement under his own command. At this time, however, Adolf Hitler was only one among many aspirants for this role.

A former army corporal, wounded and decorated in the war, Hitler was one among thousands of soldiers embittered by the humiliating end of the war. He refused to accept the idea that so many fellow Germans had lost their lives only to have a pacific democratic system imposed on Germany. Hitler was also imbued with a virulent antisemitism acquired, according to his own account, as a young would-be artist in Vienna in the decade before World War I and undoubtedly intensified by the disappointment of defeat. Filled with the conspiratorial fantasies of the radical right, he was persuaded by

Alfred Rosenberg (1893–1946), Max von Scheubner-Richter (1884–1923), and other disgruntled right-wing émigrés from the former Russian Empire that the Jews had started the war and fomented revolution to weaken the antisemitic Russian Empire, and, once this goal had been accomplished, spread "democratic Marxism" to ensure the defeat of the German Empire as well (supposedly because the German and Russian empires represented the main obstacles to the presumed goal of Jewish world domination).[13] Everything Hitler and his comrades had fought for seemed to have been lost due to what he considered the cowardice of democratic politicians. Instead of joining the Free Corps, however, Hitler took over a tiny political party that had recently been founded in Munich.

The German Workers' Party was one of many groups founded in the revolutionary period following the war to attract workers to the nationalist cause. The army encouraged the activities of such groups to combat the danger of socialism. In September 1919 Hitler was assigned by the army to monitor the party's activities. He joined the party as its 55th member. At a mass meeting in the Munich *Hofbräuhaus* on 24 February 1920, shortly before the Kapp Putsch, Hitler announced the change of the party's name to the National Socialist German Workers' Party (NSDAP). Its new Twenty-Five-Point program, written by Gottfried Feder (1883–1941), called for restrictions on the rights of Jews, the creation of a greater German Reich, censorship of the press, and a unified national community in which the common interest would prevail over individual interests. It also had a distinctly anticapitalist thrust designed to wean workers from the socialist camp. With funding from the *Reichswehr* the party was able to acquire a Munich newspaper, *Völkischer Beobachter*, which would henceforth become the official organ of the NSDAP. On 29 July 1921 Hitler was elected the new party's chairman with full dictatorial authority and the title of *Führer* (leader).

Hitler's training as a political instructor for the army at the end of the war and his leadership abilities—his sense of mission, his ability to articulate nationalist goals and grievances, and his dedication to the pursuit of power—enabled him to attract followers and build the party membership. At its first national convention in Munich in January 1923 the party numbered 20,000 members. Unlike unreconstructed monarchists such as Wolfgang Kapp, the 34-year-old Hitler (in 1923) was adept at using the vocabulary of socialism to attract a mass following. Like Mussolini's *fasci di combattimento*, Hitler's storm troopers received weapons and supplies from sympathetic army officers, including Captain Ernst Röhm (1887–1934), who helped to build up the SA while still serving in the army. By 1923 his organizational success gave Hitler considerable political leverage with the leaders of the Bavarian government, who refused to enforce the Berlin government's prohibition of the subversive activities of the radical right.

The apparent bankruptcy of the Berlin government's policy towards the French in the Ruhr set the stage for Hitler's putsch attempt. His leading fellow conspirator was none other than General Ludendorff, a strong supporter of the Kapp Putsch in 1920 and an early member of Hitler's party. Hitler was to be chancellor and Ludendorff commander-in-chief of the army in the national government the putschists intended to form. Conservative Bavarian government officials, long at loggerheads with the liberal government in Berlin, were to receive ministerial posts as well.

On the night of 8 November Hitler interrupted a nationalist rally sponsored by Kahr and proclaimed the establishment of a new national government. The model for his coup was Mussolini's "March on Rome" of the year before, in which Mussolini had been able to bluff his way into power because he enjoyed at least the tacit support of the army and leading conservatives. Hitler's effort to stage a revolution with the cooperation and permission of the authorities was not as successful, however. His party had not yet attracted the millions of followers that would make him so indispensable to conservatives ten years hence. Kahr and other Bavarian officials thought better of their alliance with the hotheaded, youthful ex-corporal after it became clear that the *Reichswehr* under Seeckt would not support the coup, even though the *Reichswehr* commander in Bavaria, General Otto von Lossow, had participated in the planning, and Seeckt had written to Kahr as late as 5 November 1923 expressing his confident expectation that the Weimar constitution would soon be changed.[14] The fact that the SPD members of Stresemann's cabinet had left the government on 2 November 1923 to protest against Stresemann's conciliatory attitude toward the Bavarian government also cooled the ardor of Bavarian officials for a clash with the national government. Hitler, however, would not be deterred. His "March on Berlin"—in the symbolic form of a march on the *Reichswehr* headquarters in Munich—was aborted on 9 November in front of the *Feldherrnhalle* (Soldiers' Memorial) by the Munich police. A column of putschists headed by Hitler and Ludendorff refused to comply with police orders to disperse. In the ensuing shootout 14 Nazis, 4 policemen, and 1 bystander were killed.

In the trial that followed, the judges allowed Hitler to use the courtroom as a platform to publicize his cause. While Ludendorff claimed not to have known of the putsch in advance, Hitler accepted full responsibility and posed as the selfless patriot who had sought only to deliver his country from the clutches of Marxists and traitors. "I cannot plead guilty," Hitler announced, "but I do confess the act. There is no such thing as high treason against the traitors of 1918."[15] For his act of high treason Hitler received the minimum sentence of five years, of which he served only eight months. His fellow conspirator Ludendorff, secure in the nimbus of a war hero, was acquitted of all charges.

In at least three respects the mild treatment accorded to Hitler contravened existing German law. First, he was tried by a friendly Bavarian court rather than the national court in Leipzig as stipulated by the "Law for the Protection of the Republic," passed only a year earlier in reaction to the Rathenau murder. Second, the court deliberately ignored the fact that Hitler had a criminal record (in May 1922 he had been convicted of disorderly conduct), which would have required him to serve his full term. Finally, the law also stipulated that foreigners convicted of high treason be deported (Hitler was still an Austrian citizen at the time).[16] Instead, Hitler was permitted to use his comfortable confinement in the minimum-security Landsberg fortress to dictate his book *Mein Kampf* (My Struggle) to his private secretary Rudolf Hess (1894–1983), who would later become deputy leader of the Nazi Party.

The lesson Hitler learned from the failure of his putsch was not to try to seize power again without making sure of army support. Henceforth he would take the legal and constitutional route to power. In 1923 the army remained conditionally loyal to the regime because the Stresemann government showed no reluctance to crack down on the left. A Communist-led uprising in the north German port city of Hamburg was crushed in October 1923. That same month the government authorized the overthrow of the democratically elected SPD–Communist coalition governments in the states of Saxony and Thuringia. Army leaders also feared Allied intervention if the Republic were destroyed by force.

Stability temporarily restored

The failure of the Hitler Putsch marked a turning point in the fortunes of the Weimar Republic. The succession of attempts to overthrow the Weimar system came to a preliminary end. Crucial to this unexpected turn for the better was the favorable resolution of the Ruhr crisis. Almost miraculously, it seemed, the government had survived the turbulent postwar years. In the Reichstag elections of December 1924 both the KPD and the radical right lost most of the seats they had gained in May of that year. The new Finance Minister Hans Luther (1879–1962) and Reich Currency Commissioner Hjalmar Schacht (1877–1970), president of Germany's central bank from 1924 to 1930 and again from 1933 to 1939, succeeded in stabilizing the German currency by the end of the year.

Stresemann's policy of fulfillment paid unexpected dividends. France found itself increasingly isolated after the end of German passive resistance, and the French economy faced increasing difficulties as a result of the French government's aggressive policies in the Ruhr. French efforts to separate the Rhineland from Germany were stymied by British and American opposition and the lack of substantial popular support for a separate state. Both Britain and the United States considered a stable German economy vital to their own trading interests. In the face of these difficulties the French had little choice but to agree to a British–American plan to reschedule the German reparations debt. The Dawes Plan, named after the American banker who headed the commission of experts, went into effect in April 1924. By spreading reparations payments over a period of several decades and calling for an American loan to enable Germany to return to the gold standard, the Dawes Plan created the foundation for economic growth and prosperity in Germany in the late 1920s.

The Locarno Pact

The diplomacy of Stresemann, who resigned as chancellor in November 1923 but served as German foreign minister until his death in 1929, also strengthened the Weimar government. In October 1925 Germany joined the western European countries in signing the Locarno Treaties, guaranteeing their common boundaries. However, no mention was made of Germany's frontiers in the east, where Stresemann wished to retain the freedom for eventual border revisions. He benefitted from British reluctance to support French demands for a German guarantee of the eastern borders as well. No German politician could afford to renounce Germany's eastern territorial losses in World War I. A major reason Stresemann pursued good relations with the west was to gain a free hand in the east. In April 1926 Stresemann signed the Treaty of Berlin with the Soviet Union, continuing the special relationship established in the Treaty of Rapallo in 1922. One basis of this relationship was the common interest of both countries in revising their borders with Poland.

Stresemann viewed the Locarno treaties as only the first step in the eventual revision of Versailles. Locarno would protect Germany from unilateral French sanctions such as the occupation of the Ruhr in 1923, which finally ended when France withdrew its last forces in July 1925. At Locarno France also agreed to the early withdrawal of the Allied occupation troops in the Rhineland, whose purpose had been to insure compliance with the terms of the Versailles Treaty. The high point of Germany's postwar rehabilitation was marked by German entry into the League of Nations with veto rights and a permanent seat on the League Council in September 1926.

Stresemann's policy of fulfillment, though aimed at an eventual revision of Versailles, infuriated radical nationalists, who accused Stresemann of treason for renouncing German claims to Alsace and Lorraine. The Nationalists (DNVP) and the radical right parties voted against Locarno in the Reichstag, as did the KPD (reflecting Soviet fears that Locarno might lead to a western alliance with Germany against the Soviet Union). But there was no disputing the success of Stresemann's strategy. Locarno helped Germany attract American investments, and the Republic entered into its most stable and prosperous phase.

The shift to the right

Despite the failures of counter-revolution in the early 1920s, the political mainstream had shifted significantly to the right since the days of the National Assembly. Undoubtedly this was due in good part to popular reactions to the Treaty of Versailles, to the burden of reparations, and to the strength of the KPD, which increased its popular support to 3.7 million votes in May 1924. Never again would the parties of the Weimar coalition (SPD, Center, and the German Democrats) gain a majority of the vote in a national election.

The fortunes of the SPD and the Democrats waned after 1920 as politics became more polarized. In the first Reichstag election in June 1920 the SPD lost nearly half of the votes the party had received in the Weimar assembly election in January 1919. Many of the SPD's supporters shifted their votes to the more militant USPD, reflecting the growing rift on the left in the wake of the government's repressive measures in 1919. The Bavarian wing of the Center Party also broke away to form an independent party more hostile to the Republic. The biggest losers, however, were the Democrats, much of whose constituency shifted to the People's Party (DVP) and the Nationalists (DNVP), the two major parties that had voted against the Weimar constitution. The elections of May and December 1924 confirmed this trend as the DNVP polled about 20 percent of the vote to become the second largest party in the Reichstag. Only the SPD with 26 percent of the vote won more seats in the December 1924 elections. Together the DNVP and the DVP gained about a third of the national vote.

Perhaps the most dramatic indication of the shift to the right was the election of General Hindenburg, at the age of 78, to the presidency following Ebert's death in February 1925. Hindenburg, the candidate of the People's Party and the Nationalists and backed by right-wing militants like Hitler as well, was willing to support the Republic only as a temporary expedient until the Hohenzollern dynasty could be restored. The election of an avowed monarchist to the highest office of the Republic underscored the continuing strength of German conservatism.

Antirepublican sentiment remained pervasive throughout German society. Leading officials of the civil service, many of them holdovers from the Imperial bureaucracy, were out of sympathy with the government whose decisions they were supposed to carry out and whose programs they administered. The judiciary, while harsh on left-wing activism, continued to mete out only token punishment to those who attacked the Republic from the right. The Junker estate owners were understandably nostalgic for the Second Empire in which they had enjoyed such extensive power and influence. Even industrialists, especially representatives of labor-intensive heavy industry, were hostile to the Republic, mainly because liberal democracy increased the bargaining power of labor, and SPD-sponsored fiscal policies and social programs threatened to reduce business profits.

Educational institutions, from the primary grades through higher education, disseminated antirepublican views. Even the churches were at best lukewarm toward the Republic, the Protestant Prussian United Church for the obvious reason that it had lost its privileged position as the established church of Prussia under its *summus episcopus*, the kaiser.[17] But Catholic leaders, too, favored a more authoritarian regime, not so much for political reasons, but because the liberal state was no longer prepared to act as the moral censor of society. The introduction of civil liberties brought with it full freedom of lifestyles and artistic expression. Standards of morality seemed to have fallen away in the creative ferment of Weimar artistic experimentation that conservatives denounced as "cultural bolshevism."

The "Conservative Revolution"

Notwithstanding the innovation and creativity in the arts for which the Weimar era is justly renowned, the dominant political climate was conservative and anti-republican. Those conservative writers and intellectuals, like Thomas Mann, who reluctantly rallied to the Republic, were in a distinct minority. More representative were the intellectuals of the so-called Conservative Revolution, who like the historian Oswald Spengler (1880–1936), the publicist Arthur Möller van den Bruck (1876–1925), or the political theorist Carl Schmitt (1888–1985) decried the shallow materialism of western civilization and called for the rebirth of German values in a "Third Reich," the euphemism for a realm from which partisan conflicts and selfish interests (read liberalism and socialism) had been purged. The German defeat in World War I gave special currency and urgency to doctrines of racial regeneration that promised the restoration of German power. *Völkisch* ideology also entered the political mainstream through the German Nationalist Party (DNVP), veterans' groups such as the *Stahlhelm* (Steel Helmet), a great variety of local and regional patriotic organizations, various groups of the Youth Movement, and publications such as the respectable conservative journal, *Die Tat*. *Völkisch* ideas reached a large audience through the works of such respected novelists as Hans Grimm (1875–1959), author of the best-selling *Volk ohne Raum* (A People Without Space), and Ernst Jünger (1895–1998), author of numerous works exalting the military state and the experience of war.

Substantial support for liberal democracy came, ironically, only from the ranks of the nominally Marxist SPD. However, the identification of Weimar democracy with SPD and labor union interests in the public mind tended to weaken middle-class support for the Republic. In the eyes of many propertied Germans the SPD remained the pariah party that had been outlawed under Bismarck and had accepted the Versailles Treaty. Many suspected the SPD of having subverted the monarchy at the end of the war. Strong support for the Republic by the SPD and the Jewish community only seemed to confirm the validity of the right-wing assertion that the Weimar system was un-German.

The changing Weimar cabinets inevitably reflected the nationalist mood and public revulsion against Versailles. If Versailles was indeed unjust, as by public consensus it was, then a policy of fulfillment could at best be a stop-gap measure. Even Stresemann, a former National Liberal and now head of the People's Party (DVP), approved of clandestine rearmament and expected Germany eventually to reclaim its lost territories in the east, if necessary by force. During the war he had favored Pan-German annexationist goals, and he had voted against the Weimar constitution in 1919. He privately referred to Locarno (and the Dawes Plan) as only an "armistice."[18]

The Republic also continued to face attacks from the radical left for its failure to introduce full social democracy. Even loyal republicans found it hard to support a government that authorized clandestine rearmament, jailed left-wing political dissidents, and seemed unable or unwilling to curb the influence of the right. Left-wing intellectuals, many of them Jewish, criticized the government for permitting militarism to endure. Ironically, supporters of the Republic could only fight for democratic principles by attacking the holders of power. Their scathing critiques of abuses of power by the Weimar establishment left them open to the later charge of having contributed to the demise of the Republic.

Right-wingers denounced the liberal system as too weak to stand up to the Allies and defend legitimate German interests. Left-wing critics, on the other hand, scorned a liberal system that was so open to the influence and control of nationalist and authoritarian elites. It seemed the liberal democratic system would only survive as long as it served the economic purposes of the dominant elites. Yet the end came sooner than even the government's critics in the late 1920s expected. The Great Depression would provide the opportunity to revert to an authoritarian regime.

7 The collapse of the Weimar Republic

The Great Depression and the rise of the Nazis

The Great Depression, the most serious crisis in the history of industrial capitalism, accelerated the fall of the Weimar Republic and made possible the triumph of the Nazis. In Germany the consequences of the depression were far more extensive than in the United States, for it led not only to changes in the free market system, many of them not dissimilar to the American New Deal, but to the destruction of political liberalism as well. The depression did not create the Nazis, of course, nor did economic grievances alone account for their striking increase in popularity among German voters. But by undermining the economic foundations of Weimar stability, the depression created the conditions under which the enemies of democracy were able to destroy the Republic.

The depression put an end to the economic growth and prosperity of the late 1920s, which by 1928 had raised the standard of living in Germany to the prewar level. After the Dawes Plan went into effect in 1924, American loans and investments stimulated the German economy and provided the funds to meet reparations payments. Under the Dawes Plan some 25 billion marks flowed into Germany in the form of bond purchases and loans to industry. The precipitous decline of prices on the New York Stock Exchange in October 1929 eliminated this source of credit, with disastrous effects on the German economy.

Even before the crash, short-term American loans to German firms were already being called in, partly because investors were attracted to the higher profits to be made in the booming stock market in New York. After the crash American investors pulled much of their remaining capital out of Germany. The drop in American demand for imported goods precipitated a slump in world prices and a slowing of business activity, until, in the depths of the depression in 1931–32, international trade came to a virtual standstill. German industrial production dropped by 39 percent between 1929 and 1932, while the registered number of unemployed reached a level of over six million. Even this figure represented only a fraction of the people in both blue- and white-collar occupations whose standard of living was drastically reduced.

Causes of the Great Depression

While the New York stock market crash that followed upon years of frenzied and unregulated speculation may have served to trigger the depression, this alone cannot explain the severity and duration of the crisis. The root cause of the malfunctioning of the industrial economies of the west in the 1930s was the unequal distribution of purchasing power, a problem the New Deal would eventually redress in the United States. Substantial segments of the population lacked the means to buy the goods that the overexpanded industries of the late 1920s produced. A disproportionately low percentage of the profits from increased industrial production in the 1920s went to farmers and workers, the potential consumers of mass-produced industrial goods. Small farmers in both the United States and Europe suffered from low agricultural prices and inadequate incomes throughout the 1920s.[1]

Industrial inventories piled up in the warehouses even before the stock market crash in New York created havoc in the financial markets of the world. Industrial overexpansion and overproduction (or underconsumption) led to the laying off of workers, thus further reducing mass purchasing power and the demand for industrial goods. Firms that had expanded on credit in the boom years of the 1920s went out of business, often bankrupting their creditors in the process. Depositors started runs on banks already weakened by the default of many of their loans. The result of this vicious cycle of business failures, growing unemployment, and financial panic was pervasive hardship, psychological insecurity, and increasing clamor for a political solution to the crisis.

By the mid- and late 1930s measures to increase broad-based purchasing power through job creation, public works projects, expansion of the social security system, unemployment compensation, farm support payments, progressive taxation, and legislation to strengthen labor unions ameliorated the worst effects of the depression in the United States. Measures similar to Roosevelt's New Deal were eventually adopted to a greater or lesser extent in most European countries and were given a theoretical rationale in the works of John Maynard Keynes.[2] Increased government spending on public works and rearmament under the Nazis helped pull Germany out of the depression. In the early 1930s, however, the cost-cutting measures adopted by both the Hoover administration in the United States and by the government of Heinrich Brüning (1885–1970) in Germany only aggravated the deflationary trend. Brüning's government cut wages, salaries, and benefits of government employees in an effort to balance the budget at a time of declining revenues. He hoped to use the economic downturn to gain a further reduction of reparations payments. His deflationary policies were supported by industrialists who wanted to reduce social and labor costs.[3] Brüning's failure to resolve the economic crisis was one of the factors leading to his replacement in 1932.

Memories of the rampant inflation of 1923 gave added impetus to the reduction of government spending in Germany. Deflationary measures also served the interests of German exporters (by keeping their prices competitive) and reflected the economic wisdom of the day. In the face of the crisis in world trade, most economists considered domestic welfare less important than international monetary stability. Cutting the costs of production by lowering wages commended itself as a means of remaining competitive in the world market. Unfortunately, as the depression deepened no country could afford to buy. Measures to discourage imports through tariffs and exchange controls further dampened world trade and overall demand, thus intensifying the worldwide slump.

The Brüning government and the 1930 Reichstag election

The depression undermined whatever confidence in economic and political liberalism still existed among middle-class Germans and polarized an electorate that now looked to radical measures to resolve the economic crisis. While increasing numbers of workers shifted their allegiance to the Communist Party (KPD), even larger numbers of middle-class Germans cast their votes for the Nazis for the first time. More and more people of all classes hoped for national salvation through a victory of the radical right.

Many voters assumed that a government encumbered by Versailles was too weak to obtain redress of German grievances and thus solve Germany's economic problems. This explanation of the crisis served the interests of Germany's economic elites. To many of the leaders of German banking and industry the crisis offered a welcome opportunity to reduce the power of labor and cut back on taxes and government social programs, and beyond that to bring about the kind of governmental restructuring that would preclude the revival of welfare-state reforms in the future. The crisis would have a silver lining if it could be used to break the power of the SPD and undermine the legitimacy of parliamentary institutions.

Economic crisis promoted the trend to political authoritarianism as a way of transcending the growing conflict over the allocation and distribution of ever scarcer resources. Conservatives in Germany hoped to use the crisis to force the SPD out of the coalition government formed under Social Democrat Hermann Müller (1876–1931) in 1928. The opportunity came in March 1930 in a dispute over government social programs. Müller's coalition collapsed as a result of the SPD's refusal to accept cuts in unemployment and social insurance benefits and the People's Party's refusal to accept increases in employers' contributions to the unemployment insurance fund.

President Hindenburg's choice to succeed Müller as chancellor was Heinrich Brüning, the conservative head of the Catholic Center Party. His appointment marked an important stage in the decline of parliamentary democracy, for Hindenburg authorized Brüning to form a presidential cabinet not formally bound to any parties or dependent on a parliamentary majority. Brüning's main aim was not the defense of Weimar democracy, but the restoration of Germany as the dominant power in Europe—a goal he shared with President Hindenburg and most military, industrial, and agrarian leaders. Brüning's immediate aim was to introduce austerity measures designed to convince Britain, France, and the United States of the need to reduce Germany's onerous reparations. Unable to gain parliamentary approval for cuts in social services, Brüning received authority from Hindenburg (who had previously refused to grant similar authority to the SPD chancellor) to enact the new budget by decree under Article 48 of the Weimar constitution. After the Reichstag voted to repeal the emergency measures in July 1930, which was tantamount to a no-confidence vote, Brüning dissolved the Reichstag and called for new elections to take place within 60 days, as required by the constitution. He might have avoided this outcome by negotiating compromise legislation with the SPD, but he could not do so without alienating his nationalist supporters. At this stage he apparently still hoped to gain a parliamentary majority for his legislative program in the elections scheduled for September 1930.

Brüning's expectations were bitterly dashed, as the election produced shocking gains for the Nazis, who increased their parliamentary representation from 12 to 107 seats. The Nazis became the second-largest party in the Reichstag as the SPD barely retained the plurality it had held since the beginning of the Weimar era. This stunning electoral triumph frustrated Brüning's efforts to govern by normal parliamentary procedure. Brüning had underestimated the extent of public impatience with government inaction. As the government increasingly relied on its emergency powers in the months that followed, the parliamentary process in Germany became virtually defunct. From 1930 to 1932 only five bills were passed by majority vote in the Reichstag, while during the same period the government issued 60 emergency decrees.[4] This dependence on emergency legislation was the vital precondition for Hitler's transition to open dictatorship in 1933.

Many of the more than five and a half million votes the Nazis gained since the previous election in June 1928 came at the expense of the conservative Nationalists (DNVP) and the economically conservative People's Party (DVP), which had been bereft of effective leadership since Stresemann's death in 1929. Millions of first-time voters also flocked to the Nazis, many of them undoubtedly to register their protest against the government's austere economic policies. The total voter turnout increased from 74 to 81 percent of the eligible electorate. The new vote included not only young people eligible to vote for the first time, but also previous nonvoters, a basically apolitical constituency easily seduced by Nazi scapegoating of Marxists and Jews and by promises of quick fixes and forceful solutions. On the left the process of radicalization took place on a somewhat lesser scale, as the Communists increased their number of deputies from 54 to 77 at the expense of the SPD, which lost ten seats.

The Nazi Party program

The Nazis' spectacular electoral gains validated Hitler's strategy of seeking power through legal and electoral means. The failure of the Beer Hall Putsch, his unsuccessful experiment in forcible revolution on the Mussolini model, had persuaded him to attempt the conquest of power by legal means instead. The open advocacy of violent overthrow of the government would only have prolonged the ban on public speaking that had been placed on him in Prussia and several other German states. Hitler's objective in refounding the National Socialist German Workers' Party (NSDAP) in February 1925 was to create a party that would generate broad mass appeal while at the same time remaining unconditionally subject to his own personal control. For this purpose Hitler required a program that appealed to a variety of social groups, including industrial workers, but that would not circumscribe his own freedom of action or commit him to specific social reforms.[5]

Much of the Nazis' 1920 Twenty-Five-Point Program resembled the program of the German Nationalists (DNVP), the party of "respectable" conservatives, which also called for an end to "the predominance of Jewry in government and public life."[6] The Nazi program differed, however, in calling for some radical economic changes. Though phrased vaguely enough to admit a variety of interpretations, a number of provisions had a distinctly anticapitalist tenor designed to attract workers in the revolutionary climate of the immediate postwar years. One provision called for the abolition of the "thraldom of interest," while another demanded the "ruthless confiscation of all war profits." The program also demanded the nationalization of trusts, the introduction of profit-sharing, and the lease of department stores to small tradesmen. Article 17 even called for the "confiscation without compensation of land for communal purposes." In the more conservative political climate of 1928 Hitler issued a declaration denying that this article posed a threat to private property. It referred only to the "creation of legal means of confiscating, when necessary, land illegally acquired, or not administered in accordance with the national welfare"; it was directed "in the first instance against the Jewish companies which speculate in land."[7]

For Hitler the program was designed to attract various discontented social groups and at the same time exercise a broad emotional appeal. Some party leaders, however, took seriously the party's proclaimed commitment to economic reform, much to Hitler's discomfiture. In the fall of 1925 Gregor Strasser (1892–1934), one of the most capable and popular young Nazis whom Hitler had appointed to head the party's Propaganda Department, circulated a draft of an extended program among party members. This program describes the kind of state some idealistic Nazis envisioned under the concept of National or German Socialism.

It was to be a corporatist state (*Körperschaftsstaat*) under the semidictatorial powers of a president elected by a National Council (consisting of the presidents of various states) and a Chamber of Estates (*Reichsständekammer*). This latter body was to be composed of representatives of occupational groups organized into five Vocational Chambers—agriculture, industry and commerce, labor, civil service and salaried (white-collar) employees, and the professions—as well as representatives from such national institutions as the churches and universities. The Chamber of Estates would not be a parliamentary body, however, as the chancellor and his ministers were to be responsible to the president alone—an arrangement not dissimilar to the Empire under Bismarck.[8]

This draft program, similar to corporatist proposals put forward by Italian Fascists and such German theorists of the "Conservative Revolution" as Arthur Möller van den Bruck, Oswald Spengler, and the Austrian corporatist Othmar Spann, was designed to prevent the lower classes and the labor movement from exercising electoral power in proportion to their numbers, as they would potentially be able to do under a democratic system of "one person, one vote." Insofar as this program also somewhat circumscribed the power of industrialists and the land-owning aristocracy, Strasser's draft reflected the hostility of many "genuine" National Socialists to both large-scale capitalism and the organized labor movement. Its overriding objective—and this was the idealistic component of National Socialism—was to create a national community from which both the Marxist class conflict and liberal individualism were eliminated.

Its antisemitic provisions and foreign policy planks were similar to the original Twenty-Five-Point Program of 1920. Nonetheless, Strasser's draft program was denounced by party hard-liners for its "Jewish–liberal–democratic–Marxist–humanitarian concept" of equal voting rights (since the representatives of the vocational chambers of the corporatist state were, after all, to be elected by their various constituencies).[9] Because Hitler viewed the party program only as a means to attract popular support and enforce ideological conformity within the party, he opposed Strasser's effort to commit the Nazis to specific social policies.

When in January 1926 Strasser met with northern party leaders to discuss his proposed revisions and to pass a resolution favoring the expropriation of former royal houses of the German states (a measure that was defeated in a nationwide popular referendum initiated by the KPD that same year), Hitler sprang into action. He countermanded Strasser's resolution on the expropriation of royal property on the grounds that every loyal German must be permitted to retain what rightfully belonged to them. "For us there are no princes," he proclaimed, "only Germans."[10] Anxious to court business support, Hitler insisted that the right to property must not be undermined.

Repeating the argument he had made in *Mein Kampf* that the public was most readily swayed by short, simple, easily comprehensible, and above all immutable dogmas, Hitler refused to permit any revision of the original Twenty-Five-Point Program. A prohibition on specific commitments to social reform was useful to Hitler's strategy of seeking business support, but it also had the advantage of ending policy debates within the party and thus ensuring his freedom of action and final authority. "The NSDAP," Hitler announced to party loyalists in 1930,

> as long as I am its leader, will never become a debating club for root-less intellectuals or chaotic parlor-Bolsheviks, but will remain what it is today: an organization of discipline, which was not created for the doctrinaire foolishness of political dilettantes, but rather for the battle

for a new Germany of the future in which class concepts will be destroyed and a new German people will determine its own fate![11]

For Hitler the tactics needed to achieve and maintain power would always take priority over principles of social or economic reform.

Hitler thus established the supremacy of the *Führerprinzip* (leadership principle) over matters of policy and succeeded in identifying the party and its program with his person. The "Heil Hitler" salute became compulsory for party members in 1926. A significant factor in Hitler's ascendancy was the defection of Joseph Goebbels (1897–1945), who had gotten his start in the party as Strasser's private secretary. Goebbels was won over to Hitler's side not, it would seem, for personal advantage or ideological reasons, but because, like so many others in the party, he felt that Hitler's forceful personality was best suited to lead the party to power. The winning of power was in the last analysis far more important to most Nazi leaders than the transformation of society in accordance with corporatist models of "German socialism."

In October 1926 Hitler appointed Goebbels *Gauleiter* (regional leader) of "Red Berlin," the SPD and Communist stronghold where the future propaganda minister could apply his demagogic talents and pseudosocialist rhetoric to bringing members of Berlin's large industrial working class into the Nazi fold. Gregor Strasser, too, now acquiesced in the personality cult that Hitler fostered in the party. However, his brother Otto and other party members who would not reconcile themselves to Hitler's opportunistic course were expelled from the party in July 1930.

The role of antisemitism

In the late 1920s Hitler, sensing perhaps the most promising sources of support, steered the party further away from an anticapitalist posture. Hitler had no concern for economic and social issues; his paramount concerns were race, national power, and national expansion. He had no vision of a new economic order to parallel the corporatist state envisioned by the Strassers and other theorists of a "Conservative Revolution." Under Hitler's command the party gave precedence to a strategy of broad emotional and psychological appeals over Strasser's conception of a program of positive plans. A virulent antisemitism served to deflect economic grievances away from structural reforms or anticapitalism. Antisemitism was also useful as a way of emphasizing the primacy of politics as the only effective way to counter the putative Jewish–democratic–Marxist threat.

A number of psychological theories have been advanced to explain Hitler's virulent antisemitism, including the suggestion that he blamed his mother's Jewish physician for her failure to recover from cancer. The documented fact, however, that Hitler intervened personally to facilitate his emigration to England after the annexation of Austria in 1938 weighs heavily against this interpretation.[12] No doubt Hitler was strongly attached to his mother and

Table 1 Sociological structure of the NSDAP prior to 1933, by occupation groups

Occupation	German Reich (1925 census)	NSDAP (Before 14 Sep 1930)	NSDAP (New members 9/14/30–1/30/33)	Percentage of NSDAP members among those employed (Before 1 Jan 1933)
Blue-collar workers	14,443,000 (45.1%)	34,000 (28.1%)	233,000 (33.5%)	1.9%
Self-employed (a) Farming	2,203,000 (6.7%)	17,100 (14.1%)	90,000 (13.4%)	4.9%
(b) Industry and crafts	1,785,000 (5.5%)	11,000 (9.1%)	56,000 (8.4%)	3.9%
(c) Commerce	1,193,000 (3.7%)	9,900 (8.2%)	49,000 (7.5%)	4.9%
(d) Professions	477,000 (1.5%)	3,600 (3.0%)	20,000 (3.0%)	4.9%
Public employees (a) Teachers	334,000 (1.0%)	2,000 (1.7%)	11,000 (1.7%)	4.0%
(b) Others	1,050,000 (3.3%)	8,000 (6.6%)	36,000 (5.5%)	
White-collar employees	5,087,000 (15.9%)	31,000 (25.6%)	148,000 (22.1%)	3.4%
Domestic workers (mostly women)	5,437,000 (17.3%)	4,400 (3.6%)	27,000 (4.9%)	0.6%
Total	32,009,000 (100%)	121,000 (100%)	670,000 (100%)	2.5%

lived in awe and fear of his severe, authoritarian father. Psychological explanations may illuminate Hitler's susceptibility to hatred, prejudice, and violence. Crucial to any explanation of Hitler's antisemitism, however, is the fact that antisemitism was so readily available as an apparently acceptable expression of personal and social discontents. Hitler's hostility to Jews may have been exacerbated by personal resentments, such as the bitterness that followed his rejection by the Vienna Academy of Arts, but more importantly, racial antisemitism had become a major component in the ideology of the radical right in both the Habsburg and Hohenzollern empires by the early twentieth century. In Vienna Hitler had ample opportunity to observe how aggressive right-wing politicians like the populist mayor of Vienna, Karl Lueger

(1844–1910), used antisemitism to discredit liberalism and wean workers from internationalist socialism. He might have been influenced by the leader of the Austrian Pan-Germans, Georg von Schönerer (1842–1921), who introduced the use of the "Heil" salute among his followers. Or perhaps he read the ubiquitous racist pamphlets of such *völkisch* sectarians as Guido von List (1848–1919) or Jörg Lanz von Liebenfels (1874–1955), both of whom used the swastika as the symbol of their esoteric Germanic cults.[13]

The traumatic defeat of World War I was the crucial experience in Hitler's decision to enter politics and seek power on the basis of a program whose antisemitic provisions resembled those of the prewar radical right and the postwar mainstream right. Like so many other German nationalists Hitler blamed the Empire's defeat on the alleged disloyalty and pacifism of Marxists and Jews. For Hitler, recovering from a gas attack at the time of the armistice, the left-wing revolutions that spread across Germany seemed to confirm the thesis that the German army had been stabbed in the back. Baltic German, Ukrainian, and Russian émigrés also helped convince Hitler that the Bolshevik Revolution had been caused by Jews to gain world domination.[14] Antisemitism was closely entwined with anti-Marxism, anticommunism, and antiliberalism in the *völkisch* ideology that animated the counter-revolutionary movement of the postwar years. The *völkisch* ideology set forth in *Mein Kampf* was neither original nor unique. A key to Hitler's demagogic success was that he voiced prejudices that were pervasive in German society. Typical of the radical right was the cynical, threatening tone embodied in Hitler's notorious suggestion that the World War could have been won if a few hundred Jews had been subjected to poison gas at the right time.[15] *Mein Kampf* went beyond the conventional right-wing literature, however, in combining ideological invective with a practical political program for the achievement of *völkisch* aims.

The Nazis' Twenty-Five-Point Program of 1920 repeated the prewar Pan-German demand for the total disfranchisement of Jews. Besides a general pledge to combat "the Jewish-materialistic spirit within and around us," the Nazi program contained several provisions aimed specifically against Jews. These stipulated that only a person of German blood, irrespective of religious denomination, could be a German citizen. Only citizens were to be eligible for public office. Noncitizens were to be placed under alien law, and, if the state should be unable to provide a livelihood for all residents, noncitizens were to be expelled from Germany. All noncitizens who entered Germany after the beginning of the war on 2 August 1914 were to be expelled, and all further immigration into Germany was to be halted.

In a closed party membership meeting chaired by Gregor Strasser in the *Bürgerbräukeller* in Munich in July 1927, Hitler set forth the antisemitic line he wanted the party to pursue. Hitler placed the onus of capitalist exploitation exclusively on "the Jew," almost always referred to in the singular to avoid any sense of differentiation between Jewish people. The Jew, Hitler contended, sought above all to gain possession of the means of production, and only polit-ical means could displace Jews from economic control. Economic competition was hopeless, Hitler contended, for economic competition was itself a Jewish idea, and Jews naturally excelled at it. The secret of Jewish success was the invention of finance capitalism and speculation in stocks. Democracy and par-liamentarianism simply facilitated Jewish efforts to secure political as well as economic power.

Historically, Hitler went on, the Jews had never been halted except when the better instinct of a race asserted itself. Because of the threat that growing racial awareness represented to Jewish interests in the twentieth century, the Jews no longer relied on democracy, but sought to maintain power by manip-ulating the masses through a dictatorship of the proletariat. Thus the Jews had introduced Bolshevism (Hitler's favored term for the less nefarious-sounding "communism" in the interwar years) in order to replace the uncer-tain majority of a democratic regime with the absolute majority assured by control of the working class. The purpose of Bolshevism was to eliminate nationalist opposition. It was true that Bolshevism socialized the means of production, but inevitably "the Jew" emerged as the administrator in a Bolshevik system, for property was depersonalized in order to be transferred to Jewry. Decades of democracy had made people cowardly and stupid and had paved the way for the Jewish offensive through Marxism. This, Hitler asserted, was the main danger in Germany today, for the SPD, despite appear-ances, was not interested in defending the Republic but only in providing the shock troops for a Red takeover.

For Hitler, then, antisemitism had the function of resolving the contradic-tion between anticapitalism and anticommunism by interpreting both liber-alism and communism as instruments of the Jewish world conspiracy. Antisemitism served as a vehicle both for legitimating (while seeming to attack) the existing economic system (by blaming its failings on the Jews) and for defaming democracy and socialism (by denouncing these as Jewish conspiracies). Through the manipulation of antisemitism the Nazis could offer their followers "positive" measures—the elimination of Jews from German life—without effecting any changes that would threaten the inter-ests of elites. The solution to Germany's problems, Hitler insisted, lay not in social reform but in a revival of national power:

> If we merely announce a social program and close our eyes to the decline of our *Volk*, then we will be nothing more than, say, a revised Marxism, but will in actuality not be able to save our *Volk*. Do not imagine that we will be able to give the German worker freedom, if the German nation sinks in chains, or that we will be able to give the German worker bread, if we become more and more international slaves.[16]

The key to reviving national power, Hitler contended, was to eradicate the influence of the Jews.

The Harzburg Front, 1931

Hitler's social conservatism and his call for a revival of national power won his party the support of large numbers of middle-class Germans in the September 1930 election. A "Manifesto from Adolf Hitler to the German People," issued on the eve of the election, read in part: "We shall see to it that the reform of our military preparedness and our foreign policy will be placed ahead of all reforms."[17] This policy also gained him the backing of non-Nazi conservatives, many of whom were nevertheless concerned about the potential economic radicalism of Hitler's followers.

The Nazis and the DNVP Nationalists had already cooperated in a losing effort to defeat the Young Plan (rescheduling Germany's reparations debt over a period of 59 years) by popular referendum in 1929. Now Hitler's electoral successes made him an attractive partner for the Nationalists, whose commitment to monarchism and aristocratic conservatism limited their own mass appeal. The Nationalists had become increasingly skeptical of Chancellor Brüning, not least because he received tacit SPD support and was evidently unwilling to enlist the Nazis as allies in the conservatives' effort to replace the Weimar system with an authoritarian regime. Instead, Brüning ruled by presidential decree under Article 48 of the constitution while relying on the support of the SPD to avoid votes of no confidence in the Reichstag. The SPD preferred to tolerate Brüning's measures, including cuts in social expenditures, rather than risk the collapse of the Brüning government and its possible replacement by a fascistic regime. SPD leaders were also concerned that the failure to tolerate Brüning would induce the Center Party to withdraw from the SPD-dominated coalition government in Prussia, Germany's largest state.

The head of the Nationalist Party (DNVP) was the industrialist Alfred Hugenberg (1865–1951), a former director of the Krupp works, owner of a giant newspaper and film cartel, and later Minister of Economics in Hitler's first cabinet. Hugenberg was particularly anxious to unify the "national opposition" to the Brüning government and the Weimar parliamentary system. Increasingly he used his communications empire to give the National Socialists favorable publicity. In October 1931 he organized a giant rally at Bad Harzburg in central Germany to demonstrate the strength and unity of the right. The DNVP leadership was joined by representatives of other conservative parties, including the German People's Party (DVP), as well as such right-wing groups as the Pan-Germans and the major veterans' organization, the *Stahlhelm*, which was closely linked to the DNVP. Leading members of industry, agriculture, and banking, including Hjalmar Schacht, president of the central *Reichsbank* and Hitler's Minister of Economics from 1934 to 1937, participated in the rally alongside such high-ranking former officers as Generals von Seeckt, von der Goltz, and von Lüttwitz. Monarchists were well represented, too, including the former kaiser's son, Prince August Wilhelm (1887–1949), who was to become a high-ranking officer in the SA.

Conservatives were delighted when Hitler agreed to participate in the Harzburg Front rally. Hitler, however, made sure that his movement would not be perceived as dependent on the conservative elite. He treated the assembled potentates with studied disdain. Some rivalry between Nationalists and Nazis was inevitable in any case as both parties contended for leadership of the right. The Nazi leadership was well aware that their capacity to attract a mass following to the nationalist cause now made them desirable partners for traditional conservatives who had previously scorned them as social inferiors and political upstarts. Part of the Nazis' attractiveness to common people was their youthful and dynamic image, untarnished by the failures of the "reactionary" elites of the old empire.

Moreover, the Nazis were widely perceived as advocates of *Mittelstand* interests against big business. It took all of Hitler's consummate demagogic and political skills to sustain this populist image while at the same time assuring himself of support from the economic elites, whose aid, both financial and political, he would need to gain power. While he could not afford to align himself too openly with "reactionaries" for fear of losing his mass base, Hitler knew that he needed to reassure the economic elites that their interests would be safeguarded under a government headed by the Nazis.

Hitler and the industrialists

In his overtures to industrialists and businessmen Hitler toned down the antisemitism that was such a prominent theme of his addresses to the party faithful at mass rallies. Instead he stressed the Nazi mission to destroy communism and social democracy in Germany. "If the advance of Bolshevism is not interrupted," Hitler told an audience of more than 600 businessmen of the prestigious *Industrieklub* in Düsseldorf in January 1932, "it will transform the entire world completely just as Christianity in the past changed the world."[18] If the Nazi Party did not exist, the question of Bolshevism or no Bolshevism in Germany would long ago have been decided in favor of the Reds. "We have made an inexorable decision," he proclaimed, "to destroy Marxism in Germany down to its very last root."[19]

Hitler told the assembled magnates of business and industry that social peace at home and economic expansion abroad could only be achieved through a powerful authoritarian state. Three factors determine the political life of a people, he said: their inner racial value, their esteem for superior personalities, and their resolve to succeed in struggle. Was it not absurd to base the economic system on personality, performance, and excellence while at the same time tolerating a political system based on the leveling principles of democracy? The leadership principle that was so essential to a productive economy must prevail in politics as well.

Hitler insisted that only a thoroughgoing political change in Germany could overcome the economic crisis. He could not concede that international factors or even the "chains of Versailles" were the primary source of

Germany's problems without thereby giving credibility to Brüning's strategy of restoring German power and prosperity by economic measures and easing the burden of reparations payments. "In contrast to our official government," Hitler said, "I cannot see any hope for the resurrection of Germany if we regard the foreign policy of Germany as the primary factor."[20] Instead, the key to German recovery was internal regeneration: the whole nation must come to share the idealism of the National Socialist Movement.

Although the business community was generally receptive to Hitler's anti-Marxism, some business leaders remained skeptical of Hitler's ability to control the unruly mass following that his demagogic oratory had mobilized. The dilemma the Nazis faced was the contradiction between their basic goals: the program of social conservatism and foreign expansion that coincided in large measure with the aims of Germany's traditional elites—and the propagandistic appeals that were required to maintain and increase the party's mass support. In urban industrial areas the Nazis frequently used anticapitalist slogans to attract worker support. To head off gains for the left in the deepening economic crisis the Nazis resorted to increasingly radical rhetoric. Conservatives valued Hitler's vote-getting ability but feared that Hitler might become the prisoner of his own populist propaganda. Too much talk of socialism and revolution could be dangerous, even if it was not seriously meant by the Nazi leadership. Hitler was forced to perform a difficult balancing act between the dominant elites and his mass constituency, for too close and too obvious links to traditional conservatives could alienate the Nazis' popular following, yet the good will of the elites was essential to his aim of acquiring power by legal methods.

The 1932 presidential election and the dismissal of Brüning

The success of Hitler's tactics, and their limitations, were demonstrated in the five nationwide elections of 1932. The presidential election in March and a runoff between the leading candidates in April were followed by state parliamentary elections at the end of April (in which the NSDAP increased its parliamentary representation in Prussia from 9 to 160 seats) and Reichstag elections in July and November of that year. In this highly politicized atmosphere of virtually nonstop campaigning the Nazis firmly established themselves as the leading party in Germany. Nazi Party membership grew from less than 100,000 in 1928 to over a million in 1932. Nonetheless, a Reichstag majority, and with it the chancellorship, continued to elude them.

Hitler was at first reluctant to cast his hat into the ring against the aging but popular war hero, President Hindenburg, whose election Hitler had backed in 1925. But because Hindenburg had now become the candidate of Brüning and supporters of the Republic, including the SPD, Hitler felt compelled to challenge his re-election. Hitler also decided to run for the largely symbolic office of president because he saw no chance of becoming chancellor in the near future. The fact that even the SPD now supported Hindenburg, an avowed monarchist, gives some indication of how far the political climate of the Weimar Republic had continued to shift to the right since the election of 1925.

The 84-year-old Reich President was himself a reluctant candidate for another six-year term. He resented having to rely on the backing of the SPD, whose politics he detested. It took all of Brüning's powers of persuasion to convince him that his candidacy was necessary to preserve public order and prevent a government headed by Hitler. Brüning's earlier plan for a constitutional amendment making Hindenburg president for life was rejected by Hitler and Hugenberg, because it would strengthen the Brüning government. Hindenburg's attitude toward Hitler was one of aristocratic disdain rather than principled opposition. He regarded a man of Hitler's lowly origin as unqualified to govern the nation, and he despised the unruly Nazi rank and file. It is ironic that his elitist attitude induced him, at this point at least, to defend the Republic he disdained against Hitler's challenge.

Hindenburg failed to gain an absolute majority in the first round of the presidential election. In the run-off on 10 April 1932 he won 53 percent of the vote, while Hitler gained 37 percent and the Communist candidate Ernst Thälmann had 10 percent. But Brüning reaped no gratitude for his tireless work in Hindenburg's campaign or for his attempt to control the Nazis by banning public demonstrations of the uniformed SA on 13 April, at the request of the Prussian and Bavarian state governments. The Communists' "Red Front" paramilitary formation had already been banned throughout the Reich in May 1929. Brüning's policy of combating street violence by restricting paramilitary cohorts ran counter to Nationalist efforts to court Nazi support. *Reichswehr* leaders, too, wanted to keep the SA as a military training ground. The head of the *Reichswehr*, General Kurt von Schleicher (1882–1934), hoped that Hindenburg's victory in the presidential election would make the Nazis more amenable to supporting or at least tolerating a Nationalist-led government. Meeting with Hitler on 7 May, he promised to work for replacement of the Brüning administration and a revocation of the ban on the SA and SS.

Schleicher found willing allies among the camarilla of aristocratic landowners and military officers who served as the president's advisers. Brüning's Minister of Defense and acting Interior Minister, General Wilhelm Groener, had already been forced out of office on 12 May for defending the government's ban on the SA in the Reichstag. Nationalists resented the fact that Brüning, rather than courting the Nazis, was apparently willing to continue to rely on the SPD for support. The SPD, in turn, had tolerated Brüning as the "lesser evil," the only viable alternative to an even more authoritarian regime. For Hindenburg's Junker advisers, including his son Oskar, who had received his military commission in the same officer-candidate class as Schleicher, the final straw seems to have been Brüning's decision to investigate the misuse of government subsidies to financially troubled aristocratic estates in eastern Germany. This program to bail out major landowners stood in stark contrast to

Brüning's deflationary policies. Estate owners accused Brüning of pandering to the SPD, which had long called for a limited redistribution of land on bankrupt estates.

The Papen coup in Prussia

Brüning's fall ended the moderate phase of the "presidential system" launched with the formation of the Brüning government in March 1930. His successors were no longer committed to the preservation of the Weimar constitution. On Schleicher's advice, Hindenburg's choice as Brüning's replacement was the Rhineland Catholic estate owner, Franz von Papen (1879–1969), whose hopelessly unrepresentative "cabinet of barons" could count only on the support of the Nationalist Party and the *Reichswehr*. Schleicher himself entered the cabinet as Papen's Minister of Defense. Papen's first two emergency decrees further reduced social services and welfare benefits, a move that endeared him to the business community, but further alienated the SPD, which refused to offer the same parliamentary toleration (a pledge not to support a no-confidence vote) to Papen as they had to Brüning. Aware of their limited popular appeal, the Nationalists hoped to bring Hitler's movement into a governing alliance in which the Nationalists would dominate.

Like other traditional conservatives, Papen shared the Nazi goal of destroying the "Weimar system," but feared the radicalism and unpredictability of Nazi methods. The economic and military elite hoped to tame the Nazis by bringing them into the government in subordinate ministerial posts. In his meeting with Schleicher in May, Hitler had made Nazi toleration of a Papen government conditional on new elections. He refused, however, to enter Papen's government in a subordinate role. Following Mussolini's example in Italy in 1922, Hitler demanded the office of chancellor for himself.[21] Papen, however, labored under the delusion that accommodation with Hitler was possible. To gain Nazi cooperation Papen dissolved the Reichstag in June 1932, rescinded the ban on the Nazi paramilitary formations, and scheduled new elections for the end of July.

On 20 July 1932, ten days before the scheduled elections and at the request of the Nazi delegation in the Prussian parliament, the Papen government struck a blow against the Republic, the importance of which can hardly be overstated. Using as a pretext the renewed political street violence that his own repeal of the ban on the SA had brought about, Papen deposed the SPD-led coalition government in Prussia, declared himself Reich Commissioner of the Prussian state, and imposed martial law in Berlin (which was not only the Prussian capital but the German capital as well). His main objective was to weaken the SPD and gain control of the Prussian bureaucracy and police preparatory to changing the Weimar constitution in a more authoritarian direction. In taking these extreme measures the Papen government dropped all pretense of adhering to the Weimar constitution, which specifically

Table 2 Reichstag elections, 1928–33

Party	20 May 1928			14 September 1930			31 July 1932			6 November 1932			5 March 1933		
	Total votes	%	No. deputies	Total votes	%	No. deputies	Total votes	%	No. deputies	Total votes	%	No. deputies	Total votes	%	No. deputies
No. eligible voters	41,224,700		491	42,957,700		577	44,226,800		608	44,373,700		584	44,685,800		647
No. valid votes cast	30,753,300	74.60		34,970,900	81.41		36,882,400	83.39		35,471,800	79.93		39,343,300	88.04	
Social Democrats (SPD)	9,153,000	29.8	153	8,577,700	24.5	143	7,959,700	21.6	133	7,248,000	20.4	121	7,181,600	18.3	120
Communist Party (KPD)	3,264,800	10.6	54	4,592,100	13.1	77	5,282,600	14.6	89	5,980,200	16.9	100	4,848,100	12.3	81
Center Party	3,712,200	12.1	62	4,127,900	11.8	68	4,589,300	12.5	75	4,230,600	11.9	70	4,424,900	11.7	74
Bavarian People's Party	945,600	3.0	16	1,059,100	3.0	19	1,192,700	3.2	22	1,094,600	3.1	20	1,073,600	2.7	18
Democrats (DDP)	1,505,700	4.9	25	1,322,400	3.8	20	371,800	1.0	4	336,500	1.0	2	334,200	0.8	5
People's Party (DVP)	2,679,700	8.7	45	1,578,200	4.5	30	436,000	1.2	7	661,800	1.9	11	432,300	1.1	2
Wirtschaftspartei	1,397,100	4.5	23	1,362,400	3.9	23	146,900	0.4	2	110,300	0.3	1	—	—	—
Nationalists (DNVP)	4,381,600	14.2	73	2,458,300	7.0	41	2,177,400	5.9	37	2,959,000	8.8	52	3,136,800	8.0	52

	Votes	%	Seats	Votes	%	Seats	Votes	%	Seats	Votes	%	Seats	Votes	%	Seats
Christlich-soz Volksdienst	—	—		868,200	2.5	14	405,300	1.1	3	412,500	1.2	5	384,000	1.0	4
Landbund	199,500	0.6	3	194,000	0.5	3	96,900	0.2	2	105,200	0.3	2	83,800	0.2	1
Christlich-natl.	581,800	1.8	10	1,108,700	3.0	19	90,600	0.2	1	46,400	0.1	—	—	—	
Bauern u. Landvolk															
Deutsch-Hannov. Partei	195,600	0.5	3	144,300	0.4	3	46,900	0.1	—	64,000	0.2	1	47,700	0.1	—
Deutsche Bauernpartei	481,300	1.5	8	339,600	1.0	6	137,100	0.3	2	149,000	0.4	3	114,000	0.3	2
National Socialists (NSDAP)	810,100	2.6	12	6,409,600	18.3	107	13,745,800	37.4	230	11,737,000	33.1	196	17,277,200	43.9	288
Other parties	1,445,300	4.8	4	828,400	2.4	4	204,400	0.6	1	336,700	0.8	—	6,800	0.0	—

prohibited the national government from removing constitutionally elected state governments from power or from their representation in the *Reichsrat* (the upper house of parliament consisting of representatives of the state governments). This was, in fact, nothing less than a forcible coup against what was left of Weimar democracy. The SPD-led government in Prussia, by far Germany's largest state, was widely regarded by the right as the linchpin that held the Weimar system in place. The Prussian government had remained in power after the parliamentary elections in April even though the Nazis had gained a plurality of 36 percent of the vote. Now the last stronghold of republicanism in Germany was breached through a legally dubious application of emergency presidential powers under Article 48.

Why was there no active resistance to the Papen government's coup? The answer to this question can help to explain why there would be so little resistance to Hitler's accession to power six months later. The SPD had long since adopted a strictly evolutionary strategy. Its dedication to legality made the party seek redress not through armed confrontation but through the judicial process. Prussian government leaders filed suit to reverse Papen's action in the Supreme Court of the Reich, which some months later predictably ruled against them. While conceding the right of the Prussian government to continue to represent the state in the *Reichsrat* (the upper chamber consisting of representatives of the states), the court nonetheless decided that the Reich government had the constitutional right to impose martial law and install a Reich Commissioner in emergency situations. It is doubtful in any case whether the Prussian police, already heavily infiltrated by Nazis, would have responded to the call to defend their government against Papen's intervention. Papen, after all, could call on the *Reichswehr* to enforce the authority of the national government. Nor was the *Reichsbanner*, the SPD's paramilitary formation (formed in 1924 in response to the Hitler Putsch), prepared to respond with force to this kind of quasilegal takeover. Primed to resist an armed Nazi putsch, the *Reichsbanner* was psychologically defenseless against a nonviolent assault on the Weimar constitution.

Labor union leaders, too, counseled SPD officials to put their faith in the courts and attempt to reverse the coup through litigation. The days of the Kapp Putsch, when a general strike could mobilize supporters of the Republic and paralyze the government, lay a long time in the past. With unemployment at over six million, a strike was not only unlikely to succeed, but might even provide a pretext for Papen to extend martial law nationwide. Widespread fatalism weakened the resolve of defenders of the Republic. The SPD also feared the cancellation of elections scheduled for 31 July, which it hoped to turn into a popular referendum on Papen's breach of the constitution.

The working class was bitterly divided by the conflict between the SPD and the Communists that had raged since the split in the world socialist movement after the Russian Revolution.[22] The bitter division on the left was rooted in the Soviet perception that Social Democratic leaders were mainly responsible for the suppression of revolutions that seemed vital to the survival of the nascent Soviet state in the immediate postwar period. SPD reformism seemed the main barrier to revolution and the establishment of a pro-Soviet regime. Since 1928 the Communist Party in Germany had followed the Comintern strategy of attacking Social Democrats (who they derided as "social fascists") for allegedly preparing the ground for fascism (thus, ironically, mimicking the Nazi attack on the SPD as the advance guard of communism). The Comintern viewed Nazism as merely the terrorist arm of a capitalist system whose mass base was provided by the SPD constituency. Underestimating the threat and the staying power of the Nazis, the Communists gave highest priority to defeating their SPD rivals for working-class support. Indeed, the KPD had gone so far as to join forces with the Nazis in an unsuccessful attempt to topple the SPD-dominated state government in Prussia in 1931. Although Communists took a more active role than Social Democrats in fighting the Nazis in the streets, the KPD leadership in effect made common cause with the Nazis in discrediting the SPD and undermining parliamentary democracy.

The Reichstag elections in July and November 1932

New opportunities for both Nazis and Communists to obstruct the parliamentary process came after the Reichstag elections at the end of July 1932. For SPD leaders who had hoped that the elections would demonstrate public support for the Weimar constitution and popular outrage at the high-handed ouster of the SPD government in Prussia, the results were a bitter disappointment. The Nazis now became the largest party in the Reichstag with 13,745,800 votes, or 37.4 percent. It was their largest plurality in any national election before Hitler became chancellor in 1933. The Communists upped their share to 14 percent of the vote—largely, it would seem, at the expense of the SPD, whose vote declined to 21.6 percent. Together the two extremist parties now controlled a majority committed to ending parliamentary government.

The Nazis again gained most of their votes at the expense of the bourgeois middle. The Democrats (now virtually defunct), the People's Party, and two conservative small-holders' parties (the *Wirtschaftspartei* and the *Christlich-Nationales Bauern und Landvolk*) lost approximately a million votes each. Those parties had shifted to the right in an attempt to save themselves during the economic crisis. This, however, only encouraged their followers to do the same, with the logical consequence that most of them shifted their votes to the Nazis. According to sociologist Jürgen Falter, the NSDAP functioned as "the representative of the formerly liberal, conservative, and special interest-oriented groups."[23] Unlike the narrow special-interest parties whose constituencies it absorbed, the Nazis had developed into a modern, well-organized, broad-based "people's party" that attracted disgruntled voters from all sectors of the electorate not bound by loyalty to Marxism or Catholicism. They did not do well in the big cities (except in the more affluent sections), in heavy industrial areas, and in the Catholic south and west, as the Catholic Center and its Bavarian affiliate held firm with about 15 percent of the vote. Upper- and upper-middle-class voters, especially the self-employed, supported the Nazis in disproportionate numbers, as did rural and small-town residents in the Protestant areas of Germany. A significant proportion of skilled, nonunionized workers also responded to the Nazi appeal.[24]

The July election results further enhanced Hitler's stature on the right and diminished that of Papen. The goal of a viable authoritarian government under conservative control now seemed unthinkable without the cooperation of Nazi leaders. Understanding that a great modern industrial nation could not be successfully governed in the long run by a small clique of officers, industrialists, and aristocrats with negligible mass support, Hindenburg met with Hitler on 13 August 1932 to sound him out on his willingness to join the Papen government as vice-chancellor.

But Hitler held fast to his all-or-nothing strategy, insisting on full power. Despite Papen's and Hindenburg's offers of ministerial positions of his choice, Hitler insisted that his party would only join the government if he were named chancellor. In early September Papen dissolved the Reichstag in an effort to prevent a vote on a Communist-sponsored no-confidence motion, but Göring as president of the Reichstag insisted on holding the vote anyway in violation of parliamentary rules. The resulting unprecedented 513 to 42 vote against Papen amounted to what historian Hans Mommsen called "a severe and irreparable loss of prestige for the Papen cabinet."[25] Undaunted nonetheless in his pursuit of a more authoritarian government, Papen called for another election in November in the hopes of bolstering his parliamentary support. The first signs of improvement in the economy following Herbert Hoover's moratorium on reparations and war debts in 1931 raised Papen's hopes of cutting into the Nazi vote.

In this last national election before Hitler took power, the Nazis did indeed suffer a stunning loss of just over two million votes. This result could be interpreted as a popular rebuff to Hitler's maximalist policy of holding out for full power. Continuing Nazi-instigated violence, including the brutal murder of a Communist worker at Potempa in Silesia in August by five SA thugs, no doubt cut into the Nazis' electoral support as well. But with 33.1 percent of the vote the Nazis remained the largest Reichstag party by a comfortable margin. The SPD held on to second place with 20.4 percent, while the Communists continued to gain at the SPD's expense. They now mustered close to six million votes, or 16.9 percent of the total. The Nationalists made only slight gains, getting fewer than three million votes, or 8.8 percent. The turnout dropped by almost one and one-half million votes, a sign of voter disaffection with the gridlock in national politics. Nonetheless voter participation remained high at close to 80 percent.

The Schleicher interlude

Despite the Nazi losses, Papen's position was even less tenable after the election than before. Around 90 percent of the vote had been cast for parties opposed to Papen. A parliamentary coalition was nowhere in sight. Papen's lack of popularity was so evident that *Reichswehr* leaders would not guarantee the army's ability to maintain order if Papen remained in power. Under these circumstances Hindenburg rejected Papen's request for emergency powers to suspend the constitution and establish an open dictatorship. "I am too old," Hindenburg told Papen in early December, "to take responsibility for a civil war at the end of my life."[26] Hindenburg also remained unwilling to entrust full power to Hitler. In this impasse, General Schleicher, Brüning's old foe and a member of Papen's cabinet, conceived the unlikely plan of forming a government based on the support of the right wing of the SPD under trade union leader Theodor Leipart and the left wing of the Nazis headed by Gregor Strasser. On 2 December 1932 Schleicher became the last chancellor of the pre-Hitler era.

The Nazi losses in the November election seemed to favor Schleicher's plan of enticing Strasser into the government. Strasser was known to be skeptical of Hitler's policy of holding out for full power. Believing that the Nazis had reached the limits of their popular support, Strasser despaired of the party ever attaining power under its current all-or-nothing strategy. Schleicher hoped that his offer of the vice-chancellorship to Strasser on 4 December would receive Hitler's blessing. Hitler, however, continued to oppose all compromises for a coalition government under any chancellor but himself. In a bitter face-to-face confrontation with Strasser, Hitler prevailed. Strasser resigned his party offices on 8 December and went on a prolonged vacation. In the blood purge of June 1934 he as well as Schleicher would fall victim to Hitler's revenge.

Unable to entice the Nazis into his government, Schleicher now in his turn requested emergency powers to dissolve the Reichstag, cancel further elections, suspend the constitution, ban both the Nazi and Communist parties, and install a military dictatorship. His motivation was not so much to prevent Hitler's accession to power as to preempt further KPD gains and a potential Communist uprising. Fear of giving the KPD further electoral ammunition also made SPD leaders unwilling to "tolerate" Schleicher as they had tolerated the presidential government under Brüning from 1930 to 1932. But having so recently denied a request for openly dictatorial powers to Papen, partly on Schleicher's own advice, and possibly fearing the danger of civil war, Hindenburg refused his chancellor's request for further emergency powers.[27] Hindenburg feared Schleicher's propensity for "socialist" experiments such as public works and work creation projects. Industrialists disliked Schleicher's cooperation with the trade unions. Hindenburg's coterie feared the revival of plans to halt the government's agrarian aid program as a result of Reichstag investigations into the misuse of funds by wealthy estate owners.

Hitler's appointment as chancellor

Schleicher's failure to muster significant political support and retain Hindenburg's confidence gave Papen the chance to turn the tables on the man who had helped oust him from office a short time before. On 4 January 1933 he met with Hitler in the house of the Rhineland banker Kurt von Schröder (1889–1965). Like many other businessmen, Schröder was convinced that only the inclusion of Hitler in the government could restore political order and avert a shift of the political momentum to the left, where the Communists were continuing to gain votes. Schröder had been one of the signatories to a letter sent by leading bankers and industrialists to Hindenburg on 19 November 1932, advocating Hitler's appointment as chancellor. Business leaders believed that the responsibilities of power would tame the Nazi movement. Strasser's departure in early December also allayed the business community's lingering concerns about anticapitalist sentiment in the Nazi ranks.

Papen did not disappoint the hopes of Germany's economic elite. He agreed to enter a Hitler cabinet as vice-chancellor and offered to secure Hindenburg's agreement to a Hitler–Papen government. Persuaded by Papen and his retinue that Hitler could be safely coopted for the conservative cause, Hindenburg overcame his earlier misgivings about the "Bohemian corporal," whom he had previously vowed never to appoint to the nation's highest governing post. Hermann Göring's (1893–1945) outstanding military record as an ace pilot in the Great War may have helped to dispel Hindenburg's doubts about the Nazis.[28] On 30 January he appointed Hitler as chancellor of a minority government that would continue to rule by presidential authority under Article 48.

Conservatives hoped that the predominance of non-Nazis in the cabinet would keep Hitler on a course of their choosing. "We're framing him in" was the way Hugenberg put it in a meeting with Papen on 26 January.[29] "What are you worried about?" Papen wrote to the wary conservative Ewald von Kleist (1881–1954), who would rise to the rank of field marshal in World War II. "I have Hindenburg's trust. In two months we will have pressed Hitler into a corner so that he'll squeal."[30] Of the 13 cabinet members only two besides Hitler were members of the Nazi Party: Wilhelm Frick (1877–1946) became Minister of the Interior while Göring joined the cabinet at ministerial rank as Deputy Reich Commissioner for Prussia and, more importantly, Prussian Interior Minister (in charge of the Prussian police). Hugenberg's appointment as Minister of Economics and Agriculture allayed conservative fears of radical social measures, as did the appointment of Franz Seldte (1882–1947), cofounder and leader of the veterans' organization *Stahlhelm*, as Minister of Labor (until the end of the war). Moreover, Papen as vice-chancellor retained his post as Reich Commissioner of Prussia and reserved for himself the right to be present whenever Hitler met with President Hindenburg. Career-officer General Werner von Blomberg (1878–1946), commander of the East Prussian military district, was Hindenburg's personal choice for the vital post of Defense Minister. Hitler's cabinet also included several holdovers from the Papen and Schleicher governments: Konstantin von Neurath (1873–1956) as Foreign Minister (until 1938); Lutz Schwerin von Krosigk (1887–1952) as Minister of Finance (until the end of the war); and Franz Gürtner (1881–1941), who had been Bavarian Minister of

Justice at the time of Hitler's Beer Hall Putsch, as Minister of Justice (until his death in 1941).

His appointment as chancellor crowned Hitler's strategy of acquiring power through electoral politics and legal means. It would be quite wrong, however, to conclude that he was swept into office by overwhelming popular support or that Hindenburg had no choice but to appoint him chancellor. The Nazis had never gained more than 37.4 percent of the vote in a national election, well short of a majority. Moreover, Hitler's appointment came at a time when the party seemed to face a serious crisis. The loss of votes in November not only ended the bandwagon effect created by rapid Nazi growth, but it also meant that the Nazis had probably reached the limits of their popularity without prospects of attaining power on Hitler's terms. Strasser's withdrawal from politics demonstrated the potential rifts in the party if Hitler persisted in his all-or-nothing strategy. An almost 40 percent loss of votes (from their July 1932 high) in parliamentary elections in the state of Thuringia in early December confirmed the party's downward slide. "The year 1932 has been one long run of bad luck," Goebbels wrote in his diary on 23 December 1932. "...The past was difficult and the future looks dark and murky; all prospects and hopes have completely disappeared."[31]

It is true that the Nazis rebounded in local elections in the state of Lippe-Detmold on 15 January 1933, adding 5,000 votes to their November results. But even in this largely rural and Protestant state the Nazis remained 2,500 votes short of the total they had received in the July elections.[32] A minuscule state with fewer than 100,000 voters, Lippe-Detmold was hardly representative of Germany as a whole. How long would Hitler have been able to retain the support of a third of the German electorate if the Nazis remained out of power? Would not the Hitler movement have been effectively stalled if Papen and his fellow conservatives had not submitted to Hitler's demands?

Ironically, the fear that the Nazi Party might continue to lose votes if Hitler continued to be excluded from power may have helped to dispel the qualms of many conservatives about a Hitler chancellorship. For whom would the Nazi constituency be likely to vote if the Hitler movement dissolved? Were not many of these radically disgruntled voters likely to shift to the Communists, who had continued to gain votes in the November elections and had not yet, it seemed, reached the limits of their electoral strength? Was not the potential affinity of Nazis and Communists, despite their street brawls, shown by their cooperation in the strike of Berlin transit workers in late 1932? For tactical reasons (to attract working-class votes in the November elections) the Nazis had decided to support the Communist-initiated and SPD-supported strike, a decision Goebbels later regretted. At the very least the breakup of the Nazi constituency threatened to strengthen the left. To worried conservatives a breakup of the NSDAP even portended a possible return to parliamentary government under the detested SPD.

Such questions and calculations led the conservatives around Hindenburg to grant Hitler power at a time when the Nazis faced problems that might have been difficult to surmount. The positive model of the Mussolini regime in Italy contributed to the willingness of Hindenburg, the *Reichswehr*, and the conservative elite to accept a Hitler government.[33]   The timely intervention of conservative leaders enabled Hitler to gain the office he had sought for so long. The leadership of government was entrusted to him despite his public pronouncements that when he achieved power "heads would roll." How different the situation was now than ten years before when conservative leaders spurned Hitler's pretensions to national leadership! Now the shoe was on the other foot. It was the conservatives who now sought out Hitler to lead the national cause.

8   The Nazi consolidation of power, 1933–34

Hitler had come to power legally, though not democratically, as the chancellor of a government ruling by presidential decree under Article 48 of the Weimar constitution. To many observers at the time, in fact, Hitler's "Government of National Concentration," the same title Papen had used for his government in 1932, seemed like just another in a line of stop-gap "presidential governments" that had ruled Germany since 1930, albeit one with greater popular support. Many of its supporters saw the new government not as a radical regime—to them Weimar was "radical"—but as a middle way between democracy and the kind of old-fashioned authoritarian regime to which Papen and Brüning had wanted to return. The Nazis had, after all, repeatedly criticized Hindenburg after the July 1932 elections for violating the Weimar constitution by failing to authorize the head of the largest party in Germany to form a presidential government. For Germany's two main democratic parties, the SPD and the Center, a military dictatorship under Schleicher seemed a greater threat to the constitution than a Hitler government hemmed in by constitutional constraints. Schleicher had, after all, violated the constitution in mid-January by refusing to schedule new elections before the coming autumn.[1] Some members of the Center Party hoped Hitler would save the constitution from Hugenberg and the DNVP. Consistently underestimating the Nazi threat, some Communist leaders also regarded the Nationalists as the dominant force in the new government. Reaction to the new regime by conservatives abroad was quite favorable as well. The *London Times* viewed Hitler as a reasonable leader overwhelmed at times by the terrorist elements in his party. French and Polish officials, too, were less disturbed by Hitler's appointment to the chancellery than by the rise of Hugenberg, whose economic imperialism seemed to present the greatest threat to the status quo at that time.[2]

The National Socialists, however, had no intention of relinquishing power again. Like Mussolini in Italy in the 1920s, Hitler used the powers of his office to establish a one-party dictatorship. The task he faced was to consolidate absolute power while retaining the good will and cooperation of the professional, business, civil service, and military elites whose support he would continue to need to achieve his goal of national expansion. Hence he had to proceed with some circumspection lest he alienate his coalition partners, the

Nationalists, and other conservative allies. It was not until after Hindenburg's death in August 1934 that Hitler fully consolidated the Nazi dictatorship.

"National rebirth"

The mood of national revival that accompanied the Nazis' entry into the government greatly abetted Hitler's task. His followers celebrated his accession to power with a dramatic torchlight parade in front of the party headquarters and the chancellery in Berlin that lasted into the early hours of the next morning. In his appeal to the German people on 1 February 1933 the new chancellor sounded a conservative revivalist theme:

> The national government regards as its first and foremost task the restoration of the unity of spirit and will of our *Volk*. It will preserve and defend the foundation on which the strength of our nation rests. It will extend its firm protection to Christianity as the basis of our moral system, and to the family as the nucleus of our *Volk* and state. It will restore to our *Volk*, beyond the divisions of rank and class, its consciousness of national and political unity and the duties this entails. It will make reverence for our great past and pride in our ancient traditions the foundation for the education of German youth. In this way it will declare a merciless war against spiritual, political, and cultural nihilism. Germany must not and will not sink into anarchistic communism. In place of turbulent instincts it will again raise national discipline to the guiding principle of our life.[3]

These were sentiments to which all conservatives could wholeheartedly subscribe.

New elections

Hitler's strategy for gaining absolute power by legal means involved dissolving the Reichstag and calling for new elections. With the resources of government now at their command, the Nazis could reasonably expect to obtain the two-thirds majority they would need to change the constitution legally. This would also have the advantage of ending his dependence on Hindenburg's presidential powers. Ironically, Hitler proposed a more constitutional path to dictatorship than Hugenberg, the Nationalist leader, who wanted to avoid new elections for fear of a Nazi majority. Hugenberg preferred a nonparliamentary cabinet based on presidential power and opposed any Nazi moves to negotiate a parliamentary majority with the Center Party.[4] Instead Hugenberg proposed expanding the governing coalition's plurality by simply outlawing the Communist Party. Hitler's more moderate course prevailed as President Hindenburg reluctantly agreed to Hitler's demand for a new election on condition that it be the last one.

On 1 February, two days after his appointment as chancellor, Hitler dissolved the Reichstag and scheduled the election for 5 March, while continuing to rule by presidential decree. The need to restore the authority of the state against the Marxist threat became the central theme of the Nazis' election campaign. In a private meeting with leading *Reichswehr* officers on 3 February Hitler assured them of his intention to eradicate pacifism, Marxism, and democracy from Germany and to reintroduce universal military service at the earliest opportunity. On 20 February he met with the leaders of business and industry to outline, in strict confidence, his plans for rearmament, an end to the parliamentary system, and the elimination of Marxists of all stripes from public life. Industrialists responded enthusiastically to Hitler's appeal by contributing some three million marks to the party coffers.

Repression of the left

In their persecution of leftists the Nazis did not need to exercise great restraint, for here they could be sure of the full support of Germany's conservatives. The first targets of officially sanctioned terror under the new regime were Social Democratic and Communist activists, many of whom were Jewish. Hermann Göring, as Prussian Minister of the Interior and head of the Prussian police, authorized the deputization of SA and SS members, who took the lead in harassing and rounding up functionaries, activists, and publicists of the left. The SA established its own prison camps, including one at Oranienburg near Berlin, the site of the Sachsenhausen concentration camp that formally opened in 1936. An emergency decree "for the protection of the German people," issued by Hitler on 4 February ostensibly in response to the Communist call for a general strike on 31 January (which went unheeded), gave the government authority to censor the Social Democratic and Communist press and curtail their right to meet. The Nazis made repeated use of this decree to ban left-wing publications, prohibit election rallies, and harass left-wing candidates. The effect of the decree was not just to eliminate the left-wing press, but also to induce centrist (i.e. liberal and republican) newspapers to practice self-censorship and suspend their criticisms of the government.

The Reichstag fire

The spectacular fire that destroyed the Reichstag building in Berlin on 27 February gave the Nazis the pretext they needed to escalate their terror against the left. The fire was set by a young Dutch ex-communist, Marianus van der Lubbe, who had been expelled from the Dutch CP and who always insisted that he had acted entirely on his own. Although the Communist Party denounced him as a Nazi provocateur, there is no firm evidence that the arsonist received any Nazi support.[5] Certainly the Nazis were the main beneficiaries of the attack. The fire destroyed the hated symbol of parliamentarism in

Germany while providing a convenient pretext for suppressing the Communist Party and suspending civil liberties in the final stages of the election campaign. Van der Lubbe was eventually executed for setting the fire, but in a much-publicized trial the government failed to convict Georgi Dmitrov, the Bulgarian head of the Comintern, of involvement in the crime.

Claiming that the fire was a signal for a Communist uprising, Hitler issued a "Decree for the Protection of People and State" the following day. The decree proclaimed a state of emergency and suspended the constitutional protection of civil liberties, including freedom of the press, the right of assembly, the right of association, the privacy of postal, telegraphic, and telephonic communications, and freedom for searches without warrant. The decree also gave the Reich government the authority to intervene in the affairs of the individual states, ostensibly to maintain law and order. The Reichstag Fire Decree led to a wave of arrests that soon overwhelmed the prison system, thereby inducing the government to set up the first official concentration camp at Dachau near Munich in March 1933 to house and "re-educate" political prisoners and other so-called "antisocials."

This Reichstag fire decree created the legal basis for the Nazi police state and was never repealed. The courts, a domain of right-wing nationalists long before the Nazis came to power, cited this decree as the basis for their refusal to limit the use of arbitrary police power. The threat of Communist subversion was used as a pretext to suppress any activity that could be interpreted as politically divisive. Indeed, the "destruction of Marxism" became the standard justification for legal terror.

Violence against the left was now perpetrated under full legal cover. According to the postwar testimony of Rudolf Diels (1900–57), who from 1930 onward headed the Prussian political police, the agency that in 1933 became the nucleus of the *Gestapo* (the secret state police), approximately 500–700 political opponents were killed in the wave of terror that engulfed Germany in the ensuing six months.[6] Communist deputies and candidates were arrested before election day. Although Communist Party property had already been confiscated and put at the disposal of the Nazi Party on 23 February, well before the Reichstag fire, the Communist Party itself was not officially banned until after the election to avoid the possibility of Communist voters shifting their support to the SPD. Despite the vicious crackdown after the Reichstag fire, almost five million Germans still voted for the KPD in the March elections. The arrest of all 81 elected Communist delegates helped to make possible the two-thirds Reichstag majority that Hitler needed for dictatorial powers.

The Enabling Act

Notwithstanding the advantages of incumbency, including financial backing by industry, official repression of political adversaries, and full use of state resources, the Nazis could do no better than 43.9 percent of the vote in the elections that followed six days after the Reichstag fire. In Berlin, stronghold of the left, the Nazis got less than a third of the vote. With their coalition partners, the Nationalists, who gained 8 percent of the vote, they had enough only for a simple majority. This would have sufficed for a normal parliamentary government, but neither Hitler nor his Nationalist partners had any intention of returning to parliamentary rule.

It was the Catholic Center Party that provided the crucial margin for the two-thirds majority needed to change the constitution. On 23 March 1933 the Reichstag passed the Enabling Act, euphemistically named the "Law for the Removal of the Distress of People and Reich," by a vote of 444 to 94. With the Communist delegates barred from taking their seats, only members of the Social Democratic Party voted against the bill. The Enabling Act furnished the legal basis for Hitler's dictatorship by conferring full legislative and executive powers upon the chancellor for a period of four years. Having fulfilled its purpose, the Reichstag was again dissolved. In November 1933 an uncontested vote returned a solid slate of Nazis. What was now a rubber-stamp Reichstag preserved the illusion of legality by extending the Enabling Act for another four years in 1937 and again in 1941.

Why did the Center Party, a bulwark of the Weimar system in the 1920s, support this quasilegal transition to dictatorship? It appears that Hitler's appointment as chancellor had created something of a bandwagon effect. The "national opposition" had legally acquired power as a government of "national redemption" in a time of apparently unending parliamentary stalemate. Communist calls for a general strike had gone unheeded. The left was too divided and demoralized to mount effective resistance to the new regime. Many critics of the regime practiced self-restraint so as not to provoke the government into violating the constitution. In any case, the left-wing parties, though maintaining their voting strength at over 30 percent in the March elections, represented only a minority of the German population. For the two-thirds of the populace who did not identify with the political left the time seemed right to bury petty differences and pull together to restore national unity, pride, and strength. Even those who personally disliked or distrusted Hitler were willing to give him a chance to lead the national revival and end the bitter partisan divisions that most middle-class Germans blamed on the unpatriotic Marxist left and on a parliamentary system that seemed to foster class-based special-interest politics.

The Center Party, which had steadily moved to the right under the leadership of Monsignor Ludwig Kaas (1881–1952) in the late 1920s and early 1930s, was not unaffected by the dominant public mood. After the November 1932 Reichstag elections Kaas had told Hindenburg: "We don't want to fall back into parliamentarism… We don't want to go backwards, but rather forwards."[7] While at the time Kaas was still ambivalent about a Hitler chancellorship, he advised Hindenburg that the Nazis would have to be included in a government of national concentration if Germany's political divisions were to be overcome. The Center Party had never opposed a parliamentary government under Hitler and had negotiated with the Nazis to form such a government in both Prussia and the Reich. By late January 1933 Kaas called for Hitler's appointment as chancellor because Schleicher lacked parliamentary backing and Hitler had pledged to seek a parliamentary majority by calling for new elections. A significant segment of the Catholic constituency favored some sort of accommodation with Hitler's new regime, as did the Church hierarchy. Meeting at Fulda on 28 March, the Conference of German Bishops retracted its earlier prohibition of Catholic membership in the NSDAP.[8] The Center's conservative Bavarian wing, the Bavarian People's Party, had never had any firm commitment to democratic government. Indeed, a number of Catholic clerics had actively promoted the early Nazi movement in Munich. Ultimately, the Catholic Center's hostility to the "godless" left outweighed its distrust of Hitler, who promised to respect the independence of the Church in Germany and to preserve its role in education. Many Center Party delegates were also reassured by a provision in the Enabling Act that the president's constitutional right to dismiss the chancellor would be respected and the continued existence of the Reichstag as an institution would not be affected.

The Day of Potsdam

The Nazis carefully orchestrated the public mood and sought to give every impression of respectability. The new Reichstag met in the historic city of Potsdam, for centuries the residence of the Prussian kings. On 21 March, the first day of spring, an elaborate opening ceremony was mounted in the venerable Garrison Church to demonstrate the union of old and new right. With the altar as a backdrop, Hitler bowed deferentially to Hindenburg, as the young chancellor and the aged president clasped hands in front of the empty seat traditionally occupied by the kaiser.

The ex-corporal at the side of the aristocratic field marshal in front of the vault of Frederick the Great: Could there be a more stirring symbol of the reconciliation of classes and the continuity of the venerable Prussian military tradition under the new regime? The ceremony was staged with full military pomp, designed to evoke the emotions of patriotism, martial pride, and national renewal. Monarchists, including the kaiser's son August Wilhelm, who had joined the Nazi Party in 1930, welcomed the new rulers in the fond expectation that Hitler would pave the way for a restoration of the Hohenzollern dynasty. The "Day of Potsdam" reinforced the impression that Hitler's regime would bring about national unity, solidarity, and rejuvenation, a new beginning for the aspirations to national greatness so painfully thwarted by defeat in the World War and by the bitter internal conflicts of the Weimar years.

Gleichschaltung

This yearning for unity and a purified, more cohesive, more powerful national community purged of its disruptive and divisive elements greatly abetted the

National Socialist effort to gain a monopoly of power and to bring all institutions of German society under their control. The official name given to this process of synchronization, coordination, and subordination was *Gleichschaltung*, the literal meaning of which is "shifting into the same gear, line, or current." The avowed aim of *Gleichschaltung* was to produce a uniform, harmonious, and militant *Volksgemeinschaft*, a national community based on cultural and "racial" kinship and pursuing the common goal of national reconstruction. Nazi egalitarianism was an outgrowth of the wartime ideology of comradeship and "brotherhood at the front." Comradeship offered a metaphor for class harmony that conveniently concealed the hierarchical structure of the Nazi movement.

The great promise of the "People's Community" was an end to debilitating class conflict and political polarization. Its great advantage to conservatives was that it did not require changing existing disparities in property or wealth. As William Sheridan Allen put it in his excellent study of the Nazi seizure of power in the north German town of Northeim, German burghers "were virtuously uplifted by the hope of creating a Volk-community without actually sacrificing their own class status."[9] The ideal of *Volksgemeinschaft* was probably the single feature of National Socialism that attracted greatest public support. Its appeal helps to account for the extraordinary willingness of substantial segments of the public to submit to *Gleichschaltung* and to participate in the dissolution of non-Nazi institutions and organizations. Many Germans also came to believe that the best way to influence the National Socialist movement was to join it rather than to oppose it.

In practice *Gleichschaltung* meant the elimination from German society of all diversity and dissent. Jews and Marxists became the special targets and primary victims of *Gleichschaltung*. Excluded by definition from the *Volksgemeinschaft*, Jews were subjected to official and unofficial persecution both as individuals and as a group (see Chapter 10). The only constraint on anti-Jewish measures was the government's fear that excessive violence might disrupt public order and damage Germany's image abroad. While a Nazi Party-sponsored boycott of Jewish businesses on 1 April was halted after one day to avoid disruptions to the economy and retaliation against German exports, the total exclusion of Jews from German society was only a matter of time.

Coordination of the state governments

The term *Gleichschaltung* was first applied to the laws, issued on 31 March and 7 April 1933, depriving the elected state governments of their authority and replacing them with governors (*Reichsstatthalter*) appointed by Hindenburg on Hitler's recommendation. This was the prelude to the abolition of state parliaments and the transfer of all authority to the Interior Ministry of the Reich. The administrative reorganization of Germany was formally enacted into law on 30 January 1934, the anniversary of Hitler's appointment as chancellor. State governments in effect became mere administrative subdivisions of the central government.[10]

The Nazi Party's own centralized nationwide administrative organization dated back to the mid-1920s. Each administrative district (called a *Gau*, an archaic term originally designating an ancient Germanic tribal region) was headed by a Nazi *Gauleiter* (district leader) who exercised absolute control in his region in accordance with the Nazis' leadership principle. Germany was divided into 32 such districts, and more were added as additional territory was annexed to the Reich. Each *Gau* was further subdivided into regional and local units. Although the line between party and government was never clearly defined, the government apparatus was eventually effectively reduced to an elaborate executive organ of the Nazi Party. In most states the same person held the offices of *Reichsstatthalter* and *Gauleiter* simultaneously. On the local level, however, *Gleichschaltung* sometimes proceeded more slowly. By a law issued in January 1935 local mayors were brought under the control of party officials, whose approval was required for all important measures.

Purge of the civil service

Gleichschaltung involved a massive purge of personnel from positions of influence in state and society. Jews, former Communists, Social Democrats, and others suspected of a negative attitude toward National Socialism were summarily removed from their posts. The legal basis for this purge was provided by the "Law for the Restoration of the Professional Civil Service" of 7 April 1933, which was based on a draft prepared by the Prussian Interior Ministry before the Nazis took power. Officials justified the purge as a necessary measure to restore the professionalism of a civil service supposedly politicized by leftists and liberals during the Weimar era. Aside from the purge of Jews and leftists, however, the vast majority of public servants, especially those occupying positions in the middle and lower levels of the bureaucracy, stayed in office after 1933. The Civil Service Law mandated the dismissal of all adherents of the left and persons of "non-Aryan descent," including after June 1933 all persons married to "non-Aryans." As a concession to President Hindenburg, the purge did not apply to combat veterans, persons who had lost close relatives in the war, and officials who had served continuously in the civil service since the start of World War I. This temporary reprieve for special-category Jews was designed to retain conservative support for the purge and would be rescinded within a year after Hindenburg's death in August 1934.

As public institutions, German schools and universities were profoundly affected by the *Gleichschaltung* of the civil service. Ironically, the need to "depoliticize" the educational system became the major justification for the purge. The dismissal of Marxist and other dissident scholars was presented as a defense, not a violation, of freedom of inquiry. The purge precipitated a major exodus of Jewish and "politically unreliable" scientists and scholars, many of whom settled in the United States and greatly enriched American intellectual life for the next several decades. Albert Einstein, whose letter to President Franklin Roosevelt in 1939 led to the launching of the Manhattan Project and the development of nuclear weapons, was only the most prominent of many hundreds of academics exiled from Germany in the wake of the Nazi takeover.[11]

The universities, purged of their Jewish faculty members and now dominated by faculty sympathetic to Nazi aims, quickly fell into line. Propaganda Minister Joseph Goebbels was present at the Opernplatz in Berlin on 10 May for a carefully planned and elaborately staged book-burning that was meant to demonstrate the new Germany's rejection of the "subversive," "degenerate," and "judaized" intellectual culture of the Weimar era. Billed as an "action against the un-German spirit," the ceremony was organized and run by the Nazi-dominated National Students' Association with Goebbels' approval and encouragement. "The era of exaggerated Jewish intellectualism is now over..." Goebbels exhorted the assembled students:

> When along with the worker you wear the same brown dress uniform, and when you march in the same ranks and files without any visible differences among you—then you are showing the whole world that Germany has once again become unified inside and out.[12]

An estimated crowd of 40,000 applauded this symbolic purification of German culture. Nazi students shouted anti-Marxist slogans and pitched books of Jewish and left-wing authors into a huge bonfire to the accompaniment of patriotic songs, marches, and cheers.

Similar demonstrations were held in university towns throughout the Reich. Most of the books consigned to the flames were taken from university libraries, but many private citizens volunteered their own copies as well. Marked for destruction was

> anything that works subversively on family life, married life or love, or the ethics of our youth or our future, or that strikes at the roots of German thought, the German home, or the driving forces in our people; any works of those who would subordinate the soul to the material; anything that serves the purpose of lies.[13]

The works of Marx and Freud headed the list of books to be destroyed. Most of the proscribed books were by Jewish authors, but in Berlin the list also included such diverse works as Helen Keller's *How I Became a Socialist*, Erich Maria Remarque's *All Quiet on the Western Front*, the plays of Bertolt Brecht, and the novels of Upton Sinclair and Heinrich and Klaus Mann, the brother and son, respectively, of the Nobel-prize winning author Thomas Mann.

The labor unions

Under *Gleichschaltung* civil associations, professional organizations, and other independent groups were eventually replaced by a single Nazi-controlled umbrella organization in every area of social life, including politics, culture,

Figure 1 A crowd of some 300,000 gives the fascist salute at the May Day celebration in the "Lustgarten," the large square in front of the Royal Palace in Berlin in 1933.

education, the professions, and the economy. There was surprisingly little resistance to this process of political and ideological coordination. Membership in many Nazi organizations did not become compulsory until 1935 or later, when large segments of the public had already been won over by propaganda and persuasion. Because most Germans supported the Nazi goal of restoring national unity and power, voluntary participation in *Gleichschaltung* was the rule rather than the exception. Much of this readiness to conform to the norms established by the new rulers came from the bandwagon effect, skillfully exploited by the Nazis through a combination of cooptation, propaganda, and repression.

The *Gleichschaltung* of the labor movement offers an instructive example of the Nazis' carrot-and-stick approach. The National Socialists staged a huge worker rally on 1 May, the traditional international Labor Day, in which the unions could hardly refuse to participate without alienating their members and appearing disloyal to the workers' cause. May Day, the day celebrated by socialists around the world, would remain a major national holiday throughout the Nazi period. Many workers genuinely believed that the Nazis had their interests at heart when they called for full working-class integration into the national community. The unions hoped that by cooperating with the regime and confining themselves to wage and benefits negotiations they would be allowed to continue functioning in the workers' interest. Yet on the very next day, 2 May 1933, police and SA deputies raided the headquarters of the free trade unions and took their leaders into "protective custody," a favorite pretext for the arrest of political opponents who had committed no crime. There were hardly any worker protests against this high-handed action. A week later the German Labor Front (DAF) was created, under party, not worker control, to replace the outlawed unions. A "Law for the Reorganization of National Labor" on 20 January 1934 prohibited the formation of competing unions. With over 25 million members, the DAF was to become the largest mass organization in Nazi Germany.

The function of the German Labor Front, headed by Robert Ley (1890–1945), was to placate a potentially restive workforce, spread Nazi ideology, and preserve labor peace rather than to represent workers' grievances. In its founding statute the German Labor Front abjured "all thoughts of class conflict."[14] Repression was tempered by inducements designed to entice industrial workers into allegiance to the regime. Under the slogan of *Kraft durch Freude* (Strength through Joy), an organization founded in November 1933, the German Labor Front offered a great variety of cultural and recreational programs, vacation tours, and entertainment to raise worker morale, as well as programs to beautify the workplace and thereby enhance productivity. To symbolize the reconciliation of classes, membership in the German Labor Front was also open to industrialists and other employers.

The political parties

The elimination of the Reichstag from the legislative process inevitably meant that the political parties would become superfluous. Their end came in June and July 1933. Parties were either suppressed by law on the grounds of treasonable activities, as in the case of the Marxist parties, the Communists, and the Social Democrats, or they dissolved themselves under the pressure of the government and public opinion, as in the case of the Nationalist Party (DNVP), the Democrats (DDP), the German People's Party (DVP), and the Catholic Center Party.

The DNVP and other non-Nazi right-wing groups such as the *Stahlhelm*, the veterans' organization founded in 1918 to combat socialism and communism, became the victims of their own oft-repeated denunciations of partisan politics and their call for a strong, authoritarian national state in which parties and parliamentary factions would become obsolete. Ironically, the Nazis benefitted from the antipolitical, antipartisan mood by posing as a movement that represented the people as a whole rather than any single class or special interest. By proceeding so vigorously against the left, the Nazis had already allayed conservative fears of their supposed "socialist" proclivities. Many prominent DNVP members, eager to support the national cause in the most effective way possible, shifted their membership to the stronger, more popular, and apparently more future-oriented NSDAP in the spring of 1933. Franz Seldte, founder of the *Stahlhelm* and Minister of Labor in Hitler's cabinet, joined the NSDAP on 26 April and offered the leadership of the *Stahlhelm* to Hitler.[15] Its younger members had already defected to the Nazis, and in 1935 the *Stahlhelm* was officially integrated into the SA.

Caught up in the enthusiasm of national renewal and eager to put the common cause ahead of the party, many DNVP members came to regard their own party as superfluous. Nationalist leader Alfred Hugenberg, who served in Hitler's cabinet as Minister of Economics and Agriculture, did not favor dissolution, but could not prevent it, as he was unable to stop the flow of defectors to the NSDAP. In trying to outdo the Nazis in radical national-ism, a tactic he had used in earlier years as well, he had simply played into the Nazi hands.

Hugenberg's extremism got him into trouble in the cabinet as well. His advocacy of a radical program of national autarky and protective tariffs at the World Economic Conference in London in June 1933 ran counter to Hitler's tactical plan of presenting a moderate face to the world. Many industrialists, too, feared foreign retaliation if Hugenberg's program of extreme economic nationalism were adopted. At odds with Foreign Minister von Neurath and Reischsbank president Hjalmar Schacht and angered by restrictions on his sphere of action, Hugenberg resigned from the cabinet in late June. He did so over Hitler's objections, who feared that Hugenberg's resignation might be perceived by the public as a move to form a national opposition to the National Socialist regime. It was partly to allay these fears that the DNVP executive voted to dissolve their party after Hugenberg's withdrawal from the government.[16]

The Center Party also dissolved itself, but did so under considerably greater duress, as did the Bavarian People's Party. It was the price German Catholic leaders were forced to pay in return for a guarantee of the adminis-trative independence of the Catholic Church in Germany. Pressure for disso-lution also came from the papacy.[17] In a concordat between the Holy See and the German government negotiated by Papen and Eugenio Pacelli, the future Pope Pius XII, and signed on 20 July 1933, the Church pledged to abstain from all political activity in Germany. In return the Church was allowed to retain its traditional parochial functions and religious rights. In November 1933 the Center Party chairman, former Chancellor Heinrich Brüning, who had opposed the dissolution of the party, left Germany for eventual exile in the United States.

The "Law Concerning the Formation of New Parties" on 14 July officially established the NSDAP as the sole political party in Germany. The one-party state was now a reality in Germany. Modeled on Mussolini's Fascists and Lenin's Bolsheviks, the Nazi Party was supposed to embody the vanguard of society, and membership was in theory open only to persons qualified to exercise leadership in the National Socialist sense. The success of the Nazis, however, precipitated a headlong rush among career-minded Germans to join the party in the spring of 1933. Party membership rose from 850,000 in January to 2.5 million by 1 May 1933. The party's rapid growth made the *Gleichschaltung* of the other parties that much easier. Opportunism and personal ambition were probably more frequent motives for joining the NSDAP than political conviction. Teachers, civil servants, and white-collar workers in particular felt their livelihood would be more secure if they joined the NSDAP. So great was the influx of new members in the spring of 1933 that the party imposed a moratorium on new memberships for several years. It was not until January 1937 that the party was again opened to deserving applicants.[18] Thereafter all public officials were expected to become party members. In 1939 party membership rose to 5.3 million. Hitler believed that the party should be grown to 7 million members—10 percent of the population. That figure was reached in 1942 and then surpassed. By 1945, Nazi Party membership stood at 8.5 million.[19]

The judicial system

Gleichschaltung of the judicial system proved to be an easy matter, although the fiction of an independent judiciary was officially maintained. Long before Hitler came to power the German Federation of Judges had already been dominated by staunch nationalists and conservatives who feared nothing so much as social democracy. The Federation of Judges was among the first professional organizations to pledge its allegiance to the new regime. On 19 March 1933 the Federation's governing board issued a declaration expressing its approval of "the will of the new government to put an end to the immense suffering of the German people" and offered its cooperation in "the task of national reconstruction."[20] It also took measures to purge its Jewish members.

On 1 April all Jewish-owned businesses and self-employed Jews were subjected to an official, one-day, nationwide boycott. That same day, even before the Law on the Civil Service went into effect, state ministries of justice suspended all Jewish judges, public prosecutors, and district attorneys. Shortly thereafter the major regional and national federations of judges, prosecutors, and lawyers voluntarily merged into the Federation of National Socialist Jurists; 10,000 lawyers took an oath pledging allegiance to Hitler at the first national convention of jurists in Leipzig in October 1933. With the completion of *Gleichschaltung* and the reopening of the NSDAP to new members in 1937, strong pressure was exerted for all judges to join the party and submit to party discipline.

Confident of the loyal cooperation of the right-wing judiciary, the Nazis could afford to leave the judicial system essentially unchanged. However, the greatly increased caseloads resulting from the criminalization of political opposition did require some innovation. Special courts were established in March 1933 with jurisdiction over all crimes listed in the Reichstag Fire Decree. Penalties for political offenses were increased, while nationalists who had committed crimes in the course of the "national revolution" were amnestied. In April 1934 a special People's Court (*Volksgerichtshof*) was established, staffed by career jurists, to provide summary justice, without chance of appeal, in cases of treason—defined broadly as any opposition to the regime. This court made a mockery of due process and became an instrument of murder against political opponents and critics of the regime. During the war it passed death sentences on persons charged with sedition for believing the war to be wrong or agitating for peace. The People's Court eventually sent more than 5,000 persons to their death.[21]

The medical profession

The medical profession provided another example of rapid and uncoerced self-coordination. Shortly after Hitler's accession to power, the chief of the German League of Medical Associations sent Hitler the following public message:

> The leading medical associations of Germany…welcome with greatest joy the determination of the Reich government of national reconstruction to create a true *Volk* community of all estates, professions, and classes, and place themselves happily in the service of this great task of our fatherland, with the promise faithfully to fulfill our duty as servants of the people's health.[22]

Although as private practitioners the vast majority of physicians were under no compulsion to join the party, almost 50 percent eventually did so—a far higher proportion than in the population at large. Meanwhile, regional medical associations took the initiative in purging their ranks of Jewish and communist or socialist members.

On 22 April 1933 the Ministry of Labor announced that health insurance claims for the services of physicians of "non-Aryan descent" or of physicians who had been active in the "communist cause" would no longer be honored. Jewish physicians were to be limited to treating Jewish patients. Leonard Conti (1900–45), the head of the National Socialist Physicians' League founded in 1929, was awarded the new title of Reich Medical Leader (*Reichsärzteführer*). The newly created *Reichsärztebund* (Reich Physicians' Association), like similar organizations in other professions, operated as a means to enforce uniformity and exclude Jews and political dissidents.

Culture and ideology

Nowhere was *Gleichschaltung* more evident than in the realm of culture and ideology. Here the party's chief propagandist and *Gauleiter* of Berlin, Joseph Goebbels, who held a Ph.D. from the University of Heidelberg, played a key role in developing and imposing the party line. Appointed by Hitler to fill the newly created post of Minister for Public Enlightenment and Propaganda in March 1933, Goebbels exercised complete control over the press, the film industry, popular music, the theater, and the arts. Censorship of the press, a provision of the original Twenty-five-Point Program, began in early February.

As in the professions, self-policing and self-censorship eased the government's task of *Gleichschaltung* in the arts. Cultural and professional organizations competed in their alacrity to rid themselves of their Jewish and left-wing members. Museum directors in various localities began to remove "degenerate" works of art long before this became mandatory. Under Goebbels' direction a new Reich Chamber of Culture with subsidiaries for literature, music, theater, radio, fine arts, the press, and the cinema was founded on 22 September 1933 as an instrument of National Socialist control. The Nazi Party newspaper *Völkischer Beobachter* became the official organ of the Chamber of Culture in 1934. Membership in the Reich Chamber of Culture, which required an "Aryan" pedigree and ideological conformity, was a precondition for the right to practice any artistic or literary vocation.

The army

Gleichschaltung of the army was hardly necessary because of the virtual identity of interests between the *Reichswehr* and the Nazi government. On the day that he assumed his new position as head of the office of War Minister Werner von Blomberg (1878–1946), Colonel (and later Field Marshal) Walter von Reichenau (1884–1942) offered the opinion that never before had there been a greater identity of interests between the army and the state.[23] In effect the army leadership and the Nazi Party formed a coalition pursuing common aims. Both the army and the party sought the restoration of German military strength, the revival of public support for universal military training, and the reawakening of Germany's "will to fight" (*Wehrwillen*). The army no longer viewed itself as unpolitical or nonpartisan. On 11 April 1933 Blomberg issued an order that the *Reichswehr* must show by its conduct that it was part of the "national movement." At a military conference on 1 June 1933 Blomberg openly supported Hitler's claim to total power and told his leading generals that the task of the *Reichswehr* was to "serve the national movement with complete dedication." The army leadership fully supported the government's purge of the left in 1933, and Blomberg took the initiative in 1934 to remove practicing Jews from the army. Hitler recognized the contributions of the army to the "national cause" on the anniversary of the Nazi takeover of power in January 1934 when he declared that the "new state" was supported by two columns, "politically by the people's community organized by the National Socialist movement, militarily by the army."[24] Yet the very identity of interests with the Nazis allowed the army to retain relative independence from outside interference. It was not until 1938 that Hitler was able to get sufficient direct control of the Wehrmacht to nullify the army's influence on policy formation. In 1934 Hitler was still somewhat dependent on the good will of army leaders. To retain their good will was one of his motives in moving to curb the expansion of the SA in June 1934.

The "Röhm Putsch"

Gleichschaltung was intended to insure total ideological conformity and eliminate all actual and potential resistance to the monopoly of Nazi rule. But not all party members were satisfied with what they regarded as the excessively slow pace of change. Many SA members, in particular, resented the need to cooperate with traditional conservatives who still occupied positions of power. They called for a "second revolution," a euphemism for the redistribution of offices and privileges to SA and party members. Some also called for the transformation of the SA into a Nazi people's army that would eventually replace or absorb the *Reichswehr* as the nation's military force.

By mid-1934 the SA had swollen to more than three million men, only a quarter of whom were actually party members (the SA continued to grow even after the temporary ban on new party members in May 1933).[25] The mass influx into the SA had a radicalizing effect. The SA harbored many unemployed or disaffected workers (some of them former communists) as well as disgruntled "old fighters" steeped in the confrontational mentality of the long years of struggle for power. Many of the storm troopers regretted that the Nazis had not come to power by force. They expected to share in the spoils of the Nazi victory and found it difficult to accept that the established authorities were no longer to be treated as enemies. Many SA thugs got used to taking the law into their own hands.

Ernst Röhm, the head of the SA, seemed all too willing to exploit this vigilante mentality to enhance his own power and independence of action. His failure to stifle talk of a "second revolution" gave rise to suspicions about his motives from inside and outside the party. Party leaders remembered that Röhm had opposed Hitler's shift to legality in 1925 in the aftermath of the failed Hitler Putsch. At the time he had left the party and accepted a position as military adviser to the Bolivian army. Party leaders also remembered that once before, in April 1931, the Berlin SA leader Walter Stennes (1899–1973) had led an unsuccessful revolt against the party leadership, whom he had accused of selling out the revolutionary aspirations of the masses by compromising with the "bourgeois" system. Although at the time Hitler had personally prevailed on Röhm to return to Germany to resolve the crisis in the SA, suspicions remained that Röhm was perhaps planning to lead a similar revolt.

Hitler was well aware of the disgruntlement in the ranks of the SA and the disaffection of conservatives who feared a "second revolution." Partly in response to the pressures of SA hard-liners, Hitler had authorized the boycott of Jewish merchants in April 1933, but SA activists continued to picket and block Jewish shops even after Hitler called off the boycott because of its potentially deleterious effects on Germany's exports abroad. In the spring of 1933 the SA had played an active role in the terror against the left, but now that the left had been effectively eliminated, the SA was no longer needed as deputy police, and SA hooliganism threatened law and order and alienated conservative opinion.

For Hitler and the party leadership the discontent and lack of discipline in the SA posed a problem, even though the loyalty of the SA leadership to Hitler was never seriously in question and no credible evidence of a Röhm conspiracy has come to light. Although the SA did not pose a threat to Hitler's rule, its insubordination and lack of restraint did threaten to turn the general public, the conservative elites, and above all the army leadership against his regime. Army leaders feared that Röhm wanted to upgrade the SA into an official fighting force that would eventually supplant the *Reichswehr*. Röhm, who entered the cabinet as minister without portfolio in December 1933, was also suspected of coveting the post of Minister of War now held by the pro-Nazi career officer, General von Blomberg. The planned introduction of universal military conscription at the earliest possible opportunity, already decided in December 1933, made the SA expendable to the *Reichswehr* leadership.[26]

Conservatives, whose main aim was to exclude the masses from decision-making, feared the undeferential and antiestablishment attitudes of rebellious storm troopers. Hugenberg told Hitler in June 1933 that he would not return to government service until the National Socialists reined in their "left wing."[27] While Hitler was quite happy to be rid of Hugenberg, he had to deal with growing conservative hostility to those aspects of Nazi rule that threatened the interests of traditional elites. Hitler also knew that many conservatives continued to hope for a restoration of the monarchy. President Hindenburg's rapid physical decline in the summer of 1934 made it urgent for Hitler to act if he hoped to retain army support for his planned consolidation of power after Hindenburg's death.

The pent-up grievances of conservatives, who had, after all, expected to use the Nazis to consolidate their own power but now found themselves increasingly playing second fiddle to the Nazis, were publicly expressed in Vice-Chancellor Papen's address at the University of Marburg on 17 June 1934. The Marburg speech revealed the dilemma of conservatives who shared the Nazis' goals but disapproved of their methods. Papen's criticisms were couched in language that constantly re-emphasized the legitimacy, desirability, and even necessity of Hitler's rule:

> An unknown soldier of the World War, who conquered the hearts of his countrymen with contagious energy and unshakable faith, has set this [German] soul free. With his Field Marshal he has placed himself at the head of a nation, in order to turn a new page in the book of German destiny and restore spiritual unity. We have experienced this unity of spirits in the exhilaration of a thousand rallies, flags and celebrations of a nation which has rediscovered itself.[28]

Though careful not to implicate Hitler himself, Papen went on to attack the revolutionary, anti-intellectual, terroristic elements of National Socialism, which many people identified with the SA. "The movement must come to a standstill some day...," he said; "have we gone through an anti-Marxist revolution in order to carry out a Marxist program?"[29] He called for greater political freedom, less propaganda and coercion, more confidence in the judgment of the German public, and a return to traditional Christian principles.

Urged on by Göring and Himmler, both of whom viewed Röhm as a dangerous rival for power in the party, Hitler now conceived of a way to assert his authority over the disruptive SA and the latent conservative opposition, as well as strengthening the allegiance of military leaders. What better way to deprive conservatives of their case against Nazi rule than by bringing the SA under firm control? On the night of 30 June 1934, later dubbed "the night of the long knives," SS detachments fanned out across the country, arresting and executing SA leaders for treason. Military units were also deployed in certain areas, although they did not take part in extra-legal executions. Hitler was present in person as Röhm and several top SA officials were roused from their beds (some with their young male lovers) in the resort town of Bad Wiessee in Bavaria. Most of the arrested officials were summarily executed. Röhm was handed a pistol and given the chance to commit suicide in a Munich prison cell. When he refused to do so and demanded to speak to the *Führer*, he was gunned down by an SS squad in his cell.

Göring and Himmler used the opportunity to settle scores with conservative opponents of the regime, including the former chancellor and head of the *Reichswehr* General von Schleicher, who was shot with his wife in his home in revenge for his opposition to a Hitler chancellorship in 1932. Other victims of the "blood purge" included Hitler's old party rival Gregor Strasser, the Bavarian President Gustav von Kahr, who had ditched Hitler in 1923, the Catholic activist Heinrich Klausener, and the conservative publicist Edgar Jung, the author of Papen's Marburg speech; 89 persons were murdered in the purge.[30] Papen himself was placed under temporary house arrest. On 3 July, three days after "the night of the long knives," he lost his post as vice-chancellor. He would continue to serve the Nazi regime, however, as ambassador to Austria (where he laid the groundwork for *Anschluss* in 1938) and Turkey (from 1939 to 1944) and as special envoy to the Vatican.

On the morning following the purge the government issued a communique asserting that immediate measures had been necessary to nip in the bud a conspiracy between Schleicher and Röhm. The government statement pointedly referred to the homosexuality of some of the SA leaders. Hitler thus successfully posed as the ever wakeful guardian of order and morality, ready to sacrifice personal comfort to protect the nation from treason and moral subversion while the unsuspecting country slept. After appointing a new SA leader, Hitler issued an order demanding absolute loyalty, obedience, and discipline from his storm troopers. He specifically prohibited all practices, such as the use of limousines, expensive meals, or unnecessary travel, that might lead the public to assume that SA leaders had access to special privileges. In a dramatic speech to the Reichstag, called into special session at the Nazi Party rally in September, Hitler proclaimed that there would be no more revolution in Germany for a thousand years.

Public reaction to the Röhm Purge was surprisingly favorable to Hitler. Most middle-class Germans disapproved of the disruptive behavior of SA thugs. Reports of SA plans for a putsch were widely accepted as genuine at the time. By curbing the socially revolutionary faction in the SA, Hitler was widely viewed as the heroic leader who had prevented, rather than perpetrated, a bloodbath.[31]

Notwithstanding the brutal murder of General Schleicher, his wife, and his closest aide General Ferdinand von Bredow (1884–1934), leading conservatives and army officers were relieved at Hitler's ruthless action against Röhm, whom they viewed as a potentially dangerous rival. Army leaders issued a statement congratulating the Führer for acting with "soldierly resolution and exemplary courage" against "traitors and mutineers."[32] Now the SA would no longer pose a threat to the army or to conservative interests. Hitler's Minister of Justice Franz Gürtner, a holdover from the Papen and Schleicher cabinets, prepared a decree retroactively legalizing the summary executions. The leading German professor of law, Carl Schmitt, provided legal justification for the purge in an essay entitled, "The Führer as the Guardian of Justice." In emergency situations, Schmitt contended, the national interest could only be protected through decisive action by the head of government.

President Hindenburg sent a telegram to Hitler congratulating him for his "gallant personal intervention" to nip treason in the bud. "You have rescued the German people from a great danger. For that I express to you my heartfelt thanks and my sincere appreciation."[33] Hindenburg telegraphed his gratitude to Göring as well. Franz Seldte, Minister of Labor in Hitler's cabinet and leader of the *Stahlhelm*, issued an order to *Stahlhelm* members pledging loyalty to the regime. "The well-being of the state will always be for us the highest law." Rather than alerting conservatives to the radical and murderous nature of the Nazi regime, the Röhm Purge had the opposite effect, convincing them that Hitler would quell any radical rebellion or revolutionary aspirations in the party, thus paradoxically deepening conservatives' trust in Hitler's rule.

The SS

But the ultimate beneficiaries of the crackdown on the SA were Himmler and the other leaders of the SS, who would see their organization eventually become the most powerful institution in Germany. The black-shirted SS (short for *Schutzstaffel*, or Protection Squad) had evolved from Hitler's personal Headquarters Guard, formed in 1922 and later expanded into the 50-man strong Hitler Assault Squad. These squads, whose function was to protect party leaders, were officially designated the SS in 1925. On 6 January 1929 Hitler appointed Heinrich Himmler, a trained agriculturalist and former chicken farmer, to head the SS with the title of *Reichsführer SS*. Under the fanatically loyal Himmler the SS developed into an elite party formation that enjoyed Hitler's full trust.

After the abortive revolt of the Berlin SA in April 1931 the SS adopted the watchword, "Thy loyalty is thine honor." By the end of 1932 the SS numbered 52,000 members, and its membership grew to over 200,000 in 1934. Candidates for SS membership were subject to a stringent racial test. As of 1935 candidates for officer positions in the SS were required to trace their "Aryan" ancestry back to 1750 (for party leadership the requirement was proof of "Aryan" descent to 1800). But in 1934 the SS was still nominally subordinate to the leader of the SA. The Röhm Purge ended this nominal subordination and paved the way for the rapid growth of the SS and the massive accumulation of power in the hands of Himmler and other SS leaders, particularly his deputy Reinhard Heydrich.[34] Appointed chief of the Bavarian political police in 1933 and deputy chief of the Prussian *Gestapo* in 1934, Himmler succeeded in gaining control of the entire state security apparatus in 1936. In June of that year the *Reichsführer SS* also became head of the German police in the Ministry of the Interior. In September 1939, after the outbreak of war, the government offices and security services were fully integrated into the SS with the establishment of the Reich Security Main Office (*Reichssicherheitshauptamt* or RSHA), the central office for the execution of Nazi terror measures including the "final solution of the Jewish Question" (see Chapter 15). The SA, on the other hand, declined in importance after the purge. By 1940 its membership had dropped below a million. It continued, however, to provide a controlled institutional outlet for the thugs attracted to the party by opportunities for aggression against Jews and political opponents. Its main function would be to provide manpower for party actions, most notoriously the pogrom of 9 November 1938, known as *Reichskristallnacht*.

Hindenburg's death

When President Hindenburg died on 2 August, Hitler reaped the benefit of his policy of cultivating the good will of army leaders. There was no opposition to Hitler's decree assuming the authority of the presidency and combining the offices of president and chancellor. Hitler thereby inherited the title of Commander in Chief of the *Reichswehr*, soon to be renamed the *Wehrmacht*. Its leaders were willing collaborators with the new regime. These career officers viewed Hitler with gratitude and admiration for his success in reconstructing the army. It was they who initiated the new requirement that all members of the armed forces swear a personal oath of loyalty to the Führer. A similar loyalty oath was required of all holders of public office on 20 August. A day earlier Hitler's new powers had been ratified by plebiscite, a form of public referendum favored by the new regime. An overwhelmingly affirmative result could be virtually assured by careful phrasing of the resolution, the absence of any positive alternative, and the full mobilization of social pressures to vote "yes." Plebiscites of this kind were useful as public displays of the agreement between government and people.

President Hindenburg's political testament, published in the *Völkischer Beobachter* on 16 August 1934, provides telling documentation of the symbiosis between old and new conservatism in the first year and a half of the new regime. The venerable Prussian *Junker*, who had once disdained Hitler because of his lowly origins and crude manners, now praised Hitler and his movement for bridging the classes and restoring internal unity to the German nation—"a decisive step of historical importance." Hindenburg quoted extensively from a message he had written in the dark days of 1919, urging his fellow Germans to retain their faith in Germany's "historical world-mission" and looking forward to the eventual restoration of the empire. In his testament he went on to condemn the Weimar constitution that he had twice been elected to uphold for failing to "correspond with the needs and characteristics" of the German people. "For a long time," he wrote, "the surrounding world has failed utterly to understand that Germany must live, not only for its own sake, but also for the sake of Europe and as the standard-bearer of Western culture." Although he refrained from explicitly naming Hitler as his successor, he ended by thanking Providence for allowing him, in the evening of his life, to be a witness to Germany's renewal.[35]

The events of the summer of 1934 marked the end of the first phase of Hitler's rule. He had successfully consolidated his power while maintaining the allegiance and support of most of the conservative elites and disciplining the potentially disruptive elements in his own ranks. The major institutions of German society had been successfully aligned with the National Socialist cause. The left-wing opposition had been brutally suppressed. The Weimar constitution had been replaced by a new authoritarian regime dedicated to restoring German pride and advancing the national interest. By 1935 the conflation of the NSDAP with German power was so complete that the Nazi Party swastika became the official German flag.

Hitler's popularity continued to grow. It was difficult even for skeptics not to be affected by the enthusiasm generated by the regime. Many Germans were genuinely convinced that the hour of national rebirth had struck. Hitler benefitted, too, from the economic upturn that accompanied his consolidation of power. Economic revival was, after all, the precondition for an active foreign policy and continued popular support. As long as the German economy prospered, his hold on power would remain secure.

9 Economy, society, and the state in the Third Reich

A major source of Hitler's growing popularity, aside from his assertion of German interests against the Allies, was the improvement of the German economy. The Nazi regime benefitted to some extent from cyclical trends in the world economy that once again reopened export markets for German goods. While it is true that the Great Depression had bottomed out in 1932 and a gradual recovery was already under way at the time that Hitler became chancellor, the Nazis could take credit for introducing deficit-spending earlier and on a larger scale than other European countries.[1] German businessmen were also much more willing to accept reflationary deficit financing from a right-wing dictatorial government that would break the power of labor than from the democratic governments of the Weimar era. The Nazis reaped the credit for the decline in unemployment from a high of over six million in 1932 to a little over one and one-half million by 1935. From 1936 on, accelerated rearmament and conscription helped to create virtually full employment and led to a labor shortage in heavy industry by 1939.

Economic policies of the Third Reich

Nazi economic policies drew on a long tradition of state-directed economic development in Germany, the roots of which can be traced back to the absolutist era and the Bismarckian Empire. The liberal notion of regulating the economy solely through market mechanisms, while popular in Britain and the United States, had never taken firm root in Germany. The economic system of the Third Reich was a form of capitalism in which the state controlled, organized, and guided production, consumption, and the distribution of income. Despite the Nazi rhetoric of "German socialism" and pervasive government regulation of the free market, however, the regime never encroached on capitalist ownership. Unlike the Communists in the Soviet Union, the Nazis never established a central planning authority (at least not until Albert Speer became Minister of Armaments and Munitions at the height of the war in 1942) nor did they wish to abolish the profit incentive of capitalism or private ownership of the means of production. Indeed, the Nazis' defense of free enterprise and

Map 2 The German Reich, 1 January 1939.

opposition to Marxism attracted business support even before Hitler's accession to power.

Hitler's economic adviser and fund-raiser Wilhelm Keppler (1882–1960), director of a chemical factory, had already organized a circle of leading bankers and industrialists in support of the Nazis in 1931. In 1933 he continued to play a key role in raising funds for the Nazis in the business community. On 20 February 1933, three weeks after his accession to power, Hitler met with leading industrialists to solicit funds and to outline his plans to suppress democracy and the left. He found a receptive audience as even industrialists who had earlier been reluctant to contribute to the Nazis for fear of their potentially revolutionary base now poured some three million RM (Reichsmark) into the party coffers. Keppler's circle eventually evolved into the much larger Circle of Friends of Heinrich Himmler, which channeled funds from the private sector into the party and the SS throughout the Nazi era.

Business enjoyed a privileged position, handsome profits, and a considerable degree of self-management in the Third Reich, on condition that it serve the political objectives established by the Nazi leadership. The "primacy of politics" was a guiding principle of Nazi economic theory and practice. As in the preliberal era, private economic interests were expected to serve the interests of the state and the nation. However, the interests of business and industry usually coincided with the interests of party and state, and economic interests certainly contributed to the expansionist thrust of the regime. Defense contracts were not dictated by the government but drawn up in collaboration with the firms involved, who based their business decisions on traditional calculations of profit.

To a considerable extent success in business depended on the private sector's willingness to submit to government mandates and to contribute to the regime's political priorities. These were to increase national power (while insuring a maximum of social stability) in order ultimately to prevail in what the Nazis regarded as an inevitable struggle for supremacy between races, peoples, and states. The Nazis adopted pragmatic economic policies that furthered or did not impede their long-term political goals. Individual profit (the goal of liberal capitalism) or social welfare (the goal of Marxism) were never ends in themselves, but only means to the more important end of strengthening the nation and the state.

Although the scope of state intervention increased markedly after 1933, there was no major structural change in the German economy. The Nazis made no attempt to reorganize the economy along the corporative model favored by Mussolini in Italy and some earlier Nazi party theorists (see Chapter 7) for fear of inhibiting productivity. Innovations such as the 1933 law to prevent the break-up of family farms or the "Strength through Joy" program for workers were designed not to bring about radical social change, but to prevent it.

The government, however, played an active supervisory role in the economy. The Reich Labor Ministry intervened in the economy to establish wage rates, monitor and prevent lay-offs, and supervise workplace regulations. In some ways the economic measures undertaken in Germany to overcome the depression and stabilize the capitalist system paralleled the "Keynesian" approach of Franklin Roosevelt's New Deal, although the spirit of the two regimes was, of course, quite different.[2] A central purpose of Nazi recovery measures was to stimulate demand through government spending and public investments.[3] Continuing a work creation program that had already been introduced by the short-lived Schleicher government in late 1932, Hitler's government sponsored wide-ranging public works projects, including construction of the *Autobahn*, a network of modern highways, which employed about 70,000 workers. The law authorizing the *Autobahn* project was signed in June 1933. The government sponsored public housing projects, programs for the restoration of public buildings, improvement of the railroad system, and mining projects. The government also introduced subsidies and tax incentives for the private sector, especially in new construction and agriculture.

Military considerations played a paramount role in the Hitler regime's approach to the problem of unemployment. The government earmarked a significant portion of work creation funds for rearmament projects, which remained largely clandestine until Hitler openly defied the Allies' proscription of rearmament in 1935. Introduction of a quasimilitary labor service for young men between the ages of 18 and 25, compulsory after the introduction of military conscription in 1935, helped to provide workers for low-wage public sector jobs. The term of service was set at six months. The duty of every able-bodied citizen to work had been part of the Nazis' original Twenty-five-Point Program, which had also guaranteed every citizen's right to a job. Nazi publications touted the Reich Labor Service (RAD) as a splendid example of "German socialism." Although Nazi attitudes toward women in the workplace were generally conservative, compulsory work service for young women, mainly in domestic and agricultural chores, was introduced in 1939.

Hjalmar Schacht (1877–1970) was back as head of the central Reichsbank (until 1939), a post he had occupied from 1923 until his resignation in protest against the adoption of the Young Plan (which rescheduled reparations payments) in 1930. Schacht, whose policies had helped to stabilize the mark after the hyperinflation of 1923, also became Hitler's Minister of Economics from 1935 to 1937 and oversaw the stabilization of the economy at a time when the Nazis' rearmament program was going into high gear. A firm believer in private enterprise and an export-driven market economy to obtain the foreign exchange needed to finance rearmament without inflation or excessive taxes, Schacht negotiated favorable trade agreements with many European countries. These bilateral agreements helped to boost German exports while making smaller neighboring countries, especially agriculture-based economies in southeast Europe, more dependent on the German market.

The Four-Year Plan

As preparations for war intensified, Schacht's conservative approach to government spending and deficit financing led to increasing conflict with the Nazi leadership. In 1937 he was replaced as Economics Minister by the more reliable Nazi Walther Funk (1890–1960), a former chief of the Party Office for Economic Policy. Funk also succeeded Schacht as head of the Reichsbank in 1939 after Schacht had warned of a looming economic crisis if the government continued to overspend on rearmament. At the annual party rally in Nuremberg in September 1936 Hitler had announced a Four-Year Plan aimed at making Germany self-sufficient in raw materials and industrial products. Autarky (economic self-sufficiency) was to make Germany immune to the kind of economic blockade that had been so effective in the Great War. Hitler himself had drawn up the plan in the summer of 1936 citing the need to be prepared for the inevitable conflict with Bolshevism, the code word for the Soviet Union. The giant IG-Farben chemical cartel provided the technical expertise and management for the plan. Administrative controls of prices, wages, and labor mobility were now tightened as the economy was increasingly harnessed to the goal of preparing Germany for war. The Four-Year Plan rested on the tacit assumption that conquest and expansion would eventually resolve the problem of the growing national debt while minimizing the sacrifices that German consumers would have to make.[4]

The Four-Year Plan ran counter to Schacht's goal of restoring and maintaining economic prosperity through production for consumption and export. In 1937 Schacht resigned as Minister of Economics because he feared the inflationary effects of the Four-Year Plan. Implementation of the plan was entrusted to Hermann Göring, who directed the economic preparations for war. The plan focused particularly on the production of synthetic substitutes for such essential materials as rubber, fuel, and textile fibers. Göring also created a new state-owned enterprise to develop the low-quality domestic ore that the steel industry was reluctant to use because of its low rate of profitability. The *Hermann Göring Works*, founded in 1937, grew into a giant state-supported enterprise producing a wide variety of war-related goods. Private steel corporations did not suffer from the new competition, however, because the high costs of producing steel from inferior ore and the increased demand for steel products as a result of rearmament tended to keep steel prices high. In any case, the new state enterprise was meant to complement private industry, not to supplant it.

Preparation for war, now the chief economic goal of the Nazi regime, was accompanied by increasing government intervention and regulatory measures. Prices, salaries, wages, rents, and interest rates were subject to regulation, and the government retained firm control over credit policy, imports, exports, and foreign exchange. Banking and the credit system were especially subject to government controls, although no effort was made to nationalize private banks; indeed, the large Dresdener Bank was reprivatized in 1937.

The government also issued directives to industry on production and investment. Manufacturers, for instance, were directed to reinvest a proportion of their profits in plant expansion and government bonds. Under the plan the state was to play a larger role in the economy, but not at the expense of private industry. "It is for the Ministry of Economics simply to set the national economic tasks," Hitler wrote, "and it is for private industry to carry them out."[5] Although the Reich now took on some of the features of a command economy, there was no effort to nationalize industry or otherwise tamper with private property rights, except for the rights of Jews. Indeed, more businesses were nationalized in the Weimar era than under the Third Reich, which favored the reprivatization of publically traded corporations rather than their nationalization. Even at the height of World War II in 1942, the newly appointed Reich Minister for Armaments and Munitions Albert Speer (1905–81) deliberately prevented Reich fiscal authorities from raiding corporate profits. British economic historian Adam Tooze has described the later stages of the war as "an alliance between Hitler's regime and the leading elements of German industrial capitalism, to secure their common survival in the life and death struggle with Stalinism."[6] The Krupp industrial empire was exempted by special law from inheritance tax and reverted from a public corporation to a family holding in 1943. The coal and steel producer Friedrich Flick (1883–1972), owner of the *Mitteldeutsche Stahlwerke*, a major arms manufacturer, built the largest industrial empire in Germany and owned a personal fortune of some three billion RM. The "Aryanization" of Jewish-owned businesses, on the other hand, was stepped up after the adoption of the Four-Year Plan. A secret memorandum to the Four-Year Plan called for the total expropriation of Jews in case of war.

Industrialists worked closely with the regime and exercised considerable influence over economic policy. Gustav Krupp von Bohlen und Halbach (1870–1950) retained his leadership position in the Association of German Industry and headed the *Adolf-Hitler-Spende*, a special industrial fund for the Nazi Party. Most industrialists supported rearmament and expansion, which offered the prospect of increased demand for their products as well as readier access to raw materials. The authority and interests of proprietors and managers were enhanced by the introduction by law of the leadership principle in all businesses in 1934. Employers assumed the title of *Betriebsführer* (enterprise leaders) and became masters in their own houses to an even greater extent than had already been the case in the Weimar Republic. Under the leadership principle executives were responsible only to their superiors, not to anyone below them in the hierarchy. All authority ultimately rested with the man at the top.

Freed from the pressure of union demands and encouraged by the regime to form monopolistic cartels in order to eliminate market instability, industrialists saw their profits rise at an even higher rate than productivity, which also rose under the relentless discipline of the new work ethic. By 1939 overall profits of limited liability companies were four times higher than they had been in 1928.[7] Industrial profits greatly outpaced wage and salary increases and the rise in the general standard of living. Whereas wages and salaries increased by 49 percent between 1933 and 1937 (and farm income by 33 percent), profits in trade and industry rose by 88 percent.

The integration of labor

Although Nazi economic policies favored employers, the labor force, deprived of its leadership and organizational independence, remained largely quiescent. Most workers could not help but feel that the availability of work represented a great improvement over the terrible uncertainties of the period from 1930 to 1933. Like so many middle-class Germans, most workers, too, were quite ready to trade personal freedom for security and order. While the elimination of independent trade unions enabled the regime to keep wages down, the German Labor Front (DAF) did exercise some pressure for an increase in the standard of living of workers. DAF leaders argued that the government could not expect the level of sacrifice and exertion that would be required for victory in war unless workers were compensated with equivalent material benefits.[8] To maintain German worker morale and prevent the work stoppages and political conflicts that had disrupted the war effort in World War I, DAF functionaries drew up generous national health insurance and pension plans at the height of the war in 1941–42. Although these did not go into effect in the few remaining years of the Third Reich, they did anticipate some of the social legislation of the Federal Republic (West Germany) after the war.

Partly as a result of DAF pressure real wages rose in the years between 1933 and 1939, though not at the rate of either productivity or profits, and in terms of actual purchasing power wages never rose to the level of 1928. During the war, however, the spoils of Nazi conquests as well as the expropriation of Jewish property throughout the Reich and occupied Europe allowed the Nazi regime to continue to offer German citizens a higher standard of living than its defeated neighbors.[9] The DAF also sponsored numerous programs to boost worker morale and spur productivity. In concert with the Reich Youth Leadership, the party office that supervised the Hitler Youth and other Nazi youth organizations, the DAF sponsored an annual vocational competition that in 1938 involved 2.2 million contestants in 1,600 vocational categories.[10] The competition was designed to enhance and reward the desire of young workers to excel in the performance of their functions. The DAF also sponsored model housing for workers and improvement in working conditions, including accident prevention programs, workplace beautification programs, and concert presentations during work breaks. Through its *Strength through Joy* (KdF) program the DAF sponsored inexpensive vacations, recreational diversions, athletic contests, and cultural events to fill the workers' leisure hours.[11] The DAF even issued savings certificates at five Marks a week toward the purchase of a new affordable people's car (*Volkswagen*) to be produced at a DAF-founded factory at Wolfsburg. Designed by Ferdinand Porsche and originally known as the "KdF-car," the Volkswagen was intended to make automobiles available to a mass public. Prototypes were ready by 1936, but more than 300,000 participants in the DAF saving program were disappointed when the factory was converted to the production of military vehicles as preparations for war went into high gear. The VW did not become available for civilian use until after the war. In the 1950s it became one of West Germany's main export products.

Propaganda, too, played a key role in integrating the work force and maintaining social peace. Through symbols, rituals, and slogans, such as "Honor of Work" (*Ehre der Arbeit*), the Nazis extolled the dignity of manual labor.[12] They never tired of propagating the fiction of a new classless society in which "workers of the fist" and "workers of the brain" enjoyed equal status. Self-employed manufacturers, tradesmen, and craftsmen belonged to the German Labor Front along with their employees, thus symbolizing the end of class war. Wage-earning workers were assured that the difference between employer and employee was only one of function, not of class. Notwithstanding their grossly differing incomes, the industrial tycoon and the manual laborer were encouraged to view themselves as equal contributors to the nation's well-being.

The Nazis used propagandistic appeals, not economic policies, to combat the potentially disruptive effects of class divisions. Through their publicity campaign for *Volksgemeinschaft* (national community) the Nazis sought to create the consciousness of a classless society. As their Twenty-five-Point Program had demanded, the selfish interests of individuals, groups, and classes were to be subordinated to the common good. The root of the problem as the Nazis described it was not economic inequality (which they viewed as a natural condition) but the perverse Marxist emphasis on the importance of class. If people would only cease to think in terms of class or economic status, the problems of class differentiation would cease to exist. The real problem was not economic inequality, as Marxists contended, but the tendency to think in materialistic terms, a "Jewish" trait common to Marxists and capitalists alike.

In their struggle for power the Nazis had frequently used the term "bourgeois" (*bürgerlich*) as a term of derision in a way that seemed to align them with Marxist critics of the bourgeoisie. By "bourgeois," however, the Nazis meant not social or economic status, but rather the materialistic consumption- and comfort-oriented attitudes that impeded the political mobilization of normal "burghers." Despite an antibourgeois rhetoric that was superficially similar to that of the left, the Nazis did not want to redistribute income or change the social and economic structure in any way that might inhibit full and efficient production. Theirs was a benign and productive capitalism, they insisted, different from the materialistic, profiteering, and exploitative "plutocracies" of the west, where money ruled.

Nazi social welfare policies

Before their assumption of power in 1933, Nazi social policies reflected the contradictions between their mass and elite constituencies. On the one hand they sought to exploit the discontent of workers alienated by cutbacks in government social services; on the other hand they courted business support by calling for a reduction of government social expenditures and an end to excessive welfare payments. Conservative policies directed toward economic recovery and rearmament tended to predominate after their assumption of power. Charity, not government social programs based on entitlement, became the preferred means of alleviating poverty. The annual party-sponsored charity drive, the *Winterhilfe* (winter relief), helped perpetuate the illusion that the selfishness of class consciousness had given way to an ethos of responsibility and mutual sacrifice for the common good. Funds were collected from firms, organizations, and residential areas, and through withdrawals from wages and salaries. Although contributions were nominally voluntary, pressure to donate was intense. The purpose of charity drives was not just to raise money, but also to inculcate a readiness to make sacrifices for the national good. In September 1933 the Winter Relief Agency, administered by the party's National Socialist Welfare Organization (NSV), introduced the practice of eating a "one-dish meal" (*Eintopf*) on the first Sunday from October to March every year to conserve food and money for those in need. The difference between the cost of *Eintopf* and the usual more elaborate Sunday dinner was to go to the Winter Relief Agency. Nazi propaganda showed the wealthy participating along with the indigent in "one-dish meals."

The NSV, originally established to provide relief to needy party members in the depression, was put in charge of all charity and welfare activities in May 1933. Partly financed by receipts from the Winter Relief Agency (which had the authority to deduct obligatory contributions from salaries and wages), the NSV was intended not to help individuals in need so much as to insure the strength and health of the German *Volk*.[13] Only those who met the regime's political, racial, and biological standards were eligible for assistance. Regular medical and dental examinations for the healthy received priority over care for the handicapped. Jews were excluded from the start and had to form their own welfare agency. In the course of *Gleichschaltung* the NSV eventually absorbed or controlled all independent relief agencies, including the charity organizations of the churches and the German branch of the International Red Cross.

Economic and technological modernization

The Nazis' pragmatic economic and social policies, designed to insure full and efficient production, often contradicted their professed aims and principles. Their "shopkeepers' socialism" had attracted support from groups who were threatened by the growth of big business and the labor movement, such as family farmers and small business proprietors (the *Mittelstand*). The Nazis effectively suppressed the independent labor movement, but for practical reasons they did not move to curtail the economic power of big business. They had pledged to reverse the disruptive social effects of the Industrial Revolution and restore a more traditional, agrarian way of life. Yet the social changes that actually took place even before the war moved Germany further away from the *völkisch* utopia of blood and soil.

National Socialists were caught in the contradiction between their ends and means. Restoration of German power, reversal of the Versailles Treaty, and conquest of living space in the east to realize their agrarian utopia required the creation of a modern army. To attain their goals the Nazis had to militarize German society and promote heavy industry and advanced technology. They could not achieve their reactionary social vision without modern technology. To bridge the contradiction between their antimodernist ideology and their need for modern technology, the Nazis claimed that, unlike the aridly rational and mercenary west, Germans infused technology with soul and spirit. This "reactionary modernism," the merging of irrationalism and technology, entailed some of the very social changes the Nazis had promised to prevent.[14]

The Nazis romanticized a rural, agrarian lifestyle and inveighed against the insidious consequences of rampant industrialization and urbanization. In practice, however, industrialization and urbanization grew at a greater rate than before. Given the militaristic priorities of the regime, the unavoidable trend in Nazi Germany was toward a reduction of the size of the agricultural sector. More people than ever before worked in large-scale industries, while the number of medium-sized and smaller enterprises declined. Members of the old *Mittelstand* of artisans, handicraftsmen, and small shopkeepers, who had expected special protection under the Nazis, continued to feel the economic squeeze. Department stores, criticized for decades by *völkisch* intellectuals as deleterious to family-owned shops, were not closed (in order to preserve jobs), and the number of small retailers continued to decline. Farm income did not keep pace with national income, and migration from the countryside to the urban centers continued. It is estimated that more than a million Germans moved from farms to cities between 1933 and 1939. Legislation designed to prevent the breakup of family farms (such as the Hereditary Farm Law of September 1933) remained ineffective; nor did other measures to discourage *Landflucht* (flight from the countryside), such as higher tariffs on agricultural imports and lowered interest rates on credit for farmers, have the desired effect. Despite the lip service paid to the ideal of striking roots in the land, occupational mobility increased. Thus the Nazis were confronted with a paradox: to overcome the putative evils of economic modernization the Nazis would have to modernize. The result was a social revolution of a very different kind than the Nazis had proclaimed. Unintentionally they contributed to precisely the modernizing trends they had always deplored. Many of the changes that occurred in Hitler's Germany anticipated (and contributed to the success of) the "Americanization" of West German society after the war.[15]

Agriculture

Ideology and practice clashed most obviously in the development of agriculture in the Third Reich. Nazi ideology and propaganda drew heavily on the rural romanticism and mystique of blood and soil that arose in reaction to rapid industrialization and urbanization in the latter part of the nineteenth century, especially among agrarian interests disadvantaged by modernizing change. Agrarian discontent with the alleged moral corruption, secularism, class strife, and social leveling of city life contributed greatly to the Nazis' electoral success in the early 1930s.[16] The Nazis continued to idealize an agrarian way of life while industrialization was accelerated under their rule. As in the case of industrial workers, however, the Nazis offered peasants, the European equivalent of subsistence farmers, more psychological compensation than material improvements. For example, the Nazis tried to endow the occupational title *Bauer* (peasant) with high status; 3 October was celebrated as the day of the peasant; and peasants were declared to be the source of the people's strength and the progenitors of pure German blood. The traditional rural virtues of loyalty, piety, honesty, morality, and patriotism and the racial purity that came from generations of regional inbreeding were to be the guarantees of a stable and hierarchical community in which everyone knew their place. The Nazis gratified such traditionally rural animosities as suspicion of foreigners and hostility to the experimental lifestyles, ethnic diversity, and progressive politics of the cosmopolitan cities, especially Berlin. Traditionally rural tastes in art and entertainment became official Nazi standards. The Nazis idealized the simple peasant-warrior as the virtuous antipode to the sophisticated, urban, Jewish intellectual. But Nazi championing of the agrarian myth also had a practical side: recovery of agricultural productivity was crucial to the achievement of autarky, and loyal peasants, they believed, make good soldiers.

Leading Nazis espoused the peasant-warrior ideology, including the former chicken farmer Heinrich Himmler, whose many offices included that of chief of the Reich Association of German Agriculturalists. His protégé Walther Darré (1895–1953), chief of the SS Main Office for Race and Resettlement and author of a book entitled *The Peasantry as the Lifespring of the Nordic Race* in 1929, was named *Reichsbauernführer* (Reich Farm Leader) in April 1933 and replaced Hugenberg as Minister of Food and Agriculture in June of that year. The farm organization headed by Darré, the *Reichsnährstand* (Reich Food Estate), was in actuality merely a front for direct government control of agriculture with the primary purpose of increasing production.

The Hereditary Farm Law of September 1933 was Darré's main attempt to put Nazi agrarian ideology into practice by stabilizing land ownership in the form of entailed property. All farms between 7.5 and 125 hectares in size (1 hectare equals 2.5 acres) were declared indivisible, unsaleable, and not subject to mortgage, and only owners of such estates were permitted to be called *Bauer* in the future. Other farmers were to be referred to as *Landwirte* (agriculturalists). Only a person of German or related blood was eligible to become a *Bauer*, a status to be documented by a certificate of descent dating back to 1800.

Yet Darré's proclaimed objective of increasing the number of small, independent farms to form a new "Germanic aristocracy of the soil" was never achieved. Although the Hereditary Farm Law was officially touted as the realization of German socialism, in practice only about 35 percent of farms were affected. It offered some advantage to farmers impoverished by the depression (by forgiving their debts and protecting them from foreclosure), but tended to become a handicap after recovery, as farmers could not freely dispose over their lands or obtain credit other than by personal loans. It had no effect on reducing the size of the great Junker estates east of the Elbe River.

Notwithstanding the Hereditary Farm Law, the tendency in Nazi Germany was toward the creation of bigger farm units to achieve self-sufficiency in foodstuffs. Point 17 of the Nazi program had called for redistribution of land to increase the number of small peasant homesteads. In actuality, however, only half as many new peasant settlements were established under the Nazis as there had been in the Weimar Republic. Most of these new homesteads were created out of land already in government hands, not out of the oversized Junker estates.[17] The better competitive position of the Junker estates, which continued to be the greatest beneficiaries of government subsidies, was left unimpaired. Although the government supported meat, dairy, and grain prices (some price supports had already been introduced under Brüning), small farmers were no better off under the Nazis than they had been before. In 1933 farm income amounted to 8.7 percent of the national income; by 1937 the figure had dropped to 8.3 percent.

The standard of living of farmers in general was much lower than that of the population at large. Larger farms were relatively better off than small farms, which were increasingly burdened by debt. In 1938 a Decree on the Welfare of the Rural Population improved the working conditions for farm laborers by offering them credits for housing and marriage loans. Yet the number of paid farm laborers fell by some 400,000 between 1933 and 1939, and despite the Nazis' pronatalist policies, the rural birthrate fell as well.[18] While new housing constructed by farmers for their employees was freed of taxation, this program discriminated against small and middle-sized farmers by making it even more difficult to retain labor in competition with larger farms. Thus the loss of farm labor was in inverse proportion to the size of the farm. What accounted for the lag in agricultural productivity on small farms, however, was not so much the lack of workers as the lack of capital to use labor efficiently. In many areas of the country, including Bavaria, small farmers still used oxen, not tractors, to till the soil. During the war the problem of rural labor shortage would be eased by the use of slave labor from countries conquered by the Germans.

The role of women

The role of women in German society offers another example of the contradiction between Nazi ideology and practice. According to Nazi ideology, the stability of the state rested on the family household, the special sphere assigned to women by nature and providence. Like other conservative groups the Nazis sought to revive and strengthen the traditional notion that women's place was in the home. *Kinder, Küche, Kirche* (children, kitchen, church) circumscribed the traditional boundaries of women's domain. Women were idealized as loyal, devoted mothers and wives and simultaneously consigned to dependence on men. Reserving the public sphere of politics and the professions for men only, the Nazis considered the political emancipation of women a mistake. Women held no leadership positions in the government or the party, except in organizations especially intended for women, such as the National Socialist Women's Organization (NSF) or the League of German Girls (*BdM*). "The phrase 'women's liberation' is a phrase invented only by Jewish intellectualism," Hitler announced in a speech to the NSF in September 1934. Shrewdly he blamed conflict between the sexes not so much on the few women who sought equal rights as on the many men who failed to exercise their authority and live up to their responsibilities as soldiers and providers. If the separation of spheres is respected, he declared, "then strife and discord can never break out between the sexes; instead they will go through life hand in hand fighting together, just the way providence intended, and for the purpose that both sexes were created."[19]

The Nazis regarded child-bearing and motherhood as the natural functions of women and rewarded these with medals and social esteem. The primary purpose of the League of German Girls was to educate girls to become housewives and mothers. Marriage and motherhood were presented not only as keys to individual happiness and fulfillment, but as obligations to the *Volk*. The Nazis' pronatalist policies were closely linked to their expansionist aims. Shortly after coming to power, the Nazis issued a call for a "war of birth" (*Geburtenkrieg*) to reverse the declining birth rate and increase the population of Germany over that of potential enemies. Tax incentives and child supplements were intended to encourage large families. Married couples who remained childless after five years paid a penalty tax. After 1938 mothers of four or more children were awarded the Mother's Cross, a medal consciously modeled on the highest military decoration for men, the Iron Cross. Mothers of four or five children received a bronze cross, mothers of six or seven children a silver cross, and mothers of eight or more children a cross in gold.[20]

The Nazis provided generous benefits for mothers, from which, however, women adjudged to be "hereditarily inferior" (for instance women with a mentally ill relative) were excluded. An auxiliary organization of the welfare agency NSV, named "Mother and Child," provided advice and support of all kinds to assist mothers in rearing their children. According to official statistics the NSV ran approximately 15,000 child-care centers in 1941.[21] Mother's Day was officially celebrated as a way of enhancing healthy family life. Eventually even single women, especially members of the National Socialist Women's Organization, were encouraged to have children through the services of *Lebensborn* (well of life), an SS agency for the care of unmarried mothers and their children established in December 1935.[22] Although *Lebensborn* certainly incorporated the principle of selective breeding, as it enabled single "Aryan" women to have children with a minimum of social stigma, it did not, as was once widely assumed, provide "breeding farms" that made men available to women who wanted to have children. Nonetheless, in announcing the founding of *Lebensborn*, Heinrich Himmler took the opportunity to remind SS men that it was their duty to have large families as part of the Nazi effort to increase the "Aryan" German population. Divorce was made easy for persons in childless marriages, and the decision not to have children was recognized as grounds for divorce. The Nazis also waged a campaign against contraception and birth control. Abortion, already restricted in the Weimar era, was now limited even more. Only a woman whose life was medically certified to be in danger was legally permitted to obtain an abortion. Punishment for physicians performing illegal abortions was greatly increased. Birth control was officially condemned as well, except for use by Jews.

Nazis blamed the feminist movement for Germany's declining birth rate in the twentieth century. To discourage women from entering the professions, a *numerus clausus* was introduced in December 1933, temporarily reducing the proportion of women admitted to universities to 10 percent. Women were permitted to enter the civil service only after the age of 35. This was not a specifically Nazi measure, as even the SPD had supported a bill for the dismissal of married female civil servants in 1932 to combat unemployment. To encourage women to stay home, the government provided marriage loans to women willing to give up their employment. The amount to be repaid was reduced by one-quarter after the birth of each child, provided the parents could prove the child was racially "pure" and healthy.

Both marriage and birth rates did in fact rise markedly in the Third Reich. But the aggressive and expansionist goals of the regime worked against the Nazis' desire to confine women to the domestic sphere. While the proportion of women in the workforce declined from 37 percent in 1933 to 31 percent in 1937, the total number of women workers actually increased as the need for workers in war-related industries grew and women with children found it necessary to work to augment their family incomes. The *numerus clausus* on the number of women students at universities was rescinded in 1936 as the need for trained professionals grew. Likewise, the ban on employment for women receiving marriage loans was revoked in 1937 as the shortage of labor became more acute. By 1939 there were seven million women in white- and blue-collar occupations. Women comprised one-third of the total German workforce in 1939, compared to 26 percent in England and only 18 percent in the United States. The shortage of labor became so acute that a decision was taken in 1939 to require a six-month work service of all young women not already employed.

Although Nazi ideals were already in conflict with reality in the 1930s, when millions of women served in the workforce, the gap between ideal and reality became ever greater during the war. The Nazi ideology of confining women to the private sphere became a liability when women were increasingly needed to keep the war economy going. Greater participation of women in the public sphere became crucial to the survival of the Nazi state in the war. By 1943, at a time that millions of college-age men were serving in the armed forces, 60 percent of German university students were women. The percentage of women physicians more than doubled, and by 1943 approximately 30 percent of all German pediatricians were women. The number of women working in industry increased to about 14.5 million in 1944, forming three-fifths of the wartime domestic labor force. Although the Nazis never made employment for German women compulsory, the regime employed a higher percentage of women in war-related industries than the western democracies.[23] Nonetheless, mobilization of women was hampered by the contradiction between the Nazis' antifeminist ideology and the exigencies of a militarized economy. The generous family allowances for German soldiers (whose families received 85 percent of the husband's peacetime earnings) had the unintended effect of reducing the number of women who volunteered for war work.

Despite their open commitment to a doctrine of male supremacy, the Nazis were quite successful in integrating women into Nazi society. The role of women in Nazi Germany and the degree of their responsibility for Nazi crimes became a controversial issue among historians of women after the war. The German historian Gisela Bock, an authority on compulsory sterilization in Germany, argued that women in Nazi Germany should be seen primarily as victims of Nazi gender policies and the structural conditions created by the Nazis, who branded women as inferior to men, did not allow women to act as responsible subjects, and tried to confine them to the private sphere. Deprived of opportunities for involvement in shaping public policy, women, Bock insisted, should not be assigned equal responsibility for Nazi crimes with German men, except, of course, in specific instances where women were directly involved as perpetrators. According to Bock, the Nazis focused more of their resources on preventing the births of "inferior" or "worthless" children than on promoting population increase. Some feminist historians even went so far as to claim that Nazi attitudes and discriminatory policies towards women resembled their attitudes and policies towards Jews. This conceptual equation of antifeminism with antisemitism as two sides of the same deadly racial policy was challenged by the American historian Claudia Koonz, who described German women as active participants in the Nazi system despite their restriction to the private sphere. On the local level the Nazis opened up new areas of activity for women in party work. While men were responsible for public policy, women provided the emotional support in family and domestic life that helped stabilize the regime. Bock in turn acknowledged that some women had contributed to Nazi crimes in their functions outside the home, but denied the guilt of women in the tradition-ally separate sphere of home and family.[24]

The polycratic state

The conventional image of Nazi Germany as a totalitarian monolith in which every aspect of life was totally controlled from the top is mislead-ing in several respects. For one thing, it implies that Nazi rule was main-tained solely by coercion rather than, as was more generally the case, by popular consensus. Nothing in Nazi Germany can be adequately explained without reference to the readiness of wide sectors of the public to collabo-rate with the regime, either out of conviction or expediency. It should be remembered that much that took place in Nazi Germany was not distinc-tively Nazi. While the Nazis created numerous new offices and the SS eventually became the most powerful organization in Nazi Germany, there was no sweeping elimination of the existing framework of government when the Nazis came to power. Old and new existed side by side. The state's administrative functions were left largely in the hands of the exist-ing civil service, purged of its Jewish and left-leaning members, just as industry was left in control of the capitalist elites, large-scale agriculture remained in the hands of the landed aristocracy, and the army continued to be run by professional officers. The émigré political scientist Ernst Fraenkel famously described Nazi Germany in the 1930s as a "dual state" in which a "normative" legal system continued to coexist with the grow-ing "prerogative state" of extra-legal party and SS rule.[25] According to a more recent study, the legal apparatus was in fact a "fundamental pillar of the Nazi dictatorship" that helped to legitimize the regime.[26] Although at the height of the war in April 1942 Hitler announced to the Reichstag his authority to override judicial decisions, the regular legal system did sur-vive and function to the very end. Nor does the model of a totalitarian monolith sufficiently acknowledge the constraints imposed on Nazi goals and plans by institutional interests, economic necessities, or regional diversity. The leadership principle, implemented at every level of govern-ment, party, and society, had the paradoxical effect of creating a kind of feudal system in which regional bosses, secure in their fiefdoms, often enjoyed considerable independence from central control. Local and regional institutions had more independence than is commonly assumed. Recent research has confirmed that orders passed down by the Reich lead-ership from party headquarters in Munich were frequently modified or ignored by officials on the regional or local level.[27]

Most importantly, perhaps, the totalitarian monolith model fails to take into account the persistence of conflict and differences within and between government, party, and societal institutions despite their hierarchical command structures. Party offices and agencies paralleled governmental bodies and often interfered in their work. Even before the start of the war the party increasingly intervened in government affairs to pressure a bureaucracy that was often perceived by party militants as too moderate or conservative in carrying out the will of the Führer. During the war the governmental bureaucracy declined in importance as the power of the party and the SS grew. The overlapping authority of party and state offices bred conflict between government and party officials, and personal rivalries among leading Nazis added to the administrative confusion of the Reich. The Nazi system offered plenty of opportunities for bullies to exercise power and lord it over others. Nazi officials were often personally corrupt, using the powers of their offices for material gain. The Social Darwinist ethos of competition and struggle that pervaded the party promoted friction and jurisdictional disputes, often resulting in inefficiency, duplication of tasks, and conflicting priorities. Government and party functionaries engaged in turf wars, jockeyed for power, and sought to expand the bureaucratic empires under their control. Historians have used the terms "bureaucratized romanticism" and "polycracy" to describe the Nazi administrative tangle resulting from overlapping jurisdictions, proliferating offices, competing authorities, and the tendency to improvise.[28] Although bonds of personal loyalty played an important role in the Nazi system, personal ambitions often clashed.

A case in point is the friction between the Chamber of Culture under Goebbels' Propaganda Ministry and the National Socialist Party's Cultural Association under Alfred Rosenberg (1893–1946) on matters of cultural policy and jurisdiction. Here as in other areas the government agencies tended to take more realistic positions than the ideologically more fanatical and uncompromising party organs. Rosenberg, author of the turgid ideological tract, *The Myth of the Twentieth Century* (1930), wanted to remold German spirituality to accord with Nazi racial ideology; Goebbels, the pragmatic realist, was more interested in achieving immediate political goals and devising a cultural program that reached a maximum number of people.

Rosenberg also headed the party's Foreign Policy Office and in that capacity clashed with Hitler's Deputy for Foreign Policy Questions, the arrogant and ambitious Joachim von Ribbentrop (1893–1946), who in turn snubbed and circumvented the Ministry of Foreign Affairs in conducting some of Hitler's diplomatic initiatives in the mid-1930s. Promoted to foreign minister in 1938, Ribbentrop also clashed with Goebbels on the management of foreign news and propaganda. The rivalry between career diplomats in the foreign ministry and Ribbentrop's party men was barely concealed. Schacht and Göring frequently clashed on economic matters. As Commissioner for the Four-Year Plan, Göring interfered in the work of the Ministries of Economics, Agriculture, Labor, and Transport. As Minister of Aviation and head of the

Luftwaffe he clashed with Admiral Erich Raeder (1876–1960), head of the navy. Robert Ley, head of the German Labor Front, clashed with Rosenberg, Darré, Schacht, and Seldte in jurisdictional disputes about the authority to set wages and working conditions. The competencies of Reich Medical Leader Leonard Conti overlapped with those of Hitler's personal physician Karl Brandt (1904–48), who headed the euthanasia program and was named Reich plenipotentiary for medical services in 1944. After the war, Reich Press Chief Otto Dietrich (1897–1952), who was himself entangled in jurisdictional disputes with Max Amann (1891–1957), president of the Reich Press Chamber, and officials of the Press Division of the Foreign Office, claimed that Hitler deliberately cultivated rivalry among his subordinates in order to concentrate all power in his own hands. "Hitler," he wrote in his self-serving postwar memoirs, "created in the political leadership of Germany the greatest confusion that has ever existed in a civilized state."[29]

The administrative chaos was less a product of a deliberate "divide-and-rule" strategy, however, than the result both of the personalized Nazi leadership principle, which tended to make powerful office-holders independent, and of Hitler's indifference to formal process or administrative detail. "A party leader and head of government less bureaucratically inclined," Hitler's biographer Ian Kershaw has written, "less committee man or man of the machine, than Hitler is hard to imagine."[30] The use of secret Führer decrees and reliance on *Sonderbeauftragte* (special representatives) and *ad hoc* organizations for devising and carrying out policies undermined orderly administration and legislation. Orders were often only given orally in face-to-face meetings. Generally, however, draft laws were circulated to concerned agencies and ministries and disputes ironed out before Hitler made the final decision. The practice of letting rivals fight it out to determine the winner was quite compatible with the Social Darwinist principles that prevailed in the party.

Up to 1941 central coordination of legislation was provided by the Reich Chancellery, whose head, Hans-Heinrich Lammers (1879–1962), controlled the information that reached the Führer and served as the main liaison between the dictator and his government ministers. During the war Lammers was a member of a "committee of three" with Martin Bormann (1900–45), Rudolf Hess's successor as head of the party chancellery after the latter's flight to England in 1941, and General Wilhelm Keitel (1882–1946), head of the High Command of the Wehrmacht (OKW). Their approval was necessary for all orders and legislation submitted to Hitler for signature. Lammers's authority to control access to Hitler diminished, however, as Bormann's powers increased in the later stages of the war. Hitler removed himself more and more from domestic affairs as he assumed personal command of the Wehrmacht during the war. The cabinet of ministers never met after 1938. The Reichstag was convened for the last time in April 1942. During the war, power accumulated in the hands of Heinrich Himmler, head of the SS, who took over the government bureaucracy as well after replacing Frick as interior minister in 1943. Besides Himmler and Bormann, others who accrued great powers during the war were Speer as minister of armaments and munitions (1942), Goebbels as plenipotentiary for total war (1944), Fritz Sauckel (1894–1946) as plenipotentiary for the mobilization of labor (1942), and Herbert Backe (1896–1947), who replaced Darré as Reich food minister in 1942, while the influence of Ribbentrop, Ley, Rosenberg, Frick, and Göring declined in the later stages of the war.

The Führer myth

The linchpin of the Nazi system of rule was Adolf Hitler, who made or approved all final decisions on matters of strategy and policy. But just how these strategies and policies were generated in the first place remains a matter of some dispute among historians. How great was the dictator's personal role in drawing up specific policies? This question was the subject of intense debate among historians of the Holocaust, as discussed in greater detail in Chapter 15. "Intentionalist" historians stressed Hitler's personal involvement in planning and initiating genocidal policies, while "structuralists" emphasized the dynamic of increasing radicalization among competing government, party, and SS leaders in the origins of the Holocaust. Historian Ian Kershaw offered a convincing way of reconciling these two interpretative extremes of an all-powerful dictator and a leader often reacting to institutional pressures and initiatives beyond his control. According to Kershaw, the key to understanding how the command system worked in Nazi Germany was the readiness, encouraged at all levels of government and party, "to work toward the Führer" by initiating measures that lower-ranking Nazis understood as implementing Hitler's political and ideological goals.[31] Nazi followers competed with each other in realizing their leader's vision in "anticipatory obedience" to the Führer's will. Thus laws, directives, and regulations were usually launched without requiring the dictator's direct mandate or intervention, but only his retroactive approval. Hitler could thus remain above the fray of day-to-day politics, embellishing his popular image as omniscient and infallible savior of his people. This image was the central element of his charismatic leadership and of the political myth that held the Nazi system together.

The Führer myth of a wise and omniscient leader who knew what was best for Germany served as a powerful integrative device. According to Kershaw, Hitler's role as a symbol and source of inspiration may have played an even more important role in Nazi Germany than his actual leadership. The major functions of the "Hitler myth" were to generate enthusiasm for the regime, stimulate popular actions against designated enemies, conceal underlying social contradictions of class and confession, and reconcile competing forces in the party and among the military, administrative, and economic elites. Hitler was widely viewed as the personification of the "national community," the leader who transcended sectional interests, personal and institutional

Figure 2 Hitler saluting the crowd at the Nuremberg Party Rally in September 1935.

rivalries, and day-to-day politics as the guarantor of national unity and strength. He was credited with Germany's economic recovery and with restoring Germany's status in the international arena. Ironically, he was widely perceived as a "moderate" who would uphold order and morality against fanatics in his own party.

The "Hitler myth" was not entirely the product of distortion and manipulation. One of the reasons for the success of Nazi propaganda is that it spoke to already existing needs, values, and attitudes in the populace. Nazi propaganda gave expression to an already well-established conservative consensus opposed to Marxism, democracy, the injustices of Versailles, and the alleged subversion of the Jews. The Hitler personality cult built on decades of popular yearning for charismatic leadership that would overcome the rifts in German society and lead the unified nation forward to the greatness it deserved and had once known. The Führer cult benefitted from popular revulsion against the partisan, special-interest politics of the Weimar years, the weakness of "leaderless" democracy, and the unaccountability of faceless bureaucrats. National salvation only seemed possible "with a leader who possessed *personal* power and was prepared to take *personal* responsibility…seeming to impose his own personal power on the force of history itself."[32]

But the will of the Führer could only effect changes that were also motivated by fears and aspirations in German society. Hitler's authority rested on the pseudodemocratic premise that he embodied and articulated the will of the people. Most of his supporters perceived the Führer not as a dictator but as the executor of the national will. Nazi propaganda presented him as a man of the people who had distinguished himself for bravery at the front during the war. He was widely revered as a truly populist chancellor who had the best interests of "ordinary people" at heart. The Führer's personal ambitions seemed entirely eclipsed by his single-minded dedication to the German cause. While lower-level party bosses were frequently the targets of popular resentments, Hitler's popularity continued to grow. Much of his popularity was due to economic recovery, which until 1939 improved the living conditions for most Germans despite the tension between production for consumption and production for war and the basic contradiction between the Nazis' archaic ideology and their pragmatic economic policies. The other great source of the Führer's popularity was his uncanny success in foreign affairs. An improbable succession of diplomatic and military triumphs gave him an aura of infallibility that did not crumble until the later stages of the war (see Chapter 12).

Coercion and consensus

The regimentation of German society was the result of both coercion and consensus. Neither the coercive power of the Nazis nor their popular support should be underestimated. Throughout the 1930s the brutal persecution of communists, Social Democrats, Jews, Gypsies, homosexuals, pacifists, "political priests," and designated "asocials" (a category that included beggars, vagrants, and habitual criminals) created a climate of fear that discouraged opposition and encouraged compliance and collaboration with the regime. The concentration camp system served not only as a means of punishment but also as a powerful deterrent to any form of opposition. Besides Dachau (1933), Sachsenhausen (1936), and numerous temporary camps, four additional permanent camps were opened before the start of the war: Buchenwald, near Weimar, in July 1937; Flossenbürg in northern Bavaria in May 1938; Mauthausen in newly annexed Austria in August 1938; and a camp for women at Ravensbrück north of Berlin in May 1939. Officially designated as camps for "political reeducation," these camps employed brutal methods of torture that were never publically acknowledged but heightened the desired deterrent effect. Political prisoners who had successfully undergone "reeducation" were sometimes released, but only on condition that they never mention their camp experiences to anyone. The number of detainees fluctuated from a high of close to 100,000 in 1933 to a fairly stable yet rotating inmate population of approximately 15,000 a year until the numbers increased again after the annexation of Austria in March 1938 and the *Reichskristallnacht* pogrom in November of that year. At the start of the war in September 1939 some 21,400 prisoners were interned in German concentration camps.[33]

After 1934, however, coercion played less of a role in inducing popular collaboration than the widespread consensus that supported Nazi rule. Because Nazi terror was directed at specifically targeted groups of victims, ordinary law-abiding Germans had little reason to fear the Gestapo, the institution charged with ferreting out political opposition and enforcing German racial laws. Its name derives from the first syllables of *Geheime Staatspolizei*, the secret state police, whose apparent omnipresence and ruthless efficiency underpinned the conventional image of a German population cowed into submission by Nazi thugs. The surveillance system seemed so pervasive that the Gestapo was thought to have agents and paid informers everywhere. In fact, however, its staff and resources were far too small to accomplish the task entrusted to it without the voluntary cooperation of wide sectors of the population. Because the Gestapo and other repressive institutions operated in the context of a broad public consensus, the use of large-scale force or coercion was not necessary to impose totalitarian controls. Historian Robert Gellately concluded that "the population at large internalized the norms of the regime to the point where they acted as unofficial extensions of the terror by keeping their eyes and ears open."[34]

Denunciations voluntarily proffered by members of the public were the key to the effectiveness of the surveillance system. Denunciations of fellow citizens played a major role in the prosecution of *Rassenschande* (racial crime) after the criminalizing of sexual relations between Germans and Jews in 1935 and between Germans and foreign workers after the start of the war. Although decrees issued in 1933 and 1934 made "malicious" criticism of the government and the party illegal and a law of August 1938 criminalized statements that weakened the will of the people to fight its enemies, no law ever required citizens to inform on each other. Yet hundreds of regulations, such as the wartime prohibition against listening to foreign broadcasts, could only be enforced if citizens were willing to inform. The leading motives for denunciation were not ideological fanaticism, however, nor fear of Gestapo reprisal, but rather opportunism, conformism, professional rivalries, personal grudges, and conflicts between neighbors. Human, all-too-human traits helped to insure the self-integration of most Germans into totalitarian society. The police state was not imposed on an unwitting population by force; it was built on a popular consensus that was largely indifferent to the fate of the outsiders who were targeted by the regime.

Integrating strategies and pressures

The Nazi regime did not only govern by fear and repression; it also offered numerous incentives to retain public support. The party offered a political track to power and wealth for ambitious men. By providing opportunities for rapid advancement regardless of social background, the Nazi regime created a new kind of meritocracy in which strength of commitment to the party and its ideology became the most important precondition for membership in the new elite. Special schools were established to train future party leaders. The most prestigious of these were the *Ordensburgen*, four military academies located in medieval castles and operated by the German Labor Front. The aspiring young leaders were referred to as *Junker*, the traditional term for young aristocrats.

The SS, too, enjoyed increasing prestige as a vehicle to power and success. It offered physically and temperamentally qualified lower-class youth the chance to rub shoulders with aristocrats and to obtain the kind of elite pre-rogatives formerly accessible only to the well-born. Members of the tradi-tional economic, professional, and military elites were specifically invited to join.[35] SS officers were trained at special officer academies at Bad Tölz in Bavaria, Braunschweig in northern Germany, and, after the *Anschluss*, at Klagenfurt in Austria. By creating a new elite open to all "pure-blooded" Germans on the basis of their genetic endowment and nationalist convictions, the Nazis seemed to make good on their promise to rid the national commu-nity of privilege and prejudice based on class.

The dynamism and energy of the Nazis seemed contagious and created a bandwagon effect that added to the pressures to conform. Pervasive propa-ganda through radio, film, and the print medium did its part to overcome latent resistance in the population. Through cinematically innovative films such as Leni Riefenstahl's (1902–2003) *Triumph of the Will*, a documentary of the 1934 Nazi party rally, the Nazis projected an image of a powerful, cohesive, and exciting movement dedicated to the renewal of the *Volk*. Lukewarm participation in the euphoria of national reconstruction became more and more suspect. Though the "German greeting" *Heil Hitler* was obligatory by law only for Nazi Party members and civil servants, failure to use it in public stamped the offending person as a political nonconformist and subjected him or her to harassment and scorn. An even more serious offense was the failure to give the Hitler salute (with arm outstretched) when the national anthem or the Nazi hymn *Die Fahne Hoch* (The Flag on High) was played. Such symbolic resistance certainly occurred, but it took considerable courage in the context of the enthusiasm and intolerance generated by the "national awakening." It must also be remembered that the full evil of Nazism became apparent only gradually. Despite the warning voices on the left, few Germans expected the national revolution to culminate in war and genocide. Only in retrospect is it clear that, as the historian Alan Beyerchen put it, "the only honorable response to National Socialism was uncompromising defiance."[36]

10 Education, culture, religion, and eugenics in the Third Reich

The Nazis enjoyed particular success in coordinating youth into the Nazi fold, though not without a measure of coercion. Although membership in the Hitler Youth was nominally voluntary until 1939, failure to join or dropping out could result in the loss of qualification for the Abitur, the entrance exam for higher education, or in the denial of apprenticeships to working youth. Uncoerced coordination, however, was the rule rather than the exception from 1933 to 1939. Youthful enthusiasm for Nazism was not only due to the natural susceptibility of children and teenagers to conform to the beliefs and behavior of their elders, but also due to adolescent rebellion against the perceived failure of the older generation to achieve nationalist goals. The Hitler Youth (open to boys aged 10–18) and the League of German Girls also appealed to youth yearning for independent activities outside the home. Moreover, their teachers in the public school system were one of the most readily coordinated groups in Nazi Germany.

Headed by the young aristocrat Baldur von Schirach (1907–74) as Reich Youth Leader, the Hitler Youth could also build on a long tradition of nationalistically minded, often antisemitic right-wing youth leagues in Germany dating back to the Youth Movement at the turn of the century. The lure of being part of a large popular, dynamic, and prestigious movement eased the Nazis' task of dissolving competing youth organizations and integrating their membership into the Nazi organizations. Leaders of rival youth organizations could be lured by promises of instant leadership positions or intimidated by threats of violent reprisal for refusing to join. Protestant groups in particular often merged voluntarily into the Hitler Youth, whose membership grew from 55,000 at the time of Hitler's accession to power to 5.5 million by the end of 1936. Catholic youth groups proved much more resistant to Nazi allure, but steadily suffered defections as well. Catholic youth groups were finally dissolved under pressure in early 1939. In March 1939 Hitler decreed that from 1940 on membership in the Hitler Youth would become mandatory for all boys at the age of 10.[1]

Education

Schooling became the primary means of integrating youth in Nazi society and indoctrinating them with the Nazi world view. Racial biology and

eugenics, along with celebratory German history and idealist German literature, formed the core curricula in educational institutions on all levels. Party
and state agencies, often in competition with each other, kept educational
materials under close surveillance to make sure that students received the
right indoctrination. The vast majority of teachers readily accommodated
themselves to the new regime. The professional organization of German secondary school teachers had actively opposed the Weimar Republic before
1933, but by 1936, 97 percent of all German teachers had joined the
National Socialist Teachers' Association and close to a third had joined the
party.[2] One of the surprising facts about Nazi Germany is that the level of
education correlated positively with the level of support for Nazism, perhaps
because education combined with membership in a Nazi organization opened
the path to better-paying jobs, higher class status, and hence to a greater
stake in the Nazi system.

The main purpose of primary and secondary education in Nazi Germany
was to inculcate a sense of discipline, duty, obedience, courage, and service to
the national cause. Critical thinking was distrusted as a liberal Jewish trait
that subverted popular faith in God, nation, and state. Since the development
of individual talent was to be for the good of the nation, not for selfish gain,
the task of the educator was to help strengthen the soul and the spirit to counteract the allegedly demoralizing effects of democratic liberalism, western
rationalism, and Jewish intellectualism. In the cause of military preparedness
the Nazis emphasized character-building and physical education more than
knowledge or intellect. Calisthenics and competitive sports, especially boxing,
track and field, and soccer, assumed a greater role in the training of youth, as
the Nazis deemed a healthy body more important than a brilliant mind. The
cult of liberal individualism had supposedly led to overspecialization and the
development of a one-sided *Gehirnmensch* (brain person) with no true connection to the community. Character-building meant inculcating the military
virtues of unquestioning respect for authority, readiness to serve the nation as
a soldier, and if necessary to sacrifice one's life on the battlefield. National
Socialism, building on the experience of solidarity at the front during the
Great War, would bring the necessary reorientation of values.

Bernhard Rust (1883–1945), a right-wing secondary school teacher who
had been dismissed from the Hanover school system for "mental imbalance"
in 1930, became Hitler's Minister of Education in 1934. Rust oversaw the
introduction of Nazi curricula in primary and secondary education. He was
also instrumental in the founding of the so-called National Political
Educational Institutes (NAPOLA), elite secondary boarding schools based on
the Italian Fascist principle of "believe, obey, and fight." Designed to serve as
models of Nazi instruction, the NAPOLAs emphasized military sports, agricultural work service, and historical field trips to Germanic sites in addition
to academic preparation. In the institutional competition that flourished in
the Third Reich the SS managed to wrest control over the NAPOLAs from
the Ministry of Education in 1940.

Art, architecture, and literature

Anti-intellectualism characterized the new regime's attitude toward art and literature as well. The Nazis rejected the principle of "art for art's sake." All aspects of aesthetic culture were to serve the national cause—the cause of national regeneration. Yet the Nazis did not think of this subordination of art to the national purpose as a politicization of art; rather they thought of it as freeing art from political instrumentalization by the left. They thought of themselves as defenders of the integrity of the fine arts against their misuse by socially or politically engaged artists and movements. What they sought was not a politicization of art—the artist engaging in political debate—so much as the aestheticizing of politics—the elimination of political debate in favor of shaping the polity according to aesthetic criteria of order, form, and "beauty." Masters of gestures, pageantry, and symbols, the Nazis practiced politics as theater. Political events, most notably the annual party rallies, were staged as theatrical spectacles to overawe and mesmerize the citizenry—and to *prevent* their actual political participation in decision-making.

Yet this typically fascist depolitization of art had a very important political function in the Third Reich. By "depoliticizing" the arts, offering the public an illusory retreat from the ruthless world of politics to the harmonious realm of aesthetics, the Nazis not only blunted the socially critical function of art but also concealed or embellished their own radically conservative political agenda. The Nazis were keenly aware of the enormous potential of art to serve, legitimate, and perpetuate power. Their sponsorship of "high culture" (as well as apolitical mass entertainment to divert the populace from thinking about political issues) enhanced their claim to nonpartisanship as the arbiters of the true national taste. Despite their anti-intellectualism, the Nazi leadership, and Hitler himself (who had earned his living as a young man from the sale of his Vienna cityscapes), were obsessed with the visual arts and presented themselves as men of culture. Many of them amassed huge art collections of their own, plundering Jewish property and museums and private collections in occupied countries during the war. Even at the height of the war Hitler pursued his pet project of creating a "Führer museum" in the Austrian city of Linz where he had grown up. "The intensity of the Führer's longing for music, theater, and cultural relaxation is enormous," Goebbels wrote in his diary in January 1942. Nazi patronage of "high art" fed the Nazi conceit of German cultural superiority and their sense of Germany's civilizing mission in the world. Art provided "the painted veil behind which they could commit whatever horrors they pleased."[3]

The Nazis understood their revolution not merely as a political changing of the guard but as a cultural transformation ultimately intended to unify the nation behind the Nazi project of national expansion and domination. Art served to conceal the contradictions and divisions in German society and to project an image of social harmony, community, and unified national purpose. Major priority was assigned to the task of reversing the alleged decline in traditional standards that conservatives in the Weimar era had already decried as "nihilism" and "cultural Bolshevism." Only a "healthy," positive, idealizing, uplifting, morally edifying, and patriotic art would henceforth be permitted. To this generalized conservative bias the Nazis added their own special emphasis on race. Authentic art was not determined by the conditions of a particular age or by changes in fashion; it was the timeless expression of the innermost character of a particular people. True art, Nazi pundits intoned, emanates from the soul of the people and expresses its eternal ideals.

The Nazis disparaged the "defective vision" of modern art in all its innovative and experimental forms and extolled instead the "clarity" and realism of "German art." They rejected the individualistic notion of self-expression and demanded that art conform to the taste of the mass of the people. Nazi cultural policies appealed to wide sectors of the public as a way of protecting the natural cultural order seemingly under attack by a self-appointed liberal cultural elite. To many ordinary citizens, modernism in music, literature, painting, and architecture represented a decline in traditional standards of beauty and form, a decline the Nazis promised to reverse. To be sure, there were some differences among the Nazi elite in their attitudes toward modernism. Goebbels, for instance, was more open to innovative trends than Rosenberg, who, as the founder of the Combat League for German Culture in 1928 and as "Delegate of the Führer for the Supervision of all Spiritual and Worldview-related Schooling and Education of the NSDAP" in 1934, wielded considerable influence in the cultural sphere. Up to the mid-1930s even modernism had its champions among the Nazi elite. Some modernist artists and architects, such as Emil Nolde (1867–1956), Ernst Barlach (1870–1938), or Ludwig Mies van der Rohe (1886–1969), sympathized with the Nazi revolution until their own works came under fire from cultural conservatives, who eventually emerged triumphant in their struggle to dominate the arts. Hitler's own personal predilection for nineteenth-century Bavarian genre painting may have doomed the modernist cause. In painting and sculpture he insisted on clarity and literal representation. "Works of art that cannot be comprehended," Hitler declaimed at the opening of the newly constructed House of German Art in Munich in 1937, "from now on will no longer be foisted upon the German people!"[4] If nonobjective artists were sincere in their deformed vision of the world, they should be declared mentally incompetent and not be allowed to reproduce; if, on the other hand, they were deliberately defrauding the public for purposes of self-promotion, they should be put behind bars!

Shortly after the opening of the House of German Art the Nazis mounted an exhibition of "degenerate art," which, ironically, enjoyed a far better attendance than the various exhibits of approved German art. The German term for degenerate is *entartet*, a term that implies deviation from the *Art*, the German word for species. The literal meaning of the term seemed to confirm the Nazi dictum that the source of degeneracy in art as in other areas of life was racial impurity and deviation from healthy Nordic stock. Jewish artists, in particular, were blamed for subverting the mental health of the public by their preoccupation with disease and deformity. In place of a socially critical art, the Nazis demanded affirmation of and enthusiastic assent to the sacred values and institutions of the Third Reich. The military virtues were particularly sacrosanct. Art that undermined religion, morality, and patriotism was to be eradicated in the same way as carriers of disease were to be removed from society. Museums were purged of "degenerate" art and replaced by works that celebrated Nordic racial perfection, masculine heroism, comradeship, and readiness for combat, and *Kinder, Küche, Kirche* for women. The purge of degenerate art paralleled the purification of the race through eugenics, each culminating in a paroxysm of senseless destruction. Thousands of banned works were eventually destroyed; many were sold abroad for profit and to acquire works by Germans from foreign museums.

The Nazi cultural program had considerable appeal to wide sectors of the public, not surprisingly so in view of the fact that Nazi artistic tastes, like their political values, reflected and flattered deep-seated popular prejudices. Just as in the political sphere the Nazi movement represented a backlash against liberal, progressive, and secular humanist values, so in the cultural sphere the Nazis could count on popular mistrust and resentment of the modernist avant-garde. The Nazis seemed to stand for a defense of the familiar and the traditional against the novelties and distortions of modernism. Much of the Nazis' popularity probably derived from the widespread perception that finally the healthy tastes and instincts of the "moral majority" were allowed to assert themselves against the degraded standards and nihilistic perspectives of a self-appointed intellectual and aesthetic elite. The Nazis helped to give prominence to an older conservative tradition of literal representation that seemed to have been overwhelmed by the innovative complexities of modern art. A key to the popularity of National Socialism was its ability to satisfy Romantic, precapitalist longings for a return to an idealized past. To many people it must have seemed as if art had once again become accessible, comprehensible, depoliticized, and useful to the common man. Nazi artists romanticized the soldier, the artisan, and the peasant-farmer tilling the soil. Typical subjects of Nazi art were "muscular figures in aggressive poses," such as the works of Hitler's favorite sculptor Arno Breker (1900–91).[5] Idealized art seemed to buttress pride and self-respect, thus counteracting the corrosive self-criticism and self-contempt of the "politicized" art of the left. Nazi artists also seemed to defend the fundamental spiritual values of morality and religion against the encroachments of materialism, rationalism, and commercialism—the deplorable modern tendencies the Nazis always ascribed to the undue growth of Jewish influence on German culture and society.

Nazism was not simply a backlash against modernism, of course, offering only a return to tradition. Rather, the Nazis offered their own vitalistic version of modernity, purged of all symptoms of degeneration and decay. Their aim, after all, was not to return to the past, but to revitalize and regenerate the *Volk*.

In this future-oriented national project all of the arts were assigned a significant role. The Nazis were quite willing to adopt aspects of modernism as well as advanced production techniques to achieve maximum aesthetic effects. Albert Speer (1905–81), for instance, Hitler's favorite architect and wartime head of arms production, created a "cathedral of light" at the annual party rallies in Nuremberg by using antiaircraft searchlights to cast beams of light into the sky to a height of 25,000 feet. This synthesis of (and tension between) aesthetic (and political) conservatism and modern technological production techniques was a central feature of Nazi culture.[6] Artists who achieved prominence in the Third Reich were by no means exclusively propagandists. Numerous talented artists of conventional tastes and conservative outlook quite willingly aligned themselves with the Nazi program of old-fashioned realism, idealized heroism, and moral renewal. As in most other fields, the ready collaboration of professionals made Nazification of the arts possible. The Nazis gave lavish support to artists who were willing to turn their talents to promoting the aesthetic policies of the regime. Artists, art dealers, and museum directors, many of whom considered themselves "apolitical," took advantage of the new opportunities opened to them. As Jonathan Petropolous has pointed out, however, idealistic beliefs and the typically Nazi "superiority complex" were just as important in explaining the support of art professionals for Nazi policies and their participation in the Nazi state as the more venal motivations usually ascribed to them.[7]

The architecture of the Third Reich revived traditional forms as well, but it also sought to achieve the functionality and dynamism of modern architecture. The House of German Art, with its rows of massive columns, was a prime example of the Nazis' predilection for the monumentalism, simplicity, and symmetry of classical styles. Hitler, whose boyhood dream was to become a master-builder, considered architecture, along with music, as one of the two queens of the arts.[8] He took a personal role in designing the New Reich Chancellery, constructed under Albert Speer's direction and completed in January 1939 to demonstrate the might of the new Reich. Visitors could gain access to Hitler's 1,300 square feet office only by walking through an imposing marble gallery almost 500 feet in length. The building was decorated with heroic, muscle-bound sculptures of "party" and "army" by Arno Breker, who achieved considerable wealth and fame after the war by supplying West Germany's corporate clients with affirmative art.[9] Architecture in the Third Reich was meant to manifest the glory, power, and dominance of the nation, state, and party. Speer's monumental, neoclassical German Pavilion at the Paris World's Fair in 1937, parts of which were destined to become permanent fixtures at the Nuremberg site of the annual party rallies, was planned to express "security, pride, self-confidence, clarity, discipline, and thereby the concept of the new Germany."[10] In his effort to create an architecture worthy of the "Thousand-year Reich," Hitler authorized Speer to draw up plans for the transformation of Berlin into the future world capital, Germania. The war prevented the realization of this megalomanic project, which would have dwarfed all previous examples of municipal architecture. The "Great Hall" that was to become the centerpiece of the new capital was to have a 300-foot ceiling and be capable of seating 180,000 persons. In the elaborate Führer bunker deep below the New Reich Chancellery Hitler took comfort in viewing the architectural model of Germania in the last days of the war.

The conservative cultural revolution launched by the Nazis extended to other fields as well. In music the Nazis favored the traditional melodic style of the Classical and Romantic eras. In literature, too, the new regime backed a reaction against such modern and socially critical literary schools as naturalism and expressionism. The Nazis promoted the traditional narrative form and heroic themes of the nineteenth-century novel and conventional rhyme and meter in poetry. Jewish writers and writers with left-wing sympathies, including Bertolt Brecht (1898–1956), Alfred Döblin (1878–1957), and Lion Feuchtwanger (1884–1958), were expelled from Germany. But even writers who sympathized with Nazism, such as, for a time, the innovative poet Gottfried Benn (1886–1956), were forced to curtail their literary experimentation. The Nazis' preferred genre, besides combat literature and historical novels exalting the German past, was *Heimatliteratur* (regional literature), a celebration of stolid rural virtues juxtaposed against the "asphalt" culture of modern urban life. Here, too, the Nazis could tap a long nativist tradition of sentimental agrarian romanticism and populist backlash against the seeming negativism and amoralism of the literary avant-garde.

Science

Even in the physical sciences the Nazis distinguished between "Aryan" and "Jewish" forms and championed a common-sense approach that dignified the familiar and disdained the abstract and abstruse. While Germanic science was supposedly based on respect for facts, exact observation, and experimentation, "Jewish" science was accused of illegitimately mixing facts with opinions. This accusation echoed the traditional anti-Enlightenment distrust of theory and reason as symptoms of the hubris of human intellect. The essential error of "Jewish physics," the defenders of a "German" science claimed, was to deny and ignore the spiritual realm of eternal truths by assuming that the workings of the universe could be explained in terms of material theories and natural science. It lacked the necessary metaphysical dimension, in the absence of which science inevitably exceeds its proper circumscribed scope and attempts to explain all of reality in material and mechanistic terms.

Nazi scientists (and conservative publicists) denounced Einstein's theory of relativity as a materialistic doctrine that attempted to explain the universe in terms of the relationship of matter to matter. Einstein, director of the Kaiser Wilhelm Institute for Physics in Berlin since 1914 and winner of the Nobel Prize for physics in 1921, symbolized for right-wing demagogues the general decline of firm patriotic values and the ascendancy of left-wing pacifism after World War I. The Nazis charged that the relativity theory (like atonal music, alienated art, or socially critical literature) could only grow in the soil of materialist Marxism. Hitler himself charged in a front-page article in the *Völkischer Beobachter* in 1921 that Jews were using science to poison the soul of the German people and bring about their internal collapse.[11] To the Germanic scientists time and space were absolute concepts rooted in intuition, not relative concepts dependent on the perspective from which they were viewed. The usefulness of given truths to political and cultural conservatives was, of course, that these did not have to be subjected to rational scrutiny. A rigid system of unshakable a priori verities provided the unassailable buttress for authoritarian politics.

The campaign for "Aryan" or "German" physics was led by the empirical physicists Philipp Lenard (1862–1947) and Johannes Stark (1874–1951), winners of Nobel prizes in physics in 1905 and 1919, respectively. Both had joined the Nazi movement well before 1933 and had polemicized against theoretical physics and Einstein's theory of relativity long before Hitler's rise to power. The champions of "German physics" denounced the semiprivate but state-supported Kaiser Wilhelm Society (KWG), the organization founded in 1911 to coordinate the work of the various Kaiser Wilhelm research institutes, as "a playground for Catholics, Socialists, and Jews."[12] After 1933 they sought to expel Jews and physicists who dissented from their right-wing views from positions of authority. By 1935, approximately one-fifth of all scientists and one-fourth of all physicists in Germany had been forced from their positions by the Nazis.[13] Stark headed the state agency funding scientific research until 1936, but lost influence thereafter as, with war approaching, practicality once again won out over ideology. Most German physicists, including Max von Laue (1879–1960), Max Planck (1858–1947), and Werner Heisenberg (1901–76), winners of Nobel prizes in 1914, 1919, and 1932, respectively, united in defense of traditional scientific principles. Persuaded by professional physicists that conventional science was indispensable to the war effort, Nazi officials gave up their support for "German physics." While the official bias against "Jewish physics" may well have played a role in the government's relative neglect of nuclear physics, a more important reason for the failure of the German nuclear weapons program was the lack of sufficient raw materials during the war.

The Churches

Many Germans expected the National Socialist revolution to lead to a revival of religion. Church membership and attendance actually grew in the early years of Nazi rule, reversing a trend of declining church membership throughout the Weimar years.[14] "There could have been no clearer sign," historian Richard Steigmann-Gall has written, "that national renewal and religious renewal were believed to be deeply connected."[15] The Christian Churches, it should be recalled, shared the Nazis' hostility toward secular liberalism and socialism and approved of their affirmation of authority, hierarchy, morality, and faith. In their 1920 program the Nazis had pledged support for "a positive Christianity," by which they meant a militant, nondenominational, fundamentalist creed tied to German nationalism and opposed to the "Jewish-materialist spirit in us and around us." Before 1933 they had traditionally opened their meetings and rallies with prayer, and leading Nazis frequently invoked God and divine providence in their speeches. Even Hitler claimed in *Mein Kampf* that he was doing the work of the Lord.

The Nazi victory in 1933 was welcomed by many Germans as not just a political turn but also as a moral turn against the secular humanist values of the Enlightenment and French Revolution. Certainly the Nazis advertised themselves as the inheritors, not the opponents, of the Christian tradition, and much of their support came from self-identified Christians.[16] In his first official proclamation on 1 February 1933, Hitler's government promised to "extend its firm protection to Christianity as the basis of our moral system, and to the family as the nucleus of our *Volk* and state."[17] Determined to show their support for religion, Nazi and SA groups frequently attended church in uniform before and after the takeover of power. Opportunism no doubt played a part in these displays of religious faith, but they also reflected the convictions of many Nazis and their leaders. They understood their movement as embodying traditional morality and religion against the "evil" forces of the Jewish-led liberal, socialist, and secular left. SS rules explicitly prohibited its members from describing themselves as atheist, as this supposedly signified an unhealthy disbelief in life's higher purposes.[18]

For all their lip-service to the importance of religion, however, the spiritual revival preached by National Socialists had little in common with the traditional doctrines of either the Catholic or Lutheran Churches. The Nazis' emphasis on nation, race, and Nordic myth and ritual, as well as their criticism of allegedly misplaced Christian humanitarianism and compassion for the weak and the poor, were bound to cause friction with the Churches. The split widened as some Nazis attempted to introduce "Life Celebrations" and party-organized marriage, birth, and funeral ceremonies in competition with traditional Church-sanctioned practices. These ceremonies attracted minimal public support, however, and in the 1930s, 95 percent of the German population remained baptized members of one of the Christian Churches. Throughout the Nazi era the state continued to collect and distribute the taxes that funded Church expenses.

Although the Nazis consciously sought to embrace both the Christian and anti-Christian wings of the *völkisch* movement, Nazi policy toward the Churches was never uniform. Even those who rejected institutional Christianity did not necessarily reject Christianity as a religion. Advocates of organized Christianity, those who were neutral toward religion, and those who were hostile to the Churches competed with each other from their various institutional perches in party and state. Had they won the war, some Nazis would certainly have wished to supplant traditional religion with their own *völkisch* cult, whether neopagan or German Protestant. In 1940 Martin Bormann, at that time still Rudolf Hess's deputy as head of the party chancellery, ordered the end of all efforts to fuse

Christianity with National Socialism in religious and ideological instruction in schools. "It will not be possible to create a Christian doctrine that would be completely compatible with the point of view of National Socialist ideology," he wrote, "just as the communities of Christian faith would never be able to accept the ideology of National Socialism in its entirety."[19] Among the reasons he cited for the impossibility of achieving a Christian–Nazi synthesis were the Churches' reluctance to embrace the Nazi racial doctrine and the inability of the various Christian denominations to agree on a common doctrine. But even Bormann believed that some form of moral education based on the Ten Commandments was necessary to insure obedience and order in the "People's Community." In his "table talk" during the war Hitler also implied that the ultimate Nazi goal was to suppress organized religion in Germany after the war. Religion "must rot like a gangrenous limb," Hitler is quoted as telling his luncheon guests at his East Prussian military headquarters in December 1941.[20]

Under the circumstances, though, Nazi leaders were forced to proceed circumspectly lest they antagonize the large number of followers of the two great Christian denominations in Germany. Well aware of the importance of his religious base, Hitler increasingly distanced himself from the *völkisch* sectarians in his party. Militant anti-Catholics like the publicist Artur Dinter (1876–1948), former *Gauleiter* of Thuringia and author of several racist tracts, was drummed out of the party long before Hitler came to power. Erich Ludendorff, too, Hitler's erstwhile accomplice in the Munich putsch, left the party in 1928 in part because he felt that the Nazis underestimated the danger posed to Germany by the universalism of the Roman Catholic Church. In deference to Church leaders Hitler refused to give official party endorsement to Rosenberg's anticlerical and anti-Catholic tract, *The Myth of the Twentieth Century*. Opponents of Christianity who tried to gain official recognition for a neo-Germanic German Faith Movement after Hitler's accession to power enjoyed a considerable following in the party, but received no encouragement from the pragmatically oriented Nazi state. In response to complaints by the Churches, the German Faith Movement was ordered by the Gestapo to confine its functions to internal membership meetings in August 1935, and SS and party members were prohibited from attending German Faith Movement functions altogether in November 1937.

The concordat that Hitler signed with the Holy See in July 1933 was designed to retain the loyalty of millions of German Catholics by guaranteeing their religious freedom. Negotiations for a concordat had begun well before Hitler came to power, but Hitler's regime made greater concessions to the Vatican than any Weimar government had been willing to do. These included Catholic religious education in public schools, expansion of Church-run schools, protection of Church property, maintenance of Catholic theological faculties at state institutions of higher learning, and the right to freely publish encyclicals in Germany. The Church in turn renounced all political activity and pledged to dissolve all its political organizations. By signing the concordat Hitler gained not only the allegiance of millions of

Catholics in Germany, but also international prestige and the end of political Catholicism.

The concordat failed to end tensions between the Catholic Church and the Nazi state, however. Although a high proportion of leading Nazis, including Hitler, Goebbels, and Himmler, had been raised as Catholics, they were also heirs to a long tradition of anti-Catholicism among German nationalists, for whom international Catholicism represented a threat to the unity and sovereignty of the German Reich. In Austria, where Hitler had grown up, Pan-German nationalists saw both the Habsburg monarchy and the Catholic Church as barriers to Austria's incorporation in a Greater German Empire. Although the concordat gave the Church the right to operate its own "charitable, cultural, or religious" organizations, the Nazis refused to recognize the independence of Catholic social and professional organizations. The Nazis sought to abolish long-standing Catholic youth and worker groups and force their members into Nazi organizations. Nazi efforts to fuse religion with race became the greatest source of conflict. The Nazis especially disdained Christian solicitude for the weak and disadvantaged and the humanitarian Catholic notion of the equality of all peoples in the eyes of God. They resented the Catholic concern for the salvation of all members of the Church, regardless of their race. The Nazis failed, however, in their efforts to compel the Church to oust its Jewish converts. Nor was the government able to persuade the Church to annul German–Jewish marriages.

The conflict between the Roman Catholic Church and the state came to a head with the publication in March 1937 of the papal encyclical "On the Condition of the Church in Germany," better known by its first three words, *"Mit brennender Sorge"* ("With Burning Anxiety"). Pope Pius XI accused the German government of failing to abide by the provision of the concordat that guaranteed the independence of the Church. He defended the integrity of traditional Catholic doctrine and denounced efforts to replace it "by arbitrary 'revelations' that certain speakers of the present day wish to derive from the myth of blood and race."[21] He reiterated the divinity of Christ and inveighed against pantheistic doctrines that identified God with the world or sought to deify any race, state, people, or leader. The pope denounced all attempts to replace a personal God with an impersonal force such as fate. He also protested against the dissolution of Catholic youth groups and organizations and called for an end to pressures on the faithful to leave the Church.

In keeping with the concordat, however, the pope did not criticize the Nazis' discriminatory legislation against Jews (who were never mentioned in the encyclical), the concentration camps, or any policies that did not directly affect the Church. Indeed the Church actively supported the antisocialist policies of the state. Almost simultaneously with *Mit brennender Sorge* the Church issued the encyclical *Divini Redemptoris*, celebrating the common mission of the Catholic Church and National Socialism to combat atheistic communism. Nonetheless, the regime responded to *Mit brennender Sorge* by seizing all available copies, incarcerating "political" priests who dared to criticize the regime from the pulpit, prosecuting priests for alleged sexual offenses, and restricting religious instruction in schools. In June 1939 Bormann also took action to reduce the number and size of theological faculties at state universities and to end state subsidies to the Church institution at Eichstädt for the training of bishops because of "extremely strong confessional activity against National Socialism."[22] The conflict between the Catholic Church and the state continued warily on both sides throughout the Nazi era, the Nazis avoiding excessively heavy-handed interventions for fear of alienating German Catholics, the Church desisting from overt political opposition (except in opposing euthanasia after the start of the war) to safeguard its institutional survival.

The Evangelical Church in Germany, long a virtual arm of the monarchical state in Prussia, proved more amenable to government interference and manipulation. The susceptibility of many German Protestants to nationalist ideology helped the Nazis in their attempts to control the Evangelical Church. Many nationalists believed that unity of purpose—the precondition for expansion—could best be achieved by the development of a specifically German national religion. Various sects in the late nineteenth and early twentieth centuries had sought to harmonize belief in Christ with *völkisch* ideology. Perhaps the most important of such efforts was the Christian Social Workers' Party founded in 1878 by Wilhelm I's court pastor, Adolf Stoecker (1835–1909), who tried unsuccessfully to use antisemitic appeals and *völkisch* religion to lure workers into the nationalist camp.

Antisemitism and authoritarianism could be traced back to Martin Luther's own virulent later writings of the sixteenth century, which were republished and widely circulated by the Nazis. Most Protestant theologians in Germany had been critical of the secularism of the Weimar Republic and supported a restoration of the monarchy or some kind of authoritarian government. Nationalists in the Evangelical Church, known as the German Christians, also benefitted from Nazi support for the unification of the 28 separate state Evangelical churches (*Landeskirchen*) into a unified central church, a *Reichskirche*. The German Christians already had won a third of the votes in the elections of representatives to the Prussian United Church synod in November 1932. In elections of representatives to a national synod of Evangelical *Landeskirchen* in July 1933 they gained two-thirds of the vote, enabling them to elect Ludwig Müller, Hitler's plenipotentiary for Evangelical Church affairs, to the newly created post of Reich Bishop. The Nazis' efforts to control the Evangelical Church appeared to have succeeded.

From the start, however, Müller was confronted by a strong movement opposed to the efforts of the German Christians to impose racist principles on the Lutheran Church. Led by the Berlin theologians Martin Niemöller (1892–1984) and Otto Dibelius (1880–1967), the Confessing Church, as this opposition group called itself, defended traditional Lutheran doctrine against nationalist infringement. The immediate occasion for the formation of this opposition was the introduction by the German Christians of the "Aryan paragraph" of the Civil Service Law into the Prussian Church in September 1933. This was followed by the attempt by German Christians to repudiate the Jewish Old Testament and to exclude "non-Aryans" from attending church services in November 1933. In response to the pressures coming from the Nazi regime, Niemöller formed the Pastors' Emergency League, a union of Protestant clergy opposed to the application of the "Aryan paragraph" in the Church. In May 1934 over 7,000 members of this league joined to form the Confessing Church, which enjoyed the support of a majority of Protestant churchgoers. Leaders of the Confessing Church directly challenged the legitimacy of Müller's German Christian-dominated church government in what came to be called the "Church Struggle."[23]

The Confessing Church was a religious movement to preserve the integrity of the Lutheran faith, not a political movement of opposition to the Nazi state. Most members of the Confessing Church enthusiastically supported the Hitler regime.[24] Indeed, Niemöller had himself joined the National Socialist Party shortly after Hitler's appointment, and both he and Dibelius had been harshly critical of the Weimar Republic. Although they denied the Nazis' authority to expel Jewish converts from offices in the Evangelical Church, both theologians were ambivalent at best about the Nazi campaign to oust Jews from positions of influence in German society. Dibelius even defended the boycott against Jewish businesses on 1 April 1933 in a broadcast to the United States.[25] Their opposition to Nazi interference in Church affairs drew its inspiration from the Lutheran separation of the worldly and spiritual realms. The doctrine of two kingdoms bred political quietism and passivity by denying that the kingdom of man might be turned into the kingdom of God. While members of the Confessing Church were prepared to uphold the traditional Lutheran values of loyalty and obedience to the state, they denied that the state had any right to determine the content of religious faith.

Anxious not to alienate their strong support among all factions of German Protestantism and conscious of the potentially damaging results that a heavy-handed intervention in the Church Struggle could provoke both at home and in the eyes of the world, the Nazi government sought to reconcile the contending factions in the German Evangelical Church. In October 1933 Rudolf Hess issued a proclamation of the party's neutrality in confessional matters, thus weakening the claims of the German Christians to sole control of the Church. In 1935 the former Prussian Minister of Justice Hanns Kerrl (1887–1941) was put in charge of a newly created Ministry for Church Affairs with a mandate to conciliate the contending factions in the Church. He failed, however, to settle the dispute, and his goal of blending Christian faith with National Socialist ideology also ran into increasing opposition from Nazi radicals, who feared the moderating influence of Christian principles on the Nazi program.

Unwilling to jeopardize the unity of the *Volksgemeinschaft* and their support among German Protestants, the Nazis eventually gave up their efforts to force Confessing Church leaders to submit to the government's will. Hitler reluctantly accepted the traditional form of Church organization and refused to appoint a successor to Kerrl after the latter's death in 1941. The Nazis would not let overt challenges to their authority go unpunished, however. Niemöller was arrested in 1937, and after a brief prison sentence spent most of the war years in "protective custody" in various concentration camps, thus providing an important symbol of resistance. Although Dibelius was acquitted by a special court of treasonable activities, his radius of action was sharply restricted. But Müller's influence and authority waned as well, and the Nazis never succeeded in bringing the Evangelical Church entirely under their control. In the face of widespread popular support for the Confessing Church, they were forced to postpone any radical action to transform traditional religious beliefs or practices until after the war. As a result of this tactically motivated moderation, the conflict between Church and state was far less damaging to Hitler's popularity than might otherwise have been the case.[26]

Racial and eugenic policies

Practical exigencies thus often led the Nazis to compromise their ideological predilections, especially in policies toward the Churches, the *Mittelstand*, agriculture, and the role of women in society. However, ideology and policy came together with a vengeance in matters relating directly to eugenics and race. The Nazis were able to build on a strong "racial hygiene" movement in Germany that had long been preoccupied with the improvement and development of the German "race." Three eminent anthropologists authored the classic German text on race science in 1921, *Outline of Human Genetics and Racial Hygiene*, a book whose ideas Hitler incorporated into *Mein Kampf*.[27] Adherents of eugenics believed that it was necessary to reverse the modern humanitarian and democratizing trends that seemed to favor the weak and the poor at the expense of the strong and the rich. German defeat in World War I not only resulted in the intensification of political antisemitism, but also led to greatly increased interest in, indeed obsession with, eugenics as a means of regenerating the German people and restoring national strength. Ironically, German racialists and eugenicists looked to legislation in the United States, including state laws prohibiting miscegenation and mandating sterilization for the mentally disabled, as well as federal laws restricting immigration from eastern Europe, as models for their own efforts.[28] A number of prominent American eugenicists, in turn, hoped to emulate Nazi legislation in the United States.

The obsession with "racial hygiene" (the application of eugenic policies toward the improvement of the race) pervaded all public policy in the Third Reich, including, as we have seen, policies directed toward workers, farmers, and women. This obsession with the purity of the German race was most evident in the discriminatory legislation against Jews (see Chapter 11). Even here, though, practical considerations inhibited hard-line measures to some extent. The official boycott of Jewish shops and stores was limited to one day,

1 April 1933, because of the opposition of industrialists who feared its disruptive effects on the production and distribution of goods. The extrusion of Jews from economic life proceeded more gradually, at least until 1938, than their exclusion from public service, cultural life, or the professions.

Nazi racial policy manifested in extreme form the determination of the new regime to apply biological principles to the solution of social problems. According to an adage attributed to Rudolf Hess, "National Socialism is nothing but applied biology."[29] The Nazis totally reversed the communist emphasis on environmental factors as the source of such social problems as crime, alcoholism, poverty, disease, or family dysfunction. From the Nazi point of view all such problems were essentially genetic in origin and could be eliminated only through measures designed to purify the gene pool (or "blood") of the nation. The regime enacted a variety of eugenic laws ostensibly designed to upgrade the quality of the German "race." The most important of these was the Law for the Prevention of Genetically Diseased Offspring issued on 14 July 1933, the same day the formation of new political parties was banned. This law, based on proposed legislation for voluntary sterilization drawn up by the Prussian Health Council in 1932, made sterilization compulsory for persons with hereditary diseases, habitual criminals, mentally retarded persons, and persons with mental illness. Hundreds of so-called Genetic Health Courts were created to determine who should be sterilized. This effort to prevent the reproduction of undesirables represented the reverse side of the pronatalist policies designed to get carriers of "pure blood" to have more children. Best estimates put the number of persons sterilized in Germany between 1933 and 1945 at close to 400,000. Most of these compulsory sterilizations were carried out before the start of the war.[30]

Sterilization of persons dependent on charity or government assistance was declared to be necessary to reduce the unacceptable costs of welfare recipients to the state. The Interior Ministry drew up elaborate charts to demonstrate that the state could not afford to allow "asocials"—persons categorized as unable to earn their own living—to reproduce. Begging and vagrancy—*prima facie* evidence of inferior racial stock—were strictly proscribed. A "Law for the Protection of Hereditary Health" in 1935 called for the registration of people deemed to be of "lesser racial value" and banned marriage between individuals suffering from "genetic infirmities."

Racial research institutes proliferated as science and academic disciplines were harnessed to the service of the regime. An Office for Kinship Research in the Ministry of the Interior issued proofs of ancestry, mandatory for candidates for Nazi Party membership. The SS agency *Ahnenerbe* (ancestral heritage), founded in 1935, promoted historical and archeological research to prove the value of "Aryan" blood. The heavily subsidized "Ethnic German Research Societies" gave right-wing racial scholars manifold opportunities to rationalize and legitimize the claims of the Nazis to proprietorship over territory in neighboring countries and the displacement of their native populations in favor of ethnically German settlers.[31] New chairs for racial biology were created at most universities and filled by reliable propagandists for the racial world view and Nordic supremacy, including such influential publicists as Hans F. K. Günther (1891–1968), author of best-selling books on race, and Fritz Lenz (1887–1976), coauthor of the leading textbook on genetics in the Weimar Republic.

Euthanasia

The Nazi regime also attempted to gain public acceptance of euthanasia, the "mercy killing" of people with incurable diseases or disabilities, and indeed the number of requests for voluntary euthanasia increased markedly in the Nazi era. A film made under the aegis of the Nazi party's Racial Policy Office, entitled *Erbkrank* ("Hereditarily Ill"), was circulated in 1936 to justify euthanasia and compulsory sterilization of "life unworthy of life." In 1941 the Nazis even sponsored a widely circulated feature film, entitled *Ich klage an* ("I accuse"), to gain acceptance for the "mercy killing" of the disabled. Involuntary euthanasia had long been a part of the public discussion in Germany, intensified by the necessity of making hard choices about scarce resources in World War I. During the war severely disabled and mentally ill persons in asylums had been allowed to starve to death as their rations were reduced to make more food available for workers in the arms industry and soldiers at the front. In 1920 an authority in constitutional law, Karl Binding, and a prominent professor of psychiatry, Alfred Hoche, teamed up to write an influential tract entitled, *Permission for the Destruction of Life Unworthy of Life*, defending involuntary euthanasia of severely handicapped persons in the interests of the community at large. "A new age will arrive," Hoche wrote, "operating with a higher morality and with great sacrifice—which will actually give up the requirements of an exaggerated humanism and overvaluation of mere existence."[32] At the very least, he asserted, "defective people" should not be allowed to reproduce. In the Third Reich these ideas received official support. The arguments in favor of eliminating the physically and mentally ill or weak gained increasing legitimacy as Germany again moved toward war in the late 1930s.

A request by parents of a disabled child to be allowed to bring about its death in the winter of 1938–39 spurred the implementation of a secret euthanasia program code-named "Aktion T-4" after the address of the building in Berlin, Tiergartenstrasse 4, from which the program was directed by the head of Hitler's private chancellery Philip Bouhler (1899–1945) and his personal physician Karl Brandt (1904–48). The program actually originated in the Führer's own chancellery but was moved out to prevent any public knowledge of its origins and administrative connections.[33] Hitler authorized the commencement of the program to coincide with the start of the war. As many as 200,000 mentally ill and physically disabled persons may have been systematically killed under the auspices of this program by the end of the war.

The T-4 program marked the first use of poison gas, in this case carbon monoxide, and many of the T-4 personnel were later actively involved in setting up the gas chambers in the death camps of the Holocaust (see Chapter 15). Under the code name "Aktion 14f13" the program had already been extended to concentration camp inmates in 1940, where victims were chosen on racial as well as on medical criteria. Despite the covert nature of the euthanasia program, knowledge of the killings began to seep out as more and more victims' relatives received word of the sudden deaths of their loved ones without any visible cause. The resultant protests, especially from members of the clergy, may have persuaded Hitler to call an official halt to the program in August 1941, at about the same time as the gassing facilities for the "Final Solution of the Jewish Question" were being prepared in occupied Poland. But despite the official end of the program, euthanasia killings, especially of disabled children, continued throughout the war.[34] In Nazi ideology the anti-semitic and eugenic traditions merged in a lethal combination as both racism and racial hygiene became official state policies. Jews and Gypsies came to be defined as carriers of social diseases, and the physically and socially disadvantaged came to be classified as being of lesser racial value than healthy or prosperous Germans.

11 Persecution of the Jews, 1933–39

Jews became the primary victims of Nazi persecution in the Third Reich. Approximately 500,000 Jews lived in Germany at the time of the Nazi takeover, comprising only three-quarters of 1 percent of the German population of 67 million. However, the Nazis were able to use the disproportionate representation of Jews in certain sectors of the economy, the professions, the press, and the entertainment industry to give credence to their conspiracy theory, according to which Jews controlled the German economy, society, and culture under the "Weimar system." The main reason for the growth of anti-semitism among German nationalists after World War I was the widespread assumption that left-wing Jews had undermined the war effort and contributed to German defeat. Nazi antisemitism also exploited popular feelings of envy, especially in the depression, and especially among the middle classes that formed the NSDAP's mass constituency. While antisemitism was not the main source of Hitler's popularity, his brutal campaign to oust Jews from German society in no way diminished his appeal to the mass of the German population. Many Germans brazenly availed themselves of the new opportunities created by the elimination of Jewish competition from the economy and the professions.

Anti-Jewish measures after the Nazi takeover

After securing full legislative power through the Enabling Act in March 1933, the Nazis acted on their pledge to remove Jews from public life. In contrast to the provisions for social and economic reform, which were generally ignored in practice, the antisemitic provisions of the Nazi program were enacted into law. Antisemitic legislation could be used to divert public attention from the absence of real social and economic reform. The Civil Service Law of 7 April 1933 removed from public employment all persons of "non-Aryan descent," defined as persons with one or more Jewish parents or grandparents. This so-called "Aryan paragraph" of the Civil Service Law was widely applied by professional organizations even before Jews were legally excluded from the professions. In the course of *Gleichschaltung* in 1933–34 Jews were excluded from employment in education, the entertainment industry, the arts, journalism, and the stock exchange. Jewish doctors and dentists were removed from health insurance panels and lost their eligibility to treat patients under the national health insurance plans. Proof of "Aryan descent" was eventually required by law even for membership in athletic clubs. A decree of February 1934 made Aryan descent a prerequisite for service in the Wehrmacht (after the Nuremberg Laws of 1935 men of mixed descent were permitted to serve in the enlisted ranks). Jews were forbidden to own farmland or deal in livestock. In April 1933, Jewish enrollment in German secondary schools and universities was restricted so that the number of newly admitted Jews did not exceed the proportion of Jews in the total population.[1] Measures to bar Jews from German universities were soon escalated. After July 1934, Jewish law students were no longer permitted to take the qualifying exams for a career in law. A similar edict was issued against Jewish medical students in February 1935.[2]

The Nuremberg Laws

This legislative campaign to exclude Jews from German society reached a preliminary climax in the Nuremberg Laws proclaimed at the annual Nazi Party Rally in September 1935 and passed by the Reichstag by acclamation. The Reich Citizenship Law reduced Jews to the status of alien subjects without any political rights. Jews were no longer even allowed to call themselves Germans. The Reich Representation of German Jews, the Jewish umbrella organization founded in 1933 under the leadership of Leo Baeck (1873–1956) to combat Nazi antisemitism, was forced to change its name to Reich Representation of Jews in Germany. A Certificate of Descent, popularly called *Ariernachweis* (Aryan certificate), was required as a precondition of German citizenship. Jews were also forbidden to display the German flag, to proffer the Hitler salute, or to give any other manifestation of membership in the German community.

A second Nuremberg Law, the so-called "Law for the Protection of German Blood and German Honor," prohibited marriage and sexual relations between Jews and ethnic Germans. This law created the new crime of *Rassenschande* (racial defilement), extended during the war to sexual relations between foreign workers and ethnic Germans as well. Violations carried a mandatory prison sentence for the males involved in the relationship (during the war foreign male workers found guilty of *Rassenschande* routinely received the death sentence). The sexual fears that fueled racism and antisemitism were evident in the provision prohibiting Jews from employing female domestic servants of German descent under the age of 45. In November 1935, a supplementary decree to the "Law for the Protection of German Blood" extended the prohibition on marriage and sexual relations to other persons of "alien blood," specifically, "Gypsies, Negroes, and their bastards."[3]

The question of how to define a Jew became the subject of bureaucratic infighting that resulted in ludicrously complicated regulations. The "Aryan paragraph" of the Civil Service Law of April 1933 had made no distinction between full and partial Jewish ancestry. Government and party functionaries could not agree, however, on whether the Aryan or Jewish "blood" predominated in persons of mixed ancestry. Some party officials wanted persons of partially Jewish descent to be subject to the same laws as full Jews (as in the Civil Service Law), while some Interior Ministry officials argued for more favorable treatment for persons in whom the German "blood" predominated.[4] In November 1935, the Interior Ministry issued a corollary to the Nuremberg Racial Laws defining a Jew as any person descended from at least three Jewish grandparents (in contrast to the Civil Service Law, which had defined "non-Aryans" as persons descended from one or more Jewish grandparents). Persons with only two Jewish grandparents were classified as Jews as well if they belonged to the Jewish religious community or were married to Jews. Despite all the effort expended on developing "racial" criteria for determining who was Jewish, even a person with four non-Jewish grandparents was considered Jewish if he or she was a member of the Jewish religious community. This was consistent with the notion long cultivated by antisemites that in cases of doubt ideology provided a reliable test of Jewish "blood."

Two categories were created for persons of mixed origin. The first category, "*Mischling* of the first degree," included any person with two Jewish grandparents who did not belong to the Jewish religion and was not married to a Jewish spouse. A person with one Jewish grandparent was classified as a "*Mischling* of the second degree." Separate marriage regulations were issued for each category. A "*Mischling* of the first degree" required official consent to marry a German or a "*Mischling* of the second degree." Marriage to another "*Mischling* of the first degree" was permitted, as was marriage to a Jew, but in that case the *Mischling* would be classified as a Jew. A "*Mischling* of the second degree," on the other hand, did not require special permission to marry a German, but was prohibited from marrying a Jew or another "*Mischling* of the second degree" and required special permission to marry a "*Mischling* of the first degree." Persons of both mixed categories continued to be excluded from the civil service and the party, and could serve in the army only as common soldiers.

The Nuremberg Laws legalized a system of segregation and, in effect, reduced Jews who remained in Germany to the legal status of the pre-emancipation era. "No past services," Winston Churchill wrote in 1935, "no proved patriotism, even wounds sustained in war, could procure immunity for persons whose only crime was that their parents had brought them into the world."[5] The Nuremberg Laws also spawned a huge variety of discriminatory regulations on the local and regional level. Municipal and district ordinances prohibited Jews from attending movie theaters or using public swimming pools, parks, and other recreational facilities. Towns and villages put up signs saying "Jews are not wanted here." While the national boycott of Jewish businesses in April 1933 was abandoned after one day at the behest of Reich economic officials, boycotts were often continued on the local level. Public employees, party members, and SA members were forbidden to patronize Jewish stores. Punitive measures sometimes extended to Germans perceived to be too friendly to Jews. Public works contracts, for instance, were withheld from contractors who did business with Jews. The steady stream of propaganda and legislation had their inevitable effect on informal social relations. On a daily basis, in countless ways, Jews faced assaults on their self-esteem—condemned to a kind of "social death."[6] Even people who were not ill-disposed to Jews broke off all social contact for fear of public scorn and ostracism. Although existing marriages were not affected by the Nuremberg Laws (a concession to the Churches), many Germans felt pressured to divorce their Jewish spouses. Nonetheless, only one in ten mixed marriages ended in divorce, and several thousand Jews were thereby able to survive the Holocaust in Germany.

If nonetheless some members of the Jewish community regarded the Nuremberg Laws with a certain sense of relief, it was because they seemed to provide a legal basis for the continued existence of Jews in Germany, even if only as an alien minority in segregated institutions. The Jewish community was still permitted to operate its own schools, newspapers, health services, and cultural institutions, and public funds were still used to pay for teachers' salaries. While not permitted to display the swastika, Jews were permitted to display the star of David. Perhaps to mollify the angry reactions that could be expected from abroad, the Nazis announced that the Nuremberg Laws marked the end of legal measures against Jews. Although few German Jews still retained the illusion that the Nazi regime would be short-lived, many hoped that the Nuremberg Laws, despite their discriminatory provisions, would put an end to the random, fitful, extralegal violence that SA and party members had directed against Jews since the beginning of the Nazi regime. The authorities, it was hoped, would now control the outrages of the radical rank and file. For a time, physical violence against Jews did in fact decline, partly as a result of the regime's efforts to project an image of normality to the world during the Olympic Games in Garmisch-Partenkirchen and Berlin in 1936. In deference to the expected influx of foreign visitors, public display of extreme antisemitic slogans was prohibited in January 1936.

Escalation of anti-Jewish measures

Even in the Olympic year, however, the flood of antisemitic decrees and regulations continued, totaling more than 2,000 in the course of the Nazi era. In March 1936, family allowances for Jewish families with more than one child were discontinued. In October 1936, Jewish teachers were prohibited from tutoring non-Jews even on a private basis. After the Olympics the Nazis again escalated their anti-Jewish campaign. On 15 April 1937, Jews were no longer permitted to earn degrees in any field at German universities. A secret decree of 12 June 1937 stipulated that Jews convicted of violating the law against sexual relations with Germans were to be interned in a concentration camp after serving their prison sentence.

The year 1938 brought a new wave of antisemitic legislation designed to force Jews to leave Germany and to identify and segregate those who remained. The intensification of the anti-Jewish campaign was linked to preparations for war. Convinced that Jews had undermined the German war effort in World War I, leading Nazis wanted to make sure that Germany would not face internal opposition in case of the resumption of hostilities. Germany's foreign policy successes and increasing economic self-sufficiency also made Germany less vulnerable to foreign retaliation. In July 1938, Jewish physicians and lawyers were forced to close their practices. Only a small minority of doctors and lawyers were permitted to continue to serve an exclusively Jewish clientele.

To prevent Jews from passing as Germans, Jews were barred from taking "German names," while parents of "Aryan" descent were prohibited from giving a child a Jewish-sounding name. The Interior Ministry issued elaborate lists of permissible and prohibited names. In August 1938, the Interior Ministry ordered all Jews who did not have recognizably Jewish first names to add "Sara" or "Israel" to their names. Jews were required to carry special identification cards and to show them at official places without being asked. In response to the Swiss government's protests against the large number of Austrian Jews seeking refuge in Switzerland after the annexation of Austria in March 1938, German authorities stamped the letter J into the passports of German Jews. This action was taken in October 1938 to head off the Swiss government's threat to no longer recognize German exit visas unless Jewish refugees were identified.

The "Aryanization" of Jewish enterprises

In 1938, the Nazis also escalated their efforts to squeeze Jews out of the German economy. In 1933, some 60 percent of German Jews earned their living through business or finance. Jews in the business sector (unlike the professions) were least affected by *Gleichschaltung* in the early years of Nazi rule because of the potentially disruptive consequences to the economy. The immediate extrusion of all Jews from German economic life would have wrecked efforts to reduce unemployment and caused havoc in both the production and distribution of goods and services. Some companies were reluctant to remove Jews from positions in which their skills and qualifications were needed. Although many Jews were in fact dismissed from the boards of major corporations after 1933, there was no central decree that obligated enterprises to dismiss their Jewish employees until 1938. Jewish-owned businesses also played a vital role in the retail economy. Hence the Nazis had opted for a gradual transfer of Jewish businesses into German hands. This process of "Aryanization," the transfer of Jewish enterprises to non-Jewish proprietors, remained nominally voluntary until the *Reichskristallnacht* pogrom in November 1938. But well before Aryanization became mandatory, pressure on Jewish businessmen to surrender ownership had become so great that they were in effect forced to sell. Aryanization was also conceived as a method of economic rationalization, reducing the competition for market share in overcrowded sectors of the retail economy and freeing up labor for the rearmament effort.

Pressure on Jewish proprietors was increasingly brought to bear by party organs, municipal officials, and opportunistic businessmen interested in acquiring Jewish property at minimal cost. Through threats, blackmail, and open violence, Jews were compelled to sell their businesses, houses, valuables, and automobiles at a fraction of their true market value. German banks made large profits on the commissions from these transactions as well as on the interest from loans to prospective buyers. A significant step toward mandatory Aryanization was the decree of April 1938 requiring Jews to register all property valued in excess of 5,000 marks. In July 1938, Jews were prohibited from conducting many kinds of commercial activities, including real estate agencies, credit reference agencies, brokerage firms, marriage agencies, and building management firms.

The *Reichskristallnacht* pogrom

The increasing radicalization of anti-Jewish policy in 1938 culminated in the murderous *Reichskristallnacht* (Reich crystal night) pogrom of 9–10 November. The term derives from the shards of broken glass that littered the streets in front of vandalized Jewish homes, businesses, and synagogues in cities and towns throughout the country on the morning of 10 November. This officially sponsored pogrom marked a turning point in German policy toward the Jews. Elated by their triumph in the Czechoslovakian crisis (see Chapter 12) and encouraged, perhaps, by the relatively muted reaction of world opinion to anti-Jewish legislation to date, the Nazi leadership apparently concluded that there was no longer any need to exercise restraint or maintain even the appearance of legality in their treatment of the Jewish population in Germany. Jews were deprived of their last legal protections and subjected to the physical violence of the Nazi-organized mobs. This relapse into barbarism, the most destructive pogrom in Central Europe since the fifteenth century, marked the transition to legalized physical violence and foreshadowed the coming annihilation.

The events that led to the November Pogrom were the result of earlier anti-Jewish policies in Germany and Poland. After the Munich Agreements that resolved the Czech crisis to Germany's advantage in October 1938, the Polish government, fearing the return to Poland of some 50,000 Polish Jews living in Germany and Austria, issued a decree that in effect revoked their Polish passports as of 31 October. The German government thereupon decided to expel all Polish Jews before the 31 October deadline. On 26 October, the SS transported trainloads of Jews to the Polish–German border and forced them to proceed on foot onto Polish territory. The Polish authorities, however, refused to accept the deportees and retaliated with repressive measures against Germans living in Poland. Thereupon the SS halted further deportations on 29 October. Most of the 17,000 deportees, however, were now caught in no-man's land, unable either to enter Poland (which eventually accepted them) or return to Germany.

Among the now homeless and stateless deportees in the Polish border area was the Grynszpan family, who in 1911 had emigrated to Germany, where their son and two daughters were born. On 3 November, the Grynszpans' 17-year-old son Hershel, who was living in Paris without a valid passport or re-entry visa to Germany, heard by postcard of his family's plight. On 7 November, exasperated by the sufferings of his family and his people, he bought a hand-gun and ammunition and headed to the German embassy, demanding to see the German ambassador. He was referred to the legation's third secretary, Ernst vom Rath. Grynszpan shot the German diplomat five times. Vom Rath died of his wounds on the evening of 9 November.

The Nazis immediately set out to exploit the assassination. Newspapers presented it as an attack by "international Jewry" against the German Reich. The pogrom that started at about midnight on 9 November was orchestrated by Propaganda Minister Goebbels. Already on 7 November, German newspaper editors had been instructed to give the assassination maximum publicity. News reports and editorials were to make the "clique of Jewish emigrants" responsible for the deed, the consequences of which would be borne by the Jews in Germany.

The annual meeting of "old fighters" in Munich on 9 November, the fifteenth anniversary of Hitler's unsuccessful putsch attempt in 1923, gave Goebbels the opportunity to set off the pogrom while maintaining the fiction that the anti-Jewish actions were spontaneous expressions of popular wrath. Goebbels used the occasion for a frenzied antisemitic tirade. He told the assembled party functionaries that the German people demanded revenge. The party, he said, would neither prepare nor organize anti-Jewish demonstrations, but would do nothing to stop them if they should occur. An internal party investigation of the events of 9–10 November later confirmed that his audience readily understood that they were to carry out the pogrom without appearing publicly as its organizers.[7]

All over Germany the word went out to local party organs and the SA, who then unleashed an orgy of sadism and destructiveness. Thirty-five Jews were killed in the course of the night, and many more committed suicide or died later as a result of their injuries. Jewish shops, synagogues, and homes were plundered, burnt, and vandalized. One hundred and seventy-seven synagogues (according to the official report, which understated the damage) and some 7,500 shops (including a number of shops that were no longer owned by Jews but had kept their former names) were destroyed. The police were ordered not to interfere except to prevent looting and to insure that non-Jewish property was not damaged. Extensive looting occurred anyway, and police raids were later conducted on suspected party members to try to recover the lost valuables. On the orders of Reinhard Heydrich (1904–42), chief of the Security Service (SD) of the SS, valuable Jewish archives were seized and thousands of Jewish men were taken into so-called "protective custody" in concentration camps. Some 30,000 Jewish men arrested after 9 November were interned at Dachau, Sachsenhausen, and Buchenwald, a camp constructed near Weimar in summer 1937. Release for the prisoners could only be obtained if their families made arrangements to emigrate.

On Goebbels's instructions the press justified the pogrom as a long overdue outburst of popular indignation against Jewish perfidy. Most of the German public disapproved of the pogrom, however, if only because of the disruption of law and order and the extensive damage to property. Some party leaders, too,

Table 3 Nazi concentration and extermination camps

Concentration camps	Date opened	Date evacuated or liberated	Satellite camps
Dachau	22 March 1933	29 April 1945	169
Sachsenhausen	August 1936	22 April 1945	61
Buchenwald	15 July 1937	11 April 1945	134
Flossenbürg	3 May 1938	23 April 1945	92
Mauthausen	June 1938	5 May 1945	56
Neuengamme	Fall 1938	29–30 April 1945	73
Ravensbrück	15 May 1939	30 April 1945	42
Stutthof (Danzig)	1 September 1939	after 27 January 1945	107
Auschwitz (I)	20 May 1940	27 January 1945	38
Gross-Rosen	2 August 1940	February 1945	99
Natzweiler-Struthof	1 May 1941	after September 1944	49
Lublin-Majdanek	October 1941	22–24 July 1944	10
Auschwitz II (Birkenau)	26 November 1941	27 January 1945	
Auschwitz III (Monowitz)	31 May 1942	27 January 1945	
Herzogenbusch-Vught	5 January 1943	5–6 September 1944	13
Riga (Latvia)	15 March 1943	after 6 August 1944	17
Bergen-Belsen	April 1943	15 April 1945	
Warsaw	15 August 1943	after 24 July 1944	
Dora-Mittelbau	27 August 1943	9 April 1945	29
Kauen (Lithuania)	15 September 1943	after 14 July 1944	8
Vaivara (Estonia)	15 September 1943	3 October 1944	10
Klooga (Estonia)	September 1943	19 September 1944	3
Krakow-Plaszow	11 January 1944	15 January 1945	

Extermination camps	Dates gas chambers or vans in operation	Number of victims (minimum numbers)
Kulmhof/Chelmno	8 December 1941–March 1943, Summer 1944	152,000
Auschwitz-Birkenau	January 1942–November 1944	over 1,000,000
Belzec	17 March 1942–Spring 1943	over 600,000
Sobibór	7 May 1942–Fall 1943	250,000
Treblinka	23 July 1942–October 1943	700,000–900,000
Lublin-Majdanek	Summer 1942–July 1944	200,000, including 60,000 Jews

were concerned about the scale of the destruction and its impact on the economy. On 10 November the *Völkischer Beobachter*, the official party newspaper, published a call to desist from any further actions and promised that redress for the murder of vom Rath would now be achieved by legislative means. Two days later, on 12 November, Hermann Göring, as head of the Four-Year Plan, convened a meeting of party and government officials to assess the results of the pogrom. "I am not going to tolerate a situation in which the [German] insurance companies are the ones to suffer," he proclaimed.[8] He announced that the Führer had requested him to resolve the Jewish question once and for all through decisive and coordinated action. The aim, he said, must be to entirely eliminate Jews from the economy as rapidly as possible, so that demonstrations that destroy property would no longer be necessary.

Aryanization was now made compulsory by law. Of the approximately 100,000 Jewish-owned businesses in Germany in 1933, some 40,000 still existed at the time of the November pogrom.[9] From 1 January 1939, Jews were officially forbidden to conduct their own businesses. Aryanization of large enterprises was carried out by the Ministry of Economics; smaller enterprises were placed under the jurisdiction of local and regional government bodies. "The destruction of the economic existence of the Jews and the step-by-step expropriation of their assets," the German historian Frank Bajohr has written, "stand as one of the largest transfers of wealth in recent European history."[10] Göring insisted that the profits of Aryanization redound to the state rather than the party, as Goebbels had wanted. The state also confiscated the insurance funds that were due to the victims of the pogrom. The Jewish community was held liable for all the damages incurred. A fine of 1 billion marks was collected by the Reich Ministry of Finance from wealthier Jews based on their ability to pay.

In the aftermath of the *Reichskristallnacht* pogrom, measures to totally separate Jews from all sectors of public life and thus pressure them to leave were enacted in a flurry of decrees. Restrictive measures previously adopted only on a local or regional level now became national law. Jews were prohibited from entering German parks, forests, theaters, concerts, or cultural exhibits. On 15 November, Jews were barred from attending German schools. In December 1938, Jews were no longer permitted to own automobiles. Forced emigration and the confiscation of Jewish property now became official policy throughout the German Reich. Jews were no longer to be tolerated as an isolated minority in Germany; they were to be removed altogether. In 1939 the Nazis quashed the last vestiges of independence of the Jewish community to conduct its own cultural, educational, and social activities. Jewish publications were banned, and Jewish community organizations came under the direct control of the Gestapo. Jewish life in Germany and Austria was to be stamped out.

Jewish emigration

The violence of the *Reichskristallnacht* pogrom was intended to further the overall aim of Nazi policy since 1933, which was to pressure Jews to leave Germany. There was no unanimity in the party, however, on just how the expulsion of Jews was to be accomplished. One faction, largely concentrated in the SA and typified by the fanatical Nuremberg *Gauleiter* Julius Streicher (1885–1946), editor of the biweekly antisemitic tabloid, *Der Stürmer*, pressed for violent methods to oust the Jews from German society. Almost immediately after Hitler became chancellor, SA-sponsored street terror and hooliganism began, with Jews as primary targets. It was mainly to appease the disgruntled SA militants that Hitler authorized the national boycott against Jewish-owned stores, lawyers, and physicians in April 1933.[11] Streicher was appointed by Hitler to head the committee planning the nationwide boycott, the announced purpose of which was to retaliate against Jewish-sponsored boycotts of German goods abroad. After the end of the official boycott physical assaults against individual Jews and Jewish businesses continued sporadically without official sanction. Perpetrators, however, almost always escaped arrest or prosecution.

Some Nazis criticized the SA's campaign of physical violence, not on humanitarian grounds, to be sure, but because it undermined discipline and order, caused property damage, provoked western charges of human rights abuses, invited retaliatory measures, and seemed an ineffective and counterproductive way of ridding Germany of its Jewish population. Hjalmar Schacht and later Hermann Göring in his capacity as chief of the Four-Year Plan deplored the adverse impact on the German economy of vandalism against Jewish stores and businesses. Some SS leaders also considered the terrorist activities of the SA and party hooligans to be crude and inefficient. They prided themselves on their superior professionalism and sought to promote emigration on a more rational and systematic basis.

The greatest obstacles to Jewish emigration from Germany were the difficulty of obtaining entry permits to other countries and the stringent limitations on German currency, foreign exchange, and personal belongings that could be taken out of the country. Many European nations had instituted immigration barriers and currency restrictions in response to the Great Depression. A flight tax had already been introduced in Germany by Chancellor Brüning at the height of the economic crisis to slow the outflow of German currency. The Nazis added further currency restrictions, which limited opportunities for Jews willing to emigrate and reinforced the reluctance of other countries to take in Jewish refugees. Even countries without anti-Jewish immigration quotas were unwilling to accept indigent Jewish refugees for fear they might become public charges. Paraguay, for instance, would only take refugees who were prepared to buy land. French and Belgian laws made it very difficult for foreigners to earn a living. This served the Nazi purposes well, as they hoped to export antisemitism by making sure that Jewish refugees would be seen as a social problem in host countries. Even if they could afford the transatlantic passage, only Jews with proof of employment or guaranteed financial support could gain entry into countries such as the United States and Australia that had traditionally welcomed foreign immigrants.

Restrictive American practices in issuing visas meant that fewer than half of the annual quota of 26,000 immigrants from Germany were admitted to the United States in the years from 1933 to 1938. Only in 1938–39 was the annual quota filled, mainly by Jewish immigrants.[12] Failure to gain admission and inhospitable conditions in countries of destination forced or persuaded some 16,000 of the 53,000 Jews who had left Germany in the first great wave of emigration in 1933–34 to return to the Third Reich.

Under pressure from his liberal supporters, President Franklin Roosevelt called an international conference to discuss the problem of Jewish refugees in 1938. However, aside from the creation of an Inter-Governmental Committee on Refugees to negotiate more favorable emigration terms with the Nazis, the conference, held at the French resort Evian-les-Bains on the Lake of Geneva in July 1938, produced minimal results. Officials justified their inaction on the grounds that they did not want to give the Germans a reason to increase their pressure on Jews to leave. The United States refused to place the subject of US quotas on the agenda, while Britain refused to discuss the question of Palestine.[13] The French, too, were more interested in finding a haven for their own refugees than in providing a refuge for German Jews. Germany, which supported Jewish emigration to Palestine but opposed the creation of a Jewish state, was not invited to the conference. The evident reluctance of states to accept Jewish refugees may have emboldened the Nazis to escalate their persecution of Jews.

Ruled by Britain under a League of Nations mandate, Palestine was the main destination of Jewish refugees from Germany before the British, under Arab pressure, restricted Jewish immigration in 1937. The British thus reversed their earlier support for Zionism, the movement to establish a Jewish state in the ancient biblical land of Israel. The Jewish community in Germany was itself divided between a minority of Zionists and a majority of assimilationist Jews who continued to regard themselves, at least until 1935, as Germans of Jewish faith. By defining Jewishness in confessional terms, the Central Association of German Citizens of Jewish Faith, the main organization of German Jews founded in 1893, hoped to invalidate the arguments of racialists who asserted that ethnic differences precluded full Jewish assimilation into German society. Assimilationist Jews thought they could negotiate with the regime to ensure their continued lawful existence in Germany. Jews who were not active on the left thought they might be safe from Nazi terror. The Federal Association of Jewish Soldiers at the Front pointed out that 12,000 German Jews had lost their lives fighting for Germany in World War I. Up to 1938 some assimilationist Jews still hoped that a viable, if segregated, Jewish community could be maintained in Germany.

The Nazis, however, favored the Zionists because they shared their central assumption that Jews constituted a separate national and ethnic group. The German authorities permitted Zionist activities in the Jewish community in the hopes that Jews would be persuaded to emigrate to Palestine rather than to one of the neighboring countries in Europe.[14] Up to 1935, however, the Zionist Organization, which operated the Palestine Office in Germany, accepted for immigration only younger Jews with the kinds of skills needed in the Jewish settlements.[15]

To promote Jewish emigration while at the same time restricting the outflow of Jewish capital, the German Economics Ministry signed the *Haavara* Agreement with the Jewish Agency in Palestine in August 1933, permitting emigrating German Jews to use a portion of their assets to purchase German products for export to Palestine. This agreement stimulated German exports and had the additional advantage of counteracting efforts to organize an international boycott of German goods in protest against anti-Jewish persecution. A similar agreement with Britain in March 1936 permitted Jewish immigrants to transfer a portion of their funds by contracting for German exports to Britain. The SS also supported efforts of Zionist leaders to arrange illegal immigration into Palestine. About 47,000 Jews found refuge in Palestine legally between 1933 and 1941, and several thousands more did so illegally.[16]

After *Reichskristallnacht*, restrictions for entry into the United States were eased, but as war approached, increasing fear of the infiltration of Nazi spies added another obstacle to immigration from Germany. Ultimately, however, the United States became the most important country of refuge, accepting more than 130,000 German and Austrian Jews. Britain took in the largest number of German Jews in Europe, over 50,000 by the start of the war. The British also organized a special children's transport to rescue Jewish children after *Reichskristallnacht*.

Role of the SS

The SS increasingly sought to force the pace of Jewish emigration and eventually succeeded in taking charge of the program from the Interior Ministry. On 24 January 1939, Göring signed an order charging Reinhard Heydrich with the task of solving "the Jewish question by emigration and evacuation in the most favorable way possible, given present conditions."[17] From late 1934 on, the leading specialist on the "Jewish Question" in the Security Service (SD) of the SS was a colorless bureaucrat by the name of Adolf Eichmann (1906–62), who, like Hitler, had grown up in Austria. In 1937, he traveled to Palestine to explore the possibilities of increased Jewish immigration. His big chance came after the annexation of Austria in 1938. In August of that year he headed the newly created Reich Central Emigration Bureau in Vienna, based on his own plans for a ruthlessly efficient central organization to expedite the emigration process. Through levies on wealthier Jews and solicitations from foreign Jewish organizations, he developed a fund to be used for poorer Jews who could not afford the transportation costs. He also used the threat of incarceration against Jews who were reluctant to emigrate. By November 1938 some 50,000 Jews (of an Austrian Jewish community of some 200,000) had left the country under duress. Similar centers for forced emigration were opened in Berlin and in the Czech capital of Prague after its occupation by the Germans in March 1939.

Yet, the Nazis' confiscatory policies and stringent restrictions on what emigrants could take with them impeded the official goal of accelerated emigration. In early 1939, supposedly to prevent the circumvention of currency restrictions by emigrants, Jews were forced to surrender all jewelry and valuables containing gold, silver, platinum, or precious stones to purchasing offices of the Economics Ministry at a fraction of their true value. Increasingly punitive taxes also reduced the funds available for travel. Nonetheless, almost 80,000 Jews still managed to leave Germany, Austria, and German-occupied Czechoslovakia (where some 5,000 German Jews had earlier sought refuge) in 1939. By the start of the war on 1 September 1939, about half of the prewar Jewish population in Germany and Austria had emigrated, many of them to neighboring countries where they would soon again fall under German control. War would obstruct the increasingly desperate efforts of Jews to leave Germany and German-controlled territories and provide the opportunity and necessary cover for systematic annihilation (see Chapter 15).

12 The origins of the Second World War

From the start of his rule Hitler was determined to achieve several major aims in foreign affairs: the reversal of the Treaty of Versailles, the creation of a greater Reich of all German-speaking peoples, the conquest of *Lebensraum* in the east, and the establishment of a new order in Europe dominated by the "Germanic race." Many of these aims, which he had stated quite openly in the two volumes of *Mein Kampf*, had the full support of the military and economic elite. They could only be achieved, however, by stages, and then only if Germany's potential enemies failed to take measures to forestall German rearmament and aggression. Yet the leaders of the victorious nations of World War I failed to take such measures while there was still a chance of avoiding war. Believing that the responsibilities of power would moderate the Nazis' radical aims, they thought that the best way to insure peace and stability in Europe was through a policy of compromise and appeasement.

The appeasement policy

"Appeasement" is an interesting example of a word whose meaning has changed as a result of historical experience. Its positive connotations of making peace and settling strife (the sense in which it was used in the Locarno Treaty in 1925) have been obscured by its negative connotation of making concessions to a potential aggressor. Yet the appeasement policy pursued by British and French leaders in the 1930s was not a policy of cowardice or passivity in the face of threats. It was an active policy of preventing war based on the premise that Europe could not survive another bloodbath of the kind that had occurred from 1914 to 1918. Since memories of the Great War were still very much alive in the 1930s, appeasement was at least in part the result of a history lesson too well learned. By the late 1920s most educated people subscribed to the view that the Great War was a tragic accident that could have been prevented if only the great powers had not cut short the diplomatic process by a premature resort to arms. At the heart of appeasement, then, lay the conviction that differences between nations can and must be resolved by negotiation rather than the use of force. This principle was embodied in the Covenant of the League of Nations, which committed member nations not to go to war before submitting their disputes to arbitration.

A second motive for appeasement was the growing disillusionment with the Treaty of Versailles in Britain and to a lesser extent in France. By the late 1920s even non-German historians were writing that guilt for the Great War could not be pinned on the Germans alone, and by 1933 it was generally acknowledged that some of Germany's grievances were justified.[1] Some British leaders, having concluded that Versailles was an instrument of French ambitions, opposed French military intervention to force German compliance out of fear of provoking a new round of fighting.

Most importantly, Versailles came to be widely viewed as the primary cause of the Nazi ascendancy. If Nazism was a disease caused by Versailles, would not modification of its terms bring about a remission? Proponents of appeasement assumed that the radical nationalism of the Germans would abate once their legitimate national grievances and aspirations were met. From that perspective it seemed prudent to avoid any actions—including rearmament—that might provoke a hostile German response.

But appeasement would not have gone as far as it did if it had not been for a third important motive, the fear of communism. Appeasement was the policy of British and French conservatives who feared communism even more than they disliked fascism. Their slogan, "Better Hitler than Stalin," which was actually used in a British election campaign, captures the basic political orientation of western conservatives. In the French parliamentary elections in 1936 right-wing opponents of the socialist candidate Leon Blum (1872–1950) even used the slogan, "Better Hitler than Blum." Much as they might have disdained fascism as a political system in their own countries, many British and French conservatives recognized its value as a bulwark against communism in central Europe. A strong National Socialist Germany and Fascist Italy seemed the best guarantee against the expansion of Soviet influence in the heart of Europe. Ultimately the appeasers hoped to integrate Nazi Germany into a stable European order that would keep the Soviet menace at bay. Appeasement was not a generalized unwillingness to fight against dictatorship: it was a specific unwillingness to fight against right-wing authoritarianism for fear that this would encourage the spread of communism.

The Conservative Party under Prime Ministers Stanley Baldwin (1867–1947) and, from 1937 to 1940, Neville Chamberlain (1869–1940) dominated British politics in the 1930s. It is often forgotten that appeasement enjoyed strong public support in Britain. Indeed, Chamberlain was welcomed back from his meeting with Hitler at the Munich Conference in October 1938 as a hero who had secured "peace for our time."[2] While the French were more divided on the efficacy of appeasement, the realities of power obliged them to follow the British lead in diplomatic relations with Germany.

The Popular Front

There was a left-wing alternative to appeasement, but it had limited public support in France and virtually none in Britain. This was the strategy of uniting all center to left political factions into an antifascist front. The "Popular Front" strategy originated with the Communist Party in France and was subsequently adopted as the official policy of the Moscow-directed Communist International (Comintern). To make cooperation more palatable to potential allies on the left the communists pledged to renounce revolutionary aims for the duration of the broader struggle against fascism.

Popular Front coalitions won elections in France and Spain in 1936, but in Britain the communists were too weak to play a significant role in public affairs. Its communist connections made the Popular Front anathema not only to conservatives but to many liberals and social democrats as well. The Comintern's official 1935 definition of fascism as "the openly terrorist dictatorship of the most reactionary elements of finance capitalism," though somewhat more nuanced than its earlier definition of fascism as simply "the terrorist dictatorship of big capital," was hardly suited to attract much support in the west. Western socialists committed to peace and disarmament suspected communists of wanting to precipitate a war against Germany, while Trotskyists accused Stalinists of turning their backs on social revolution, particularly in Spain, where the Popular Front government was defeated in a bitter civil war—a war that foreshadowed the horrors of the coming war in Europe. Leon Blum, who was elected to head a Popular Front government in France in May 1936, was forced to resign under pressure from right and left in June 1937. Criticism of appeasement from the ranks of the British Labor Party was muted by strong currents of pacifism and opposition to any preparations for war. Perhaps the most outspoken critic of appeasement was the maverick Conservative and defender of British imperial interests, Winston Churchill. But even Churchill, a strong British nationalist, admired Hitler's leadership in restoring German national pride after the humiliation of World War I.[3]

The end of reparations

Well before Hitler came to power the victors of World War I had already made some important concessions to Germany. The Allies had ended their occupation of the Rhineland in 1930, five years before the date fixed in the Versailles Treaty. In 1931 the American President Herbert Hoover announced a one-year moratorium on reparations and war debts as a measure to revive the international economy. Payments were never resumed (although after World War II Germany was held accountable for the repayment of interest on the loans that the German government had taken to pay reparations). Germany had paid less than a fifth of its original debt. Thus Hitler had the advantage of coming to power at a time when the urge to conciliate a peaceful Germany was strong.

In the first year of his rule Hitler did his best to present a moderate and reasonable face to the world. In February 1933 the German delegation, which had been withdrawn by the Papen government in September 1932, returned to disarmament negotiations in Geneva. To be sure, there was little effort to conceal the internal Nazi campaign of terror against the left. But virulent anti-Marxism could, after all, be construed as evidence of the essentially conservative and constructive nature of the regime. Persecution of Jews, too, was carried out under the guise of combating political disloyalty and subversion. In the early years Jews were arrested primarily on the pretext of safeguarding law and order from the alleged subversion of the left. The rationale used to gain Hindenburg's approval for the removal of Jews from the Civil Service in April 1933 was the necessity of safeguarding state secrets. Of course, the regime could not afford to entirely ignore the potentially adverse reaction of foreign governments to repression in Germany. That is why the official boycott of Jewish-owned stores ended after only one day, although Goebbels threatened to extend it if retaliatory measures were taken to boycott German goods abroad.

The Geneva Disarmament Conference

Why did not the Allies prevent the Germans from rearming when they had the power to do so? Arms control was the most important international issue of the years 1932 and 1933. The charter of the League of Nations, which Germany had joined after signing the Locarno Treaty in 1925, called for the mutual disarmament of all nations. At the international disarmament conference convened in Geneva in February 1932 the Brüning government demanded that all nations reduce their arms to the level imposed on Germany by Versailles, but in September the German delegation was withdrawn in protest against the unwillingness of the Allies to treat Germany as an equal. Indeed, by calling for a reduction of French troops to the German level, the German government could claim to be more genuinely committed to disarmament than the western countries.

In December 1932, in response to the German withdrawal, which lasted until Hitler resumed negotiations in March 1933, the western powers had accepted the right of Germany to military parity on condition of German adherence to a system of collective security. Hitler's efforts to free Germany from arms restrictions did not, therefore, seem to mark a departure from previous German policy; nor were these efforts necessarily perceived to be in conflict with his declarations of peaceful intentions. The Germans could, after all, plead their case for parity on the principle of the equal right of all nations to ensure their own security. The threat of Soviet communism, revived during the Great Depression, also served as a credible argument for a strong German defense.

In March 1933 Hitler accepted a plan drawn up by Britain's Conservative-dominated government of National Union under former Labour leader Ramsay MacDonald, which called for the limitation of troop strength in both France and Germany to 200,000. This would have doubled the ceiling on German forces and simultaneously reduced French forces by two-thirds (although the French were to be permitted an additional 200,000 troops in their colonies). It was the latest manifestation of a British tendency, dating back to the French occupation of the Ruhr in 1923, to view French ambitions as a potentially greater threat to continental stability than the revisionist demands of Germany. British leaders believed that collective security could only function if the defeated nations of World War I were integrated into the international system on an equal basis. Ironically, the victor nations now seemed ready to grant Hitler the parity they had denied to his predecessors. In July 1933 on Mussolini's instigation, Italy, Germany, England, and France signed a four-power peace pact in Rome, reaffirming their resolve to avoid war. However, the pact never entered into force due to Germany's withdrawal from the League.

Germany leaves the League of Nations

As the brutality and aggressiveness of the Nazi regime became more apparent in the spring and summer of 1933, the British government began to retreat from the MacDonald Plan. In negotiations in Geneva no agreement could be reached on the role of the paramilitary SA, which more and more resembled an unofficial army. The newly introduced Labor Service, though still voluntary, was also recognized by the British and French as a concealed form of military training. Reports of Germany's clandestine rearmament, including aircraft construction, which had been going on for years, called into question the credibility of the regime's claims of peaceful intent. In October 1933, under French pressure, the British presented a more restrictive version of the MacDonald Plan. It lifted the ceiling on German troop strength to 200,000, but the Versailles restrictions on heavy weaponry would remain in force, and France and Britain would be permitted to maintain their military superiority for a period of eight years. After that time, if Germany complied with the agreement, other nations were to reduce their troops in Europe to 200,000 and destroy their heavy weaponry as well.

The Germans used the opportunity afforded by this toughening of British terms to scuttle negotiations altogether. They responded with a dramatic move that had been prepared well in advance. On 14 October 1933, with Hindenburg's approval and the strong support of the *Reichswehr* leadership, which was absolutely committed to rearmament, Germany withdrew from the Disarmament Conference and from the League of Nations, thus following the example of Japan, which had quit the League in March 1933 in response to criticism of its aggression in Manchuria. At the same time Hitler again proclaimed Germany's peaceful intentions and promised that Germany would disarm totally if other nations did the same. He blamed the collapse of the disarmament talks on the failure to grant Germany full equality, thus banishing the specter of disarmament while at the same time maintaining the moral high ground as the advocate of parity and fairness.

The British hoped to salvage negotiations by acknowledging that their proposal was dead. Foreign Secretary John Simon (1873–1954) publicly conceded that durable international agreements could not be achieved against the will of so important a nation as the German Reich. The French might have been willing to take military action against the increasingly overt rearmament that could be expected now that the Reich had left the League and dissociated itself from all disarmament efforts. But they were not willing to do so without British support, not least because of the memories of the failed intervention in the Ruhr in 1923.

Hitler used this foreign policy coup to shore up support for the Nazi regime at home. It strengthened his hand in relations with the military and industrial elites as they became increasingly dependent on the National Socialist government to guarantee the international conditions for speedy German rearmament, as well as for financing the arms build-up and for legitimating it in the eyes of the German public.[4] Most Germans fully accepted the government's view that the League of Nations served as an instrument of British and French interests. Germans rejoiced that for the first time their government had successfully stood up to the victor powers and had gained the upper hand. In a plebiscite on 12 November 1933, 96 percent of eligible voters went to the polls, and 95.1 percent of these approved the government's decision to leave the League. Meanwhile, an unopposed slate of Nazi candidates was "elected" to the new Reichstag by the same overwhelming percentage. Henceforth the "coordinated" Reichstag would serve only as a convenient public forum for official speeches and pronouncements.

The Soviet Union and collective security

A ten-year nonaggression treaty with Poland in January 1934 seemed to confirm Hitler's peaceful intentions, though it was primarily intended to weaken Polish ties with France and prevent any preemptive moves against German rearmament. The Nazi government was quite nervous about potential Polish intervention and had issued instructions not to wear SA uniforms in public in Danzig or in Polish border areas.[5] The nonaggression treaty with Poland was also based on mutual hostility to Soviet Russia. Some months earlier Hitler had ended the special arrangement, dating back to 1926, under which the *Reichswehr* provided special training to the Red Army in return for the opportunity to test new and proscribed weaponry in the isolation of the vast and distant Russian steppes. The 1926 Treaty of Berlin, which had called for cooperation with the USSR, had expired in 1931 and was never renewed.

Originally the Soviets had viewed Hitler's rise to power with some ambivalence, for although he was the sworn enemy of communism, his adamant opposition to Versailles and hostility to liberal democracy seemed to offer the prospect of splitting the capitalist camp. Under instructions from the Comintern, German communists had often supported the Nazis' attacks on the Weimar parliamentary system and had cooperated with the Nazis in attempts to dislodge the SPD government in Prussia. Captive to their ideology, the Soviets refused to believe that Hitler could remain in power for long without strong working-class support. They expected a communist regime to follow the early collapse of Hitler's government. It did not take long to disabuse Stalin of this notion, however. Hitler's rapid consolidation of power and the virulence of Nazi Germany's hostility to Soviet communism convinced the Soviet leadership of the need to break out of their international isolation.

Germany's departure from the League of Nations paved the way for Soviet entry into that body in September 1934. For the next several years the Soviets would try to forge an antifascist front with the western powers, a direct challenge to the appeasement policy. Led by Foreign Minister Maxim Litvinov (1876–1951), the Soviets called for collective security against the fascist threat and for cooperation with bourgeois parties in forming Popular Front coalitions. Their efforts, however, had little success, as the western powers sought to avoid any actions that might provoke Germany into greater militancy. Western distrust of the Soviet Union and their loss of faith in the Versailles Treaty played into Hitler's hands, for the Germans could rationalize their need for arms on the basis of the growing Bolshevik threat.

Austro-fascism

The Germans could also point to a basic contradiction in the postwar settlement: It was ostensibly based on the principle of national self-determination, but it failed to grant self-determination to ethnic Germans outside the Reich. For many Germans the *Anschluss* (union) with Austria was a top priority. Hitler himself was of Austrian birth, and the Pan-German movement in Austria had helped to form his worldview. After the collapse of the Habsburg Empire, German Austrians had voted for union with Germany in March 1919, for the small German Austrian rump state, now deprived of its hinterlands, no longer seemed economically viable. Article 61 of the Weimar constitution provided for union with "German Austria" and granted German Austrians the right to participate in the deliberations in the Reichstag.[6] The Allies, however, refused to permit a move that would in any way strengthen the defeated German nation. The Versailles Treaty prohibited the union of Austria with Germany, and the Treaty of Saint-Germain in August 1919 obligated the Austrians to maintain their independence. The French also blocked the Brüning government's proposal for a customs union between Austria and Germany in March 1931, a measure designed to promote German economic recovery at the height of the Great Depression. The success of the Nazis in Germany, however, contributed to the growth of the Nazi Party in Austria and renewed agitation for union with the German Reich.

While most Austrians probably favored union with Germany in principle, only a minority were prepared to become part of a National Socialist German state. Opposing the Nazis were not just the Austrian Social Democrats, who had strongly supported *Anschluss* with a democratic Germany, but also the Catholic-based Christian Social Party under Chancellor Engelbert Dollfuss (1892–1934). To counter the Nazi pressure for *Anschluss* Dollfuss turned to Mussolini, who advised him to crush the Social Democratic Party to deprive Hitler of any pretext for intervening in the name of saving Austria from "Bolshevism." In February 1934 the Austrian army used labor unrest as a pretext to strike against the Social Democrats. Using heavy artillery against worker apartment blocks constructed by the Social Democratic Vienna city government after the war, the army decimated the Social Democratic strongholds with the loss of hundreds of lives.[7]

Dollfuss established a quasifascist, authoritarian regime in which both the Social Democratic and the National Socialist parties were outlawed. Driven underground but supported by the German government, the Austrian Nazis made an armed bid for power in July 1934. Dollfuss was shot and fatally wounded as the Austrian Nazis attempted to seize the chancellery in Vienna. The coup failed, however, as the Austrian army remained loyal to the government. Mussolini moved a number of Italian divisions to the Austrian border to dissuade Hitler from intervening. The monarchist Kurt von Schuschnigg (1897–1977), Minister of Justice in Dollfuss's cabinet, became his successor and stabilized the Austrian regime.

Foiled by this first attempt to seize power in Austria, Hitler was forced to adopt a waiting game. He was unwilling to allow the Austrian question to disrupt good relations with Fascist Italy, whose support he would need to bolster his claims against the western democracies. At their first meeting in Venice in June 1934 Hitler assured Mussolini that Austria would not be annexed. It was not until Mussolini became embroiled in Ethiopia in late 1935 that the prospects for *Anschluss* once again improved.

Return of the Saarland and remilitarization

The Nazis had greater success in regaining German control of the contested Saar region by peaceful methods. The Saar was a small, coal-rich territory placed under French control for a period of 15 years after World War I, its final status to be decided by plebiscite. This plebiscite, held in January 1935, resulted in a 90.8 percent vote in favor of full reincorporation into the German Reich. The outcome of the vote in the Saar was hardly surprising as its population was entirely German. Nonetheless it demonstrated to the world the popularity of the Hitler regime. The Führer received an enthusiastic reception when he traveled to Saarbrücken on the day of its transfer from French to German control.

Buoyed by this triumph and firmly in the saddle at home, Hitler decided the time was right to openly renounce the restrictive military clauses of the Versailles Treaty, which had long been breached in practice in any case. Rearmament was the cause that cemented the alliance between Hitler and the military leadership. In March 1935, preempting a British disarmament plan drawn up to induce the Germans to re-enter the League, Hitler announced that Germany would reintroduce universal military training and build up the *Wehrmacht* to a strength of 36 divisions—more than three times the number permitted under the Versailles Treaty. The decision for rearmament had been made long before; however, its open implementation was delayed until conditions were favorable. The construction of an air force (the *Luftwaffe*), banned under the terms of Versailles but secretly under way for years, was now openly acknowledged. Hitler rationalized rearmament on the grounds that the Allies had failed to disarm as called for in the Versailles Treaty, and Germany had to be prepared to confront the growing Soviet army of close to a million men.

Hitler had correctly foreseen that the French government would not undertake military action to prevent German rearmament. In October 1934 the tough-minded French Foreign Minister Louis Barthou had been assassinated by the Ustase, a Croatian fascist organization, while he was escorting the king of Yugoslavia on a state visit to France. Barthou was replaced by the more appeasement-minded Pierre Laval (1883–1945) who would become the main French political leader to collaborate with the Nazis during the war. At this time, however, Laval was more interested in appeasing Mussolini in an effort to gain his support against Hitler. The French called a conference with British and Italian leaders to deliberate on common measures to meet Germany's new assertiveness. The three nations, meeting at the Italian resort of Stresa in April 1935, reaffirmed the Locarno Treaty of 1925 and condemned any unilateral breach of treaty obligations. But Italy's aggressive designs on Ethiopia (at that time still known as Abyssinia) would soon lead to a break in the common front. In May 1935 the French government also negotiated mutual assistance pacts with the Soviet Union and Czechoslovakia to forestall German eastward expansion.

The Anglo-German Naval Agreement

A League of Nations resolution condemned German rearmament, but French calls for sanctions against Germany were of no avail in the absence of full British support. To the consternation of the French, the British preferred to negotiate a new naval arms limitation agreement with Germany that implicitly recognized the eclipse of Versailles and retroactively sanctioned German militarization. Signed in June 1935 without prior consultation with France, this agreement permitted Germany to build up its navy to one-third the size of the British navy. It also gave Germany full parity with Britain in submarine tonnage.

The Anglo-German Naval Agreement seemed to diminish the threat of another naval arms race of the kind that had poisoned German–British relations in the period leading up to the Great War (a 3:1 ratio in naval strength was in fact what Britain had unsuccessfully sought before World War I), but the strength of the German navy allowed under the agreement substantially exceeded the ceilings imposed by the Treaty of Versailles. The agreement set limits only on tonnage, not on the kinds of ships that were permitted. Nothing could demonstrate more clearly the loss of British resolve in enforcing the postwar settlement. Yet the agreement was celebrated in Britain as a guarantee of British naval predominance. It also reinforced the confidence of British leaders that negotiations with the Hitler regime were possible and could lead to positive results.

The invasion of Ethiopia

Mussolini took advantage of the temporary Franco-British rift by launching an all-out attack on Ethiopia in October 1935. The British and French response followed a familiar pattern of appeasement. The two west European powers condemned the attack and voted in favor of League sanctions against

Italy, but failed to follow this up with effective action. The embargo on oil was never enforced, and neither nation was prepared to intervene militarily to defend the League Covenant. The former wartime allies had a greater interest in retaining Italy as a member of the "Stresa Front" against renewed German efforts to annex Austria or bring about other territorial changes in Europe. Indeed, the decision to continue to supply Italy with oil, which was vital to the Italian campaign in Ethiopia, was taken in the hopes of gaining Italian support against Hitler's move into the Rhineland in March 1936.

While some British and French politicians, including Pierre Laval, were prepared to sacrifice Ethiopia, public opinion in both countries, outraged by Italian atrocities, forced them to offer at least token condemnation of Italian aggression and delay official recognition of the Italian conquest until 1938. The German government, however, labored under no such constraints and gave Mussolini its full support. The most immediate benefit accruing to the Germans from Mussolini's war was a freer hand for intervention in Austrian affairs, as the Duce pulled out of the Stresa Front in January 1936, taking back his guarantee of Austrian independence in return for German support of his policy in Ethiopia. Inept British and French diplomacy in the Ethiopian crisis led to the worst possible outcome: it alienated Italy without preventing the conquest of Ethiopia, which was formally annexed in May 1936. The ineffectiveness of the League of Nations, which voted to end sanctions against Italy after the fall of Ethiopia, was now clearly demonstrated to the rest of the world. The moribund organization would play an insignificant role in later events.

Remilitarization of the Rhineland

The rift caused by Mussolini's Ethiopian adventure between the signatories of the Locarno Treaty now enabled Hitler to achieve his goal of reoccupying the Rhineland sooner than he had originally envisaged. On 7 March 1936 he sent a force of some 20,000 men across the Rhine to re-establish full German sovereignty over the left bank. This was more than a breach of the Versailles Treaty; it violated the Locarno Treaty as well, which had provided for a permanently demilitarized buffer between Germany and France. Hitler rationalized his action on the grounds that the Franco-Soviet Security Pact, which the French parliament had finally ratified at the end of February after long and bitter debate, violated the spirit of Locarno and changed the balance of power in Europe to Germany's disadvantage. Hitler assured the western governments that Germany was merely defending itself against the ever-present Soviet threat to peace. Not only did he offer to negotiate new demilitarized zones on both sides of the border with France, he even offered German re-entry into the League of Nations once the latter had been suitably reformed.

With Germany's military strength still substantially inferior to France's, German army leaders had their doubts about the wisdom of Hitler's Rhineland action, but Hitler's intuition proved correct. Despite a French warning a week earlier against any German move, the French failed to intervene. There were several reasons for this. For one thing, at the end of January the government of Pierre Laval had fallen as a result of the Ethiopian crisis. Moreover, France was in the midst of a bitterly fought election campaign that would culminate in the victory of the Popular Front coalition under the socialist Leon Blum in May. The mutual assistance pact with the Soviets, which gave Hitler his pretext for sending troops into the Rhineland, was unpopular among French conservatives and the military. Plagued by disunity, the interim French government was in no position to act decisively.

A third factor in France's failure to intervene was the lack of confidence at the top of the French military leadership. A defensive mentality predominated, symbolized by the construction, from 1929 to 1934, of the immobile and immobilizing Maginot Line, a series of military fortifications along the Franco-German border from Belgium to Switzerland. Chief of Staff General Maurice-Gustave Gamelin (1872–1958) greatly overestimated the strength of the German forces. It would not be the last time that western leaders were taken in by Hitler's exaggerations and boasts. Gamelin made a successful military operation in the Rhineland contingent on British support. This, however, was not forthcoming. The British were determined to avoid a military clash on an issue they did not regard as vital to their interests. In the end they even avoided economic sanctions, though the League passed a resolution condemning the German treaty violation. Some British politicians openly defended the German action. Indeed, public opinion in Britain favored the Germans more than the French. All the Germans had done, defenders of the Rhineland action said, was to reclaim their own backyard and strengthen their border defenses.

In retrospect it is clear that the remilitarization of the Rhineland marked an important milestone on the path to war. Some historians even suggest that it was the last time that German aggression could have been stopped short of war. Yet even at this time intervention would probably have led to some form of armed clash. Hitler had ordered his troops to make a fighting withdrawal if the French should intervene. As it was, the Germans were able to score an important victory without having to fire a shot. Politically and psychologically, the balance of power now shifted in Germany's favor. French allies reconsidered their interests in the light of the new situation. The Belgians moved toward a neutral posture and abandoned their earlier intention of extending the Maginot Line along their border with Germany. For Hitler this successful blow against the postwar settlement meant an enormous boost in prestige and popularity at home. The German people gave him 99 percent backing in the plebiscite that followed the Rhineland coup.

The civil war in Spain

Appeasement also gave the fascist powers the opportunity to intervene in the Spanish Civil War, which broke out when units of the Spanish army, including the colonial army in North Africa under General Francisco Franco (1892–1975), took up arms against the democratically elected, left-wing Popular Front government in Madrid in July 1936. The pretext for this right-wing revolt was the alleged inability of the government to maintain law and order in the politically divided country. But in reality the Spanish Civil War was a class war between right and left, rich and poor, the propertied and the dispossessed. The fascist powers supported the right-wing rebellion. For Mussolini, fresh from his Ethiopian triumph, the war offered a chance to expand his power in the Mediterranean. Close to 50,000 Italian troops were eventually dispatched to fight on the side of Franco's forces.

Germany sent no ground troops to Spain, but its contributions were highly important to Franco's cause nonetheless. German aircraft helped to ferry Franco's forces from Morocco to the mainland early in the war. For the *Wehrmacht* Spain provided an ideal testing ground for the modern weapons of war. German bombers of the notorious Condor Legion tested the effects of air attacks on civilian populations. A savage attack on the northern Spanish town of Guernica in April 1937 inspired one of Picasso's most famous paintings and came to symbolize the barbarism of air war. German submarines participated clandestinely in attacks on Spanish government vessels in the Mediterranean as well.[8]

Hoping to forestall fascist intervention, the western powers called for a moratorium on all outside aid. Britain's and France's seemingly even-handed policy of nonintervention in fact tipped the balance in favor of the fascist side. It left the Spanish government unable to procure arms in the western nations to defend itself. The Blum government in France had compelling reasons not to provide open support for their fellow Popular Front government in Spain. The French polity was so polarized that any intervention in Spain risked spreading the war into France. Volunteer units from the west, including the American Abraham Lincoln Brigade, helped to stave off defeat of the Spanish government for a time. The Soviet Union became the main source of support for government loyalists, with the consequence that communist functionaries soon came to dominate the loyalist side. The effect of communist domination, however, was to dampen the revolutionary idealism of defenders of the Popular Front.

The Spanish government's ties to the Soviet Union enabled Hitler to continue to pose as the defender of European civilization against the Bolshevik threat. The war was so useful to his purposes that he did not want it to end too soon. It served to distract the Western governments, leaving Hitler free to pursue his major ambition of territorial expansion in eastern Europe. It also deepened the gulf between Italy and the West, thus driving Mussolini further into the German embrace.

One outcome of the increasingly cordial relationship between Italy and Germany was Mussolini's official announcement of the "Berlin–Rome axis" in November 1936. Even before that Hitler had gained an important concession in Austria. In July 1936, with Mussolini's acquiescence, he signed an agreement with Austrian Chancellor Schuschnigg bringing Austria into closer alignment with Germany. In return for a German pledge of nonintervention, the Austrian chancellor promised to pursue a policy "based always on the principle that Austria acknowledges herself to be a German state."[9] Schuschnigg also promised to grant a greater role in Austrian affairs to the "national opposition," which in effect meant those who favored *Anschluss* with Germany.

The Olympic Games

The appeasement mentality manifested itself in less formal ways as well. There was no move, for instance, to boycott the Olympic Games in Berlin in August 1936, despite the openly antisemitic policies of the regime. In fact, some teams, including the Americans, kept Jewish athletes out of certain events, apparently out of deference to the racial prejudices of their German hosts. To be sure, the Nazis removed antisemitic signs and placards in Berlin for the duration of the games to polish their image abroad. Indeed, the games turned into a public relations triumph for the Germans, who ended up winning more medals than any other nation. Even the four gold medals won by the American sprinter Jesse Owens hardly tarnished the impression of Germany's athletic prowess. Hitler attended the opening and closing ceremonies and some of the track and field events. He left early on the day of Owens' victories, however, thus avoiding the congratulatory handshake he had previously proffered to the winners of other events. There was some speculation that Hitler might have been unwilling to acknowledge the superiority of an African-American athlete.

An array of foreign dignitaries visited Germany and came away favorably impressed by the achievements of the Nazi regime. Among them was David Lloyd George (1863–1945), British prime minister from 1916 to 1922, who visited Hitler at his alpine retreat in Berchtesgaden. Former British King Edward VIII (1894–1972) and his American-born wife Wallis Simpson (1896–1986), the Duchess of Windsor, visited Germany in 1937 and expressed their warm admiration of the new order. The Anti-Comintern Pact that Germany signed with Japan in November 1936 and that Italy joined in November 1937 was particularly reassuring to those who viewed fascism as a lesser evil than communism. Germany's new respectability abroad in turn enhanced Hitler's popularity at home.

Germany's enhanced status strengthened the hands of the British appeasers. Neville Chamberlain, the political leader most closely identified with the appeasement policy, replaced Baldwin as British prime minister in May 1937 with a pledge to preserve peace in Europe. Advocates of appeasement played a leading role in his administration. In November 1937 Minister of War Lord Edward Halifax (1881–1959) visited Hitler on Chamberlain's behalf with a conciliatory message. Halifax assured Hitler that Britain would not oppose some border rectifications in east-central Europe (he specifically mentioned Austria, Czechoslovakia, and Poland) on condition that all changes be effected by peaceful means. French Foreign Minister Yvon Delbos, who was known to be unhappy with the Franco-Soviet Pact, also indicated that France would have no objections to a further merging of German and Austrian domestic institutions.[10]

The Hossbach Memorandum

What the advocates of appeasement failed to take into account was that Hitler had more far-reaching goals than merely restoring the German borders of 1914 or assimilating all ethnic Germans to the Reich. He never lost sight of his ultimate goal, the conquest of *Lebensraum*. Driven by the Social Darwinist notion of unavoidable and unceasing struggle between peoples and races in which nature and providence favored "superior" races, Hitler had written in *Mein Kampf*, "The right to possess soil and territory can become a duty, if decline seems to threaten a great nation unless it extends its territory."[11] As early as February 1933, shortly after his assumption of power, Hitler had told his generals in strict confidence that Germany's living space was too small for its population.[12] In a meeting with his top military and diplomatic officials on 5 November 1937 the Führer outlined his goals with remarkable candor. The minutes of the meeting have survived in the form of the so-called Hossbach Memorandum, named after Hitler's adjutant Colonel Friedrich Hossbach (1894–1980), who took the notes. The other participants in the meeting, all pledged to strict secrecy, were Minister of War Werner von Blomberg; the heads of the three branches of the *Wehrmacht*, General Werner von Fritsch (1880–1939), Admiral Erich Raeder (1876–1960), and Hermann Göring; and Foreign Minister Konstantin von Neurath (1873–1956).

Hitler told his assembled leaders that the only solution to Germany's long-term economic, security, and population problems lay in the expansion of German living space, and this in turn could only be achieved by force. A solution must be achieved by the years 1943–45, for if Germany failed to act by that time, her relative power vis-à-vis other major powers would begin to decline. Any delay beyond this time frame also entailed the danger that Germany's modern armaments would become obsolescent and would have to be replaced. Moreover, Hitler feared that the dynamism of the Nazi movement would eventually diminish as its present leadership aged. He was convinced that he alone had the requisite will and determination to lead Germany to the fulfillment of its world mission.

While Hitler acknowledged that France and Britain opposed his plans for expansion in the east, he believed the threat from the west could be met by building up a position of overwhelming strength. His immediate objectives were to strengthen Germany's strategic position through the annexation of Austria and the destruction of Czechoslovakia, a state with considerable economic resources, military potential, and close ties to France and the Soviet Union. He believed that the governments of Britain and France had already tacitly written off Austria and the Czech state. An opportunity to liquidate Czechoslovakia might come as soon as 1938, he asserted, if France should be disabled by internal strife or if Britain and/or France should become embroiled in a war with Italy. Hence Hitler favored prolongation of the war in Spain to keep tensions in the Mediterranean alive.[13]

While none of the military leaders objected to the planned destruction of Czechoslovakia, Blomberg and Fritsch expressed their misgivings about a policy that might lead to war with Britain and France before Germany was sufficiently prepared. They also drew Hitler's attention to the strength of Czech fortifications, which might not be as easy to breach as Hitler apparently assumed. Neurath added the reservation that there was no indication of an imminent Anglo-French–Italian conflict. But Hitler dismissed their objections by reiterating his conviction that Britain and France would not intervene to save Czechoslovakia. In this he would prove to be more perspicacious than his generals.

The ouster of Blomberg and Fritsch

Hitler's generals had no fundamental objections to a policy of territorial expansion in the east. But their caution could hamper or slow down the attainment of his goals. This was probably the reason Hitler decided to strengthen his control of the *Wehrmacht*. The initiative to purge the High Command, however, came from Göring, head of the *Luftwaffe*, and Himmler, head of the SS, both of whom had long resented the army elite for blocking the expansion of their own respective fiefdoms. In February 1938 they took advantage of Blomberg's marriage to a former prostitute to force the general to retire. His cabinet position of minister of war was abolished. Hitler himself took over the functions of war minister and assumed the title of Supreme Commander. A new military staff was created for the Führer, the High Command of the *Wehrmacht* (OKW), headed by the obsequious Wilhelm Keitel (1882–1946) with Alfred Jodl (1890–1946) as chief of operations from 1939 on. Both men would retain their posts until the end of the war. Fritsch, too, was cashiered on a trumped-up charge of homosexuality and replaced by the more amenable Walter von Brauchitsch (1881–1948). Sixty generals were eventually retired in what amounted to the culmination of the *Gleichschaltung* of the army that had begun in 1933–34. Skeptics and doubters were now being replaced by reliable subordinates ready to collaborate in Hitler's plans for expansion and conquest.

   Parallel changes occurred in the Foreign Ministry, where the vain and sycophantic Joachim Ribbentrop (1893–1946) replaced the old-school diplomat Konstantin von Neurath (who was not invited to join the Nazi Party until 1937). As head of the party's Foreign Affairs Department, Ribbentrop had long functioned as a shadow foreign minister, helping to negotiate the Naval Treaty with Britain and the Anti-Comintern Pact with Japan, which was later broadened into the Berlin–Rome–Tokyo Axis. From 1936 until his appointment as foreign minister in 1938, Ribbentrop was ambassador to Britain. He came to regard the British with that mixture of resentment and contempt so typical of the attitude of Germans who could not understand why an ostensibly Nordic people rejected partnership with Germany in a worldwide division of spoils.

The *Anschluss* of Austria

Ribbentrop helped to persuade Hitler that while Britain might remain hostile to German expansion in eastern Europe, they would not go to war to prevent it. The replacement of Anthony Eden (1897–1977) as British Foreign Secretary by Lord Halifax in February 1938 seemed to confirm this impression, for Eden was an opponent of appeasement who had come into office in 1936 as a result of the government's failure in the Ethiopian crisis. Nothing, it seemed, now stood in the way of *Anschluss* (union), except the opposition of the Austrian government. On 12 February 1938 Hitler summoned Schuschnigg to Berchtesgaden and berated him for failing to live up to the terms of the 1936 agreement. Hoping to obtain German recognition of Austrian independence, Schuschnigg agreed to Hitler's demand for greater Nazi representation in the Austrian government. He amnestied hundreds of Nazi prisoners in Austria, legalized the party, and on 16 February appointed Arthur Seyss-Inquart (1892–1946) as minister of the interior with complete control over police and internal security.

Armed with these powers, Seyss-Inquart prepared for a Nazi takeover. This came sooner than even Hitler seems to have anticipated. As Nazi-inspired demonstrations and disturbances spread in Austria, Schuschnigg gambled on one last effort to change the momentum toward *Anschluss*. Defying the Nazis, he called for a popular plebiscite on Austrian independence, scheduled for 13 March. The referendum was to be worded in a way that would assure a positive outcome. Most Austrians would have found it hard to vote against a proposition that called for "a free and a German Austria, an independent and a social Austria, a Christian and a united Austria."[14]

To prevent a referendum that they were likely to lose, the Nazis decided to intervene. Using Seyss-Inquart's formal request for German aid as legal cover, German troops crossed the Austrian borders on 12 March to the welcome of enthusiastic crowds. The crushing of the Social Democrats and the liberal left in 1934 had left Schuschnigg's "Austrofascist" regime without a mass base to oppose German intervention. The next day the Austrian government, now under Seyss-Inquart, decreed the "reunion" of Austria with the German Reich. Two days later Hitler himself made a triumphant entry into Vienna, the city he had left as a penniless sidewalk artist a quarter century earlier. Before hundreds of thousands of people in the city's main square on 15 March he proclaimed the formation of the Greater German Reich. Many Germans welcomed the *Anschluss* as the long overdue completion of German unification. What Bismarck had failed to accomplish in 1871 and what was barred by the victors in 1919, Hitler achieved without firing a shot. His popularity soared to new heights. A plebiscite throughout the new Greater Reich approved the *Anschluss* by 99 percent. While this vote was obviously skewed by government pressures, the absence of a true secret ballot, and threats of reprisals against those who refused to participate, there can be no doubt but that *Anschluss* enjoyed overwhelming popular support.

The Czechoslovakian crisis

A wave of nationalist fervor now also swept through the German minority in neighboring Czechoslovakia. Some three and a half million ethnic Germans lived in the border region known as the Sudetenland, ringing the Czech part of the country. Despite its heavily German population, the Sudetenland was included in the new state of Czechoslovakia in the postwar settlement, because it had always been part of the Habsburg Empire out of which Czechoslovakia was formed. The mountain ranges that marked the ancient Habsburg borders also gave Czechoslovakia reasonably defensible frontiers.

But the Germans had the advantage of being able to invoke the principle of national self-determination, the main rationale for the creation of new states in the peace settlement that followed World War I. Statistical evidence also seemed to bear out the charge that the Sudeten German minority of 3.2 million (about a third of the Czech population) had substantially fewer opportunities for employment and advancement than the Czech majority. The leader of the Nazi-subsidized Sudeten German Party, Konrad Henlein (1898–1945), accused the Czech state of discrimination and demanded self-rule and eventual autonomy for the German-populated region. Hitler encouraged these demands as a means toward the ultimate destruction of the Czech state, an objective he had already announced to *Wehrmacht* leaders in November 1937. Cession of the well-fortified border territory would render Czechoslovakia defenseless. The German demands were deliberately escalated to thwart any possibility that partial Czech concessions to its German minority might defuse the crisis. The Czechoslovak government, however, stood firm against the Sudeten German demand for full autonomy. To underscore its readiness to defend itself, the government mobilized its forces on 20 May. This gave rise to the most serious war scare in Europe since Hitler's accession to power.

Unsure whether the French would stand by their treaty obligations to the Czechs, which would also have activated the Soviets (who by the terms of the treaty were bound to come to the defense of Czechoslovakia only if France did so), Hitler was not yet ready to risk a military confrontation in May 1938. But the defiant stance of the Czechs only reinforced his determination to take military action at the earliest favorable opportunity. On 30 May he informed his military leaders of his "unalterable decision to smash Czechoslovakia by military action in the near future" and ordered them to draw up the requisite plans for attack.[15]

A firm western pledge of support for Czechoslovakia might have deterred Hitler from an attack in the foreseeable future, all the more so as the Soviet Union seemed ready to honor its treaty obligations to Czechoslovakia if France did so. Hitler was pragmatic enough to want to avoid a repetition of the two-front war that had fatally overextended German forces in the Great War. But a change of government in France in April 1938 brought to power a more conservative regime that was even less willing to cooperate with the Soviet Union than the previous government under Leon Blum. The new premier, Edouard Daladier (1884–1970), and his foreign minister, Georges Bonnet, adhered closely to the appeasement policy that had now become dominant in Britain.

Fearing that French treaty obligations to Czechoslovakia might lead to a war from which Britain could not stand aside, Chamberlain's government was determined to find a peaceful solution to the Czech crisis. With the British urging the Czechs to take a conciliatory course in negotiations with the Sudeten Germans, Hitler took full advantage of the unmistakable desire of the western powers to avoid war. In September 1938, after Henlein had broken off negotiations with the Czech government on German instructions and riots had broken out in the Sudetenland, Hitler used the annual Nazi Party rally in Nuremberg as a forum to announce that a final resolution of the crisis was imminent.

The threat of imminent war spurred Chamberlain into action. In an extraordinary example of personal diplomacy at the highest levels, Chamberlain flew to Germany three times in the span of two weeks to meet with Hitler and attempt to resolve the dispute. At Berchtesgaden on 15 September he agreed, over the heads of Czechoslovakia's dismayed leaders, to the cession of the Sudetenland in principle, but reserved a final commitment until he had consulted his cabinet and the French government. Under pressure from Britain and France the Czechoslovakian government was forced to accept a proposal for the immediate cession of all territories with a German population of more than 50 percent.

But when Chamberlain returned to Germany a week later to deliver this concession, he found that Hitler had upped his demands. Hitler now insisted on the immediate military occupation of all territories designated by the German government, to be followed by a plebiscite to determine the final Czech–German frontier. This transparent device to deprive Czechoslovakia of all its strategic frontier territory was totally unacceptable to the Czechs, who rightly saw it as tantamount to a surrender of their nation's independence.

The Munich Agreement

The Czechs again mobilized their armed forces, and once again headlines throughout Europe proclaimed the imminent prospect of war. But Chamberlain refused to give up his quest for peace. He informed the Germans that the Czech rejection was not the last word, and then appealed to Mussolini to help persuade Hitler to enter a further round of negotiations. Hitler was forced to agree to meet lest it become too obvious that his goal was not the solution of the Sudeten question but the destruction of Czechoslovakia. Moreover, the public mood in Germany was clearly unenthusiastic about war.

Chamberlain and Daladier met with Hitler and Mussolini at Munich on 29 September and agreed to all of Hitler's demands. Hitler's only concession was to extend the deadline for completing the occupation of the Sudetenland to 10 October. The Czech government, which was not represented at Munich, had no choice but to accept these draconian terms or fight a war it would surely lose. In addition to the loss of territory, Czechoslovakia lost its frontier fortifications, important economic resources, and over a million people of Czech or Slovak origin. It was now also faced by territorial claims from Poland and Hungary and independence movements that would lead within weeks to virtual autonomy for Slovakia and the Ruthenian province of Carpatho-Ukraine. The promised plebiscites in the Sudetenland were never held. The

Czech state was reduced to virtual satellite status well before German troops marched into Prague on 15 March 1939, the anniversary of Hitler's triumphant celebration of the *Anschluss* in Vienna the year before.

At Munich Chamberlain also persuaded Hitler to sign a declaration of Anglo-German friendship as a token of "the desire of our two peoples never to go to war with one another again."[16] The declaration included a provision for mutual consultations on questions of concern to the two countries. It was this declaration that led Chamberlain on his return to assure the British public that he had secured "peace for our time." The French signed a similar pact with Germany in December 1938. At the same time, however, rearmament was speeded up in both Britain and France. Talks between their respective military staffs opened on 1 February 1939.

Apologists for Munich would later argue that the peaceful resolution of the Czech crisis had at least gained time for the west to improve its military preparedness. Critics of Munich, however, would point out that the military capacity of the Czechs and the likely involvement of the Soviet Union made the constellation of forces arrayed against Germany stronger in 1938 than in 1939. Yet there is considerable evidence that Hitler did not regard the Munich Agreement as an unalloyed triumph. He may have been concerned that another result of Munich, the reduction of tensions between Italy and Britain in the Mediterranean, would inhibit his predatory plans in the east. Hitler must also have been frustrated by the fact that compliance with the terms of the agreement would certainly tie his hands in the future. The western willingness to accommodate genuine German grievances made it more difficult to find a credible pretext for a war of conquest. The following year he would make sure that no last-minute offer of mediation would deprive him of the opportunity to launch the war against Poland.

At Munich appeasement reached its apogee. In later years "Munich" would become a virtual synonym for abject surrender to dictatorial demands. Its consequences were indeed little short of disastrous. The last surviving democracy in east-central Europe passed into the German sphere. France had to accept the disintegration of its alliance system in eastern Europe. The "Little Entente" of Czechoslovakia, Romania, and Yugoslavia was shattered, and the latter two countries, suppliers of vital raw materials to the Reich, were increasingly drawn into the German orbit. All grounds for a possible military revolt in Germany against Hitler's reckless rush to war were effectively removed. However, Munich also seems to have persuaded Hitler that Britain was likely to resist any further German advance to the east. Certainly he could no longer hope to enlist Britain as an ally in the racial struggle against the Jews and the Slavs as he had envisioned in *Mein Kampf*. The realization that Britain would never accept German expansion to the east beyond minor rectifications of the Polish–German borders brought about a reorientation of German policy toward the west. In September 1938 he issued secret instructions to the Wehrmacht to prepare for war against England with a target date of 1942.[17]

The acquiescence of the western powers to Hitler's demands at Munich reinforced Hitler's reputation for infallibility—and his own sense of it. The triumphalist post-Munich mood also contributed to the re-escalation of the internal campaign against Jews that culminated in the terrible *Kristallnacht* pogrom in November 1938. Jews were to be forced out of the Greater German Reich and their property confiscated before the start of a major war. Most significant of all, the Soviet dictator Joseph Stalin seems to have concluded from the Munich Agreement that the west was not serious about fighting fascism or containing Nazi Germany. Munich fed Stalin's overriding fear—not entirely irrational—that the west was prepared to give Germany the free hand it sought to turn its military machine against the USSR. The Soviets feared that the Hitler–Chamberlain agreement for mutual consultations would lead to the creation of an anti-Soviet front. It ultimately convinced Stalin that the Soviet Union needed to make some arrangement with Nazi Germany to avoid a war in which the Soviets would have to fight the Germans alone.

The destruction of Czechoslovakia

Hitler viewed the Munich Agreement as a stepping stone to the liquidation of the Czech state. In October 1938 he issued orders to the *Wehrmacht* to prepare plans to invade the rump Czech state in case the Czechs pursued "anti-German" policies.[18] The plans were prepared on the assumption that the Czechs would put up no resistance. Hitler's strategy was to foment disorder in Czechoslovakia, which would then enable him to occupy the country on the pretext of restoring order. He found willing tools among nationalists in the autonomous province of Slovakia under Monsignor Jozef Tiso (1887–1947), a Roman Catholic priest and head of the fascist Slovak People's Party.

Under German prodding, the Tiso government proclaimed its full independence from Prague on 14 March 1939. German troops occupied the Czech–Slovak border to counter any Czech military moves. In the hopes of preventing the final dismemberment of Czechoslovakia, Czech President Emil Hacha (1874–1945) now asked for a personal audience with Hitler in Berlin. This was a bad mistake, for it enabled Hitler to give his destruction of the Czech state an appearance of legality. Hitler presented Hacha with two alternatives: Either request German intervention and enjoy limited autonomy under Germany's benign protection or face a full-scale military invasion and the subsequent loss of all vestiges of autonomy for the Czech people. To spare his people the latter fate, Hacha gave in and signed the German terms.

The following morning German troops entered Prague. Hitler himself arrived in Prague later that day to reclaim the ancient Habsburg provinces of Bohemia and Moravia for the German Reich. Hacha remained as nominal president of the new Reich protectorate throughout the war. Slovakia retained its nominal independence under Tiso as a German satellite state. Meanwhile Hungary, which had only recently joined the Anti-Comintern Pact, seized the Carpatho-Ukrainian province of Ruthenia with German blessings.

The Polish question

Why did Hitler deliberately flout the Munich Agreements and thus undermine the appeasement policy from which he had gained so much benefit? If instead of seizing Prague he had immediately turned to negotiating a return of the German territories lost to Poland, he might have continued to enjoy the rewards of British and French appeasement. Probably he did not anticipate the vehemence of the western response to the occupation of Prague. He may have concluded that the west had already implicitly agreed to the loss of Czechoslovakian independence at Munich as long as it occurred without war. Hacha's request for German intervention, though obtained under duress, offered at least the appearance of legitimacy.

The most likely explanation for Hitler's failure to exercise more patience, however, is that he had already made up his mind to launch a war of conquest in the east in the near future to take advantage of Germany's lead in rearmament and the weakness of Britain's and France's current leadership. Germany's comparative advantage in military technology was likely to decline in the years to come. As historian Adam Tooze has convincingly shown, in an arms race with the western democracies "time was clearly not on Germany's side." With more than 20 percent of national income going to military spending, "Germany's 'wartime economy at peace' had reached a critical threshold" in 1939.[19] The liquidation of Czechoslovakia was a precondition for the successful prosecution of an eastern campaign as it greatly strengthened Germany's economic and military resources while eliminating an adversary that harbored many German émigrés and cultivated close ties with the Soviet Union.

The British guarantee to Poland

Less than a week after the occupation of Prague, Ribbentrop issued the German demand for the return of Danzig (now Polish Gdansk), a free city under the governance of a high commissioner appointed by the League of Nations. The Germans also demanded an extra-territorial highway across the Polish Corridor to connect the Reich with East Prussia. In return the Germans offered to guarantee Poland's independence. In a sense these demands were less unreasonable than their earlier claim to the Sudetenland, which had not been a part of Germany before World War I. Moreover, the Lithuanians provided a precedent for negotiated border rectifications by returning the city of Memel (now the Lithuanian city of Klaipeda) to Germany on 23 March in return for a German guarantee of their national independence. Under British pressure Lithuania had already turned over direction of local affairs in Memel to ethnic Germans in 1935.

But for the Poles, fearful of sharing the fate of Czechoslovakia (though they had participated in Czech partition by seizing the principality of Teschen), the return of the territories acquired from Germany after World War I was not negotiable. Although Danzig was a predominantly German city, its port facilities were important to the Polish economy and to its security. British and French leaders, under the pressure of public outrage against the surrender of Czechoslovakia, were now determined not to repeat the mistake of Munich or, for that matter, of July 1914, when the British failed to give swift and clear warning of their intention to fight. On 31 March 1939 they offered a guarantee of unconditional military support in the event that Poland was forced to go to war to defend its independence. The British guarantee was also a function of growing British fears that Poland might remain neutral in a war between Germany and the west.

The effect of the unconditional guarantee, extended to Romania and Greece after Mussolini attacked Albania on 7 April, was to reinforce the Polish refusal to negotiate territorial revisions with Germany. The Germans responded to the unconditional guarantee by declaring the Anglo-German Naval Agreement invalid and abrogating the 1934 nonaggression pact with Poland. On 11 April 1939 Hitler ordered the Wehrmacht to prepare plans for an attack on Poland with a target date of 26 August. On 22 May Germany and Italy concluded a firm military alliance, known as the Pact of Steel, promising mutual support in case of war. A day later Hitler summoned military leaders to the chancellery and told them of his decision to attack Poland at the first suitable opportunity. "Danzig is not what it is about at all," he told the assembled Wehrmacht brass. "It is a question of expanding our living space in the east and of securing our food supplies, as well as the settlement of the Baltic problem."[20]

Whether anything could have deterred Hitler from using force against Poland from this point on is an open question. Critics of Britain's abrupt turnaround in March 1939 have pointed out that Poland, a quasidictatorship with aggrieved Ukrainian and Belorussian minorities, was less defensible than democratic Czechoslovakia had been in the previous year. Britain and France failed to follow up their guarantee to Poland with tangible military support. Most critically, Britain and France failed to forcefully pursue the one option that might have deterred a German attack: an alliance with the Soviet Union.[21]

The Nazi–Soviet Nonaggression Treaty

Soviet policy toward the west had undergone an important shift in 1934 when the USSR, alarmed by the National Socialist consolidation of power in Germany, joined the League of Nations and ended nearly 17 years of international isolation. The Stalinist policy of eliminating the SPD had contributed to the collapse of the Weimar Republic and played into Nazi hands. Stalin had welcomed the split in the capitalist camp that Hitler's accession to power seemed to presage. By 1934, however, he recognized that the Nazi regime represented a far greater threat to the USSR than the western capitalist states. In 1935 Stalin told British Foreign Minister Anthony Eden that "the only way to meet the present situation was by some scheme of pacts. Germany must be made to realize that if she attacked any other nation she would have Europe against her."[22] For several years, it seems, the Soviets were quite sincere in seeking a military commitment from the west that would provide some security against the German threat. Under Foreign Minister Maxim Litvinov the Soviets championed collective security against fascism while supporting the western communists' Popular Front policy of collaboration with Social Democrats and liberals. At a meeting of the Communist International in July 1935 the Soviet Union pledged to support the western democracies against fascism. Under the sway of the appeasement mentality, however, western leaders rebuffed Soviet overtures for fear of provoking the fascist rulers. While the French did sign a defensive pact with the Soviet Union in response to German rearmament in 1935, they dragged their heels in implementing its provisions for military cooperation, and it became a dead letter after the Munich Agreement in 1938.

Munich must have shaken whatever confidence Stalin still had in a collective security policy. Nonetheless he renewed his proposal of a military alliance with the west in the wake of the Nazi occupation of Prague. At the same time, however, the Soviets dropped increasing hints to the Germans that they would welcome a rapprochement. Denunciations of fascism were toned down in official speeches and in the Soviet press. The clearest signal to the Germans was the replacement of Litvinov, who was Jewish and strongly identified with the collective security policy, by Vyacheslav Molotov (1890–1986) as Soviet Foreign Minister on 3 May.

Stalin may in fact have been hoping for an agreement with Germany for some time, despite the continued unrelenting hostility of the Nazi regime. The Great Purges of 1936–38, which also targeted the top Soviet military leadership, may have been motivated in part by Stalin's desire to eliminate left-wing critics and opponents who might stand in the way of closer relations with Germany. The phasing-out of Soviet aid for the Spanish loyalists, which led to Franco's triumph in the spring of 1939, removed a further obstacle to an understanding with Germany. It also, however, removed an obstacle to negotiations with the western powers, who had always been critical of the Soviet intervention in Spain.

But the Chamberlain government was clearly reluctant to conclude a military treaty with the USSR. It was not until 23 July that Britain entered into military negotiations. The British negotiating team that took the long route by ship to Russia was made up of low-ranking officials without plenipotentiary powers. They were authorized to talk only about general principles, not specific military agreements. Confident, perhaps, that the Soviet Union would never be able to bridge its differences with Germany, the British attached no great urgency to the negotiations.

Ideological revulsion against any form of cooperation with "Bolsheviks" played a part in reinforcing British reluctance to conclude an alliance with the Soviets. But there were other factors as well that made such a partnership unappealing. British military leaders had a low regard for the military capacity of the Red Army, weakened as it was by the recent purge of its officer corps. They saw little advantage in tying their military fortunes to an ally who was more likely to need help than to provide it. From the British point of view the worst possible scenario was to be dragged into a war with Germany to save the USSR.

There were practical difficulties as well. The beneficiaries of British guarantees of support, Poland and Romania, were adamant in refusing to allow Soviet troops to cross their territories, as they would have to do to defend against a German attack, because the Soviet Union had no common border with Germany. Polish and Romanian fear of Soviet encroachment was at least as great as their fear of a German attack. Nor were the British willing to consign the Baltic states, Estonia, Latvia, and Lithuania, to the Soviet sphere. This would not only violate the principle of national self-determination, but also eliminate the *cordon sanitaire* that was intended to serve as a buffer against the expansion of communist influence in Europe.

Some historians have speculated that Stalin's main motive for entering into negotiations with Britain was to lure Hitler into an agreement. Stalin, in turn, suspected the British of using the talks to get Hitler to negotiate with them. Both the British and the Soviets feared being forced into a war against Germany. Indeed, for the Soviet Union a nonaggression pact with Germany offered a number of advantages over an alliance with Britain. It would secure their European flank at a time when the Soviets were actively engaged in military skirmishes with strongly anticommunist Japan on the Manchurian border. Clashes between Soviet and Japanese troops had already taken place in July and August 1938. An agreement with Germany would keep the Soviets out of a European war, at least for a time, whereas an alliance with Britain and France, if it failed to deter Hitler, would immediately involve the Soviets in war. An agreement with Germany would not only gain time for the Soviets, but also space, as Hitler did not share the British qualms about ceding the independence of the Baltic states. An understanding with Germany seemed the optimal way to insure Soviet security in the short term. The prospect of splitting the capitalist camp gave the Soviets added incentive to negotiate an agreement with Hitler.

Alarmed, perhaps, by the possibility that a Franco-British–Soviet alliance might yet foil his plan to attack Poland and unable at this stage to persuade Japan to commit itself to a formal military alliance with Germany and Italy, Hitler decided in August 1939 to pick up on the Soviet feelers for improved relations. Frustrated by British opposition to his plans in the east, Hitler told C. J. Burckhardt, the High Commissioner for Danzig, on 11 August that if Britain could not be made to understand that Germany's efforts were ultimately directed against the Jewish–Bolshevik threat in the east, then Hitler would be forced to make a temporary agreement with the Soviet Union.[23] For Hitler a nonaggression pact with the Soviets offered the prospect of a free hand in Poland. Suppression of Polish independence and division of Polish territory had provided the historical basis for Russo-German partnership since the eighteenth century. Hitler could not believe that Britain and France, having failed to fight for a militarily strong and democratic Czechoslovakia a year before despite the assurance of Soviet aid, would now fight to save a militarily weak and undemocratic Poland without the prospect of Soviet aid. But even if the pact failed to deter Britain and France from intervening to prevent a German invasion of Poland, it would in any case make Germany immune to the kind of economic and naval blockade that had brought the nation to its knees in World War I.

Ribbentrop took the initiative in working out the details of the nonaggression pact. On 21 August he flew to Moscow to sign the agreement, and on 23 August the Nazi–Soviet Pact was announced to a stunned world. It called for each nation to remain neutral in case the other was involved in war, no matter who initiated that war. Mutually beneficial trade arrangements were also negotiated, whereby Germany was to send industrial products to the Soviet Union in return for raw materials and foodstuffs. A secret protocol called for the division of eastern Europe into German and Soviet spheres of interest. Latvia and Estonia, Bessarabia, and the eastern portion of Poland, acquired by the Poles during the Russian Civil War in 1920 and largely populated by Belorussians and Ukrainians, fell to the Soviet sphere. In agreeing to the partition of Poland Hitler may have wrongly assumed that the British guarantee of Polish territorial integrity would be in force against the Soviet Union as well, thus making an alliance between Britain and the Soviet Union impossible. Hitler no doubt regarded the territorial concessions to the USSR as only temporary in any case, in view of his long-term plans for the conquest of *Lebensraum* in the east.

The German attack on Poland

The Nazi–Soviet Nonaggression Pact set the stage for the German invasion of Poland. Conditions seemed ideal for reversing the most abhorrent legacy of Versailles—the loss of the eastern territories. On 22 August a day before the signing of the pact, Hitler told his military leaders assembled at his alpine retreat in Berchtesgaden that war with Poland was imminent. He knew that his generals had no objections to the conquest of Poland. Their only fear was a premature clash with the western powers. Hence he sought to reassure them that they need not fear British or French intervention. "Our enemies are little worms," he said. "I saw them at Munich."[24]

The expectation of British and French neutrality was one reason Hitler was determined to force the issue now. In any case, he told his generals, the risk of war with the west had to be accepted. Germany could not afford not to fight, he said, because of its need for resources. "We have nothing to lose; we can only gain," he exhorted his audience. "Our economic situation is such, because of our austerity measures, that we can only hold out for a few more years."[25] Conditions for war with the west were far more favorable than in World War I, because the Nazi–Soviet Pact made an economic blockade impossible. Hitler was in a hurry because he regarded his own leadership as indispensable to success. Having reached the age of 50 in April 1939, he was plagued by premonitions of an early death. The potential problems of an economy geared to preparations for war rather than to raising the standard of living through production for export and consumption also influenced Hitler's decision to go to war sooner rather than later.

Hitler hesitated only briefly when the British and French made clear their intention to stand by their commitment to Poland despite the Nazi–Soviet Pact. The invasion of Poland, originally scheduled for 26 August, was put off to 1 September. Through the mediation of Birger Dahlerus, a Swedish businessman and personal friend of Göring's, Hitler sought to drive a wedge between Poland and Britain that might yet induce the British to stay out of the war. Hitler offered to form an alliance with Britain once the Polish question was satisfactorily resolved. His terms to the Poles were relatively mild—the return of Danzig and a plebiscite to decide the fate of the Corridor—but he demanded that a Polish emissary with full plenipotentiary powers appear in Berlin before midnight on 30 August to accept these terms. The British urged the Poles to accede to Hitler's demands, but promised to stand by Poland if Hitler resorted to force. The Poles declared their readiness to negotiate, but refused to bow to a German ultimatum. If Hitler had been patient he might yet have gained concessions without resorting to war. But the freedom of action he wanted in Poland could only be achieved by force, and time was of the essence as a further delay might compel a postponement of the invasion to the following year. "I shall give a propagandist reason for starting the war," he told his generals and admirals, "no matter whether it is plausible or not. The victor will not be asked afterwards whether he told the truth or not."[26] Shortly after noon on 31 August he gave the final order for attack. Still unsure what Britain and France would do, he ordered the *Wehrmacht* to refrain from attacking them first.

A staged raid by specially recruited SS men in Polish uniforms on a German radio station in the border town of Gleiwitz was intended to create the impression that the Poles had started the fighting. The corpse of a convicted criminal dressed as a radio station employee was left behind to give the incident credence in the eyes of the German public. Hitler appeared in the Reichstag in military uniform on the morning of 1 September and cynically announced that as of early that morning the Germans were "returning fire." The record of appeasement apparently convinced him that he need not fear resolute military action from the western countries, even if they did declare war. Indeed, Chamberlain and Halifax still hoped for a negotiated solution to the crisis. But Parliament and public opinion forced the government to issue an ultimatum to the Germans to halt their advance into Poland. When the ultimatum ran out on 3 September without a German response, the British and French found themselves at war.

Historians have debated the degree of Soviet culpability for allowing Hitler to start the war under favorable conditions. It was indeed ironic that just at the time the western countries were renouncing appeasement, the Soviet Union turned to appeasing Hitler. Events in Munich led them to the reasonable conclusion that they could not rely on the west for support. Even so staunch an anticommunist as Winston Churchill described the Nazi–Soviet Nonaggression Pact as "the culminating failure of British and French foreign policy and diplomacy."[27] Chamberlain's policies had resulted in war under far less favorable circumstances for Britain than would have been the case a year before. The Allies' unwillingness to fight in 1938 can be partly explained by the reluctance of liberals and conservatives to fight alongside the Soviets against the German Reich. After the Nazi–Soviet Pact, however, this reservation was removed, and the Nazi claim of providing a bulwark against communism lost its credibility. In this respect, at least, the Nazi–Soviet Pact, which was intended by Hitler to restrain Britain and France from going to war, may ironically have made it easier for them to do so.

13 The Second World War

From European to global war, 1939–41

What began as a war that the Germans hoped to keep localized in Poland ended as the most widespread and destructive war of all times. The war can be divided into three major phases. From 1939 to 1941 the European phase of the war unfolded. In 1941 the German assault on the Soviet Union and the Japanese attack on the United States spread the war across the globe and ushered in the period of greatest Axis ascendancy in the summer of 1942. For several months the war hung in the balance. The tide turned in late 1942 and early 1943 with Allied victories in Russia, North Africa, and the Pacific, inaugurating the final phase of the war. But two more years of bitter fighting were required before the Germans and Japanese were defeated in 1945.

The Polish campaign and the "Phony War"

From 1939 to 1941 the German Wehrmacht seemed invincible. The Polish campaign provided a textbook example of what came to be called *Blitzkrieg* (lightning war), a strategy in effect forced on Germany by its relative economic inferiority to the west and consequent disadvantage in a long war. Yet none could doubt that German military technology and preparedness were vastly superior to that of the Poles. Supported by heavy artillery and squadrons of dive bombers, German armored and motorized columns rapidly pierced the Polish lines and encircled the enemy forces. The Germans also made innovative use of paratroopers dropped behind enemy lines. The infantry followed to carry out mopping-up operations. Some 60 German divisions (a division numbered approximately 18,000 soldiers) participated in the invasion. German troops reached Warsaw on 9 September, and by 16 September the capital was surrounded. The following day the Soviet army crossed Poland's eastern borders to claim the share of Polish territory allotted to the USSR in the Nazi–Soviet Pact. This area had been seized by Poland during the Russian Civil War, and a majority of its population was not Polish, but Ukrainian, Belorussian, and Jewish. On 27 September Warsaw surrendered after heavy German bombardment. The last Polish military units surrendered on 5 October 1939, five weeks after the German invasion.

In the west, on the other hand, the war took the form of what Germans called *Sitzkrieg* (sitting war) and in the west was referred to as the "Phony War." Despite a substantial, if temporary, superiority in numbers and materiel, the French did not venture out of their defensive positions on the Maginot Line, for the experience of World War I had convinced French military leaders that defense was superior to offense. Their unwillingness to launch an offensive was also a product of the continuing illusion that actual fighting might yet be avoided, if only the Germans were not provoked. The fear of aerial retaliation against civilian targets was another deterrent, as was the well-fortified, 400-mile West Wall (also called Siegfried Line) that the Germans had constructed from the Swiss border to north of the city of Aachen before the start of the war. The Allies believed that time was on their side and that an Allied blockade would eventually bring about a German collapse.

After the successful completion of the Polish campaign, Hitler offered peace in return for Allied acquiescence in the German occupation of Poland. By offering at the same time to guarantee the British Empire Hitler hoped to drive a wedge between Britain and France. When his offer was rejected Hitler favored an immediate attack on the western front. Several considerations persuaded Hitler of the need to seek a rapid resolution of the war in the west: Soviet and American neutrality might not endure; Italy and Japan—both of which were dismayed by Hitler's pact with the Soviet Union—might waver in their allegiance; and the western countries were likely to gain in military strength. Weather conditions, however, as well as the accidental loss of German battle plans in Belgium in January, forced a postponement of the attack until the following spring.

The "Winter War" and the Scandinavian campaign

The Soviet Union, meanwhile, moved to shore up its military presence in the areas ceded to it under the Nazi–Soviet Pact. The Baltic countries of Estonia, Latvia, and Lithuania were pressured into signing treaties of friendship and cooperation in September and October 1939, which permitted the Soviet Union to station troops on their soil. Finland, however, resisted Soviet demands for territorial concessions in the Karelian Isthmus that Soviet leaders hoped would strengthen the country's defenses around Leningrad. This dispute led to the outbreak of the so-called Winter War on 30 November as the Soviet Union sought to take the territory by force. For this act of aggression the Soviet Union was expelled from the League of Nations on 14 December. The western Allies promised to aid the Finns, but very little aid was actually forthcoming, as Norway and Sweden were reluctant to grant transit rights for fear of being drawn into the war. Yet the Finns put up an unexpectedly strong defense, inflicting heavy losses on the numerically far superior Red Army. In the peace that was signed on 13 March 1940 the Soviets achieved only a part of their objective. Their losses of some 200,000 killed exceeded Finnish losses by about eight to one.[1] The poor performance of the Red Army in the Winter War, coupled with the military purge of 1937, would help to persuade Hitler and German military leaders that the Soviet Union would crumble before a German attack.

The Winter War shifted the focus of both German and British military planners to Scandinavia, which became the next theater of war. Norway served as the conduit of French and British aid for the Finns in the Winter War, although very little of that aid actually arrived in Finland. The Germans feared, not without reason, that the Allies were planning to open a second front against Germany in Scandinavia. Thus on 9 April 1940 German troops invaded Denmark and Norway to prevent the British from occupying these countries and disrupting the flow of iron ore from neutral Sweden, which was vital to the German war economy. Denmark fell within 12 hours, but the Norwegian army fought tenaciously, with Allied support, for several weeks. Final resistance did not end until 10 June when the German campaign against France was already in full swing. In Norway the Germans established a client regime under the former Norwegian defense minister Vidkun Quisling (1887–1945), whose name would become a symbol for abject collaboration.

The campaign in the west

On 10 May 1940 German forces launched an all-out attack on Holland, Belgium, Luxembourg, and France with the same ruthless efficiency they had previously demonstrated in Poland. The Germans proclaimed their invasion of the Low Countries as necessary to forestall a supposedly imminent Allied attack, but their real reason was to lure French and British troops to the north in order to weaken the Allied flank. The decisive German breakthrough came against French troops in the Ardennes Forest on terrain considered unsuitable for mechanized warfare. On 13 May the German army crossed the Meuse River near Sedan and headed toward the Channel ports in the north, successfully surrounding the French and British troops in Belgium and northern France. The spectacular success of the German campaign was not due to technical superiority, superior equipment, or even to better morale. Victory was achieved by a combination of the greatest possible concentration of forces and the greatest possible surprise. It was a gamble that worked despite Hitler's initial doubts and the caution of the military leadership. Ironically, however, it would inspire Hitler to take similar gambles later in the war that failed disastrously and contributed to German defeat.[2]

The German advance in the Low Countries was made easier by the earlier failure of Holland and Belgium to coordinate their defenses with France and Britain for fear of compromising their neutrality. Holland surrendered on 15 May after the massive bombardment of Rotterdam. Brussels fell on 17 May. The Belgian surrender on 28 May imperiled the French and British forces that had moved to the north to meet the German advance. For a time it seemed as if the British expeditionary force, trapped near the French coastal town of Dunkirk, would be destroyed, but a temporary halt in the German advance on 24 May gave the British enough time to organize their defenses and launch a massive evacuation by sea. By the time Dunkirk was finally taken by the Germans on 4 June more than 338,000 British, French, and Belgian troops had been transported back across the Channel by every available seagoing vessel. This spectacular rescue operation turned a major defeat into something of a moral triumph.

Dunkirk gave rise to later speculations that Hitler may have deliberately allowed the British army to escape in order to leave the door open for peace negotiations. There were more plausible practical reasons, however, for the German failure to press home the attack. Their rapid advance had overextended German supply lines. With supplies running low a further advance in terrain inhospitable to armored vehicles might have exposed the troops to needless risks. The decision to advance was left in the hands of Army Group Commander General Gerd von Rundstedt (promoted to Field Marshal in July 1940), who feared a French attack on the flank. Besides, the tanks were now needed for the push against the major French armies around Paris to the south. Hitler had no reason to doubt Göring's assurance that the *Luftwaffe* could finish off the Allied forces at Dunkirk. But overcast skies and the spirited resistance of Royal Air Force (RAF) fighter planes left the Luftwaffe unable to make good on Göring's boast. Nonetheless, Dunkirk was a major military defeat for the Allies. The bulk of the British expeditionary force and over 120,000 French and Belgian soldiers were ferried across the Channel to safety, but they were forced to leave most of their heavy equipment and transport behind. The RAF lost 177 aircraft in the nine days of the evacuation; the navy lost several destroyers.

The fall of France

The German troops now pursued the French forces retreating to the south. Anxious to get in on the spoils, Mussolini (who a year earlier had informed Hitler that Italy would not be ready for war until 1943) declared war on France and Britain on 10 June. Paris fell to the Germans on 13 June. On 17 June the French Premier Paul Reynaud (1878–1966), who wanted to continue the war from North Africa, was replaced by the aged hero of the battle of Verdun in World War I, Marshal Henri-Philippe Pétain (1856–1951), whose staunchly conservative views often coincided with those of the Nazis and made him less reluctant to negotiate with them. Indeed, Pétain was convinced that the defeat of his country was due to the demoralizing effects of Marxist and leftist ideas over the course of the past 20 years.

The Franco-German armistice was signed on 22 June in the very same railroad car in the forest clearing near Compiègne in which the Germans had signed the armistice ending World War I. The northern and western parts of the country were to be occupied by German troops with their headquarters in

Paris. The rest of France, about two-fifths of the land area, was to remain independent under a new authoritarian government with its temporary capital in the provincial town of Vichy. Pétain assumed the presidency of this collaborationist regime, which replaced the revolutionary slogan of liberty, equality, and fraternity with the conservative triad of work, family, and fatherland. Under Premier Pierre Laval (1883–1945), who guided Vichy policies from June to December 1940 and again from April 1942 until the liberation of France in 1944, the Vichy regime formed an active partnership with Nazi Germany directed primarily against communism and the Soviet Union.

In the hopes of preventing the French colonies from joining the British, the Germans permitted the French to retain their naval fleet. But the British were not prepared to risk the possibility that the powerful fleet, fourth largest in the world, might fall into German hands. After failed negotiations with the French commander, a British naval squadron attacked and destroyed a major part of the fleet in the Algerian naval base of Mers-el-Kébir on 3 July 1940. The incident cost over 1,200 French lives and led to a break in diplomatic relations between Vichy France and Britain on 8 July. It also exacerbated relations between the Vichy regime and the Free French movement under General Charles de Gaulle (1890–1970), who tried to rally the French from his headquarters in London to continue the fight on the British side.

For Hitler the French surrender represented the greatest triumph of his life. Most Germans shared his sense of elation. Wilhelm Keitel, one of 12 generals promoted to field marshal in July 1940, called Hitler "the greatest battlefield commander of all time." With the Nazis staging massive military parades in Berlin and Paris to celebrate their victory, the humiliation of 11 November 1918 was erased. Alsace and parts of Lorraine were once again restored to the Reich, and Britain, the last remaining enemy, had been driven from the continent. Peace on German terms seemed within easy grasp. With all hope of victory now apparently dispelled and their own island domains in mortal danger, it was inconceivable to most Germans that the British would want to continue the war.

The Battle of Britain

On 19 July Hitler triumphantly addressed the Reichstag and again called on the British to end the war on the basis of a global share-out. Britain would retain its imperial possessions in return for conceding continental supremacy to Germany. Hitler's only territorial demand outside of Europe was the restoration of the colonies lost in World War I. Peace with Britain would allow Hitler to accomplish his primary goal, the conquest of *Lebensraum* in the east. But in Britain the accession of Winston Churchill to the post of prime minister on 10 May 1940 marked the end of all lingering illusions that a deal could still be made to avoid all-out war. In a memorable speech Churchill offered his countrymen only "blood, sweat, toil, and tears" and exhorted them to stand firm against the German tide. It was not just the desire to avoid humiliation that strengthened British resolve, but the long-term danger to democracy all over the world from any settlement that left Hitler the master of Europe. Hitler's seemingly generous offer of peace to Britain was delivered in his usual aggressive, sarcastic tone that belied his real intention: to prepare the German people for the coming Battle of Britain. On 16 July Hitler issued orders for the preparation of "Operation Sea Lion," the projected invasion of Britain, with a target date of 15 September. Throughout the summer of 1940 this operation received the highest priority in resources and material.

A necessary precondition for success, however, was German control of the air above the Channel and the British Isles. In early August the Luftwaffe launched massive attacks against British air and naval bases and other strategic targets. The Royal Air Force fought back doggedly with the help of their recently perfected early-warning radar system. But German attacks on RAF airfields took a devastating toll. For weeks the battle for air supremacy hung in the balance.

In early September, possibly in retaliation for an unexpected RAF bombing raid on Berlin on 25 August, the Germans launched an all-out "blitz" against residential areas in London and other major cities. Although the blitz took some 60,000 British lives, this shift from military to civilian targets turned out to be a mistake. Far from undermining British morale, it actually strengthened the British will to resist. The blitz would later justify the far more destructive bombardment of German cities while galvanizing world opinion on the British side.

The Luftwaffe's shift from military to civilian targets enabled the RAF to retain mastery of the skies. The RAF inflicted heavy losses on the German bomber fleets. In the air war over Britain the Germans lost almost twice as many aircraft as the British. It became increasingly apparent that the conditions for a successful implementation of Operation Sea Lion could not be created. German military planners could not agree on such vital questions as the length and location of landing sites on the British coast. Hitler, whose territorial ambitions lay in the east, was also inclined to caution. In early October, after several postponements of the target date, the invasion was put off until the following spring. By then Operation Sea Lion would serve primarily as a camouflage for the impending war against Soviet Russia. Operation Sea Lion was not officially rescinded, however, until February 1942.

Hitler's military options

Without mastery of the air the invasion of Britain posed too great a risk for the Germans. The destruction of an invading force might set back the German war effort by ten years and encourage Russian and/or American intervention. The Führer now faced the dilemma of how to defeat the British or at least persuade them to end the war. One option was to deprive Britain of its last potential continental ally by eliminating Russia. Hitler believed that the British would refuse to come to terms as long as they could hope for Soviet intervention. "With Russia smashed," Hitler told General Franz Halder (1884–1972), the Army Chief of Staff, "Britain's last hope would be shattered."[3] On 22 July 1940, the same day the British rejected his demand to end the war, Hitler ordered the Wehrmacht to prepare plans for the invasion of Russia. At that time he still hoped to conquer Britain before launching an attack on the Soviet Union. On 31 July, while the invasion of Britain was still very much in the works, Hitler told his generals to be ready for an attack on the USSR in spring 1941.

War against the Soviet Union was not the only option Hitler considered after the Battle of Britain ended inconclusively in the fall of 1940. Another possibility was to strike at Britain through a Mediterranean campaign with the objective of seizing Gibraltar, the Suez Canal, and British imperial possessions in the Middle East. This strategy was favored by Grand Admiral Erich Raeder (1876–1960), the commander in chief of the German navy until 1943, who insisted on the neces- sity of defeating England before launching an attack on the Soviet Union. A high priority in either case was to keep the United States in its neutral status. On 27 September 1940 Hitler joined with Japan and Italy to sign the Tripartite Pact, which was designed primarily to deter American entry into the war. The signatories pledged to assist each other in case of attack by a power not presently involved in the European or Chinese–Japanese wars. Germany's anticommunist central European and Balkan satellites, including Hungary, Romania, Bulgaria, Slovakia, and eventually Croatia, signed on to the pact as well.

In late October Hitler traveled to southern France for separate talks with Pétain and Spain's Francisco Franco in the hopes of persuading them to coop- erate more actively in the war against Britain. Among the obstacles to such cooperation, however, were the conflicting colonial claims of Italy, Spain, and Vichy France in North Africa. Spain's active participation was particularly crucial to a successful campaign against Britain in the Mediterranean. At the height of Germany's military success in France in June, Franco had changed Spain's official status from neutrality to nonbelligerency on the side of his fas- cist patrons. But Franco, who was known to be unhappy with the Nazi– Soviet Pact and who had just won a bitter civil war that left the country devastated, refused to commit Spain to a more active role in the war until a number of conditions were met. To offset the losses suffered in the Spanish Civil War Franco submitted a list of military and industrial requests so long as to virtually preclude their fulfillment. Not even Hitler's personal diplomacy could overcome Franco's cautious wait-and-see attitude. A full-fledged Mediterranean strategy was never a realistic alternative in any case, given Hitler's commitment to acquiring territory in the east.[4]

The Italian invasion of Greece

The escalation of German involvement in the Mediterranean was eventually necessitated by defeats suffered by their Italian allies in Libya in January 1941 as well as by an earlier act of Italian aggression that Hitler had neither desired nor foreseen. On 28 October 1940 Mussolini's forces had invaded Greece without warning from their bases in occupied Albania. Not content to play the role of Hitler's subordinate, Mussolini wanted a triumph in the Balkans to match the steady expansion of German influence in Romania. Now ruled by the notoriously corrupt and widely despised King Carol II (1893–1953), Romania had previously had close ties to the west but increasingly gravitated into the German orbit under the impact of Germany's military success and fear of the Soviet Union.

From the German point of view the opening of a new Balkan front at this time was a blunder, and not just because the Greeks successfully resisted the Italian advance. Hitler had previously written to Mussolini requesting him to postpone any action in the Balkans until after the American presidential election, in which Roosevelt was elected to a third term.[5] The violation of Greek neutrality would also adversely affect German efforts to bring the other Balkan states, particularly Yugoslavia (upon whom Italy also had territorial designs) and Bulgaria, into the German orbit in preparation for the coming campaign against the Soviet Union. The most unfortunate effect of the Italian invasion from the German point of view was to draw Britain into the Balkans as the guarantors of Greek independence. From bases in Greece Britain could threaten the Romanian oil fields, the most important source of oil for the Wehrmacht.

Negotiations with the Soviet Union

Another potential threat to the oil fields came from the Soviet Union, which in June 1940 had occupied not only the Romanian territory of Bessarabia allotted to it in the secret protocol of the Nazi–Soviet Pact, but also northern Bukovina, an area not mentioned either in the pact or in the follow-up Treaty of Friendship and Demarcation of September 1939. In June 1940, at the height of the German campaign in France, the Soviets also sent troops into Lithuania, Latvia, and Estonia. Soon afterwards the Baltic states "voted" to become Soviet Socialist Republics and were formally annexed by the Soviet Union in August 1940. The forced incorporation of Bessarabia/Bukovina resulted in the flight of the Romanian king, Carol II, and the dictatorship of Ion Antonescu (1882–1946), who was to become Hitler's most reliable ally in the war against the USSR. The Germans had not expected the Soviets to move quite so precipitously in consolidating control of the areas assigned to their sphere of influence. Still, with the exception of northern Bukovina, all of the Soviet moves were in line with the Nazi–Soviet Pact and the subsequent demarcation treaty, to which Stalin scrupulously adhered. In the fall of 1940 Hitler appears to have considered closer collaboration with the Soviets as a further option in his efforts to persuade the British to come to terms. The formation of a continental bloc against Britain and the United States was an option apparently favored by Ribbentrop. Perhaps the Soviets could even be persuaded to actively join in the war against Britain.

In November 1940 Molotov traveled to Berlin, where he was subjected to German pressure and cajolery. The Germans sought to tempt the Soviets with offers of British imperial possessions in the Near and Far East, including Iran and Afghanistan. While this effort to incite the Soviets to expand at the expense of the British Empire was no doubt intended to involve the Soviet Union in war with Britain, it would have the added advantages of diverting Soviet ambitions from territorial objectives in Europe and deceiving them about Hitler's ultimate expansionist aims in the east. Indeed, it is highly unlikely that Hitler ever envisioned collaboration with the Soviet Union as anything but a temporary gambit to defeat Britain in preparation for an attack on his former partner.

In consultations with Molotov, Hitler and Ribbentrop invited the Soviets to join the Tripartite Pact, which had specifically reaffirmed the special relationship established in the Nazi–Soviet Pact. The fact that Soviet adherence to the Tripartite Pact—the German–Japanese–Italian alliance that had its origins in the Anti-Comintern Pact in 1936—could become a topic of serious discussion attests to how greatly the Nazi–Soviet Pact had altered relations between Germany and the USSR. But the Soviets were not about to be manipulated into war against Britain or to be diverted from what they regarded as their essential interests in Europe. In fact they demanded an extension of their European sphere to cover Bulgaria, Finland, the Bosporus, and the Baltic Sea.[6] Molotov's hand may have been strengthened by the fact that at one point the talks had to be adjourned to an air raid shelter in the basement because of a British raid. "Isn't it a bit soon," Molotov is said to have asked, "to be dividing up the British Empire?" The talks ended without agreement and confirmed Hitler's doubts about the benefits of continuing the unnatural partnership with the Soviet Union. In December Hitler made his decision. He issued a directive to implement the plan for the invasion of Russia, now code-named "Operation Barbarossa," even before the end of the war against Britain.

Why did Hitler attack the Soviet Union?

The decision to attack the Soviet Union was one of those overdetermined historical events for which a number of different reasons can be adduced, each of which would seem to have been a sufficient cause. Basic to the decision were mutually reinforcing ideological, racial, and geopolitical assumptions, all already presaged in *Mein Kampf*. Here he had written: "But if we speak of new soil and territory in Europe today, we can think primarily only of Russia and of the subject states bordering it."[7] As late as 11 August 1939, two weeks before signing the Nazi–Soviet Pact, Hitler told Carl J. Burckhardt, the League of Nations high commissioner in Danzig:

> Everything I do is directed against Russia. If the West is too blind and stupid to understand that, I shall have to come to terms with the Russians, defeat the West and then turn with all my forces against the Soviet Union. I need the Ukraine so that we can never again be starved out as we were in the last war.[8]

According to historian Adam Tooze, the German invasion of the Soviet Union is best understood as "the last great land-grab in the long and bloody history of European colonialism."[9]

Hitler had also pledged to destroy Marxism in Europe. The tactical nonaggression pact with the Soviet Union in no way diminished the Nazis' fundamental opposition to communism. How better to accomplish the destruction of communism than to strike at its source in the Soviet Union? That communism should have taken root in the Soviet Union was no coincidence, in the view of Germanic supremacists, for only a racially inferior people would adopt a social system that favored the weak and inferior at the expense of the healthy and strong. And what could be a more appropriate objective to satisfy the superior German race's need for *Lebensraum* than the wide-open steppes, populated by Slavic "subhumans" who pledged allegiance to an ideology that threatened to destroy all human creativity and enterprise? Antisemitism was closely tied to anticommunism, for according to Nazi dogma communism was an international system concocted by Jews to destroy national leadership elites and to control and manipulate the working masses of all nations. Nazis as well as traditional conservatives considered "Jewish Bolshevism" the main threat to European culture and civilization.

For Hitler the attack on the Soviet Union was the fulfillment of his life's mission. Since the end of World War I he had often expressed his belief in the inevitability of a violent reckoning with Bolshevism, the most extreme culmination from his point of view of the movement of political sedition that had started with the French Revolution. In a letter announcing the start of Operation Barbarossa to Mussolini, who was not informed in advance of the German plans, Hitler conveyed the sense of relief that he felt at finally being able to sever his purely opportunistic partnership with the Soviets. "Since I struggled through to this decision," he wrote, "I again feel spiritually free."[10]

The actual timing of the attack on the USSR was the result of practical considerations as much as ideology. Foremost among these was the expectation that the defeat of the Soviet Union would finally extinguish all British hopes of victory and induce them to come to terms. There was no indication that Britain would make peace as long as the Soviet Union remained independent, even if the Soviet Union greatly increased its shipments of supplies to Germany. Hitler no doubt was also aware that it might become more difficult to mobilize popular support for war against Russia once a settlement had been reached in the west. With Britain for the moment unassailable in her island fortress but incapable of offensive action, and the United States still precariously neutral, the time for Operation Barbarossa seemed right. The conquest of Russia would make the European continent impregnable and allow Germany to mobilize all her forces for the eventual showdown with the Anglo-American powers. The attack on the Soviet Union was intended to *prevent* a two-front war, not to bring one about.

Operation Barbarossa offered the prospect of neutralizing the United States in another way. The Germans hoped that defeat of the Soviet Union would free up Japan to strike at British and American interests in Asia and thus keep the United States from intervening in Europe. There were economic considerations as well. Although the Soviets provided essential resources to the Germans and scrupulously abided by the terms of the Nazi–Soviet trade agreements, they demanded prompt payment in war materiel and manufactured goods, and they were in a position to cut off supply shipments at any time. Shortages in copper and aluminum made the delivery of manufactured goods particularly irksome to the Germans. The conquest of Russia, Hitler believed, would end this state of dependency and presumably make Soviet resources available to Germany on a much larger scale. Finally, a military campaign against the Soviet Union would help to combat the potential disaffection of countries like Italy and Spain where the nonaggression pact with the Soviets was widely viewed as a betrayal of the fascist cause. Italy had already withdrawn its ambassador from Moscow in January 1940, although full relations were again restored after Italy's entry into the war against the western powers in June of that year.[11]

The German government justified its violation of the nonaggression treaty to the German public on the grounds that the Soviet Union, in collusion with the British, was planning to attack Germany. A preventive war was allegedly necessary to save Europe from the Bolshevik scourge. Certainly the Germans were nervous about the potential Soviet military threat to the Romanian oil fields, the build-up of Soviet troops in the western provinces of the USSR, and the Soviet refusal to abandon their territorial ambitions (or security concerns) in eastern Europe in exchange for the prospect of sharing in the division of the British Empire. The Soviets were obviously trying to build up their forces in preparation for the eventuality of war. It is also true that Soviet military plans called for an offensive in case of war, but this was because the Soviets adhered to the doctrine (which proved to be flawed) that a rapid drive into central Europe offered the best chance of defending the homeland in case of war.[12] What the Soviets lacked was the political will for a war of aggression. Stalin adamantly rejected the advice of those of his military leaders, including Marshals Georgi Zhukov (1896–1974) and Semyon Timoshenko (1895–1970), who proposed a preventive war against Hitler. His mood was predominantly cautious and defensive. So anxious was the Soviet leader to avoid war with Germany that he even ignored secret intelligence reports of an impending German invasion. Stalin may have considered war with Germany unavoidable in the long run, but he was determined to avoid a military confrontation in the summer of 1941.

Central to the German decision to strike was the assumption of Soviet weakness. The massive purge of the Red Army leadership in 1937 and its poor performance in the Winter War against Finland seemed to bear out this assumption. Archival documents reveal that German intelligence considered the Red Army incapable of offensive war. An early draft (5 August 1940) of the German plan of attack was based on the premise that "the Russians will not do us the favor of attacking us."[13] On 7 April 1941 the German naval attaché in Moscow reported that the Soviet army was not strong enough to undertake war against Germany. As late as 9 April 1941 General Franz Halder (1884–1972), chief of the army general staff between 1938 and 1942, issued a secret situation report that pronounced the Soviet troop build-up in the border areas as "purely defensive."[14] German intelligence was not inaccurate. Historian David M. Glantz describes the Red Army in June 1941 as "a Colossus with feet of clay."[15]

In World War I Germany had defeated the Russian armies and occupied the entire Ukraine despite the terrible war of attrition on the western front. Was there any reason to think that the mobile and powerful Wehrmacht, freed of a front in France, would be unable to do at least as well against an opponent weakened by internal strife and more than two decades of communist rule? How could communism, an ideology of and for the weak, possibly confer fighting strength? It was the communists who had been the pacifists and "defeatists" in World War I. The Germans expected the Soviet system to collapse rapidly under the pressures of war. Hitler thought that compared to the campaign in France a Blitzkrieg against the Soviet Union would be like a "sandbox game."[16] His generals agreed that the Red Army could be crushed with one decisive blow. German soldiers were told that the Soviet enemy was "unsuited for modern warfare" and "incapable of decisive resistance."[17] Army Commander Walther von Brauchitsch (1881–1948) estimated the campaign would be over in four to six weeks. Hitler was more realistic and thought it would take from four to six months. It certainly did not seem possible that Germany could be defeated. A Russian campaign seemed like far less of a gamble than an attempt to invade the British Isles. Indeed, for German leaders, victory in the east seemed like a sure thing.

The Balkan campaign

Before the attack on the Soviet Union could begin, however, the Germans had to secure their position in southeastern Europe. By the middle of November 1940 it was clear that the Italians would need German assistance in subduing Greece, a necessity if Britain, which had already occupied the island of Crete, was to be prevented from acquiring a foothold in the Balkans. The military regimes in Hungary, a member of the Anti-Comintern Pact since February 1939, and Romania, which under Antonescu adhered to the Tripartite Pact in November 1940, were firmly committed to the German side. Bulgaria, too, under intense German pressure, acceded to the Tripartite Pact in March 1941.

In Yugoslavia, however, a revolt by military officers who feared the partition of their country overthrew the pro-German government on 27 March 1941. The new government opened negotiations with the Soviets for a security pact. The Germans responded by mounting simultaneous invasions of Yugoslavia and Greece on 6 April with the cooperation of Hungary, Romania, and Bulgaria, where German forces were based. Exploiting the nationalities conflict in

Yugoslavia by promising Croatian autonomy, the Germans crushed the Yugoslav army in 11 days. A week later Greek army resistance also ended. A spectacular German airborne assault at the end of May drove the Greek government and British expeditionary forces from the island of Crete as well. The Balkans were now firmly under German control. Pacification of the Balkans, however, may have delayed the attack on the Soviet Union by several weeks. This delay would prove costly when the onset of winter weather slowed the German advance in the fall of 1941.

On 30 April Hitler fixed the date for the German invasion on 22 June. The massive build-up of German forces in the weeks preceding the attack could hardly escape detection. But the Germans assured the Soviets that troop movements in the east were intended as a decoy for their impending invasion of Britain. Deployment of troops in areas as far apart as Scandinavia and the Balkans could be explained away as necessary to the war effort against Britain. The Germans also concealed their intentions by continuing to ship industrial products to the USSR on schedule.

Stalin did not believe the Germans would risk opening a second front before the end of the war in the west. He thought that the increasing number of German reconnaissance flights over Soviet territory was an attempt by the Germans to pressure the Soviets into further trade concessions. He angrily accused his own intelligence service of having fallen prey to German disinformation. Soviet intelligence unwittingly contributed to Stalin's self-delusion by indicating that while the Wehrmacht sought war in June 1941, Hitler hoped to achieve his aims through negotiations.[18] Stalin also failed to give credence to repeated British and American warnings of an impending German attack. The British had been wrong once before, after all, when they forecast a German invasion in May, shortly before the successful German attack on the British-occupied island of Crete.[19]

Stalin feared that the western powers were trying to provoke a Russo-German war. He was probably confirmed in his suspicions by the mysterious flight of Hitler's deputy Rudolf Hess to Scotland on 10 May 1941, undertaken without Hitler's authorization, apparently in the hope of persuading British leaders to make peace before the Germans attacked the USSR. Hess seems to have thought he could make use of his good contacts with aristocratic British political figures who had favored the appeasement policy before the war. Although Hess was interned by the British, and the German government—forced to dissociate itself from the failed effort—declared him insane, this peculiar incident revived Soviet suspicions about Anglo-German collusion and the possibility of a new Munich-style agreement. Three days after Hess landed in Britain the Soviets deployed additional forces on their western borders.

The Churchill government never intended to negotiate with Hess, but it was quite prepared to make use of his flight to encourage Soviet suspicions and undermine cooperative relations between Stalin and Hitler. Perhaps Hess's defection could be used to draw the Soviets to the British side. By maintaining strict silence on negotiations with Hess, the British government hoped to put pressure on Stalin to accept British offers of closer cooperation in preparation for an impending German attack.[20] But the effect on the Soviets of Britain's calculated silence seems to have been quite different from what British leaders had hoped. Stalin apparently concluded that the British had not yet decided whether to accept Hess's terms. As long as there was no change in the British government to indicate that a deal had been struck with the Germans, the Soviets could feel relatively secure that there would not be a German attack. At any rate Stalin was determined not to be goaded into war. Soviet troops were instructed to avoid all provocations. While already under attack in the early morning of 22 June, some front-line units still waited obediently for permission to return fire.

The invasion of the Soviet Union

Without a declaration of war the Germans invaded on a 2,000 mile front with a force of more than three and a half million men, 2,770 aircraft, and 3,600 tanks. Hitler called it "the greatest battle in the history of the world."[21] Romania, Hungary, and Finland, as well as the Nazi-sponsored states of Slovakia and Croatia, joined in the war against the Soviet Union; Italy sent its crack units and Spain sent a 47,000-man strong "Blue Division" to fight on the eastern front; French, Dutch, Danish, and Belgian volunteers joined units raised by the SS. Bulgaria, a Slavic country with designs on Greek Macedonia, declared war on Britain (the protector of Greece), but did not participate in the war against the Soviet Union.

The German army made spectacular gains in the first few weeks of the war, encircling entire Soviet armies with rapid pincer movements and capturing hundreds of thousands of prisoners. The Soviets' earlier deployment of large units close to the borders now played into German hands. Soviet border fortifications had not yet been completed at the time of the attack. By the end of the year more than three million prisoners had fallen into German hands. Most of them were doomed to perish by deliberate starvation in army or SS camps. Of the 5.7 million Soviet soldiers taken prisoner during the war, 3.5 million died in German camps.[22]

Hitler had instructed his generals to fight the war without regard for the accepted rules of combat. Unlike the war in the west, this was to be a racial and ideological war of the utmost savagery. The Nazis fought not to liberate people from the Stalinist yoke, but to gain territory for themselves and to destroy the possibility of creating a successful communist society. The cities of Moscow and Leningrad were to be razed to the ground. In a secret directive dated 6 June 1941 and signed for the chief of the OKW Wilhelm Keitel by Deputy Chief of Operations General Walter Warlimont (1894–1976), Hitler ordered the immediate execution of all captured commissars, communist officers responsible for the political indoctrination of Soviet units. "To act in accordance with international rules of war is wrong," this so-called "Commissar Decree" announced, "and endangers both our own security and the rapid pacification of conquered territory."[23] The Wehrmacht was instructed to cooperate with special SS task forces, the infamous *Einsatzgruppen* (mobile task forces), whose mission was to round up and kill Jews and communist officials in conquered areas on the pretext of fighting partisans (see Chapter 15). By November 1941, when the "Final Solution of the Jewish Question" went into effect, perhaps as many as 500,000 Soviet Jews had already been murdered by the *Einsatzgruppen*.

Nazi occupation policies

In the Baltic countries, which had been forcibly incorporated into the Soviet Union a year before, the German troops were greeted by many people as liberators and initially received widespread popular support. The same was true in the Ukraine, where nationalists welcomed the opportunity to throw off Soviet rule. Substantial numbers of people did in fact collaborate with the conquerors, and thousands of Ukrainian volunteers were recruited into SS units that eventually manned some of the defensive positions on the coast of northern France. But the predatory practices of the Wehrmacht and the draconian occupation policies under Nazi Reich Commissioner Erich Koch (1896–1986) helped to turn the bulk of the population against the Germans.

Alfred Rosenberg, promoted to Minister of the Occupied Eastern Territories in November 1941, sought to enlist minority nationalities in the anticommunist crusade. Rosenberg was also critical of the Wehrmacht's brutal treatment of Soviet POWs, which he regarded as a serious obstacle to the efforts to encourage desertions and exploit anti-Soviet sentiment among the "liberated" population.[24] But Hitler rejected his proposal to establish independent states in the east. Vast tracts of eastern territory, including the Baltic States and the Crimean peninsula, were slated for eventual annexation to the Reich. To the Nazis all Slavic peoples were "subhuman," fit only to serve the needs of the German master race. As in Poland, schools in the Ukraine were shut down on the assumption that education was an unnecessary luxury for a people whose main function was to provide physical labor. Hundreds of thousands were drafted into involuntary servitude in Germany. In the next two and a half years some 2.5 million Soviet civilians were transported to Germany to work in industry and agriculture—an average of 20,000 a week.[25]

Conquered areas were exploited in every way for the benefit of the German economy. The Wehrmacht's dependence on the agricultural products of occupied areas condemned millions of indigenous civilians to famine. Eventually the Nazis planned to forcibly remove Ukrainians and Russians from vast stretches of land to make them available for German settlement. The so-called General Plan for the East (*Generalplan Ost*), drawn up in 1941 for Heinrich Himmler in his capacity as Reich Commissioner for the Strengthening of German Ethnicity, called for the removal of over 30 million inhabitants of Poland, the Baltic region, and the Soviet western territories to Siberia to make way for settlers from the Reich and other non-Slavic countries. Only "re-Germanizable" Balts and Ukrainians would be permitted to participate in the Germanization of the East.

But ultimately the Nazis' repressive policies were counterproductive as they were forced to cope with an ever-increasing number of partisans sabotaging the German war effort behind the lines. Because of active and passive resistance and the destruction of war, the Germans were not even able to extract as much grain from the occupied areas as they had received in trade from the Soviet Union under the Nazi–Soviet Pact. The occupied areas of the Soviet Union produced only 10 percent of their prewar industrial output and only half of their agricultural yield.[26]

In the late summer and fall of 1941, however, it seemed as if German victory was just around the corner. Despite fierce Soviet resistance, the Germans captured Smolensk, just 200 miles west of Moscow, in August, and completed the encirclement of Leningrad by the middle of September. They planned to starve the former imperial capital into surrender. Meanwhile, the drive toward Moscow was temporarily stalled when Army Group Center outran its supply lines and German forces, including General Heinz Guderian's (1888–1954) Second Panzer Group, were diverted south to capture the Ukraine. The Ukrainian capital of Kiev fell on 19 September and Kharkov on 24 October. The attack on Moscow, code-named "Operation Typhoon," resumed in October, and by the middle of the month German troops stood only 60 miles from the Soviet capital. Soviet government offices were evacuated to the east, although Stalin himself remained in Moscow. The collapse of the Soviet Union seemed imminent.

Even sympathetic American observers did not expect the Red Army to be able to hold out for long. Indeed, some State Department officials argued against American aid to the Soviets on the grounds that theirs was a lost cause. US Secretary of War Henry L. Stimson (1867–1950) reported to President Roosevelt that in the view of the American Joint Chiefs of Staff the German campaign in Russia would last a maximum of three months.[27] Until late 1944 American and British officials would be far more worried about a Soviet collapse than about Soviet expansion. Nazi press chief Otto Dietrich proclaimed the final defeat of the Russians in October 1941. So confident were the Germans of victory in the fall of 1941 that Hitler issued an order to shift industrial production from materiel needed for the land war to naval and antiaircraft weaponry in anticipation of the coming showdown with the Anglo-American powers.

The American role in the war

Since the outbreak of war and particularly since the German victory in France in the summer of 1940 the United States had been moving steadily toward greater involvement on the British side. In September 1939 President Franklin D. Roosevelt had issued a declaration of neutrality, but refused, unlike Woodrow Wilson in 1914, to ask Americans to remain neutral in thought as well. The American embargo on arms sales to belligerent nations was lifted on 4 November 1939, and by June 1940 the United States was shipping surplus arms to the British. However, when French Prime Minister Paul Reynaud (1878–1966) appealed for immediate US intervention at the height of the German attack in June 1940, Roosevelt was forced to say no, for the American polity was far too divided between liberal interventionists and conservative isolationists to make decisive action possible.

Nonetheless, the growing Nazi threat induced Congress to approve the first peacetime military conscription in the history of the United States in September 1940. After winning re-election to a third term in November 1940, Roosevelt called upon the United States to become the "arsenal of democracy." The Lend-Lease Act of March 1941 empowered the president to provide war supplies without payment to any nation whose survival was deemed vital to American interests. On 10 April US forces occupied Greenland, nominally a possession of German-occupied Denmark, in order to use it as a base for delivering supplies to Britain. The Germans responded to these measures by expanding their area of submarine activity and attacking American convoys to Britain. Clashes between German submarines and American patrol boats on the Atlantic became more frequent.

On 27 May 1941 Roosevelt declared an unlimited national emergency in the face of the U-boat war. All German consulates in the United States were closed and German assets seized in June. On 24 June two days after the onset of "Operation Barbarossa," the United States pledged all possible aid to the USSR. On 7 July American forces relieved British and Canadian troops in Iceland even though Germany had declared the island a combat zone. On 14 August, meeting on the American cruiser Augusta off Newfoundland, Roosevelt and Churchill signed the Atlantic Charter, a declaration of goals that included the "final destruction of the Nazi tyranny." This charter was to form the basis of the United Nations Declaration signed by China, Britain, the Soviet Union, and the United States on 1 January 1942. A further escalation of German submarine warfare in the late summer of 1941 was followed by the sinking of more American ships. On 11 September American ships and planes were authorized to fire at Axis warships on sight. For all practical purposes Germany and the United States were already at war in the Atlantic well before the Japanese attack on Pearl Harbor on 7 December.

Why did Germany declare war on the United States?

What role did the Germans play in the attack on Pearl Harbor, and why did Hitler formally declare war on the United States on 11 December? The war might have taken an entirely different course if the Japanese had joined in the attack on the Soviet Union instead. The Germans, however, had not informed the Japanese in advance of their invasion plans, believing they would not need Japanese assistance in defeating the Red Army. In view of Japan's long-standing hostility to the USSR and their military clashes in the Far East, the Germans may have expected Japan to enter the war on its own. From the German point of view, however, Japan's most important function was to deter and prevent American involvement in the war in Europe. This was the major purpose of the Tripartite Pact of September 1940, which contained an article affirming that the pact was not directed against the Soviet Union. Rather than coordinating "Operation Barbarossa" with the Japanese in the spring of 1941, which might have put the secrecy of the operation at risk, the Germans urged Japan to attack British bases in the Far East. This would have the effect of tying down British forces as well as diverting American attention from Europe to the Pacific. The success of "Operation Barbarossa" would also free up Japan to attack the United States.[28]

As early as July 1941, however, Germany belatedly sought to enlist Japanese support in the Russian war. Anxious to create a Eurasian bloc that could successfully confront the United States, Ribbentrop instructed the German ambassador in Tokyo on 10 July "to employ all available means in further insisting upon Japan's entry into the war against Russia at the soonest possible date."[29] It is indeed likely that a Japanese attack from the east would have spelled the defeat of the USSR. It would have prevented the Soviet deployment of fresh troops from the Far East in the successful defense of Moscow in December 1941. But an attack on the Soviet Union at this time had very little appeal to Japanese leaders, who had followed the German example in signing their own nonaggression pact with the Soviet Union in April 1941. It was the United States, not the Soviet Union, that was aiding China and blocking Japanese access to the raw materials of Southeast Asia. A war in Siberia on vast and inhospitable terrain might tie down even more Japanese troops than were presently engaged in China without significantly advancing Japan's imperialist aims. Moreover, a Japanese attack on the USSR and interference with American arms shipments to Vladivostok were as likely to provoke American intervention as a Japanese drive to the oil fields of Southeast Asia. The Japanese may also have been wary of becoming dependent on Germany, an unwelcome possibility, should the Germans gain too rapid a victory over the Soviet Union. It was the apparently imminent Soviet collapse that determined the timing of the Japanese attack on the United States.

The failure of Ribbentrop's efforts to persuade Japan to enter the war against the Soviet Union made it all the more imperative, from the German perspective, to involve Japan in war against the United States. The one eventuality that had to be prevented at all costs was a Japanese–American rapprochement. The Germans feared that Japan might use withdrawal from the Tripartite Pact as a bargaining chip to gain the cessation of American aid to China. A peaceful conclusion to the Japanese–American negotiations in the summer and fall of 1941 would free the United States to devote all its efforts to supplying military aid to Britain and the Soviet Union. Hence Ribbentrop sought to disrupt these negotiations by encouraging Japan to ignore American opposition to Japanese expansion in China and Southeast Asia. He sought to assure Japanese leaders of America's lack of military preparedness and continuing isolationist sentiment. He urged them to take advantage of America's alleged weakness and indecision.

Indeed, the Nazis were convinced that American fighting strength was fatally compromised by democratic government, humanitarian values, and, above all, racial mixing. On 28 November Ribbentrop promised immediate German participation in case of war between Japan and the United States. By that time the Japanese task force had already left its home base to strike at Pearl Harbor.

Three days after the Japanese attack on Pearl Harbor, the Germans honored their commitment to Japan by declaring war on the United States, even though they were not technically obligated to do so under the Tripartite Pact, which called for military assistance only if war was initiated by an outside power. Although in retrospect his declaration of war on the United States may seem like Hitler's greatest blunder, at the time it seemed to underscore the success of his strategy of using Japan as a counterweight to the United States. The attack on Pearl Harbor lifted German morale at a time when the offensive to capture Moscow had unexpectedly bogged down in the outskirts of the city. The Germans had failed to prepare adequately for the severe winter weather that now favored the Russian defense. In early December the Soviets launched a counterattack that caught the Germans by surprise and resulted in a crushing German defeat. But for the Germans the good news from the Far East seemed to more than offset the bad news from the Russian front: Japanese entry into the war seemed almost like a deliverance. Surely the United States would now be unable to intervene in Europe or continue to provide aid to Britain and Russia, as Japan would keep the Americans tied down in Asia. What better way to bolster Japanese commitment to the war than to pledge Germany's all-out support? By declaring war on the United States, Hitler could also share in the credit for Japan's expected victories. Indeed, for reasons of public morale Hitler was anxious to declare war before the United States had a chance to do likewise.

In any case a declaration of war only formalized an already existing state of war on the high seas. On 9 December the German submarine fleet was ordered to launch an all-out attack on American shipping. German naval leaders, in particular, favored a formal declaration of war in the hopes of now getting a greater share of military resources, the bulk of which was going into the war against Russia. It was time, they contended, that the navy received due recognition for its heroic role in the undeclared war in the Atlantic. Withholding a declaration of war would not lessen the horrendous sacrifices German submarine crews were being asked to make, but it might adversely affect their fighting morale.

In the United States there was no illusion about the fact that war with Japan meant war with her Axis partners as well. But it might have been difficult to press a declaration of war through Congress if Germany (and Italy, which followed suit) had not acted first. And it might have been more difficult to convince the American public of the need to send troops to Europe rather than concentrating all efforts on the defeat of Japan. As it was, the American government decided to give priority to the European theater of war. This was partly a result of Churchill's influence, who arrived in Washington for extensive consultations with Roosevelt on 22 December 1941, but other factors entered into the decision as well. Germany was thought to have the greater technological capacity to develop new weapons. The fear of a Soviet collapse and the danger that the Soviets might be forced by military reversals to make a separate peace also contributed to the decision to give top priority to the defeat of Germany.

14 The Second World War

From triumph to defeat, 1942–45

The Japanese attack on Pearl Harbor turned out to benefit the Russians more than the Germans, as it relieved the Russians of the threat in the Far East while drawing a powerful new ally into the war. December 1941 marked a preliminary turning point, not only because of American entry into the war but also because of the failure of Hitler's Blitzkrieg strategy to bring victory in Russia. Hitler had successfully gambled in 1939 that Britain and France would not go on the offensive to save Poland from defeat. He successfully gambled again in 1940 in launching a militarily risky attack on France through the Ardennes Forest. In 1941, however, his luck ran out. His gamble on the quick defeat of the USSR through Operation Barbarossa failed.

The Battle of Moscow

Informed by their secret agent in the German embassy in Tokyo, the communist Richard Sorge, that there would be no Japanese attack on the USSR, the Soviets were able to mass three million men for the defense of Moscow in late autumn of 1941. On 5 December, two days before Pearl Harbor, the Red Army went on the attack. With much of their equipment immobilized by the severe cold, the Germans were forced to retreat from their advance positions in the outskirts of Moscow before they were able to stabilize their lines some 90 miles west of the city in January 1942. With his once invincible German army having suffered a major defeat, Hitler now had to face the fact that the war in Russia would last considerably longer than the German planners had foreseen.

Hitler attributed the setback at Moscow to a failure of will on the part of his leading generals. On 19 December he dismissed Brauchitsch as the army's commander in chief and assumed direct operational command of the army himself. From the *Wolfsschanze* (wolf's lair), his secret, well-fortified field headquarters in a forest in East Prussia from June 1941 to November 1944, Hitler determined not only the overall strategy, but frequently day-to-day tactics as well. His almost mystical faith that willpower could overcome material or numerical inferiority and his determination to avoid withdrawal even in the face of destruction—principles that may indeed have helped to stabilize the German lines outside of Moscow in the winter of 1941–42—brought him into increasing conflict with his generals, whose judgment he overrode with often disastrous results. Field Marshal Fedor von Bock (1880–1945), commander of Army Group Center, was relieved of his command in early 1942. Despite his doubts about Hitler's strategy, General Halder remained as army chief of staff until September 1942, shortly before the Battle of Stalingrad was joined.

German conquests in 1942

In 1942, despite the defeat at Moscow and the formidable power now arrayed against them, the initiative still lay with the Axis powers. General Erwin Rommel's (1891–1944) Africa Corps, first dispatched to bail out the Italians in February 1941, resumed their offensive against the British in North Africa in early 1942. Although outnumbered and outgunned by the British, the Germans more than made up for these deficiencies with aggressiveness and brilliant tactical maneuvers. The success of the North African campaign earned Rommel the reputation of "desert fox" and a promotion to field marshal. In June 1942 the Africa Corps captured Tobruk and drove the British back into Egypt. By the beginning of July the Germans had reached El Alamein, only 60 miles from Alexandria and the Nile Delta and within striking range of the Suez Canal. Here, however, Rommel's advance was stopped due to lack of reinforcements and supplies. The men and materiel that might have won the North African campaign were needed in the battle for Russia, which for the Germans had a far higher military priority than the Mediterranean front.

In spring 1942 the Germans again seized the offensive in Russia. Rather than trying to take the heavily reinforced city of Moscow, the Germans aimed their offensive south through the fertile southern plains toward the industrial cities along the Don and Volga rivers and the oil fields of the Caucasus. Army Group South completed the conquest of the Crimea in July, captured Rostov-on-Don on 23 July, and crossed the Don River in August, reaching the outskirts of Stalingrad on the Volga in early September. The main German force headed toward the Caucasus, seized the destroyed oil fields at Maikop, and sent advance units within 50 miles of the Chechen city of Grozny. By September the Germans had advanced more than a thousand miles from the 1941 Polish–Soviet border. By the end of 1942, 40 percent of the prewar Soviet population and 75 percent of its productive capacity had come under German occupation. The German advance marked the high point of German military success on the eastern front, unleashing a new wave of optimism among the German leadership and public. Once again the Soviet Union seemed on the point of collapse.[1]

German submarine warfare reached its greatest effectiveness as well in the summer of 1942, sinking Allied ships at the rate of one every four hours. The Allies lost some five million tons of shipping in 1942 alone. In the Far East the Japanese, despite their loss of initiative at sea after the Battle of Midway in June, had captured the Philippines, Indonesia, and Malaya and were

Map 3 The height of German expansion, November 1942.

threatening to attack India through Burma and China. The war hung in the balance, as the German pincers in North Africa and the Caucasus threatened to sweep through the British-controlled Mideast and link up in Syria or Iraq. In his monologues at the dinner table in his field headquarters Hitler indulged in fantasies of linking up with the Japanese in India.

El Alamein, the Allied invasion of North Africa, and the Battle of Stalingrad

The decisive turning of the tide came in late October and November 1942. On 23 October the British army under General Bernard Montgomery (1887–1976) counterattacked at El Alamein and sent the Africa Corps into retreat. On 8 November American and British forces under General Dwight D. Eisenhower (1890–1969) landed on the North African coast at Casablanca, Oran, and Algiers, meeting little resistance from the Vichy French troops in Morocco and Algeria despite Pétain's order to combat the Allied invasion. In fact, the successful Allied landing induced French leaders in North Africa to switch sides. Admiral Jean Francois Darlan (1881–1942), commander of the Vichy forces in French North Africa and a former premier of Vichy France, now called on the French to fight on the side of the Allies.

The Germans responded by ending the independence of Vichy France, occupying it, and sending reinforcements to Africa, but it was too little too late. The Africa Corps was driven out of Egypt in November and out of Libya in January 1943. Besieged by the British from the east and the Americans from the west, they made their last stand in Tunisia. Rommel himself returned to Germany in March, but Hitler refused to accept his advice to withdraw the remaining German forces. In early May some 250,000 Axis troops surrendered to the Allies at Tunis.

The greatest blow of all to the German war effort was the destruction of the German Sixth Army at Stalingrad in one of the most horrific battles in the history of warfare—a battle that was decisive for the outcome of the war. On 19 November 1942, after weeks of ferocious house-to-house combat for control of the city, the Soviets unexpectedly launched major offensives to the north and south of Stalingrad that rapidly broke through lines defended by inadequately armed Romanian troops. By 25 November some 300,000 battle-hardened German troops under General Friedrich Paulus were surrounded in the ruined city. Efforts to relieve the encircled troops through the air and on the ground failed, yet Hitler denied Paulus's urgent request for permission to attempt a break-out through Soviet lines to the rear. Lack of fuel, ammunition, and transport made such a break-out problematical in any case.

Intense fighting continued in the rubble of Stalingrad for several more weeks as the Soviets tightened the noose. The Luftwaffe's attempts to supply the beleaguered German troops by air came to an end when the Soviets captured the last remaining airfield. To prevent the surrender of the Sixth Army Hitler promoted Paulus to the rank of field marshal on 31 January 1943. No

German field marshal had ever surrendered in battle. Two days later Paulus became the first one in history to do so. The Sixth Army had run out of ammunition and food and had resorted to eating horsemeat and even cats. Two-thirds of the Sixth Army had died in the battle, many of them by starving or freezing to death. Fewer than 100,000 survivors marched or limped into Soviet captivity. Only a small fraction of that number would ever see their homeland again.

German naval defeat

The turn of the war in the Atlantic came in early 1943 as well. As Allied anti-submarine technology improved, the German U-boats were hunted down in ever-increasing numbers. Lacking aerial reconnaissance because of the overextension of the Luftwaffe in Russia and the Mediterranean, the German submarine fleet could no longer defend itself adequately against the growing number of Allied ships and planes. In the first five months of 1943 the Germans lost more submarines than they had lost in all of 1942; 242 submarines with more than 10,000 crew members were lost in the course of the year. In May 1943 alone the Germans lost 42 submarines while sinking 44 Allied vessels, a ratio of hardly more than one to one. In late May Admiral Karl Dönitz (1891–1980), who had replaced Raeder as commander in chief of the navy in January 1943, pulled his submarine fleet out of the North Atlantic in an effort to reduce losses. Production, which had reached a high of 15 new U-boats per month in 1942, could no longer keep pace with the losses; yet U-boats continued to be sent out on virtually suicidal missions for the remainder of the war. Their crews were assured they were contributing to victory by diverting Allied air forces from the main theaters of war.

The air war

Contributing to the crisis was the Allied intensification of the air war over Germany itself. Already in 1940 Winston Churchill is quoted as saying that the only way to win the war was through "an absolutely devastating, exterminating attack by very heavy bombers from this country upon the Nazi homeland."[2] In February 1942 the RAF Bomber Command under General Arthur Harris received the go-ahead for a saturation area bombing campaign designed to undermine the morale of the civilian population and spur popular revolt against the Nazi regime. Area bombing was the easier alternative to the precision bombing of industrial targets originally favored by the American Air Force. Precision bombing was in fact quite imprecise, at least in 1941, with only one bomb in five landing within a five-mile radius of its target.[3] Area bombing (also referred to as carpet bombing) was also less risky than precision bombing because it could be conducted at night. Area bombing was conceived in part as retaliation for the German blitz against English cities, including a devastating raid on Coventry in November 1940, and the so-called "Baedeker raids" (named after a popular tourist guidebook) against English tourist centers from April to June 1942. The "Baedeker raids" were themselves under-taken in retaliation for RAF raids on the picturesque north German cities of Lübeck and Rostock in March and April 1942.[4] These were followed by "thousand-bomber raids" on Cologne and Essen in May and June 1942.[5]

By 1943, with the Germans needing their shrinking fighter aircraft force to support the ground troops in Russia, the Allies were increasingly able to launch daylight raids at will. A daylight raid on Berlin on 30 January 1943 disrupted the tenth anniversary celebrations of Hitler's regime. Nighttime raids by the RAF were coordinated with daytime raids by the rapidly grow-ing USAF with increasingly devastating results. From March to July 1943 the RAF launched a sustained series of attacks against all the major industrial cities of the Ruhr Valley, greatly inhibiting German production and trans-port. The air war reached a preliminary climax with a massive incendiary attack on Hamburg, code-named "Operation Gomorrha," at the end of July 1943. Approximately 42,000 civilians were killed in the ensuing firestorm, the highest casualty toll for a single series of raids during the war. The bomb-ing of Dresden in February 1945 took approximately 35,000 lives. More than half a million civilians are estimated to have been killed in the Allied bomb-ing campaign over Germany during the war.

While the bombing slowed industrial production and diverted German resources, it was less successful in undermining the popular will to continue the war. If anything the air raids created a kind of defiant solidarity as people helped each other cope with their terrible ordeal. Moreover, it created the conditions that enabled the Nazi party to consolidate its control over every aspect of municipal government and services. Party members took a leading role in rescuing survivors, organizing relief, and maintaining order. Housing and furnishings seized from Jewish households all over Europe were distrib-uted to Germans who had lost their homes, helping to sustain public morale. In Hamburg, concentration camp inmates were used to clear the rubble from the streets. The bombing did not halt military and industrial production, but it certainly slowed it down. While vital installations were rapidly rebuilt, production facilities had to be moved underground or into reinforced bunkers, disrupting the production process and forcing a reallocation of scarce resources. Nonetheless, German military production actually reached its peak in August 1944. In March 1945 Germany was still turning out more tanks than in the first year of the war.

The German economy during the war

It was not until 1942, if then, that the German economy was converted to full military production. Nazi leaders were always acutely aware that the bulk of the German population entered the war without anything resembling the patriotic enthusiasm that had accompanied the start of World War I. Enthusiasm grew with military success, of course. In the summer of 1940 Hitler reached the height of his popularity in Germany. But Hitler was reluctant to demand too many economic sacrifices lest they lead to public disaffection as was the case in World War I. Although strict rationing was already introduced in 1939, existing industrial plant capacity was not significantly expanded, and production of consumer goods continued until well into the war. Civilian food rations were actually temporarily increased in 1942. German historian Götz Aly has controversially argued that Hitler deliberately bought the loyalty of the German people through low taxation and social welfare policies, made possible by the ruthless expropriation of Jews and economic exploitation of occupied countries. However, his analysis understates the economic sacrifices actually required of the German people, and he is certainly wrong to claim that the regime was unwilling to impose the full costs of the war on its citizenry.[6] As long as the Blitzkrieg was successful, the German public could enjoy the economic spoils of conquest, and the policy of "guns *and* butter" could continue. But Germany simply did not have the material resources for a protracted war.

The failure of the Blitzkrieg in Russia and the entrance of the United States into the war made increased military production mandatory. In February 1942 Hitler appointed Albert Speer (1905–81), his favorite architect, as Reich Minister for Armaments and Munitions (later Armaments and War Production). Speer inherited from his predecessor Fritz Todt (1892–1942), who was killed in a plane crash, the so-called *Organization Todt*, an organization of almost one and a half million construction workers, most of them by this time forced laborers and prisoners of war. Under Speer's direction armaments production grew substantially from 1942 to 1944, partly as a result of measures already introduced by Todt and Field Marshal Erhardt Milch (1892–1972), the head of aircraft production. Although in his self-serving memoirs after the war Speer credited this "armaments miracle" to increased rationalization and more efficient organization, in actual fact the production gains were primarily due to the Nazis' increased resort to coercion and slave labor.[7]

Heinrich Himmler's SS played an increasingly active role in the economy, not only making its concentration camp prisoners available to industry, but also running its own industrial enterprises. From 1942 on the German camps that had originated as detention and re-education camps for political prisoners increasingly supplied labor for the German war machine. Oswald Pohl (1892–1951), whom Himmler appointed to head the SS Economics and Administration Main Office in February 1942, oversaw not only the allocation of concentration camp inmates to private industry but also the growing SS economic empire of mining, construction, and armament firms. Pohl was the official primarily responsible for implementing the SS racial policy of "destruction through labor," which cost some 500,000 camp prisoners their lives through a combination of overwork, abuse, disease, and malnutrition. However, the war-induced turn to more production-oriented policies did, for a time, markedly decrease the mortality rate among working concentration camp prisoners from around 10 percent a month throughout 1942 to around 2 or 3 percent in 1943.[8] The growing need for labor to make up for the potential labor lost to Himmler's extermination policies and to replace German armaments workers inducted into the Wehrmacht put great power into the hands of Fritz Sauckel (1894–1946), a trained engineer who took charge of the mobilization of slave labor from occupied areas in March 1942. Sauckel procured 5.3 million foreign workers for forced employment in German industry and agriculture. If war prisoners and camp inmates are included in the total, some 7.8 million foreign workers, a fifth of the entire workforce (and a third of all workers in the arms industry), toiled to make the German war economy run in the summer of 1944.[9]

Despite the Nazis' negative attitude toward women in the workplace, Hitler finally authorized the mobilization of women for factory work in January 1943, but this policy was never fully implemented. A further drastic effort to mobilize the German civilian population for the war effort came in the wake of the defeat at Stalingrad. The Allied decision at the Casablanca Conference in January 1943 to demand Germany's "unconditional surrender" ironically may have made it easier for the Nazis to spur greater public involvement in the war effort. On 18 February 1943, less than three weeks after the loss of the Sixth Army at Stalingrad, Propaganda Minister Goebbels gave one of his most infamous but effective addresses to prepare the German people for greater sacrifices to come. Goebbels announced the propaganda line that the Nazis would repeat for the rest of the war: only Germany was capable of defending western culture and civilization against the spread of savage Bolshevism. Germany's territorial ambitions in the east, a major motive for the attack on the Soviet Union, were never mentioned in public once the tide of war turned against the Germans. "Total war" was the euphemism for demanding 100 percent participation of every German citizen in the war effort, which was now justified as a European struggle for independence and survival. Before a packed house of party members (including Speer, Sauckel, and Robert Ley) in the *Sportspalast*, Berlin's largest indoor athletic arena, Goebbels whipped his audience into a frenzy of enthusiasm. When he asked, with rhetorical flourish, "Do you *want* total war?" his audience responded with exuberant assent.

The Battle of Kursk

Despite the disastrous defeat at Stalingrad and the subsequent retreat of Army Group South under Field Marshal Erich von Manstein (1887–1973), the Germans managed to stabilize the front, retake Kharkov, and amass a tank and infantry reserve for another major offensive in the spring of 1943. The failure of this offensive, code-named Operation Citadel, in July 1943 confirmed that the military initiative in the east had now permanently passed to the Soviet armies. Forewarned by military intelligence of the German plans to attack the Soviet salient at Kursk, 450 miles south of Moscow, the Soviets were well prepared when the Germans struck. For once, the Germans lacked a key element of their earlier military successes, the element of surprise. The qualitative superiority of the new German Tiger and Panther tanks was not enough to overcome the vast numerical superiority of the Soviets, who were able to assemble a force of highly mobile T-34 tanks and assault guns twice the size of the German attacking force.

German defeat in the Battle of Kursk, the largest tank battle in history, spelled the end of the Wehrmacht's offensive capability. From then on the German army was forced into an increasingly defensive role. Although the new German Panther and Tiger tanks were equipped with greater firepower, they proved to be less maneuverable than their smaller Soviet counterparts and in any case were heavily outnumbered. Increased production in factories beyond the Urals along with a steady stream of American supplies enabled the Russians to replace their losses at a far more rapid rate than the Germans. The Soviets were increasingly able to take the initiative, set the terms of battle, and go on the offensive. By the end of 1943 the Russians had regained two-thirds of the territory they had lost to the Germans in the war. The Red Army recaptured Smolensk on 25 September and Kiev on 6 November. On 27 January 1944 the Russians managed to lift the siege of Leningrad after 865 days.

The fall of Mussolini

On the Mediterranean front the Allies also scored important gains in July 1943. The imminent invasion of the Italian mainland and the threat of large-scale destruction finally undid the Mussolini regime. On 10 July, a day after the Germans launched their ill-fated Operation Citadel in Russia, the Allies landed in Sicily and two weeks later entered the city of Palermo. For the first time in the war the Allies bombed the city of Rome. The Allied threat to Italy forced Hitler to withdraw some elite SS units from the eastern front. On 25 July the Fascist Grand Council and King Victor Emmanuel ousted Mussolini in favor of Marshal Pietro Badoglio (1871–1956), who secretly initiated talks with the Allies on conditions for Italy's surrender. The Italians signed an armistice on 3 September, the same day that Allied troops landed on the southern tip of the Italian mainland. On 13 October 1943 the Italian government officially switched sides and declared war on Germany.

Italy's defection did not catch the Germans unprepared. They immediately put into operation their contingency plan to disarm the Italian army and occupy the country. With Mussolini freed from Italian captivity in a daring SS commando raid on 12 September, the Germans reinstalled him as dictator of a Fascist republic in northern Italy with its capital at Salò on Lake Garda. Here he ended his days as head of a rump state entirely dependent on German support. Modeled on Nazi Germany, the Salò Republic had little public support and increasingly ruled the population through terror. Mussolini was captured and shot by Italian partisans on 28 April 1945, two days before Hitler's own death in the bunker of the chancellery in Berlin.

The Allied military advance in Italy was costly and slow as troops and reinforcements were diverted to England in preparation for the Normandy invasion. Although Naples fell on 1 October 1943, Rome was not taken until 4 June

1944, two days before the Normandy invasion. At the end of the war the Allied army had still not advanced beyond the Po Valley in northern Italy. But by pinning down some 25 German divisions the hard-fought Italian campaign helped to insure the success of the Allied cross-channel invasion in 1944.

D-Day

The long-anticipated D-Day Allied invasion of northern France on the early morning of 6 June 1944, code-named "Operation Overlord," was the largest amphibious operation in history. Yet both the timing and the location caught the Germans by surprise. Stormy weather conditions seemed to make the day unsuitable for a major landing. The Germans expected the invasion to occur at Calais, the point at which the distance between England and the continent, and the route to the German industrial center, were the shortest. Instead it came on the coast of Normandy where the German defenses were weakest. Over 150,000 Allied soldiers landed on the first day of the attack. They met intense fire at "Omaha Beach," but encountered relatively little resistance at four other landing sites. The Germans hesitated to dispatch reinforcements from other sites along the coast for fear that the invasion in Normandy was intended as a diversion from the main landing site. For several days the German commanders continued to expect the major attack to come at the Pas de Calais, from where the Germans had planned to launch "Operation Sea Lion" some four years before.

Virtually unchallenged air superiority enabled the Anglo-American forces to expand their beachheads against stiff German resistance in the days and weeks that followed. On 27 June Cherbourg became the first major port city to fall to the Allies. But Allied progress was slower than anticipated. The city of Caen, less than 20 miles from the coast, was supposed to have been taken on D-Day according to Allied plans. It finally fell on 10 July, and St. Lo, 25 miles inland, on 18 July. The decisive breakthrough in Normandy came at the end of July and the early part of August with the American encirclement of large German forces in the so-called Falaise pocket. Now the road to the east was clear.

On 15 August the Allies launched a second invasion in the south of France and met little German resistance. General Pétain, who refused to leave Vichy in the face of the Allied advance, was forcibly evacuated to Germany by the SS. The French underground resistance forces now participated actively in the liberation of their country as well. Paris was liberated even before the arrival of Allied troops. Contrary to Hitler's orders, the German occupiers withdrew without destroying the city. On 25 August General de Gaulle made a triumphant entry into the French capital.

On the eastern front, where the Soviets renewed their offensive on 22 June, three years to the day after the German invasion, the situation, too, went from bad to worse for the Germans. Army Group Center crumbled under the blows of the huge Soviet assault. The Belorussian capital of Minsk was liberated on

4 July, the Polish city of Lublin and its extermination camp at Majdanek (see Chapter 15) were freed on 23 July, and the Red Army reached the outskirts of Warsaw by the end of the month. On 18 August 1944 the Soviets reached the German borders in East Prussia. Romania signed an armistice with the Soviets and declared war on the Germans on 25 August. On 31 August the Soviets seized Bucharest and cut off the Germans from the vital oil fields at Ploesti. Finland, which had gone into a purely defensive mode after regaining the territory it had lost in the Winter War of 1939–40, concluded an armistice with the Soviets on 19 September 1944.

The German rocket program

Hitler, who visited the western front only once, 11 days after the Normandy invasion, refused to recognize the reality of impending defeat. He rejected the advice of his generals to fall back to more defensible lines along the Seine and once again accused them of lacking will. He temporarily dismissed his western commander Gerd von Rundstedt (1875–1953) on 3 July, and his successor, Hans von Kluge (1882–1942), on 17 August without, however, effecting any improvement in the military situation. More and more he pinned his hopes on the development of new miracle weapons. On 12 June the first of the self-propelled V-1 rocket bombs (the V stood for *Vergeltungswaffe*—reprisal weapon) were launched against the city of London from sites along the French coast. By September, however, all of the launching sites had either been captured or destroyed by bombing. Of some 9,000 launched V-1 missiles, only about 2,000 reached their target area.

The V-2 missile, which went into operation from launching sites in Belgium on 8 September, was more accurate and had a much longer range than the V-1, but the damage it inflicted was also disproportionately small in comparison to its cost. Over 3,500 missiles were fired before the launching sites fell to the Allied advance. Under SS Major Wernher von Braun (1912–77), the organizing genius behind the American aerospace program after the war and future American citizen, German engineers pioneered the technology of space exploration, but missile development was hampered by the interdepartmental rivalry so typical of the Nazi regime, and the military significance of the rocket program was minor.

The military benefits might have been greater if the funds invested in the V-2 had been spent on the development of jet aircraft instead, in which German scientists and engineers also played a pioneering role. But here, too, Hitler's fixation on vengeance and reprisal had a deleterious effect on the military usefulness of the new weaponry. Instead of developing jet fighters that might have contested Allied air superiority over the continent, Hitler ordered the construction of slower and more expensive jet bombers. Yet when jet aircraft became operational toward the end of the war, they could not be used for lack of fuel.

The German military resistance

The Allied landings in Normandy and the resumption of devastating Soviet offensives in the east finally convinced a number of Hitler's generals that the war was irretrievably lost. Field Marshal Rommel, who now commanded an army group on the western front, sought to persuade Hitler to sue for peace in the west in order to reinforce the eastern front. Rommel believed that continuation of the war could only end in the total destruction of his country. Hitler, however, refused to listen to any suggestions of peace without victory. Rommel was among a number of high-ranking officers who were prepared to seize power by force if Hitler failed to take appropriate action to avert the impending catastrophe. On 17 July 1944, however, he was severely wounded in the battle raging at Caen in France and was unable to play a part in the unfolding military conspiracy.

The leader of the military resistance was Colonel Claus von Stauffenberg (1907–44), who had access to Hitler as newly appointed chief of staff of the German Reserve Army in July 1944. The young battle-scarred veteran had lost an eye, his right hand, and two fingers of his left hand on the North African front in April 1943. After his recovery, Stauffenberg joined the already existing military conspiracy under General Friedrich Olbricht (1888–1944), head of the troop replacement office in the OKW. Together they reworked an already existing contingency plan against domestic unrest, code-named "Operation Valkyrie," into a plan to unseat the Nazi government. On 20 July 1944 Stauffenberg planted a bomb under a conference table in Hitler's East Prussian headquarters bunker during a briefing session. Everything, however, went wrong in the long-delayed assassination attempt. Although four persons were killed, Hitler survived the blast with only minor injuries.

The plot might still have succeeded if Stauffenberg's fellow conspirators had acted expeditiously in Berlin. Instead they waited until Stauffenberg's return some four hours later before issuing orders for Operation Valkyrie to begin. By that time telephone lines to Hitler's headquarters had been reopened. Propaganda Minister Goebbels, the highest ranking Nazi official in Berlin, was able to dissuade the officer sent to arrest him from carrying out his orders by convincing him that Hitler was still alive. Only in occupied France were the conspirators' orders to arrest SS and Gestapo leaders successfully carried out. For a few hours, at least, the conspirators under General Karl Heinrich von Stülpnagel (1886–1944) were in control in Paris, while General von Kluge, still commander in chief of the western front at the time, adopted a wait-and-see attitude that would later cost him his life. In Berlin the plot rapidly collapsed once it became evident that Hitler had not been killed. Stauffenberg's superior, Commander of the Reserve Army General Friedrich Fromm (1888–1945), who had refused to commit himself to the conspiracy until its success was assured, now cast his lot with the Nazi regime. That same evening Stauffenberg and his leading coconspirators were shot by a hastily assembled firing squad in the courtyard of the army headquarters building in Berlin.

Why did the military resistance fail to unseat Hitler? The vast majority of high-ranking officers remained loyal to the regime. There were a number of reasons for this. Most officers owed their promotions to Hitler's rapid expansion of the armed forces in the 1930s and during the war. To have violated their oaths of personal loyalty to Hitler would have constituted a breach of traditional standards of military honor. Even more of a deterrent was the stigma of committing an act of high treason in wartime. For many officers the Allied policy of unconditional surrender seemed to leave no alternative but to continue the fight. Others believed that a change of government would only reveal Germany's weakness and disunity, thereby eliminating any chance of negotiating a compromise peace. Typical was the attitude of General Manstein, who was critical of Hitler's leadership but refused to support efforts to overthrow him.

Even the leaders of the military resistance were inhibited by a fatal ambivalence toward the Nazi regime. Most dissident officers were authoritarian nationalists who helped to plan Hitler's campaigns, cheered his successes, and shared his goal of a powerful and expanded German Reich. For many of them, though not all, it was only the prospect of overwhelming German defeat that finally induced them to try to overthrow the regime. Even Stauffenberg's enthusiasm for the war did not wane until 1942. The ambivalence of members of the military resistance in no way diminishes their personal courage, but it does help to explain the failure of many resistance figures, such as Admiral Wilhelm Canaris (1887–1945), the head of the counterintelligence service in the OKW, to take a clear-cut stance until the loss of the war galvanized them into action.

Most of the conspirators hoped to conclude peace with the western Allies in order to hold the line against Soviet communism. They received no encouragement from the Allies, however, who were skeptical about the chances of a military coup and determined to avoid the reappearance of a stab-in-the-back legend in Germany after the war. The unconditional surrender policy precluded the possibility of negotiating a separate peace. In the heat of the battle Allied leaders were not inclined to see much difference between Prussian militarism and National Socialism. When Churchill was told of the coup attempt he is said to have responded, "Let dog eat dog."

Distrustful of populism and democracy, the members of the 20 July plot envisioned a conservative–authoritarian government in a postwar Germany that would retain its 1938 boundaries, including Austria and the Sudetenland. Some members of the resistance, such as the diplomat Ulrich von Hassell (1881–1944), even expected to retain the Polish Corridor. Stauffenberg's conditions for a negotiated peace, discovered by the Gestapo after the failure of the plot, included restoration of Germany's 1914 borders, the retention of Austria and the Sudetenland, and continuation of the war, if necessary, in the east.[10] Their vision of a compromise peace with the western Allies was strangely out of touch with reality. General Ludwig Beck (1880–1944), who had retired as army chief of staff in August 1938 to protest

Hitler's Czechoslovakian policy, was slated to become the head of the new state with retired Field Marshal Erwin von Witzleben (1881–1944) as commander in chief of the Wehrmacht and Olbricht as minister of war. Beck had already hatched plans to depose Hitler in 1938 on condition that the British stand firm on Czechoslovakia, but he had received no encouragement from the appeasement-minded British Foreign Office.[11] Most of the conspirators had welcomed the Nazis in the early years of the regime. The former mayor of Leipzig, Carl Goerdeler (1884–1945), slated to become chancellor in the event of the coup's success, opposed Nazi violence against Jews but favored some measures to restrict the rights of Jews in Germany.

With the collapse of the coup attempt the Nazis rapidly regained control. Their reprisals were brutal and sweeping. Beck was shot on the night of 20 July after bungling a suicide attempt, while Goerdeler, Witzleben, and other leading conspirators were subjected to humiliating sham trials before the People's Court and later hanged in particularly grizzly fashion with piano wire on meat hooks. Their death agony was filmed for Hitler's sadistic pleasure. The vacillating Fromm, who had aborted the plot when he learned that Hitler was alive, was executed by firing squad in March 1945. But the anti-Hitler conspiracy proved to be much larger than anticipated. In the months that followed the suppression of the plot approximately 700 persons, some only loosely connected to the resistance, were arrested. The People's Court passed close to 200 death sentences on persons connected to the plot. Members of the conspirators' families were imprisoned or placed in concentration camps. Measures were also taken to place the army under party control. Regional *Gauleiter* now assumed the responsibilities of "Reich Defense Commissioners." Already appointed Reich interior minister in August 1943, Heinrich Himmler assumed command of the German Reserve Army on 21 July 1944 (and of several army groups in 1945), while Goebbels took over the new post of "plenipotentiary for total war" in August. The Nazi salute replaced the military salute in the army three days after the failure of the coup.

Other resistance to Hitler

Another center of predominantly conservative resistance with links to the military resistance was the Kreisau Circle of professional people and army officers who met at the estate of Count Helmuth von Moltke (1907–45), a descendant of a long line of Prussian military heroes including a former chief of the German General Staff (his great-uncle). Members of the Kreisau Circle differed on the form a post-Nazi Germany would take but agreed in their hatred of Hitler. However, most of its members were inspired by religious ideals that ruled out assassination as a legitimate method of bringing down the regime. This did not save them from the wrath of the Nazis, however, as they, too, were caught in the massive dragnet cast out by the SS after the failure of the 20 July plot. Moltke had already been arrested in January 1944 and was executed in January 1945. The Jesuit priest Alfred Delp (1907–45) and the Protestant theologian Dietrich Bonhoeffer (1906–45), clerical activists loosely connected with the Kreisau Circle, were put to death in April 1945. Bernhard Lichtenberg (1875–1943), the Catholic prior of St. Hedwig's Cathedral in Berlin and one of the few leading church figures to openly criticize Nazi policies against the Jews, died while being transported to Dachau in November 1943.

It is not surprising that the only serious threat to the Nazi regime came from disgruntled conservatives who feared that Hitler's leadership would lead to the total ruination of their country. All other potential sources of resistance had been subjected to thorough and devastating repression since 30 January 1933. This is particularly true of the socialist and communist underground, which nonetheless managed to function under extreme duress even in the war years. In 1942 the main communist espionage group referred to by the Gestapo as the *Rote Kapelle* (Red Orchestra) was broken up and 50 of its members were executed. The group had previously provided valuable intelligence information to the Soviet Union. Some Social Democratic dissidents had close links to the 20 July conspirators, including the former Reichstag deputy Julius Leber (1891–1945) and the former interior minister of the state of Hessen, Wilhelm Leuschner (1890–1944), both of whom were slated for ministerial posts in the new government. Leber and Leuschner were among the hundreds executed after the failure of the plot.

There were also isolated acts of resistance in the general population, including incidents of industrial sabotage, work slowdowns, and clandestine aid to Jews, foreign workers, or Allied prisoners of war. On 8 November 1939 the Swabian carpenter Georg Elser (1903–45) planted a bomb in the *Bürgerbräukeller*, where Hitler was scheduled to give an address on the anniversary of the Munich putsch. Seven persons died, but Hitler had left the hall ten minutes before the bomb went off. An example of great courage and commitment was provided by the religiously inspired students Sophie (1921–43) and Hans Scholl (1918–43), who organized a resistance circle at Munich University under the name of "The White Rose." Apprehended for distributing leaflets that called upon German youth to rise up against the Nazi regime, the Scholls and their fellow conspirator Christoph Probst (1919–43) were executed by guillotine in February 1943. Their Catholic mentor Kurt Huber (1893–1943) and several other student members of the White Rose were executed later that year.

Resistance in occupied Europe

Resistance to Nazism was particularly difficult in Germany, especially in wartime, because it involved treason against one's own country. The same did not, of course, apply to countries occupied by the Nazis, where resistance was an expression of patriotism. While in most countries of occupied Europe collaborators at first outnumbered resisters, the changing fortunes of war soon tipped the scales the other way. Resistance forces played a significant role in a number of countries, particularly Yugoslavia, where guerilla fighters under Marshal Josip Tito (1892–1980) tied down a number of German divisions throughout the war and succeeded in liberating the country before the arrival of the Red Army in Belgrade in late October 1944.

In Poland, on the other hand, the underground Home Army under the control of the Polish government in exile in London failed in its attempt to free the country from its German invaders. The Warsaw uprising that began on 1 August 1944 (not to be confused with the Warsaw Ghetto uprising of April 1943, which is discussed in the following chapter) was timed to coincide with the arrival of Soviet troops on the banks of the Vistula within striking distance of Warsaw. The Polish exile government in London intended to liberate the capital before the arrival of the Red Army in order to prevent the communists from dominating Poland after the war, but the execution of this plan was disastrous.

Diplomatic relations between the London Poles and the Soviet Union had been broken off after the German discovery of mass graves of Polish officers in the forest of Katyn in April 1943. Although the Soviets blamed the Germans for the massacre at the time and even persuaded the Allies to include it among the charges against the Nazi leadership at the Nuremberg war crimes trials in 1945, the atrocity was actually committed by the Soviet secret service (NKVD) in 1940 to eliminate opposition to communist rule in Poland. This conflict between the Soviets and the anticommunist London Poles explains why the Soviets were not informed of the planned uprising in advance. The uprising was directed militarily against the Germans, but politically against the Soviets. The Red Army withheld all assistance to the Home Army while the Germans applied massive force to crush the revolt. After two months of savage fighting that cost close to 200,000 Polish lives, the Warsaw rebels surrendered on 2 October. Only then did the Red Army move to occupy the destroyed city, which fell to the Russians in January 1945.

All across Europe the anti-Nazi resistance was divided between communist and noncommunist or anticommunist factions. In some countries, such as Yugoslavia and Greece (and China), the two factions clashed, but in most countries communist and noncommunist resistance fighters cooperated in the common struggle. After the German invasion of the Soviet Union, communists throughout Europe formed the most militant factions in underground movements and were often more ready to take risks and do battle than their noncommunist counterparts. This was the case, for instance, in Yugoslavia, where the British originally backed the noncommunist resistance movement under the Serbian nationalist Colonel Dragoljub Mihajlovic (1893–1946), but shifted their support to Tito in 1943 when it became apparent that his partisans were more vigorous and effective in fighting the Germans.

Partisans played an increasingly important military role as the war progressed. The vast forested areas of the Soviet Union were particularly favorable for partisan warfare. Guerilla bands disrupted German supply lines and tied down German troop units behind the front lines. In the west the resistance had less military significance, though it did supply the Allies with important intelligence information. By 1944 the resistance movement in France could count on some 200,000 partisans whose activities were coordinated with the Allied armies. In Italy partisans succeeded in capturing and executing Mussolini in the closing days of the war.

Nazi reprisals against partisan warfare assumed draconian proportions. The notorious "Night and Fog" decrees of July 1941, signed by Field Marshal Keitel, authorized the seizure and deportation to Germany of any person in occupied Europe suspected of anti-German activity. To discourage popular support for resistance fighters the Germans adopted the practice of executing hostages and destroying entire villages in retaliation for acts of resistance. Among the most savage reprisals was the destruction of the Czech village of Lidice and the execution of all its male inhabitants after the assassination of top SS official Reinhard Heydrich (1904–42), *Reichsprotektor* of Bohemia and Moravia, by Czech underground agents in May 1942. In March 1944, 335 Italian prisoners were massacred in the caves of Via Ardeatina, near Rome, in retaliation for the ambush of German troops by partisans.[12] On 10 June 1944, four days after the Allied landing in Normandy, a unit of the SS tank division "Das Reich" murdered all 642 inhabitants of the French village Oradour-sur-Glane. The toll of victims included 207 children.[13]

Germany's defeat

By the middle of October 1944 the Allied offensives in east and west had reached the borders of the German Reich. On 21 October Aachen became the first German city captured by the Allies. It appeared that the war would end within a matter of weeks, but in mid-December the Germans mounted one last desperate offensive in the west in an effort to stave off impending defeat. A German spearhead drove 50 miles into the Allied lines in the Belgian Ardennes in what came to be known as the Battle of the Bulge. By the end of the month the German offensive was halted well short of its objective of the port city of Antwerp. German tanks and assault vehicles were stranded for lack of fuel. It took several weeks, however, before Allied forces recaptured the lost terrain. But the Germans were now left without any effective reserves. The withdrawal of German units from the east for the Battle of the Bulge had weakened defenses against the Red Army, which rapidly advanced into East Prussia in January 1945, precipitating huge columns of refugees frantically seeking refuge in the west.

In January 1945 the Allied forward drive on the western front resumed. Cologne fell on 6 March, and a day later American forces seized a railway bridge over the Rhine at Remagen that the retreating Germans had failed to destroy. Although the bridge collapsed on 17 March, the Germans were unable to dislodge the Allied bridgehead on the east bank of the Rhine. On 19 March Hitler issued his so-called "Nero order" for the total destruction of the infrastructure necessary to the survival of the civilian population in areas

Map 4 Germany after 1945, showing territorial losses following World War II.

lost to the Allies, but his order was ignored in practice. In April American troops reached the Elbe River in central Germany, the demarcation line between Soviet and western occupation zones agreed upon at the Yalta Conference of the Big Three (Roosevelt, Churchill, and Stalin) in February. American and Soviet troops met at Torgau on the Elbe on 25 April, effectively cutting the country in two. American forces might well have beaten the Soviets to Prague and Berlin, as Churchill urged them to do for political reasons, but Eisenhower continued to give highest priority to the military goal of defeating the enemy as rapidly as possible. His foremost objective was not to capture territory, but to destroy enemy forces in order to end the war in the shortest possible time. Another consideration in his decision to halt American troops short of Berlin or Prague was the fact that supply lines had been stretched thin by the rapid advances of the preceding weeks. The possibility that Hitler might try to establish a fortified redoubt in the Bavarian Alps could not be ignored, either. An elaborate network of well-equipped underground bunkers and fortifications had been constructed in Berchtesgaden, but Hitler decided to remain in Berlin.

In mid-April the Soviets mounted their final offensive against the German capital, fanatically defended by vastly outnumbered, ill-equipped, and largely under- or overaged German troops. In the closing stages of the war the Nazis drafted boys as young as 15 to fill the depleted ranks of the *Wehrmacht*. Men too old or disabled to serve in the regular army were organized into a civil defense force called *Volkssturm* (people's storm), equipped mainly with anti-tank bazookas. After two weeks of intense house-to-house combat Red Army units fought their way into the center of Berlin. From his elaborate and well-fortified bunker under the chancellery Hitler frantically ordered phantom armies to come to the relief of the city. He was briefly buoyed by the news of President Roosevelt's death on 12 April, which he hoped would lead the Americans to end their alliance with the Soviets. This, too, turned out to be a delusion.

On 30 April Hitler committed suicide with his faithful companion Eva Braun, whom he had married the day before. The fanatically loyal Josef Goebbels, who continued to exhort the German people to fight to the last man, committed suicide with his wife after poisoning their six young children to spare them from having to live in a post-Nazi world. In his terse political testament Hitler showed no change of heart or remorse. He blamed the war on the Jews and exhorted Germans to continue building a National Socialist state. Enraged by their unsuccessful last-minute attempts to negotiate a separate peace with the western powers, Hitler stripped Göring and Himmler of all their offices. It was left to Grand Admiral Karl Dönitz, Hitler's designated successor, to organize Germany's unconditional surrender on 8 May 1945. The surrender documents were signed at the Allied headquarters in Rheims on 7 May and at Soviet headquarters in Berlin shortly after midnight the following day. The European phase of the most destructive war in history had come to a close.

Losses

More than three million Germans had lost their lives in combat, most on the eastern front. Between June 1941 and June 1944 more than 90 percent of all German army battle casualties were inflicted by the Russians. Another million German prisoners of war failed to return from Soviet captivity. It is estimated that almost 3 million German civilians lost their lives, at least 1.5 million of these in the mass migration of refugees from the war in the east. This westward migration continued in the months following the war as a result of the expulsion of Germans from territories annexed by Poland and the Soviet Union. More than half of all German losses came after 20 July 1944, the day of the failed officers' revolt that was intended to end or at least shorten the war.

The total number of deaths resulting from the war is today estimated to have been close to 55 million, a majority of them civilians.[14] Soviet casualties are difficult to pin down precisely because of the reluctance of the Soviet state to admit heavy losses. Estimates of Soviet losses based on the latest data from Soviet archives range from 27 million to 40 million.[15] Approximately 9 million Soviet soldiers lost their lives, including some 3.5 million prisoners of war deliberately starved to death or killed by other means in camps run by the *Wehrmacht* or SS. Poland suffered even greater losses in proportion to their population. Some 6.5 million Polish citizens lost their lives, half of them Jewish. Yugoslavia, too, suffered a high toll, with about 1.5 million dead. In contrast, Britain suffered losses of about 400,000, and the United States approximately 350,000 on both the European and far eastern fronts. France, which had lost 1.5 million men in World War I, suffered much lighter losses in World War II.

The German defeat in World War II is a classic case of a country done in by its own odious supremacist ideology and unrealistic imperial ambitions. In political and military terms, Hitler made three fatal miscalculations. His first was the assumption that after the defeat of France, Britain would have no choice but to make peace. His second miscalculation was his assumption that the Soviet armies would not fight or could not fight effectively. His third major misjudgment was his egregious underestimation of the will and capacity of the United States to wage war. Hitler was the victim of his ideological delusions, rooted in his conviction of the superiority of the German race. From 1942 on he was gradually forced to renounce all of the objectives for which he had started the war. One goal, however, he was determined to accomplish even in defeat: the destruction of the European Jews.

15 The Holocaust

Hitler's Germany perpetrated the most notorious genocide in history: the mass murder of Europe's Jews. The Holocaust was central to the Nazis' wide-ranging program of destruction. The victims of lethal Nazi persecution included Gypsies (or Roma), the mentally and physically disabled, homosexuals, pacifists (Jehovah's Witnesses), and political opponents, especially Communists. The Nazis also systematically killed millions of Soviet prisoners of war as well as potential leadership elites (including priests, intellectuals, military officers, and politicians) in Poland and other occupied areas in the east. But no group was massacred more single-mindedly or on a greater scale than the Jews. At the height of the war, besieged by Allied armies on all fronts, the Nazi government diverted valuable resources from military uses to complete the destruction of the European Jews. Approximately six million, two-thirds of the Jewish population in Europe and fully a third of world Jewry, lost their lives in the Holocaust. How can genocide on such a scale be explained? How and why did the discrimination and persecution of the 1930s escalate into the systematic genocide of the 1940s? Historians have long wrestled with these questions without coming to full consensus.

Intentionalist and structuralist interpretations

For many years the historiographical debate on how Nazi policies for the destruction of Europe's Jews were formed and implemented have been based on the distinction between two broad categories: "intentionalist" interpretations which stress the centrality of Hitler's role and believe that the Holocaust was a step-by-step implementation of Hitler's long-standing, preconceived plan to kill the Jews; and "functionalist" (or "structuralist") interpretations, according to which the Holocaust was primarily the result of increasingly radical efforts by competing Nazi agencies and leaders to "solve" the "Jewish problem"—the allegedly excessive political, economic, and cultural influence of Jews in German and European society—under the specific circumstances of the war.[1] Did Hitler always intend the physical extinction of the Jews or was this decision reached only after the alternatives of emigration and resettlement proved unworkable? At issue is not just *when* but also *how* the decision for the "final solution of the Jewish problem" was reached. Intentionalists stressed the importance of Hitler's and the top Nazi leadership's own long-term plans, will, and intentions in bringing about the Holocaust; functionalists stressed the "cumulative radicalization"[2] of policy driven by a bureaucracy charged with finding a workable solution to the "Jewish problem" under the increasingly inflexible conditions of war. Functionalists contended that there was no pre-existing grand design; rather, the Holocaust resulted from the failure or unfeasibility of increasingly radical projects to extrude Jews and from the loosening of all constraints against mass murder in the war.

The intentionalism vs. functionalism (or structuralism) debate had implications for other aspects of the history of Nazi Germany as well. One important issue it raised was the extent of Hitler's power. Intentionalists tended to stress Hitler's total control of decision-making and the centralized hierarchical structure of the regime, while functionalists tended to emphasize the "polycratic," decentralized, fragmented nature of Nazi rule, in which overlapping agencies and middle-level bureaucrats competed with each other to implement broad policy directives (such as the extrusion of the Jews) received from on high.

Another issue raised by the intentionalist–functionalist debate involves the role of ideology in Nazi rule. Was ideology the sole or primary determinant in Nazi decision-making, as intentionalists contend, or was it one among several factors, such as regional or local initiatives, competition between party and state agencies, and other more or less contingent factors that explain the radicalization of the Nazis' antisemitic policies, as functionalist interpretations suggest?

Most importantly, it is also a debate about historical responsibility. Was Hitler primarily to blame for the Holocaust or was it his underlings who were primarily responsible for this most heinous historical crime? The issue is so contentious because interpretations that stress contingencies, social structures, or bureaucratic dynamics seem to disperse responsibility for the Holocaust and conceal the human actors within a bureaucratic structural system. Any diminution of Hitler's central role seems to diffuse responsibility and makes ultimate responsibility for the Holocaust that much harder to pin down.[3]

As is often the case in historical interpretation, there are extra-historical issues at stake here as well. If the physical extermination of the Jews was not planned in advance but was the result of a contingent, unsystematic, or improvised process of policy formation—if the road to Auschwitz was twisted, not straight—the image of Nazism as absolute evil appears to be somewhat tempered.[4] Intentionalists criticize functionalist interpretations for giving too much weight to contingent circumstances and *ad hoc* processes, thereby understating the lethal purposes inherent in the Nazi movement and its ideology from the start. Intentionalists accuse functionalists of diluting the unique criminality of the Holocaust by offering seemingly rational explanations for how and why it happened. Functional explanations—explanations that seek the causes of the Holocaust in the Nazi system, structure, or bureaucratic dynamic or in the broader developments of modern western civilization—may seem to downplay the moral question of personal responsibility and guilt by attributing rational and utilitarian motives to the perpetrators. But intentionalism, too, is susceptible to a form of apologetics. By attributing causation of the Holocaust too exclusively to Hitler and a small clique of Nazi leaders at the top, intentionalist interpretations have been used (or mistakenly understood as being used) to exculpate other sectors of German society, including lower-level and non-Nazi elites and institutions. Much of the functionalist scholarship on the structure and dynamic of the Nazi regime demonstrated the wide-ranging complicity of Germany's bureaucratic, military, and economic elites and institutions in the Holocaust.

Despite the acrimony of the debate, in recent years a consensus has developed among historians of the Holocaust that the distinction between intentionalism and functionalism (or structuralism) is no longer fruitful. Both interpretative perspectives need to be taken into account, for no simple explanation can account for so massive and lethal a program as the "Final Solution of the Jewish Question." As Ian Kershaw has pointed out, it is impossible to separate intentions from the impersonal conditions under which intentions are realized in practice.[5] Ideology set the crucial parameters within which the various agencies dealing with Jewish policy operated, but it did not provide a step-by-step program of how to resolve the Nazi-defined "Jewish question." From the very start the Nazis were committed to the total exclusion of Jews from German society—the creation of a *judenrein* Reich. They also were committed to the deadly eugenic principle of exterminating what they defined as "life unworthy of life." These two main tracks of Nazi policy—antisemitism and racial hygiene—merged to produce the Holocaust under the favorable conditions for institutionalized murder created by war. Although there was no master plan for how the destruction of the Jewish community in Germany was to be accomplished, physical extermination was always inscribed in the logic of Nazi antisemitism. Throughout the 1930s, however, persecution, isolation, and degradation of the Jews proceeded fitfully through various stages (see Chapter 11), thus repeatedly fanning hopes in the Jewish community that the worst was finally over. Few were able to foresee the terrible end of a process that now stands clearly revealed as a step-by-step path to total annihilation.

War and genocide

In their anti-Jewish policies (as in their foreign policy) during the 1930s the Nazis were constrained by certain practical realities, not least of which were the potentially adverse effects of antisemitic measures on the German economy and the potentially hostile reaction of foreign states. There were constraints on eugenic policies as well, foremost among them the likelihood of public opposition to institutionalized euthanasia. It was the war that freed the Nazis of all restraints on violence and provided the necessary cover to implement, first, their program to kill the disabled, and then their "final solution," the physical destruction of the Jews.

War also gave spurious credibility to Nazi charges that the Jews constituted dangerous enemies of the Reich. According to Nazi conspiracy theory, propagated for two decades, the Jews had been responsible for World War I, German defeat, and the Bolshevik Revolution. On 30 January 1939, after the Munich Agreement but before the occupation of Prague, Hitler addressed the Reichstag:

> Today I shall once more be a prophet. If the international Jewish financiers inside and outside Europe should again succeed in plunging the nations into another world war, then the result will not be the Bolshevization of the world and thus a victory for Jewry, but the annihilation of the Jewish race in Europe...[6]

Hitler probably hoped that his threat would put pressure on the west to make additional concessions to German expansionism.[7] Already in the 1920s radical antisemites had proposed treating Jews as hostages to prevent Allied intervention to enforce the Versailles Treaty. But Hitler's threat was not intended only as a tactical move. Central to the paranoid Nazi vision was the myth that Jews had declared war on Germany and were bent on its destruction. German Jews were to be held responsible for the damage caused to Germany by the hostile attitudes of western nations. Well before the German attack on Poland on 1 September 1939 Jews were officially stigmatized as the enemies of the German nation and were treated as such.

For the 350,000 Jews still remaining in the greater Reich the outbreak of war brought new and ever-increasing restrictions. Already before the war measures had been taken to concentrate Jews in residential blocks and apartment houses for easier surveillance. If before the war the official reason given was that Germans could not be expected to live in the same buildings with Jews, after the start of the war such draconian measures could be rationalized as necessary for public safety. Suppression of the internal enemy was declared to be vital to victory in the war.

Beginning in 1940, a nightly curfew was imposed on Jews. All radios owned by Jews were confiscated on the pretext that they were needed for the war effort. Jews received reduced food rations (rationing was introduced at the start of the war) and as of July 1940 were permitted to shop only at certain hours. They were no longer permitted to have a telephone service, own household pets, or use public libraries. The invasion of the Soviet Union in 1941 ushered in the final escalation of anti-Jewish measures in Germany. On 1 September 1941 all Jews in Germany over the age of six were required to wear the yellow Star of David. A similar decree had already been introduced in occupied Poland in November 1939. On 23 October 1941 all further Jewish emigration from areas controlled by the German Reich was prohibited, and the deportation of German Jews to the killing sites of the "final solution" began.

Ghettoization

The German invasion of Poland had transformed the nature and scope of the self-created "Jewish problem" for the Nazis. The overall goal of German policy remained what it had been before the war: to remove the Jewish population from all German and German-controlled areas. But the acquisition of Polish territories with a far greater Jewish population than Germany itself raised the question how this goal could possibly be accomplished. By the end of the Polish campaign almost two million Polish Jews, many of them impoverished, had fallen into German hands. Eastern Jewry had been the particular target of antisemitic prejudices in Germany and Austria since the late nineteenth century. Hostility to these *Ostjuden* was also fed by anti-Polish prejudice and resentment of the poor. In the Nazi catalog of "subhuman" races, Polish and Russian Jews ranked at the bottom.

The German invasion was accompanied by antisemitic excesses committed by soldiers as well as ethnic Germans living in Poland. Special SS task forces (*Einsatzgruppen*) were formed to enforce anti-Polish, anti-Jewish, and anti-Communist policy in the occupied areas. Among their assigned tasks was the liquidation of the Polish elite of political and clerical leaders and intellectuals, many of them Jewish. About 7,000 Jews are estimated to have been murdered before the end of 1939.[8] On 21 September 1939 Heydrich, chief of the Security Service of the SS and second in authority only to Himmler, ordered the concentration of all Polish Jews in cities and towns with railway connections in order to facilitate large-scale and rapid population transfers to as yet unspecified and undetermined destinations. In each ghetto Jewish councils were formed on German orders whose chief responsibility would be to administer and execute occupation decrees.

The concentration of Jews in urban ghettos was clearly intended as an interim measure pending a decision on the final disposition of the Jewish population. The occupiers confined Jews to ghettos in every Polish city. The largest such ghetto was located in the prewar capital of Warsaw, home before the war to the second-largest Jewish community in the world after New York. German officials in occupied Poland vied with each other in their eagerness to clear their regions of Jews. Plans in Berlin originally called for the transfer of Jews from the "incorporated territories," the western Polish territories directly annexed to the Reich as the *Wartheland*, to the so-called *Generalgouvernement*, the occupied portion of central Poland administered by the Germans from the provincial capital of Krakow. A Jewish reservation was to be created in the *Generalgouvernement* around the area of Lublin. Governor-General Hans Frank (1900–46) adamantly opposed this plan, however, as he, too, pursued a vision of ridding his territory of Jews. After sparring with officials of the "incorporated territories" for several months and pleading his case in Berlin, he succeeded in halting the influx of Jews into the *Generalgouvernement* in July 1940. This meant that the ghettos in the "incorporated territories," originally intended as way stations to resettlement in Lublin, would have to remain for a time. The largest of these ghettos was located in Lodz (renamed Litzmannstadt by the Germans), the second-largest city in Poland.

Conditions in the ghettos grew progressively worse for their humiliated, impoverished, and savagely exploited inhabitants. In November 1940 the Warsaw ghetto was walled in. Residents of the ghetto were no longer permitted contact with anyone outside. Other ghettos, including the Lodz ghetto, were sealed off with barbed wire. Jews caught outside the ghettos were shot on the spot. Many ghetto inhabitants were forced to work in factories making supplies for the German army. As Jews from the countryside were forcibly relocated into the ghetto, the population of the Warsaw ghetto swelled to over 400,000, and 160,000 Jews were crammed into the Lodz ghetto without adequate running water or sewage system. The spread of epidemics as a result of overcrowding, inadequate food supplies, and the lack of sanitation served as rationales for ever more extreme measures of segregation and isolation. With excruciating poverty, hunger, and disease driving up the mortality rate, more than 800,000 Jews lost their lives in the ghettos of German-occupied eastern Europe.[9]

The Jewish Councils, responsible for food, housing, health, and welfare in the ghettos, found themselves in what would ultimately become an impossible dilemma. Humiliated by the SS and forced to carry out German orders, council members and members of the Jewish police were often scorned and distrusted by the Jewish population, who saw them as instruments of the German administration. Yet communal life continued in the ghettos to a remarkable degree. Schools, hospitals, and cultural organizations continued to function under the most adverse conditions right up to the deportation of the remaining ghetto residents to the death camps in 1942–43.

Resettlement plans

For the radical right in Germany the ideal "solution" to the "Jewish problem" had always been to eliminate Jewish influence, and therefore the Jewish presence, from German society. The official policy of expulsion and forced emigration continued after the start of the war. In October 1939 a plan drawn up by Adolf Eichmann's office to deport German and Austrian Jews into the Soviet sector of Poland failed after more than 2,000 Viennese Jews had been driven across the San River, despite Soviet protests. The program was halted for lack of railroad cars, as the necessary cooperation of the *Wehrmacht* and the *Reichsbahn* (Reich Railway) had not yet been secured.[10] Despite vastly restricted opportunities, 15,000 German and Austrian Jews were still able to emigrate in 1940, and 8,000 more in 1941. But emigration could never solve the "problem" of the far greater number of Jews in German-occupied Poland

and western Europe. On 24 June 1940, two days after the armistice in France, the head of the Reich Security Main Office Reinhard Heydrich wrote to Foreign Minister Ribbentrop to make sure that he would be included in any decisions involving a territorial solution to deal with the 3.75 million European Jews who now fell under German control.

In the latter part of 1940 the German Foreign Office seriously considered using the French colonial island of Madagascar off the East African coast as a site for Jewish resettlement. The collapse of plans to create a Jewish reservation around Lublin made an alternative to deportation to the *Generalgouvernement* necessary, and the fall of France seemed likely to make Madagascar available. The Madagascar proposal had already surfaced in the antisemitic literature of the nineteenth century and was also discussed by British authors as an alternative to Palestine in the interwar years. Moreover, the Polish government had shown some interest in exploring the possibility of a Jewish homeland in Madagascar in 1937 and had actually sent a commission to Africa to consider its suitability. The commission found, however, that the island could provide adequate settlement for only a few thousand persons. The leading Nazi Jew-baiter Julius Streicher propagated a Madagascar plan in his antisemitic journal *Der Stürmer* in 1938. Addressing foreign correspondents in February 1939, Nazi ideologist Alfred Rosenberg made it clear that Madagascar's isolation was the source of its attraction to the Nazis: Palestine was not an acceptable Jewish homeland because it would give Jews a Middle Eastern power base from which they could expand their power worldwide.

On 15 August 1940 Eichmann, to whom had been delegated the task of working out the details of Jewish resettlement, submitted his plan for the "final solution" of the Jewish problem. An island solution was preferred to prevent Jewish contact with non-Jewish people. The Jewish homeland was to be structured as a police state under German authority. The Madagascar Plan already contained some essential elements of the genocidal "final solution": it called for the forced collaboration of Jewish organizations, the confiscation of all Jewish property, and the transport and resettlement of four million Jews under concentration camp-like conditions that were expected to decimate their numbers. The project was to be financed by western Jewish communities under terms of the peace treaty that Britain was still, in the summer of 1940, expected to sign.

The genesis of the "final solution"

The Madagascar Plan depended on an essential precondition that was not forthcoming: victory over Britain. Up to 1941 German plans appear to have been predicated on the assumption that the "final solution" of the Jewish question would not come until the end of the war. In the course of 1941, as it became evident that the war would not end soon, the Nazis turned to a policy of complete physical annihilation, even as the fiction of "resettlement" was maintained to deceive both victims and bystanders. Physical destruction was always inherent in resettlement schemes in any case and was certainly implicit in the logic of Nazi antisemitism.

Whether there was a specific "Führer order" for the "final solution," i.e. for the systematic killing of all European Jews, and when that decision was made (as well as why it was made at that time) are matters of continuing scholarly debate.[11] Some historians, including Martin Broszat, Hans Mommsen, and Peter Longerich, argue that a Führer order or even a specific decision was not necessary to account for the launching of the "final solution." "The history of the Holocaust," Longerich argued,

> is not the history of an extermination program that progressed without deviation as a result of a single order, but is rather the history of a process, in the course of which various interests were weighed, priorities established, and decisions made—a process that was, in short, the result of a policy, but shaped by politics.[12]

For obvious reasons the Nazis did not leave a paper trail, but some evidence points to key decisions as early as spring 1941, when preparations for "Operation Barbarossa" were in full swing. Certainly mass murder of Soviet Jews was planned as part of the attack on the Soviet Union in June 1941. This was to be a racial and ideological war without concern for the internationally accepted rules of war, and Soviet Jews as well as Communist Party officials were specifically targeted in plans drawn up as early as March and April 1941.

But what about the millions of Polish Jews, the German Jews, and the Jews of the other occupied countries of Europe? While Soviet Jews were being murdered in the summer of 1941, Jews in occupied western Europe were still being permitted to emigrate if they had the means. Coordination of overall policy fell to Reinhard Heydrich who had been put in charge of Jewish emigration from Germany in 1939. In a memorandum probably written by Heydrich himself and dated 31 July 1941, Heydrich obtained from *Reichsmarschall* Göring the authorization to carry out all necessary preparations "for a total solution of the Jewish question in the German sphere of influence in Europe." Heydrich was charged with submitting "an overall plan showing the preliminary organizational and financial measures for the execution of the intended final solution of the Jewish question."[13] In the light of what followed it seems clear that here the term "final solution" already refers to physical extermination. Yet even after the SS *Einsatzgruppen* had murdered hundreds of thousands of Russian Jews in June and July 1941, some SS officials evidently still expected the "final solution" to involve the resettlement of European Jews in the newly conquered Soviet areas to the east.

There is no documentary evidence to tell us precisely when and how the decision to murder all the Jews under German control was made. We do know from a document discovered by the German scholar Christian Gerlach in the newly opened Soviet archives in 1997 that Hitler formally announced the killing program to assembled regional party leaders in Berlin on 12 December 1941, the day after the German declaration of war on the United States.[14] It may be that American entry into the war removed the last restraints on the "final solution." However, it is more likely that the decision was already made and approved by Hitler by October 1941 at the latest, for at that time preparations for systematic gassing operations were well under way in Poland. In the same month emigration of Jews was prohibited throughout occupied Europe, and preparations for the commencement of Jewish deportations from Germany were put into place.[15]

The *Einsatzgruppen*

In late March 1941, in preparation for Operation Barbarossa, the German Wehrmacht officially agreed to provide all necessary logistical support to special units of the SS (the *Einsatzgruppen*) who were to follow closely behind the front-line troops to "carry out of their own accord executionary measures toward the civilian population."[16] The official task of these mobile killing units was to execute *"weltanschauliche Gegner"* (ideological opponents), including functionaries of the Communist Party, "Jews in party and state positions," and other "radical elements." The *Einsatzgruppen* sought to exploit indigenous antisemitism and incite pogroms, which could then be attributed to spontaneous popular wrath. Local resentment against the Soviet repression that preceded the German invasion was often directed against Jews, particularly in the Baltic States. More than 1,500 Jews were clubbed to death by Lithuanians in the city of Kovno (Kaunas) in one such pogrom at the end of June 1941. The killings were extended by order of the SS on 11 July to include "all male Jews between 17 and 45 years of age convicted of looting" with the decision as to who was guilty left up to SS commanders.[17] The need to pacify vast areas after the initial success of Operation Barbarossa provided the necessary cover to extend the killings to "anyone who even looks sideways at us," as Hitler put it in a meeting with Nazi leaders on 16 July.[18] By the end of July the killings were extended to women and children as well. The four *Einsatzgruppen* of about 750 men each operated in different theaters of war: Group A in the Baltic, Group B in White Russia (today Belarus), Group C in the Ukraine, and Group D in the Crimea. Between June 1941 and April 1942 they murdered at least 560,000 people, including virtually the entire remaining Jewish population of the conquered areas (some one and a half million Soviet Jews fled inland before the German advance). "Men, women, and children were driven into forests and fields, shot, and buried in mass graves."[19]

The Nazis regarded the *Einsatzgruppen* as an elite troop with an ideological mission. The leadership included a high proportion of men with advanced academic degrees. The commander of Group A, Dr. Franz Walther Stahlecker, had 11 lawyers on his staff, 9 with doctoral degrees. The personnel of the

Einsatzgruppen were recruited from the Security Police (combining Gestapo and criminal police), the SD, and the *Waffen-SS*, the military arm of the SS. They were supported by auxiliary police units and paramilitary groups recruited from Latvians, Lithuanians, Belorussians, and Ukrainians. The greatest single massacre perpetrated by the *Einsatzgruppen* occurred at Babi Yar on the outskirts of Kiev on 29 and 30 September 1941, ten days after the German capture of the city. According to the official report, a *Sonderkommando* (special unit) of Group C killed 33,771 Jews in two days. The Jews were told to assemble at a freight station in the city, ostensibly for resettlement, and instructed to bring along papers, money, valuables, and clothing. Once assembled, the Jews were marched on foot to a ravine a few miles outside the city and forced to undress. The terrified victims were herded through a narrow entrance in the ravine, forced to lie on the corpses in front of them, and shot in the back of the neck. This "action" received the explicit approval of the *Wehrmacht* which provided support in blocking off traffic, furnishing security, and later in removing all traces of the massacre. Ukrainian auxiliary police provided additional support.[20]

Units of the German Order Police, an auxiliary force recruited mainly from men over the age of military service, also participated in shooting Jews in eastern Europe and in rounding up Jews for the transports to the death camps. The approximately 500 men of one such unit, Auxiliary Police Battalion 101 stationed in Poland, perpetrated over 83,000 murders on Polish territory in 1942–43.[21] Mass shootings of Jews were also perpetrated in other occupied areas of Europe, especially Yugoslavia, where the German army played an even more active genocidal role than in eastern Europe under the pretext of combating partisans.

In November and December 1941 *Einsatzgruppe* A and other killing units in Riga and Minsk murdered the first trainloads of Jews deported from inside the Reich. Systematic mass shootings continued throughout the war, particularly in Poland, even after the death camp killing centers had gone into operation. One of the bloodiest shooting operations of the war occurred on 3 November 1943 at Lublin, where 18,000 Jews from the Majdanek camp were murdered by SS thugs in an operation code-named "Harvest Festival." It is estimated that as many as one and a half million persons, a quarter of all the Jews killed in the Holocaust, were murdered in open-air shootings by the *Einsatzgruppen*, order police and other SS killing units, the *Wehrmacht*, and their eastern European accomplices during the war.

The death camps

Murder by shooting was psychologically debilitating for the perpetrators and inefficient in terms of the ratio of kills to the number of executioners and the time invested. Himmler himself visited the site of an *Einsatzgruppen* action in Minsk in August 1941 and became physically ill at the sight of the bloodshed. Physical and psychological problems proliferated among the members of the killing units to the point of reducing their capacity to kill. Alcoholism became rampant. Clearly a more efficient method of mass murder was needed if the extermination campaign was to be extended from the Soviet Jews to all the Jews of Europe. In the late summer of 1941 experiments in the use of poison gas were conducted by the SS at various locations in eastern Europe. Carbon monoxide had already been used in the clandestine euthanasia program, code-named T-4, that was run by Philip Bouhler from the Führer Chancellery beginning in October 1939 (see Chapter 10). At several institutions for the mentally and physically disabled, gassings took place in specially constructed chambers disguised as shower rooms. Under the code name 13f14 in 1940, the killing program had already been extended to Jews in concentration camps deemed incapable of work.

The experience gained in the euthanasia program was put to use in the war against the Jews. Mobile gas vans were used to kill the wives and children of Jewish hostages in Serbia in October 1941. In the same month preparations began for the use of mobile gas vans at Chelmno (known to the Germans as Kulmhof), 40 miles northwest of Lodz in the western Polish territory incorporated into the Reich as the Wartheland (or Warthegau). The Chelmno gas vans were put into systematic operation on 8 December 1941 to murder the Jews of the Wartheland. Chelmno was the first of the six Nazi killing centers in Poland to go into operation. More than 150,000 Jews, mostly from the Lodz ghetto, were gassed at Chelmno in 1942. The use of a different kind of gas, a powerful pesticide known as Cyclon B, was tested at another camp located on formerly Polish territory at Oswiecim, known to the Germans as Auschwitz. Here 900 Soviet prisoners of war were killed in the first test of Cyclon B on 3 September 1941. Four other killing centers, Belzec, Sobibor, Treblinka, and Majdanek, went into operation in 1942.

The Wannsee Conference

The preparations for mass murder by gas in Auschwitz and Chelmno in September and October 1941 suggest that the decision to extend the killing campaign from Soviet Jews to all European Jews was made in these months. In November 1941 Heydrich called a conference of representatives from all the government and party agencies whose cooperation in the "final solution" would be required for smooth operations. The conference at a luxurious villa now used as a guest house for SS Security Service personnel in the Berlin suburb of Wannsee was originally scheduled for 8 December the same day the gas vans went into operation at Chelmno, but the unexpected Russian offensive at Moscow and the Japanese attack on Pearl Harbor made senior civil servants temporarily unavailable and forced a postponement until 20 January 1942. By the time of the Wannsee Conference daily gassings had already taken place at Chelmno for more than six weeks. The purpose of the conference was not to determine the nature of the "final solution"—that had already been decided at a higher level—but rather to coordinate departmental policies, allocate tasks associated with the projected European-wide deportations, and remove any bureaucratic obstacles that might impede the SS in its implementation of the extermination program. The meeting was also designed to commit the civilian bureaucracy to the program of racial extermination and to establish their shared complicity in the murder of the Jews.[22]

The conference, chaired by Heydrich, was attended by high-ranking career civil servants from the Foreign Office, the Ministry of the Interior, and the Ministry of Justice; representatives from the *Generalgouvernement*, the Occupied Eastern Territories, the Office of the Four-Year Plan, and the Reich and Party chancelleries; and leading officials from the SS and the Reich Security Main Office.[23] Heydrich opened the meeting by announcing his appointment by Göring as Plenipotentiary for the Preparation of the Final Solution and explaining the scope of the program. Eichmann, now responsible for all Jewish affairs in the Reich Security Main Office of the SS, provided the statistics. Eleven million Jews throughout Europe were to be included, an inflated figure that included some 330,000 British Jews and overstated by about two million the number of Soviet Jews expected to come under German control (the actual Jewish population in Europe before the final solution is estimated at around nine to ten million). The minutes of the meeting are couched in euphemistic language that refers to the killing machinery in veiled terms, but it is clear that none of the participants had any doubt about the murderous intent of the "final solution." Jews were to be "evacuated" to the east and subjected to hard labor, "in which task a large part will undoubtedly disappear through natural diminution."

> The remnant that may eventually remain, being undoubtedly the part most capable of resistance, will have to be appropriately dealt with, since it represents a natural selection and in the event it is set free is to be regarded as the germ cell of a Jewish revival. (Note the experience of history.)[24]

In plain language, Jews were to be worked to death, and those that survived were to be killed by other means.

One question that needed to be addressed was the degree of cooperation or resistance to be expected from the governments and institutions of countries whose Jews were to be subjected to the "final solution." The Foreign Office representative, Under-secretary of State Martin Luther, foresaw no great difficulties in southeastern and western Europe. Opposition, however, could be expected in the Scandinavian states. For that reason (and because the number of Jews in these countries was much smaller) he proposed postponing the implementation of the "final solution" in the Scandinavian countries for the time being.

The question whether to include Jews in mixed marriages and persons of partially Jewish descent in the "final solution" gave rise to lengthy discussions. Their fate inevitably raised issues of public morale, as the reaction of their "Aryan" German relatives had to be taken into account. The bureaucratic problem of defining who was a Jew emerged once again and would have to be resolved on a case-by-case basis. To avoid "endless administrative labor," the Secretary of State in the Interior Ministry Dr. Wilhelm Stuckart, who had helped draft the Nuremberg Laws and their later amendments, suggested compulsory sterilization for all first-degree *Mischlinge* and all second-degree *Mischlinge* deemed equal to Jews (which included those whose appearance was deemed "especially unfavorable in racial terms" and those who conducted themselves like Jews). To simplify "the mixed-marriage problem" he proposed dissolving all such marriages by legislative fiat. No final decision was reached at the Wannsee Conference on these matters. But when the Gestapo rounded up Jews in mixed marriages in Berlin in February 1943, a protest demonstration by their German spouses may have caused Goebbels to order their release.[25] Although discussions on what categories of Jews to include in the "final solution" took up about half of the time of the Wannsee Conference, they affected only Jews in the Reich. It is one of the ironies of the Holocaust that part-Jews and Jews in mixed marriages had a better chance of survival in Germany than in areas under German occupation, where the reaction of victims' relatives was never considered an obstacle to murder.

"Operation Reinhard"

At the Wannsee Conference the representative of the *Generalgouvernement*, Dr. Josef Bühler, requested that the Jews of the *Generalgouvernement* be the first to be subjected to the "final solution." He argued that most ghetto inhabitants were no longer capable of productive work. The ghettos also created the danger of epidemics. And, as the "final solution" was to be carried out in the east, transportation would be less of a problem than in countries located at a greater distance from the killing sites. By the time of the Wannsee Conference, preparations were in fact already well under way under the Lublin SS and Police Leader Odilo Globocnik, a former *Gauleiter* of Vienna who had been ousted from his office because of corruption. The murder of the Jews of the *Generalgouvernement* received the code name *Aktion Reinhard* to commemorate Reinhard Heydrich after his assassination by the Czech underground in May 1942. The term *Aktion Reinhardt* had originally referred to the operations of Fritz Reinhardt (1895–1969), the official in the Reich Finance Ministry in charge of administering the valuables, including dental gold, extracted from the victims before their death.

The Nazis established three killing centers for the implementation of Operation Reinhard: Belzec, Sobibor, and Treblinka. All three camps were located in the eastern part of the *Generalgouvernement* in isolated areas close to railroad lines. Each camp was used primarily to kill the Jewish population of the geographical area in which it was located. Personnel recruited from the T-4 program, the program to kill the disabled that was formally ended in fall 1941, brought their technical expertise to the killing centers of Operation Reinhard. SS major Christian Wirth (1885–1944), who had conducted the first gassings of Germans certified as incurably insane in 1939 and was promoted to head the euthanasia institutions throughout Germany in 1940, was named the first commandant of the Belzec death camp in December 1941 and inspector of the three Operation Reinhard death camps in August 1942.

The first transports of Polish Jews arrived at Belzec in February 1942. In contrast to Auschwitz, where the killing was done with Cyclon B, Wirth decided to use carbon monoxide in order to be independent of suppliers. Specially trained Ukrainian volunteers participated in the murders; 600,000 Jews perished at Belzec before it was dismantled at the end of 1942. Sobibor went into operation in April 1942 under the Austrian Commandant Franz Stangl (1908–71), formerly a member of the staff at Hartheim, a euthanasia center in Germany, and later the commandant at Treblinka; 250,000 Jews died at Sobibor before it ceased operations in 1943. Exhaust gasses from captured Soviet tanks were used at Treblinka, the most efficient of the three Operation Reinhard camps. Located only 45 miles from Warsaw, Treblinka was the site where most of the Jews of the Warsaw ghetto were killed. The death toll of 900,000 at Treblinka was second only to that of Auschwitz. There was no selection here. Victims were taken straight to the gas chambers. To speed the killing process they were made to run so that they would take deeper breaths when inhaling the gas. The extermination facilities at Treblinka operated from July 1942 to August 1943.

Most victims of Operation Reinhard were Polish Jews (and several thousand Poles killed for aiding Jews), but they also included Jewish transports from Holland, France, Austria, Greece, Slovakia, and Theresienstadt, the camp created by the Nazis in November 1941 as a "ghetto" for elderly Jews and certain categories of privileged German Jews (including war veterans, individuals of distinction, and former senior civil servants) in the Czech town of Terezin, 35 miles from Prague in what was now the "Protectorate of Bohemia and Moravia." Theresienstadt was supposed to be the "model camp" that could be used to conceal the true nature of the camp system from the public; it was the only camp opened to the inspection of representatives of the International Red Cross in July 1944. In reality, however, Theresienstadt served more as a transit camp for Jews destined for the death camps further east.

In spring 1943 Himmler ordered the total liquidation of all ghettos in Poland, including workers in ghetto factories that manufactured supplies for the German army. The Warsaw ghetto, decimated by the deportations that began in July 1942, was razed to the ground after a last desperate rebellion by its remaining inmates in April 1943. The Lodz ghetto was the last ghetto to be liquidated in August 1944. Operation Reinhard was officially ended on 19 October 1943, ten months after the original target date set by Himmler for completing the killing of the Jews of the *Generalgouvernement*. The three death camps, Belzec, Sobibor, and Treblinka, were dissolved. The last few months were devoted to removing all traces of the killing operations. Bodies at mass burial sites were exhumed and burned. Belzec was the first camp to be closed at the end of 1942. Sobibor was transformed into a camp for the storage and sorting of captured munitions. At Treblinka the last commando of work Jews dismantled barracks and fences before they, too, were shot. After the end of the killing operations, Ukrainian camp personnel were lodged in newly constructed housing on the site.

Auschwitz

The Operation Reinhard killing centers were no longer needed because of the growing capacity of Auschwitz in the course of 1942. Auschwitz was located not far from Krakow in the part of Poland that had been absorbed by Austria-Hungary in the nineteenth century. In September 1939 the area was incorporated into the German Reich. A concentration camp was constructed here in spring 1940 around a core of former Polish and before that Austro-Hungarian military barracks. Originally planned as a transit camp to points further east, Auschwitz, in the four and a half years of its existence, became the largest forced labor and extermination complex in the German imperium.

There were three main camps in the Auschwitz complex. The base camp first served as a concentration camp for Poles (political leaders, priests, intellectuals, and other actual and potential opponents of the Nazi regime), who constituted the majority of camp inmates until the fall of 1941. Also, it was here that the first gas chamber was constructed for testing purposes in the basement of one of the camp blocks in September 1941. At Auschwitz-Monowitz, with its 38 satellite labor camps, German industry, particularly the I. G. Farben synthetic rubber and oil plants, exploited the labor of inmates who were forced to work until they died.

In a rural area two miles northwest of the base camp was the killing center of Auschwitz-Birkenau, erected in November 1941 complete with tracks and a selection ramp to serve both as a camp to house slave labor and as an extermination factory. Up to 100,000 inmates could be housed in the barracks constructed at Birkenau. In January 1942 the first gas chamber was constructed at Birkenau; a second one was added in June. In December 1942 the original gas chamber was dismantled and replaced by a technologically updated crematory with two gas chambers. Crematories obviated the problems associated with mass burials and the open-air incineration of corpses as originally practiced at Auschwitz and in the Operation Reinhard camps. By 1944 four crematories were in use at Auschwitz. The gas chambers were camouflaged as shower rooms and victims were told they were to be disinfected, a technique already used in the T-4 euthanasia program from 1939 to 1941. Adjoining barracks were used for undressing and the storage of suitcases, glasses, hair, shoes, and other personal effects.

Transports carrying Jews arrived at Auschwitz-Birkenau from all over Europe beginning in spring 1942. Men and women were lined up separately in rows of five abreast. SS officers asked questions about age, vocation, and health. Those selected as capable of work were registered, tattooed, and given prison clothing. Those selected as incapable of work (up to 90 percent of each transport) were sent directly to the gas chambers without further bureaucratic processing. SS physicians also selected candidates for medical experiments. A part of the camp at Birkenau was cordoned off to house Gypsies, the only other group of Nazi victims selected solely on the basis of race. The Gypsy camp was liquidated in August 1943. It is estimated that as many as half a million Gypsies may have died in the Holocaust—more than 100,000 at Auschwitz.

The last large group to be murdered at Auschwitz were Hungarian Jews, who fell under German control after the Germans occupied Hungary in March 1944. More than 400,000 Jews were deported to Auschwitz before the Hungarian government, under pressure from western countries, succeeded in halting the deportations in July 1944. The number of victims who died at Auschwitz between January 1942 and November 1944, when Himmler ordered the destruction of the gas chambers, is today estimated at roughly one million, the largest death toll of any of the six Nazi killing camps in Poland. Thousands more died, many from starvation and cold, as all remaining inmates fit to walk were marched into Germany to elude the advancing Soviet armies in winter 1944–45. These death marches represented a deliberate continuation of the killings by other means.[26]

Original estimates of the death toll at Auschwitz ran much higher than one million, due in part to the testimony of Rudolf Höss (1900–47), who was the camp commandant until November 1943 before moving up to become deputy chief of the SS Economic and Administrative Main Office, the highest administrative unit of the camp system.[27] At the Nuremberg Trials Höss gave a figure of two and a half million deaths at Auschwitz. The Soviet government gave an even higher figure, declaring that four million had died at the camp. Discrepancies like these have allowed right-wing extremists to sow doubts about whether there was a systematic program to murder Jews and Gypsies by gas at Auschwitz. Of that there can be no doubt, despite the paucity of written records. Little documentary evidence survived, due in part to Himmler's order to leave no trace of the extermination sites. The Red Army liberated Auschwitz in January 1945, finding only those survivors who had been left behind because they were unfit to walk.

The other Nazi killing center in Poland that originated as a concentration camp was the Lublin camp, established as a prisoner of war camp for the *Waffen-SS* in the fall of 1941. The gassing facilities were located at Majdan on the outskirts of Lublin. At Majdanek both Cyclon B and carbon monoxide, supplied in portable tanks, were used. Some 200,000 persons were killed here, including at least 60,000 Jews, between the summer of 1942 and July 1944, when the camp was liberated by the Soviets.[28]

Although the goal of the "final solution," the killing of all of the European Jews, was not achieved, it claimed approximately six million Jewish victims—roughly two-thirds of the prewar Jewish population in Europe and one-third of world Jewry—thus making the Holocaust unique in scope among the genocides of history. Approximately half of these deaths occurred in the systematic killing operations in the death camps. Approximately one and a half million died in open-air shootings at the hands of the *Einsatzgruppen* and other killing units. Another estimated one and a half million Jews died of disease, starvation, and brutal mistreatment in the ghettos and concentration camps. The death toll included at least 2.7 million Polish Jews, 2.2 million Soviet Jews, a half million Hungarian Jews, 230,000 German and Austrian Jews, 140,000 Jews from Czechoslovakia, more than 100,000 from the Netherlands, 60,000 each from Yugoslavia and Greece, more than 30,000 from France, and smaller numbers from Belgium, Italy, Albania, Norway, Luxembourg, Denmark, and Bulgaria. At least 200,000 Jews were killed in pogroms and camps in Romania and Transnistria (the part of the Ukraine annexed by Romania in 1941), most at the hands of Germany's Romanian allies.[29]

How much did the German public know?

Secrecy and deception were central to the killing operations of the Holocaust. The Nazis had an obvious interest in keeping all information on the killings from the Allies. It would not have been in the Nazis' military interest to provide their enemies with an issue that could only have turned world opinion against Germany. The killings took place many miles from where the victims lived. The euphemism of "resettlement" was always used for the deportations to the death camps, the aspect of the "final solution" most visible to the general public both in Germany and occupied Europe. The policy of secrecy was probably motivated less by fear of public opposition than by desire to avert panic among the victims. There were many possibilities for the German public to learn of the Holocaust; in fact, it was difficult *not* to know that Jews were being put to death on a horrendous scale. Hundreds of thousands of ordinary Germans participated in some capacity in the machinery of murder.[30] Many more Germans had direct knowledge of one or another facet of the "final solution." Although perpetrators were under strict orders not to talk about their work, even Höss, the commandant at Auschwitz, told his family about the nature of the camp. The massacres on the Soviet front could not be concealed from the rank and file of the Wehrmacht, many of whom wrote home about them. The concentration camps and ghettos and their liquidation could not be concealed from the public eye.

There were other ways of knowing about the "final solution" as well. On 16 November 1941 Goebbels wrote in *Das Reich*, a Nazi weekly with a circulation of 500,000, that Hitler's prophecy of 30 January 1939 was now being fulfilled.[31] After eight years of escalating antisemitic persecution, at a time of war for which the Jews were officially blamed, it must have been clear to Goebbels' readers that he was not using the term *Vernichtung* (destruction) in a purely metaphorical sense. Hitler, too, in a speech to the Reichstag on 30 January 1942, made reference to his earlier prophecy and announced that it was now being fulfilled. Julius Streicher wrote in *Der Stürmer* on 19 March 1942 that "in this war not the Aryan race will be destroyed, but the Jew will be exterminated."[32] On 4 November 1943 *Der Stürmer* carried the following report:

> It is really the truth that the Jews have disappeared, so to speak, from Europe and that the Jewish "reservoir" of the East, from which the Jewish plague has for centuries beset the people of Europe, has ceased to exist... The Führer of the German people at the beginning of the war prophesied what has now come to pass...[33]

The wartime speeches of Nazi leaders were full of allusions to the killing program. But very few Germans had exact knowledge of the nature and scope of the killings. While Nazi leaders spoke openly about the destruction of Jews, they treated the details of the death camps as a state secret. By announcing the extermination program without revealing its full scale and barbarity, the Nazis ensured the complicity of the German public while avoiding the potentially demoralizing effects of that knowledge on the war effort. One purpose of treating the "final solution" as an "open secret" was to convince the German people that there was no alternative to fighting the war to the bitter end. Shared liability would "make people realize that there was no way back."[34] Most Germans probably did not want to know about the death camps and the gas chambers. Ignorance could serve as a convenient shield for the moral conscience. It is not at all clear that there would have been significant popular opposition even if the details of the killing camps had become public knowledge. Preoccupied with their own difficulties in a time of total war, most ordinary Germans were at best indifferent to the fate of the Jews.[35]

The Allies and the Holocaust

The Holocaust could not have occurred without the apathy and indifference of bystanders. The appeasement policy (and isolationism in the United States) had muted western criticism of Germany's anti-Jewish policy before the war. Historians still debate the degree of Allied culpability in failing to do more to rescue victims and halt the killings during the war. By June 1942 western leaders had been informed of the extermination camps by emissaries of the Polish underground. There was some reluctance to believe these reports, however, not least because much of the atrocity propaganda of World War I had turned out to be exaggerated. There was no precedent in history for genocide on such a scale. The Allies were also reluctant to single out any victim group by acknowledging that Jews faced special treatment at the hands of the enemy. Nonetheless, in November 1942 Allied leaders issued a public warning to the Nazis to stop the killing of the Jews or face the consequences of their crime after the war.

In January 1944 President Roosevelt established the War Refugee Board, which contributed to the rescue of several thousand Hungarian Jews, largely through the efforts of Swedish diplomat Raoul Wallenberg (1912–47), who issued protective passports after his posting to Budapest in July 1944. Yet, despite appeals by the World Jewish Congress in August 1944 and a successful raid on the I. G. Farben plant at Auschwitz-Monowitz that same month, the killing installations at Auschwitz-Birkenau were not bombed, as both British and American military planners were disinclined to divert aircraft from military targets. Officials argued that the rescue of civilian populations must not be allowed to delay the winning of the war by the most rapid means.[36] On 26 June 1944 the US War Department responded to a proposal to bomb the railroad lines leading to Auschwitz by stating that "the early defeat of the Axis" provided "the most effective relief of the victims."[37] Opinion is divided on whether any of the proposed options for military actions or rescue operations were realistic and had any reasonable chance of success. Any attempt to take out the gas chambers faced considerable technological difficulties. Historian William D. Rubinstein has pointed out that if the Allies had bombed Auschwitz-Birkenau, they would have been criticized for murdering Jews. In any case, the priority given to the extermination of the Jews by the Nazis made it highly unlikely that destruction of the gas chambers would have ended the killing program.[38]

The role of the Church

The Roman Catholic Church under Pius XII (Eugenio Pacelli [1876–1958]) has also been criticized for failing to issue an explicit denunciation of the Holocaust during the war. There is no question that the Church hierarchy was fully informed of the mass murder by an unrivaled network of informants. But the Church was committed to political neutrality between the two power blocs to safeguard its interests and maintain an environment in which the Church could operate freely. Pius XII's Christmas Message of 1942 condemning racial policies and the mistreatment of civilians never specifically named the Nazis nor did it specifically mention the Jews:

> Mankind owes that vow [to bring men back to the law of God and service of neighbor] to the hundreds of thousands of persons who, without any fault on their part, sometimes only because of nationality or race, have been consigned to death or to a slow decline.[39]

Pacelli later justified his failure to issue a more explicit condemnation of the Holocaust on the grounds that it might have made matters even worse for the victims, as indeed seemed to have been the case after protests by Catholic leaders in Nazi-occupied Holland in February 1942 failed to slow the deportation of Dutch Jews. More importantly, he claimed, he wanted his moral indictment of crimes against civilians to include Soviet atrocities as well.

Historians attribute the Pope's failure to issue any public protest against the Holocaust, despite the request for papal intervention by the Catholic Bishop of Berlin Konrad von Preysing (1875–1950) in 1943, mainly to his fear of thereby facilitating a communist victory in Europe. "In his mind," historian Michael Phayer has written, "Germany was and would remain the European bulwark against Russian communism."[40] As papal nuncio in Munich at the end of World War I, Pacelli had become convinced that Jews played a disproportionate role in the aborted revolution in that city in 1919. Certainly his uncompromising opposition to communism contrasted markedly to his conciliatory attitude toward fascism. All the major fascist or fascist-sympathizing leaders in Europe, including Hitler, Mussolini, Franco, Pétain, the Hungarian regent Miklós Horthy (1868–1957), the Croatian Ustasha leader Ante Pavelic (1889–1959), and the Portuguese dictator António Salazar (1889–1970), were Catholics and supported the German crusade against Bolshevism.

Whatever his specific motives and objectives may have been, Pius XII clearly preferred behind-the-scenes diplomacy as a means of influencing events to any overt attempt to mobilize public opinion against the Nazis. The Church was committed to a policy of conciliation and reserve toward the warring nations in which the Church played an active public role.[41] No doubt fears that the Church would not be permitted to continue its public religious functions in a murderous war in which the Church was responsible to Catholics on both sides of the conflict reinforced the Pope's reluctance to issue a public statement specifically denouncing the Nazi genocidal policies toward the Jews. Failure to issue such a protest could not help but tarnish the image of the Church in the eyes of those who considered its fundamental moral obligations to be more important than its immediate institutional interests.

Although Pius XII did not publicly condemn German deportations of the Jews of Rome in October 1943, his defenders have pointed out that the Church leadership did take actions that resulted in the rescue of thousands of Jews, particularly converts to Catholicism. Hundreds were hidden in the Vatican itself; others found refuge in monasteries, convents, and safe houses in Catholic countries, as well as in Catholic homes; 30,000 Jews survived in Catholic Poland, where, unlike in the west, aid to the Jews was punishable by death. Courageous individual clerics such as Bernhard Lichtenberg (1875–1943), provost of St. Hedwig's Cathedral in Berlin, and the Jesuit priest Alfred Delp (1907–45) were martyred for protesting the persecution of the Jews.[42] But most priests followed the lead of the Vatican in remaining silent on the Nazis' anti-Jewish policies. Even clerical leaders like Bishop Clemens von Galen (1878–1946), who had protested the killing of the disabled from the pulpit and had filed a criminal complaint with the Ministry of Justice in 1941, failed to speak out against the killing of the Jews. What effect an explicit papal denunciation of Nazi crimes against the Jews would have had remains a matter of speculation and dispute. It is virtually certain, however, that at the height of the killings in 1942 no force on earth could have prevented the Nazi juggernaut from implementing its murderous vision of a world without Jews.

16 Continuities and new beginnings

The aftermath of National Socialism and war

Germans sometimes refer to the collapse of Nazi Germany in May 1945 as *"Stunde Null"* (zero hour), suggesting an entirely new beginning. It did indeed mark more than just the end of the Nazi regime. It marked the end of the great-power status achieved under Bismarck in the previous century and the end of Germany's imperialist ambitions. The degree of destruction exceeded anything the Allies could have imagined. German cities lay in ruins—the greatest heaps of rubble the world had ever seen. The country's economic infrastructure was devastated. Not only was Germany defeated and occupied, it had ceased to exist as a sovereign state. The *Wehrmacht* and the Nazi Party were dissolved. The Dönitz government carried on at the convenience of the western Allies for another two weeks before its members were formally arrested in Flensburg on the Danish border on 22 May. Some leading Nazis sought to escape detection by blending in with the population. It was not until 23 May that Heinrich Himmler was discovered in the uniform of an ordinary enlisted man in a British detention camp for *Wehrmacht* soldiers in northern Germany. He committed suicide by swallowing a poison capsule implanted in his teeth. His end was not unusual, as historian Richard Lakowski estimated that more than 100,000 Germans committed suicide in the spring of 1945.[1]

Former foreign minister Ribbentrop was not identified and arrested in Hamburg until 14 June. It is estimated that as many as 80,000 lower-ranking Nazi leaders may have successfully changed their identities in the chaos of the immediate postwar period.[2] Adolf Eichmann, whose identity and role in the Holocaust were not yet well known, escaped from American captivity in 1946 and fled to Argentina in 1950 with the help of papers supplied by the right-wing Austrian Catholic Bishop Alois Hudal (1883–1963), who was finally forced to resign his office by the Vatican in 1952.[3] In 1960 Eichmann was abducted and taken to Israel, where he was tried and executed in 1962. Werner Heyde (1902–64), the SS physician who headed the T-4 euthanasia program and was sentenced to death in absentia in 1946, was discovered practicing medicine under an assumed name in northern Germany in 1959. He committed suicide while awaiting a new trial in 1964. Josef Mengele (1911–79), the SS physician who carried out selections and conducted medical

experiments on inmates at Auschwitz, was among the hundreds of incriminated SS officials who took refuge in Argentina after the war with the help
of falsified papers. He reputedly died in a swimming accident in Brazil in
1979.

One result of the Nazis' fanatical fight to the end, a decision fortified by the
Allies' unconditional surrender policy, was that conditions following World War
II were quite unlike the situation after World War I. The victorious Allies
resolved not to repeat the mistakes of the past. Germany was to be occupied,
demilitarized, denazified, deindustrialized, and democratized. The totality of
destruction paradoxically enhanced the prospects for democratization in
Germany, for the conservative elites who had blocked democracy in the Weimar
Republic were either destroyed or gravely weakened, partly by the Nazis themselves. Gone were the remnants of particularism and privilege. The Prussian
state, associated for centuries with militarism, was formally abolished in 1947.
For the time being, at least, the hierarchical, militarist, and chauvinist values of
the past were entirely discredited.

Except for isolated acts of murder by die-hard Nazis against German civilians ready to cooperate with the Allies, the underground resistance movement
planned by the Nazis under the code name "Werewolf" never materialized.
Although only anti-Nazis experienced the Allied victory as political liberation, most Germans were nonetheless relieved to be liberated from the terrible burdens of a war that increasingly came to be perceived as senseless and
wrong. Perhaps the most important legacy of World War II was the almost
universal revulsion against an ideological system that had wreaked such terrible havoc on so many people. For the rest of the century Nazism would
become for most people, in Germany as much as elsewhere, the embodiment
of evil. The demonization of Nazism and top Nazi leaders, however, also
helped sustain the fiction that Nazism was imposed on an essentially inno-
cent population by force.

Although the victor powers were united in their rejection of fascism, they
had different definitions of democracy and could not agree on the form it
should take. Now rivals rather than allies, the Soviet Union and the western
occupying powers (the United States, Britain, and France) could not agree on
common governing institutions for Germany nor on the terms of a formal
peace settlement. Although the division of Germany into occupation zones
(and the capital of Berlin into sectors) was intended to be temporary, the onset
of the Cold War resulted in the formation of two rival German states that were
not reunited until the collapse of communism in 1989–90.

The division of Germany and Berlin was the most visible manifestation of
the conflict between Soviet authoritarian socialism and western liberal capitalism that took center stage after the end of the war and was not resolved
until the communist collapse. On both sides the passions of the recently
ended war were soon channeled into the East–West confrontation. As a result
of the Cold War both *Vergangenheitsbewältigung* (coming to terms with the
past) and the implementation of democratic reforms in Germany were more

limited than might otherwise have been the case. The Cold War had the effect of mitigating efforts to root out Nazism and to conscientiously confront questions of personal responsibility. On both sides of the Cold War divide the need to restore order and stability eventually took precedence over the need to institute change or take responsibility for the past.

The Nuremberg Trials

Although the Allies had already agreed in 1942 on the need to punish the major Nazi leaders, it was not until August 1945 that the actual procedure was decided. Supporters of a formal trial, mainly American, ultimately prevailed over those, like Stalin, who advocated summary executions as the appropriate form of punishment on the grounds that a judicial proceeding might leave the victors open to the potentially embarrassing charge of trying the Nazis under laws that did not exist or were not binding at the time. The International Military Tribunal formed to try the Nazi leadership consisted of one judge and one alternate from each of the four victor powers (United States, USSR, Britain, and France). Prosecutorial duties were also shared among representatives of the four countries. The trial ran from October 1945 to November 1946. There were four counts in the indictment: first, conspiracy (plans to wage wars of aggression); second, crimes against peace (wars of aggression and violations of international treaties); third, war crimes (violations of international agreements on the conduct of war, such as the Hague and Geneva Conventions on the treatment of POWs and civilians); and fourth, crimes against humanity. The latter count, a response to the unprecedented scale of Nazi atrocities, provided the main grounds for the death penalties that were eventually handed down. It invalidated the defense that genocidal policies did not formally violate German law during the Nazi period.

Twenty-four leading Nazis were indicted, but only 21 were in the dock when the proceedings began. Robert Ley committed suicide before the trial began, the industrialist Gustav Krupp was too ill to stand trial, and Martin Bormann could not be located. It was later determined that Bormann had been killed attempting to escape from Berlin in the last days of the war.

After a lengthy trial in which most of the defendants attempted to place all responsibility for the crimes of the Nazi period on Hitler, 12 of the leading Nazis were sentenced to death, including Göring, Ribbentrop, Rosenberg, Frick, Sauckel, Streicher, Bormann (in absentia), Seyss-Inquart (who had served as governor of Holland during the German occupation), Hans Frank (governor-general of occupied Poland), Ernst Kaltenbrunner (Heydrich's successor as head of the SS police apparatus), and Generals Keitel and Jodl. Rudolf Hess, Walther Funk (Schacht's successor as Economics Minister), and Admiral Raeder received life sentences, although only Hess served his full term (until his suicide in 1987). Albert Speer and Hitler Youth Leader Baldur von Schirach, both of whom showed some contrition, received terms of 20 years. Former foreign minister Neurath and Admiral Dönitz received 15 and 10 years, respectively.

Despite strenuous Soviet objections, Franz von Papen and Hjalmar Schacht, the old conservatives who had been so instrumental in the Nazis' rise to power, were acquitted, as was Hans Fritzsche, head of the Radio Division in Goebbels' Propaganda Ministry. The Soviets also dissented against the tribunal's failure to convict three of the organizations originally indicted. The SS, including the Gestapo and SD, and the Leadership Corps of the Nazi Party were branded criminal organizations while charges against the SA, the Reich Cabinet, and the General Staff and High Command of the *Wehrmacht* (OKW) were dropped. The SA was exempted because of its relatively insignificant role after 1934, while the cabinet never met after 1937. The verdict of historians on the criminal role of the *Wehrmacht* in the Holocaust, however, has been far harsher than the verdict of the Nuremberg tribunal.

Despite their imperfections, unavoidable in a process in which four victor powers with differing systems of justice provided both judges and prosecutors, the Nuremberg Trials served a very important purpose in documenting the horrors of Nazi crimes. The stark revelations of the extermination system were as shocking to many Germans as they were to the rest of the world. The atrocities revealed at the trials helped to discredit the Nazis and thus assure that there would be no repeat of the dangerous myths and fantasies that had fed right-wing radicalism after World War I. The trials thus helped to reinforce the genuine antifascism that developed among the populations of both West and East Germany after the war. The information brought to light at Nuremberg fills 42 bulky volumes, an invaluable resource for historians of the Third Reich. The Nuremberg Trials were also important for providing a precedent for the prosecution of human rights abuses under international law. Codified by the United Nations in 1950, the Nuremberg Principles have been adopted as part of the legal system of most major nations of the world. However, except for the UN-sponsored military tribunal to prosecute crimes committed in the war in Yugoslavia in the 1990s, no similar tribunal has been established for any other of the many smaller wars of the second half of the twentieth century and the first eight years of the twenty-first century. The UN-sponsored International Court in The Hague to adjudicate differences between nations and prosecute war crimes has been gravely weakened by the refusal of the world's leading military power, the United States, to participate in its functions or adhere to its decisions.

American occupation authorities conducted 12 subsequent trials at Nuremberg against administrative, military, medical, and judicial figures of the Third Reich; once-powerful industrialists, including steel magnate Friedrich Flick and the major executives of the I. G. Farben combine and the Krupp steel concern; officials of the Foreign Office and other leading civil servants (known as the Wilhelmstrasse trial); *Einsatzgruppen* leaders; and SS officers involved in the administration of concentration camps and slave labor programs. Of the 185 defendants, 131 were convicted, 24 were sentenced to death, and 12 were executed. Similar trials were held in the British, French, and Soviet zones of occupation, as well as in neighboring countries. In the western zones about 5,000 persons were convicted, of whom 486 were executed.[4] Rudolf Höss was tried in Poland and executed at Auschwitz in 1947.

With the founding of the Federal Republic of Germany (FRG) in the west and the German Democratic Republic (GDR) in the east in 1949 further prosecution of Nazi war crimes devolved to the German successor states. However, Adenauer's government was more interested in obtaining amnesty for convicted war criminals than in initiating new trials against persons accused of war crimes. Systematic legal investigation into Nazi war crimes did not begin again in the FRG until the founding of a Central Judicial Office in Ludwigsburg in 1958 under pressure from journalists and intellectuals of the left. The trial of 21 former SS guards at Auschwitz in 1963 resulted in 6 life terms and 11 further convictions. More importantly, this trial (and the Eichmann trial in Jerusalem in 1961) contributed to a renewed public consciousness of and scholarly research into the atrocities of the Nazi regime. Partly in response to international pressure the West German legislature (*Bundestag*) abolished the statute of limitations for crimes of murder and genocide altogether in 1979. West German judicial proceedings against Nazi crimes between 1945 and 1992 resulted in over 6,000 convictions; in East Germany the official figure stood at 12,000, while in Austria, where the Allies encouraged the dubious notion that Austria had been Hitler's first victim, some 14,000 convictions were handed down.[5] But far larger numbers of perpetrators escaped prosecution or were acquitted.[6] Convicted war criminals rarely served their full sentences; by 1956 all of the 120 perpetrators sentenced by the US tribunal in the secondary Nuremberg trials had been released—including those sentenced to life imprisonment.[7]

Denazification

At the Yalta Conference in February 1945 and again at the Potsdam Conference in July and August 1945 the United States, Soviet Union, and Britain resolved not only to punish Nazi crimes, but also to rid Germany of all vestiges of Nazi influence. This was not an easy matter, as almost nine million Germans had joined the Nazi Party and millions of others had become members of Nazi-affiliated groups. Party membership did not necessarily mean participation in the crimes of the regime. Even some members of the resistance, such as the diplomat Adam von Trott zu Solz (1909–44), who was executed for his role in the 20 July plot, had been a party member. Many others who played an active role in the crimes of the Third Reich had never joined the party. Even so high-ranking a Nazi as Gestapo chief Heinrich Müller (1900–45) had not joined the NSDAP until 1939, although he had been a member of the SS since 1934.

The Law for the Liberation from National Socialism and Militarism, enacted in the American zone in March 1946 and extended by the Allied Control Council (the supreme commanders of the four occupying armies) to the other zones later that year, called for the assignment of all former Nazis into five categories ranging from "major offender," "offender," and "minor offender" to "fellow traveler" and "exonerated." American and British authorities required virtually all adults in their occupation zones to fill out lengthy questionnaires that would serve as the basis for further action, including criminal prosecution where it was judged to be warranted. Persons who had joined the Nazi Party or one of its affiliates before 1937 were prohibited from employment until they had undergone denazification procedures. Originally conceived as a program to permanently exclude unreconstructed Nazis from positions of influence to complement efforts at re-educating Germans in democracy, denazification was soon transformed into a process of rehabilitating former Nazis. In the course of this transformation the very meaning of the term "denazification" changed. In his analysis of the denazification process at the University of Heidelberg in the postwar years, American historian Steven Remy spoke of "the evolution of the entire denazification program from one that aimed primarily at purging former Nazis from positions of influence and authority to one that aimed only to remove the 'taint' of Nazism."[8] The objective of weeding out "genuine" Nazis without penalizing those who had only joined the party because of careerist or conformist pressures left the process open to considerable abuse.

In the western zones the Allies turned the process over to the Germans by establishing appeal boards staffed by non-Nazi Germans (mostly representatives of the refounded political parties) to implement denazification. Allied expectations that most Germans would welcome the opportunity for a fundamental purge of Nazi influence proved misplaced, however. Instead, the appeals process gradually allowed the return of former Nazis to positions of influence in both the private and public sectors. Because persons in one of the "offender" categories could almost always get their status demoted to "fellow traveler" (*Mitläufer*), a category that carried no penalty, the entire process came to be known as a *Mitläuferfabrik* (a factory for producing fellow travelers).[9] Of the 3.6 million party members who underwent denazification in the American zone, only 1,654 were found to be "major offenders."[10] The old nationalist leader Alfred Hugenberg, who had been so instrumental in Hitler's rise to power and had served as Hitler's "economic dictator" for the first six months of the Hitler regime, was classified as a "fellow traveler." Even mid-level members of the Nazi terror apparatus, the SD, Gestapo, or special courts, were often classified as mere "fellow travelers."

Those who were originally categorized as "fellow travelers" found it relatively easy to get their status further reduced to "exonerated." Of the over six million persons affected by denazification in the western zones, almost 98 percent were categorized as either "fellow travelers" or "exonerated."[11] As the denazification process grew more lenient, former Nazis could prove their lack of commitment to Nazism simply by demonstrating their Christian beliefs, which they could do, for instance, by offering evidence of their practice of saying prayers before meals. The churches were particularly generous in providing affidavits of innocence to members of their faith. If the assumption was made that the person under review did not truly share Nazi beliefs, then even pro-Nazi activities could be made to appear as clandestine resistance. Joining the Nazi Party could be rationalized as an effort to exercise a moderating influence on the regime.

Former Nazi university faculty members criticized denazification as an unwarranted politicization of the university, thus employing in their defense the same criticism the Nazis had leveled against leftists in their purge of the universities in the 1930s. The older generation of conservatives who had collaborated with the Nazis but were eventually displaced by younger Nazis could exonerate themselves by pointing out that they had been ousted by Nazi Party members. These younger party members could in turn exonerate themselves by insisting that they had helped rid the university of a big-name collaborator. The competitive nature of Nazi political culture and the personal confrontations and enmities it produced gave former Nazis plenty of opportunity to claim that they had suffered some form of professional discrimination in the Third Reich.[12] Most former party members presented themselves as "victims" of the Nazi regime. Appeals boards often used contradictory arguments to justify lenient verdicts. In some cases the "idealism" that led some people to join the party was cited as a mitigating factor, in others "opportunism" was adduced as evidence of a lack of true Nazi convictions. Almost everyone could point to an extenuating circumstance of some kind.

Rarely did anyone take responsibility for their actions or declare guilt or remorse. All looked for loopholes and alibis. There were no more Nazis in Germany, and it almost seemed as if there had never been any. A favorite mode of evasion was to put all blame on superiors in the chain of command, a tactic already employed by the defendants at Nuremberg. Perhaps this was inevitable since those who acknowledged their complicity, far from receiving absolution, faced the loss of their livelihood. For many Germans repression and distortion of the past became the precondition for a successful postwar career.

Although denazification may have failed to generate a full and honest appraisal of popular complicity in the Nazi system, it did have the effect of reinforcing the stigma of the Nazi label. Nobody could hope for exoneration by defending Nazism, only by denying adherence to it. Denazification certainly contributed to the public rejection of Nazi ideology and its elimination from public discourse. The proclamation of personal innocence became an established pattern, but underlying this pattern was a healthy popular consensus that Nazism and racism were evil. In that sense, at least, denazification, despite its rehabilitative function, was a success. The rehabilitation of former Nazis did not mean the rehabilitation of Nazi ideology. Instead it turned former Nazis into avowed democrats, at least in their public posture.

Some defenders of the process have argued that by permitting the rapid reintegration of former Nazis into German society, denazification actually strengthened postwar democracy in the FRG. National Socialism was now discredited even among most of its former supporters. Because of their sheer numbers, so the argument goes, the permanent exclusion of former Nazis would have posed a far greater threat to democracy by creating a hostile and potentially subversive force in postwar Germany.[13] As it was, the consensus that emerged in the 1950s in support of the Federal Republic included most former Nazis. The western-style parliamentary form of government that had been so bitterly rejected by segments of the German public in the Weimar era was now fully accepted.

Both the German public, and, more importantly, the occupying powers, grew increasingly weary of the denazification process. Many Germans empathized more with the "victims" of denazification than with the victims of German aggression. The painful economic deprivations which many Germans suffered up to the currency reform of 1948 contributed to this sense of victimization.[14] In general the non-Nazi right in West Germany criticized denazification as excessively harsh while the left considered it too lenient.[15] But even anti-Nazi Germans criticized the unfairness of a program in which relatively minor offenders who were processed early on received tough penalties whereas those guilty of much greater offenses later got off scot-free. In 1947 the newly revived parties of the left, the Social Democrats and the Communists, dropped their earlier support for denazification when it became clear that continued support would cost them too many votes. In early 1948 both churches demanded termination of the denazification program.

German public opinion was only one of the factors that led to increasing Allied leniency and their eventual abandonment of denazification in the western zones. More important was the growing realization that the technical and professional expertise of former Nazis was needed if German institutions were to function smoothly again. A series of amnesties and amendments to the denazification law in the US zone in 1946 and 1947 greatly reduced the number of incriminated offenders. Most crucial to the end of denazification, however, was the impact of the incipient Cold War. Western leaders were quite aware that thoroughgoing denazification risked losing support among German voters for Konrad Adenauer's conservative Christian Democratic Union (CDU), the party that favored close alignment with the west. Under pressure from members of Congress who became convinced that denazification was impeding West German recovery and the establishment of liberal democracy, the American military government simply reclassified 90 percent of remaining offenders to the category of "fellow travelers" in 1948.[16]

Denazification effectively ended with the founding of the Federal Republic in 1949. An amendment to Article 131 of the new West German constitution in 1951 called for the reinstatement of all civil servants who had lost their positions as a result of denazification, except those who were charged with actual crimes. This led to the rapid return of former Nazis to positions of influence in the Federal Republic. In 1952, 43 percent of senior officials in the West German Foreign Ministry had been members of the Nazi Party.[17] About 70 percent of the 15,000 judges and prosecutors in the Federal Republic in 1950 were holdovers from the Third Reich.[18] Included in that number were more than 100 jurists who had participated in one or more of the more than 27,000 death sentences handed down by German courts between 1933 and 1945.[19] One of the most notable beneficiaries of the amended Article 131 was Hans Globke (1889–1973), who was appointed to the highest administrative post in Konrad Adenauer's Federal Chancellery despite having authored some of the Interior Ministry commentaries to the Nuremberg racial laws in 1935. "You don't throw out dirty water," Adenauer commented at the time, "as long as you have no clean water to replace it."[20] In February 1953 a Munich denazification court went so far as to posthumously exonerate General Alfred Jodl, who at Nuremberg had been found guilty on all four counts and was subsequently executed.[21]

The purge of the economic and civil service elites was far more thorough in the Soviet zone, where 520,000 former Nazis were dismissed from positions of authority up to 1948 as part of a thoroughgoing transformation of the social and economic order.[22] The abolition of the capitalist economic system entailed a far greater institutional break with the past than was the case in the west. But the revival of authoritarian political structures, despite the differences between Nazi and communist ideologies, led to continuity of a different kind in the East: the continued suppression of free speech and political opposition. Denazification could serve as a convenient tool to suppress all forms of opposition to communism. Middle-class opponents of communism stood accused of fascist sympathies and of collaborating with the Nazis' anticommunist crusade even if they had played only marginal roles in the Nazi regime.

The absence of democratic process in the East also left fewer opportunities for former Nazis to cite mitigating circumstances in their defense, as was so often the case in the western denazification process. But in 1948 the exclusion of former Nazis from employment in positions of influence came to an end in the Soviet zone, too, for the same reason as in the West: the growing need for the professional expertise of former Nazis in the construction of a new society. Politically sensitive professions such as the legal profession were thoroughly purged of former Nazis in the GDR, but the same was not true, for instance, of medicine, where the need for public health prevailed over the imperative for political change. In 1954 over 45 percent of professors of medicine in the GDR were former members of the Nazi Party.[23]

The Cold War in Germany

In both East and West Germany former Nazis, including some suspected war criminals, benefitted from the rise of the Cold War, particularly if they had useful skills. After 1946 both sides were increasingly prepared to overlook the Nazi past of individuals who could provide services to enhance their respective competitive positions in the East–West conflict. In July 1947 General Lucius Clay (1897–1978), military governor of the American zone, announced that suspected war criminals would no longer be extradited from the American zone, and British officials soon followed suit.[24] Competition over the recruitment of scientists and secret agents played a role in the erosion of trust between East and West as early as 1945.[25] Hundreds of former Nazi scientists, engineers, and technicians were brought to the United States by the army, sometimes in contravention of American immigration law.[26] Their proven anticommunism and the skills first applied in the war on the eastern front made Nazi intelligence operatives, military researchers, and other specialists particularly useful to the United States. Former Nazis and Nazi collaborators throughout Europe, sometimes including known war criminals, were secretly recruited into US-sponsored covert operations against the Soviet Union in the late 1940s and early 1950s. American intelligence officials even helped suspected war criminals avoid trial, as in the case of Klaus Barbie (1913–91), the wartime head of the Gestapo in the city of Lyons, France, whom French authorities eventually tracked down in Bolivia and sentenced to life imprisonment in 1987.[27]

The inability to agree on a common policy for Germany was both a cause and a result of the Cold War. At Yalta and again at Potsdam tenuous agreement had been reached on a punitive policy toward the defeated Reich. The Soviet Union was particularly committed not only to demilitarization and denazification, but also to deindustrialization, which would not only prevent the revival of Germany as a threat to peace but also make ample reparations available to compensate for the enormous losses suffered by the USSR during the war. At Potsdam each occupying power was authorized to extract reparations in capital goods from its own zone. But because the Soviet Union had suffered by far the greatest losses and because Germany's industrial center, the Ruhr, was located in the British zone, the western powers agreed to make industrial equipment that was not needed for peaceful production available to the Soviets as well (some of it in exchange for agricultural goods from the Soviet side). In early 1946, however, as US–Soviet relations deteriorated and it became increasingly clear that joint administration of Germany by powers with such vastly different social systems was unworkable, the western powers called an abrupt halt to reparations shipments to the East. In 1947, with the Cold War in full swing, the United States and Britain launched a major effort to revive the economy in their zones. This initiative eventually resulted in the establishment of a separate West German state.

The shift in American policy that led to the division of Germany was not solely a result of growing Cold War tensions. It was also a practical response to the increasingly desperate economic situation in Germany in 1945–46. The deterioration of the standard of living in Germany did not stop at the end of the war. Indeed, for most Germans the two years after the end of the war were the years of greatest deprivation. Malnutrition, disease, and infant mortality were widespread, and the black market governed a barter economy in which cigarettes constituted the main means of exchange.

Adding to the acute food and housing shortages was the unanticipated influx of millions of Germans expelled from territories annexed by Poland and the Soviet Union east of the new boundary on the Oder and Neisse rivers. The expulsion of over seven million Germans from these regions began in summer

1945 and was followed by expulsions of some three million ethnic Germans from Czechoslovakia (the Sudetenland), and lesser numbers from Hungary, Romania, Yugoslavia, and Poland proper.[28] Most sought refuge in the western zones, and many of those who originally settled in the Soviet zone later came west as refugees as well.

Because food imports were needed to maintain the expanded West German population at the same time as industrial plant was being dismantled for shipment to the East, American taxpayers were in effect being asked to underwrite reparations to the Soviet Union. Under normal circumstances the United States, the only power to emerge from the war with a strengthened economy, might have acceded to this form of indirect aid to their wartime ally, but the growing rift between the two powers, particularly over the imposition of communism in eastern Europe, made all cooperation illusory.

The Soviets viewed the halt of reparations payments and the American shift to a policy of economic reconstruction of a separate West Germany as violations of the Yalta and Potsdam Agreements. The Berlin Blockade of 1948–49 was a desperate and unsuccessful Soviet effort to prevent the formation of a separate West German state (or, failing that, to force the western powers out of Berlin on the grounds that Berlin had been divided into four sectors only because it was intended to serve as the capital of a unified German state). The United States was able to thwart the Soviet blockade with a dramatic round-the-clock airlift that supplied the beleaguered West Berlin population and galvanized world opinion against the Soviet tactics of intimidation. The currency reform of 1948 provided the foundations for the "economic miracle" that would make the revived West German economy one of the strongest in the world for decades to come.

Repression of the past

Confrontation with the communist East made National Socialism appear in a different light in the West and facilitated repression of the past. The political imperatives of the Cold War discouraged continued preoccupation with a movement that no longer seemed a danger. After all, it was the Nazis' most bitter opponents that now constituted the major threat to the West. Anticommunism provided the ideological bond for the full reintegration of many former Nazis into West German society and for the integration of a reformed and restored West Germany into the NATO alliance. In their commitment to the destruction of communism former Nazis could even claim to have been ahead of their time.

Some aspects of *völkisch* ideology needed only minimal changes to be refashioned for use in the Cold War.[29] The Nazis, after all, had also employed the rhetoric of freedom (most cynically in the slogan, "Work makes one free" [*Arbeit macht frei*], that adorned the entrances to concentration camps), even if their conception of freedom was quite different from liberal individualism. Freedom could, after all, be readily invoked to justify a Social Darwinist system in which the rich and the strong were not encumbered by legal protections for the poor and the weak. Theodor Oberländer, former *Reichsführer* of the *Bund deutscher Osten* (League for the German East) during the Third Reich, had no trouble recycling some of his earlier writings about the need to liberate eastern Europe from communism while serving as Adenauer's Minister for the Expelled from 1956 until 1960, when revelations about his past forced him from office. Former Nazis who sought the right to publish their views formed the so-called Society for a Free Journalism (*Gesellschaft für freie Publizistik*) in 1960, a group that gave precedence to the "preservation of the *Volk*" over the free development of the individual.

Both sides instrumentalized Nazism to gain an advantage in the Cold War. The continuities in German anticommunism and the prevalence of ex-Nazis in positions of public trust gave the GDR many opportunities to tar the Federal Republic with the Nazi brush. Western publicists reciprocated by pointing out the structural continuities between the Nazi and Stalinist dictatorships in the GDR, all differences in ideology notwithstanding. Interpreting Nazism as the product of materialist, collectivist, and anti-Christian ideology, as West German Chancellor Konrad Adenauer (1876–1967) did in a speech in 1948, served not only to discredit communism and the left, but it also implicitly exonerated Christian conservatives from complicity in the Nazi debacle. In 1950 Adenauer went so far as to tell a CDU party convention that "the pressure that National Socialism exercised through the Gestapo, the concentration camps, and the court system was moderate in comparison to what is currently happening in the 'Eastern Zone.'"[30] Meanwhile, East German revelations of the Nazi past of public figures such as Globke or Oberländer could be dismissed as mere communist propaganda.

While endeavoring to associate the other side with the negative characteristics of Nazism, both German states made every effort to demonstrate their own complete break with the past. In that sense, at least, the Cold War reinforced Germans' postwar repudiation of Nazism as a normative set of values and ideas. Antifascism, in fact, became a major ideological element in the GDR's desperate quest for popular legitimation. But formal repudiation of the past could also mask a substantive repression of the past. By simply declaring that their new state represented the "other" Germany, the left wing that had always opposed Nazism, the East German regime enabled its citizens to avoid a full-scale critical appraisal of their own role in the Nazi era. Identification with the communist opposition to fascism also enabled the regime to avoid financial restitution to Jewish victims by denying any responsibility for Nazi crimes.[31]

Rejection of antisemitism

In West Germany Nazism was defined not by its anticommunism, which liberals generally shared, but by its antisemitism and suppression of individual rights. Defining Nazism by its antisemitism rather than its anticommunism made it easier to repudiate any connections with the Nazi past.[32] The Federal Republic distanced itself from Nazism through unequivocal rejection of antisemitism and through *Wiedergutmachung*, restitution payments to the Jewish victims of the Holocaust and to the state of Israel, enacted into law in 1952. East German leaders, on the other hand, dismissed these restitution payments as merely a way of concealing the ubiquitous presence of Nazi perpetrators in West German society.[33] This Cold War-inspired attack on West German motives was wide of the mark, however. Since 1945 the official rejection of racism and antisemitism formed a key component of West Germany's postwar democratic identity. The new state of Israel, too, enjoyed strong official and popular support in the FRG.

In both East and West Germany, the traditional antisemitism that was so crucial to Germany's self-definition in the earlier part of the century played no role in the public sphere after 1945 except as a belief system to be excoriated. Antisemitic statements became punishable offenses in both East and West, and in the reunited Germany after 1990 Holocaust denial would be criminalized as well. Whatever elements of German national identity may have survived the German defeat in 1945, the public acceptability of antisemitism was not one of them. In both East and West Germany antisemitism lost its function as a political ideology and was banished to the sphere of private resentments. Of course, privately held antisemitic attitudes continued despite the official taboo, especially in the FRG, but public opinion polls showed that even these diminished substantially with the passing of the older generations of Nazis and Nazi sympathizers, at least until the revival of right-wing radicalism among disaffected German youth in the 1990s.[34] However widespread traditional anti-Jewish prejudices may still be, antisemitism lacks all institutional support in contemporary Germany and can no longer be politically mobilized into an effective mass movement.

Ausländerfeindlichkeit

The racist theories based on biology and genetics that were so prevalent in Germany even before 1933 found no public acceptance after 1945. Overt racism was suppressed in the GDR, and rejection of racism was very much a part of the legitimizing popular consensus in the FRG as well. However, while antisemitism remained heavily stigmatized, a culturally based racism re-emerged among some sectors of the West German population in the 1970s and 1980s in the form of hostility to foreign workers and demands for their repatriation. Guest workers had been recruited from Turkey, Yugoslavia, Italy, Spain, and other southern European countries for the booming West German economy after erection of the Berlin Wall cut off the supply of refugee labor from the East in 1961. As the West German economy slowed after the "oil shock" in 1973 guest workers faced increasing hostility and discrimination. The growing Turkish immigrant population, in particular, became targets of revived right-wing demagoguery and terror in the 1980s and early 1990s. Because German citizenship was still defined by ethnic origin, even the descendants of foreign-born residents who grew up in Germany and spoke perfect German had difficulty obtaining German citizenship, while ethnic Germans arriving from the former USSR were often easily naturalized.

Ausländerfeindlichkeit (hostility to foreigners) and anti-immigrant fervor was further fanned by popular resentments against the large numbers of refugees seeking political asylum in Germany under the liberal constitutional provision adopted by the Federal Republic in 1949 in reaction to the political persecutions of the Nazi years. The number of asylum seekers increased greatly in the turbulent years following the fall of communism and dissolution of the Soviet bloc from 1989 to 1991. Although only a small fraction of asylum requests were approved by the German government, applicants were maintained at public expense during an evaluation process that could take several years. The influx of asylum seekers, which reached a peak of some 438,000 in 1992, declined after the constitution was amended to make asylum much more restrictive in 1993.[35] The new law, upheld by the Federal Constitutional Court in 1996, no longer granted political asylum to emigrants from countries whose human rights records have not been officially certified as unsatisfactory. Opponents of the constitutional change deplored the fact that in effect the new law facilitated right-wing efforts to exclude foreigners from German society.

Radical right-wing parties in the Federal Republic

Preoccupation with the *"Ausländerproblem"* and intolerance of ethnic diversity were hallmarks of the radical right-wing parties that re-emerged in the Federal Republic after the war. But the war and the Holocaust had so thoroughly discredited Nazism and antisemitism that even those Germans who continued to hold radical right-wing attitudes disclaimed these labels for fear of losing all credibility in the postwar era. Radical right-wing parties found it necessary to eschew open antisemitism and adopt the vocabulary of democracy to gain a hearing with the public. A case in point was the National Democratic Party (NPD), the first radical right-wing party of any significance in the Federal Republic. An earlier party established by former Nazis in 1949, the Socialist Reich Party, which rejected the Bonn Republic, was banned by the Federal Constitutional Court in 1952. To spare itself the same fate, the NPD did not take the same openly rejectionist stance toward democracy. Founded in 1964 with 12 former Nazis on its 18-member executive committee, the NPD gained 4.3 percent of the vote in the 1969 *Bundestag* elections, short of the 5 percent required for parliamentary representation under the federal constitution. Benefitting from the conservative backlash against the protest movements of the 1960s, the NPD did gain representation in the parliaments of 7 of the 11 federal states in the late 1960s, but support for the party declined thereafter.[36]

Extreme right-wing parties failed to overcome the 5 percent hurdle in any state or federal election after 1968 until the German People's Union (DVU) climbed over the 5 percent mark in the elections to the city parliament in Bremen in 1987. That same decade a new Bavarian-based party on the far right adopted the name of an American party, the Republicans, in an evident attempt to project an image of moderation. While racism still formed the core of the "New Right" ideology, it was packaged now as the defense of the interests not just of Germans or Nordics but of Europeans and the "white race." The Republicans sought to exploit *Ausländerfeindlichkeit* directed at guest workers and asylum seekers. Although they gained over two million votes (7.1 percent) in the elections to the largely powerless European Parliament in June 1989, they, too, failed to overcome the 5 percent barrier in the five national elections in the newly reunited Germany up to the present. Founded by a former SS officer, the Republicans did receive more than the required 5 percent in some municipal and state elections, as the NPD had also done. However, in 1998 it was the resurrected DVU that raised greatest concern by securing almost 13 percent in elections in Saxony-Anhalt, one of the new states of the former GDR. Their success was widely attributed to their ability to exploit hostility to alien residents, who displaced Jews as the main scapegoats of German society in the postwar and postunification era. However, no radical right-wing party in Germany achieved the success of Jörg Haider's anti-immigrant "Freedom Party" in Austria, which gained enough votes in national elections to join a coalition government with the conservative Austrian People's Party in February 2000.

Although German neofascist parties remained marginal on the national level, their effect was to encourage mainstream parties to adopt anti-immigrant policies to retain the right-wing vote. While radical right-wing parties propagated a barely concealed racism and celebrated various aspects of the Third Reich, their interest in gaining popular support forced them to downplay any direct link to Nazism, which remained totally discredited in public discourse. For tactical reasons if nothing else, parties that seek to succeed in German electoral politics today cannot afford to openly acknowledge their Nazi sympathies.

Neo-Nazism

No such scruples inhibited militantly right-wing extra-parliamentary groups and skinheads who openly proclaimed their Nazi sympathies and engaged in violence against dark-skinned foreigners, Jews, gays, left-wing activists, the homeless, and other outsiders. An outbreak of antisemitic vandalism in 1959–60 embarrassed the Adenauer government and induced it to take more stringent actions against the extreme right. Militant neo-Nazism emerged again on the right-wing fringe in West Germany in the late 1970s and 1980s, coinciding with a more general shift to the right in West German politics.

The fall of communism in 1990 contributed to the re-emergence of radical right-wing activism in East Germany as well, particularly among young, underemployed men. Their susceptibility to right-wing ideology was a result both of their disenchantment with the communist ideology of the failed GDR and of the harsh economic consequences of the abrupt, uncushioned transition to a market economy. Alienated youth, overwhelmingly male, vented their rage on foreigners and other visible scapegoats at the bottom of the social scale whom they viewed as illegitimate competitors for scarce jobs and benefits. Neo-Nazi violence reached an unprecedented level in four days of rioting against a refugee hostel in the East German city of Rostock in August 1992. In the weeks that followed, however, hundreds of thousands of Germans took to the streets in the major cities to protest right-wing violence and reassure Germany's foreign community, which today numbers over 7 million of a total population of 80 million.

The attraction of disaffected youth to Nazi slogans and symbols can be partly explained by their shock value in a society where the open display of Nazi symbols violates a taboo that has been firmly in place since 1945. Use of the swastika, the Hitler salute, Nazi songs, and antisemitic slogans remain criminal offenses in Germany today, and alienated youth in Germany as elsewhere flaunt these symbols precisely because they represent an outrageous form of provocation to the established order. For many young people neo-Nazi ideology is not the cause of disaffection so much as it is a means of expressing their disaffection in a way that is sure to gain maximum public attention.

Right-wing extremism continues to form an international subculture that feeds on social discontent at the start of the twenty-first century. Particularly in eastern Europe the revival of ethnic nationalism after the collapse of the Soviet bloc contributed to at least a temporary resurgence of the radical right. Although its appearance in Germany raised particular concerns in the light of German history, such extremism does not appear to be any stronger in Germany than in other European countries (or the United States, for that matter, from where right-wing publications, illegal in Germany, are often imported by American extremists). Neo-Nazism is more of a fringe phenomenon in Germany today than neofascism is in Italy. At the height of the terror campaign against immigrants and social outcasts in 1992, when 17 deaths were attributed to neo-Nazi and skinhead attacks, the number of activists in militant neo-Nazi organizations in Germany was estimated at about 6,400. However, official government estimates of the number of violence-prone skinheads and neo-Nazis in Germany rose to over 13,000 by 2001.[37]

Even though the neo-Nazi segment of the population is proportionately no larger than other countries, the memory of Germany's past understandably gives rise to greater international concern. The Nazis, so the argument goes, were a fringe group at the start as well. However, analogies to the relative insignificance of the Nazis in the early 1920s are inappropriate, because from the start the Nazis proclaimed political views that were shared by a large number of mainstream nationalists. This was not the case in the reunited

Federal Republic where the political climate remained inhospitable to right-wing extremism. Nor are the skinheads of the late twentieth and early twenty-first centuries the street force of an organized party as the SA was in the years of the Nazis' struggle for power. The vast majority of Germans today are quite aware that it is in their own best interests to prevent a return to the hypernationalist policies that brought ruin and destruction in the past.

Nonetheless, neo-Nazism could serve an apologetic function by diverting attention from more insidious mainstream racism. The response of the German government to right-wing terrorism against foreigners, refugees, and other marginalized groups was widely perceived as a test of the strength of German commitment to democracy and of the genuineness of Germany's break with its authoritarian, racist, and imperialist past. In the early 1990s critics of the government, the judiciary, and the police accused the authorities of failing to combat the excesses of the radical right with the same uncompromising resolve they had brought to bear against the left-wing terrorism of the Red Army Faction in the 1970s or, for that matter, against antinuclear protesters. In the 1992 riots in Rostock the police failed to intervene to prevent attacks on the refugees, who were eventually bussed to another location. By giving higher priority to limiting the influx of foreign refugees than to containing the right-wing violence or confronting the social problems that generated youthful disaffection, the government seemed to legitimate the view that the presence of foreigners was the primary source of the problem. The message conveyed seemed to be that right-wing radicalism would not be a problem if only foreign refugees could be kept out of Germany.

The readiness of the German government to downplay the seriousness of right-wing radicalism is no different from the reluctance of governments in France, Britain, or the United States to acknowledge the prevalence of racism and hostility to immigrants in their own countries. But because of the stigma of the Nazi past the need to project a positive image to the world and to deny manifestations of right-wing extremism is more strongly felt in Germany than elsewhere. Paradoxically, the need to repudiate Nazism has tended to encourage denial of pathological symptoms in the present. Precisely because the rejection of Nazism has become such an integral part of Germany's postwar identity, German national pride requires affirmation and confirmation that Germany is indeed a reformed, a changed, a reborn society. The break with the past is a source of national pride, but it has also encouraged repression of a past that has placed on Germans a most unwelcome burden of guilt. In no other country has historical memory played such a key role in national consciousness. How Germans sought to come to terms with the past and its burden is the subject of the concluding chapter.

17 The historians' debate

The place of Hitler's Reich in German history and memory

Repudiation of Nazism became a fundamental element of public consciousness in both postwar Germanys. But precisely because of its significance as a negative foil to both democracy in West Germany and socialism in East Germany, the interpretation of National Socialism has been hotly contested in the political arena and in historiography. In both East and West the historiography of Nazism has been closely linked to political practice.

Antifascism in the German Democratic Republic

In the now defunct East German state there was little deviation from the orthodox Marxist–Leninist contention, dating back to the 1930s, that Nazism was merely the political arm of "monopoly capitalism." Long discredited in the West, this officially sanctioned interpretation suffered the same fate after 1989 as the communist regimes it supported. But for 40 years the antifascist doctrine inherited from the 1930s provided the main legitimating ideology in the GDR. Standing for more than merely opposition to a fascist revival in Germany, antifascism was particularly useful as an ideological weapon in the Cold War. It defined fascism as the most dictatorial, terroristic, and imperialistic form of capitalism, thus putting the western states into close proximity to fascism. Socialist states, according to antifascist doctrine, had cleansed themselves of fascist contamination by eliminating the capitalist economy. And indeed, because of the wholesale change in the government and economic system, the removal of former Nazis from leadership positions in the bureaucracy was much more comprehensive in the GDR than in the Federal Republic (FRG).

The founders of the GDR drew their moral authority from their active participation in the resistance against the Nazis. Walter Ulbricht (1893–1973), effectively the leader of the GDR from its founding in 1949 until 1971, directed communist resistance from exile in Moscow, but a number of his associates were survivors of Nazi concentration camps. His successor Erich Honecker (1912–94) had been incarcerated in Germany from 1937 to 1945. Long-time German Communist Party (KPD) leader Ernst Thälmann (1886–1944), who was killed at Buchenwald, was officially celebrated in the GDR as a heroic martyr to the antifascist cause. To get the population to identify itself with its communist leadership, East Germans were encouraged by the ruling Socialist Unity Party (SED) to think of themselves as part of the winning, not the losing, side in the war, thus allowing them to evade responsibility for the Nazi debacle.

GDR propaganda sought to encourage the popular belief that the antifascist struggle was ongoing. Unpopular measures could be justified as essential to combating the still-present fascist threat from the West. Thus the Berlin Wall, erected in August 1961 to stop the migration of East Germans to the West, was officially labeled a "*Schutzwall*" (protective wall) against fascism. History books extolled the leading role that communists played in the struggle against Nazism. No mention was made of the contributions that communist denunciations of Social Democrats made to the triumph of the Nazis in 1933. In its official self-understanding the GDR represented a total break with the Third Reich. The only lines of continuity that were officially acknowledged linked the GDR with the glorious antifascist resistance and with the Soviet cause.

In West Germany, on the other hand, the links to the past, though sometimes distorted, were never entirely denied. From the start the Federal Republic understood itself as the true Germany, the official heir of the German state that had collapsed in 1945. This posture was useful in marginalizing the GDR as an illegitimate state imposed by the Soviet occupying power. But it also meant having to accept responsibility for Germany's past, including the Holocaust. As in the East, interpretation of the Nazi past was essential to constructing a viable postwar West German identity. But unlike the GDR, the West German state decided to make amends through restitution payments to Jewish victims and the state of Israel in 1952 and to other victims of Nazism in 1956. Meanwhile, the GDR's surviving industrial base was dismantled by the USSR, the victor power that had suffered the greatest losses during the war, while the FRG benefitted from American largesse under the Marshall Plan after 1947.

Historiography in the Federal Republic

Historical interpretation of the National Socialist experience went through three clearly discernible phases up to 1990, mirroring major political developments and changes in political consciousness in the Federal Republic. In the first decade and a half after the end of the war the historiography of National Socialism in Germany reflected the conservative political climate of the Adenauer era (1949–63) and the ideological imperatives of the Cold War. A generational shift to the left marked the second phase that culminated in Willy Brandt's (1913–92) Social Democratic coalition government from 1969 to 1974, followed by Helmut Schmidt's (b. 1918) more centrist chancellorship from 1974 to 1982. This political shift to the left and the US–Soviet détente that accompanied the winding down of the Vietnam War in the 1970s was paralleled in the historiography of Nazism, as the generational revolt of the student movement gave rise to a critical historiography that directly challenged the silence and evasiveness of the parent generation about their own roles in the Nazi catastrophe.

The third phase was marked by a swing of the political pendulum back to more conservative rule in the 1980s. The moderate right represented by the Christian Democratic Union (CDU) enjoyed a revival under Helmut Kohl (b. 1930), who became chancellor in 1982, presided over German reunification in 1990, and served as head of government until 1998. The neoconservative reaction to the progressive agenda of the 1960s and 1970s led to the bitter "historians' dispute" (*Historikerstreit*) in the months leading up to the *Bundestag* election in January 1987. Some of the issues raised in this dispute lost their relevance with the end of the Cold War, the collapse of communism in eastern Europe in 1989, the *Wende* (change of government) in the GDR in 1990, and the break-up of the Soviet Union in 1991; others continued to animate the "cultural wars" in a reunited Germany in the 1990s and the first decade of the twenty-first century. German reunification also brought new pressures to face the Nazi past: the end of German division eliminated a favorite tactic in both the FRG and the GDR to avoid issues of guilt by blaming the other side for past and present ills.[1]

The postwar era, 1945–61

Psychic repression and denial of the past characterized the public mood in West Germany in the immediate postwar era and helped to make a sham of the denazification process. As we have seen in the previous chapter, repudiation of Nazism was not necessarily synonymous with frank acceptance of responsibility for the past. Ritualistic condemnation of Nazism could serve as a means of avoiding a critical examination of personal involvement in the Nazi system and personal complicity in Nazi crimes. Indeed, ever more forceful repudiation of Nazi ideology could serve to cover up the growing retreat from denazification.[2] In a controversial book published in 1987, the German-Jewish journalist Ralph Giordano provocatively labeled the repression and denial of personal responsibility after 1945 as Germany's "second guilt."[3]

The demonization of Hitler and the top Nazi leadership often served a convenient apologetic function. A favorite strategy of denial by some conservative historians was to blame the catastrophe entirely on Hitler and a small clique of gangsters who had taken advantage of the German people for their own despicable ends. Typically drawing a sharp line between their own conservatism and the radicalism of the Nazis, such historians presented Nazism as an accidental and untypical aberration in German history and as a movement that originated in sources outside Germany. For example, the eminent historians Friedrich Meinecke (1862–1954) and Gerhard Ritter (1888–1967), who had lived through the Third Reich and had shared its nationalist premises while opposing its excesses, published works that associated Nazism with the rationalizing and democratizing trends emanating from the Enlightenment and the French Revolution.[4] Meinecke and Ritter established the framework for numerous published attempts by German conservatives to explain and condemn Nazism without implicating their own conservative values. Indeed, for Meinecke and Ritter Nazism was an expression of the putative cultural and spiritual crisis of western civilization corrupted by the arrogant Enlightenment idea of rational, worldly progress.

The Cold War reinforced the conservative mood of the Federal Republic in the 1950s. One of the ideological features of the Cold War was the contest between East and West for the right to claim greater distance and difference from National Socialism. Just as East German historians found it difficult to concede that the single greatest challenge to Hitler had come from the old elites on 20 July 1944, so West German historians celebrated the conservative resistance to Hitler while ignoring the much more uncompromising resistance of the German left, which was widely equated with treason.[5] Whereas in the GDR the Cold War reinforced antifascist orthodoxy, in the FRG it helped to give credence to the totalitarianism school that emphasized the structural similarities between Nazism and Soviet Communism. These included a millenarian ideology, a single party dictatorship, the suppression of individual rights, a state monopoly on arms and communications, central economic planning, and the use of terror against political opponents.[6]

The term "totalitarianism" was coined by both opponents and supporters of Italian Fascism in the 1920s to criticize or praise Mussolini's quest for total power. It was used polemically by conservatives, liberals, and some Social Democrats to link Nazism with communism in the 1930s. Although the Nazi and Soviet regimes pursued very different social goals, both fascism and communism differed sharply from liberal democracy in making total claims on their respective societies. The "Great Retreat" under Stalin to more nationalist and conservative policies in the mid-1930s and the signing of the Nazi–Soviet Nonaggression Pact in 1939 had already persuaded many disillusioned liberals and socialists that the Soviet Union was as much of an enemy of western democracy as Nazi Germany. Totalitarianism theory offered a way of validating and promoting anticommunism without in any way embracing its fascist antithesis. It also had the advantage of at least partially exculpating the German people by identifying manipulation and mobilization of the atomized masses by a monolithic dictatorship as a central feature of totalitarian regimes. The implied distinction between a villainous leadership and a duped and disabled public would be useful in the 1950s to rehabilitate a people whose cooperation was now sought in the confrontation with the remaining totalitarian regime, the Soviet Union, and its satellites.

The Cold War shifted the focus of public attention from the Nazi enemy of the past to the communist enemy of the present. The interest of the western powers in building up West Germany as an ally against the Soviet Union eased pressures for the prosecution of war crimes and encouraged the suppression of memory of the recent past. Preoccupation with past crimes would only hinder the rearmament of West Germany—sought by the United States after the start of the Korean War—and its full integration into the western alliance. Many Americans feared that the burden of guilt for the Nazi past would weaken the will of West Germans to resist Soviet pressures.

Evasion of the questions of guilt and responsibility was characteristic of the treatment of Nazism in German schools, where former Nazis had little difficulty retaining or reclaiming their teaching positions.[7] History courses on the primary and secondary level in West Germany in the 1950s generally ended with World War I.[8] When the Third Reich was discussed at all, it was generally presented as a tyranny imposed on the German people by Hitler's demonic powers of propaganda and seduction. Most histories of the Third Reich demonized the Nazis but exculpated traditional conservatives. When in 1955 the political scientist Karl Dietrich Bracher showed how Hindenburg and Chancellor Brüning had manipulated Article 48 to undermine the parliamentary system, most German historians defended Brüning's policies as the only viable strategy to save a failed parliamentary system.[9]

The 1960s and 1970s

The dramatic turn to the left in the political climate of the 1960s after Adenauer's resignation as chancellor in 1963 left its mark on the historiography of Nazism as well. In all European countries and the United States a youthful student-based movement protested the Vietnam War, called for solidarity with Third World peoples, and demanded democratizing reforms in government, education, and society. All over the western world (and to a lesser extent in the east as well) the protest movements of the 1960s contributed to the development of a new political culture that was highly critical of established authority. In West Germany the student movement challenged the repression of the Nazi past by members of the parental generation who had lived through the Third Reich. The revival of interest in the origins and causes of Nazism was reflected in a variety of new historical works that ended the relative silence about the recent past in the postwar years. A younger generation of historians in Germany called attention to historical continuities that were ignored or downplayed in the conservative 1950s.

The most important historiographical breakthrough had already come in 1961 with the appearance of the Hamburg historian Fritz Fischer's (1908–99) *Griff nach der Weltmacht* (translated as *Germany's Aims in the First World War*), which unleashed the first major historiographical controversy in postwar Germany.[10] On the basis of a thorough examination of the German Foreign Office archives opened in 1953, Fischer concluded that the German government had deliberately manipulated the crisis in 1914 to bring about a showdown with Russia and France with the aim of consolidating Germany's dominance in Europe and expanding German borders. In Fischer's judgment Germany bore greater responsibility for the start of World War I than any other major power. More provocative still was Fischer's contention that German plans to annex territory in eastern and western Europe enjoyed the backing of industry and finance and foreshadowed the Nazis' aims in World

War II. Fischer followed up this path-breaking book with works that traced the continuities in German history back to the founding of the German Empire and forward to the Third Reich.[11] Influenced by his years of study in the United States and Britain in the 1950s, Fischer introduced a methodological innovation into postwar German historiography as well. By stressing the economic interests behind the formation of foreign policy Fischer linked social and diplomatic history, which traditional adherents of the "primacy of foreign policy" had tended to treat in isolation from each other.

The "Fischer thesis" of German responsibility for World War I was greeted with scorn by the older generation of German historians, including Gerhard Ritter, who wrote a highly critical review of Fischer's first book in Germany's major historical journal.[12] It was well received, however, in other countries and exercised a strong influence on a younger generation of German historians who rejected the conservative apologetics of the 1940s and 1950s. Fischer's work launched a decisive break with Germany's tradition of conservative and nationalist historiography. A new critical spirit dominated historical analyses of the Third Reich in the 1960s and 1970s. The totalitarianism model that had undergirded the Cold War gave way to a variety of left-liberal and neo-Marxist interpretations that sought the causes of Nazism in the structural flaws of German society. Younger historians refused to be satisfied with explanations that pinned all the blame on the leading Nazis while sparing Germany's conservative elites. They rejected the older generation's assertion that Nazism was an accidental aberration or inconsequential episode in German history that had now been overcome. Instead they investigated the roles that social, economic, and political interest groups in Imperial Germany and the Weimar Republic played in undermining democracy and preparing the ground for Nazism. They also investigated whether and how the ideological forces and institutions that undermined democracy might have outlived the collapse of the Nazi regime and survived into the present.

The most important center of critical social history in Germany developed at the newly founded University of Bielefeld under the leadership of historians Hans-Ulrich Wehler, Jürgen Kocka, and Hans-Jürgen Puhle in the early 1970s. The "Bielefeld School" of younger critical historians applied the methods and insights of the social sciences, particularly sociology and political science, to the study of German history to a greater degree than had been the practice in traditional German historiography, which concentrated on the actions and decisions of a few major political leaders and was more concerned with the analysis of state documents than of social structures and processes. From the work of this younger generation of critical social historians a new interpretation emerged that viewed Germany's deviation from the western pattern of democratic development as a major source of the tragic crises of the first half of the twentieth century. The Bielefeld School criticized the authoritarian tradition in Germany, the antidemocratic values of traditional elites, the excessive nationalism and lack of restraint of *Weltpolitik* under Wilhelm II, and the failure of Germany's political institutions to keep pace with economic modernization and liberalization in the nineteenth century.[13] For the Bielefeld School the German *Sonderweg*, Germany's political deviation from the democratic west, once a source of pride to German idealists and nationalists, was the key to the overextension of German power in the twentieth century.

The work of the Bielefeld School and other critical historians was driven by an unequivocal commitment to the liberal democratic values of the west, which served as the standard against which German historical development came to be judged. In some respects the work of the "Bielefeld School" and other critical historians brought German historiography of Nazism into congruence with liberal interpretive models that had long been dominant in Anglo-American scholarship. The 1960s also gave rise to more radical interpretations that implicated some of the institutions of the Federal Republic in the Nazi debacle, such as the judiciary with its many holdovers from the Third Reich. Although few radicals endorsed the simplistic communist "agent theory" of fascism (the Nazis as agents of monopoly capitalism), they were willing to give East German historians a much more sympathetic hearing in the late 1960s and early 1970s than they had received before.

There were other factors that contributed to a more critical perspective on the past in the 1960s as well, including the trial of Adolf Eichmann in 1961 and the well-publicized trial of former Auschwitz guards in Frankfurt in 1963, which greatly increased public awareness of the scale and barbarity of Nazi genocide. Consciousness of Nazi-instigated genocide grew in the 1960s, although the term "Holocaust" did not gain general currency in Germany until 1979 after the showing of a widely viewed American television play by that title. Under the pressure of both domestic and foreign opinion the West German *Bundestag* extended the 20-year statute of limitations on Nazi murders in 1965 and in 1979 abolished the statute entirely. By the mid-1970s critical confrontation with the German past and frank acceptance of German responsibility informed the self-understanding of the Federal Republic, despite the continued agitation (and terrorism) of left-wing radicals who felt that West Germany's reformation had not gone far enough. Chancellor Willy Brandt's spontaneous *Kniefall* (act of kneeling) in front of the memorial to the victims of the Warsaw Ghetto during his state visit to Poland in December 1970 movingly symbolized German contrition.

The conservative revival in the 1980s

But the critical confrontation with the German past that set in in the 1960s never went uncontested. Conservatives who opposed Chancellor Brandt's *Ostpolitik* (the policy of normalizing relations with the Eastern Bloc by renouncing the territorial losses of World War II and recognizing the GDR as a separate German state) feared that preoccupation with the Nazi past would weaken the Federal Republic's voice in the NATO alliance and compromise public commitment to victory in the Cold War. Excessive focus on Nazi crimes would allegedly only strengthen the officially sponsored antifascist ideology of the GDR. Prominent conservative politicians such as Franz Josef Strauss, the leader of the Bavarian wing of the Christian Democratic Union (CDU), called on Germans to cast off their "burden of guilt" in order to play a more active role in combating the communist menace.

From the mid-1970s to the fall of the SPD government in 1982 the swing to the right was fed by a backlash against the left-wing militancy of the so-called "Red Army Faction" (RAF), a terrorist group that was widely perceived as an extreme result of the general reorientation of values to the left in the 1960s. Appalled by what they viewed as the continuation of fascist attitudes and institutions in the Federal Republic, members of the RAF thought of themselves as playing the same role in the FRG as the German resistance had played in Hitler's Germany. Through a campaign to assassinate leading representatives of government and industry the RAF hoped either to unleash a socialist revolution or, failing that, to salvage German honor by providing a symbol of resistance as underground fighters had done in Nazi Germany. Although the declared intention of the RAF was to actively combat the vestiges of Nazism in West Germany in order to prevent a neofascist restoration and to impede western imperialism, their resort to violence and terrorism ironically, and tragically, reproduced typically Nazi methods. Blinded by fanatical antifascism they completely misjudged the mood of the population, which swung against them with a vengeance. The leaders of the RAF committed suicide in prison in 1977.

The discovery of an East German agent among Brandt's closest advisers led to Brandt's resignation as chancellor in 1974 and contributed to the rightward trend. The shift to the right in the Federal Republic was also a part of a more general rejection of "socialist" welfare-state policies in the western world, as exemplified by the electoral victories of the staunchly antisocialist free market advocates Margaret Thatcher in Britain in 1979 and Ronald Reagan in the United States in 1980. The accession of CDU leader Helmut Kohl to the chancellorship in 1982 signaled the triumph of the new conservatism in the Federal Republic.

Bitburg

The neoconservative tide brought with it a new determination not to allow shame and guilt about the past to inhibit successful prosecution of the Cold War against the Soviet Union. In the United States this search for a usable past took the form of overcoming the so-called "Vietnam syndrome," the sense of guilt about American involvement and failure in Vietnam that supposedly led to irresolution in the Cold War and a reluctance to apply American power in the anticommunist cause. In West Germany, with its far greater burden of guilt and shame, the neoconservative campaign to remove the stigma of the past and free up public energies for the struggle against Soviet communism was bound to create greater controversy.

If Brandt's *Kniefall* in Warsaw was emblematic of left-wing willingness to achieve an understanding with the Soviet bloc and to fully accept the geopolitical consequences of the Nazi debacle (including the existence of the GDR), then Kohl's decision to host President Reagan for a wreath-laying ceremony at the Bitburg military cemetery in May 1985 was emblematic of neoconservative efforts to bury the Nazi trauma and demonstrate a united front in the newly revived Cold War. The ceremony in a military cemetery that was the burial site not only of *Wehrmacht* soldiers but of members of the *Waffen SS* (the military arm of the SS) as well was planned by Kohl's government as a symbolic act of reconciliation between the Federal Republic and the United States on the fortieth anniversary of the end of World War II. To its critics, however, the ceremony seemed to symbolize the suppression of the antifascist alliance of the past in order to strengthen the anticommunist alliance of the present. Conservatives defended the ceremony by arguing that the young, conscripted members of the *Waffen SS* buried there were as much victims of Nazism as the inmates of concentration camps. The suggestion that fallen German soldiers and murdered Jews were equally victims of Hitler seemed to trivialize the genocidal role of the SS and deny the exceptionality of the Holocaust. Bitburg remained a symbol of the desire to downplay the significance of Nazi atrocities and anticipated the bitter dispute among West German historians known as the *Historikerstreit*.[14]

The *Historikerstreit*

As always, historiographical trends in Germany reflected and reinforced the general reorientation of political values. From the late 1970s on historical works appeared in the FRG with a distinctly more conservative tenor than those of the Bielefeld School. Conservative historians rejected what they considered to be the excessively self-flagellating historiography of the 1960s and called for a halt to the tendency to view all of the German past through the lens of the Nazi trauma. The historian Thomas Nipperdey, for instance, published a highly praised and widely read work in 1983 that stressed the positive continuities in German history and refused to accept 1933 as the vantage point from which to examine earlier German history.[15]

One of the most assertive revisionists was Michael Stürmer, a historian with close ties to the ruling Christian Democratic party. Stürmer argued that a revival of national pride and self-confidence was necessary if the Federal Republic was to avoid debilitating social conflict and remain a reliable partner in NATO. Stürmer warned against the "obsession with guilt" about the Nazi past, for which he blamed not only Marxist historians of the GDR but also left-liberal historians of the 1960s upheaval in the Federal Republic. "The cultural policies of the 1960s sowed the wind," he wrote, "and today we are reaping the tempest."[16] A revival of national consciousness was needed to prevent the kind of social conflict that doomed the Weimar Republic. Stürmer went so far as to make communists and left-wing intellectuals primarily responsible for Weimar's collapse.[17]

Stürmer assigned to historians the task of creating a unified and positive national identity to counteract pacifism among German youth and promote social harmony and integration, prerequisites for winning the cold war against the GDR. "In a land without history," he wrote, "the future is controlled by those who determine the content of memory, coin the concepts, and interpret the past."[18] Only if historians provided a positive picture of the German past to counter the fixation of the left on Germany's historical guilt would the Federal Republic emerge triumphant in its contest with the GDR for German hearts and minds. By stressing Germany's exposed central location in the heart of Europe as the major reason for its tragic involvement in continental wars, Stürmer sought to divert or weaken the focus of historians on the personal responsibility of German leaders for World Wars I and II. Through a kind of geographical determinism Germans could again reclaim a positive historical identity freed of their debilitating obsession with the Nazi period.[19]

It was the social philosopher Jürgen Habermas (b. 1929), one of West Germany's leading public intellectuals, who first called public attention to the new revisionism and thus precipitated the bitter *Historikerstreit* in the summer of 1986. In an article in the liberal weekly *Die Zeit* he accused Stürmer and like-minded historians of rewriting history to build a national consensus in support of neoconservatism.[20] The main target of his criticisms, however, was the historian Ernst Nolte (b. 1923), whose article, "The Past That Will Not Pass," published in the conservative *Frankfurter Allgemeine Zeitung* a month earlier, had asserted that Nazi atrocities were no worse than the earlier Bolshevik and Stalinist crimes on which they were allegedly modeled and that the Holocaust represented an understandable preemptive response by the Nazis to the perceived communist threat.[21] Nolte asserted that Stalin's crimes not only equaled or exceeded those of Hitler, but provoked them as well.

In denying the uniqueness of Nazism and the Holocaust, Nolte contradicted his own much-acclaimed *Three Faces of Fascism*, published in the very different political climate of 1963. Here he had written that the annihilation of the Jews "differed essentially from all other extermination actions, both as to scope and to intention."[22] Now, however, Nolte called for the same dispassionate treatment of the Nazi experience that all other past events have eventually received. Only the Nazi past, Nolte lamented, seemed to be excluded from this normalization process, apparently because it provided a conveniently unambiguous target for pacifists, feminists, and anti-imperialists and because it served the interests "of the persecuted and their descendants in having a permanent special status and the privileges that go with it." Nolte went on to pose a series of rhetorical questions that seemed to defend Nazi motives and shifted the primary blame for the mass killings of the twentieth century on to the communists:

Did the National Socialists or Hitler perhaps commit an "Asiatic" deed merely because they considered themselves and their kind to be potential victims of an "Asiatic" deed? Was the Gulag Archipelago not prior to Auschwitz? Was the Bolshevik murder of an entire class not the logical and factual precedent for the "racial murder" of National Socialism?[23]

Nolte's apologetics and Habermas' intervention provoked a fiercely polemical public debate that eventually involved virtually every historian of modern German history (and of other fields) in the Federal Republic as well as a number of prominent journalists and public figures. The fact that in Germany interpretation of National Socialism has formed an important component of political education in democratic values since 1945 added to the rancor of the dispute. The controversy coincided with a bitterly contested election campaign (won by a narrow margin by Kohl's CDU in January 1987) and divided the historical profession along political lines. Both sides accused the other of instrumentalizing history for political purposes. Liberals and the left accused conservatives of attempting to "normalize" the Nazi past and "relativize" Nazi crimes to gain a public consensus for more conservative foreign and domestic policies. Normalization of Nazism would permit the rehabilitation of Germany's conservative political tradition that had been damaged by its association with the Nazi trauma. Conservatives, on the other hand, charged that the dispute was started by left-wing intellectuals in their desperate efforts to counteract the loss of their dominance of politics and public opinion since the late 1960s. Conservatives argued that the left's obsessional focus on German guilt and responsibility had the effect, whether intended or not, of weakening West Germany's psychological defenses against the continuing ideological threat from the socialist East.[24]

Conservative historiography in reunified Germany

While the defense against communism lost its immediate relevance with the collapse of the Soviet system and the unification of Germany in 1989–90, the debate on the appropriate interpretation of the Nazi past and its meaning for Germans today continued into the 1990s. The end of the Cold War and the collapse of communism from 1989 to 1991 was bound to give more conservative perspectives on the Third Reich at least a temporary boost while diminishing the credibility of Marxist interpretations. For many Germans the need to come to terms with the communist past now took welcome precedence over the increasingly irksome obligation of continuing to wrestle with the moral and political implications of the Nazi past. Indeed, the rapidity with which legal, social, and political measures were put into effect to redress the wrongs of the GDR stood in marked contrast to the foot-dragging with which the two Germanys, especially the FRG, had faced up to the Nazi past.[25] The massive dismissal of East German historians from their university positions contributed to what Stefan Berger has called "the renationalisation of German historiography" in the wake of reunification. The Munich-based *Institut für Zeitgeschichte*, founded in 1950 with the specific task of researching the Nazi era, increasingly turned to investigations of the GDR after 1989 and was joined by a number of new and well-funded institutes founded specifically for the historical study of the GDR or of "totalitarianism."[26] Conservatives sought to shift the focus of *Vergangenheitsbewältigung* from the Nazi regime to the misdeeds of the communist dictatorship. They called on the left to undertake the kind of penitential reappraisal that for so many years had been demanded of the right. Revelations of the pervasive internal spying of the *Stasi*, the vast state security system of the former GDR, allowed invidious comparisons to Nazi Germany, where the secret police system had indeed been much smaller because the Third Reich had enjoyed far greater popular support than did the postwar communist regime in East Germany.

The conservative triumphalism that accompanied reunification at least temporarily strengthened the voices of those who, like Nolte, called for a *Schlussstrich* (bottom line), an end to public discussion of the crimes of the Nazi past and to what Nolte called the "mea-culpa mentality" of the left.[27] Nolte saw the collapse of communism as a vindication of the revisionist view of National Socialism that had been so bitterly contested in the *Historikerstreit*. In the long struggle against communism in the twentieth century, the National Socialists, however misguided their methods, were now seen by Nolte to have been on the right side. In a series of books Nolte set forth his revisionist thesis that National Socialism was a justified, if excessively radical, response to the greater menace of Soviet communism.[28] According to Nolte, the revolutionary excesses of communism inevitably provoked an equally totalizing response on the right. Insofar as it opposed communism, now revealed in its full horror, National Socialism could no longer be considered uniquely criminal, nor could it be equated with absolute evil.

Nolte considered Nazism a *less* radical and therefore more defensible movement than communism, for the communists sought a far more thoroughgoing transformation of society than the Nazis. Nolte shrewdly reversed the fronts: if in the 1930s communism attracted many followers because of its uncompromising opposition to fascism, now Nolte portrayed fascism as retroactively attractive because of its uncompromising opposition to communism. He defended his philosophical mentor Martin Heidegger's option for National Socialism as the only reasonable alternative to communism from the perspective of well-meaning Germans in 1933.[29] Ultimate responsibility for the disasters of the twentieth century had to be borne by what Nolte called the "eternal left," the urge to reject existing social and institutional arrangements in the name of a higher normative code of reason or justice.[30]

Germany's new right

While Nolte's revisionist paradigm of Nazism as an at least partially justified reaction to the greater evil of Soviet communism attracted a number of followers among Germany's new right in the 1990s, some conservatives were uncomfortable with Nolte's frank avowal of Hitler's partisanship for the threatened bourgeoisie. Rainer Zitelmann (b. 1957), for instance, a leading representative of the younger generation of German conservatives, preferred the earlier conservative emphasis on the antibourgeois and antielitist aspects of Hitler's ideology. The tension in new right historiography derived from the contradiction between, on the one hand, their efforts to gain sympathy and understanding for the conservatives who supported the Nazis to counter the communist threat and, on the other hand, their desire to attribute Nazi abuses of power to the left-wing features of the Nazi program. Zitelmann portrayed Hitler as a left-wing revolutionary and Nazism as no less a progressive, modernizing movement than communism.[31] Unconvincing though his interpretation may have been, its obvious aims were to at least partially rehabilitate Nazism while at the same time incriminating and discrediting the left.

Viewing National Socialism as a modernizing, predominantly left-wing movement also permitted the new right to retain the older conservative postulate that fascism as well as communism originated in the French Revolution (not the royalist counter-revolution) and represented a revolt of the masses. Zitelmann emphasized the allegedly progressive social legislation of the Nazi era (such as support for large families, generous old-age pensions, and maternity benefits) and portrayed Hitler as a genuinely egalitarian social reformer who came to regret his tactical alliance with the elites and created new opportunities for upward mobility for the lower-class members of the *Volksgemeinschaft*. According to Zitelmann, the modernizing effects of the Nazi dictatorship were not achieved *despite* Nazi ideology, as traditional historiography would have it, but *because of* Nazi commitment to progressive policies. He denied that Hitler's social program was designed to serve his foreign policy and war; rather, his foreign policy and war were designed to achieve his socialist utopia. Zitelmann went so far as to claim that the prevention of Hitlerian socialism was one of the main motives of the conservative resistance.[32]

Thus, ironically, the fall of communism abetted the revival of totalitarianism theory, partly because of the virtual disappearance of countervoices on the Marxist left. By portraying Nazism as socialist and stressing the commensurability of Nazi and Soviet crimes, conservative revisionists sought to integrate the Nazi period into German history in a way that minimized the burden of German guilt. If earlier apologetics had aimed primarily at dissociating conservatism from Nazism, the new right sought more boldly to show Nazism in a more positive light as a movement with many "progressive" features heroically dedicated to the destruction of communism. Anticommunism became the great alibi for Nazism. No longer was it necessary to repress the memory of Nazism or to deny complicity, modes of evasion favored by German nationalists and conservatives after the war and attacked and rejected by the generation of the 1960s. Nor was it necessary to make such outlandish claims as denying the Holocaust, a stance that Nolte criticized for failing to take Hitler's ideas seriously enough (and because he could not believe that German officers who testified to the killings would lie under oath). "Moderate" revisionism presented itself as objective mainstream scholarship, but its aim was to neutralize and trivialize Nazi crimes. A positive view of German history was an essential ingredient in the new conservative ethos that Nolte, Zitelmann, and their allies hoped to create.

The Goldhagen controversy

The *Historikerstreit* was only the most striking example of inextricable interrelationship between history and politics in Germany (or elsewhere, for that matter). If in the *Historikerstreit* the Cold War was still the primary political issue, in the 1990s the foremost source of political conflict was probably the issue of multiculturalism and the inclusiveness of German society. The cultural wars between left and right in Germany resembled very similar conflicts and debates in industrialized countries facing massive immigration from eastern Europe or the "Third World." In Germany, however, the debate inevitably involves the memory of the German past—and the interpretation of Nazism. It would be wrong, however, to exaggerate the influence of the "new right" in a united Germany. On the whole, the debate unleashed in the *Historikerstreit* of the 1980s reinforced public awareness that the Nazi era cannot simply be "normalized" to enhance German national pride. Contrary to widely expressed fears at the time, the transition of 1989–90 did not have the effect of displacing Nazism either in public memory or in the field of historical studies. In fact the focus of research shifted dramatically to the Holocaust in the wake of the questions raised about its singularity and causation in the *Historikerstreit*.

Perhaps the most important example of the renewed focus on the Nazi past, the Holocaust, and the antisemitic ideology that propelled it was the wide readership attracted by Daniel J. Goldhagen's (b. 1959) emotionally charged bestseller, *Hitler's Willing Executioners*, published in the United States and Germany in 1996.[33] The young author received a surprisingly favorable public reception especially from younger Germans on a book tour in September 1996. The book's graphic descriptions of horrific acts of murder differed sharply from the emotionally detached, "objective" style with which historians had traditionally presented the brutal details of the genocide. Goldhagen did his research in Germany in the late 1980s when Nolte's brazen revisionism first achieved notoriety. His book offered a salutary antidote to the efforts of Germany's "new right" to "relativize" the Holocaust, "normalize" the Nazi era, and distance themselves from the past. *Hitler's Willing Executioners* served to refocus the debate on the question of German responsibility and guilt. But Goldhagen's blanket rejection of any interpretation that might seem to diminish specifically German responsibility for the Holocaust led him to the opposite extreme of an overly narrow determinism. Goldhagen contended that the Holocaust was a German "national project" perpetrated with the full knowledge and approval of the German public. As the ultimate source of this "voluntary barbarism" Goldhagen identified an "eliminationist" antisemitic hatred so deeply rooted in

German history and culture as to have become part of the common sense of the average German. Goldhagen went so far as to recommend using the methods of anthropology to understand how radically different prewar German society and culture had been from western norms.

Goldhagen's book was severely criticized by German, American, British, and Israeli historians for exaggerating German exceptionalism, offering an overly simplistic, monocausal explanatory model for the origins of the Holocaust, neglecting the political context in which Nazism arose, generalizing from a sample of hard-core perpetrators to the German population as a whole, insisting that antisemitism had been more pervasive in Germany than in other countries without providing any comparative data, and for overstating the novelty of his thesis that antisemitism was the root cause of the Holocaust. One would never have known from Goldhagen's book that there was an active German left, which, though anticapitalist, was fundamentally opposed to antisemitism. As the American historian Doris Bergen (b. 1960) wrote in a searching critique, "Goldhagen neglects both the non-German perpetrators and the nonperpetrator Germans."[34]

As his subtitle, *Ordinary Germans and the Holocaust*, made clear, Goldhagen directly challenged American historian Christopher Browning's (b. 1944) findings on perpetrator motivation in his path-breaking book, *Ordinary Men: Reserve Police Battalion 101 and the Final Solution in Poland* (1992). While Browning had called attention to the many situational factors that can turn ordinary human beings, whether German or not, into willing and even eager killers in time of all-out war, Goldhagen insisted that only Germans' irrational hatred of Jews could explain the brutality of the killings and the fact that the Holocaust occurred in Germany. There was a paradoxically reassuring aspect to Goldhagen's emphasis on the uniqueness and pervasiveness of German eliminationist antisemitism: while the thrust of Browning's analysis was to warn against the possibility of a future recurrence of genocide with different perpetrators and different victims, the logic of Goldhagen's revival of the notion of a peculiarly aberrant German political culture seemed to relegate the Holocaust safely to the past.[35]

Goldhagen's castigation of Germany's pre-Nazi political culture also marked a departure from the imperatives and conventions of the Cold War up to 1989. Goldhagen virtually obliterated the previously almost obligatory distinction between criminal Nazis and ordinary Germans—the benign myth that had facilitated the integration of West Germany into the western alliance during the Cold War. The western interest in courting West German support for the NATO alliance was not well served by incriminating ordinary Germans or burdening them with an undue sense of guilt about their past. Goldhagen himself understood this potential damage to western unity by assuring his readers that Germany's endemic antisemitism had not survived beyond 1945.[36] His readiness to attest to the complete success of the Federal Republic's conversion to democracy after 1945 may have helped to make many middle-aged and younger Germans particularly receptive to his blanket indictment of Germany's wartime and prewar generations. Ironically, Goldhagen's favorable assessment of the Federal Republic pleased the German nationalist right while disappointing German progressives who had welcomed his book for galvanizing public attention on German responsibility for Nazi atrocities and thus strengthening the ethos of democratic citizenship in Germany.[37]

The continuing debate

In the culture of the Federal Republic of Germany the questions of the complicity of Germans in Nazi crimes and the place of the Nazi experience in German history continued to be highly divisive issues. How best to commemorate the end of the war on 8 May 1945 is a case in point. On the 40th anniversary in 1985, the West German president Richard von Weizsäcker had delivered a powerful address to the *Bundestag*, referring to the end of the war as a day of liberation and urging his fellow Germans to accept personal responsibility for remembering the atrocities of the Nazi regime. In contrast to the symbolic reconciliation staged by Chancellor Kohl at the Bitburg military cemetery that same year, Weizsäcker called on his listeners to internalize the memory of Nazi crimes as a moral debt to the victims of the Holocaust. "What we need," he said, "is a memorial of thinking and feeling within ourselves."[38] Yet ten years later, in April 1995, an advertisement signed by some 300 conservative public figures and published in Germany's leading conservative newspaper, the *Frankfurter Allgemeine Zeitung*, called on Germans to commemorate the 50th anniversary of the end of the war in Europe not only as the end of Nazi tyranny but as the beginning of communist tyranny. A storm of protest greeted what seemed to be a renewed attempt to divert public attention from the horrors of Nazism to the supposedly equivalent (or greater) horrors of communism.

Another recent example of the passions generated by the questions of German guilt and responsibility was the controversy that surrounded a traveling photographic exhibit of Wehrmacht crimes during the war. Sponsored by the left-liberal Hamburg Institute for Social Research (HIS), the exhibit, which opened in Hamburg in March 1995, took aim at the national myth of a "clean Wehrmacht," untainted by the crimes and atrocities committed by the SS. The exhibit's many gruesome photos of killings committed by regular army soldiers, and its display of incriminating orders and guidelines issued by the army High Command, gave the lie to the myth that the army had not participated in the killing of Jews. Historians have long known that the Wehrmacht had been deeply involved in Nazi war crimes, but the myth of the untainted Wehrmacht was slow to die in the minds of the German public.[39] The exhibit, which attracted close to a million viewers nationwide, provoked protests in major German cities, particularly in Munich in 1997. Neo-Nazis marched in the streets to protest the exhibition, but more significantly, mainstream political figures from the Christian Social Union (CSU), the Bavarian wing of the Christian Democrats (CDU), also objected to this alleged slur on the reputation of German soldiers.

The exhibit was forced to shut down in November 1999 when right-wing critics of the exhibit seized on some minor inaccuracies to discredit its purpose and dispute Wehrmacht involvement in the Holocaust. The strongly anti-Soviet Polish historian Bogdan Musial accused the organizers of the exhibit of having attributed several photographs of mass killings in the Polish-Ukrainian town of Zloczow in July 1941 to the Wehrmacht rather than to the Soviet NKVD. While an independent commission of scholars convened by the HIS recommended in November 2000 that 20 out of 1,433 photographs be withdrawn because of inaccurate labeling, the commission also concluded that the vast majority of Zloczow photographs were indeed of Jews killed by the Nazis and that the basic thesis of the "Crimes of the Wehrmacht" exhibition was correct. Nonetheless, under conservative pressure, the HIS abandoned plans to show the exhibit in other cities, including in New York, where it had been scheduled to open in December 1999.[40]

Another dramatic example of the disputes inspired by the challenge of coming to terms with the past was the prolonged public discussion throughout the 1990s on the feasibility, location, and design of a central Holocaust memorial in the new and former capital of Berlin. Although construction of such a memorial was decided by the *Bundestag* in 1988, before the fall of the wall, it was not finally completed and opened until 2005. A number of prominent German public figures opposed any kind of national memorial dedicated solely to the Holocaust. In a speech in October 1998 the well-known German novelist Martin Walser (b. 1927) referred to the planned memorial as the "monumentalization of shame" and a prime example of the use of the Holocaust as a "moral cudgel" by the left to inhibit the development of a positive sense of German national identity.[41] Conservatives preferred the kind of memorial that lumped all victims together as casualties of war, on the model of the *Neue Wache*, the national memorial to "the victims of war and the rule of violence" reopened in Berlin by the Kohl government in 1993 and featuring a famous sculpture of a grieving mother, which the renowned artist Käthe Kollwitz (1867–1945) had originally created to commemorate the loss of her son in World War I. But criticism of a Holocaust memorial was not limited only to the political right. What kind of design could possibly do justice to such an unparalleled crime? Even critics associated with the political left expressed fear that the erection of a giant monument could serve as a substitute rather than an incentive for continuing moral and intellectual engagement with the meaning of the Holocaust.[42]

In the end, however, supporters of a national Holocaust memorial in Berlin won out. Ironically, Walser's speech, and especially the enthusiastic reception it received on the right, convinced the SPD government under Chancellor Gerhard Schröder that opposing the project would now be perceived as support for far-right extremism. The memorial, based on an impressive design by architect Peter Eisenman, features a maze of concrete slabs of widely varying sizes intended to give visitors a sense of the loss of moorings that Jews experienced in the Holocaust. Its huge scale and its prominent location near the

Brandenburg Gate reinforce the sense of how central the Holocaust has become to German national memory.[43]

The culture of national contrition is even stronger in a united Germany than it was before the end of the division of Germany, when the two Germanys in differing ways routinely shifted responsibility for the past to the other side. In no other country has there been such soul-searching about the Nazi past as in Germany, where debates about the Nazi past are not academic debates, nor merely political debates, but debates about national identity and the moral bases of politics. While after reunification the overwhelming majority of Germans agreed that consciousness and memory of the crimes of the Nazi past must be preserved as part of German national identity, there was no consensus on whether national or transnational, right-wing or left-wing, West German or East German historical interpretations of Nazism and fascism should prevail. Conservative revisionism is based on the assumption that a positive depiction of German history is needed if Germans are to play a constructive role in the world. Their left-wing critics counter by arguing that only active commemoration of Nazism's unspeakable crimes can provide that positive identity. For conservatives Nazism distorts and blocks the view of the past they wish to reclaim. For their critics on the left the living memory of Nazism is essential to sensitize German citizens to the need to defend democratic principles. As the last members of the generation that experienced the Nazi era in full consciousness die out and the Nazi era is inevitably relegated to the sphere of history and memory, the debate is more relevant to contemporary concerns than ever.

Notes

Introduction

1 The term "Nazi" is formed from the first two syllabi of "National Socialist" as it is pro-nounced in German. It was first used as a term of mild disparagement by opponents of the National Socialist Party, in the same way that "Sozi" was used to designate members of the Social Democratic Party. In this book I use the terms Nazi and National Socialist inter-changeably.

2 A sensationalistic, moralizing, and nonanalytical approach dominated much of the early popular literature on Nazism. Even so thoroughly documented a study as the still useful best-seller by William L. Shirer, *The Rise and Fall of the Third Reich: A History of Nazi Germany*, New York, Simon and Schuster, 1960, adopted a strongly moralistic tone.

3 For a cursory survey of the historiography of Nazism, see my *Routledge Companion to Nazi Germany*, New York and London, Routledge, 2007, pp. 22–53.

4 In accordance with conventional practice, I use "fascism" in the lower case to refer to the generic concept, under which the various national forms of fascism, including National Socialism (or Nazism), were subsumed. I capitalize Fascism when referring specifically to the Italian movement or to other fascist parties that used "Fascism" in their names. The same principle applies to communism, which I capitalize only when referring to a particu-lar party.

5 The best discussion of the major controversies about Nazism in English is Ian Kershaw, *The Nazi Dictatorship: Problems and Perspectives of Interpretation*, 4th ed., London, Hodder Arnold, 2000. In German, see Wolfgang Wippermann, *Umstrittene Vergangenheit: Fakten und Kontroversen zum Nationalsozialismus*, Berlin, Elefanten Press, 1998.

6 This is the title of a book by Zeev Sternhell, *Neither Right nor Left: Fascist Ideology in France*, trans. David Maisel, Princeton, NJ, Princeton University Press, 1986.

7 This is the title of a book by the chief critics of the *Sonderweg* thesis, David Blackbourn and Geoff Eley, *The Peculiarities of German History: Bourgeois Society and Politics in Nineteenth-Century Germany*, Oxford, Oxford University Press, 1984.

8 This is the title of a book by the British historian A. J. P. Taylor, *The Course of German History: A Survey of the Development of German History since 1815* (1946), repr. London, Routledge, 2001, which, written in the closing months of World War II, emphasizes Germany's undemocratic development and, despite its war-induced exaggerations, remains useful today.

9 For an excellent recent discussion of equality as the determining criterion for the left–right distinction see Norberto Bobbio, *Left and Right: The Significance of a Political Distinction*, trans. Allan Cameron, Chicago, University of Chicago Press, 1996, esp. pp. 60–71.

10 For the definitive critique of the *Sonderweg* theory, see Blackbourn and Eley, *The Peculiarities of German History*. For recent discussions of the *Sonderweg*, see Reinhard Kühnl, "The German *Sonderweg* Reconsidered: Continuities and Discontinuities in Modern German History," in Reinhard Alter and Peter Monteath, eds., *Rewriting the German Past: History and Identity in the New Germany*, Atlantic Highlands, NJ, Humanities Press, 1997, pp. 115–28, and Jürgen Kocka, "German History before Hitler: The Debate about the German 'Sonderweg,' " *Journal of Contemporary History* 23 (1988), 3–16, and "German Identity and Historical Comparison: After the *Historikerstreit*," in Peter Baldwin, ed., *Reworking the Past: Hitler, the Holocaust, and the Historians' Debate*, Boston, Beacon Press, 1990, esp. pp. 283–93. See also the exchange between Volker R. Berghahn, "The German Empire 1871–1914: Reflections on the Direction of Recent Research," which offers a response to the critics of the *Sonderweg*, and Margaret Lavinia Anderson, "Reply to Volker Berghahn," *Central European History* 35 (2002), 75–81, 83–90, respectively.

11 See for instance Shulamit Volkov, *The Rise of Popular Antimodernism in Germany: The Urban Master Artisans, 1873–1896*, Princeton, NJ, Princeton University Press, 1978, esp. pp. 297–325. A good summary of Nazism as an antimodernizing movement is Henry A. Turner, "Fascism and Modernization," in *Reappraisals of Fascism*, New York, New Viewpoints, 1975, pp. 117–39.

12 Jeffrey Herf, *Reactionary Modernism: Technology, Culture and Politics in Weimar and the Third Reich*, Cambridge, Cambridge University Press, 1984.

13 For a good overview of the debate see Mark Roseman, "National Socialism and Modernization," in Richard Bessel, ed., *Fascist Italy and Nazi Germany: Comparisons and Contrasts*, Cambridge, Cambridge University Press, 1996, pp. 197–229.

14 See James A. Gregor, *The Ideology of Fascism: The Rationale of Totalitarianism*, New York, Free Press, 1969; *Interpretations of Fascism*, New Brunswick, NJ, Transaction, 1974; and *Italian Fascism and Developmental Dictatorship*, Princeton, NJ, Princeton University Press, 1979.

15 Ralf Dahrendorf, *Society and Democracy in Germany*, New York, Doubleday, 1967, and David Schoenbaum, *Hitler's Social Revolution: Class and Status in Nazi Germany, 1933–1939*, New York, Norton, 1980, argue that the Nazis unintentionally contributed to Germany's modernization by destroying the traditional institutions that had blocked such social aspects of modernization as vocational mobility, the weakening of class status, the liberalization of the economy, and the loosening of traditional ties to region and religion. Rainer Zitelmann, a representative figure of Germany's "new right," claimed that Hitler's regime was intentionally a modernizing dictatorship. See his essay, "Die totalitäre Seite der Moderne," in Michael Prinz and Rainer Zitelmann, eds., *Nationalsozialismus und Modernisierung*, Darmstadt, Wissenschaftliche Buchgesellschaft, 1991, pp. 1–20.

16 The phrases are taken from Detlev J. K. Peukert, *Inside Nazi Germany: Conformity, Opposition, and Racism in Everyday Life*, trans. Richard Deveson, New Haven, Yale University Press, 1987, p. 243, and *The Weimar Republic: The Crisis of Classical Modernity*, trans. Richard Deveson, New York, Hill and Wang, 1992. See also his "The Genesis of the 'Final Solution' from the Spirit of Science," in David F. Crew, ed., *Nazism and German Society, 1933–1945*, London, Routledge, 1994, pp. 274–99.

17 Martin Broszat, "Plädoyer für eine Historisierung des Nationalsozialismus," *Merkur* (May 1985), 373–85; English translation in "A Plea for the Historicization of National Socialism," in Baldwin, *Reworking the Past*, pp. 77–87. For a trenchant critique of Broszat's article, see Saul Friedländer, "Some Reflections on the Historicization of National Socialism," and Broszat and Friedländer, "A Controversy about the Historicization of National Socialism," in Baldwin, *Reworking the Past*, pp. 88–134. Friedländer feared that the "historicization" of Nazism would lead to its trivialization and to the revival of the uncritical methods of

German historicism, which placed a premium on empathizing with leading historical actors rather than on normative judgment and critique.

18 At a symposium on the significance of Martin Broszat's historical writings in December 2006 Friedländer argued that Broszat's plea for historicization was motivated by his concern that the perspective of Jewish victims of the Holocaust would eventually displace his own generation's perspective of the Nazi era in historical memory. See Saul Friedländer, "Ein Briefwechsel, fast zwanzig Jahre später," in Norbert Frei, ed., *Martin Broszat, der "Staat Hitlers" und die Historisierung des Nationalsozialismus*, Göttingen, Wallstein Verlag, 2007, pp. 188–94.

19 See, for instance, Nolte's *Streitpunkte: Heutige und künftige Kontroversen um den Nationalsozialismus*, Berlin, Propyläen Verlag, 1993, pp. 19, 84, 391, and his *Lehrstück oder Tragödie? Beiträge zur Interpretation der Geschichte des 20. Jahrhunderts*, Cologne, Böhlau Verlag, 1991, pp. 9, 14.

1 Fascism and the conservative tradition

1 Recent analyses of fascist doctrines and movements are Michael Mann, *Fascists*, Cambridge, Cambridge University Press, 2004; Robert O. Paxton, *The Anatomy of Fascism*, New York, Alfred A. Knopf, 2004; Kevin Passmore, *Fascism: A Very Short Introduction*, Oxford, Oxford University Press, 2002; Dave Renton, *Fascism: Theory and Practice*, London, Pluto Press, 1999; George L. Mosse, *The Fascist Revolution: Toward a General Theory of Fascism*, New York, Howard Fertig, 1999; Roger Eatwell, *Fascism: A History*, New York, Viking Penguin, 1996; and Roger Griffin, *The Nature of Fascism*, London, Routledge, 1993. For empirical surveys of fascist movements, see Stanley G. Payne, *A History of Fascism, 1914–1945*, Madison, WI, University of Wisconsin Press, 1995, and F. L. Carsten, *The Rise of Fascism*, 2nd ed., Berkeley, CA, University of California Press, 1980. For a variety of interpretations, see Roger Griffin with Matthew Feldman, eds., *Fascism: Critical Concepts in Political Science*, 5 vols., London and New York, Routledge, 2004; Roger Griffin, ed., *International Fascism: Theories, Causes and the New Consensus*, London, Oxford University Press, 1998; and Walter Laqueur, ed., *Fascism: A Reader's Guide*, Berkeley, University of California Press, 1976.

2 For arguments defending the validity of the left–right distinction, see Norberto Bobbio, *Left and Right: The Significance of a Political Distinction*, trans. Allan Cameron, Chicago, University of Chicago Press, 1996.

3 See in particular Zeev Sternhell, *Neither Right Nor Left: Fascist Ideology in France*, trans. David Maisel, Princeton, NJ, Princeton University Press, 1986. For a countervoice see Robert J. Soucy, "The Debate over French Fascism," in Richard J. Golsan, ed., *Fascism's Return: Scandal, Revision, and Ideology Since 1980*, Lincoln, NB, University of Nebraska Press, 1998, pp. 130–51. For a convincing plea not to define fascism by its ideology or propaganda but by its functions at different stages of development, see Robert O. Paxton, "The Five Stages of Fascism," *The Journal of Modern History* 70 (March 1998), 1–23.

4 For readers of German, an excellent analysis of the commonalities (and differences) between monarchists, aristocrats, and fascists is Stephan Malinowski, *Vom König zum Führer: Deutscher Adel und Nationalsozialismus*, Frankfurt, Fischer Taschenbuch Verlag, 2004, esp. pp. 47–114 and 476–609.

5 Bobbio, *Left and Right*, p.19. For a brief, but still useful interpretation of fascism as a "conservative revolution," see John Weiss, *The Fascist Tradition: Radical Right-Wing Extremism in Modern Europe*, New York, Harper & Row, 1967, esp. pp. 1–30. For a contrary view, interpreting fascism as a mixture of right and left, see Eugen Weber, *Varieties of Fascism: Doctrines*

of Revolution in the Twentieth Century, New York, Van Nostrand Reinhold, 1964, esp. pp. 24–5.

6 Soucy, "Debate over French Fascism," p. 138.

2 The problem of German unity

1 The classic account of German history as a special case is A. J. P. Taylor's *The Course of German History: A Survey of the Development of Germany Since 1815*, New York, Coward-McCann, 1946. For the most authoritative version of the *Sonderweg* thesis, see Hans-Ulrich Wehler, *The German Empire, 1871–1918* (1973), trans. Kim Traynor, Providence, RI, Berg, 1985, and more recently, *Deutsche Gesellschaftsgeschichte*, especially Vol. 3, *Von der "Deutschen Doppelrevolution" bis zum Beginn des Ersten Weltkrieges, 1849–1914*, Munich, C. H. Beck, 1995, esp. pp. 461–86. For concise summaries of Wehler's arguments in English, see his essay "The German 'Double Revolution' and the *Sonderweg*, 1848–1879," in Reinhard Rürup, ed., *The Problem of Revolution in Germany, 1789–1989*, Oxford and New York, Berg, 2000, pp. 55–65, and Jürgen Kocka, "German History before Hitler: The Debate about the German *Sonderweg*," *Journal of Contemporary History* 23 (1988), 3–16. See also Ian Kershaw, "The Essence of Nazism: Form of Fascism, Brand of Totalitarianism, or Unique Phenomenon?," in *The Nazi Dictatorship: Problems and Perspectives of Interpretation*, 3rd ed., London, Edward Arnold, 1993, pp. 17–39. For another version of the *Sonderweg* thesis, see Ralf Dahrendorf, *Society and Democracy in Germany*, New York, Doubleday, 1967. For a forceful statement of the differences in the English and German political systems, see Paul Kennedy, *The Rise of the Anglo-German Antagonism, 1860–1914*, London, Allen and Unwin, 1982.

2 The most important critics of the German *Sonderweg* thesis are David Blackbourn and Geoff Eley, *The Peculiarities of German History: Bourgeois Society and Politics in Nineteenth-Century Germany*, Oxford, Oxford University Press, 1984. See also Geoff Eley, "What Produces Fascism: Pre-industrial Traditions or a Crisis of the Capitalist State?," in *From Unification to Nazism: Reinterpreting the German Past*, Boston, Unwin Hyman, 1986, pp. 254–82. For excellent introductions to the *Sonderweg* discussion, see Charles S. Maier, *The Unmasterable Past: History, the Holocaust, and German National Identity*, Cambridge, MA, Harvard University Press, 1988, pp. 109–15, and Shelley Baranowski, "East Elbian Landed Elites and Germany's Turn to Fascism: The Sonderweg Controversy Revisited," *European History Quarterly* 26 (1996), 209–49. For an interpretation critical both of the *Sonderweg* thesis (for understating the stability of the Wilhelmian constitutional system) and of its critics (for understating the differences between the German and western models), see Mark Hewitson, "The *Kaiserreich* in Question: Constitutional Crisis in Germany before the First World War," *Journal of Modern History* 73 (December 2001), 725–80. Hewitson does not believe that maintenance of the political status quo was the main motive of German leaders in going to war in 1914.

3 Geoffrey Barraclough, *The Origins of Modern Germany* (1946), repr. New York, Norton, 1984, esp. pp. 355–466, offers many insights into the enduring effects of Germany's delayed unification.

4 Hans Rosenberg, *Bureaucracy, Aristocracy, and Autocracy: The Prussian Experience, 1660–1815*, Cambridge, MA, Harvard University Press, 1958, pp. 160 and 190.

5 Koppel S. Pinson, *Modern Germany: Its History and Civilization*, 2nd ed., Prospect Heights, IL, Waveland Press, 1966, p. 58.

6 A. J. P. Taylor, *The Course of German History*, p. 68.

7 The best discussion of these issues in English is Theodore Hamerow, *Restoration, Revolution, Reaction: Economics and Politics in Germany, 1815–1871*, Princeton, NJ, Princeton University Press, 1958, esp. pp. 117–95.

8 For a critique of moralizing indictments of the German bourgeoisie for failing to fight for liberal democracy, see Blackbourn and Eley, *Peculiarities*, esp. pp. 13–14 and 51–61.

9 This analysis is based on the definitive work on Bismarck in English, Otto Pflanze's *Bismarck and the Development of Germany*, esp. Vol. I, *The Period of Unification, 1815–1871*, Princeton, NJ, Princeton University Press, 1963. See also Theodore S. Hamerow, *The Social Foundations of German Unification, 1858–1871: Ideas and Institutions*, Princeton, NJ, Princeton University Press, 1969.

10 See Ernst Fraenkel, "Historical Obstacles to Parliamentary Government in Germany," in Theodor Eschenburg, Ernst Fraenkel, Kurt Sontheimer *et al.*, *The Path to Dictatorship, 1918–1933*, trans. John Conway, New York, Frederick A. Praeger, 1967, pp. 19–31.

11 James W. Gerard, *My Four Years in Germany*, New York, George H. Doran, 1917, p. 41. See also Bernadotte Everley Schmitt, *England and Germany, 1740–1910*, Princeton, NJ, Princeton University Press, 1918, pp. 38ff.

3 The German Empire

1 For the notion of a Thirty Years' War see, for instance, William R. Keylor, *The Twentieth-Century World: An International History*, Oxford, Oxford University Press, 1984, pp. 43ff., and P. M. H. Bell, *The Origins of the Second World War in Europe*, London and New York, Longman, 1986, pp. 14–30.

2 For "bourgeois feudalization," see Michael Stürmer, ed., *Das kaiserliche Deutschland: Politik und Gesellschaft 1870–1918*, Düsseldorf, Droste, 1970, esp. pp. 265ff., and Gerhard A. Ritter and Jürgen Kocka, eds., *Deutsche Sozialgeschichte: Dokumente und Skizzen*, Vol. 2, *1870–1914*, Munich, C. H. Beck, 1974, pp. 77ff. For "feudalization" as reflected in German literature, see Ernest K. Bramstead, *Aristocracy and the Middle Classes in Germany: Social Types in German Literature, 1830–1900* (1937), repr. Chicago, University of Chicago Press, 1964, pp. 228ff.

3 David Blackbourn and Geoff Eley, *The Peculiarities of German History: Bourgeois Society and Politics in Nineteenth-Century Germany*, Oxford, Oxford University Press, 1984, p. 13.

4 Hans-Ulrich Wehler, *The German Empire, 1871–1918*, trans. Kim Traynor, Providence, RI, Berg, 1985, pp. 90–4.

5 See Henning Sietz, "In New York wird die grösste Panik ausbrechen: Wie Kaiser Wilhelm II die USA mit einem Militärschlag niederzwingen wollte," *Die Zeit*, 8 May 2002.

6 Ibid., pp. 94–9.

7 Geoff Eley, *Reshaping the German Right: Radical Nationalism and Political Change after Bismarck*, New Haven, CT, Yale University Press, 1980, esp. pp. 41–98.

8 Roger Chickering, *We Men Who Feel Most German: A Cultural Study of the Pan-German League, 1886–1914*, Boston, George Allen & Unwin, 1984, esp. pp. 230–45 and 299ff.

9 David Blackbourn, *Class, Religion, and Local Politics in Wilhelmine Germany: The Center Party in Württemberg before 1914*, New Haven, CT, Yale University Press, 1980, pp. 58–60.

10 See Richard E. Frankel, *Bismarck's Shadow: The Cult of Leadership and the Transformation of the German Right, 1898–1945*, Oxford and New York, Berg, 2005, especially pp. 49–86.

11 V. R. Berghahn, *Germany and the Approach of War in 1914*, London, Macmillan, 1973, pp. 145–214, and *Imperial Germany, 1871–1914: Economy, Society, Culture, and Politics*, Providence, RI, Berghahn Books, 1995, esp. pp. 274–6.

12 Berghahn, *Imperial Germany*, pp. 290ff. See also Fritz Fischer, *Germany's Aims in the First World War*, New York, Norton, 1967, pp. 3–49; *From Kaiserreich to Third Reich: Elements of Continuity in German History, 1871–1945*, trans. Roger Fletcher, London, Allen & Unwin, 1986, esp. pp. 39–55; *War of Illusions: German Policies from 1911 to 1914*, New York, Norton, 1975; and

World Power or Decline: The Controversy over Germany's Aims in the First World War, trans. Lancelot L. Farrar, Robert Kimber, and Rita Kimber, New York, Norton, 1974, pp. 3–19.

13 This is Fischer's conclusion in *Germany's Aims in the First World War*, pp. 87–92. His findings were most recently corroborated by Mark Hewitson, *Germany and the Causes of the First World War*, Oxford, Berg, 2004, particularly p. 3.

4 Germanic idealogy

1 Robert Anchor, *Germany Confronts Modernization: German Society and Culture, 1790–1890*, Lexington, MA, D. C. Heath, 1972, pp. 3–58.

2 For a fuller development of this idea, see Roderick Stackelberg, *Idealism Debased: From Völkisch Ideology to National Socialism*, Kent, OH, Kent State University, 1981, esp. pp. 1–15.

3 See Fritz Stern, "The Political Consequences of the Unpolitical German" (1960), in *The Failure of Illiberalism: Essays on the Political Culture of Modern Germany*, New York, Columbia University Press, 1992, pp. 3–25.

4 Paul de Lagarde, *Deutsche Schriften*, 5th ed., Göttingen, Dieterich'sche Universitäts-Buchhandlung, 1920, p. 408.

5 The standard works on *völkisch* ideology are Fritz Stern, *The Politics of Cultural Despair: A Study in the Rise of Germanic Ideology*, Garden City, NY, Doubleday Anchor, 1965, and George L. Mosse, *The Crisis of German Ideology: Intellectual Origins of the Third Reich*, New York, Grosset & Dunlap, 1964.

6 Peter G. J. Pulzer, *The Rise of Political Anti-semitism in Germany and Austria*, rev. ed., Cambridge, MA, Harvard University Press, 1988, pp. 3–16.

7 See Franklin H. Littell, *The Crucifixion of the Jews*, New York, Harper & Row, 1975, p. 32.

8 Artur Comte de Gobineau, *Essai sur l'inégalité des races humaines*, 4 vols., Paris, Firmin-Didot, 1853–55.

9 See Uriel Tal, *Christians and Jews in Germany: Religion, Politics, and Ideology in the Second Reich, 1870–1914*, trans. Noah Jonathan Jacobs, Ithaca, NY, Cornell University Press, 1975, esp. pp. 223ff.

10 Richard S. Levy argues that the essential distinction is not between religious and racial antisemitism but between what he calls "conventional" and "revolutionary" antisemites. Conventional antisemites aimed for discriminatory legislation through parliamentary means while revolutionary antisemites despaired of constructing their racial utopias through existing Imperial institutions. See *The Downfall of the Anti-semitic Political Parties in Imperial Germany*, New Haven, Yale University Press, 1975, p. 2. Daniel Jonah Goldhagen, *Hitler's Willing Executioners: Ordinary Germans and the Holocaust*, New York, Alfred A. Knopf, 1996, applies the designation "eliminationist antisemitism" to both the religious and racial varieties. A more convincing study of how German antisemitism could develop such lethal force is John Weiss, *Ideology of Death: Why the Holocaust Happened in Germany*, Chicago, Ivan Dee, 1996. See also Paul Lawrence Rose, *German Question/Jewish Question: Revolutionary Antisemitism from Kant to Wagner*, Princeton, NJ, Princeton University Press, 1990, p. xvii.

11 See Steven E. Aschheim, "The Jew Within: The Myth of 'Judaization' in Germany," in *Culture and Catastrophe: German and Jewish Confrontations with National Socialism and Other Crises*, New York, New York University Press, 1996, pp. 45–67.

12 Heinrich Class, "If I Were the Kaiser" (1912), in Roderick Stackelberg and Sally A. Winkle, eds., *The Nazi Germany Sourcebook: An Anthology of Texts*, London and New York, Routledge, 2002, pp. 20–6.

13 See Wolfgang J. Mommsen, "Der Geist von 1914: Das Programm eines politischen 'Sonderwegs' der Deutschen," in *Nation und Geschichte: Über die Deutschen und die deutsche Frage*, Munich, Piper, 1990.

5 The First World War

1 See Omer Bartov, "Defining Enemies, Making Victims: Germans, Jews, and the Holocaust," *American Historical Review* 103 (June 1998), esp. 772–81. On the effect of World War I in extending the responsibilities of the state, see Belinda J. Davis, *Home Fires Burning: Food, Politics, and Everyday Life in World War I Berlin*, Chapel Hill, University of North Carolina Press, 2000.

2 Roger Chickering and Stig Förster, eds., *Great War, Total War: Combat and Mobilization on the Western Front, 1914–1918*, Cambridge and New York, Cambridge University Press, 2000, p. 6.

3 George L. Mosse, *Masses and Man: Nationalist and Fascist Perceptions of Reality*, New York, Howard Fertig, 1980, pp. 263–83. See also Mosse's *The Nationalization of the Masses: Political Symbolism and Mass Movements in Germany from the Napoleonic Wars through the Third Reich*, New York, Howard Fertig, 1975.

4 See Jeffrey Verhey, *The Spirit of 1914: Militarism, Myth, and Mobilization in Germany*, Cambridge and New York, Cambridge University Press, 2000.

5 Mark Hewitson, *Germany and the Causes of the First World War*, Oxford, Berg, 2004, p. 3. Even military leaders who were quite aware that this would not be a short war, such as Chief of the General Staff Helmuth von Moltke (1848–1916), favored going to war, the sooner, the better. See Stig Förster, *Der doppelte Militarismus: Die deutsche Heeresrüstungspolitik zwischen Status-Quo-Sicherung und Aggression 1890–1913*, Stuttgart, Franz Steiner Verlag, 1985, especially pp. 247–74; Holger Afflerbach, "Planning Total War? Falkenhayn and the Battle of Verdun, 1916," in Chickering and Förster, *Great War, Total War*, pp. 113–31; and Robert T. Foley, *German Strategy and the Path to Verdun: Erich von Falkenhayn and the Development of Attrition, 1870–1916*, Cambridge and New York, Cambridge University Press, 2005.

6 Hajo Holborn, *A History of Modern Germany, 1840–1945*, New York, Alfred A. Knopf, 1969, p. 429.

7 Gerhard Ritter, *The Schlieffen Plan: Critique of a Myth*, trans. Andrew and Eva Wilson, New York, Frederick A. Praeger, 1958. Terence Zuber, *Inventing the Schlieffen Plan: German War Planning 1871–1914*, Oxford and New York, Oxford University Press, 2002, criticizes Ritter for distorting the flexibility of German war planning and speculates that the Schlieffen Plan was "invented" by *Reichswehr* leaders after the war to deflect blame for defeat from the German General Staff. The actual document was destroyed during World War II. None of Zuber's speculative arguments affect the critique of Germany's military strategy presented here.

8 Fritz Fischer, *Germany's Aims in the First World War*, New York, W. W. Norton, 1967, p. 103.

9 See, for example, the recently published diaries of Vice Admiral Albert Hopman, *Albert Hopman: Das ereignisreiche Leben eines "Wilhelminers,"* Michael Epkenhans, ed., Munich, R. Oldenbourg, 2004.

10 See Rafael Scheck, *Alfred von Tirpitz and German Right-Wing Politics, 1914–1920*, Atlantic Highlands, NJ, Humanities Press, 1998.

11 On Ludendorff's pursuit of an eastern empire and on the precedent that the German occupation of eastern territories in World War I set for later ethnic cleansing, see Vejas Gabriel Liulevicius, *War Land on the Eastern Front: Culture, National Identity, and German Occupation in World War I*, Cambridge and New York, Cambridge University Press, 2000.

12 Harry R. Rudin, *Armistice 1918*, New Haven, CT, Yale University Press, 1944, pp. 24–88.

13 Quoted by Ernst Nolte, *Die Weimarer Republik: Demokratie zwischen Lenin und Hitler*, Munich, Herbig, 2006, p. 28, from the documentary collection, *Ursachen und Folgen. Vom deutsche Zusammenbruch 1918 und 1945 bis zur staatlichen Neuordnung Deutschlands in der Gegenwart*, Vol. II, *Der militärische Zusammenbruch und das Ende des Kaiserreiches*, Herbert Michaelis and Ernst Schraepler, eds., Berlin, n.d.

14 A. J. Ryder, *The German Revolution of 1918: A Study of German Socialism in War and Revolt*, Cambridge, Cambridge University Press, 1967.

6 The Weimar Republic and the weakness of liberal democracy

1 Robert G. L. Waite, *Vanguard of Nazism: The Free Corps Movement in Postwar Germany, 1918–1923*, Cambridge, MA, Harvard University Press, 1952, p. 7.

2 Koppel S. Pinson, *Modern Germany: Its History and Civilization*, 2nd ed., New York, Macmillan, 1966, p. 411; Carl E. Schorske, "Weimar and the Intellectuals," *New York Review*, 7 May 1970, p. 24.

3 Hans Mommsen, *Aufstieg und Untergang der Republik von Weimar 1918–1933*, Berlin, Ullstein, 1997, pp. 61–2; *The Rise and Fall of Weimar Democracy*, trans. Elborg Forster and Larry Eugene Jones, Chapel Hill, University of North Carolina Press, 1996, pp. 42–3.

4 Ibid., p. 69.

5 Waite, *Vanguard of Nazism*, p. 36.

6 Ibid., p. 161.

7 Michael Kellogg, *The Russian Roots of Nazism: White Émigrés and the Making of National Socialism 1917–1945*, Cambridge, Cambridge University Press, 2005, p. 105.

8 Waite, *Vanguard of Nazism*, p. 162.

9 Klaus Schwabe, ed., *Die Ruhrkrise 1923: Wendepunkt der internationalen Beziehungen nach dem Ersten Weltkrieg*, Paderborn, Schöningh, 1985, esp. pp. 89–97.

10 Ibid., pp. 68ff.

11 Mommsen, *Aufstieg und Untergang*, p. 175; *Rise and Fall of Weimar Democracy*, pp. 133–4. For the roots of the German inflation, see Gerald D. Feldman, *The Great Disorder: Politics, Economics, and Society in the German Inflation, 1914–1924*, New York and Oxford, Oxford University Press, 1993. For the effects of inflation on German culture and society, see Bernd Wittig, *Culture and Inflation in Weimar Germany*, Berkeley, University of California Press, 2001.

12 Eric D. Weitz, *Creating German Communism, 1890–1990: From Popular Protests to Socialist State*, Princeton, Princeton University Press, 1997, p. 98.

13 Richard S. Levy, ed., *Antisemitism in the Modern World: An Anthology of Texts*, Lexington, MA, D. C. Heath, 1991, pp. 213–21. See also Kellogg, *Russian Roots of Nazism*, pp. 63–76.

14 Gordon A. Craig, *Germany, 1866–1945*, New York and Oxford, Oxford University Press, 1978, p. 465.

15 Office of the US Chief of Counsel for Prosecution of Axis Criminality, *Nazi Conspiracy and Aggression*, Vol. V, Washington, DC, US Government Printing Office, 1946, p. 74.

16 Uwe Wesel, "Doch ein kolossaler Kerl, dieser Hitler! Wie Münchens Justiz 1924 einen rechtsradikalen Terroristen hofierte und ihm damit den Weg an die Macht ebnete," *Die Zeit*, 3 May 2001, p. 84.

17 Daniel R. Borg, *The Old-Prussian Church and the Weimar Republic: A Study in Political Adjustment, 1917–1929*, Hanover, NH, University Press of New England, 1984, esp. pp. 56ff.

18 Fritz Fischer, *Hitler war kein Betriebsunfall: Aufsätze*, Munich, C. H. Beck, 1993, p. 15.

7 The collapse of the Weimar Republic

1 John Kenneth Galbraith, *The Great Crash 1929* (1954), reprinted Boston, Houghton Mifflin, 1988, pp. 174ff.; John A. Garraty, *The Great Depression: An Inquiry into the Causes, Course, and Consequences of the Worldwide Depression of the Nineteen-Thirties, as Seen by Contemporaries and in the Light of History*, New York, Harcourt Brace Jovanovich, 1986, pp. 2–25.

2 John Maynard Keynes, *The General Theory of Employment, Interest and Money* (1936), reprinted London, Macmillan, 1951.

3 Hans Mommsen, *The Rise and Fall of Weimar Democracy*, trans. Elborg Forster and Larry Eugene Jones, Chapel Hill, University of North Carolina Press, 1996, pp. 364–5, 372–6. On the controversial question whether there were any viable alternatives to Brüning's economic policies, see Theo Balderston, *Economics and Politics in the Weimar Republic*, Cambridge, Cambridge University Press, 2002, pp. 88–98.

4 Heinrich August Winkler, *Weimar, 1918–1933: Die Geschichte der ersten deutschen Demokratie*, Munich, C. H. Beck, 1993, pp. 324–74.

5 Dietrich Orlow, *The History of the Nazi Party: 1919–1933*, Pittsburgh, PA, University of Pittsburgh Press, 1969, pp. 69–75.

6 Geoffrey G. Field, *Evangelist of Race: The Germanic Vision of Houston Stewart Chamberlain*, New York, Columbia University Press, 1981, p. 413.

7 Gottfried Feder, *Hitler's Official Programme and Its Fundamental Ideas* (1934), reprinted New York, Howard Fertig, 1971, p. 41.

8 Gregor Strasser, Joseph Goebbels, and others, "Draft of a Comprehensive Program of National Socialism," in *Nazi Ideology before 1933: A Documentation*, trans. Barbara Miller Lane and Leila J. Rupp, Austin, TX, University of Texas Press, 1970, pp. 83–7. See also Reinhard Kühnl, *Die nationalsozialistische Linke, 1925–1930*, Meisenheim am Glan, Verlag Anton Hain, 1966, and Peter Stachura, *Gregor Strasser and the Rise of Nazism*, London, Allen and Unwin, 1983.

9 NSDAP Hauptarchiv, Reel 44, Folder 896.

10 Jeremy Noakes, "Conflict and Development in the NSDAP, 1924–1927," *Journal of Contemporary History* I (October 1966), p. 30.

11 NSDAP Hauptarchiv, Reel 69, Folder 1508.

12 Ernst Nolte, *Die Weimarer Republik: Demokratie zwischen Lenin und Hitler*, Munich, Herbig, 2006, p. 390, note 27.

13 Brigitte Hamann, *Hitler's Vienna: A Dictator's Apprenticeship*, trans. Thomas Thornton, New York, Oxford University Press, 1999, pp. 404–6.

14 Michael Kellogg, *The Russian Roots of Nazism: White Émigrés and the Making of National Socialism, 1917–1945*, Cambridge, Cambridge University Press, 2005, pp. 136–7.

15 Adolf Hitler, *Mein Kampf*, trans. Ralph Manheim, Boston Houghton Mifflin, 1971, p. 679.

16 NSDAP Hauptarchiv, Reel 3, Folder 81/82.

17 H. Michaelis, E. Schraepler, and G. Scheel, eds., *Ursachen und Folgen vom deutschen Zusammenbruch 1918 und 1945 bis zur staatlichen Neuordnung Deutschlands in der Gegenwart. Eine Urkunden- uns Dokumentensammlung zur Zeitgeschichte*, Vol. VII, Berlin, Dokumenten-Verlag Dr. Herbert Wendler, 1962, p. 372.

18 Louis L. Snyder, ed., *Hitler's Third Reich: A Documentary History*, Chicago, Nelson-Hall, 1981, p. 64.

19 "Hitler's Speech to the Industry Club in Düsseldorf, 27 January 1932," in R. Stackelberg and S. A. Winkle, eds., *The Nazi Germany Sourcebook: An Anthology of Texts*, London and New York, Routledge, 2002, p. 111.

20 Ibid., p. 112.

21 Wolfgang Schieder, "Das italienische Experiment, Der Faschismus als Vorbild in der Krise der Weimarer Republik," *Historische Zeitschrift* 262 (February 1996), p. 123.

22 Eric D. Weitz, *Creating German Communism, 1890–1990: From Popular Protests to Socialist State*, Princeton, NJ, Princeton University Press, 1997, pp. 84–98.

23 Jürgen W. Falter, "The Social Bases of Political Cleavages in the Weimar Republic, 1919–1933," in Larry Eugene Jones and James Retallack, eds., *Elections, Mass Politics, and Social Change in Modern Germany: New Perspectives*, Cambridge, Cambridge University Press, 1992, p. 394.

24 Richard Hamilton, Thomas Childers, and Jürgen Falter, *Hitlers Wähler*, Munich, C. H. Beck, 1991. The latest scholarship on Nazi voters stresses the party's appeal across class lines as a broad-based protest movement. There is agreement, however, that Protestants and members of the middle classes, both upper and lower, were over-represented. Falter describes the NSDAP as "a people's party with a middle-class bulge." For an interesting argument that the Nazis attracted a wide constituency by appealing to people's material interests, see William Brustein, *The Logic of Evil: The Social Origins of the Nazi Party, 1925–1933*, New Haven, Yale University Press, 1996.

25 Mommsen, *The Rise and Fall of Weimar Democracy*, p. 471.

26 Winkler, *Weimar 1918–1933*, p. 556.

27 Dirk Blasius, *Weimars Ende: Bürgerkrieg und Politik 1930–1933*, Göttingen, Vandenhoeck und Ruprecht, 2005, emphasizes fear of civil war as a major factor in the motivation of the leading figures in the events leading up to Hitler's appointment as chancellor.

28 Martin Broszat, *Hitler and the Collapse of Weimar Germany*, trans. V. R. Berghahn, Leamington Spa, Berg, 1987, p. 141.

29 Wolfgang Michalka and Gottfried Niedhart, eds., *Deutsche Geschichte 1918–1933: Dokumente zur Innen- und Aussenpolitik*, Frankfurt, Fischer Taschenbuch Verlag, 2002, p. 239.

30 Ibid., p. 242.

31 Ibid., p. 230.

32 Henry Ashby Turner, *Hitler's Thirty Days to Power: January 1933*, Reading, MA, Addison-Wesley, 1996, p. 64.

33 Schieder, "Das italienische Experiment," p. 124.

8 The Nazi consolidation of power, 1933–34

1 See Dirk Blasius, *Weimars Ende: Bürgerkrieg und Politik, 1930–1933*, Göttingen, Vandenhoeck und Ruprecht, 2005.

2 Pierre Ayçoberry, *The Nazi Question: An Essay on the Interpretations of National Socialism (1922–1975)*, trans. Robert Hurley, New York, Pantheon, 1981, p. 15; John A. Leopold, *Alfred Hugenberg: The Radical Nationalist Campaign against the Weimar Republic*, New Haven, Yale University Press, 1977, p. 138.

3 "Proclamation of the Reich Government to the German People," in R. Stackelberg and S. A. Winkle, eds., *The Nazi Germany Sourcebook: An Anthology of Texts*, London and New York, Routledge, 2002, p. 127.

4 Leopold, *Alfred Hugenberg*, p. 124.

5 Gestapo Chief Rudolf Diels and Chief of the Army General Staff Franz Halder both implicated Göring in the Reichstag Fire in testimony given at the Nuremberg Trials after the war. See William M. Shirer, *The Rise and Fall of the Third Reich: A History of Nazi Germany*, New York, Simon & Schuster, 1960, pp. 192–3. The Swiss historian Walter Hofer is the main critic of the claim that van der Lubbe acted alone. See Walter Hofer *et al.*, *Der Reichstagbrand: Eine*

wissenschaftliche Dokumentation, ed. Alexander Bahar, Freiburg, Ahriman Verlag, 1992. For a defense of the thesis that van der Lubbe acted alone, see Fritz Tobias, *The Reichstag Fire*, New York, Putnam, 1964. The latest biographer of Marianus van der Lubbe, the Dutch journalist Martin Schouten, also believes he acted on his own: see Martin Schouten, *Marinus van der Lubbe: Eine Biographie*, Frankfurt am Main, Verlag Neue Kritik, 1999.

6 Testimony of Rudolf Diels, first head of the Gestapo, at the Nuremberg War Crimes trial. Office of the US Chief of Counsel for the Prosecution of Axis Criminality, *Nazi Conspiracy and Aggression*, Washington, DC, US Govt. Printing Office, 1946, Vol. 5, doc. no. 2544-PS, pp. 288–90.

7 Wolfgang Michalka and Gottfried Niedhart, eds., *Die Ungeliebte Republik: Dokumentation zur Innen- und Aussenpolitik Weimars, 1918–1933*, Munich, Deutscher Taschenbuch Verlag, 1980, p. 342.

8 Eva Gottschaldt, ed., *Antifaschismus und Widerstand: Der Kampf gegen den deutschen Faschismus 1933–1945. Ein Überblick*, Heilbronn, Distel Verlag, 1985, p. 136.

9 William Sheridan Allen, *The Nazi Seizure of Power in a Single German Town*, rev. ed., New York, Franklin, Watts, 1984, p. 236.

10 Martin Broszat, *The Hitler State: The Foundation and Development of the Internal Structure of the Third Reich*, New York, Longman, 1981, pp. 96–132.

11 See H. Stuart Hughes, *The Sea Change: The Migration of Social Thought, 1930–1965*, New York, Harper & Row, 1975, esp. pp. 1–34.

12 Helmut Heiber, ed., *Goebbels-Reden*, Vol. 1, *1932–1939*, Düsseldorf, Droste Verlag, 1972, pp. 108–12.

13 *New York Times*, 11 May 1933, as cited in Louis L. Snyder, ed., *Hitler's Third Reich: A Documentary History*, Chicago, Nelson-Hall, 1981, p. 116.

14 Christian Zentner and Friedemann Bedürftig, eds., *The Encyclopedia of the Third Reich*, trans. Amy Hackett, New York, Da Capo Press, 1997, p. 333.

15 Broszat, *The Hitler State*, p. 87.

16 Leopold, *Alfred Hugenberg*, pp. 151–63.

17 John Cornwell, *Hitler's Pope: The Secret History of Pius XII*, New York, Viking, 1999, pp. 144–7.

18 Norman Rich, *Hitler's War Aims: Ideology, the Nazi State, and the Course of Expansion*, New York, Norton, 1973, p. 42.

19 Norbert Frei, *National Socialist Rule in Germany: The Führer State 1933–1945*, trans. Simon B. Steyne, Oxford, Blackwell, 1993, pp. 42, 167.

20 Ingo Müller, *Hitler's Justice: The Courts of the Third Reich*, trans. Deborah Lucas Schneider, Cambridge, MA, Harvard University Press, 1991, pp. 36–9.

21 Ibid., pp. 140–52.

22 Cited in Robert N. Proctor, *Racial Hygiene under the Nazis*, Cambridge, MA, Harvard University Press, 1988, p. 70.

23 Jürgen Förster, "Das Verhältnis von Wehrmacht und Nationalsozialismus im Entscheidungsjahr 1933," *German Studies Review* 18 (October 1995), 471–2.

24 Ibid., 477–8.

25 Frei, *National Socialist Rule*, p. 9.

26 Michael Geyer, "Traditional Elites and National Socialist Leadership," in Charles Maier, Stanley Hoffmann, and Andrew Gould, eds., *The Rise of the Nazi Regime: Historical Reassessments*, Boulder, CO, Westview, 1986, p. 628.

27 Leopold, *Alfred Hugenberg*, p. 161.

28 "Vice-Chancellor Franz von Papen's Speech at Marburg, 17 June 1934," in Stackelberg and Winkle, *The Nazi Germany Sourcebook*, p. 170.

29 Ibid., p. 171.

30 Frei, *National Socialist Rule*, p. 23.

31 Ian Kershaw, *The "Hitler Myth": Image and Reality in the Third Reich*, New York, Oxford, 1987, p. 85.

32 *Der 30. Juni 1934. Hitlers Sieg über Rebellion und Reaktion*, Berlin, Verlagsanstalt Paul Schmidt, 1934, pp. 13–14.

33 Cited in Louis Snyder, ed., *Hitler's Third Reich: A Documentary History*, Chicago, Nelson Hall, 1981, p. 192.

34 Frei, *National Socialist Rule*, pp. 101–8.

35 "Hindenburg's Political Testament, August 1934," in Stackelberg and Winkle, *The Nazi Germany Sourcebook*, pp. 174–6.

9 Economy, society, and the state in the Third Reich

1 Avraham Barkai, *Nazi Economics: Ideology, Theory, and Policy*, New Haven, CT, Yale University Press, 1990, pp. 1ff. See also C. Edmund Clingan, *Finance from Kaiser to Führer: Budget Policies in Germany, 1912–1934*, Westport, CT, Greenwood Press, 2000.

2 See John A. Garraty, "The New Deal, National Socialism, and the Great Depression," *American Historical Review* 78 (1973), 907–44.

3 R. J. Overy, *The Nazi Economic Recovery 1932–1938*, 2nd ed., Cambridge, Cambridge University Press, 1996, p. 38.

4 Adam Tooze, *The Wages of Destruction: The Making and Breaking of the Nazi Economy*, London, Allen Lane, 2006, esp. pp. 285–304; Dieter Petzina, *Autarkiepolitik im Dritten Reich*, Stuttgart, Deutsche Verlagsanstalt, 1968, pp. 48–53; Peter Hayes, *Industry and Ideology: I.G. Farben in the Nazi Era*, Cambridge, Cambridge University Press, 1987, pp. 164–7.

5 "Hitler's Memorandum on the Four-Year Plan, August 1936," in R. Stackelberg and S. A. Winkle, eds., *The Nazi Germany Sourcebook*, London and New York, Routledge, 2002, p. 199.

6 Tooze, *The Wages of Destruction*, pp. 567, 571.

7 Ian Kershaw, *The Nazi Dictatorship: Problems and Perspectives of Interpretation*, 3rd ed., London, Edward Arnold, 1993, p. 88.

8 Timothy W. Mason, *Social Policy in the Third Reich: The Working Class and the "National Community,"* Jane Caplan, ed., trans. by John Broadwin, Providence, RI, Berg Publishers, 1993, pp. 19ff.

9 Joseph W. Bendersky, *A History of Nazi Germany*, Chicago, Nelson-Hall, 1985, p. 141. Götz Aly argues in his controversial book, *Hitler's Beneficiaries: Plunder, Racial War, and the Nazi Welfare State*, New York, Metropolitan, 2007, that Hitler bought the consent of the German people by his generous social programs and tax relief, financed by systematic plunder of Jewish property and ruthless exploitation of occupied territory. While Aly rightly stresses the Nazis' thievery and destruction, he overstates the improvement in the German standard of living and understates the economic sacrifices required for war. According to Tooze, *The Wages of Destruction*, p. 256, Germany was the most heavily taxed society in Europe in the late 1930s. See also Tooze's refutation of Aly's arguments in "Economics, Ideology and Cohesion in the Third Reich: A Critique of Goetz Aly's *Volksstaat*," posted at <www.hist.cam.ac.uk-academic-staff/further_details/tooze.html>.

10 Christian Zentner and Friedemann Bedürftig, *The Encyclopedia of the Third Reich*, trans. Amy Hackett, New York, Da Capo Press, 1997, p. 789.

11 See Shelley Baranowski, *Strength through Joy: Consumerism and Mass Tourism in the Third Reich*, Cambridge, Cambridge University Press, 2004.

12 Alf Lüdtke, "The 'Honor of Labor': Industrial Workers and the Power of Symbols under National Socialism," in David F. Crew, ed., *Nazism and German Society, 1933–1945*, London, Routledge, 1994, pp. 67–109, and "What Happened to the 'Fiery Red Glow?' Workers' Experiences and German Fascism," in Alf Lüdtke, ed., *The History of Everyday Life: Reconstructing Historical Experiences and Ways of Life*, trans. William Templer, Princeton, NJ, Princeton University Press, 1995, pp. 198–251.

13 Michael Burleigh and Wolfgang Wippermann, *The Racial State: Germany 1933–1945*, Cambridge, Cambridge University Press, 1991, pp. 70–3.

14 Jeffrey Herf, *Reactionary Modernism: Technology, Culture and Politics in Weimar and the Third Reich*, Cambridge, Cambridge University Press, 1984, pp. 189–216.

15 David Schoenbaum, *Hitler's Social Revolution: Class and Status in Nazi Germany, 1933–1939* (1966), reprinted New York, Norton, 1980, p. 285.

16 Shelley Baranowski, *The Sanctity of Rural Life: Nobility, Protestantism, and Nazism in Weimar Prussia*, New York and Oxford, Oxford University Press, 1995.

17 Schoenbaum, *Hitler's Social Revolution*, p. 159.

18 Tooze, *The Wages of Destruction*, pp. 262, 264.

19 "Hitler's Speech to the National Socialist Women's Organization, September 1934," *The Nazi Germany Sourcebook*, p. 182.

20 Irmgard Weyrather, *Muttertag und Mutterkreuz: Der Kult um die "deutsche Mutter" im Nationalsozialismus*, Frankfurt, Fischer, 1993, p. 55.

21 Lisa Pine, *Nazi Family Policy, 1933–1945*, Oxford, Berg, 1997, pp. 23, 28ff.

22 Ibid., esp. pp. 38–43.

23 Tooze, *The Wages of Destruction*, p. 515. See also Burleigh and Wippermann, *The Racial State*, pp. 242–66.

24 For a good summary of the controversy see Adelheid von Saldern, "Victims or Perpetrators? Controversies over the Role of Women in the Nazi State," in David F. Crew, ed., *Nazism and German Society*, London and New York, Routledge, 1994, pp. 143–65. See also Gisela Bock, "Antinatalism, Maternity and Paternity in National Socialist Racism," *Nazism and German Society*, pp. 110–40, and Claudia Koonz, *Mothers in the Fatherland: Women, the Family, and Nazi Politics*, New York, St. Martin's, 1987. Bock also contributed a chapter, "Racism and Sexism in Nazi Germany: Motherhood, Compulsory Sterilization and the State," to the path-breaking volume, *When Biology Became Destiny: Women in Weimar and Nazi Germany*, Renate Bridenthal, Atina Grossmann, and Marion Kaplan, eds., New York, Monthly Review Press, 1984, pp. 271–96. See also Jill Stephenson, "Women, Motherhood and the Family in the Third Reich," in Michael Burleigh, ed., *Confronting the Nazi Past: New Debates on Modern German History*, New York, St. Martin's Press, 1996, pp. 167–83.

25 Ernst Fraenkel, *The Dual State: A Contribution to the Theory of Dictatorship*, trans. E. A. Shils, Edith Lowenstein, and Klaus Knorr, New York, Octagon, 1941.

26 Nikolaus Wachsmann, *Hitler's Prisons: Legal Terror in Nazi Germany*, New Haven, CT, Yale University Press, 2004, p. 373.

27 Carl-Wilhelm Reibel, *Das Fundament der Diktatur: Die NSDAP-Ortsgruppen 1932–1945*, Paderborn, Ferdinand Schöningh, 2004, p. 382.

28 Dietrich Orlow, *The History of the Nazi Party, 1919–1933*, Pittsburgh, PA, University of Pittsburgh Press, 1969; Martin Broszat, *The Hitler State: The Foundation and Development of the Internal Structure of the Third Reich*, London, Longman, 1981, pp. 294–323.

29 Otto Dietrich, *Hitler*, Chicago, IL, Regnery, 1955, p. 113.

30 Ian Kershaw, "Hitler as Dictator: 'Working towards the Führer.' Reflections on the Nature of the Hitler Dictatorship," in Christian Leitz, ed., *The Third Reich: The Essential Readings*, Malden, MA, Blackwell, 1999, p. 235.

31 See Ian Kershaw, "Hitler: 'Master in the Third Reich' or 'Weak Dictator'?" *The Nazi Dictatorship: Problems and Perspectives of Interpretation*, 3rd ed., London, Edward Arnold, 1993, pp. 59–79.

32 Ian Kershaw, *The "Hitler Myth": Image and Reality in the Third Reich*, Oxford, Oxford University Press, 1987, p. 255.

33 Office of the US Chief of Counsel for Prosecution of Axis Criminality, *Nazi Conspiracy and Aggression*, Vol. VIII, Washington, DC, US Government Printing Office, doc. R-129, 1946, p. 199.

34 Robert Gellately, *The Gestapo and German Society: Enforcing Racial Policy 1933–1945*, Oxford, Clarendon Press, 1990, pp. 7–8, and *Backing Hitler: Consent and Coercion in Nazi Germany*, Oxford, Oxford University Press, 2001, p. 259. See also Eric A. Johnson, *Nazi Terror: The Gestapo, Jews, and Ordinary Germans*, New York, Basic Books, 1999, esp. p. 17; and Klaus-Michael Mallmann and Gerhard Paul, "Omniscient, Omnipotent, Omnipresent? Gestapo, Society and Resistance," in Crew, *Nazism and German Society*, pp. 166–96.

35 Gunnar C. Boehnert, "The Third Reich and the Problem of 'Social Revolution': German Officers and the SS," in Volker R. Berghahn and Martin Kitchen, eds., *Germany in the Age of Total War*, London, Croom Helm, 1981, pp. 203–17.

36 Alan D. Beyerchen, *Scientists under Hitler: Politics and the Physics Community in the Third Reich*, New Haven, CT, Yale University Press, 1977, p. 69.

10 Education, culture, religion, and eugenics in the Third Reich

1 Michael H. Kater, *Hitler Youth*, Cambridge, MA, Harvard University Press, 2004, pp. 13–28. See also Lawrence D. Walker, *Hitler Youth and Catholic Youth, 1933–1936: A Study in Totalitarian Conquest*, Washington, DC, Catholic University of America Press, 1970.

2 Reiner Lehberger, "Die Mühen des aufrechten Ganges," *Die Zeit*, 15 February 1991.

3 Frederick Spotts, *Hitler and the Power of Aesthetics*, Woodstock and New York, Overlook Press, 2004, pp. 10, 12.

4 Benjamin Sax and Dieter Kunz, *Inside Hitler's Germany: A Documentary History of Life in the Third Reich*, Lexington, MA, D. C. Heath, 1992, p. 229.

5 Jonathan Petropolous, *Art as Politics in the Third Reich*, Chapel Hill, NC, University of North Carolina Press, 1996, p. 283.

6 See Karen A. Fiss, "In Hitler's Salon: The German Pavilion at the 1937 Paris Exposition Internationale," in Richard A. Etlin, ed., *Art, Culture, and Media in the Third Reich*, Chicago, University of Chicago Press, 2002, p. 327.

7 Jonathan Petropolous, *The Faustian Bargain: The Art World in Nazi Germany*, Oxford and New York: Oxford University Press, 2000.

8 Adolf Hitler, *Mein Kampf*, trans. Ralph Manheim, Boston, MA, Houghton Mifflin, 1971, p. 303.

9 See Jonathan Petropolous, "From Seduction to Denial: Arno Breker's Engagement with National Socialism," in *Art, Culture, and Media in the Third Reich*, esp. p. 207.

10 Peter Reichel, "Bildende Kunst und Architektur," in Wolfgang Benz, Hermann Graml, and Hermann Weiss, eds., *Enzyklopädie des Nationalsozialismus*, Munich, Deutscher Taschenbuch Verlag, 1997, p. 160.

11 Carsten Könneker, "Wie die Nazis Einstein für ihre Zwecke missbrauchten," *Spiegel Online*, 19 January 2005.

12 Kristie Macrakis, *Surviving the Swastika: Scientific Research in Nazi Germany*, Oxford, Oxford University Press, 1993, p. 98.

13 Alan D. Beyerchen, *Scientists under Hitler: Politics and the Physics Community in the Third Reich*, New Haven, CT, Yale University Press, 1977, p. 41.

14 Shelley Baranowski, *The Sanctity of Rural Life: Nobility, Protestantism, and Nazism in Weimar Prussia*, Oxford, Oxford University Press, 1995, p. 87; see also Robert P. Ericksen, *Theologians under Hitler: Gerhard Kittel, Paul Althaus, and Emanuel Hirsch*, New Haven, CT, Yale University Press, 1985, p. 46.

15 Richard Steigmann-Gall, *The Holy Reich: Nazi Conceptions of Christianity, 1919–1945*, Cambridge, Cambridge University Press, 2003, p. 114.

16 Richard Steigmann-Gall, "Rethinking Nazism and Religion: How Anti-Christian were the 'Pagans'?" *Central European History* 36 (2003), 75–105.

17 "Proclamation of the Reich Government to the German People, 1 February 1933," in Roderick Stackelberg and Sally A. Winkle, eds., *The Nazi German Sourcebook*, London and New York, Routledge, 2002, p. 127.

18 Michael Burleigh, *Ethics and Extermination: Reflections on Nazi Genocide*, Cambridge and New York, Cambridge University Press, 1997, p. 22.

19 Letter of Martin Bormann to Alfred Rosenberg, 24 February 1940, in *The Nazi Germany Sourcebook*, p. 238.

20 Henry Picker, *Hitlers Tischgespräche im Führerhauptquartier: Entstehung, Struktur, Folgen des Nationalsozialismus*, 2nd ed., Berlin, Ullstein, 1997, p. 109.

21 Pope Pius XI, Encyclical Letter, "The Church in Germany," 14 March 1937, *The Nazi Germany Sourcebook*, p. 210.

22 Office of the US Chief of Counsel for Prosecution of Axis Criminality, *Nazi Conspiracy and Aggression*, Vol. III, doc. 123-PS, 1946, p. 178.

23 "Theological Statement" issued by the Confessing Synod of the German Evangelical Church in Wuppertal-Barmen, 29–31 May 1934, *The Nazi Germany Sourcebook*, pp. 168–9.

24 Ericksen, *Theologians under Hitler*, p. 48.

25 Peter Matheson, ed., *The Third Reich and the Christian Churches*, Edinburgh, T & T Clark, 1981, pp. 63–4.

26 Ian Kershaw, *The "Hitler Myth": Image and Reality in the Third Reich*, Oxford, Oxford University Press, 1987, p. 106.

27 The three authors were Erwin Bauer, Eugen Fischer, and Fritz Lenz. Henry Friedlander, *The Origins of Nazi Genocide: From Euthanasia to the Final Solution*, Chapel Hill, NC, University of North Carolina Press, 1995, p. 13.

28 Stefan Kühl, *The Nazi Connection: Eugenics, American Racism, and German National Socialism*, New York and Oxford, Oxford University Press, 1994, p. 16.

29 Cited in Edwin Black, *War against the Weak: Eugenics and America's Campaign to Create a Master Race*, New York, Thunder's Mouth Press, 2003, p. 270.

30 On the sterilization law, see particularly Robert N. Proctor, *Racial Hygiene: Medicine under the Nazis*, Cambridge, MA, Harvard University Press, 1988, pp. 95–117; see also Michael Burleigh and Wolfgang Wippermann, *The Racial State: Germany 1933–1945*, Cambridge, Cambridge University Press, 1991.

31 Michael Fahlbusch, "The Role and Impact of German Ethnopolitical Experts in the SS Reich Security Main Office," in Ingo Haar and Michael Fahlbusch, eds., *German Scholars and Ethnic Cleansing, 1919–1945*, New York and Oxford, Berghahn Books, 2005, pp. 28–50.

32 Karl Binding and Alfred Hoche, "Permitting the Destruction of Unworthy Life: Its Extent and Form," trans. Walter E. Wright and Patrick G. Derr, *Issues in Law and Medicine*, Vol. VIII, 2 (1992), 264–5.

33 Michael Burleigh, *Death and Deliverance: Euthanasia in Germany 1900–1945*, Cambridge, Cambridge University Press, 1994, pp. 122–3.

34 Friedlander, *Origins of Nazi Genocide*, p. 136.

11 Persecution of the Jews, 1933–39

1 Lucy Dawidowicz, *A Holocaust Reader*, West Orange, NJ, Berman House, 1976, pp. 42–3; Saul Friedländer, *Nazi Germany and the Jews*, Vol. I, *The Years of Persecution, 1933–1939*, New York, HarperCollins, 1997, p. 30.

2 Wolfgang Benz, ed., *Die Juden in Deutschland 1933–1945: Leben unter nationalsozialistischer Herrschaft*, Munich, C. H. Beck, 1988, *passim*.

3 Friedländer, *Nazi Germany and the Jews*, Vol. I, *The Years of Persecution*, p. 153.

4 Nora Levin, *The Holocaust: The Destruction of European Jewry, 1933–1945*, New York, Schocken, 1973, pp. 131–2.

5 Winston Churchill, "Hitler and his Choice," in *Great Contemporaries*, New York, G. P. Putnam's Sons, 1937, p. 231.

6 Marion A. Kaplan, *Between Dignity and Despair: Jewish Life in Nazi Germany*, New York, Oxford University Press, 1998, p. 5. See also David Bankier, ed., *Probing the Depths of German Antisemitism: German Society and the Persecution of the Jews, 1933–1941*, New York, Berghahn Books, 2000, and "Jewish Society through Nazi Eyes," *Holocaust and Genocide Studies* 6 (1991), 111–27.

7 Wolfgang Benz, *Der Holocaust*, Munich, C. H. Beck, 1995, p. 27; English version, *The Holocaust: A German Historian Examines the Genocide*, trans. Jane Sydenham-Kwiet, New York, Columbia University Press, 1999.

8 Benjamin Sax and Dieter Kuntz, *Inside Hitler's Germany: A Documentary History of Life in the Third Reich*, Lexington, MA, D. C. Heath, 1992, p. 414.

9 Benz, *The Holocaust*, p. 39.

10 Frank Bajohr, "Expropriation and Expulsion," in Dan Stone, ed., *The Historiography of the Holocaust*, New York, Palgrave Macmillan, 2004, p. 52.

11 Karl Schleunes, *The Twisted Road to Auschwitz: Nazi Policy toward German Jews 1933–1938*, Urbana, University of Illinois Press, 1970, p. 73.

12 William D. Rubinstein, *Why the Democracies Could Not Have Saved More Jews from the Nazis*, London, Routledge, 1997, p. 20.

13 Yehuda Bauer, *A History of the Holocaust*, New York, Franklin, Watts, 1982, pp. 123–9.

14 Heinz Höhne, *The Order of the Death's Head*, New York, Ballantine, 1977, p. 37.

15 Abraham Margaliot, "The Problem of the Rescue of German Jewry during the Years 1933–1939: The Reasons for the Delay in Their Emigration from the Third Reich," *Rescue Attempts During the Holocaust*, Jerusalem, Yad Vashem, 1977, pp. 253–5.

16 Benz, *The Holocaust*, p. 36.

17 Dawidowicz, *Holocaust Reader*, pp. 72–3.

12 The origins of the Second World War

1 See, for instance, Sydney B. Fay, *The Origins of the World War*, 2nd ed., New York, Macmillan, 1930.

2 Koppel S. Pinson, *Modern Germany: Its History and Civilization*, 2nd ed., New York, Macmillan, 1966, p. 520.

3 Winston S. Churchill, *Great Contemporaries*, New York, G. P. Putnam's Sons, 1937, p. 228.

4 Michael Geyer, "Traditional Elites and National Socialist Leadership," in Charles S. Maier, Stanley Hoffmann, and Andrew Gould, eds., *The Rise of the Nazi Regime: Historical Reassessments*, Boulder, CO, Westview Press, 1986, pp. 57–73.

5 Office of the US Chief of Counsel for Prosecution of Axis Criminality, *Nazi Conspiracy and Aggression*, Vol. V, Washington, DC, US Government Printing Office, 1946, p. 672.

6 *Nazi Conspiracy and Aggression*, Vol. IV, p. 674.

7   Norman Rich, *Hitler's War Aims: Ideology, the Nazi State, and the Course of Expansion*, New York, W. W. Norton, 1973, pp. 90ff.

8   Bodeo Herzog, "Piraten vor Malaga," *Die Zeit*, 6 December 1991. See also Hannes Heer, "Strasse um Strasse: Vor 70 Jahren zerstörten deutsche und italienische Flieger die baskische Stadt Guernica. Ihr Ziel war es, den totalen Bombenkrieg zu testen," *Die Zeit*, 19 April 2007.

9   Gordon A. Craig, *Germany, 1866–1945*, New York, Oxford University Press, 1978, p. 694.

10 Rich, *Hitler's War Aims*, p. 98.

11 Adolf Hitler, "Mein Kampf," in R. Stackelberg and S. A. Winkle, eds., *The Nazi Germany Sourcebook: An Anthology of Texts*, New York and London, Routledge, 2002, p. 93.

12 "Hitler's remarks on his political goals to army and navy commanders, 3 February 1933," *The Nazi Germany Sourcebook*, p. 129.

13 *Nazi Conspiracy and Aggression*, Vol. III, doc. 386-PS, pp. 295–305.

14 Rich, *Hitler's War Aims*, p. 99.

15 Ibid., p. 105.

16 Donald Cameron Watt, *How War Came: The Immediate Origins of the Second World War, 1938–1939*, New York, Pantheon Books, 1989, p. 29.

17 Adam Tooze, *The Wages of Destruction: The Making and Breaking of the Nazi Economy*, London, Allen Lane, 2006, p. 288.

18 Rich, *Hitler's War Aims*, p. 111.

19 Tooze, *The Wages of Destruction*, pp. 310, 315.

20 "Minutes of conference on 23 May 1939," *The Nazi Germany Sourcebook*, p. 232.

21 A strong critique of the British failure to conclude a military alliance with the Soviet Union to deter Hitler is provided in A. J. P. Taylor's controversial *The Origins of the Second World War*, Greenwich, CT, Fawcett Publications, 1961. A contrary view is Keith Eubank's *The Origins of World War II*, 2nd ed., Arlington Heights, IL, Harlan Davidson, 1990. Adam Tooze accepts the sincerity of western efforts to reach an agreement with the Soviets, but points out that the unconditional guarantee to Poland made a deal with the Soviets impossible. See *The Wages of Destruction*, p. 306.

22 Anthony Eden, *Facing the Dictators*, Boston, Houghton Mifflin, 1962, p. 173; cited in Hugh Ragsdale, *The Soviets, the Munich Crisis, and the Coming of World War II*, Cambridge, Cambridge University Press, 2004, p. 191.

23 Tooze, *The Wages of Destruction*, p. 320.

24 "The Führer's speech to the Commanders of the Wehrmacht, 22 August 1939," *The Nazi Germany Sourcebook*, p. 245.

25 Ibid., p. 243.

26 "Second speech by the Führer, 22 August 1939," *The Nazi Germany Sourcebook*, p. 246.

27 Winston Churchill, *The Second World War*, Vol. I, *The Gathering Storm*, Boston, Houghton Mifflin, 1948, pp. 393–4.

13 The Second World War: from European to global war, 1939–41

1   I. C. B. Dear and M. R. D. Foot, eds., *The Oxford Companion to World War II*, Oxford, Oxford University Press, 1995, pp. 372–5.

2   An excellent analysis of the campaign in France is offered by Adam Tooze, *The Wages of Destruction: The Making and Breaking of the Nazi Economy*, London, Allen Lane, 2006, pp. 270–80. See also Ernest R. May, *Strange Victory: Hitler's Conquest of France*, New York, Hill and Wang, 2000, esp. pp. 448–64.

3 "The Halder War Diary, 1940," in R. Stackelberg and S. A. Winkle, eds., *The Nazi Germany Sourcebook*, London and New York, Routledge, 2002, p. 267.

4 Ian Kershaw, "Did Hitler Miss His Chance in 1940?," in Neil Gregor, ed., *Nazism, War and Genocide: Essays in Honour of Jeremy Noakes*, Exeter, University of Exeter Press, 2005, pp. 110–30.

5 Office of the US Chief of Counsel for Prosecution of Axis Criminality, *Nazi Conspiracy and Aggression*, Vol. V, Washington, DC, US Government Printing Office, 1946, p. 410.

6 For Soviet objectives, see Geoffrey Roberts, "Ideology, Calculation, and Improvisation: Spheres of Influence and Soviet Foreign Policy 1939–1945," in Gordon Martel, ed., *The World War II Reader*, New York and London, Routledge, 2004, pp. 85–104.

7 Adolf Hitler, *Mein Kampf*, trans. Ralph Manheim, Boston, Houghton Mifflin, 1971, p. 654.

8 Cited in Karl Hildebrand, *The Third Reich*, trans. P. S. Falla, London, Allen and Unwin, 1984, p. 37.

9 Tooze, *The Wages of Destruction*, p. 462.

10 Cited in William L. Shirer, *The Rise and Fall of the Third Reich: A History of Nazi Germany*, New York, Simon & Schuster, 1960, p. 851.

11 Gabriel Gorodetsky, *Grand Delusion: Stalin and the German Invasion of Russia*, New Haven, Yale University Press, 1999, p. 25.

12 See Nikolaj M. Romanicev, "Militärische Pläne eines Gegenschlags der UdSSR," in Gerd R. Ueberschär and Lev A. Bezymenskij, eds., *Der deutsche Angriff auf die Sowjetunion 1941: Die Kontroverse um die Präventivkriegsthese*, Darmstadt, Primus Verlag, 1998, pp. 92–3. For a repudiation of the "preventive war" thesis, see Wolfram Wette and Gerd Überschär, *"Unternehmen Barbarossa": der deutsche Überfall auf die Sowjetunion, 1941*, Paderborn, F. Schöningh, 1984. The myth of an impending Soviet attack is also decisively refuted by David Glantz and Jonathan House, *When Titans Clashed: How the Red Army Stopped Hitler*, Lawrence, KS, University Press of Kansas, 1995.

13 Hans-Erich Volkmann, "Die Legende vom Präventivkrieg. Alle Informationen der Regierung und der Wehrmacht stimmten überein: Sowjetrussland war 1941 zum Angriffskrieg weder fähig noch willens," *Die Zeit* 25 (20 June 1997).

14 Gerd R. Ueberschär, "Die militärische Planung für den Angriff auf die Sowjetunion," in Ueberschär and Bezymenskij, *Der deutsche Angriff*, p. 29. For a good overview of the historiography of the Nazi–Soviet war, see Rolf-Dieter Müller and Gerd Überschär, *Hitler's War in the East 1941–1945: A Critical Assessment*, trans. Bruce D. Little, Providence and Oxford, Berghahn Books, 1997, particularly pp. 3–41. German version: Rolf-Dieter Müller and Gerd Überschär, *Hitlers Krieg im Osten 1941–1945: Ein Forschungsbericht*, Darmstadt, Wissenschaftliche Buchgesellschaft, 2000.

15 David M. Glantz, *Barbarossa: Hitler's Invasion of Russia 1941*, Charleston, SC, Tempus, 2001, p. 205.

16 Wolfgang Melanowski, "Rücken an Rücken oder Brust an Brust?" *Der Spiegel* 10 (1989), 148.

17 Cited in Richard Overy, *Russia's War*, New York, Penguin, 1998, p. 327.

18 Gorodetsky, *Grand Delusion*, p. 321.

19 Michael Burleigh, "'See You Again in Siberia': The German–Soviet War and Other Tragedies," in *Ethics and Extermination: Reflections on Nazi Genocide*, Cambridge, Cambridge University Press, 1997, p. 38. A full list of 34 separate intelligence warnings provided to Stalin from 27 August 1940 through 21 June 1941 is given in David E. Murphy, *What Stalin Knew: The Enigma of Barbarossa*, New Haven, Yale University Press, 2005, pp. 261–3.

20 See the article by Rainer F. Schmidt, "Ein Geschenk vom Himmel," *Die Zeit* (10 December 1993), which is based on the British Hess documents opened to scholars for the first time in June 1992.

21 Ueberschär, "Die militärische Planung," p. 32.

22 Ulrich Herbert, *Arbeit, Volkstum, Weltanschauung: Über Fremde und Deutsche im 20. Jahrhundert Arbeit*, Frankfurt, Fischer, 1995, p. 125.

23 Helmut Krausnick, Hans Buchheim, Martin Broszat, and Hans-Adolf Jacobsen, eds., *Anatomy of the SS State*, trans. Richard Barry, Marian Jackson, and Dorothy Long, New York, Walker & Co., 1968, pp. 532–4.

24 Rosenberg's Letter to Wilhelm Keitel, 28 February 1942, in *Nazi Conspiracy and Aggression*, Vol. III, pp. 126–8.

25 Herbert, *Arbeit, Volkstum, Weltanschauung*, p. 126.

26 Omer Bartov, *Hitler's Army: Soldiers, Nazis, and War in the Third Reich*, New York, Oxford University Press, 1992, p. 75.

27 Cited in Overy, *Russia's War*, p. 327.

28 Norman Rich, *Hitler's War Aims: Ideology, the Nazi State, and the Course of Expansion*, New York, Norton, 1973, p. 230.

29 *Nazi Conspiracy and Aggression*, Vol. V, pp. 564–5.

14 The Second World War: from triumph to defeat, 1942–45

1 Adam Tooze, *The Wages of Destruction: The Making and Breaking of the Nazi Economy*, London, Allen Lane, 2006, pp. 585–6.

2 Cited in Ian Buruma, "The Destruction of Germany," *New York Review*, 21 October 2004, p. 10.

3 Ibid.

4 I. C. B. Dear and M. R. D. Foot, eds., *The Oxford Companion to World War II*, Oxford, Oxford University Press, 1995, p. 101. See also Lothar Gruchmann, *Totaler Krieg: Vom Blitzkrieg zur bedingungsloser Kapitulation*, Munich, Deutscher Taschenbuch Verlag, 1991.

5 Tooze, *The Wages of Destruction*, p. 597. See also Wolfgang Paul, *Der Heimatkrieg 1939 bis 1945*, Esslingen am Neckar, Bechtle, 1980, pp. 105–17.

6 Götz Aly, *Hitler's Beneficiaries: Plunder, Racial War, and the Nazi Welfare State*, New York, Metropolitan, 2007. For a refutation, see Tooze, *The Wages of Destruction*, pp. 642–8.

7 For a demolition of Speer's self-proclaimed "economic miracle" see Tooze, *The Wages of Destruction*, pp. 552–89, 627–8. See also Dan van der Vat, *The Good Nazi: The Life and Lies of Albert Speer*, Boston, Houghton Mifflin, 1997; and Michael Thad Allen, *The Business of Genocide: The SS, Slave Labor, and the Concentration Camps*, Chapel Hill, University of North Carolina Press, 2002, esp. pp. 171–7.

8 Allen, *The Business of Genocide*, p. 188. See also Walter Naasner, *Neue Machtzentren in der deutschen Kriegswirtschaft 1942–1945*, Boppard am Rhein, Harald Boldt, 1994.

9 Ulrich Herbert, *Arbeit, Volkstum, Weltanschauung: Über Fremde und Deutsche im 20. Jahrhundert*, Frankfurt, Fischer, 1995, p. 128. See also Herbert's *Hitler's Foreign Workers: Enforced Foreign Labor in Germany under the Third Reich*, trans. William Templer, Cambridge, Cambridge University Press, 1997, pp. 127–92.

10 "Gestapo Report on Stauffenberg's Relations with Foreign Countries, 1 August 1944," in R. Stackelberg and S. A. Winkle, eds., *The Nazi Germany Sourcebook*, London and New York, Routledge, 2002, p. 312. See also Theodore Hamerow, *On the Road to the Wolf's Lair: German Resistance to Hitler*, Cambridge, MA, Harvard University Press, 1997, p. 285.

11 See Patricia Meehan, *The Unnecessary War: Whitehall and the German Resistance to Hitler*, London, Sinclair-Stevenson, 1992.

12 *The Oxford Companion to World War II*, p. 50.

13 "Manche Hände zittern noch," *Die Zeit*, 5 October 1990.

14 Rolf-Dieter Müller and Gerd R. Ueberschär, *Kriegsende 1945: Die Zerstörung des deutschen Reiches*, Frankfurt, Fischer Taschenbuch Verlag, 1994, p. 140.

15 Gerd R. Ueberschär and Lev A. Bezymenskij, eds., *Der deutsche Angriff auf die Sowjetunion 1941: Die Kontroverse um die Präventivkriegthese*, Darmstadt, Primus Verlag, 1998, p. 60. Rolf-Dieter Müller and Gerd R. Ueberschär, *Hitler's War in the East, 1941–1945: A Critical Assessment*, trans. Bruce D. Little, Providence, RI, Berghahn Books, 1997, pp. 142–3, put Soviet losses at 27 million, including 9 million soldiers. Richard Overy, *Russia's War*, New York, Penguin Books, 1998, p. 288, puts Soviet military dead at 8,668,400.

15 The Holocaust

1 This distinction was first introduced to English-speaking readers by Tim Mason, "Intention and Explanation: A Current Controversy about the Interpretation of National Socialism," in G. Hirschfeld and L. Kettenacker, eds., *Der "Führerstaat": Mythos und Realität*, Stuttgart, Klett, 1981.

2 The phrase was coined by Hans Mommsen, a leading "structuralist" historian, in his essay, "Die Realisierung des Utopischen: Die 'Endlösung der Judenfrage' im 'Dritten Reich,'" *Geschichte und Gesellschaft* 9 (1983), p. 387. English version: "The Realization of the Unthinkable: The 'Final Solution of the Jewish Question' in the Third Reich," *From Weimar to Auschwitz: Essays in German History*, London, Blackwell, 1991, pp. 224–53. See also his essay, "Cumulative Radicalization and Progressive Self-Destruction as Structural Determinants of the Nazi Dictatorship," in Ian Kershaw and Moshe Lewin, eds., *Stalinism and Nazism: Dictatorships in Comparison*, Cambridge, Cambridge University Press, 1997, pp. 75–87; and Ian Kershaw, "'Cumulative Radicalisation' and the Uniqueness of National Socialism," in Christian Jansen, Lutz Niethammer, and Bernd Weisbrot, eds., *Von der Aufgabe zur Freiheit. Politische Verantwortung und bürgerliche Gesellschaft im 19. und 20. Jahrhundert: Festschrift für Hans Mommsen zum 5. November 1995*, Berlin, Akademie Verlag, 1995, pp. 323–36.

3 For a good discussion of the intentionalist–structuralist debate, see Charles S. Maier, *The Unmasterable Past: History, Holocaust, and German National Identity*, Cambridge, MA, Harvard University Press, 1988, esp. p. 95.

4 The metaphor of the "twisted road" is a reference to the book by Karl A. Schleunes, *The Twisted Road to Auschwitz: Nazi Policy toward German Jews, 1933–1939*, Urbana, IL, University of Illinois, 1970.

5 Ian Kershaw, *The Nazi Dictatorship: Problems and Perspectives of Interpretation*, 4th ed., London, Hodder Arnold, 2000, pp. 93–133. See also Richard Bessel, "Functionalists vs. Intentionalists: The Debate Twenty Years On *or* Whatever Happened to Functionalism and Intentionalism?" *German Studies Review* 26/1 (2003), 16–20. Christopher R. Browning argues for a "moderate functionalism" in his essay, "Beyond 'Intentionalism' and 'Functionalism': The Decision for the Final Solution Reconsidered," in *Paths to Genocide: Essays on Launching the Final Solution*, Cambridge, Cambridge University Press, 1992, pp. 86–121. Philippe Burrin represents what might be called a "conditional intentionalism" by arguing that ever since Germany's defeat in 1918 Hitler intended to kill the Jews if another world war should break out. See *Hitler and the Jews: The Genesis of the Holocaust*, trans. Patsy Southgate, London, Edward Arnold, 1994, esp. pp. 149–53.

6   Norman H. Baynes, ed., *The Speeches of Adolf Hitler, April 1922–August 1939*, New York, Howard Fertig, 1969, p. 741.

7   For a discussion of Hitler's motives in making his threat against the Jews, see Hans Mommsen, "Hitler's Reichstag Speech of 30 January 1939," in *Passing into History: Nazism and the Holocaust beyond Memory*, special issue of *History and Memory* 9 (Fall 1997), 147–61. See also "Realisierung des Utopischen," pp. 395ff.

8   Dieter Pohl, "Die Ermordung der Juden im Generalgouvernement," in Ulrich Herbert, ed., *Nationalsozialistische Vernichtunspolitik 1939–1945: Neue Forschungen und Kontroversen*, Frankfurt, Fischer Taschenbuch Verlag, 1998, p. 99.

9   Raul Hilberg, *The Destruction of the European Jews*, Student Edition, New York, Holmes & Meier, 1985, p. 338. See also the section on "Ghetto Formation," *Destruction of the European Jews*, New Haven, Yale University Press, 2003, pp. 217–37.

10 Hans Safrian, *Eichmann und seine Gehilfen*, Frankfurt, Fischer Taschenbuch Verlag, 1995, pp. 68–81.

11 Richard Breitman, *The Architect of Genocide: Himmler and the Final Solution*, Hanover, NH, University Press of New England, 1992, pp. 145ff., places the decision in spring 1941. Browning, "Beyond 'Intentionalism' and 'Functionalism,'" believes the decision was not made until August 1941 in the euphoria of battlefield successes in the east; see also his essay, "From 'Ethnic Cleansing' to Genocide to the 'Final Solution': The Evolution of Nazi Jewish Policy, 1939–1941," in *The Holocaust: A Reader*, Simone Gigliotti and Berel Lang, eds., Malden, MA, Blackwell, 2005, pp. 143–66. Philippe Burrin, *Hitler and the Jews*, p. 147, dates the decision to the middle of September, but believes it was the result of the failure of Operation Barbarossa, not its success. Götz Aly, *Final Solution: Nazi Population Policy and the Murder of the European Jews*, trans. Belinda Cooper and Allison Brown, London, Arnold, 1999, contends that while the decision to deport the European Jews to the east was made in March 1941, the decision for extermination did not come until later. In the original German version of his book, *Endlösung: Völkerverschiebung und der Mord on den europäischen Juden*, Frankfurt, Fischer, 1995, p. 358, he offered the first two weeks of October 1941 as the probable date for an official decision about systematic murder. Arno Mayer, *Why Did the Heavens Not Darken? The "Final Solution" in History*, New York, Pantheon, 1990, also places the decision in the fall of 1941, and believes the decision was made because of impending defeat in the east. Christian Gerlach argues that the decision was made as a result of the US entry into the war in December 1941. See note 14, below. Richard Rhodes, *Masters of Death: The SS Einsatzgruppen and the Invention of the Holocaust*, New York, Vintage, 2003, p. 48, places the decision in December 1941 as well.

12 Peter Longerich, *Policy of Destruction: Nazi Anti-Jewish Policy and the Genesis of the "Final Solution,"* Washington, DC, Center for Advanced Holocaust Studies, United States Holocaust Memorial Museum, 2001, p. 21.

13 Office of the US Chief of Counsel for Prosecution of Axis Criminality, *Nazi Conspiracy and Aggression*, Vol. III, Washington, DC, US Government Printing Office, 1946, doc. 710-PS, pp. 525–6.

14 Christian Gerlach, "The Wannsee Conference, the Fate of the German Jews, and Hitler's Decision on Principle to Exterminate All European Jews," *Journal of Modern History* 70 (1998), 759–812. Christopher Browning, *The Origins of the Final Solution: The Evolution of Nazi Jewish Policy, September 1939–March 1942*, Lincoln, University of Nebraska Press, 2004, p. 540, disputes Gerlach's conclusion: "What he interprets as Hitler's basic decision, I see as an official initiation of party leaders to a decision taken several months earlier."

15 Browning, "Beyond 'Intentionalism' and 'Functionalism,'" pp. 115–21.

16 Wolfgang Benz, *The Holocaust: A German Historian Examines the Genocide*, trans. Jane Sydenham-Kwiet, New York, Columbia University Press, 1999, p. 75.

17 Rhodes, *Masters of Death*, p. 48.

18 Cited in Browning, *The Origins of the Final Solution*, p. 309.

19 Benz, *The Holocaust*, p. 75.

20 Ibid., pp. 76–84.

21 Christopher R. Browning, *Ordinary Men: Reserve Police Battalion 101 and the Final Solution in Poland*, New York, HarperCollins, 1992.

22 See Mark Roseman, *The Wannsee Conference and the Final Solution: A Reconsideration*, New York, Metropolitan Books, 2002, esp. pp. 79–140.

23 "Minutes of the Wannsee Conference, 20 January 1942," in R. Stackelberg and S. A. Winkle, eds., *The Nazi Germany Sourcebook: An Anthology of Texts*, London and New York, Routledge, 2002, pp. 346–52.

24 Ibid., p. 349.

25 Guenter Lewy, *The Catholic Church and Nazi Germany*, New York, McGraw-Hill, 1964, p. 289. Nathan Stolzfus, *Resistance of the Heart: Intermarriage and the Rosenstrasse Protest in Nazi Germany*, New York, Norton, 1996, argues that the success of this protest showed that public resistance to Nazi policies was possible. Wolf Gruner, however, denied that this was the proper conclusion to draw, as the Nazis never intended to deport this particular group of Jewish men. See his article, "The Factory-Action and the Events at the Berlin Rosenstrasse: Facts and Fiction about 27 February 1943—Sixty Years Later," *Central European History* 36, 2 (2003), 179–208.

26 Daniel Jonah Goldhagen, *Hitler's Willing Executioners: Ordinary Germans and the Holocaust*, New York, Alfred A. Knopf, 1996, pp. 327–71.

27 Rudolf Höss, *Kommandant in Auschwitz: Autobiographische Aufzeichnungen*, ed. Martin Broszat (1963); repr. Munich, Deutscher Taschenbuch Verlag, 1998, p. 251. English version: *Commandant of Auschwitz: The Autobiography*, trans. Constantine Fitz Gibbon, London, Weidenfeld and Nicolson, 1959.

28 Wolfgang Benz, Hermann Graml, and Hermann Weiss, eds., *Enzyklopädie des Nationalsozialismus*, Munich, Deutscher Taschenbuch Verlag, 1997, p. 573.

29 Wolfgang Benz, ed., *Die Dimension des Völkermords: Die Zahl der jüdischen Opfer des Nationalsozialismus*, Munich, R. Oldenbourg, 1991, pp. 15–16.

30 Goldhagen, *Hitler's Willing Executioners*, pp. 164–78.

31 Siegfried Maruhn, "Das deutsche Volk war eingeweiht," *Die Zeit*, 2 June 1995.

32 *Nazi Conspiracy and Aggression*, Vol. VIII, doc. M-31, p. 19. See also Karlheinz Weissmann, *Der Weg in den Abgrund: Deutschland unter Hitler 1933–1945*, Berlin, Propyläen Verlag, 1995, p. 426.

33 *Nazi Conspiracy and Aggression*, Vol. IV, doc. 1965-PS, p. 602.

34 David Bankier, "German Public Awareness of the Final Solution," in David Cesarani, ed., *The Final Solution: Origins and Implementation*, London, Routledge, 1994, p. 225. See also Peter Longerich, *"Davon haben wir nichts gewusst!" Die Deutschen und die Judenverfolgung 1939–1945*, Munich, Siedler, 2006.

35 This is the conclusion of Kershaw, *The Hitler Myth: Image and Reality in the Third Reich*, Oxford, Oxford University Press, 1987, esp. pp. 248–52.

36 David Wyman, *The Abandonment of the Jews: America and the Holocaust, 1941–1945*, New York, Pantheon Books, 1984, pp. 288ff.; Walter Laqueur, *The Terrible Secret: Suppression of the Truth about Hitler's "Final Solution,"* New York, Penguin, 1980, pp. 65–100.

37 Cited in William D. Rubinstein, *The Myth of Rescue: Why the Democracies Could Not Have Saved More Jews from the Nazis*, London and New York, Routledge, 1997, p. 161.

38   Rubinstein, *Myth of Rescue*, p. x, argues that

> no Jew who perished during the Nazi Holocaust could have been saved by any action
> which the Allies could have taken at the time, given what was actually known about the
> Holocaust, what was *actually proposed* at the time and what was realistically possible.

39   John F. Morley, *Vatican Diplomacy and the Jews During the Holocaust 1939–1943*, New York,
     KTAV Publishing House, 1980, p. 300, n. 188.

40   Michael Phayer, *The Catholic Church and the Holocaust, 1930–1955*, Bloomington, Indiana
     University Press, 2000, p. 58. An even stronger indictment of Pacelli's indifference to the
     mass murder of the Jews is offered by John Cornwell, *Hitler's Pope: The Secret History of Pius
     XII*, New York, Viking, 1999, esp. pp. 278–97.

41   Michael R. Marrus, *The Holocaust in History*, New York, Meridian, 1987, pp. 179–83.

42   Henry Friedlander, *The Origins of Nazi Genocide: From Euthanasia to the Final Solution*, Chapel
     Hill, NC, University of North Carolina Press, 1995, pp. 115–16.

16 Continuities and new beginnings

 1   Cited by Klaus Wiegrefe, "Im Bunker des Bösen," *Der Spiegel*, 23 August 2004, p. 60.

 2   See "Illegal bis in den Tod," *Der Spiegel*, 13 April 1998, pp. 50–2.

 3   Michael Phayer, *The Catholic Church and the Holocaust, 1930–1965*, Bloomington, IN,
     University of Indiana Press, 2000, p. 166.

 4   Wolfgang Benz, Hermann Graml, and Hermann Weiss, eds., *Enzyklopädie des Nationalsozialismus*,
     Munich, Deutscher Taschenbuch Verlag, 1997, p. 593; A. J. Ryder, *Twentieth-Century Germany:
     From Bismarck to Brandt*, New York, Columbia University Press, 1973, p. 471.

 5   Konrad Kwiet, "Nazi War Crimes Trials and Investigations," in Dieter K. Buse and
     Juergen C. Doerr, eds., *Modern Germany: An Encyclopedia of History, People, and Culture,
     1871–1990*, New York, Garland, 1998, p. 709.

 6   John Weiss, *The Ideology of Death: Why the Holocaust Happened in Germany*, Chicago, Ivan R.
     Dee, 1996, pp. 380–97.

 7   *Enzyklopädie des Nationalsozialismus*, p. 593. See also Norbert Frei, *Adenauer's Germany and
     the Nazi Past: The Politics of Amnesty and Integration*, trans. Joel Golb, New York, Columbia
     University Press, 2002, esp. pp. 67–91.

 8   Steven P. Remy, *The Heidelberg Myth: The Nazification and Denazification of a German
     University*, Cambridge, MA, Harvard University Press, 2002, pp. 175–6; see also Rebecca
     L. Boehling, *A Question of Priorities: Democratic Reforms and Economic Recovery in Postwar
     Germany*, Providence, RI, Berghahn Books, 1996, p. 239.

 9   Lutz Niethammer, *Die Mitläuferfabrik: Die Entnazifizierung am Beispiel Bayerns*, Berlin,
     Dietz, 1982.

10   Lothar Kettenacker, *Germany since 1945*, Oxford, Oxford University Press, 1997, p. 17.

11   Christian Zentner and Friedemann Bedürftig, *The Encyclopedia of the Third Reich*, trans. Amy
     Hackett, New York, Da Capo Press, 1997, p. 190. See also Richard L. Merritt, *Democracy
     Imposed: U.S. Occupation Policy and the German Public, 1945–1949*, New Haven, Yale
     University Press, 1995, esp. the chapter on denazification, pp. 179–207.

12   See, for instance, Hannjost Lixfeld, *Folklore and Fascism: The Reich Institute for German
     Volkskunde*, ed. and trans. James R. Dow, Bloomington, IN, Indiana University Press, 1994,
     p. 46.

13   See, for instance, Hermann Lübbe, "Der Nationalsozialismus im Bewusstsein der deutschen
     Gegenwart," in *Die Aufdringlichkeit der Geschichte: Herausforderungen der Moderne vom Historismus
     bis zum Nationalsozialismus*, Graz, Verlag Styria, 1989, pp. 334–50.

14 Robert G. Moeller, "War Stories: The Search for a Usable Past in the Federal Republic of Germany," *American Historical Review* 101 (October 1996), 1008–48.

15 John H. Herz, "The Fiasco of Denazification in Germany," *Political Science Quarterly* LXII, 4 (1948), p. 579.

16 Boehling, *Question of Priorities*, p. 237.

17 David Childs, "The Far Right in Germany since 1945," in L. Cheles, R. Ferguson, and M. Vaughan, eds., *The Far Right in Western and Eastern Europe*, 2nd ed., London, Longman, 1995, p. 293. See also Hans-Jürgen Döscher, *Verschworene Gesellschaft: Das Auswärtige Amt unter Adenauer zwischen Neubeginn und Kontinuität*, Berlin, Akademieverlag, 1995.

18 Ryder, *Twentieth-Century Germany*, p. 473.

19 Michael Kohlatruck, "Das Zweite Ende der Nachkriegszeit: Zur Veränderung der politischen Kultur um 1960," in Gary S. Schaal and Andreas Wöll, eds., *Vergangenheitsbewältigung: Modelle der politischen und sozialen Integration in der bundesdeutschen Nachkriegsgeschichte*, Baden-Baden, Nomos Verlagsgesellschaft, 1997, p. 119. See also Marc von Miquel, "Juristen: Richter in eigener Sache," in Norbert Frei, ed., *Karrieren im Zwielicht: Hitlers Eliten nach 1945*, Frankfurt, Campus Verlag, 2002, pp. 181–237.

20 Cited in the news report, "Globke, Filbinger, Fassbinder, Walser, Flick: Der Skandal um Günter Grass hat Vorläufer," *Berlin Tagesspiegel*, 23 August 2006.

21 Hermann Weiss, ed., *Biographisches Lexikon zum Dritten Reich*, Frankfurt, Fischer Taschenbuch Verlag, 1999, p. 242.

22 Kettenacker, *Germany since 1945*, pp. 18–19.

23 Mary Fulbrooke, *Anatomy of a Dictatorship: Inside the GDR 1949–1989*, Oxford, Oxford University Press, 1995, p. 81.

24 Claudia Mosel, *Frankreich und die deutschen Kriegsverbrecher: Politik und Praxis der Strafvervolgung nach dem Zweiten Weltkrieg*, Göttingen, Wallstein, 2004.

25 Christopher Simpson, *Blowback: America's Recruitment of Nazis and Its Effects on the Cold War*, New York, Weidenfeld & Nicolson, 1988, pp. 277ff.

26 See Linda Hunt, *Secret Agenda: The United States Government, Nazi Scientists, and Project Paperclip, 1945 to 1990*, New York, St. Martin's Press, 1991.

27 Timothy Naftali, "The CIA and Eichmann's Associates," in Richard Breitman, ed., *US Intelligence and the Nazis*, Washington, DC, National Archives Trust Fund Board for Nazi War Crimes and Japanese Imperial Government Record Interagency Working Group, 2004, pp. 337–74; on Barbie, see Norman J. W. Goda, "Manhunts: The Official Search for Notorious Nazis," esp. pp. 426–30.

28 Müller and Ueberschär, *Kriegsende*, p. 123; Wolfgang Benz, ed., *Die Vertreibung der Deutschen aus dem Osten: Ursachen, Ereignisse, Folgen*, Frankfurt, Fischer Taschenbuch Verlag, 1995, p. 14. See also Norman M. Naimark, *Fires of Hatred: Ethnic Cleansing in Twentieth-Century Europe*, Cambridge, MA, Harvard University Press, 2001.

29 Michael Burleigh, *Germany Turns Eastwards: A Study of Ostforschung in the Third Reich*, Cambridge, Cambridge University Press, 1988, pp. 300–21.

30 Cited in Frei, *Karrieren im Zwielicht*, p. 239.

31 Jeffrey Herf, *Divided Memory: The Nazi Past in the Two Germanys*, Cambridge, MA, Harvard University Press, 1997, pp. 69–105.

32 See Charles S. Maier, *The Unmasterable Past: History, Holocaust, and German National Identity*, Cambridge, MA, Harvard University Press, 1988, pp. 89–91.

33 Herf, *Divided Memory*, p. 194.

34 Werner Bergmann and Rainer Erb, *Anti-Semitism in Germany: The Post-Nazi Epoch since 1945*, New Brunswick, NJ, Transaction Publishers, 1997, pp. 306–7.

35 Lee McGowan, *The Radical Right in Germany 1870 to the Present*, London, Longman, 2002, p. 165.

36 R. Kühnl, R. Rilling, and C. Sager, *Die NPD: Struktur, Ideologie und Funktion einer Neo-Faschistischen Partei*, Frankfurt, Suhrkamp, 1969, p. 226; McGowan, *The Radical Right*, p. 156.

37 Christopher T. Husbands, "Militant Neo-Nazism in the Federal Republic of Germany in the 1990s," in Cheles, Ferguson, and Vaughan, *The Far Right in Western and Eastern Europe*, p. 329; "Rechtsextremistische Gewalttaten 1992," Report of the Federal Ministry of the Interior, 6 February 1993; and McGowan, *The Radical Right*, p. 179.

17 The historians' debate

1 Bill Niven, *Facing the Nazi Past: United Germany and the Legacy of the Third Reich*, London, Routledge, 2002, p. 2. See also Bill Niven, ed., *Germans as Victims: Remembering the Past in Contemporary Germany*, New York, Palgrave Macmillan, 2006.

2 Norbert Frei, *Adenauer's Germany and the German Past: The Politics of Amnesty and Integration*, trans. Joel Golb, New York, Columbia University Press, 2002, p. 303. See also his *Karrieren im Zwielicht: Hitlers Eliten nach 1945*, Frankfurt, Campus Verlag, 2002, esp. pp. 304–35.

3 Ralph Giordano, *Die Zweite Schuld, oder von der Last Deutscher zu sein*, Hamburg, Rasch und Röhring, 1987. For a conservative response, see Manfred Kittel, *Die Legende von der "Zweiten Schuld": Vergangenheitsbewältigung in der Ära Adenauer*, Berlin, Ullstein, 1993.

4 Friedrich Meinecke, *The German Catastrophe: Reflections and Recollections*, trans. Sidney B. Fay, Cambridge, MA, Harvard University Press, 1950; Gerhard Ritter, "The Historical Foundations of the Rise of National Socialism," in International Council for Philosophy and Humanistic Studies, *The Third Reich*, London, Weidenfeld & Nicolson, 1955, pp. 385ff.; "The Fault of Mass Democracy," in John Snell, ed., *"The Nazi Revolution: Germany's Guilt or Germany's Fate*, New York, D. C. Heath, 1959; "The European Context" and "Militarism and Nazism," in John Snell and Alan Mitchell, eds., *The Nazi Revolution: Hitler's Dictatorship and the German Nation*, 2nd ed., Lexington, MA, D. C. Heath, 1973, pp. 22–34, 164–70.

5 Gerhard Ritter, *The German Resistance: Carl Goerdeler's Struggle against Tyranny*, trans. R. T. Clark, New York, Praeger, 1959; Hans Rothfels, *The German Opposition to Hitler*, Hinsdale, IL, Regnery, 1948.

6 See Carl J. Friedrich and Zibigniev K. Brzezinski, *Totalitarian Dictatorship and Autocracy*, New York, Praeger, 1967. See also Wolfgang Wippermann, "'Totalitäre Diktaturen'? Trivialisierung durch Vergleich," in *Wessen Schuld? Vom Historikerstreit zur Goldhagen-Kontroverse*, Berlin, Elefanten Press, 1997, pp. 10–23. For a balanced critique of totalitarianism theory, see Ian Kershaw, *The Nazi Dictatorship: Problem and Perspectives of Interpretation*, 4th ed., London, Hodder Arnold, 2000, esp. pp. 34–40.

7 See Benjamin Ortmeyer, *Schulzeit unterm Hitlerbild: Analysen, Berichte, Dokumente*, Frankfurt, Fischer Taschenbuch Verlag, 1996, pp. 141ff. See also Rolf Gutte and Freerk Huisken, *Alles bewältigt, nichts begriffen! Nationalsozialismus im Unterricht: Eine Kritik der antifaschistischen Erziehung*, Berlin, Edition Ost, 1997.

8 Ernst Nolte, *Die Deutschen und ihre Vergangenheit: Erinnerung und Vergessen von der Reichsgründung Bismarcks bis heute*, Berlin, Propyläen, 1995, p. 116.

9 Fritz Fischer, *Hitler war kein Betriebsunfall: Aufsätze*, Munich, C. H. Beck, 1992, pp. 16–17. For a recent defense of Brüning's policies that denies Brüning's own claim that he sought a monarchical restoration in 1931–32, see William L. Patch, Jr., "Heinrich Brüning's Recollections of Monarchism: The Birth of a Red Herring," *Journal of Modern History* 70 (June 1998), 340–70. According to Patch, Brüning only advocated restoration of the monarchy in order to rally Germany's conservative elites against the Nazis. See *Heinrich Brüning and the Dissolution of the Weimar Republic*, Cambridge, Cambridge University Press, 1998, pp. 135, 302.

10 Fritz Fischer, *Griff nach der Weltmacht: Die Kriegszielpolitik des kaiserlichen Deutschlands 1914–1918* (1961); trans. *Germany's Aims in the First World War*, New York, Norton, 1967.

11 Fritz Fischer, *World Power or Decline: The Controversy over Germany's Aims in the First World War* (1965), New York, Norton, 1974; *War of Illusions: German Policies from 1911–1914* (1969), New York, Norton, 1975; *From Kaiserreich to Third Reich: Elements of Continuity in German History, 1871–1945* (1979), London, Allen & Unwin, 1986. See also *Hitler war kein Betriebsunfall: Aufsätze*, Munich, C. H. Beck, 1992. For Fischer's impact on the German historical profession, see Stefan Berger, *The Search for Normality: National Identity and Historical Consciousness since 1800*, Providence, RI, Berghahn Books, 1997, pp. 56–76.

12 Gerhard Ritter, "Eine neue Kriegsschuldthese? Zu Fritz Fischers Buch *Griff nach der Weltmacht*," *Historische Zeitschrift* 194 (1962), 646–88.

13 Hans-Ulrich Wehler, *The German Empire, 1871–1918* (1973), trans. Kim Traynor, Providence, RI, Berg, 1985, and *Deutsche Gesellschaftsgeschichte*, Vol. 3, *Von der "Deutschen Doppelrevolution" bis zum Beginn des Ersten Weltkrieges 1849–1914*, and Vol. 4, *Vom Beginn des Ersten Weltkriegs bis zur Gründung der beiden deutschen Staaten 1914–1949*, Munich, C. H. Beck, 1995–2003. See also Wolfgang Mommsen, "Die Deutschen und ihre Geschichte," in *Nation und Geschichte: Über die Deutschen und die deutsche Frage*, Munich, Piper, 1990, pp. 175–6.

14 See Geoffrey H. Hartman, ed., *Bitburg in Moral and Political Perspective*, Bloomington, IN, Indiana University Press, 1986.

15 Thomas Nipperdey, *Deutsche Geschichte 1800–1866: Bürgerwelt und starker Staat*, Munich, 1983, and *Deutsche Geschichte 1866–1918*, 2 vols., Munich, C. H. Beck, 1990–92.

16 Michael Stürmer, *Dissonanzen des Fortschritts: Essays über Geschichte und Politik in Deutschland*, Munich, R. Piper, 1986, p. 276.

17 Stürmer, "Kein Eigentum der Deutschen: Die Deutsche Frage," in Werner Weidenfeld, ed., *Die Identität der Deutschen*, Munich, C. Hanser, 1983, pp. 83–101, and "Nation und Demokratie," *Die Politische Meinung* 230 (1987), 22.

18 Stürmer, "Geschichte im geschichtslosen Land," *Frankfurter Allgemeine Zeitung*, 25 April 1986. Translation in "History in a Land without History," in *Forever in the Shadow of Hitler? Original Documents of the Historikerstreit, the Controversy Concerning the Singularity of the Holocaust*, trans. James Knowlton and Truett Cates, Atlantic Highlands, NJ, Humanities Press, 1993, p. 16.

19 Stürmer, "Deutsche Identität: Auf der Suche nach der verlorenen Nationalgeschichte," in *Dissonanzen des Fortschritts*, pp. 201–9.

20 Jürgen Habermas, "Eine Art Schadensabwicklung: Die apologetischen Tendenzen in der deutschen Zeitgeschichtsschreibung," *Die Zeit*, 18 July 1986. The major documents of the *Historikerstreit* have been collected in *"Historikerstreit"—Die Dokumentation der Kontroverse um die Einzigartigkeit der nationalsozialistischen Judenvernichtung*, Munich, Piper, 1987. The English translation *Forever in the Shadow of Hitler?* contains numerous errors and should be checked against the German original.

21 Ernst Nolte, "Vergangenheit, die nicht vergehen will," *Frankfurter Allgemeine Zeitung*, 6 June 1986; translated as "The Past That Will Not Pass: A Speech That Could Be Written but Not Delivered," in *Forever in the Shadow of Hitler?*, pp. 18–23.

22 Nolte, *Three Faces of Fascism: Action Française, Italian Fascism, National Socialism*, trans. Leila Vennewitz, New York, Holt, Rinehart and Winston, 1966, p. 399.

23 Ibid., pp. 19, 22.

24 For a discussion of the major issues of the *Historikerstreit*, see Charles S. Maier, *Germany's Unmasterable Past: History, Holocaust, and German National Identity*, Cambridge, MA, Harvard University Press, 1988; Richard J. Evans, *In Hitler's Shadow: West German Historians and the Attempt to Escape from the Nazi Past*, New York, Pantheon Books, 1989;

and Peter Baldwin, ed., *Reworking the Past: Hitler, the Holocaust, and the Historians' Debate*, Boston, Beacon Press, 1990.

25 Niven, *Facing the Nazi Past*, p. 6.

26 Berger, *The Search for Normality*, pp. 124, 157. On the political organizations, think tanks, press organs, and publicists that comprise Germany's "New Right," see Roger Woods, *Germany's New Right as Culture and Politics*, New York, Palgrave Macmillan, 2007.

27 Interview with Nolte, "'Ein historisches Recht Hitlers'?" *Der Spiegel* 40 (3 October 1994), p. 99.

28 See especially Nolte's *Der europäische Bürgerkrieg 1917–1945: Nationalsozialismus und Bolschewismus*, Berlin, Propyläen Verlag, 1987; *Lehrstück oder Tragödie? Beiträge zur Interpretation der Geschichte des 20. Jahrhunderts*, Cologne, Böhlau Verlag, 1991; *Streitpunkte: Heutige und künftige Kontroversen um den Nationalsozialismus*, Berlin, Propyläen Verlag, 1993; *Die Deutschen und ihre Vergangenheiten: Erinnerung und Vergessen von der Reichsgründung Bismarcks bis heute*, Berlin, Propyläen Verlag, 1995; and most recently, *Die Weimarer Republik: Demokratie zwischen Lenin und Hitler*, Munich, Herbig, 2006.

29 Nolte, *Martin Heidegger: Politik und Geschichte im Leben und Denken*, Berlin, Propyläen Verlag, 1992, pp. 123, 296; see also the chapter on Heidegger in *Geschichtsdenken im 20. Jahrhundert: Von Max Weber bis Hans Jonas*, Berlin, Propyläen Verlag, 1991, pp. 471–82.

30 Nolte, *Streitpunkte*, pp. 323–34.

31 Rainer Zitelmann, *Hitler: Selbstverständnis eines Revolutionärs*, Hamburg, Berg, 1987, and *Adolf Hitler: Eine politische Biographie*, Göttingen, Muster-Schmidt Verlag, 1989. See also his essays, "Die totalitäre Seite der Moderne," in Michael Prinz and Rainer Zitelmann, eds., *Nationalsozialismus und Modernisierung*, Darmstadt, Wissenschaftliche Buchgesellschaft, 1991, pp. 1–20, and "Nationalsozialismus und Antikommunismus: Aus Anlass der Thesen von Ernst Nolte," in Uwe Backes, Eckhard Jesse, and Rainer Zitelmann, eds., *Die Schatten der Vergangenheit: Impulse zur Historisierung des Nationalsozialismus*, Berlin, Propyläen Verlag, 1990, pp. 229–30.

32 Zitelmann, *Adolf Hitler*, pp. 119ff., 149ff.

33 Daniel J. Goldhagen, *Hitler's Willing Executioners: Ordinary Germans and the Holocaust*, New York, Alfred A. Knopf, 1996. For critiques, see Franklin H. Littell, ed., *Hyping the Holocaust: Scholars Answer Goldhagen*, East Rockaway, NY, Cummings & Hathaway, 1997; Julius H. Schoeps, ed., *Ein Volk von Mördern? Die Dokumentation zur Goldhagen-Kontroverse um die Rolle der Deutschen im Holocaust*, Hamburg, Hoffmann & Campe, 1996; and Norman G. Finkelstein and Ruth Bettina Birn, *A Nation on Trial: The Goldhagen Thesis and Historical Truth*, New York, Henry Holt, 1998. A less publicized but better book on the same topic as Goldhagen's book appeared in the same year: John Weiss, *Ideology of Death: Why the Holocaust Happened in Germany*, Chicago, Ivan R. Dee, 1996.

34. Doris L. Bergen, "Controversies about the Holocaust: Goldhagen, Arendt, and the Historians' Conflict," in Hartmut Lehmann, ed., *Historikerkontroversen*, Göttingen, Wallstein, 2000, p. 158.

35 Ulrich Herbert, "Extermination Policy: New Answers and Questions about the History of the 'Holocaust' in German Historiography," in Ulrich Herbert, ed., *National Socialist Extermination Policies: Contemporary German Perspectives and Controversies*, New York, Berghahn Books, 2000, p. 2.

36 Daniel Jonah Goldhagen, "*Modell Bundesrepublik*: National History, Democracy, and Internationalization in Germany," in Robert R. Shandley, ed., *Unwilling Germans? The Goldhagen Debate*, Minneapolis, University of Minnesota Press, 1998, pp. 275–85.

37 Geoff Eley, "Ordinary Germans, Nazism, and Judeocide," in Geoff Eley, ed., *The "Goldhagen Effect": History, Memory, and Nazism—Facing the German Past*, Ann Arbor, University of Michigan Press, 2000, pp. 1–31.

38 Cited in Niven, *Facing the Nazi Past*, p. 107.

39 See Omer Bartov, *Hitler's Army: Soldiers, Nazis, and War in the Third Reich*, New York, Oxford University Press, 1992, and "Whose History Is It Anyway? The Wehrmacht and German Historiography," in Hannes Heer and Klaus Naumann, eds., *War of Extermination: The German Military in World War II, 1941–1944* (1995), New York, Berghahn, 2000. The role of Hitler's generals in atrocities on the eastern front was recently confirmed by Johannes Hürter, *Hitlers Heerführer: Die deutschen Oberbefehlshaber im Krieg gegen die Sowjetunion 1941/1942*, Munich, Oldenbourg Verlag, 2006.

40 Omer Bartov *et al.*, *Bericht der Kommission zur Überprüfung der Ausstellung "Vernichtungskrieg: Verbrechen der Wehrmacht 1941 bis 1944,"* cited in Niven, *Facing the Nazi Past*, p. 173.

41 Cited in Niven, *Facing the Nazi Past*, p. 194. See also, U. Heimrod, G. Schlusche, and H. Seferens, *Der Denkmalstreit—das Denkmal? Die Debatte um das Denkmal für die ermordeten Juden Europas: Eine Dokumentation*, Berlin, Philo, 1999.

42 See "Vom Mahnmal zum Wahnmal," *Der Spiegel*, 24 August 1998, pp. 170–8.

43 For a thorough discussion of the issues involved, see the chapter, "The Holocaust Memorial," in Niven, *Facing the Nazi Past*, pp. 194–232.

Bibliography

Even a partial listing of works relevant to the subject matter of this book would fill several volumes. The following list includes only a selection of the most useful and important books in English. Many of the best historical works in German are now available in English translation as well. The list includes most of the older classic texts as well as the more recent literature on specialized topics.

The bibliography is organized into eight categories:

1 General and theoretical works on fascism and National Socialism
2 General German history
3 The German Empire, 1871–1918
4 The Weimar Republic, 1918–33
5 The Nazis and the Third Reich
6 World War II
7 The Holocaust
8 The aftermath of National Socialism

1 General and theoretical works on fascism and National Socialism

Arendt, Hannah, *The Origins of Totalitarianism* (1951), new ed., New York, Harcourt, Brace & World, 1966.

Bessel, Richard, ed., *Fascist Italy and Nazi Germany: Comparisons and Contrasts*, Cambridge, Cambridge University Press, 1996.

——, *Nazism and War*, New York, Modern Library, 2004.

Bobbio, Norberto, *Left and Right: The Significance of a Political Distinction*, trans. Allan Cameron, Chicago, University of Chicago Press, 1996.

Carsten, F. L., *Fascist Movements in Austria: From Schönerer to Hitler*, London, Sage, 1977.

——, *The Rise of Fascism*, 2nd ed., Berkeley, CA, University of California Press, 1980.

Cassels, Alan, *Fascism*, New York, Thomas Y. Crowell, 1975.

De Grand, Alexander J., *Fascist Italy and Nazi Germany: The "Fascist" Style of Rule*, London, Routledge, 1995.

Durham, Martin, *Women and Fascism*, London and New York, Routledge, 1998.

Eatwell, Robert, *Fascism: A History*, New York, Viking, 1996.

Fenner, Angelica, and Weitz, Eric D., eds., *Fascism and Neofascism: Critical Writings on the Radical Right in Europe*, New York, Palgrave Macmillan, 2004.

Friedrich, Karl, and Brzezinski, Zibigniev, *Totalitarian Dictatorship and Autocracy*, New York, Praeger, 1967.

Gellately, Robert, *Lenin, Stalin, and Hitler: The Age of Social Catastrophe*, New York, Alfred A. Knopf, 2007.

Gregor, James A., *The Ideology of Fascism: The Rationale of Totalitarianism*, New York, Free Press, 1969.

——, *Interpretations of Fascism*, Morristown, NJ, General Learning Press, 1974.

——, *Italian Fascism and Developmental Dictatorship*, Princeton, Princeton University Press, 1979.

——, *Phoenix: Fascism in our Time*, Brunswick, NJ, Transaction, 1999.

——, *The Faces of Janus: Marxism and Fascism in the Twentieth Century*, New Haven, Yale University Press, 2000.

——, *Fascist Intellectuals: Fascist Social and Political Thought*, Princeton, Princeton University Press, 2005.

Gregor, Neil, Roemer, Nils, and Roseman, Mark, eds., *German History from the Margins*, Bloomington, University of Indiana Press, 2006.

Griffin, Roger, *The Nature of Fascism*, London, Routledge, 1993.

——, ed., *International Fascism: Theories, Causes and the New Consensus*, London, Oxford, 1998.

——, ed., *Fascism, Totalitarianism, and Political Religion*, London and New York, Routledge, 2005.

——, *Modernism and Fascism: The Sense of a Beginning under Mussolini and Hitler*, London, Palgrave Macmillan, 2007.

——, and Feldman, Matthew, eds., *Fascism: Critical Concepts in Political Science*, 5 vols., London and New York, Routledge, 2004.

——, Loh, Werner, and Umland, Andreas, eds., *Fascism Past and Present, West and East: An International Debate on Concepts and Cases in the Comparative Study of the Extreme Right*, Stuttgart, ibidem-Verlag, 2006.

Griffiths, Richard, *An Intelligent Person's Guide to Fascism*, London, Duckworth, 2000.

Guerin, Daniel, *Fascism and Big Business*, trans. Frances and Mason Merrill, New York, Pathfinder Press, 1973 (1936).

Hamilton, Alastair, *The Appeal of Fascism: A Study of Intellectuals and Fascism 1919–1945*, New York, Macmillan, 1971.

Kirk, Tim, and McElligott, Anthony, eds., *Opposing Fascism: Community, Authority and Resistance in Europe*, Cambridge, Cambridge University Press, 1999.

Kitchen, Martin, *Fascism*, London, Macmillan, 1976.

Laqueur, Walter, *Fascism: A Reader's Guide*, Berkeley, University of California Press, 1976.

Mann, Michael, *Fascists*, Cambridge, Cambridge University Press, 2004.

Morgan, Philip, *Fascism in Europe, 1919–1945*, London, Routledge, 2003.

Mosse, George L., *Nationalism and Sexuality: Respectability and Abnormal Sexuality in Modern Europe*, New York, Howard Fertig, 1985.

——, *The Fascist Revolution: Toward a General Theory of Fascism*, New York, Howard Fertig, 1999.

Nolte, Ernst, *Three Faces of Fascism: Action Francaise, Italian Fascism, National Socialism*, trans. Leila Vennewitz, New York, Holt, Rinehart and Winston, 1966.

——, *Marxism, Fascism, Cold War*, Atlantic Highlands, NJ, Humanities Press, 1982.

Passmore, Kevin, *Fascism: A Very Short Introduction*, Oxford, Oxford University Press, 2002.

——, ed., *Women, Gender, and Fascism in Europe, 1919–1945*, New Brunswick, NJ, Rutgers University Press, 2003.

Pauley, Bruce F., *Hitler, Stalin, and Mussolini: Totalitarianism in the Twentieth Century*, Wheeling, IL, Harlan Davidson, 1997.

Paxton, Robert O., *The Anatomy of Fascism*, New York, Alfred A. Knopf, 2004.

Payne, Stanley G., *A History of Fascism, 1914–1945*, Madison, WI, University of Wisconsin Press, 1995.

——, Sorkin, David J., and Tortorice, John S., eds., *What History Tells: George L. Mosse and the Culture of Modern Europe*, Madison, University of Wisconsin Press, 2004.

Renton, Dave, *Fascism: Theory and Practice*, London, Pluto Press, 1999.

Roberts, David, *The Totalitarian Experiment in the Twentieth Century: Understanding the Poverty of Great Politics*, New York, Routledge, 2006.

Soucy, Robert, *French Fascism: The First Wave, 1924–1933*, New Haven, Yale University Press, 1986.

——, *French Fascism: The Second Wave, 1933–1939*, New Haven, Yale University Press, 1995.

Sternhell, Zeev, *Neither Right nor Left: Fascist Ideology in France*, trans. David Maisel, Princeton, NJ, Princeton University Press, 1986.

Trotsky, Leon, *The Struggle against Fascism in Germany*, New York, Pathfinder, 1971.

Turner, Henry Ashby, Jr., ed., *Reappraisals of Fascism*, New York, New Viewpoints, 1975.

Weber, Eugene, *Varieties of Fascism: Doctrines of Revolution in the Twentieth Century*, New York, Van Nostrand Reinhold, 1964.

Weiss, John, *The Fascist Tradition: Radical Right-Wing Extremism in Modern Europe*, New York, Harper & Row, 1967.

Woolf, S. J., ed., *The Nature of Fascism*, New York, Random House, 1969.

——, ed., *Fascism in Europe*, London, Methuen, 1981.

2 General German history

Anchor, Robert, *Germany Confronts Modernization: German Society and Culture, 1790–1890*, Lexington, MA, D. C. Heath, 1972.

Applegate, Celia, *A Nation of Provincials: The German Idea of Heimat*, Berkeley, University of California Press, 1990.

Balfour, Michael, *Germany: The Tides of Power*, London, Routledge, 1992.

Barraclough, Geoffrey, *The Origins of Modern Germany* (1946), repr. New York, Norton, 1984.

Bellon, Bernard P., *Mercedes in Peace and War: German Automobile Workers, 1903–1945*, New York, Columbia University Press, 1990.

Berdahl, Robert M., *The Politics of the Prussian Nobility: The Development of a Conservative Ideology 1770–1848*, Princeton, NJ, Princeton University Press, 1988.

Berger, Stefan, *The Search for Normality: National Identity and Historical Consciousness in Germany since 1800*, Providence, RI, Berghahn Books, 1997.

Berghahn, V. R., *Modern Germany: Society, Economy and Politics in the Twentieth Century*, 2nd ed., Cambridge, Cambridge University Press, 1987.

Blackbourne, David, *The Long Nineteenth Century: A History of Germany, 1780–1918*, New York, Oxford University Press, 1998.

Buse, Dieter K., and Doerr, Juergen C., eds., *Modern Germany: An Encyclopedia of History, People, and Culture, 1871–1990*, 2 vols., New York, Garland, 1998.

Calleo, David, *The German Problem Reconsidered: Germany and the World Order, 1870 to the Present*, Cambridge, Cambridge University Press, 1978.

Carr, William, *A History of Germany, 1815–1945*, 2nd ed., New York, St. Martin's, 1979.

Carsten, F. L., *Princes and Parliaments in Germany: From the Fifteenth to the Eighteenth Century*, Oxford, Clarendon Press, 1959.

Childs, David, *Germany in the Twentieth Century*, 3rd ed., New York, HarperCollins, 1991.

Cocks, Geoffrey, and Jarausch, Konrad H., eds., *German Professions 1800–1950*, New York, Oxford University Press, 1990.

Craig, Gordon A., *The Politics of the Prussian Army 1640–1945*, Oxford, Clarendon Press, 1955.

——, *Germany, 1866–1945*, New York and Oxford, Oxford University Press, 1978.

——, *The Germans*, New York, Putnam, 1982.

——, and Roth, Jack Joseph, eds., *World War I, a Turning Point in Modern History: Essays on the Significance of War*, New York, Knopf, 1967.

Dahrendorf, Ralf, *Society and Democracy in Germany*, New York, Doubleday, 1967.

Dehio, Ludwig, *Germany and World Politics in the Twentieth Century*, trans. Dieter Pevsner, New York, Norton, 1967.

Eghigian, Greg, and Berg, Matthew Paul, eds., *Sacrifice and National Belonging in Twentieth-Century Germany*, College Station, TX, Texas A & M University Press, 2002.

Elon, Amos, *The Pity of It All: A History of the Jews in Germany 1743–1933*, New York, Metropolitan, 2002.

Epstein, Klaus, *The Genesis of German Conservatism*, Princeton, Princeton University Press, 1966.

Evans, Richard J., *Rereading German History: From Unification to Reunification 1800–1996*, London, Routledge, 1997.

Fullbrooke, Mary, *The Divided Nation: A History of Germany 1918–1990*, New York and Oxford, Oxford University Press, 1992.

——, ed., *German History since 1800*, London, Arnold, 1997.

Goerlitz, Walter, *History of the German General Staff, 1657–1945*, trans. Brian Battershaw, New York, Praeger, 1953.

Gregor, Neil, Roemer, Nils, and Roseman, Mark, eds., *German History from the Margins*, Bloomington, University of Indiana Press, 2006.

Hamerow, Theodore, *Restoration, Revolution, Reaction: Economics and Politics in Germany, 1815–1871*, Princeton, NJ, Princeton University Press, 1958.

Hardach, Karl, *The Political Economy of Germany in the Twentieth Century*, Berkeley, University of California Press, 1980.

Hermand, Jost, *Old Dreams of a New Reich: Volkish Utopias and National Socialism*, trans. Paul Levesque, Bloomington, IN, Indiana University Press, 1992.

Holborn, Hajo, *A History of Modern Germany 1840–1945*, New York, Alfred A. Knopf, 1969.

Hughes, Michael, *Nationalism and Society: Germany, 1800–1945*, London, Arnold, 1988.

Iggers, Georg, *The German Conception of History: The National Tradition of Historical Thought from Herder to the Present*, Middletown, CT, Wesleyan University Press, 1968.

Jarausch, Konrad H., *The Unfree Professions: German Lawyers, Teachers, and Engineers, 1900–1950*, New York, Oxford University Press, 1990.

——, and Jones, Larry Eugene, eds., *In Search of Liberal Germany: Studies in the History of German Liberalism from 1789 to the Present*, New York, Berg, 1990.

Jones, Larry Eugene, *Elections, Mass Politics, and Social Change in Modern Germany: New Perspectives*, Washington, DC, German Historical Institute, 1992.

——, and Retallack, James, eds., *Between Reform, Reaction, and Resistance: Studies in the History of German Conservatism from 1789 to 1945*, Oxford, Berg, 1993.

Keylor, William R., *The Twentieth-Century World: An International History*, Oxford, Oxford University Press, 1984.

Kitchen, Martin, *A Military History of Germany: From the Eighteenth Century to the Present Day*, Bloomington, IN, Indiana University Press, 1975.

——, *The Political Economy of Germany, 1815–1914*, London, Croom Helm, 1978.

——, *A History of Modern Germany 1800–2000*, Malden, MA, Blackwell, 2006.

Kohn, Hans, *The Mind of Germany: The Education of a Nation*, New York, Charles Scribner's, 1960.

Krieger, Leonard, *The German Idea of Freedom: History of a Political Tradition*, Chicago, University of Chicago Press, 1957.

Lepenies, Wolf, *The Seduction of Culture in German History*, Princeton, Princeton University Press, 2006.

Lukács, György, *The Destruction of Reason*, trans. Peter Palmer, Atlantic Highlands, NJ, Humanities Press, 1981.

MacDonogh, Giles, *Prussia: The Perversion of an Idea*, London, Mandarin, 1994.

McGowan, Lee, *The Radical Right in Germany: 1870 to the Present*, London, Pearson, 2002.

Martel, Gordon, ed., *Modern Germany Reconsidered 1870–1945*, London, Routledge, 1992.

Mayer, Arno J., *Dynamics of Counterrevolution in Europe, 1870–1956: An Analytic Framework*, New York, Harper & Row, 1971.

——, *The Persistence of the Old Regime: Europe to the Great War*, New York, Pantheon, 1981.

Mosse, George L., *The Nationalization of the Masses: Political Symbolism and Mass Movements in Germany from the Napoleonic Wars through the Third Reich*, New York, Howard Fertig, 1975.

——, *Masses and Man: Nationalist and Fascist Perceptions of Reality*, New York, Howard Fertig, 1980.

Orlow, Dietrich, *A History of Modern Germany, 1871 to Present*, Englewood Cliffs, NJ, Prentice-Hall, 1987.

Pasley, Malcolm, ed., *Germany: A Companion to German Studies*, London, Routledge, 1988.

Pauley, Bruce F., *From Prejudice to Persecution: A History of Austrian Anti-Semitism*, Chapel Hill, NC, University of North Carolina Press, 1992.

Pinson, Koppel S., *Modern Germany: Its History and Civilization*, 2nd ed., Prospect Heights, IL, Waveland Press, 1989.

Pulzer, Peter, *The Rise of Political Anti-Semitism in Germany and Austria*, rev. ed., Cambridge, MA, Harvard University Press, 1988.

——, *Jews and the German State: The Political History of a Minority, 1848–1933*, Oxford, Blackwell, 1992.

——, *Germany 1870–1945: Politics, State Formation, and War*, Oxford, Oxford University Press, 1997.

Raff, Diether, *A History of Germany from the Medieval Empire to the Present*, trans. Bruce Little, Oxford, Berg, 1988.

Rosenberg, Hans, *Bureaucracy, Aristocracy, and Autocracy: The Prussian Experience 1660–1815*, Cambridge, MA, Harvard University Press, 1958.

Rürup, Reinhard, ed., *The Problem of Revolution in Germany, 1789–1989*, Oxford, Berg, 2000.

Ryder, A. J., *Twentieth-Century Germany: From Bismarck to Brandt*, New York, Columbia University Press, 1973.

Schmitt, Bernadotte E., *England and Germany 1740–1914*, Princeton, Princeton University Press, 1918.

Sheehan, James J., *German Liberalism in the Nineteenth Century*, Chicago, University of Chicago Press, 1978.

Snyder, Louis L., *Roots of German Nationalism*, Bloomington, Indiana University Press, 1978.

Taylor, A. J. P., *The Course of German History: A Survey of the Development of Germany since 1815* (1946), repr. London, Routledge, 2001.

Vogt, Hannah, *The Burden of Guilt: A Short History of Germany 1914–1945*, trans. Herbert Strauss, New York, Oxford University Press, 1964.

Weitz, Eric D., *Creating German Communism, 1890–1990: From Popular Protests to Socialist State*, Princeton, NJ, Princeton University Press, 1997.

Williamson, George S., *The Longing for Myth in Germany: Religion and Aesthetic Culture from Romanticism to Nietzsche*, Chicago, University of Chicago Press, 2004.

Winkler, Heinrich August, *Germany: The Long Road West*, Vol. I, *1789–1933*, trans. Alexander J. Sager, Oxford, Oxford University Press, 2006.

3 The German Empire, 1871–1918

Balfour, Michael, *The Kaiser and His Times*, New York, Norton, 1972.

Berghahn, V. R., *Germany and the Approach of War in 1914*, London, Macmillan, 1973.

——, *Imperial Germany, 1871–1914: Economy, Society, Culture, and Politics*, Providence, RI, Berghahn Books, 1994.

Blackbourne, David, *Class, Religion, and Local Politics in Wilhelmine Germany: The Center Party in Württemberg before 1914*, New Haven, Yale University Press, 1980.

——, and Eley, Geoff, *The Peculiarities of German History: Bourgeois Society and Politics in Nineteenth-Century Germany*, Oxford, Oxford University Press, 1984.

Bramstead, Ernest K., *Aristocracy and the Middle Classes in Germany: Social Types in German Literature, 1830–1900* (1937), repr. Chicago, University of Chicago Press, 1964.

Cecil, Lamar, *Wilhelm II*, Vol. 1, *Prince and Emperor, 1859–1900*; Vol. 2, *Emperor and Exile, 1900–1941*, Chapel Hill, NC, University of North Carolina Press, 1989, 1996.

Chickering, Roger, *We Men Who Feel Most German: A Cultural Study of the Pan-German League, 1866–1914*, Boston, George Allen & Unwin, 1984.

——, *The Great War and Urban Life in Germany: Freiburg, 1914–1918*, Cambridge, Cambridge University Press, 2007.

——, and Förster, Stig, eds., *Great War, Total War: Combat and Mobilization on the Western Front, 1914–1918*, Cambridge, Cambridge University Press, 2000.

Clingan, C. Edmund, *Finance from Kaiser to Führer: Budget Policies in Germany, 1912–1934*, Westport, CT, Greenwood Press, 2000.

Crankshaw, Edward, *Bismarck*, New York, Viking, 1981.

Crew, David F., *Town in the Ruhr: A Social History of Bochum, 1860–1914*, New York, Columbia University Press, 1979.

Daniel, Ute, *The War from Within: German Working-Class Women in the First World War*, Oxford, Berg, 1997.

Davis, Belinda J., *Home Fires Burning: Food, Politics, and Everyday Life in World War I Berlin*, Chapel Hill, University of North Carolina Press, 2000.

Eley, Geoff, *Reshaping the German Right: Radical Nationalism and Political Change after Bismarck*, New Haven, Yale University Press, 1980.

——, *From Unification to Nazism: Reinterpreting the German Past*, Boston, Unwin Hyman, 1986.

Evans, Richard J., ed., *Society and Politics in Wilhelmine Germany*, London, Croom Helm, 1978.

Fay, Sidney B., *The Origins of the World War*, 2nd ed., New York, Macmillan, 1930.

Feldman, Gerald D., ed., *German Imperialism, 1914–1918: The Development of a Historical Debate*, New York, Wiley, 1972.

——, *Army, Industry, and Labor in Germany, 1914–1918* (1966), Providence, RI, Berg, 1992.

Field, Geoffrey G., *Evangelist of Race: The Germanic Vision of Houston Stewart Chamberlain*, New York, Columbia University Press, 1981.

Fischer, Fritz, *Germany's Aims in the First World War*, New York, Norton, 1967.

——, *World Power or Decline: The Controversy over Germany's Aims in the First World War*, trans. Lancelot L. Farrar, Robert Kimber, and Rita Kimber, New York, Norton, 1974.

——, *War of Illusions: German Policies from 1911 to 1914*, New York, Norton, 1975.

——, *From Kaiserreich to Third Reich: Elements of Continuity in German History, 1871–1945*, trans. Roger Fletcher, London, Allen & Unwin, 1986.

Foley, Robert T., *German Strategy and the Path to Verdun: Erich von Falkenhayn and the Development of Attrition, 1870–1916*, Cambridge, Cambridge University Press, 2005.

Frankel, Richard E., *Bismarck's Shadow: The Cult of Leadership and the Transformation of the German Right, 1898–1945*, Oxford and New York, Berg, 2005.

Gall, Lothar, *Bismarck: The White Revolutionary*, trans. J. A. Underwood, London, Allen & Unwin, 1985.

Gerard, James W., *My Four Years in Germany*, New York, George H. Doran, 1917.

Goodrick-Clarke, Nicholas, *The Occult Roots of Nazism: Secret Aryan Cults and Their Influence on Nazi Ideology*, New York, New York University Press, 1993.

Haffner, Sebastian, *The Ailing Empire: Germany from Bismarck to Hitler*, trans. Jean Steinberg, New York, Fromm International Publishing, 1989.

Hamann, Brigitte, *Hitler's Vienna: A Dictator's Apprenticeship*, trans. Thomas Thornton, New York, Oxford University Press, 1999.

Hamerow, Theodore, *The Social Foundations of German Unification, 1858–1871: Ideas and Institutions*, Princeton, Princeton University Press, 1969.

Herwig, Holger H., *The German Naval Officer Corps: A Social and Political History, 1890–1918*, Oxford, Clarendon Press, 1973.

——, *"Luxury" Fleet: The Imperial German Navy, 1888–1918*, London, Ashfield Press, 1987.

——, *The First World War: Germany and Austria-Hungary, 1914–1918*, London, Arnold, 1997.

Hewitson, Mark, *Germany and the Causes of the First World War*, Oxford, Berg, 2004.

Horne, John N., and Kramer, Alan, eds., *German Atrocities, 1914: A History of Denial*, New Haven, Yale University Press, 2001.

Hull, Isabel V., *Absolute Destruction: Military Culture and the Practices of War in Imperial Germany*, Ithaca, NY, Cornell University Press, 2005.

Jarausch, Konrad H., *Students, Society, and Politics in Imperial Germany: The Rise of Academic Illiberalism*, Princeton, Princeton University Press, 1982.

Kauders, Anthony, *German Politics and the Jews: Düsseldorf and Nuremberg 1910–1933*, Oxford, Clarendon Press, 1996.

Kehr, Eckart, *Economic Interest, Militarism, and Foreign Policy: Essays on German History*, trans. Grete Heinz, Berkeley, CA, University of California Press, 1977.

Kelly, Alfred, *The Descent of Darwin: The Popularization of Darwinism in Germany, 1860–1914*, Chapel Hill, University of North Carolina Press, 1981.

Kennedy, Paul, *The Rise of the Anglo-German Antagonism, 1860–1914*, London, Allen and Unwin, 1982.

Kitchen, Martin, *The German Officer Corps, 1890–1914*, Oxford, Oxford University Press, 1968.

——, *The Silent Dictatorship: The Politics of the German High Command under Hindenburg and Ludendorff, 1916–1918*, New York, Holmes & Meier, 1976.

Kocka, Jürgen, *Facing Total War: German Society, 1914–1918*, trans. Barbara Weinberger, Cambridge, MA, Harvard University Press, 1984.

——, and Mitchell, Alan, eds., *Bourgeois Society in Nineteenth-Century Europe*, Oxford, Berg, 1993.

Kohut, Thomas A., *Wilhelm II and the Germans: A Study in Leadership*, New York, Oxford University Press, 1991.

Kurlander, Eric, *The Price of Exclusion: Ethnicity, National Identity, and the Decline of German Liberalism, 1898–1933*, New York, Berghahn Books, 2006.

Laqueur, Walter, and Mosse, George L., eds., *1914: The Coming of the First World War*, New York, Harper & Row, 1966.

Levy, Richard S., *The Downfall of the Anti-semitic Political Parties in Imperial Germany*, New Haven, Yale University Press, 1975.

Liulevicius, Vejas Gabriel, *War Land on the Eastern Front: Culture, National Identity, and German Occupation in World War I*, Cambridge, Cambridge University Press, 2000.

Lowry, Bullitt, *Armistice 1918*, Kent, OH, Kent State University Press, 1996.

Marchand, Suzanne, and Lindenfeld, David, eds., *Germany at the Fin de Siècle: Culture, Politics, and Ideas*, Baton Rouge, Louisiana State University Press, 2004.

Mommsen, Wolfgang, *Imperial Germany 1867–1918: Politics, Culture, and Society in an Authoritarian State*, trans. Richard Deveson, London, Arnold, 1995.

Mosse, George L., *The Crisis of German Ideology: Intellectual Origins of the Third Reich*, New York, Grosset & Dunlop, 1964.

——, *Germans and Jews: The Right, the Left, and the Search for a "Third Force" in Pre-Nazi Germany*, New York, Grosset & Dunlap, 1970.

Pflanze, Otto, *Bismarck and the Development of Germany*, Vol. 1, *The Period of Unification, 1815–1871*; Vol. 2, *The Period of Consolidation, 1871–1880*; Vol. 3, *The Period of Fortification, 1880–1898*, Princeton, NJ, Princeton University Press, 1990.

Repp, Kevin, *Reformers, Critics, and the Paths of German Modernity: Anti-Politics and the Search for Alternatives, 1890–1914*, Cambridge, MA, Harvard University Press, 2000.

Rich, Norman, *Great Power Diplomacy since 1914*, New York, McGraw-Hill, 2003.

Ringer, Fritz K., *The Decline of the German Mandarins: The German Academic Community, 1890–1933*, Cambridge, MA, Harvard University Press, 1969.

Ritter, Gerhard, *The Schlieffen Plan: Critique of a Myth*, trans. Andrew and Eva Wilson, New York, Frederick A. Praeger, 1958.

Röhl, John C. G., *Germany without Bismarck: The Crisis of Government in the Second Reich, 1890–1900*, Berkeley, University of California Press, 1967.

——, *From Bismarck to Hitler: The Problem of Continuity in German History*, New York, Barnes & Noble, 1970.

——, *The Kaiser and His Court: Wilhelm II and the Government of Germany*, trans. Terence F. Cole, Cambridge, Cambridge University Press, 1995.

Rosenberg, Arthur, *Imperial Germany: The Birth of the German Republic, 1871–1918* (1931), trans. Ian F. D. Morrow, Boston, Beacon Press, 1964.

Rudin, Harry R., *Armistice 1918*, New Haven, Yale University Press, 1944.

Rüger, Jan, *The Great Naval Game: Britain and Germany in the Age of Empire*, Cambridge, Cambridge University Press, 2007.

Scheck, Rafael, *Alfred von Tirpitz and German Right-Wing Politics, 1914–1920*, Atlantic Highlands, NJ, Humanities Press, 1998.

Schorske, Carl E., *German Social Democracy, 1905–1917: The Development of the Great Schism*, Cambridge, MA, Harvard University Press, 1955.

——, *Fin-de-Siècle Vienna: Politics and Culture*, New York, Alfred A. Knopf, 1981.

Sheehan, James J., ed., *Imperial Germany*, New York, Franklin Watts, 1976.

Smith, Helmut Walser, *German Nationalism and Religious Conflict: Culture, Ideology, Politics, 1870–1914*, Princeton, Princeton University Press, 1995.

Smith, Woodruff D., *The Ideological Origins of Nazi Imperialism*, New York, Oxford University Press, 1986.

Stachura, Peter, *The German Youth Movement, 1900–1945*, New York, St. Martin's, 1981.

Stackelberg, Roderick, *Idealism Debased: From Völkisch Ideology to National Socialism*, Kent, OH, Kent State University, 1981.

Stern, Fritz, *The Politics of Cultural Despair: A Study in the Rise of the Germanic Ideology*, Garden City, NY, Doubleday Anchor, 1965.

——, *Gold and Iron: Bismarck, Bleichröder and the Building of the German Empire*, New York, Alfred A. Knopf, 1977.

——, *Dreams and Delusions: The Drama of German History*, New York, Vintage Books, 1989.

——, *The Failure of Illiberalism: Essays on the Political Culture of Modern Germany*, New York, Columbia University Press, 1992.

Strong, George V., *Seedtime for Fascism: The Disintegration of Austrian Political Culture, 1867–1918*, Armonk, NY, M. E. Sharpe, 1998.

Struve, Walter, *Elites against Democracy: Leadership Ideals in Bourgeois Political Thought in Germany, 1890–1933*, Princeton, Princeton University Press, 1973.

Szejnmann, Claus-Christian, *Nazism in Central Germany: The Brownshirts in "Red" Saxony*, New York, Berghahn Books, 1999.

Tal, Uriel, *Christians and Jews in Germany: Religion, Politics, and Ideology in the Second Reich, 1870–1914*, trans. Noah Jonathan Jacobs, Ithaca, NY, Cornell University Press, 1975.

Taylor, A. J. P., *Bismarck: The Man and the Statesman*, New York, Alfred A. Knopf, 1955.

Turda, Marius, *The Idea of National Superiority in Central Europe, 1880–1918*, Lewiston, NY, Edwin Mellen, 2004.

——, and Weindling, Paul, eds., *"Blood and Homeland": Eugenics and Racial Nationalism in Central and Southeast Europe, 1900–1940*, Budapest and New York, Central European University Press, 2007.

Verhey, Jeffrey, *The Spirit of 1914: Militarism, Myth, and Mobilization in Germany*, Cambridge, Cambridge University Press, 2000.

Volkov, Shulamit, *The Rise of Popular Antimodernism in Germany: The Urban Master Artisans, 1873–1896*, Princeton, Princeton University Press, 1978.

Wehler, Hans Ulrich, *The German Empire, 1871–1918*, trans. Kim Traynor, Providence, RI, Berg, 1985.

Weindling, Paul, *Health, Race, and German Politics*, Cambridge, Cambridge University Press, 1993.

Wiese, Christian, *Challenging Colonial Discourse: Jewish Studies and Protestant Theology in Wilhelmine Germany*, trans. Barbara Harshav and Christian Wiese, Leiden and Boston, Brill, 2005.

Wildenthal, Lora, *German Women for Empire, 1884–1945*, Durham, Duke University Press, 2001.

Zuber, Terence, *Inventing the Schlieffen Plan: German War Planning, 1871–1914*, Oxford, Oxford University Press, 2002.

4 The Weimar Republic, 1918–33

Abraham, David, *The Collapse of the Weimar Republic: Political Economy and Crisis*, 2nd ed., New York, Holmes & Meier, 1986.

Bahr, Ehrhard, *Weimar on the Pacific: German Exile Culture in Los Angeles and the Crisis of Modernism*, Berkeley, University of California Press, 2007.

Balderston, Theo, *Economics and Politics in the Weimar Republic*, Cambridge, Cambridge University Press, 2002.

Baranowski, Shelley, *The Sanctity of Rural Life: Nobility, Protestantism, and Nazism in Weimar Prussia*, Oxford, Oxford University Press, 1995.

Bessel, Richard, *Germany after the First World War*, Oxford, Clarendon Press, 1993.

Bookbinder, Paul, *Weimar Germany: The Republic of the Reasonable*, Manchester, Manchester University Press, 1996.

Borg, Daniel R., *The Old-Prussian Church and the Weimar Republic: A Study in Political Adjustment, 1917–1929*, Hanover, NH, University Press of New England, 1984.

Breitman, Richard, *German Socialism and Weimar Democracy*, Chapel Hill, University of North Carolina Press, 1981.

Brenner, Michael, *The Renaissance of Jewish Culture in Weimar Germany*, New Haven, Yale University Press, 1996.

Broszat, Martin, *German National Socialism, 1919–1945*, trans. Kurt Rosenbaum and Inge Pauli Boehm, Santa Barbara, CA, Clio Press, 1966.

——, *Hitler and the Collapse of Weimar Germany*, trans. V. R. Berghahn, Leamington Spa, Berg, 1987.

Brustein, William, *The Logic of Evil: The Social Origins of the Nazi Party, 1925–1933*, New Haven, Yale University Press, 1996.

Caldwell, Peter C., and Scheuerman, William E., *From Liberal Democracy to Fascism*, Boston, Humanities Press, 2000.

Caplan, Jane, *Government without Administration: State and Civil Service in Weimar and Nazi Germany*, Oxford, Clarendon Press, 1988.

Carsten, F. L., *Revolution in Central Europe 1918–1919*, Berkeley, University of California Press, 1972.

——, *The Reichswehr and Politics 1918–1933*, Berkeley, University of California Press, 1973.

Childers, Thomas, *The Nazi Voter: The Social Foundations of Fascism in Germany, 1919–1933*, Chapel Hill, University of North Carolina Press, 1983.

——, ed., *The Formation of the Nazi Constituency 1919–1933*, Totowa, NJ, Barnes & Noble, 1986.

Deak, Istvan, *Weimar Germany's Left-Wing Intellectuals: A Political History of the Weltbühne and Its Circle*, Berkeley, University of California Press, 1968.

Diehl, James M., *Paramilitary Politics in Weimar Germany*, Bloomington, Indiana University Press, 1977.

Dobkowski, Michael N., and Wallimann, Isidor, eds., *Towards the Holocaust: The Social and Economic Collapse of the Weimar Republic*, Westport, CT, Greenwood Press, 1983.

——, eds., *Radical Perspectives on the Rise of Fascism in Germany 1919–1945*, New York, Monthly Review Press, 1989.

Dorpalen, Andreas, *Hindenburg and the Weimar Republic*, Princeton, NJ, Princeton University Press, 1964.

Eschenburg, Theodor, Fraenkel, Ernst, Sontheimer, Kurt, *et al.*, *The Path to Dictatorship 1918–1933*, trans. John Conway, New York, Frederick A. Praeger, 1967.

Feldman, Gerald D., *The Great Disorder: Politics, Economics, and Society in the German Inflation, 1914–1924*, New York, Oxford University Press, 1997.

Fritzsche, Peter, *Rehearsals for Fascism: Populism and Political Mobilization in Weimar Germany*, New York, Oxford University Press, 1990.

——, *Germans into Nazis*, Cambridge, MA, Harvard University Press, 1998.

Galbraith, John Kenneth, *The Great Crash 1929* (1954), repr. Boston, Houghton Mifflin, 1988.

Garraty, John A., *The Great Depression: An Inquiry into the Causes, Course, and Consequences of the Worldwide Depression of the Nineteen-Thirties, as Seen by Contemporaries and in the Light of History*, New York, Harcourt Brace Jovanovich, 1986.

Gay, Peter, *Weimar Culture: The Outsider as Insider*, New York, Harper & Row, 1968.

Gerwarth, Robert, *The Bismarck Myth: Weimar Germany and the Legacy of the Iron Chancellor*, Oxford, Clarendon Press, 2005.

Gordon, Harold J., *The Reichswehr and the German Republic, 1919–1926*, Princeton, Princeton University Press, 1957.

——, *Hitler and the Beer Hall Putsch*, Princeton, Princeton University Press, 1972.

Grathwol, Robert P., *Stresemann and the DNVP: Reconciliation or Revenge in German Foreign Policy 1924–1928*, Lawrence, The Regents Press of Kansas, 1980.

Grunberger, Richard, *Red Rising in Bavaria*, New York, St. Martin's, 1973.

Haffner, Sebastian, *Failure of a Revolution: Germany 1918–1919*, trans. Georg Rapp, Chicago, Banner Press, 1973.

Harsch, Donna, *German Social Democracy and the Rise of Nazism*, Chapel Hill, University of North Carolina Press, 1993.

Heberle, Rudolf, *From Democracy to Nazism: A Regional Case Study on Political Parties in Germany*, New York, Grosset & Dunlap, 1970.

Herf, Jeffrey, *Reactionary Modernism: Technology, Culture and Politics in Weimar and the Third Reich*, Cambridge, Cambridge University Press, 1984.

Holborn, Hajo, *Republic to Reich: The Making of the Nazi Revolution*, New York, Pantheon, 1972.

Hughes, Michael L., *Paying for the German Inflation*, Chapel Hill, NC, University of North Carolina Press, 1988.

Jelavich, Peter, *Berlin Alexanderplatz: Radio, Film, and the Death of Weimar Culture*, Berkeley and Los Angeles, University of California Press, 2006.

Jones, Larry Eugene, *German Liberalism and the Dissolution of the Weimar Party System, 1918–1933*, Chapel Hill, University of North Carolina Press, 1988.

Kaes, Anton, Jay, Martin, and Dimendberg, Edward, eds., *The Weimar Republic Sourcebook*, Berkeley, University of California Press, 1994.

Kellogg, Michael, *The Russian Roots of Nazism: White Émigrés and the Making of National Socialism, 1917–1945*, Cambridge, Cambridge University Press, 2005.

Kershaw, Ian, ed., *Weimar: Why Did Weimar Democracy Fail?*, New York, St. Martin's, 1990.

Keynes, John Maynard, *The General Theory of Employment, Interest and Money* (1936), repr. London, Macmillan, 1951.

Klemperer, Klemens von, *Germany's New Conservatism: Its History and Dilemma in the Twentieth Century*, Princeton, Princeton University Press, 1957.

Knox, MacGregor, *On the Threshold of Power, 1922/1933*, Vol. I, *Origins and Dynamics of the Fascist and National Socialist Dictatorships*, Cambridge, Cambridge University Press, 2008.

Koshar, Rudy, ed., *Splintered Classes: Politics and the Lower Middle Classes in Interwar Europe*, New York, Holmes & Meier, 1990.

Lane, Barbara Miller, and Rupp, Leila J., eds., *Nazi Ideology before 1933: A Documentation*, Austin, University of Texas Press, 1978.

Large, David Clay, *Where Ghosts Walked: Munich's Road to the Third Reich*, New York, Norton, 1997.

Lebovics, Herman, *Social Conservatism and the Middle Classes in Germany, 1914–1933*, Princeton, Princeton University Press, 1969.

Lee, Marshall M., and Michalka, Wolfgang, *German Foreign Policy 1917–1933: Continuity or Break?*, Leamington Spa, Berg, 1987.

Leopold, John A., *Alfred Hugenberg: The Radical Nationalist Campaign against the Weimar Republic*, New Haven, Yale University Press, 1977.

McElligott, Anthony, *Contested City: Municipal Politics and the Rise of the Nazis in Altona, 1917–1937*, Ann Arbor, University of Michigan Press, 1998.

——, *Rethinking the Weimar Republic: Citizens and State in Germany, 1916–1936*, New York, Arnold, 2001.

——, *Rethinking the Weimar Republic: Authority and Authoritarianism, 1916–1936*, London, Hodder Arnold, 2005.

McNeil, William C., *American Money and the Weimar Republic: Economics and Politics on the Eve of the Great Depression*, New York, Columbia University Press, 1986.

Maier, Charles S., *Recasting Bourgeois Europe: Stabilization in France, Germany, and Italy in the Decade after World War I*, Princeton, Princeton University Press, 1975.

Mayer, Arno, *Politics and Diplomacy of Peacemaking: Containment and Counter-Revolution at Versailles*, New York, Knopf, 1967.

Mitchell, Allan, *Revolution in Bavaria, 1918–1919: The Eisner Regime and the Soviet Republic*, Princeton, Princeton University Press, 1965.

Mommsen, Hans, *From Weimar to Auschwitz*, trans. Philip O'Connor, Princeton, Princeton University Press, 1991.

——, *The Rise and Fall of Weimar Democracy*, trans. Elborg Forster and Larry Eugene Jones, Chapel Hill, University of North Carolina Press, 1996.

Niewyk, Donald L., *Socialist, Anti-Semite, and Jew: German Social Democracy Confronts the Problem of Anti-Semitism, 1918–1933*. Baton Rouge, Louisiana State University Press, 1971.

Nolan, Mary, *Visions of Modernity: American Business and the Modernization of Germany*, New York, Oxford University Press, 1994.

Patch, William L., *Heinrich Brüning and the Dissolution of the Weimar Republic*, Cambridge, Cambridge University Press, 1998.

Peukert, Detlev J. K., *The Weimar Republic: The Crisis of Classical Modernity*, trans. Richard Deveson, New York, Hill and Wang, 1992.

Potter, Pamela M., *Most German of the Arts: Musicology and Society from the Weimar Republic to the End of Hitler's Reich*, New Haven, Yale University Press, 1998.

Pridham, Geoffrey, *The Nazi Movement in Bavaria, 1923–1933*, New York, Harper & Row, 1973.

Ryder, A. J., *The German Revolution of 1918: A Study of German Socialism in War and Revolt*, Cambridge, Cambridge University Press, 1967.

Sneeringer, Julia, *Winning Women's Votes: Propaganda and Politics in Weimar Germany*, Chapel Hill, University of North Carolina Press, 2002.

Taylor, Simon, *Prelude to Genocide: Nazi Ideology and the Struggle for Power*, New York, St. Martin's, 1985.

Turner, Henry Ashby, Jr., *Stresemann and the Politics of the Weimar Republic*, Princeton, Princeton University Press, 1963.

Waite, Robert G. L., *Vanguard of Nazism: The Free Corps Movement in Postwar Germany, 1918–1923*, Cambridge, MA, Harvard University Press, 1952.

Watt, Richard M., *The Kings Depart: The Tragedy of Germany, Versailles and the German Revolution*, New York, Simon and Schuster, 1968.

Weitz, Eric D., *Weimar Germany: Promise and Tragedy*, Princeton, Princeton University Press, 2007.

Wheeler-Bennett, John W., *The Nemesis of Power: The German Army in Politics, 1918–1945*, London, Macmillan, 1953.

Woods, Roger, *The Conservative Revolution in the Weimar Republic*, New York, St. Martin's, 1996.

5 The Nazis and the Third Reich

Adam, Peter, *The Arts of the Third Reich*, New York, Harry N. Abrams, 1992.

Allen, William Sheridan, *The Nazi Seizure of Power in a Single German Town*, rev. ed., New York, Franklin, Watts, 1984.

Aly, Götz, *Hitler's Beneficiaries: Plunder, Racial War, and the Nazi Welfare State*, New York, Metropolitan Books, 2006.

——, Chroust, Peter, and Pross, Christian, *Cleansing the Fatherland: Nazi Medicine and Racial Hygiene*, Baltimore, Johns Hopkins University Press, 1994.

Amkraut, Brian, *Between Home and Homeland: Youth Aliyah from Nazi Germany*, Tuscaloosa, University of Alabama Press, 2006.

Anderson, Mark M., ed., *Hitler's Exiles: Personal Stories of the Flight from Nazi Germany to America*, New York, New Press, 1998.

Ayçoberry, Pierre, *The Nazi Question: An Essay on the Interpretations of National Socialism (1922–1975)*, trans. Robert Hurley, New York, Pantheon, 1981.

——, *The Social History of the Third Reich 1933–1945*, trans. Janet Lloyd, New York, New Press, 1999.

Baird, Jay W., *To Die For Germany: Heroes in the Nazi Pantheon*, Bloomington, Indiana University Press, 1992.

——, *Hitler's War Poets: Literature and Politics in the Third Reich*, Cambridge, Cambridge University Press, 2007.

Bajohr, Frank, *"Aryanization" in Hamburg: The Economic Exclusion of Jews and the Confiscation of Their Property in Nazi Germany*, New York, Berghahn, 2002.

Baranowski, Shelley, *The Confessing Church: Conservative Elites and the Nazi State*, New York, Edwin Mellen, 1986.

——, *Strength through Joy: Consumerism and Mass Tourism in the Third Reich*, Cambridge, Cambridge University Press, 2004.

Barkai, Avraham, *Nazi Economics: Ideology, Theory, and Policy*, trans. Ruth Hadass-Vashitz, New Haven, Yale University Press, 1990.

Baynes, Norman H., ed., *The Speeches of Adolf Hitler, April 1933–August 1939*, 2 vols., New York, Howard Fertig, 1969.

Bendersky, Joseph W., *A History of Nazi Germany*, Chicago, Nelson-Hall, 1985.

Bergen, Doris L., *Twisted Cross: The German Christian Movement in the Third Reich*, Chapel Hill, University of North Carolina Press, 1996.

Bergerson, Andrew Stuart, *Ordinary Germans in Extraordinary Times: The Nazi Revolution in Hildesheim*, Bloomington, University of Indiana Press, 2004.

Bessel, Richard, ed., *Life in the Third Reich*, Oxford, Oxford University Press, 1987.

Beyerchen, Alan D., *Scientists under Hitler: Politics and the Physics Community in the Third Reich*, New Haven, Yale University Press, 1977.

Bracher, Karl Dietrich, *The German Dictatorship: The Origins, Structure, and Effects of National Socialism*, trans. Jean Steinberg, New York, Praeger, 1970.

Bramstead, Ernest K., *Goebbels and National Socialist Propaganda, 1925–1945*, East Lansing, Michigan State University Press, 1965.

Bridenthal, Renate, Grossmann, Atina, and Kaplan, Marion, eds., *When Biology Became Destiny: Women in Weimar and Nazi Germany*, New York, Monthly Review Press, 1984.

Broszat, Martin, *German National Socialism, 1919–1945*, trans. Kurt Rosenbaum and Inge Pauli Boehm, Santa Barbara, CA, Clio Press, 1966.

——, *The Hitler State: The Foundation and Development of the Internal Structure of the Third Reich*, New York, Longman, 1981.

Bukey, Evan Burr, *Hitler's Austria: Popular Sentiment in the Nazi Era, 1938–1945*, Chapel Hill, University of North Carolina Press, 1999.

Bullock, Alan, *Hitler: A Study in Tyranny*, rev. ed., New York, Harper & Row, 1964.

——, *Hitler and Stalin: Parallel Lives*, New York, Alfred A. Knopf, 1992.

Burleigh, Michael, *Germany Turns Eastwards: A Study of Ostforschung in the Third Reich*, Cambridge, Cambridge University Press, 1988.

——, *Death and Deliverance: Euthanasia in Germany 1900–1945*, Cambridge, Cambridge University Press, 1994.

——, *The Third Reich: A New History*, New York, NY, Hill and Wang, 2000.

——, and Wippermann, Wolfgang, *The Racial State: Germany 1933–1945*, Cambridge, Cambridge University Press, 1991.

Campbell, Bruce, *The SA Generals and the Rise of Nazism*, Lexington, The University Press of Kentucky, 1998.

Carr, William, *Arms, Autarky and Aggression: A Study in German Foreign Policy, 1933–1939*, New York, W. W. Norton, 1973.

Carsten, F. L., *The German Workers and the Nazis*, Aldershot, Scolar Press, 1995.

Chandler, Andrew, ed., *The Moral Imperative: New Essays on the Ethics of Resistance in National Socialist Germany, 1933–1945*, Boulder, CO, Westview, 1998.

Childers, Thomas, and Caplan, Jane, eds., *Reevaluating the Third Reich*, New York, Holmes & Meier, 1993.

Churchill, Winston S., *Great Contemporaries*, New York, G. P. Putnam's Sons, 1937.

Clinefelder, Joan L., *Artists for the Reich: Culture and Race from Weimar to Nazi Germany*, Oxford, Berg, 2005.

Conway, John S., *The Nazi Persecution of the Churches, 1933–1945*, New York, Basic Books, 1968.

Cornwell, John, *Hitler's Pope: The Secret History of Pius XII*, New York, Viking, 1999.

——, *Hitler's Scientists: Science, War, and the Devil's Pact*, New York, Viking, 2003.

Crew, David F., ed., *Nazism and German Society, 1933–1945*, London, Routledge, 1994.

Cuomo, Glen R., ed., *National Socialist Cultural Policy*, New York, St. Martin's, 1995.

Deichmann, Ute, *Biologists under Hitler*, Cambridge, MA, Harvard University Press, 1996.

Diner, Dan, *Studies on Germany, Nazism, and the Holocaust*, Berkeley, University of California Press, 2000.

Dülffer, Jost, *Nazi Germany 1933–1945: Faith and Annihilation*, trans. Dean Scott McMurry, London, Arnold, 1996.

Eberle, Henrik, and Uhl, Matthias, eds., *The Hitler Book: The Secret Dossier Prepared for Stalin from the Interrogations of Hitler's Personal Aides*, trans. Giles MacDonogh, New York, Public Affairs, 2005.

Engelmann, Bernt, *In Hitler's Germany: Daily Life in the Third Reich*, trans. Krishna Winston, New York, Pantheon, 1986.

Ericksen, Robert P., *Theologians under Hitler: Gerhard Kittel, Paul Althaus, and Emanuel Hirsch*, New Haven, Yale University Press, 1985.

Etlin, Richard A., ed., *Art, Culture, and Media under the Third Reich*, Chicago, University of Chicago Press, 2002.

Evans, Richard J., *The Coming of the Third Reich*, London, Penguin Books, 2003.

——, *The Third Reich in Power*, London, Penguin Books, 2005.

Farquharson, J. E., *The Plough and the Swastika: N.S.D.A.P. and Agriculture in Germany, 1928–1945*, Bloomington, IN, Indiana University Press, 1976.

Feder, Gottfried, *Hitler's Official Programme and Its Fundamental Ideas* (1934), repr. New York, Howard Fertig, 1971.

Fest, Joachim C., *The Face of the Third Reich: Portraits of the Nazi Leadership*, trans. Michael Bullock, New York, Pantheon, 1970.

——, *Hitler*, trans. Richard and Clara Winston, New York, Vintage Books, 1975.

——, *Inside Hitler's Bunker: The Last Days of the Third Reich*, trans. Margo Bettauer Dembo, New York, Picador, 2004.

Fischer, Conan, *The Rise of the Nazis*, Manchester, University of Manchester Press, 1995.

Fischer, Klaus P., *Nazi Germany: A New History*, New York, Continuum, 1995.

Fraenkel, Ernst, *The Dual State: A Contribution to the Theory of Dictatorship*, New York, Octagon, 1969.

Frei, Norbert, *National Socialist Rule in Germany: The Führer State 1933–1945*, trans. Simon B. Steyne, Oxford, Blackwell, 1993.

Friedländer, Saul, *Pius XII and the Third Reich: A Documentation*, New York, Alfred A. Knopf, 1966.

——, *Reflections of Nazism: An Essay on Kitsch and Death*, New York, Harper & Row, 1984.

Gellately, Robert, *The Gestapo and German Society: Enforcing Racial Policy 1933–1945*, Oxford, Clarendon Press, 1990.

——, *Backing Hitler: Consent and Coercion in Nazi Germany*, Oxford, Oxford University Press, 2001.

——, and Stolzfus, Nathan, eds., *Social Outsiders in Nazi Germany*, Princeton, Princeton University Press, 2001.

Geyer, Michael, and Boyer, John W., eds., *Resistance against the Third Reich, 1933–1990*, Chicago, University of Chicago Press, 1994.

Giles, Geoffrey J., *Students and National Socialism in Germany*, Princeton, Princeton University Press, 1985.

Gispen, Kees, *Poems in Steel: National Socialism and the Politics of Inventing from Weimar to Bonn*, New York, Berghahn Books, 2002.

Graml, Hermann, *Antisemitism in the Third Reich*, trans. Tim Kirk, Oxford, Blackwell, 1992.

——, et al., *The German Resistance to Hitler*, Berkeley, University of California Press, 1970.

Gregor, Neil, ed., *Nazism, War and Genocide: Essays in Honour of Jeremy Noakes*, Exeter, University of Exeter Press, 2005.

Griech-Polelle, Beth A., *Bishop von Galen: German Catholicism and National Socialism*, New Haven, Yale University Press, 2002.

Grunberger, Richard, *The 12-Year Reich: A Social History of Nazi Germany 1933–1945*, New York, Holt, Rinehart and Winston, 1971.

Gruner, Wolf, *Jewish Forced Labor under the Nazis: Economic Needs and Racial Aims, 1938–1944*, trans. Kathleen M. Dell'Orto, New York, Cambridge University Press, 2006.

Guenther, Irene, *Nazi Chic? Fashioning Women in the Third Reich*, Oxford, Berg, 2004.

Haffner, Sebastian, *The Meaning of Hitler*, trans. Ewald Osers, Cambridge, MA, Harvard University Press, 1983.

Hamilton, Richard F., *Who Voted for Hitler?*, Princeton, Princeton University Press, 1982.

Hayes, Peter, *Industry and Ideology: IG Farben in the Nazi Era*, Cambridge, Cambridge University Press, 1987.

——, *From Cooperation to Complicity: Degussa in the Third Reich*, Cambridge, Cambridge University Press, 2004.

Heilbronner, Oded, *Catholicism, Political Culture, and the Countryside: A Social History of the Nazi Party in South Germany*, Ann Arbor, University of Michigan Press, 1997.

Helmreich, Ernst Christian, *The German Churches under Hitler: Background, Struggle, and Epilogue*, Detroit, Wayne State University Press, 1979.

Herzog, Dagmar, *Sexuality and German Fascism*, New York, Berghahn, 2005.

Hiden, John, and Farquharson, John, *Explaining Hitler's Germany: Historians and the Third Reich*, Totowa, NJ, Barnes & Noble, 1983.

Hildebrand, Klaus, *The Foreign Policy of the Third Reich*, trans. Anthony Fothergill, London, Batsford, 1973.

——, *The Third Reich*, trans. P. S. Falla, London, George Allen & Unwin, 1984.

Hillgruber, Andreas, *Germany and the Two World Wars*, trans. William C. Kirby, Cambridge, MA, Harvard University Press, 1981.

Hitler, Adolf, *Mein Kampf*, trans. Ralph Manheim, Boston, Houghton Mifflin, 1971.

Hoffmann, Peter, *German Resistance to Hitler*, Cambridge, MA, Harvard University Press, 1988.

———, *Stauffenberg: A Family History, 1905–1944*, Cambridge, Cambridge University Press, 1995.

Höhne, Heinz, *The Order of the Death's Head*, New York, Ballantine, 1977.

Hughes, H. Stuart, *The Sea Change: The Migration of Social Thought, 1930–1965*, New York, Harper & Row, 1975.

International Council for Philosophy and Humanistic Studies, *The Third Reich*, London, Weidenfeld & Nicolson, 1955.

Jäckel, Eberhard, *Hitler's World View: A Blueprint for Power*, trans. Herbert Arnold, Cambridge, MA, Harvard University Press, 1981.

Jacobsen, Hans-Adolf, and Smith, Arthur L., Jr., *The Nazi Party and the German Foreign Office*, London, Routledge, 2007.

James, Harold, *The Nazi Dictatorship and the Deutsche Bank*, New York, Cambridge University Press, 2004.

Johnson, Eric A., *Nazi Terror: The Gestapo, Jews, and Ordinary Germans*, New York, NY, Basic Books, 1999.

———, and Reuband, Karl-Heinz, *What We Knew: Terror, Mass Murder, and Everyday Life in Nazi Germany*, New York, NY, Basic Books, 2005.

Kater, Michael H., *The Nazi Party: A Social Profile of Members and Leaders, 1919–1945*, Cambridge, MA, Harvard University Press, 1983.

———, *Doctors under Hitler*, Chapel Hill, NC, University of North Carolina Press, 1989.

———, *Hitler Youth*, Cambridge, MA, Harvard University Press, 2004.

Kershaw, Ian, *Popular Opinion and Political Dissent in the Third Reich: Bavaria 1933–1945*, Oxford, Clarendon Press, 1983.

———, *The "Hitler Myth": Image and Reality in the Third Reich*, Oxford, Oxford University Press, 1987.

———, *Hitler*, London, Longman, 1991.

———, *Hitler*, Vol. 1, *1889–1936: Hubris*, Vol. 2, *1936–1945: Nemesis*, New York, Norton, 1999–2000.

———, *The Nazi Dictatorship: Problems and Perspectives of Interpretation*, 4th ed., London, Hodder Arnold, 2000.

———, *Making Friends with Hitler: Lord Londonderry, the Nazis, and the Road to War*, New York, Penguin, 2004.

———, and Lewin, Moshe, eds., *Stalinism and Nazism: Dictatorships in Comparison*, Cambridge, Cambridge University Press, 1997.

Kirk, Tim, *The Longman Companion to Nazi Germany*, London and New York, Longman, 1995.

———, *Nazism and the Working Class in Austria: Industrial Unrest and Political Dissent in the National Community*, Cambridge, Cambridge University Press, 1996.

Klemperer, Victor, *I Will Bear Witness: A Diary of the Nazi Years*, Vol. 1, *1933–1941*, Vol. 2, *The Nazi Years*, trans. Martin Chalmers, New York, Random House, 1998–99.

———, *The Language of the Third Reich: LTI-Lingua Tertii Imperii: A Philologist's Notebook*, trans. Martin Brady, London, Athlone Press, 2000.

Koonz, Claudia, *Mothers in the Fatherland: Women, the Family and Nazi Politics*, New York, St. Martin's, 1987.

———, *The Nazi Conscience*, Cambridge, MA, Harvard University Press, 2003.

Koshar, Rudy, *Social Life, Local Politics, and Nazism, 1880–1935*, Chapel Hill, NC, University of North Carolina Press, 1986.

Krausnick, Helmut, *et al.*, *Anatomy of the SS State*, trans. Richard Barry, Marian Jackson, and Dorothy Long, New York, Walker and Company, 1968.

Kühl, Stefan, *The Nazi Connection: Eugenics, American Racism, and German National Socialism*, New York, Oxford University Press, 1994.

Large, David Clay, *Between Two Fires: Europe's Path in the 1930s*, New York, Norton, 1991.

——, ed., *Contending with Hitler: Varieties of German Resistance in the Third Reich*, Cambridge, Cambridge University Press, 1991.

Leitz, Christian, *The Third Reich: The Essential Readings*, Malden, MA, Blackwell, 1999.

Lewy, Günter, *The Catholic Church and Nazi Germany*, New York, McGraw-Hill, 1964.

Lixfeld, Hannjost, *Folklore and Fascism: The Reich Institute for German Volkskunde*, ed. and trans. James R. Dow, Bloomington, IN, Indiana University Press, 1994.

Lochner, Louis P., ed., *The Goebbels Diaries*, New York, Doubleday, 1948.

Lüdtke, Alf, ed., *The History of Everyday Life: Reconstructing Historical Experiences and Ways of Life*, trans. William Templer, Princeton, NJ, Princeton University Press, 1995.

Lukacs, John, *The Hitler of History*, New York, Alfred A. Knopf, 1997.

McElligott, Anthony, and Kirk, Tim, eds., *Working towards the Führer: Essays in Honour of Sir Ian Kershaw*, Manchester, Manchester University Press, 2003.

McFarland-Icke, Bronwyn Rebekah, *Nurses in Nazi Germany: Moral Choice in History*, Princeton, Princeton University Press, 1999.

McKale, Donald M., *The Nazi Party Courts: Hitler's Management of Conflict in His Movement, 1921–1945*, Lawrence, University Press of Kansas, 1974.

Macrakis, Kristie, *Surviving the Swastika: Scientific Research in Nazi Germany*, New York and Oxford, Oxford University Press, 1993.

Maier, Charles S., Hoffmann, Stanley, and Gould, Andrew, eds., *The Rise of the Nazi Regime: Historical Reassessments*, Boulder, CO, Westview, 1986.

Mason, Timothy, *Social Policy in the Third Reich: The Working Class and the "National Community," 1918–1939*, Jane Caplan, ed., trans. John Broadwin, Oxford, Berg Publishers, 1993.

Matheson, Peter, ed., *The Third Reich and the Christian Churches*, Edinburgh, T & T Clark, 1981.

Meissner, Hans-Otto, *Magda Goebbels: The First Lady of the Third Reich*, trans. Gwendolen Mary Keeble, New York, Dial Press, 1980.

Michaud, Eric, *The Cult of Art in Nazi Germany* (1996), Stanford, Stanford University Press, 2004.

Miercejewski, Alfred, *Hitler's Trains: The German National Railway and the Third Reich*, Chapel Hill, University of North Carolina Press, 2000.

Mommsen, Hans, ed., *The Third Reich between Vision and Reality: New Perspectives on German History 1918–1945*, Oxford and New York, Berg, 2001.

Mosse, George, ed., *Nazi Culture: Intellectual, Cultural, and Social Life in the Third Reich*, New York, Grosset and Dunlap, 1966.

Mühlberger, Detlev, *Hitler's Followers: Studies in the Sociology of the Nazi Movement*, London, Routledge, 1991.

——, *Hitler's Voice: Der Völkische Beobachter, 1920–1933*, Bern, Peter Lang, 2004.

Müller, Ingo, *Hitler's Justice: The Courts of the Third Reich*, trans. Deborah Lucas Schneider, Cambridge, MA, Harvard University Press, 1991.

Neumann, Franz, *Behemoth: The Structure and Practice of National Socialism 1933–1944* (1944), repr. New York, Harper & Row, 1966.

Nicosia, Francis R., *The Third Reich and the Palestine Question*, Austin, University of Texas Press, 1985.

Noakes, Jeremy, *The Nazi Party in Lower Saxony, 1921–1933*, Oxford, Oxford University Press, 1971.

——, and Pridham, Geoffrey, eds., *Nazism 1919–1945: A History in Documents and Eyewitness Accounts*, Vol. 1, *The Nazi Party, State and Society, 1919–1939*; Vol. 2, *Foreign Policy, War and Racial Extermination*, New York, Schocken, 1983–88.

——, *Nazism 1919–1945: A Documentary Reader*, 4 vols., Exeter, University of Exeter Press, 1998.

Office of United States Chief of Counsel for Prosecution of Axis Criminality, *Nazi Conspiracy and Aggression*, 8 vols., Washington, DC, US Government Printing Office, 1946.

Orlow, Dietrich, *The History of the Nazi Party, 1919–1933*, Pittsburgh, University of Pittsburgh Press, 1969.

——, *The History of the Nazi Party, 1933–1945*, Pittsburgh, University of Pittsburgh Press, 1973.

Overy, R. J., *War and Economy in the Third Reich*, Oxford, Clarendon Press, 1994.

——, *The Nazi Economic Recovery 1932–1938*, 2nd ed., Cambridge, Cambridge University Press, 1996.

——, *The Penguin Historical Atlas of the Third Reich*, London, Penguin, 1996.

——, *The Dictators: Hitler's Germany and Stalin's Russia*, New York, W. W. Norton, 2004.

Padfield, Peter, *Dönitz: The Last Führer*, New York, Harper & Row, 1984.

Paret, Peter, *An Artist against the Third Reich: Ernst Barlach, 1933–1938*, Cambridge, Cambridge University Press, 2003.

Pauley, Bruce F., *Hitler and the Forgotten Nazis: A History of Austrian National Socialism*, Chapel Hill, University of North Carolina Press, 1981.

Peterson, Edward N., *The Limits of Hitler's Power*, Princeton, Princeton University Press, 1969.

Petropolous, Jonathan, *Art as Politics in the Third Reich*, Chapel Hill, University of North Carolina Press, 1996.

——, *The Faustian Bargain: The Art World in Nazi Germany*, Oxford, Oxford University Press, 2000.

——, *Royals and the Reich: The Princes von Hessen in Nazi Germany*, Oxford and New York, Oxford University Press, 2006.

Peukert, Detlev J. K., *Inside Nazi Germany: Conformity, Opposition and Racism in Everyday Life*, trans. Richard Deveson, New Haven, Yale University Press, 1987.

Pine, Lisa, *Nazi Family Policy, 1933–1945*, Oxford, Berg, 1997.

——, *Hitler's National Community: Society and Culture in Nazi Germany*, London, Hodder Arnold, 2007.

Proctor, Robert N., *Racial Hygiene: Medicine under the Nazis*, Cambridge, MA, Harvard University Press, 1988.

——, *The Nazi War on Cancer*, Princeton, Princeton University Press, 1999.

Redles, David, *Hitler's Millennial Reich: Apocalyptic Belief and the Search for Salvation*, New York, New York University Press, 2005.

Renneberg, Monika, and Walker, Mark, eds., *Science, Technology and National Socialism*, Cambridge, Cambridge University Press, 1994.

Ritter, Gerhard, *The German Resistance: Carl Goerdeler's Struggle against Tyranny*, trans. R. T. Clark, New York, Praeger, 1959.

Rosenbaum, Ron, *Explaining Hitler: The Search for the Origins of his Evil*, New York, Random House, 1998.

Rothfels, Hans, *The German Opposition to Hitler: An Appraisal*, trans. Lawrence Wilson, Chicago, Henry Regnery, 1962.

Sax, Benjamin, and Kuntz, Dieter, *Inside Hitler's Germany: A Documentary History of Life in the Third Reich*, Lexington, MA, D. C. Heath, 1992.

Schoenbaum, David, *Hitler's Social Revolution: Class and Status in Nazi Germany, 1933–1939* (1966), repr. New York, Norton, 1980.

Scholder, Klaus, *The Churches and the Third Reich*, Vol. 1, *Preliminary History and the Time of Illusions, 1918–1934*, trans. John Bowden, Philadelphia, Fortress Press, 1988.

Shirer, William L., *The Rise and Fall of the Third Reich: A History of Nazi Germany*, New York, Simon and Schuster, 1960.

Smelser, Ronald, *Robert Ley: Hitler's Labor Front Leader*, Oxford, Berg, 1988.

Snell, John, ed., *The Nazi Revolution: Germany's Guilt or Germany's Fate*, New York, D. C. Heath, 1959.

——, and Mitchell, Alan, *The Nazi Revolution: Hitler's Dictatorship and the German Nation*, 2nd ed., Lexington, MA, D. C. Heath, 1973.

Snyder, Louis L., *Hitler's Third Reich: A Documentary History*, Chicago, Nelson-Hall, 1981.

——, *Encyclopedia of the Third Reich*, New York, Paragon House, 1989.

Sofsky, Wolfgang, *The Order of Terror: The Concentration Camp*, trans. William Templer, Princeton, NJ, Princeton University Press, 1997.

Speer, Albert, *Inside the Third Reich: Memoirs*, trans. Richard and Clara Winston, New York, Macmillan, 1970.

Spicer, Kevin P., *Resisting the Third Reich: The Catholic Clergy in Hitler's Berlin*, DeKalb, Northern Illinois University Press, 2004.

Spotts, Frederic, *Hitler and the Power of Aesthetics*, Woodstock and New York, Overlook Press, 2004.

Stachura, Peter, *Gregor Strasser and the Rise of Nazism*, London, Allen & Unwin, 1983.

Stackelberg, Roderick, *The Routledge Companion to Nazi Germany*, New York and London, Routledge, 2007.

——, and Winkle, Sally, eds., *The Nazi Germany Sourcebook: An Anthology of Texts*, London, Routledge, 2002.

Steigmann-Gall, Richard, *The Holy Reich: Nazi Conceptions of Christianity, 1919–1945*, Cambridge, Cambridge University Press, 2003.

Steinweis, Alan E., *Art, Ideology, and Economics in Nazi Germany: The Reich Chambers of Music, Theater, and the Visual Arts*, Chapel Hill, University of North Carolina Press, 1993.

——, *Studying the Jew: Scholarly Antisemitism in Nazi Germany*, Cambridge, MA, Harvard University Press, 2006.

——, and Rogers, Daniel E., eds., *The Impact of Nazism: New Perspectives on the Third Reich and Its Legacy*, Lincoln, NB, University of Nebraska Press, 2003.

Stephenson, Jill, *Women in Nazi Society*, New York, Barnes & Noble, 1975.

——, *The Nazi Organisation of Women*, London, Croom Helm, 1981.

——, *Hitler's Home Front: Württemberg under the Nazis*, New York, Hambledon Continuum, 2006.

Stern, J. P., *Hitler: The Führer and the People*, rev. ed., Berkeley, University of California Press, 1992.

Stibbe, Matthew, *Women in the Third Reich*, London, Arnold, 2003.

Stolzfus, Nathan, *Resistance of the Heart: Intermarriage and the Rosenstrasse Protest in Nazi Germany*, New York, Norton, 1996.

Stone, Dan, *Responses to Nazism in Britain, 1933–1939*, New York, Palgrave Macmillan, 2003.

Stone, Norman, *Hitler*, Boston, Little, Brown, 1980.

Szöllösi-Janze, Margit, ed., *Science in the Third Reich*, Oxford and New York, Berg, 2001.

Taylor, Telford, *Munich: The Price of Peace*, Garden City, NY, Doubleday, 1979.

Tilton, Timothy Alan, *Nazism, Neo-Nazism, and the Peasantry*, Bloomington, IN, Indiana University Press, 1975.

Tobias, Fritz, *The Reichstag Fire*, New York, Putnam, 1964.

Tooze, Adam, *The Wages of Destruction: The Making and Breaking of the Nazi Economy*, London, Allen Lane, 2006.

Traverso, Enzo, *The Origins of Nazi Violence*, New York, New Press, 2003.

Turner, Henry Ashby, Jr., *German Big Business and the Rise of Hitler*, New York, Oxford University Press, 1985.

——, *Hitler's Thirty Days to Power: January 1933*, Reading, MA, Addison-Wesley, 1996.

van der Vat, Dan, *The Good Nazi: The Life and Lies of Albert Speer*, Boston, Houghton Mifflin, 1997.

Von Lang, Jochen, *The Secretary Martin Bormann: The Man Who Manipulated Hitler*, trans. Christa Armstrong and Peter White, New York, Random House, 1979.

Von Maltitz, Horst, *The Evolution of Hitler's Germany: The Ideology, the Personality, the Moment*, New York, McGraw-Hill, 1961.

Wachsmann, Nikolaus, *Hitler's Prisons: Legal Terror in Nazi Germany*, New Haven, Yale University Press, 2004.

Walker, Lawrence D., *Hitler Youth and Catholic Youth, 1933–1936: A Study in Totalitarian Conquest*, Washington, DC, Catholic University of America Press, 1970.

Weikart, Richard, *From Darwin to Hitler: Evolutionary Ethics, Eugenics, and Racism in Germany*, New York, Palgrave Macmillan, 2004.

Weinberg, Gerhard L., *The Foreign Policy of Hitler's Germany: Diplomatic Revolution in Europe, 1933–1936*, Chicago, University of Chicago Press, 1970.

——, *The Foreign Policy of Hitler's Germany: Starting World War II, 1937–1939*, Chicago, University of Chicago Press, 1980.

Weitz, John, *Hitler's Banker: Hjalmar Horace Greeley Schacht*, Boston, Little, Brown, 1997.

Welch, David, ed., *Nazi Propaganda: The Power and the Limitations*, London, Croom Helm, 1983.

——, *The Third Reich: Politics and Propaganda*, London, Routledge, 1993.

Williams, Maurice, *Gau, Volk, and Reich: Friedrich Rainer and the Paradox of Austrian National Socialism*, Klagenfurt, Verlag des Geschichtsvereins für Kärnten, 2005.

Wistrich, Robert S., *Who's Who in Nazi Germany*, London, Routledge, 1995.

Zentner, Christian, and Bedürftig, Friedemann, eds., *The Encyclopedia of the Third Reich*, trans. Amy Hackett, New York, Da Capo Press, 1997.

Ziegler, Herbert F., *Nazi Germany's New Aristocracy: The SS Leadership, 1925–1939*, Princeton, Princeton University Press, 1989.

Zitelmann, Rainer, *Hitler: The Politics of Seduction*, trans. Helmut Bogler, London, London House, 1999.

6 World War II

Bartov, Omer, *Hitler's Army: Soldiers, Nazis, and War in the Third Reich*, New York, Oxford University Press, 1992.

——, Grossmann, Atina, and Nolan, Mary, eds., *Crimes of War: Guilt and Denial in the Twentieth Century*, New York, The New Press, 2002.

Beevor, Antony, *The Fall of Berlin, 1945*, New York, NY, Penguin, 2002.

Bell, P. M. H., *The Origins of the Second World War in Europe*, London and New York, Longman, 1986.

Berghahn, Volker R., and Kitchen, Martin, eds., *Germany in the Age of Total War*, London, Croom Helm, 1981.

Berkhoff, Karel C., *Harvest of Despair: Life and Death in Ukraine under Nazi Rule*, Cambridge, MA, Harvard University Press, 2004.

Boyce, Robert, and Maiolo, Joseph A., eds., *The Origins of World War Two: The Debate Continues*, New York, NY, Palgrave Macmillan, 2003.

Churchill, Winston, *The Second World War*, 6 vols., Boston, Houghton Mifflin, 1948–1953.

Crowe, David M., *Oskar Schindler: The Untold Account of His Life, Wartime Activities and the True Story behind the List*, Cambridge, MA, Westview, 2004.

Davies, Peter, *Dangerous Liaisons: Collaboration and World War Two*, Harlow, England, Pearson Longman, 2004.

Dear, I. C. B., and Foot, M. R. D., *The Oxford Companion to World War II*, Oxford, Oxford University Press, 1995.

DiNardo, Richard, *Germany and the Axis Powers: From Coalition to Collapse*, Lawrence, University Press of Kansas, 2005.

Eubank, Keith, *The Origins of World War II*, 2nd ed., Arlington Heights, IL, Harlan Davidson, 1990.

Finney, Patrick, ed., *The Origins of the Second World War*, London, Arnold, 1997.

Friedländer, Saul, *Prelude to Downfall: Hitler and the United States 1929–1941*, New York, Alfred A. Knopf, 1967.

Fritz, Stephen G., *Endkampf: Soldiers, Civilians, and the Death of the Third Reich*, Lexington, University Press of Kentucky, 2004.

Garrett, Stephen A., *Ethics and Airpower in World War II: The British Bombing of German Cities*, New York, St. Martin's, 1993.

Glantz, David M., *Barbarossa: Hitler's Invasion of Russia 1941*, Charleston, SC, Tempus, 2001.

——, and House, Jonathan, *When Titans Clashed: How the Red Army Stopped Hitler*, Lawrence, University of Kansas Press, 1995.

Gorodetsky, Gabriel, *Grand Delusion: Stalin and the German Invasion of Russia*, New Haven, Yale University Press, 1999.

Hancock, Eleanor, *National Socialist Leadership and Total War, 1941–1945*, New York, St. Martin's, 1991.

Harvey, Elizabeth, *Women and the Nazi East: Agents and Witnesses of Germanization*, New Haven, Yale University Press, 2003.

Heer, Hannes, and Naumann, Klaus, *War of Extermination: The German Military in World War II, 1941–1944*, New York, Berghahn Books, 2000.

Heiber, Helmut, and Glantz, David M., eds., *Hitler and His Generals: Military Conferences 1942–1945*, New York, Enigma Books, 2003.

Herf, Jeffrey, *The Jewish Enemy: Nazi Propaganda during World War II and the Holocaust*, Cambridge, MA, Harvard University Press, 2006.

Hoare, Marko Attila, *Genocide and Resistance in Hitler's Bosnia: The Partisans and the Chetniks, 1941–1943*, New York, Oxford University Press, 2006.

Kay, Alex J., *Exploitation, Resettlement, Mass Murder: Political and Economic Planning for German Occupation Policy in the Soviet Union, 1940–1941*, New York, Berghahn Books, 2006.

Keegan, John, *The Second World War*, New York, Viking, 1989.

Kershaw, Ian, *Fateful Choices: Ten Decisions that Changed the World 1940–1941*, New York, Penguin, 2007.

Kitchen, Martin, *A World in Flames: A Short History of the Second World War in Europe and Asia 1939–1945*, London, Longman, 1990.

——, *Nazi Germany at War*, London, Longman, 1995.

Kochavi, Arieh J., *Confronting Captivity: Britain and the United States and Their POWs in Nazi Germany*, Chapel Hill, University of North Carolina Press, 2005.

Kreis, Georg, ed., *Switzerland and the Second World War*, London, Frank Cass, 2000.

Leckie, Robert, *Delivered from Evil: The Saga of World War II*, New York, Harper & Row, 1987.

Liddle, Peter, Bourne, John, and Whitehead, Ian, eds., *The Great World War 1914–1945*, 2 vols., London, HarperCollins, 2000–01.

Lukacs, John, *Five Days in London: May 1940*, New Haven, Yale University Press, 1999.

——, *June 1941: Hitler and Stalin*, New Haven, Yale University Press, 2006.

Mackenzie, S. P., *The Colditz Myth: The Real Story of POW Life in Nazi Germany*, Oxford, Oxford University Press, 2006.

Martel, Gordon, ed., *The World War Two Reader*, New York and London, Routledge, 2004.

Meehan, Patricia, *The Unnecessary War: Whitehall and the German Resistance to Hitler*, London, Sinclair-Stevenson, 1992.

Militärgeschichtliches Forschungsamt, *Germany and the Second World War*, 7 vols., New York, Oxford University Press, 1900–2006.

Mineau, André, *Operation Barbarossa: Ideology and Ethics against Human Dignity*, Amsterdam and New York, Rodopi, 2004.

Mosse, George, *Fallen Soldiers: Reshaping the Memory of the World Wars*, New York, Oxford University Press, 1990.

Müller, Rolf-Dieter, and Ueberschär, Gerd R., *Hitler's War in the East 1941–1945: A Critical Assessment*, trans. Bruce D. Little, Providence, RI, Berghahn, 1997.

Murphy, David E., *What Stalin Knew: The Enigma of Barbarossa*, New Haven, Yale University Press, 2005.

Overy, Richard J., *The Air War 1939–1945*, Chelsea, MI, Scarborough House, 1980.

——, *Why the Allies Won*, New York, Norton, 1995.

——, *Russia's War*, New York, Penguin, 1997.

——, and Wheatcroft, Andrew, *The Road to War*, London, Macmillan, 1989.

Paxton, Robert O., *Vichy France: Old Guard and New Order, 1940–1944*, New York, Columbia University Press, 1982.

Payne, Stanley G., *Franco and Hitler: Spain, Germany, and World War II*, New Haven, Yale University Press, 2008.

Powers, Thomas, *Heisenberg's War: The Secret History of the German Bomb*, New York, Alfred A. Knopf, 1993.

Reinhardt, Klaus, *Moscow—The Turning Point: The Failure of Hitler's Strategy in the Winter of 1941–1942*, trans. Karl B. Keenan, Oxford, Berg, 1992.

Rich, Norman, *Hitler's War Aims*, Vol. 1, *Ideology, the Nazi State, and the Course of Expansion*; Vol. 2, *The Establishment of the New Order*, New York, Norton, 1973–74.

Robertson, E. M., *Hitler's Pre-war Policy and Military Plans, 1933–1939*, New York, Citadel Press, 1967.

Rose, Paul Lawrence, *Heisenberg and the Nazi Atomic Bomb Project: A Study in German Culture*, Berkeley, University of California Press, 1998.

Scheck, Raffael, *Hitler's African Victims: The German Army Massacres of Black French Soldiers in 1940*, Cambridge, Cambridge University Press, 2006.

Schulte-Sass, Linda, *Entertaining the Third Reich*, Durham, Duke University Press, 1996.

Shepherd, Ben, *War in the Wild East: The German Army and Soviet Partisans*, Cambridge, MA, Harvard University Press, 2004.

Smith, Arthur L, Jr., *Hitler's Gold: The Story of the Nazi War Loot*, Oxford, Berg, 1996.

Stargardt, Nicholas, *Witnesses of War: Children's Lives under the Nazis*, New York, Alfred A. Knopf, 2005.

Steinert, Marlis G., *Hitler's War and the Germans: Public Mood and Attitude during the Second World War*, trans. Thomas E. J. De Witt, Athens, OH, Ohio University Press, 1977.

Taylor, A. J. P., *The Origins of the Second World War*, Greenwich, CT, Fawcett Publications, 1961.

Watt, Donald Cameron, *How War Came: The Immediate Origins of the Second World War, 1938–1939*, New York, Pantheon Books, 1989.

Weinberg, Gerhard L., *A World at Arms: A Global History of World War II*, New York and Cambridge, Cambridge University Press, 1994.

——, *Germany, Hitler, and World War II: Essays in Modern German and World History*, New York and Cambridge, Cambridge University Press, 1995.

——, *Visions of Victory: The Hopes of Eight World War II Leaders*, New York, Cambridge University Press, 2005.

Westermann, Edward B., *Hitler's Police Battalions: Enforcing Racial War in the East*, Lawrence, University Press of Kansas, 2005.

Wette, Wolfram, *The Wehrmacht: History, Myth, Reality*, trans. Deborah Lucas Schneider, Cambridge, MA, Harvard University Press, 2006.

Wright, Gordon, *The Ordeal of Total War 1939–1945*, New York, Harper & Row, 1968.

Zumbro, Derek S., *Battle for the Ruhr: The German Army's Final Defeat in the West*, Lawrence, University Press of Kansas, 2006.

7 The Holocaust

Allen, Michael Thad, *The Business of Genocide: The SS, Slave Labor, and the Concentration Camps*, Chapel Hill, NC, University of North Carolina Press, 2002.

Aly, Götz, *Final Solution: Nazi Population Policy and the Murder of the European Jews*, New York, Oxford University Press, 1999.

——, and Heim, Susanne, *Architects of Annihilation: Auschwitz and the Logic of Destruction*, Princeton, Princeton University Press, 2002.

Aronson, Shlomo, *Hitler, the Allies, and the Jews*, Cambridge, Cambridge University Press, 2004.

Baer, Elizabeth R., and Goldenberg, Myrna, eds., *Experience and Expression: Women, the Nazis, and the Holocaust*, Detroit, Wayne State University Press, 2003.

Bankier, David, *The Germans and the Final Solution: Public Opinion under Nazism*, Oxford, Blackwell, 1992.

——, ed., *Probing the Depths of Antisemitism: German Society and the Persecution of the Jews, 1933–1941*, Jerusalem, Yad Vashem, 2000.

Bard, Mitchell G., *Forgotten Victims: The Abandonment of Americans in Hitler's Camps*, Boulder, CO, Westview, 1994.

Barkai, Avraham, *From Boycott to Annihilation: The Economic Struggle of German Jews, 1933–1943*, Hanover, NH, University Press of New England, 1989.

Barnett, Victoria J., *Bystanders: Conscience and Complicity during the Holocaust*, Westport, CT, Greenwood, 1999.

Barnow, David, and Van der Strom, Gerrold, *The Diary of Anne Frank: The Critical Edition*, trans. Arnold J. Pomerans and B. M. Mooyaart-Doubleday, New York, Doubleday, 1989.

Bartov, Omer, *Murder in Our Midst: The Holocaust, Industrial Killing, and Representation*, New York, Oxford University Press, 1996.

——, ed., *The Holocaust: Origins, Implementation, Aftermath*, London, Routledge, 2000.

——, *Germany's War and the Holocaust: Disputed Histories*, Ithaca, NY, Cornell University Press, 2003.

——, and Mack, Phyllis, eds., *In God's Name: Genocide and Religion in the Twentieth Century*, Oxford, Berghahn, 2001.

Bauer, Jehuda, *A History of the Holocaust*, New York, Franklin, Watts, 1982.

——, *Rethinking the Holocaust*, New Haven, CT, Yale University Press, 2001.

Bauman, Zygmunt, *Modernity and the Holocaust*, Ithaca, NY, Cornell University Press, 1989.

Benz, Wolfgang, *The Holocaust: A German Historian Examines the Genocide*, trans. Jane Sydenham-Kwiet, New York, Columbia University Press, 1999.

Black, Edwin, *IBM and the Holocaust*, New York, Crown Publishers, 2001.

——, *War against the Weak: Eugenics and America's Campaign to Create a Master Race*, New York, Thunder's Mouth Press, 2004.

Braham, Randolph I. (with Scott Miller), ed., *Last Victims: The Holocaust in Hungary*, Detroit, Wayne State University Press, 1997.

Breitman, Richard, *The Architect of Genocide: Himmler and the Final Solution*, Hanover, NH, University Press of New England, 1992.

——, *Official Secrets: What the Nazis Planned, What the British and Americans Knew*, New York, Hill and Wang, 1998.

Browning, Christopher, *Ordinary Men: Reserve Police Battalion 101 and the Final Solution in Poland*, New York, HarperCollins, 1992.

——, *Paths to Genocide: Essays on Launching the Final Solution*, Cambridge, Cambridge University Press, 1992.

——, with Matthäus, Jürgen, *The Origins of the Final Solution: The Evolution of Nazi Jewish Policy, September 1939–March 1942*, Lincoln, NB, University of Nebraska Press, 2004.

Burleigh, Michael, *Ethics and Extermination: Reflections on Nazi Genocide*, New York, Cambridge University Press, 1997.

Burrin, Philippe, *Hitler and the Jews: The Genesis of the Holocaust*, trans. Patsy Southgate, London, Edward Arnold, 1994.

——, *Nazi Anti-Semitism: From Prejudice to the Holocaust*, trans. Janet Lloyd, New York, The New Press, 2005.

Cesarani, David, ed., *The Final Solution: Origins and Implementation*, London, Routledge, 1994.

——, *Becoming Eichmann: Rethinking the Life, Crimes, and Trial of a "Desk Murderer,"* Cambridge, MA, Da Capo Press, 2006.

Corni, Gustavo, *Hitler's Ghettos: Voices from a Beleaguered Society*, New York, Oxford University Press, 2002.

Dawidowicz, Lucy, *The War against the Jews 1933–1945*, New York, Holt, Rinehart, and Winston, 1975.

——, *A Holocaust Reader*, West Orange, NJ, Berman House, 1976.

Ericksen, Robert P., and Heschel, Susannah, eds., *Betrayal: German Churches and the Holocaust*, Minneapolis, Fortress Press, 1999.

Finkelstein, Norman G., and Birn, Ruth Bettina, eds., *A Nation on Trial: The Goldhagen Thesis and Historical Truth*, New York, Henry Holt, 1998.

Fleming, Gerald, *Hitler and the Final Solution*, Berkeley, University of California Press, 1984.

Friedlander, Henry, *The Origins of Nazi Genocide: From Euthanasia to the Final Solution*, Chapel Hill, NC, University of North Carolina Press, 1995.

Friedländer, Saul, ed., *Probing the Limits of Representation: Nazism and the "Final Solution,"* Cambridge, MA, Harvard University Press, 1992.

——, *Nazi Germany and the Jews*, Vol. 1, *The Years of Persecution, 1933–1939*, Vol. 2, *The Years of Extermination, 1939–1945*, New York, HarperCollins, 1997, 2007.

Friling, Tuvia, *Arrows in the Dark: David Ben Gurion, the Yishuv Leadership, and Rescue Attempts during the Holocaust*, Madison, University of Wisconsin Press, 2005.

Gigliotti, Simone, and Lang, Berel, eds., *The Holocaust: A Reader*, Malden, MA, Blackwell, 2005.

Gilbert, Martin, *The Holocaust: A History of the Jews of Europe during the Second World War*, New York, Holt, Rinehart, and Winston, 1986.

——, *Holocaust Journey: Travelling in Search of the Past*, New York, Columbia University Press, 1997.

——, *The Righteous: The Unsung Heroes of the Holocaust*, New York, Henry Holt, 2003.

——, *Kristallnacht: Prelude to Destruction*, New York, Harper Perennial, 2006.

Goldhagen, Daniel Jonah, *Hitler's Willing Executioners: Ordinary Germans and the Holocaust*, New York, Alfred A. Knopf, 1996.

——, *A Moral Reckoning: The Role of the Catholic Church in the Holocaust and Its Unfulfilled Duty of Repair*, New York, Alfred A. Knopf, 2002.

Gutman, Israel, and Zuroff, Efraim, eds., *Rescue Attempts during the Holocaust*, Jerusalem, Yad Vashem, 1977.

Gutman, Yisrael and Berenbaum, Michael, *Anatomy of the Auschwitz Death Camp*, Bloomington and Indianapolis, Indiana University Press, 1994.

Haar, Ingo, and Fahlbusch, Michael, eds., *German Scholars and Ethnic Cleansing, 1919–1945*, New York and Oxford, Berghahn Books, 2005.

Hayes, Peter, ed., *Lessons and Legacies: The Meaning of the Holocaust in a Changing World*, Evanston, IL, Northwestern University Press, 1991.

Herbert, Ulrich, ed., *National Socialist Extermination Policies: Contemporary German Perspectives and Controversies*, New York, Berghahn, 2000.

Hilberg, Paul, *Perpetrators, Victims, Bystanders: The Jewish Catastrophe 1933–1945*, New York, HarperCollins, 1992.

——, *The Destruction of the European Jews* (1961), 3rd ed., 2 vols., New Haven, Yale University Press, 2002.

Höss, Rudolf, *Commandant of Auschwitz: The Autobiography of Rudolf Hoess*, trans. Constantine Fitz Gibbon, London, Weidenfeld and Nicolson, 1959.

Jones, Adam, *Genocide: A Comprehensive Introduction*, London and New York, Routledge, 2006.

Kaplan, Marion A., *Between Dignity and Despair: Jewish Life in Nazi Germany*, New York, Oxford University Press, 1998.

Katz, Jacob, *From Prejudice to Destruction: Anti-semitism, 1700–1933*, Cambridge, MA, Harvard University Press, 1980.

Kertzer, David, *The Popes against the Jews*, New York, Alfred A. Knopf, 2001.

Kiernan, Ben, *Blood and Soil: A World History of Genocide and Extermination from Sparta to Darfur*, New Haven, Yale University Press, 2007.

Klee, Ernst, Willi Dressen, and Volker Riess, eds., *"The Good Old Days": The Holocaust as Seen by Its Perpetrators and Bystanders*, trans. Deborah Burnstone, New York, Konecky & Konecky, 1991.

Landau, Ronnie S., *Studying the Holocaust: Issues, Readings, and Documents*, London, Routledge, 1998.

Laqueur, Walter, *The Terrible Secret: Suppression of the Truth about Hitler's "Final Solution,"* New York, Penguin, 1980.

——, and Baumel, Judith Tydor, eds., *The Holocaust Encyclopedia*, New Haven, Yale University Press, 2001.

Levin, Nora, *The Holocaust: The Destruction of European Jewry 1933–1945*, New York, Schocken, 1973.

Levy, Richard S., *Antisemitism in the Modern World: An Anthology of Texts*, Lexington, MA, D. C. Heath, 1991.

Lewy, Guenter, *The Nazi Persecution of the Gypsies*, Oxford, Oxford University Press, 2000.

Lifton, Robert J., *The Nazi Doctors: Medical Killing and the Psychology of Genocide*, New York, 1986.

Littell, Franklin H., *The Crucifixion of the Jews*, New York, Harper & Row, 1975.

——, and Locke, Hubert G., eds., *The German Church Struggle and the Holocaust*, Detroit, Wayne State University Press, 1974.

Longerich, Peter, *Policy of Destruction: Nazi Anti-Jewish Policy and the Genesis of the "Final Solution,"* Washington, DC, Center for Advanced Holocaust Studies, United States Holocaust Memorial Museum, 2001.

——, *The Unwritten Order: Hitler's Role in the Final Solution*, Stroud, Tempus, 2001.

Lower, Wendy, *Nazi Empire-Building and the Holocaust in Ukraine*, Chapel Hill, University of North Carolina Press, 2005.

Marrus, Michael, *The Holocaust in History*, New York, Meridian, 1987.

Mayer, Arno J., *Why Did the Heavens Not Darken? The "Final Solution" in History*, New York, Pantheon, 1990.

Morley, John F., *Vatican Diplomacy and the Jews during the Holocaust 1939–1943*, New York, KTAV Publishing House, 1980.

Mosse, George L., *Toward the Final Solution: A History of European Racism*, New York, Howard Fertig, 1977.

Müller-Hill, Benno, *Murderous Science: Elimination by Scientific Selection of Jews, Gypsies, and Others, Germany 1933–1945*, Oxford, Oxford University Press, 1988.

Phayer, Michael, *The Catholic Church and the Holocaust, 1930–1965*, Bloomington: Indiana University Press, 2000.

Postone, Moishe, and Santner, Eric, eds., *Catastrophe and Meaning: The Holocaust and the Twentieth Century*, Chicago, University of Chicago Press, 2003.

Pringle, Heather, *The Master Plan: Himmler's Scholars and the Holocaust*, New York, Viking, 2006.

Reitlinger, Gerald, *The Final Solution: The Attempt to Exterminate the Jews of Europe 1939–1945*, London, Valentine, Mitchell, 1968.

Rhodes, Richard, *Masters of Death: The SS Einsatzgruppen and the Invention of the Holocaust*, New York, Vintage, 2003.

Rittner, Carol, and Roth, John K., *From the Unthinkable to the Unavoidable: American Christian and Jewish Scholars Encounter the Holocaust*, Westport, CT, Greenwood, 1997.

Rose, Paul Lawrence, *German Question/Jewish Question: Revolutionary Antisemitism from Kant to Wagner*, Princeton, Princeton University Press, 1990.

Roseman, Mark, *A Past in Hiding: Memory and Survival in Nazi Germany*, New York, Metropolitan Books, 2000.

——, *The Villa, the Lake, the Meeting: Wannsee and the Final Solution*, London, Allen Lane, 2002.

——, *The Wannsee Conference and the Final Solution: A Reconsideration*, New York, Metropolitan Books, 2002.

Rosenbaum, Alan S., ed., *Is the Holocaust Unique? Perspectives on Comparative Genocide*, Boulder, CO, Westview, 1996.

Rubinstein, William D., *Why the Democracies Could Not Have Saved More Jews from the Nazis*, London, Routledge, 1997.

Schleunes, Karl, *The Twisted Road to Auschwitz: Nazi Policy toward German Jews 1933–1939*, Urbana, IL, University of Illinois Press, 1970.

Sereny, Gitta, *Into that Darkness: From Mercy Killing to Mass Murder*, New York, McGraw-Hill, 1974.

Sofsky, Wolfgang, *The Order of Terror: The Concentration Camp*, trans. William Templer, Princeton, NJ, Princeton University Press, 1997.

Stark, Tamás, *Hungarian Jews during the Holocaust and after the Second World War, 1939–1949: A Statistical Review*, Boulder, CO, East European Monographs, 2000.

Stone, Dan, *Responses to Nazism in Britain, 1933–1939: Before War and Holocaust*, New York, Palgrave Macmillan, 2003.

——, ed., *The Historiography of the Holocaust*, New York, Palgrave Macmillan, 2004.

Weiss, John, *The Ideology of Death: Why the Holocaust Happened in Germany*, Chicago, Ivan R. Dee, 1996.

——, *The Politics of Hate: Anti-semitism, History, and the Holocaust in Modern Europe*, Chicago, Ivan R. Dee, 2003.

Weitz, Eric D., *A Century of Genocide: Utopias of Race and Nation*, Princeton, Princeton University Press, 2003.

Wistrich, Robert S., *Hitler and the Holocaust*, New York, Modern Library, 2001.

Wyman, David, *The Abandonment of the Jews: America and the Holocaust, 1941–1945*, New York, Pantheon Books, 1984.

Yahil, Leni, *The Holocaust: The Fate of European Jewry*, trans. Ina Friedman and Haya Galai, New York, Oxford University Press, 1990.

Zertel, Idith, *Israel's Holocaust and the Politics of Nationhood*, trans. Chaya Galai, Cambridge, Cambridge University Press, 2005.

Zuccotti, Susan, *Under His Very Windows: The Vatican and the Holocaust in Italy*, New Haven, Yale University Press, 2002.

8 The aftermath of National Socialism

Alter, Reinhard, and Monteath, Peter, eds., *Rewriting the German Past: History and Identity in the New Germany*, Atlantic Highlands, NJ, Humanities International Press, 1997.

Annas, George J., and Grodin, Michael A., eds., *The Nazi Doctors and the Nuremberg Code: Human Rights in Human Experimentation*, New York, Oxford University Press, 1992.

Arad, Gulie Ne'eman, ed., *Passing into History: Nazism and the Holocaust beyond Memory*, special issue of *History & Memory*, Vol. 9 (Fall 1997).

Aschheim, Steven E., *Culture and Catastrophe: German and Jewish Confrontations with National Socialism and Other Crises*, New York, New York University Press, 1996.

Baldwin, Peter, ed., *Reworking the Past: Hitler, the Holocaust, and the Historians' Debate*, Boston, Beacon Press, 1990.

Balfour, Michael, *West Germany: A Contemporary History*, New York, St. Martin's, 1982.

Barnouw, Dagmar, *Germany 1945: Views of War and Violence*, Bloomington, IN, Indiana University Press, 1996.

Bergmann, Werner, and Erb, Rainer, *Anti-Semitism in Germany: The Post-Nazi Epoch since 1945*, New Brunswick, NJ, Transaction Publishers, 1997.

Bessel, Richard, and Schumann, Dirk, eds., *Life after Death: Approaches to a Social and Cultural History of Europe During the 1940s and 1950s*, Cambridge, Cambridge University Press, 2003.

Biess, Frank, *Homecomings: Returning POWs and the Legacies of Defeat in Postwar Germany*, Princeton, Princeton University Press, 2006.

Bloxham, Donald, *Genocide on Trial: War Crimes Trials and the Formation of Holocaust History and Memory*, Oxford, Oxford University Press, 2001.

Boehling, Rebecca L., *A Question of Priorities: Democratic Reforms and Economic Recovery in Postwar Germany*, Providence, RI, Berghahn Books, 1996.

Bower, Tom, *The Pledge Betrayed: America and Britain and the Denazification of Postwar Germany*, Garden City, NY, Doubleday, 1982.

Bredthauer, Karl D., and Heinrich, Arthur, *Aus der Geschichte lernen/How to Learn from History*, Bonn, edition Blätter 2, 1997.

Breitman, Richard, *et al.*, *U.S. Intelligence and the Nazis*, Washington, DC, National Archives Trust Fund Board, 2004.

Brown-Fleming, Suzanne, *The Holocaust and Catholic Conscience: Cardinal Aloisius Muench and the Guilt Question in Germany*, Notre Dame, University of Notre Dame Press, 2006.

Burleigh, Michael, ed., *Confronting the Nazi Past: New Debates on Modern German History*, New York, St. Martin's, 1996.

Buruma, Ian, *The Wages of Guilt: Memories of War in Germany and Japan*, New York, Farrar Straus Giroux, 1994.

Cheles, L., Ferguson, R., and Vaughan, M., eds., *The Far Right in Western and Eastern Europe*, 2nd ed., London, Longman, 1995.

Chin, Rita, *The Guest Worker Question in Postwar Germany*, Cambridge, Cambridge University Press, 2007.

Cole, Tim, *Selling the Holocaust: From Auschwitz to Schindler: How History Is Bought, Packaged, and Sold*, New York, Routledge, 1999.

Confino, Alon, *Germany as a Culture of Remembrance: Promises and Limits of Writing History*, Chapel Hill, University of North Carolina Press, 2006.

——, and Fritzsche, Peter, eds., *The Work of Memory: New Directions in the Study of German Society and Culture*, Urbana, University of Illinois Press, 2002.

Conot, Robert E., *Justice at Nuremberg*, New York, Harper & Row, 1983.

Dahrendorf, Ralf, *The Unresolved Past: A Debate in German History*, New York, St. Martin's, 1990.

Davidson, Eugene, *The Death and Life of Germany: An Account of the American Occupation*, New York, Alfred A. Knopf, 1961.

De Mildt, Dick, *In the Name of the People: Perpetrators of Genocide in the Reflection of Their Post-war Prosecution in West Germany: The "Euthanasia" and "Aktion Reinhard" Trial Cases*, The Hague, Martinus Nijhoff, 1996.

Diefendorf, Jeffry M., Frohn, Axel, and Rupieper, Hermann-Josef, eds., *American Policy and the Reconstruction of West Germany, 1945–1955*, Cambridge, Cambridge University Press, 1993.

Eley, Geoff, ed., *The "Goldhagen Effect": History, Memory, Nazism—Facing the German Past*, Ann Arbor, University of Michigan Press, 2000.

Evans, Richard J., *In Hitler's Shadow: West German Historians and the Attempt to Escape from the Nazi Past*, New York, Pantheon Books, 1989.

——, *Telling Lies about Hitler: The Holocaust, History, and the David Irving Trial*, London, Verso, 2002.

Fehrenbach, Heide, *Race after Hitler: Black Occupation Children in Postwar Germany and America*, Princeton, Princeton University Press, 2005.

Frei, Norbert, *Adenauer's Germany and the Nazi Past: The Politics of Amnesty and Integration*, trans. Joel Golb, New York, Columbia University Press, 2002.

Friedländer, Saul, *Memory, History, and the Extermination of the Jews in Europe*, Bloomington, IN, Indiana University Press, 1993.

Frommer, Benjamin, *National Cleansing: Retribution against Nazi Collaborators in Postwar Czechoslovakia*, Cambridge, Cambridge University Press, 2005.

Fulbrooke, Mary, *Anatomy of a Dictatorship: Inside the GDR 1949–1989*, Oxford, Oxford University Press, 1995.

——, *German National Identity after the Holocaust*, Cambridge, Polity Press, 1999.

Garton Ash, Timothy, *In Europe's Name: Germany and the Divided Continent*, New York, Random House, 1993.

Gassert, Philipp, and Steinweis, Alan E., eds., *Coping with the Nazi Past: West German Debates on Nazism and Generational Conflict, 1955–1975*, New York, Berghahn Books, 2006.

Geller, Jay Howard, *Jews in Post-Holocaust Germany, 1945–1953*, Cambridge, Cambridge University Press, 2005.

Gimble, John, *The American Occupation of Germany: Politics and the Military, 1945–1949*, Stanford, CA, Stanford University Press, 1968.

Goda, Norman J. W., *Tales from Spandau: Nazi Criminals and the Cold War*, New York, Cambridge University Press, 2006.

Goldensohn, Leon, *Nuremberg Interviews: An American Psychiatrist's Conversations with the Defendants and Witnesses*, Robert Gellately, ed., New York, Vintage Books, 2005.

Gollancz, Victor, *In Darkest Germany*, Hinsdale, IL, Henry Regnery, 1947.

Golsan, Richard J., ed., *Fascism's Return: Scandal, Revision, and Ideology since 1980*, Lincoln, University of Nebraska Press, 1998.

Grossmann, Atina, *Jews, Germans, and Allies: Close Encounters in Occupied Germany*, Princeton, Princeton University Press, 2006.

Habermas, Jürgen, ed., *Observations on "The Spiritual Situation of the Age": Contemporary German Perspectives*, trans. Andrew Buchwalter, Cambridge, MA, MIT Press, 1984.

——, *The New Conservatism: Cultural Criticism and the Historians' Debate*, trans. Sherry Weber Nicholsen, Cambridge, MA, MIT Press, 1989.

——, *A Berlin Republic: Writings on Germany*, trans. Steven Rendall, Lincoln, NB, University of Nebraska Press, 1997.

Hamburger Institut für Sozialforschung, *The German Army and Genocide: Crimes against War Prisoners, Jews and Other Civilians, 1939–1944*, New York, New Press, 1999.

Harms, Kathy, Reuter, Lutz R., and Dürr, Volker, *Coping with the Past: Germany and Austria after 1945*, Madison, University of Wisconsin Press, 1990.

Harris, Geoffrey, *The Dark Side of Europe: The Extreme Right Today*, Edinburgh, Edinburgh University Press, 1994.

Hartman, Geoffrey H., ed., *Bitburg in Moral and Political Perspective*, Bloomington, Indiana University Press, 1986.

Heineman, Elizabeth D., *What Difference Does a Husband Make? Women and Marital Status in Nazi and Postwar Germany*, Berkeley, University of California Press, 1999.

Herf, Jeffrey, *Divided Memory: The Nazi Past in the Two Germanys*, Cambridge, MA, Harvard University Press, 1997.

Herzog, Dagmar, *Sex after Fascism: Memory and Morality in Twentieth-Century Germany*, Princeton, Princeton University Press, 2005.

——, ed., *Lessons and Legacies VII: The Holocaust in International Perspective*, Evanston, Northwestern University Press, 2006.

Hilberg, Raul, *The Politics of Memory: The Journey of a Holocaust Historian*, Chicago, Ivan Dee, 1996.

Hockenos, Matthew D., *A Church Divided: German Protestants Confront the Nazi Past*, Bloomington, IN, Indiana University Press, 2004.

Hockenos, Paul, *Joschka Fischer and the Making of the Berlin Republic: An Alternative History of Postwar Germany*, New York, Oxford University Press, 2007.

Hoffmann, Christhard, ed., *Preserving the Legacy of German Jewry: A History of the Leo Baeck Institute 1955–2005*, Tübingen, Mohr, Siebeck, 2005.

Hunt, Linda, *Secret Agenda: The United States Government, Nazi Scientists, and Project Paperclip, 1945–1990*, New York, St. Martin's, 1991.

Iggers, Georg, ed., *The Social History of Politics: Critical Perspectives in West German Historical Writing since 1945*, New York, St. Martin's, 1986.

Independent International Commission of Experts, *Switzerland, National Socialism, and the Second World War*, Zurich, Pendo, 2002.

Judt, Tony, *Postwar: A History of Europe since 1945*, New York, Penguin, 2005.

Kansteiner, Wulf, *In Pursuit of German Memory: History, Television, and Politics after Auschwitz*, Athens, Ohio University Press, 2006.

Kattago, Siobhan, *Ambiguous Memory: The Nazi Past and German National Identity*, Westport, CT, Praeger, 2001.

Kettenacker, Lothar, *Germany since 1945*, Oxford, Oxford University Press, 1997.

Koshar, Rudy, *Germany's Transient Pasts: Preservation and National Memory in the Twentieth Century*, Chapel Hill, University of North Carolina Press, 1998.

——, *Monuments to Traces: Artifacts of German Memory, 1870–1990*, Berkeley, University of California Press, 2000.

Kurthen, Hermann, Bergmann, Werner, and Erb, Rainer, eds., *Antisemitism and Xenophobia in Germany after Unification*, New York and Oxford, Oxford University Press, 1997.

Lang, Berel, *The Future of the Holocaust: Between History and Memory*, Ithaca, NY, Cornell University Press, 1999.

Langer, Lawrence L., *Using and Abusing the Holocaust*, Bloomington, University of Indiana Press, 2006.

Levy, Daniel, and Sznaider, Natan, *The Holocaust and Memory in the Global Age*, trans. Assenka Oksiloff, Philadelphia, Temple University Press, 2005.

Levy, Daniel, and Weiss, Yfaat, eds., *Challenging Ethnic Citizenship: German and Israeli Perspectives on Immigration*, New York, Berghahn Books, 2002.

Littell, Franklin H., ed., *Hyping the Holocaust: Scholars Answer Goldhagen*, East Rockaway, NY, Cummings & Hathaway, 1997.

Low, Alfred D., *The Third Reich and the Holocaust in German Historiography: Toward the Historikerstreit of the Mid-1980s*, Boulder, CO, East European Monographs, 1994.

MacDonogh, Giles, *After the Reich: The Brutal History of the Allied Occupation*, New York, Basic Books, 2007.

Maier, Charles S., *The Unmasterable Past: History, the Holocaust, and German National Identity*, Cambridge, MA, Harvard University Press, 1988.

Marcuse, Harold, *Legacies of Dachau: The Uses and Abuses of a Concentration Camp, 1933–2001*, Cambridge, Cambridge University Press, 2001.

Marrus, Michael R., *The Nuremberg War Crimes Trial 1945–46: A Documentary History*, Boston, Bedford Books, 1997.

Meinecke, Friedrich, *The German Catastrophe: Reflections and Recollections*, trans. Sidney B. Fay, Cambridge, MA, Harvard University Press, 1950.

Merritt, Richard L., *Democracy Imposed: U.S. Occupation Policy and the German Public, 1945–1949*, New Haven, Yale University Press, 1995.

Moeller, Robert G., *War Stories: The Search for a Usable Past in the Federal Republic of Germany*, Berkeley, University of California Press, 2001.

Moses, A. Dirk, *German Intellectuals and the Nazi Past*, Cambridge, Cambridge University Press, 2007.

Naimark, Norman M., *The Russians in Germany: A History of the Soviet Zone of Occupation, 1945–1949*, Cambridge, MA, Harvard University Press, 1995.

Niven, Bill, *Facing the Nazi Past: United Germany and the Legacy of the Third Reich*, London, Routledge, 2002.

——, ed., *Germans as Victims: Remembering the Past in Contemporary Germany*, New York, Palgrave Macmillan, 2006.

Novick, Peter, *The Holocaust in American Life*, Boston, Houghton Mifflin, 1999.

Olick, Jeffrey K., *In the House of the Hangman: The Agonies of German Defeat, 1943–1949*, Chicago, University of Chicago Press, 2005.

Overy, Richard, *Interrogations: The Nazi Elite in Allied Hands, 1945*, London, Penguin Books, 2001.

Pendas, Devin O., *The Frankfurt Auschwitz Trial, 1963–1965: Genocide, History, and the Limits of the Law*, New York, Cambridge University Press, 2006.

Pick, Hella, *Guilty Victim: Austria from the Holocaust to Haider*, London, I.B. Tauris, 2000.

Posner, Gerald L., *Hitler's Children: Sons and Daughters of Leaders of the Third Reich Talk about Their Fathers and Themselves*, New York, Random House, 1991.

Rapaport, Lynn, *Jews in Germany after the Holocaust: Memory, Identity, and German–Jewish Relations*, Cambridge, Cambridge University Press, 1997.

Remy, Steven P., *The Heidelberg Myth: The Nazification and Denazification of a German University*, Cambridge, MA, Harvard University Press, 2002.

Rosenfeld, Alvin H., *Thinking about the Holocaust: After Half a Century*, Bloomington, University of Indiana Press, 1997.

Rosenfeld, Gavriel D., *Munich and Memory: Architecture, Monuments, and the Legacy of the Third Reich*, Berkeley, University of California Press, 2000.

——, *The World Hitler Never Made*, Cambridge, Cambridge University Press, 2005.

Rousso, Henry, *The Vichy Syndrome: History and Memory in France since 1944*, trans. Arthur Goldhammer, Cambridge, MA, Harvard University Press, 1991.

Sa'adah, Anne, *Germany's Second Chance: Trust, Justice and Democratization*, Cambridge, MA, Harvard University Press, 1998.

Sereny, Gitta, *Albert Speer: His Battle with the Truth*, New York, Knopf, 1995.

——, *The Healing Wound: Experiences and Reflections on Germany, 1938–2001*, New York, W.W. Norton, 2001.

Shandley, Robert R., ed., *Unwilling Germans? The Goldhagen Debate*, Minneapolis, University of Minnesota Press, 1998.

Sichrovsky, Peter, *Born Guilty: Children of Nazi Families*, trans. Jean Steinberg, New York, Basic Books, 1988.

Simpson, Christopher, *Blowback: America's Recruitment of Nazis and Its Effects on the Cold War*, New York, Weidenfeld & Nicolson, 1988.

Smith, Arthur L., Jr., *The War for the German Mind: Re-educating Hitler's Soldiers*, Providence, RI, Berghahn Books, 1996.

Smith, Bradley F., *Reaching Judgment at Nuremberg*, New York, Basic Books, 1977.

Smyser, W. R., *From Yalta to Berlin: The Cold War Struggle over Germany*, New York, St. Martin's, 2000.

Steinweis, Alan E., and Rogers, Daniel E., eds., *The Impact of Nazism: New Perspectives on the Third Reich and Its Legacy*, Lincoln, University of Nebraska Press, 2003.

Teschke, John P., *Hitler's Legacy: West Germany Confronts the Aftermath of the Third Reich*, New York, Peter Lang, 1999.

Tetens, T. H., *The New Germany and the Old Nazis*, London, Secker & Warburg, 1961.

The Dilemmas of Commemoration: German Debates on the Holocaust in the 1990s, Special Issue of *German Politics and Society*, Vol. 17 (Fall 1999).

Trachtenberg, Marc, *A Constructed Peace: The Making of the European Settlement, 1945–1963*, Princeton, Princeton University Press, 1999.

Vogt, Timothy R., *Denazification in Soviet-Occupied Germany: Brandenburg, 1945–1948*, Cambridge, MA, Harvard University Press, 2000.

Watson, Alan, *The Germans: Who Are They Now?*, Chicago, Edition Q, 1992.

Wiesen, Jonathan S., *West German Industry and the Challenge of the Nazi Past, 1945–1955*, Chapel Hill, University of North Carolina Press, 2002.

Wittmann, Rebecca, *Beyond Justice: The Auschwitz Trial*, Cambridge, MA, Harvard University Press, 2005.

Woods, Roger, *Germany's New Right as Culture and Politics*, New York, Palgrave Macmillan, 2007.

Wrench, John, and Solomos, John, eds., *Racism and Migration in Western Europe*, Oxford, Berg, 1993.

Index